Lt.

SEC / EWS

Duty Phone 2370

DWIGHT L. GENTRY, Ph.D., University of Illinois, is Assistant Dean and Professor of Business Administration in the College of Business and Public Administration at the University of Maryland. He previously taught at the University of Miami, the University of Illinois, and Wake Forest College. Dr. Gentry has served as a consultant to industry and is a member of the local and regional Advisory Councils of the Small Business Administration. He is co-author of two other books in the business area and has written numerous articles in professional and academic journals.

CHARLES A. TAFF, Ph.D., University of Maryland, is Professor and Head of the Department of Business Administration in the College of Business and Public Administration at the University of Maryland. He also serves as a consultant to business, the Department of Defense, and the Council of Economic Advisers. He previously taught at Kent State University and Virginia Polytechnic Institute and is the author of three other books and numerous articles in the areas of marketing, management, and transportation.

ELEMENTS OF
BUSINESS ENTERPRISE

DWIGHT L. GENTRY

and

CHARLES A. TAFF
Both University of Maryland

SECOND EDITION

THE RONALD PRESS COMPANY • NEW YORK

Library of Congress Catalog Card Number: 66–16843
PRINTED IN THE UNITED STATES OF AMERICA

Preface

The management of business is an exciting and challenging field. Its rewards can be substantial both in satisfaction of accomplishment and in monetary return. And the opportunities for success are available to everyone whose efforts are purposefully directed. The broad aim of the Second Edition of this book, like that of its predecessor, is to provide the beginning student with the basic knowledge of the field of business. It has been written for the first course in business and provides solid substance without sacrificing simplicity of presentation. For those students who take only a single course in the subject, this book offers a comprehensive examination of the theory and practice of business.

The scope of business activities, the types of business organizations, the relationship of business and government, business ethics, and the interdisciplinary approach to the management of business are all discussed to demonstrate the role of business enterprise not only in the economic life but in the social, political, and moral life of our nation as well. The various aspects of business included in the usual curriculum are presented in sufficient depth to give the student an effective survey of business management. These topics include finance and accounting, statistics, personnel management and organized labor, marketing, transportation, law, and research.

In business management, as in many activities, the trend is toward the scientific approach and the analytical solution. Therefore, in this edition, the student is introduced to the concepts of the quantitative and behavioral areas of business management. The growing development of electronic data processing and the applications of computer technology in all facets of business activity are reflected in the substantial emphasis given these subjects in this book.

To aid the student in the selection of his career objectives, the authors have included a section in each chapter devoted to outlining the opportunities available in each area and suggested courses for advanced study in the subject. Discussion questions and case problems at the end of each chapter also enable the student to apply the material he has studied to realistic business situations.

The authors would like to express their gratitude to all those who have assisted in the preparation of the book, especially Professor Arthur Patrick, who read and offered suggestions on the information management material. We are indebted also to the many teachers in various colleges and universities who have been kind enough to pass along suggestions.

DWIGHT L. GENTRY
CHARLES A. TAFF

College Park, Maryland
    March, 1966

Contents

I

BUSINESS MANAGEMENT BACKGROUND

1

Our Business Enterprise Economy

We generally think of *business enterprise* as a term referring to the firms, and the activities of firms, concerned with the production and distribution of goods and services. Perhaps most people think of business enterprise in relation to privately owned and operated organizations; and it is true that our economy is predominantly one of private enterprise. We should, however, bear in mind that considerable quantities of goods and services are produced and distributed by the public sector of the economy. In this text we shall concentrate upon those activities commonly associated with privately owned and operated concerns. Many of the principles applicable to the management of the private firm are also pertinent to the enterprise owned and operated through the agency of government. The *businessman* is usually thought of as one primarily concerned with the activities involved in producing, buying, and selling. In the broad sense, the term distinguishes him from the farmer, the professional man, or the institutional employee. The full scope of the activities of the businessman will unfold for the student as he progresses through this text and others dealing with business management.

THE EVOLUTION OF BUSINESS ENTERPRISE IN AMERICA

Early Developments

The first settlers to reach America found themselves in a life and death struggle for existence. The problem was to wrest from nature the bare essentials of food and clothing. The family as a unit was forced to be as nearly self-sufficient as possible. As the colonies grew, some trade developed with England and other countries—notably Holland. Initially, this consisted of trading raw products for certain manufactured essentials that the colonists could not make at home. At this stage it is probable that very little incentive existed for the colonists to trade among themselves. Such "industry" as existed has been described as being in the *home stage.*[1] The father of the family was a Jack-of-All-Trades who processed hides and made shoes, kitchen utensils, furniture, and other items used by the family. Spinning, weaving, and the making of clothing were carried on by the women of the family.

Business Transactions Develop

The human tendency for one to specialize in what he does best made itself felt among the early colonists. It is logical to assume that some men gained a reputation for being proficient in making certain items while others became known as experts in performing other functions. This created a natural environment for some type of exchange or trade. It appears that some of the more proficient craftsmen emerged from the home and began working on an itinerant basis—traveling from village to village offering their services. Among the first of the itinerant craftsmen were the shoemakers. Shoemakers, as well as other craftsmen, bartered their services for food, clothing, or other produce.[2]

As transportation and communications improved, the itinerant craftsman ceased traveling and established a shop at a convenient location. Customers now came to the craftsman and sought his services. Work was done on a "custom" basis, and hence the shop operator did not carry an inventory of finished goods or have a problem of selling. It should be noted that in this stage the maker of the product and the user of the product were meeting face-to-face. No middlemen were involved; however, the middleman was soon to appear.

The merchant, or storekeeper, made his appearance when sufficient concentrations of population justified his services. Initially, his business was largely a barter transaction; he handled items and produce from the colonies as well as a limited line of imported items. In his quest for inventory, the merchant soon turned to the craftsman. He frequently supplied the craftsman with raw materials and then took over the responsibility of selling the finished product. This arrangement benefited the craftsman in that it made him less dependent upon the

[1] Donald L. Kemmerer and C. Clyde Jones, *American Economic History* (New York: McGraw-Hill Book Co., 1959), Chap. 9.
[2] *Ibid.*, p. 161.

sporadic demand arising from a custom, or "be-spoke," type of operation. From the merchant's point of view, there were disadvantages in
this relationship. The craftsmen were scattered and it was difficult to
maintain contact with the small shops. Also, the problem of controlling
the quality of work was a difficult one. This led to the emergence of
what is known as the *factory stage*.

The effort of merchants to bring craftsmen together under one roof
was especially notable in the early stages of the shoe industry. This act
of bringing together workmen not only enabled better control, but it
presented the opportunity to capitalize on the various degrees of specialization existing among the workmen. Also, apprentices or workers
of limited skill could be utilized by delegating the more difficult work
to the more experienced. This assembling of workers under one roof
and, to a degree, a centralized management with some emphasis on the
division of labor marks the beginning of a factory concept. In later
years as machinery developed in the shoe industry, and in other industries as well, the need for the assembly of a workforce became increasingly evident. The individual craftsman could not afford the initial cost
and maintenance of a complex machine that he might use to a small
extent of its capacity.

The Industrial Revolution

The industrial revolution may be said to have begun in England early
in the eighteenth century. Certain inventions in the textile field had
succeeded in revolutionizing that industry by the end of the eighteenth
century. It was also during this period (1769) that James Watt developed
the steam engine. This made available a source of power that expanded
the factory system and introduced a new way of life throughout much
of the civilized world. By the start of the nineteenth century the industrial revolution had begun in the United States. While under the
dominance of the British, the American colonies had not been allowed
freedom in industrial development. England had sought to use the
colonies as a source of raw materials while forbidding the development
of manufacturing that would be in competition with English sources.
Now that the United States had emerged a free nation, the urge to become increasingly self-sufficient was especially strong.

Fortunately, the United States was blessed with abundant resources.
Sources of water power in New England were harnessed as that section
led in the development of manufacturing. A diverse climate and soil
provided a wide variety of raw materials from agricultural sources, and
extractive industries such as fishing and mining soon were of importance. Population in the United States had grown and was soon to swell

from the rush of immigration. A new nation with resources and dedicated to the concept of free enterprise offered an ideal setting for industrial development.

The Age of Big Business

The development of industry—the demands for materials, power, and specialized skills—soon led to industrial concentrations. Initially, the movement toward bigness was undoubtedly prompted by the desire to take advantage of certain economies of operation that were available only to the large-scale operator. The trend to bigness was especially apparent during the last half of the nineteenth century. During this period, mergers were accomplished and trusts were formed. The economy, which had relied upon completion as a regulating device, was now threatened by declining competition. The corporation, which had become a predominant form of business enterprise, lent itself well to the processes of expansion and acquisition. As a result of the trend toward bigness and some of the abuses inherent therein, the federal government began to take regulatory action. The development of large-scale industry has continued but so has the regulatory function of government in an effort to protect competition.

THE BUSINESS ENVIRONMENT

The Free-Enterprise System

One well-known authority has described four elements as being essential to the free-enterprise system.[3] First, there is the private ownership of property and the means of production and distribution. Second, the free-enterprise system accepts the goal of profit-making as an economic and justifiable endeavor. Third, competition is considered the most desirable inducement to efficiency. The fourth element is an assurance of freedom from interference insofar as possible in order that superior effort and ability may be rewarded. The extent to which these elements exist in an unmodified state in our present economy may be a subject of debate. Ironically, while competition is an efficient regulator up to a point, if left completely free of interference it has a tendency to destroy itself. Generally speaking, the early efforts of the government to regulate industry were aimed at the preservation of competition. The emergency conditions arising from war and the mainte-

[3] Marshall E. Dimock, *Business and Government* (3rd ed.; New York: Henry Holt & Co., 1957), p. 9.

nance of national defense have further restricted the free play of forces traditionally considered basic to free enterprise.

Regardless of the way in which basic concepts have been modified, we are still blessed with the fundamental advantages of a free-enterprise system. Except in periods of national emergency, our resources are allocated to a great extent according to the conditions of supply and demand. Our resources are devoted to the needs of the people as expressed in the market place. This is in contrast to conditions in the totalitarian states where resources are allocated by administrative mandate. Closely allied to the freedom of allocation in our economy is the factor of *consumer's choice*. In our system, the consumer is free to make a choice—to buy or not to buy—and when the decision to buy is made, the consumer may choose from the products of many producers. The success of the producer is contingent upon his ability to detect and meet the needs and desires of the consumer. At the same time, the producer is free to attempt to influence the consumer to prefer his product. The avenue of influence is a two-way street; but it suffices to say that the producer, in the long run, must deliver a product that satisfies a need if he is to survive competition. The role of consumer's choice is further intensified as a result of the fact that we normally live in a *buyers' market*. A *buyers' market* for a product is said to exist when, at a given point, there is more of the product available than that amount required to meet immediate demand. Conversely, a *sellers' market* exists when there is not enough of a product available to meet the immediate demand. Today, if one wants to purchase a television set, he may pick and choose from a countless variety of models, sizes, and prices. This is characteristic of a buyers' market. In a sellers' market, one would consider himself fortunate to find a television set available and, consequently, would not be inclined to express very much choice. The privilege of consumer's choice is fundamental in a free-enterprise system.

Our system permits one to enter whatever business or profession he chooses as long as his choice does not conflict with laws established for the preservation and protection of society. He is free to direct his efforts toward making a profit, assuming ethical conduct and operations within the scope of existing laws. It is in the area of profit-making that some may feel that restrictions contrary to the spirit of free enterprise are encountered. In this respect, high taxation is a principal factor in limiting individual profit. However, the demands for public service are great, and the cost of national defense has become a necessity and not just a matter of policy. All in all, we have preserved many of the virtues of free enterprise while having to give up some of its privileges. At the same time, it has been necessary to bring some aspects of the free-enterprise system under the supervision of regulatory bodies in order to safeguard the system.

A Changing Economy

The great depression of the early 1930's marked a turning point in the American economy. The role of government in business increased with the measures taken to relieve economic conditions. There soon followed the impetus of World War II and the industrial expansion that has always characterized periods of war. The postwar period has found the economy operating at a high level and under the influence of both governmental and economic philosophies vastly different from those operative prior to the 1930's. The standard of living enjoyed by the American people has risen rapidly. The rise may be attributed to many factors: the stimulus of war and continued defense preparation, changing economic and political philosophy, and the normal progress expected from an advancing technology are among the reasons. Perhaps one of the most significant changes from a business viewpoint has been the change in the distribution of income. A leveling in the distribution of income has seen the postwar emergence of a huge middle class and the opening up of vast markets for a variety of goods previously considered within reach of only the more well-to-do citizens. The explosive growth of the American economy can be noted in Figure 1-1. The *Gross National Product* may be roughly described as the total value of all final goods and services produced by the nation's economy. Since 1940 the economy has grown at a rate, and achieved a level, that would have amazed our forefathers. By looking ahead as shown in Figure 1-2, the growth potential is reflected in expected increases to 1975 for gross national product, per capita income, labor force, and population.

The industrial economy has been characterized by the development of large-scale enterprise, and this may have marked the decline of competition in the traditional sense, but accompanying the trend to bigness has been an increase in regulatory measures by the government. A development of particular note in our changing economy has been the growth of powerful organizations representing various interest groups. Especially prominent has been the growth and development of organized labor. The rapid development of education and communications has resulted in an increased ability on the part of the masses to express themselves through the democratic processes. The effect of a more extensive democracy has made itself felt in our economic policies. An example of this is the popular demand that the federal government take action to prevent severe fluctuations in the business cycle. The future of our economy may well rest upon the ability of the masses to realize that authority carries with it the counterpart of responsibility.

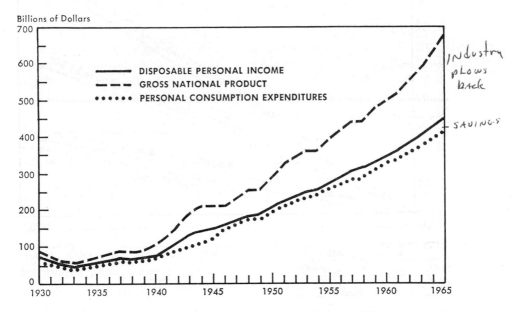

Fig. 1–1. This chart shows the rapid expansion of the American economy, 1930–1965. (U.S. Department of Commerce, Bureau of the Census.)

The possible influence of technological developments upon the business environment of the future staggers one's imagination. New sources of power and new and improved methods of transportation and communication will come into use. Electronic computers have achieved revolutionary accomplishments. The business environment is changing and presenting new problems and new challenges year by year.

THE WIDE RANGE OF INDUSTRY

A Diversified Economy

The United States has been among the more fortunate nations with an abundance of resources, both human and material. Sources of power in terms of water power, coal, and petroleum have been fundamental to our industrial growth. An ample supply of iron ore combined with a ready supply of coal permitted the development of the world's greatest steel industry. Although the United States continues as the leading producer of steel, there is concern over the possible depletion of the

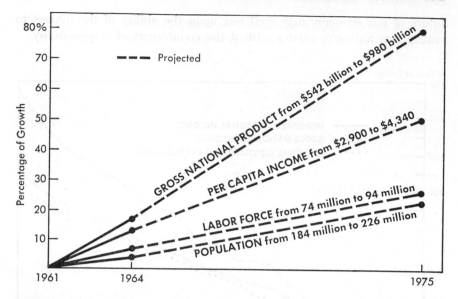

Fig. 1–2. Expected growth of the American economy, 1964–1975. (Courtesy, *Newsweek* magazine, June 14, 1965, p. 87; source data, Department of Commerce and Council of Economic Advisers.)

sources of ore. As the economy has grown more complex, there has arisen a demand for an ever widening variety of mineral products. Thus, we have grown more dependent upon other nations to supply some of the items of which we are deficient.

Table 1–1 shows a breakdown of total employment into major occupational groups by sex. The breakdown is by the type of work performed and thus cuts across many specific industries. We are accustomed to use the term *industry* in several ways: we speak of all business activity collectively as industry, while we also refer to individual lines of endeavor as industries. Accordingly, we speak of the agricultural industries, the manufacturing industries, the distributive industries, and so on through the list. Our industries continually undergo changes as technology and social customs change, and employment frequently shifts from one industry to another. Space limitations will permit only a few references at this point.

Agriculture. At one time the economy of the United States was predominantly agricultural; however, the twentieth century has seen a growing shift of the population away from farms and into non-farm employment. In 1910 approximately 13,555,000 persons were employed on farms. By 1940 this figure had declined to 10,979,000; by 1950 to

9,342,000; and by 1965 it was down to 6,518,000.[4] This does not imply a decline in the production of agricultural commodities. Improvements in machinery, fertilization, and the science of farming in general have kept production high while demanding less labor. The shift of population away from the farm has seen the decline of the family-type farm and the growth of large-scale commercial farming.

Manufacturing. Beginning with the industrial revolution, manufacturing has experienced growth and has gained relative to agriculture. By 1965 manufacturing was three times as important as farming (in terms of employment).[5] More recently, manufacturing employment rose from 15,051,000 in 1942 to an average of 17,035,000 in 1965. Average weekly earnings in manufacturing rose from $44.39 per week in

Table 1–1. U.S. Major Occupation Groups by Sex

Major occuption group Week of July 12–18, 1964	Both sexes	Male	Female	Per cent distribution		
				Both sexes	Male	Female
Professional technical and kindred workers	7,897	5,236	2,663	10.9	10.9	11.0
Farmers and farm managers	2,488	2,336	153	3.4	4.9	.6
Managers, officials and proprietors, except farm	7,471	6,386	1,085	10.3	13.3	4.5
Clerical and kindred workers	10,970	3,423	7,547	15.2	7.1	31.1
Sales workers	4,553	2,781	1,772	6.3	5.8	7.3
Craftsmen, foremen and kindred workers	9,364	9,138	225	12.9	19.0	.9
Operatives and kindred workers	13,140	9,483	3,657	18.1	19.7	15.1
Private household workers .	2,285	70	2,215	3.2	.1	9.1
Service workers, except private household	7,088	3,290	3,797	9.8	6.8	15.7
Farm laborers and foremen	2,970	1,947	1,023	4.1	4.0	4.2
Laborers, except farm and mine	4,179	4,073	106	5.8	8.5	.4
Total employed	72,405	48,164	24,241	100.0	100.0	100.0

SOURCE: Bureau of Labor Statistics (estimates in thousands of persons 14 years old and over).

1945 to approximately $99.38 per week in 1963.[6] New inventions, improved transportation, and a growing population have been factors in the growth of manufacturing. As a result of increased mechanization and improved technology, the productivity of manufacturing has in-

[4] Economic Research Service, Department of Agriculture, Washington, D.C., 1964.
[5] Economic Research Service, Department of Agriculture, and Bureau of Labor Statistics, U.S. Department of Labor, Washington, D.C., 1964.
[6] Bureau of Labor Statistics, U.S. Department of Labor, Washingon, D.C., 1964.

creased much faster than the rate of growth of employment in manufacturing would indicate. Table 1–2 shows the growth of employment in non-agricultural establishments and enables a comparison of manufacturing with other areas.

Distribution of Goods and Services. A significant development in our economy has been the increasing proportion of employed persons engaged in the distribution of goods and services. It is now estimated that at least one out of every four persons employed is engaged in some manner in the marketing processes. Further inspection of Table 1–2 will show that employment in wholesale and retail trade has grown rapidly over recent decades. This represents a long-term trend. Between 1900 and 1950, the number of people engaged in the production of goods increased at a slower rate than those engaged in retail and wholesale trade.[7] This situation may be explained by the fact that the distributive industries have not been able to mechanize and use mass productive techniques as successfully as the production industries. Also, the consumer has demanded more and more in the way of services from the marketing system. The tendency of industry to specialize and locate in areas where conditions are favorable to the type of industry has increased the distance between the producer and consumer, and this has added to distribution costs.

Other Industries. Employment in mining has shown a decline in recent years. This is partly due to the development of machines that replaced some of the manual labor previously required. Also, the substitution of fuels such as petroleum and natural gas for coal has had an effect. The construction industry has grown as a result of the postwar boom in family formations. Higher standards of living have also been a factor in a rising demand for better housing. Industrial building has grown in response to an expanding economy. Transportation, public utilities, and other service industries have reflected the growth of the economy and growing demands on the part of the consuming public. Accompanying the growth of the past two decades has been a steady increase in the number of persons employed in government services.

Specialization of Management

The great variety found in the types of industries, coupled with the trend toward the large-scale enterprise, have contributed to an ever increasing amount of specialization in the functions of production and distribution. We have seen how the shoemaker in colonial days dealt

---

[7] Historical Statistics of the U.S.—Colonial Times to 1957 (U.S. Department of Commerce), Chapter D.

Table 1–2. Employees in Non-agricultural Establishments (Annual Average), by Industry Group, 1919–1964 (in thousands)

Year or month	Total	Mining	Contract construction	Manu-facturing	Transportation and public utilities	Wholesale and retail trade	Finance, insurance, and real estate	Service and miscellaneous	Government
1940	32,376	925	1,294	10,985	3,038	6,750	1,502	3,681	4,202
1945	40,394	836	1,132	15,524	3,906	7,314	1,497	4,241	5,944
1950	45,222	901	2,333	15,241	4,034	9,386	1,919	5,382	6,026
1951	47,849	929	2,603	16,393	4,226	9,742	1,991	5,576	6,389
1952	48,825	898	2,634	16,632	4,248	10,004	2,069	5,730	6,609
1953	50,232	866	2,623	17,549	4,290	10,247	2,146	5,867	6,645
1954	49,022	791	2,612	16,314	4,084	10,235	2,234	6,002	6,751
1955	50,675	792	2,802	16,882	4,141	10,535	2,335	6,274	6,914
1956	52,408	822	2,999	17,243	4,244	10,858	2,429	6,536	7,277
1957	52,904	828	2,923	17,174	4,241	10,886	2,477	6,749	7,626
1958	51,423	751	2,778	15,945	3,976	10,750	2,519	6,811	7,893
1959	53,404	732	2,960	16,675	4,011	11,127	2,594	7,115	8,190
1960	54,370	712	2,885	16,796	4,004	11,391	2,669	7,392	8,520
1961	54,224	672	2,816	16,327	3,903	11,337	2,731	7,610	8,828
1962	55,841	652	2,909	16,859	3,903	11,582	2,798	7,949	9,188
1963	57,174	634	3,029	17,035	3,913	11,865	2,866	8,297	9,535
March .	55,714	616	2,556	16,756	3,847	11,497	2,825	8,076	9,541
1964, March (prel.) .	57,375	610	2,756	17,054	3,885	11,921	2,895	8,414	9,840

SOURCE: Department of Labor, Bureau of Labor Statistics.

directly with his customer. We also know that as the shoemaker's market expanded, he found it difficult to handle both the production and selling functions. In order to fully capitalize upon his skill as a producer, the selling function was transferred to merchants who could specialize in that activity. The division of production and selling has been followed by further division along functional lines.

The skill required in the formation and use of capital has led to the administration of *finance* as a specialized function. The modern factory is a highly specialized operation designed to accommodate the production processes. The function of *industrial management* utilizes specialists from engineering, business administration, and other physical and social sciences. Closely associated with industrial management are those devoting their efforts to *personnel management and labor relations.* Our complex industrial society needs the services of the student of human relations. If we are to continue to produce goods, they must be distributed; and this calls for the skills of the *marketing* specialists. Sales, advertising, and marketing research demand persons of education and experience. The departments of *transportation and traffic management* concentrate upon the movement of goods and thus play a vital role in distribution. The departments of *accounting and statistical management* supply management with a flow of data essential to the decision-making processes. Thus, it can be seen that with the growth of business enterprise and the emergence of the large-scale firm, the overall management job has been subdivided to make use of particular talents and skills.

Professional Management

As may be seen from the foregoing pages, there are many problems of management that are common to all firms irrespective of the type of business. In areas such as finance, industrial and personnel management, marketing, transportation, accounting, and statistics, the problems—especially those encountered at the higher levels of management—tend to be similar. This has given rise to the concept of *professional management;* basically, the idea that a person trained and experienced in the management of one firm can, with some indoctrination, transfer his services to another firm in a different line and still perform as a valuable executive. The shifts of management personnel from one company to another, often in unrelated lines, would seem to support the validity of the concept. The emergence of the professional manager has advanced the teaching of business management in colleges and universities. If business firms have sufficient problems in common to permit executives to shift from one to another, it would seem to indicate that certain *principles of management* exist and that these principles can be discovered and successfully taught.

The foregoing does not imply that experience is no longer an important part of management. There is still no substitute for on-the-job experience, but the experience gained in one company may enable the executive to perform creditably in another. The old idea that an executive had to "grow up in a business" and understand all of its technology to be successful as a manager has declined in recent years.

Your Career in Business

This chapter has introduced the scope of business activity. The diversity of what we commonly refer to as "business" is immense. There is something in the world of business to challenge the ability, interest, ambition, and spirit of every individual. Unfortunately, many young people enter some phase of business without understanding what is involved. The fact that jobs in business cover such a wide area of activity makes it a formidable task to choose the right one. Young people are advised to proceed with caution in picking a particular career in business. It is a major purpose of books such as this to assist the student in gaining some insight into our system of business enterprise and the activities involved in its management.

The proper education for one planning a career in business is still a matter of much debate. The techniques and philosophies of business management change, and schools alter their curriculum in business to reflect such changes. It is perhaps safe to point out that a sound education for a career in business is more a matter of capable teachers and interested students than it is a matter of course titles or textbooks. Our entire concept of education for business has come in for some critical examination. This is a healthy development, and much may be gained from self-examination.

TOPICS FOR DISCUSSION

1. What do you feel would be a definition of an "economy"?
2. Prior to the Civil War, businessmen concentrated on what major problem areas?
3. In the United States, anyone who owns or can accumulate the necessary financial resources can start a business firm. To survive, the American entrepreneur must meet the test of economics. What is this test?
4. How do you distinguish between the terms *entrepreneur* and *executive?*
5. Do you feel that the tremendous size of some firms has contributed to the increasing difficulty of business management?
6. How much profit is a business firm entitled to make?
7. The field of retailing is characterized by a high failure rate. It has been suggested that the government should establish certain requirements that a person would have to meet in order to open a retail store. Do you feel that this should be a function of government?
8. Are certain business activities such as production management, selling, and advertising entitled to be referred to as professions?
9. What do you feel will be the effects of increasing automation on the United States economy?
10. Will the businessman of tomorrow have to be more specialized or less specialized than his present counterpart?

CASE 1–1

CHANGES IN THE AMERICAN ECONOMY

Over the past twenty-five years, we have witnessed remarkable changes in the American economy. Our population has increased rapidly during this period of time. In 1940, the population was 132,594,000; in 1950, it was up to 152,271,000; and, by 1964, it was up to 192,119,000. Our gross national income has increased while the share of that income taken for taxes has also increased. However, our disposable personal income (personal income less tax and non-tax payments), stated in dollars current for each date shown, has increased at a remarkable rate. In 1940, our disposable personal income was $76,100,000,000; in 1950, it was $207,700,000,000; and, in 1964, it was $431,800,000,000.

As can be seen from the above statistics, our population and our total disposable personal income have been increasing. In order to determine the extent, if any, to which the standard of living of the American people has improved since 1940, we need to know something of the way in which the purchasing power of the dollar has changed during the period of time in question. The Statistical Abstract of the United States, from which the foregoing figures were taken, also tells us that the purchasing power of the dollar has changed. For instance, using the years 1957–1959 as a base (1957–1959 equal to $1.00), we find that the purchasing power of the 1940 dollar was $2.05; the 1950 dollar, $1.19; and the 1964 dollar was worth 93 cents when compared to the average dollar for 1957–1959.

1. From an analysis of the above data, would you conclude that the standard of living of the American people in the present year is higher or lower than in 1940?

2. Can you think of problems that may arise from the changing value of the American dollar?

SELECTED REFERENCES

Allen, L. A. *The Management Profession.* New York: McGraw-Hill Book Co., 1964.
Bach, G. L. *Economics: An Introduction to Analysis and Policy.* 4th ed. Englewood Cliffs, N.J.: Prentice-Hall, Inc., 1963.
Kemmerer, D. L., and C. C. Jones. *American Economic History.* New York: McGraw-Hill Book Co., 1959.
Redford, E. S. *American Government and the Economy.* New York: The Macmillan Co., 1965.

2

Economics and the Study
of Business Enterprise

ECONOMICS AND BUSINESS

In very general terms, we may think of *economics* as a body of
knowledge that deals with the creation and appropriation of goods and
services in the never ending process of satisfying human wants. Mankind has always been concerned with the problems of allocating limited
resources in an effort to meet what often appear to be unlimited needs.
The economist is involved in studying theories relating to demand and
supply relationships, and in studying and working with a wide range
of activities that often begin in theoretical analysis and terminate in
application. The scope of the study of economics is very broad, and
students of the subject find it practical to concentrate on divisions of the
subject. Thus, there are economists who specialize in monetary problems, pricing theory, labor problems, international trade, and many
other subject areas. Although the businessman usually does not have
the depth of training possessed by the professional economist, it is
essential that he have a general knowledge of many phases of the subject in order that he may draw upon this as background knowledge.
The methodology and discipline encountered in the study of economics
can become valuable parts of the businessman's education.

The development of economics as an area of study led eventually to a
division of the subject into courses of a theoretical nature and those
of a more applied nature. Courses in business administration evolved

more directly from the study of economics than from any other area. It was not until comparatively recent times that courses such as marketing, management, finance, and transportation emerged as independent study courses. Even today many schools offer such courses as a part of a general economics program.

THE DEVELOPMENT OF ECONOMIC THOUGHT

Influence of the Social Order

As one studies the evolution of economic thinking, he realizes the great extent to which the economist is influenced by the world in which he lives. Economic theories have grown out of man's effort to explain how he obtains a living—or more properly perhaps, to explain why he doesn't achieve a better living. In an age when government was oppressive in preventing the people from obtaining the goods and services desired, economic doctrine advocating the freedom of commerce from interference developed. In a later age when man had created the conditions conducive to the business cycle, economic doctrine advocating government intervention appeared on the scene. Many of our economic theories that were pertinent when introduced have fallen by the wayside as technology, education, and other achievements marked the road of progress. It is impossible to include here more than a passing reference to the great ideas characterizing the evolution of our economic thinking.

Mercantilism

Among the earliest of the economic doctrines was that of mercantilism. This term has been used to describe the economy of countries such as England and France in the sixteenth and seventeenth centuries. In brief, the advocates of mercantilism viewed the nation as an extension of the individual merchant. Thus, the nation, like the merchant, could become successful only by taking in more by selling than is paid out through buying. In practice, the system attempted by various regulations to maintain an excess of exports over imports and to collect the difference in the form of precious metals that could be used in building up the power and prestige of the state.

The doctrine of mercantilism promoted the welfare of manufacturing at the expense of labor, agriculture, and the colonies. Wages were suppressed in order to offer favorable prices in competing for foreign markets. The prices of agricultural products were held down in order to furnish food as cheaply as possible to low-paid laborers. The goods that could be produced and traded by the colonies were restricted to avoid competition with the mother country. The suppression of manufacturing in the American colonies during the early period is an example of the policy. The doctrine of mercantilism engendered powerful opposition through its suppression of large segments of the economy. This opposition led to the formulation of economic theories counter to the mercantilistic principle.

The Physiocrats

About the middle of the eighteenth century, a group of French statesmen and philosophers developed what is often referred to as the first complete and self-contained view of the economic order as a whole. The doctrine developed by this group became known as *physiocracy*.[1] The physiocrats maintained that all wealth was derived from the land. Without food, fiber, wood, minerals, and stone, man could not exist. The husbandman was thus the only valid producer. It was held that the husbandman produced a surplus above his own needs, and from this surplus he could commission the craftsmen whose services he needed. But the craftsmen were entitled only to the amount necessary to satisfy their wants; they could not accumulate wealth unless the state intervened in their behalf. Propertyless wage earners could receive only that which was necessary to keep them alive. The theory maintained that the more intelligent and thrifty farmers would save their surplus and buy up the land of the less industrious. The less industrious would then have no recourse but to work for the more industrious and would be entitled to wages only to the extent of subsistence.

The physiocrats viewed the above doctrine as being in conformity with "natural law." Any intervention in the working of the natural law was considered undesirable. It was from the teachings of the physiocrats that the concept of laissez faire emerged. This concept viewed the laws of nature as a regulating device and opposed the idea of government interference. The theory emphasized the landowner as the primary factor in the economy and reduced manufacturing, distribution, and other functions to a subsidiary role as facilitating agencies. Naturally, the physiocrats were opposed to mercantilism, which had exalted manufacturing at the expense of agriculture. While the doctrine of the physiocrats never prevailed to a great extent in actual practice, it did mark the decline of mercantilism and paved the way for the emergence of what was to be known as the *classical theory*.

---

[1] Overton Taylor, *A History of Economic Thought*. New York: McGraw-Hill Book Co., 1960. This is one of many texts that the student may consult in pursuing the development of economic thought.

The Classical Theory

The founder of the classical school of economics (i.e., the group who developed what has become known as classical theory) was Adam Smith. Smith's famous book, *The Wealth of Nations,* appeared in 1776 and is regarded as a milestone in economic thought. In the book, Smith opposed the doctrine of mercantilism. He held that the doctrine placed the interest of the consumer secondary to that of the producer. This he viewed as wrong, since consumption was the sole end and purpose of all production. He presented a strong case for a policy of free trade between nations—indicating that if trade within a nation is desirable, it could be just as desirable between nations. Smith accepted some of the doctrine of the physiocrats but stopped short of their extreme positions. He thought agriculture to be of prime importance, but he also saw industry and trade as being productive. He also did not go as far as the physiocrats in restricting the role of government. While undoubtedly adhering to the principle of laissez faire, he ascribed to government the responsibility of public works, education, and the protection of foreign commerce. It was the duty of government to provide for national defense, but Smith thought a strong industry to be a basic element in defense and felt that the government should have regard for the economy.

Other economists contributed to the development and refinement of the classical theory. Ricardo, Malthus, John Stuart Mill, and Jean Baptiste Say were among those whose contributions stand out. In brief, the classical theory embraces the concept that man's self-interest is a guiding force. Man's economic behavior is then generalized in the statement of certain principles or laws that are regarded as being universally applicable. The classical economists, as did the physiocrats, place strong reliance upon the concept of natural law. There is the feeling that government should not intervene in economic life. The belief in the ownership of private property and the freedom of the individual to maximize his gains are fundamental to the classical theory. The classical economists constructed a theory centering around cause and effect relationships. Through a process of assumption, conditions were established to permit a pattern of logical reasoning. A weakness in the system derived from the fact that the assumed conditions underlying economic relationships tended to remove the doctrine far afield from reality.[2] The classical theory was to survive for many years, but eventually other theories emerged to challenge the classicists.

[2] Dudley Dillard, *The Economics of John Maynard Keynes* (Englewood Cliffs, N.J.: Prentice-Hall, Inc., 1948), Chap. 2. This is a good summary of the criticisms of the classical theory.

The Socialists

Before continuing to trace the main stream of the development of economic ideas, it is desirable to consider certain social and economic thinking that influenced these developments. Initially, the doctrine of socialism did not come into practice on a wide scale. In comparatively recent years, various types of socialism have become predominant in certain economies. As classical theory merged into the neoclassical period, socialism was perhaps more active as a stimulant for change than as a threat to replace existing systems.

It is difficult to summarize socialism as an economic doctrine. The term has been applied to numerous systems, some of which are not at all alike. The term has been, and continues to be, confused with communism. The countries now described as communistic are perhaps more accurately described as examples of national socialism. Generally, socialism is thought of as referring to a collective system whereby the means of production (capital goods) and the operation of such production facilities are controlled by the government. Thus, a country may be partially, or completely, socialized.

Karl Marx is considered to have been the leading exponent of modern socialism. Marx drew heavily upon classical theory to show the exploitation of the worker. While the physiocrats saw land as the principal source of value, Marx saw labor as the principal source of value. The classical theory had contended, along with the physiocrats, that labor under the "natural law" would derive only its subsistence. Marx contended that the true value of a product was the value of the labor that went into its manufacture. When the employer sold the product to the consumer, he was receiving the true value of labor; but since he paid the worker a minimum subsistence wage, the difference in what the worker receives and the consumer pays is a surplus appropriated by the employer—or capitalist—as Marx contended. This he saw as exploitation of the worker. The instruments of production (equipment, etc.) used by the worker were equal in value to the labor that went into their production, and these instruments should be owned by the worker. In short, Marx denied that the capitalist had a legitimate economic function.

Marx predicted that eventually there would exist a small group of capitalists on one hand, and on the other hand would be the masses of the propertyless working class—or proletariat. As a result of the abuses of the capitalists, the proletariat would revolt and come into power. The doctrine of Marx did not devote much attention to the manner in which society would operate after the proletariat came into power. He seemed to feel that once the capitalistic system was replaced, universal happiness would automatically prevail.

The predictions of Marx have not come to pass. He foresaw an increasing tendency toward the exploitation of labor. Changes in technology, and in economic thinking, have resulted in the continuous improvement of the state of the working class. The standard of living enjoyed by the average American worker would undoubtedly prove both startling and unbelievable to Marx. The fact that Marx did not concern himself greatly with a plan for society after the rise of the proletariat has particular significance for us at this time. In the countries where the doctrine of Marx provided the spur for revolution, the end result has been the formation of a totalitarian state with the suppression of the masses in social and economic matters.

The Neoclassical Period

The economists of the nineteenth century were predominantly concerned with a refinement of the classical theory. The writings of Socialists such as Marx were leveling attacks against the classical theory and were prompting its adherents to re-examine certain precepts. The neoclassicists led by Alfred Marshall and others worked to buttress the doctrine against major criticisms. The belief in the finality of "natural law" was tempered, and other aspects of the theory were admittedly subject to limitations. All in all, the neoclassicists clung to the basic elements of classical theory and concerned themselves with certain refinements of the doctrine.

The Institutionalists

Among the many theories of economic behavior, that of institutional economics should be mentioned. The institutionalists rejected the concept of natural law and developed a doctrine that stressed the influence of social forces on man's economic actions. It was felt that institutions such as private property, monopoly, and production restraints were often used to the disadvantage of the nation as a whole. This made it essential that other institutions such as labor unions, consumer organizations, and regulatory bodies emerge to counter these forces. The institutionalists viewed the economic system as the product of the organizations and social forces prevailing. Institutions were considered products of their time and history; they evolve and expand or contract and die from the impact of other institutions. While the classicists saw the economic system as a product of natural law and thus not in need of social control, the institutionalists saw the economic system as a product of social action and thus subject to social direction.

Keynesian Economics

The classical theory, with its many refinements, presented a neat package in logical analysis; but critics continued to point out that the network of assumptions upon which the theory rested tended to remove it from all reality. Despite refinements, the belief in natural law remained a primary tenet of the theory. This precluded any action by the government that might be termed significant interference with the workings of the economy. The periods of recession in England and elsewhere following World War I brought increasing criticism of the hands-off policy of the classicists.

The blow that was to stagger classical theory came from a British economist, John Maynard Keynes. In 1936, Keynes published his *General Theory of Employment, Interest and Money.* Keynes renounced the classical doctrine as sterile because of the assumptions upon which it was based, and he proposed to develop a theory for which unrealistic assumptions would be unnecessary.[3] The theory developed by Keynes, with certain additions and refinements added by his followers, has in many quarters replaced classical doctrine and has come to be considered a more realistic explanation of certain aspects of economic behavior.

A major element of the Keynesian theory was the injection of government into the workings of the economy. In depression, when private business will not invest because of a poor economic outlook, government can step in and invest funds. A significant part of the Keynesian theory was the contention that money invested was subject to a *multiplier* effect; i.e., money invested will create income in an amount several times that of the original investment. In depression, government can invest because it does not have to earn a profit. The money so invested, and subject to the multiplier effect, will stimulate the economy. Improved business conditions will in turn stimulate private investors to again become active.

Many of the plans of our own government to prevent depression —such as standby plans for public works—are in harmony with the Keynesian theory. The Keynesian theory is often associated with a depression economy since much of his doctrine concerned measures calculated to relieve economic depression. In times of depression, Keynes advocated that a government should spend more than it collected if needed; he saw no calamity in deficit financing. On the other hand, in times of inflation, Keynes advocated that the government collect more than it spent, thus having a surplus. Unfortunately, many who claim

[3] *Ibid.*

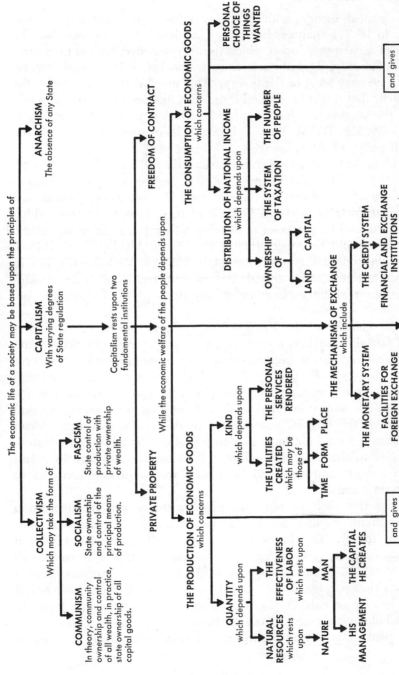

Fig. 2–1. A summary of economic systems, with emphasis on functions in a capitalistic society. (By permission from *Dictionary of Economics*, by H. S. Sloan and A. J. Zurcher. Copyright, 1953, Barnes & Noble, Inc., New York.)

24

to be disciples of Keynes recommend his measures in depression but conveniently forget his recommendations for action during inflation. In summary, however, one may say that the theories of Keynes in one form or another are predominant in much of the economic thinking of today throughout the free world.

ECONOMIC SYSTEMS

Systems Are Mixed

A problem in discussing economic systems is the difficulty in citing clearly defined examples. Any given system is likely to have characteristics borrowed from another. Capitalism has borrowed from socialism and vice versa. The situation is further confused by the fact that the name applied to a given economic system may not be truly indicative of the type of system existing. An effort to understand the economic system prevailing in a country calls for an analysis of the internal organization and functioning of the system. In this section of the text, an effort will be made to summarize the outstanding features of some of the more common systems that have existed, or are at present active. Bear in mind that the systems described are not likely to be found existing in a pure state, rather they are likely to be modified by the adoption of features from other systems. The student is urged to study the diagram shown in Figure 2-1. This diagram summarizes major systems with detailed attention paid to the capitalistic system. For convenience we may group the collective systems for discussion and then discuss our own system.

The Collective Systems

Collective systems stressing state ownership, or strict control, of the means of production are exemplified by *communism* and *socialism*. These terms are often confused and used to describe certain systems erroneously. For example, the system of the Soviet Union is often referred to as communism when it is perhaps more accurately described as a type of state socialism. Communism is correctly defined as a system advocating government or community ownership of all wealth. Rights to private property are abolished. Theoretically, in a communist system, each should produce according to his ability and consume according to his need. This system, which basically denies the right of an individual to profit from superior ability or effort, has never successfully operated for any significant period of time. Apparently, the conflict with human nature is too much to overcome.

Socialism may also be defined as the collective ownership and operation of the means of production.[4] This usually implies government ownership. As generally used, the term *socialism* describes a system that stops short of the communal existence inherent in communism. The individual is permitted rights of personal property, and individual initiative can be rewarded. Emphasis is on the state ownership of basic production facilities such as mines, manufacturing, and transportation. In Russia, state ownership has extended to include the land and to control the system for distributing goods as well as production.

In some respects, various collective systems have appealed to those who sought to improve the lot of mankind through encouraging cooperation and sacrifice for the common good. Often those of an idealistic nature, who are attracted to a seemingly moral and desirable endeavor, are victimized by those who proceed to use them as a means of gaining personal power. Historically, socialistic ventures seem to exhibit a tendency toward terminating in a system of dictatorial control in which the people lose their individual freedom without receiving the material blessings promised.

Capitalism

In its pure state, capitalism is a system stressing the private ownership of property, including the means of production. The freedom of the individual to engage in economic activities for the purpose of making a profit is emphasized. Government interference with economic activity is considered justified only to the extent of protecting the public from abuse. The system draws heavily upon the concept of natural law as a regulator of economic behavior. Since capital goods are owned by individuals, there is incentive for the accumulation of funds to purchase these goods. In the capitalistic system, the accumulation of funds is an economic function and deserving of reward.

It is doubtful that an economy operating under the doctrine of pure capitalism could be found today. The United States, considered the bulwark of the capitalistic system, could accurately be described as an example of modified capitalism. As will be seen in Chapter 3, it became necessary early in our history to place restrictions upon certain economic activities that grew out of a laissez faire type of capitalism. Through a succession of wars and economic crises, we have seen the role of government become more and more interwoven into the web of our economic life. The role of government has expanded in response to the increasing demands by the people for public service and security

---

[4] H. S. Sloan and A. J. Zurcher, *A Dictionary of Economics* (3rd ed.; New York: Barnes and Noble, Inc., 1962), p. 110. This book, available in paperback, provides a means of quick reference for many of the terms that the beginning student may encounter.

from economic uncertainties. Also, the government has ventured into the ownership of some of the means of production, notably in the electric-power field. These changes have all marked a departure from the original concepts of capitalism. Although changes have occurred, we have retained the primary elements of the system. The ownership of private property, the freedom to enter a calling of one's choice, and the freedom to earn a profit are still to be enjoyed. Especially significant is the fact that the resources of our nation are allocated largely on the basis of consumer choice.

ECONOMIC ANALYSIS

Studying Economic Behavior

Our economy may be compared to a complex machine consisting of many component parts. These parts may be thought of as "elements" such as demand, supply, price, cost, competition, monopoly, and similar factors. Economic analysis involves the study of the parts of our economy and the relationship of the parts to one another. Much of our economic behavior can be explained in terms of a cause-effect relationship. For example, a change in *demand* may influence the *supply* of the product, which in turn influences the *cost* of producing it. The relative degree of competition or monopoly present will have to be considered by the economist in analyzing these relationships.

In his study of economic behavior, the economist may focus his attention on the firm, the industry, or the entire economy as a whole. Economic analysis dealing with the firm, or industry, is referred to as *microeconomics*, while analysis dealing with national aggregates is termed *macroeconomics*. The classical economists tended to work under the assumption of perfect competition or complete monopoly and to concentrate upon the analysis of the firm and the industry. The economic behavior of the whole economy was then regarded as a projection of the behavior of the firms and industries therein. The more recent schools of economic thought have more or less rejected the approach of micro-analysis on the grounds that the assumptions necessary to such analysis impose severe limitations. They prefer the approach of macroanalysis —the study of the behavior of aggregates—as being more representative of the true nature of the economy. Although it is true that our economy does not exemplify a model of perfect competition, competition does play a vital role in its functioning. There is still enough competition in our economy to justify an understanding of economic behavior as influenced by competition. It is not the purpose of this text to involve the student in the study of intricate economic relationships, but a few special cases will be cited as illustrative of the techniques used in economic analysis.

The Study of Demand

A basic area of economic analysis is the study of demand. The economist seeks to explain, measure, and forecast the demand for goods and services. In Figure 2–2 the solid line *D* shows the demand for the product of an industry under competitive conditions. Note that the line is a curve slanting to the right and downward. The vertical axis of the diagram reflects price, and the horizontal measures quantity. The fact that the curve slants to the right and downward means that different amounts will be taken off the market at different prices; i.e., generally speaking, as the price is lowered the quantity taken will increase. The dashed line *D'* shown in Figure 2–2 illustrates the type of demand faced by an individual seller in a competitive industry. Here the individual seller is faced by a single price regardless of the quantity that he may offer for sale. One of the conditions of a competitive market is that no individual seller will be able to influence price. Under the conditions illustrated, price becomes the only element of competition among buyers and sellers. Advertising and other aspects of sales promotion—often characterized as non-price competition—are ruled out through the as-

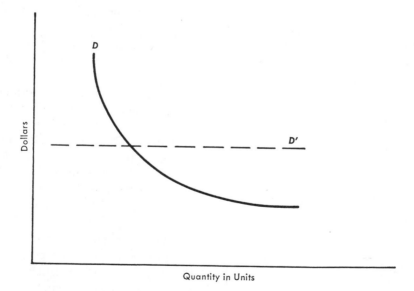

Quantity in Units

Fig. 2–2. The status of demand under competitive conditions. Curve *D* shows the demand curve faced by the industry while *D'* shows the demand curve faced by an individual seller.

sumptions upon which the analysis is based. At this point, the student will begin to see some of the objections to this type of analysis as a sole explanation of how the economy works.

The nature of the demand for a product or service may be *elastic* or *inelastic*. In Figure 2–3, the solid curve D pictures an elastic demand. At certain points along this curve, a small change in price will result in a proportionately larger quantity taken in the market. The demand for certain luxury items is said to be elastic; since people can do without the item, they will buy only when the price is considered favorable. The dashed curve in Figure 2–3 shows the demand as relatively inelastic. Here, changes in price do not have a great effect upon the quantity demanded. The demand for medicines might be described as inelastic since when needed they will be purchased within the total limits of the buyer's funds. Products having an inelastic demand are less subject to fluctuating sales as a result of business conditions.

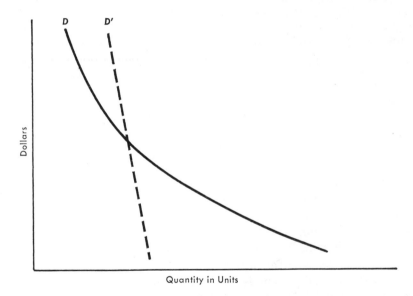

Fig. 2–3. Demand may be relatively elastic or inelastic. Curve D shows a relatively elastic demand while curve D′ shows a relatively inelastic demand.

Another aspect of demand analysis involves the different concepts of the term. When the economist refers to "demand," he is usually talking about a demand schedule. A demand schedule is represented by a curve that shows the different amounts that will be taken at the different prices. Thus, when the economist talks about a change in demand, he is referring to the movement of the entire demand curve. An increase in demand is reflected by a shifting of the curve to the right, as shown in Figure 2–4. Curve *D* shows the original demand for the product, and curve *D'* shows the demand after the increase. A decrease in demand would be shown by a corresponding shift of the curve to the left. Changes in the demand schedule occur as a result of changes in the buying and consuming habits of people. When large numbers of women began smoking cigarettes, the influence on industry demand would have been to shift the curve to the right. The increase in demand came about as a result of social change rather than a change in price.

When the quantity taken in the market changes as a result of a price change, we say there has been a change in *market demand*. The demand schedule remains the same, but the price-quantity relationship has moved from one place to another on the curve. A change in market demand may be identified by the fact that it occurs in response to a price change. If the demand for a product is *elastic*, market demand will increase with a lowering of price and decrease when prices are increased. Figure 2–5 shows a change in market demand as a result of a decrease in price.

Demand, Supply, and Price

In the foregoing discussion, we have seen that the demand curve for the product of an industry under competitive conditions is represented by a curve that slants right and downward. This implies that as price decreases, the market will be willing to take more of the product. The supply curve of an industry under competitive conditions appears as the converse of the demand curve. The supply curve would slant upward and to the right. The consumer will buy more if prices are lowered, but the supplier will supply more if the prices are raised. In a competitive market, these two opposing forces come into adjustment at a point where the amount the supplier is willing to supply is equal to the amount that the buyers are willing to take. This point of adjustment marks the price at which the goods will exchange hands. In Figure 2–6, the adjustment is marked at the point where the demand and supply curves intersect. At this point, *X* quantity will be exchanged at price *P*.

Cost, Price, and the Size of the Firm

Mass production and its corresponding economies have played a great role in our economy. The concept of mass production rests upon several factors—one being the principle that production costs are lowered if the production facility is fully utilized. Another principle has to do with the idea that a plant may be more efficient when operated at one

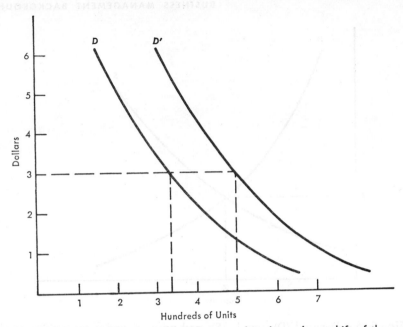

Fig. 2–4. An increase in schedule demand is shown by a shift of the curve to the right (note that price does not change, but more units are purchased).

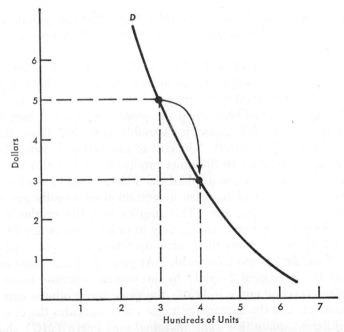

Fig. 2–5. A change in market demand (*D*) resulting from a change in price (note that a decrease in price has resulted in more units being demanded).

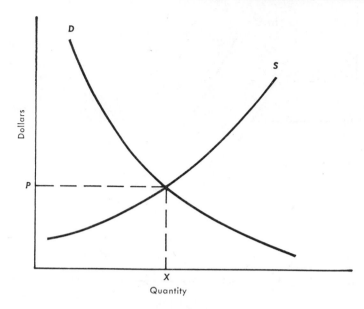

Fig. 2–6. Demand (D), supply (S), and price (P) under competitive conditions (an industry).

size than another. Both these principles imply that the producer should strive to determine the optimum size facility and then operate it at full capacity.

The full utilization of a facility involves a consideration of *fixed* and *variable* costs. Fixed costs are such items as rent, heat, light, certain taxes, etc. The fixed costs are not influenced by plant output; the light bill may be just as high when the plant is running at half capacity as when running at full capacity. Variable costs are those that vary directly with the plant output. The cost of raw materials would be likely to vary in direct relation to the units produced. It has also been found that total costs may decrease as plant size increases up to a certain point; thereafter, unit costs will increase as certain diseconomies are encountered from an increasing size. This implies that the producer is constantly seeking the optimum size facility in order to maximize his profits. Figure 2–7 shows a competitive firm operating at a point where the position of the firm is most favorable. At point *P,* the average unit cost curve (*AUC*) is tangent (equal) to the average revenue curve (*AR*). The average revenue curve indicates the price the producer can receive for his product, and the average unit cost curve indicates the cost of producing different quantities. The marginal cost curve (*MC*) shows the cost of producing each additional unit. In the diagram, the seller faces one price and, hence, his marginal revenue (*MR*) curve does not deviate from the average revenue curve. Marginal revenue is the revenue received from the last unit sold, and under conditions of monopoly this could vary as the monopolist may vary his price.

In Figure 2–7, the producer will operate at a point where his average unit cost and his marginal cost are equal and where they are both equal to his average revenue. This is possible because in the language

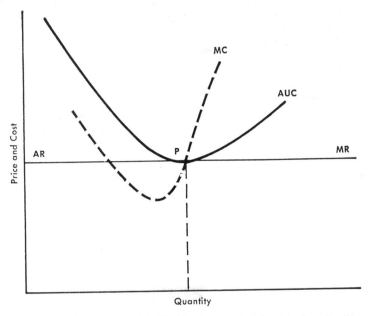

Fig. 2–7. The relationship of costs, price, and output for the firm under competitive conditions. Average unit cost (*AUC*), marginal cost (*MC*), marginal revenue (*MR*), and average revenue (*AR*) are in adjustment at the point (*P*) indicating the amount that the firm will produce and sell at the prevailing price.

of the economist, the producer's profit is contained in the definition of average unit cost. Under competitive conditions, the producer could not realize an average revenue higher than cost.

Monopoly

In economic analysis, a discussion of demand, supply, cost, and price under conditions of monopoly is developed paralleling that of the competitive situation. Since our purpose in this text is merely to illustrate some of the more common approaches in economic analysis, we will not develop a discussion of monopoly. The area of monopolistic competition in which the combined influences of competition and monopoly are studied is also an important area of analysis.

Macroanalysis

As previously indicated, many present-day economists feel that competitive analysis does not afford an adequate basis for understanding economic behavior. In an effort to find a more realistic approach, the trend has been toward analysis in the area of macroeconomics. Statistics dealing with aggregates of individuals and groups of commodities—as well as aggregates dealing with consumption, employment, and income—are utilized. The techniques of input-output analysis seek to understand the movement of factors in our economic life. Economic relationships such as investment and consumption are studied through the collection and analysis of statistical data rather than through the abstract logic featured in the classical approach. The student should be reminded that this does not imply that competitive analysis no longer has a place in economic theory; rather, it indicates that competitive analysis is now considered one of many approaches to be used in efforts to explain the functioning of our economy.

Forecasting

A major objective of the economist concerns his efforts to forecast economic behavior. Business, government, and the individual consumer would all like to know what to expect in the way of economic conditions. The operation of a business enterprise entails much in the way of advanced planning, and there is a constant search on the part of industry to determine the markets of the future, the labor supply, the state of raw material resources, etc. It is through the collection and analysis of data on the economy that we seek to pierce the veil of the future. The methodology and techniques of forecasting are becoming highly developed and will afford an area of interest to the advanced student in economics.

YOUR CAREER IN ECONOMICS

The Tools of Economics

At one time the study of economics was included in the area described as political economy. The economist still finds it difficult to study economic factors apart from the political environment in which they operate. In addition, the economist must draw heavily upon areas such as sociology and psychology in his efforts to interpret economic behavior.

Thus, the study of economics must rest heavily upon the foundation of a liberal education. More recently, with a growing emphasis on macro-economics, the economist needs a command of statistical techniques and methods of statistical interpretation. It is also apparent that modern economics has moved in the direction of applying mathematical analysis to the study of economic relationships. Mathematics has contributed in defining, through symbolism, certain economic relationships; and it has also facilitated the manipulation of variables to permit a type of analysis not widely used in previous years. While there are certain advantages in the mathematical approach, there are also limitations. In shaping data for mathematical analysis, it is often necessary to qualify through a web of assumption. This may take the economist back to the criticisms faced by his classical predecessors. Another objection to overreliance on the mathematical approach is that in making the subject so dependent, it moves it from the grasp of those not qualified in mathematics. It would perhaps be advisable for the student desiring to major in economics to take courses in mathematics up through the level of calculus.

Job Opportunities

The student with an undergraduate major in economics has a background often desired in areas such as banking, finance, and government service. Also, many industrial firms regard training in economics as a good background for the training offered by the company. The student who desires to become a professional economist will usually find it necessary to take graduate work, generally to the extent of acquiring the Ph.D. degree. The professional economist is widely employed in government service and also by many of the larger industrial firms. In private industry, he is concerned with business research, the analysis of statistical data, and planning and forecasting. There is also a strong demand for well-qualified teachers of economics in colleges and universities.

TOPICS FOR DISCUSSION

1. What revenue implications does the elasticity of demand concept have for the individual firm?

2. The economist in discussing demand theory considers separately consumer demand and producer demand. What distinction can be made between these two types of demand?

3. Could micro-economic theory also be called the theory of pricing and production?

4. Why do United States government agencies attempt to exercise control over monopolies?

5. Would the price system that exists in the United States be adaptable to the economic system of the Union of Soviet Socialist Republics?

6. "If left unchecked, competition tends to destroy itself." Explain this statement.

7. It is quite common for firms in an industry to sell similar products at the same or nearly the same price. Competition is said to take the form of *meeting the competitor's price but with a better product.* Is this a socially desirable form of competition?

8. If all manufacturers of steel quoted the same prices, would that be evidence of competition—or the lack of it?

9. Should a man who aspires to a political career study economics?

10. Mr. X, a rather critical observer, commented as follows: "Karl Marx thought that labor was the only source of value, and that the working man was entitled to receive a majority of the goods and services produced. He also thought that the working man should control the country. At the present time these conditions more nearly prevail in the United States than in any country since the dawn of history." Comment—agreeing or disagreeing.

CASE 2–1

A STUDY IN THE DEMAND FOR HAMILTON PENS

The Hamilton Pen Company was organized in 1955 to manufacture and market a new type of ball-point pen. The unique feature of the Hamilton pen was protected by a patent, and as a result the company has enjoyed some protection from the direct competition of other ball-point pens. The Hamilton pen was distributed through drugstores, variety stores, and supermarkets, and sold at retail for $2.49. In 1964, the company sold 900,000 pens at an average price to the dealer of $2.00 each. The cost of producing and marketing the pen amounted to $1.90 each; thus the firm realized a profit of 10 cents per pen, or a total of $90,000.

Executives of the Hamilton Pen Company were aware of the fact that, if volume could be increased, the per-unit cost of production could be lowered. Several suggestions were made for increasing the sales volume, including the suggestion that the price of the pen to the customer be reduced. The advocates of a price reduction argued that the demand for the pen was an elastic one, and that a reduction in price would produce an immediate increase in sales volume and profits. Executives of the company were uncertain regarding the elasticity of the demand for the product. Finally, it was decided that tests should be conducted in four market areas, to be designated as areas A, B, C, and D. The areas chosen for the tests were thought to be as nearly alike as possible. The tests were run simultaneously, and over a period of four months.

In area A, the pens were continued for sale at the customary price of $2.49 each. In area B, the price was reduced to $2.40; in area C, to $2.30; and in area D, to $2.25. A careful record was kept of sales in each of the four areas. While the market tests were going on, the production department made a careful analysis of the way in which increased volume might affect per-unit production costs. Studies were also made of the influence of volume on marketing costs. On the basis of information learned in the market tests, and from the cost studies made, executives were able to make the following estimates of price, cost, and volume relationships:

Hamilton Price to Dealers	Hamilton Cost Per Unit	Hamilton Volume to Dealers (Units)	Dealer's Price to Customer (Per Unit)
$2.00	$1.90	900,000	$2.49
1.95	1.85	1,000,000	2.40
1.89	1.80	1,250,000	2.30
1.85	1.77	1,350,000	2.25

The Hamilton Pen Company had never had any trouble in controlling the price at which its pens retailed. It was assumed that dealers would not resist the reduced retail price, in view of the plans of the company to reduce their prices to the dealers.

1. Assuming the above estimates of the relationship between price, cost, and volume to be correct, at what price should the Hamilton Pen be marketed?

2. Would you consider the demand for the Hamilton Pen to be elastic or inelastic? (You may need to draw a diagram showing the shape of the demand curve for Hamilton pens.)

SELECTED REFERENCES

Bach, G. L. *Economics: An Introduction to Analysis and Policy.* 4th ed. Englewood Cliffs, N.J.: Prentice-Hall, Inc., 1963.

Dillard, Dudley. *The Economics of John Maynard Keynes.* Englewood Cliffs, N.J.: Prentice-Hall, Inc., 1948.

Harris, C. Lowell. *The American Economy, Principles, Practices, and Policies.* Homewood, Ill.: Richard D. Irwin, Inc., 1962.

Morris, Ruby T. *Fundamentals of Economics.* New York: The Ronald Press Co., 1961.

Samuelson, Paul A. *Economics.* 6th ed. New York: McGraw-Hill Book Co., 1964.

3

Business Enterprise
and the Regulatory
Role of Government

HISTORICAL BACKGROUND

The early American colonies were settled by people who sought relief from oppression, often oppression at the hands of government. It is not surprising that the colonists were fearful of government, and, when it came time to frame a Constitution for the United States, powerful safeguards were formulated to protect the rights of the individual. While going to great length to assure individual rights, the Constitution was not conceived as a static document. Provisions for amendment were included in it, and this has made it possible for our Constitution to reflect changing philosophies of government.

In the early days of our country, the authority of the federal government was very restricted. With the passage of time, however, the authority of centralized government has been expanded through amendments to the Constitution and through judicial interpretation of existing laws. The expansion of centralized authority has not proceeded at a uniform rate; in fact, the greater part of federal regulatory activity has developed over the past four decades. It is felt that the majority of Americans agree on the need for some degree of regulatory activity in the area of business enterprise. The people are not agreed, however, as to what constitutes a desirable amount of regulation. Some seem to feel that the federal government has not moved rapidly enough, and far enough, in exercising control over commercial practices. Others are equally strong in the belief that we are overburdened with regulation, and that the strength and initiative of the economy are being throttled. Fortunately, we shall not be called upon to resolve the issue in this book.

The framers of the Constitution realized the need for federal control over interstate and foreign commerce. Accordingly, the states were restricted to the regulation of commerce within their borders. The provision giving the federal government control over commerce has been broadly interpreted, and perhaps this grant of power to the federal government may be said to be one of the most important found in the Constitution. The fact that individual states have been prohibited from levying tariffs and otherwise interfering with the flow of trade has been most important in the development of the United States as a strong nation.

In the early years of our nation's history, the role of government tended to promote an environment conducive to the development of private property and free enterprise. The federal and state governments exercised certain police powers concerned with health, safety, and morals. Police powers are generally reserved to the states, but the federal government has become more and more active in this area. The Civil War marked a turning point in the growth of a strong federal government. A major issue in the war involved the rights of the states versus a strong federal union. The victory of the federal forces strengthened the drive toward a strong centralized government. Following the war there occurred a period of rapid growth in business enterprise, and this was accompanied by a corresponding growth in the scope of government.

The growth of large-scale business enterprise marked a decline in competition and the development of certain monopoly abuses. This brought demands that the government should offer some protection against the excesses of large-scale enterprise. One authority remarks on the sentiment for regulatory action as follows:

As the more powerful business interests became even stronger, complaints were heard from farmers, small businessmen, workers, and consumers about the growing domination of large corporations. At first these weaker groups sought regulatory legislation at their state capitals, but soon they were hammering on the doors of Congress for railroad and antitrust legislation, arguing that only the Federal government was sufficiently strong . . . to deal with the national problems that the big corporations were beginning to create.[1]

[1] Marshall E. Dimock, *Business and Government* (3d ed.; New York: Holt, Rinehart & Winston, Inc., 1957), pp. 47–48.

Thus, it was by popular demand that the federal government found itself thrust more and more into a regulatory role. World War I, the depression of the 1930's, and World War II saw an ever increasing trend in the growth of government and its regulatory role. Apparently, the unrestricted competition characterizing the early days of our economy led to a situation in which competition itself was threatened, and it became necessary that government take a hand in preserving a healthy business environment.

The continued growth of democracy and the development of institutions through which the masses of the people exercise a voice are also factors influencing the increasing role of government in business. Critics of government intervention often lose sight of the fact that such intervention usually comes as a result of public demand. In a democracy, the government is the people and the regulatory role of government could not be imposed against the public will. This is not to say that regulatory measures are desirable simply because the public demands them. In fact, the demands made upon government may reflect a public that exercises authority without an accompanying sense of responsibility.

THE REGULATORY POWERS OF GOVERNMENT

The Government's Role

The role of government in its relationship with business may vary from a laissez faire policy of non-intervention to the other extreme whereby the government owns many of the facilities of production. As seen in an earlier chapter, in a socialistic state the government ownership of major production facilities is an inherent part of the system. In the United States, the private ownership of the facilities of production still predominates; however, in a few areas such as electric-power production, the federal government has ventured into the ownership of facilities. It has been contended that the government has ventured into ownership of facilities only in those cases in which private ownership would find the project undesirable, or where the capital outlay would be prohibitive to the private concern. The government ownership of electric-power facilities, such as the Tennessee Valley Authority, has been associated with flood control and other conservation measures. In the forthcoming development of atomic power, it is probable that the government will directly, or indirectly, play a major role. The size of the investment required and the risk inherent in the development of atomic power may restrict private development; however, private companies have expressed the intent to develop atomic power, and many of them are busily engaged in research.

At the present time, the role of government in business may be described as a middle ground between the two extremes mentioned above. In its regulatory role, the government has become an active influence in all phases of business. It stands by as rule-maker and referee for business activities such as consolidations and mergers, labor-management relations, the pricing of products and services, advertising, and many other activities. The development of programs such as social security and unemployment compensation, coupled with the fact that the business firm also serves as a tax collector, has virtually made the government a "partner" in every business operation.

The Government's Power To Act

As previously stated, the increasing role of government in business enterprise has come largely as a result of public demands. In each case, as the government extended its powers, it met a legal challenge from those who most keenly felt the impact of growing regulation. The powers of government may be extended in two ways: (1) through legislative action, even to the extent of amending the Constitution if necessary and (2) through judicial interpretation of existing laws. Through the process of judicial interpretation of the Constitution, the powers of the government to regulate have been established without requiring specific legislation. For example, in the famous case of *Munn* v. *Illinois*, 94 U.S. 113 (1876), the Supreme Court held that a business vested with a public interest (in this case a grain elevator) could be subjected to rate regulation without depriving the owners of their property rights protected by the due process clause of the 14th Amendment. This case was a milestone in establishing the rights of government to regulate public utilities. It is interesting to note that as public opinion became more favorably disposed toward regulation, the courts became more liberal in interpreting the right of the government to regulate.[2] Undoubtedly this tendency relieved the necessity for new legislation in many instances.

The tendency of the judiciary to extend the regulatory rights of the federal government was not sufficient to meet all the demands for regulatory measures. The legislative branch of the government is most directly attuned to the sentiments of the public; and as the demand arose

[2] For example, in the case *Lochner* v. *New York*, 198 U.S. 45 (1905), the Supreme Court held unconstitutional a state law fixing the maximum working day in bakeries at ten hours. The majority opinion held that such a law unreasonably limited freedom of contract as protected by the 14th Amendment. Then in 1917, in the case *Bunting* v. *Oregon*, 243 U.S. 426, the Supreme Court upheld a state statute limiting the working day in certain industries to ten hours and also prescribing time and a half for hours worked in excess of ten hours. This was considered a reversal of the *Lochner* v. *New York* decision.

for government action, it was expressed through legislative acts. Thus, from the close of the Civil War until the present time, both the legislative and judicial branches of our government have, in general, moved in the direction of extending the participation of the federal government in the conduct of business.

Examples of Federal Laws Affecting Business

To trace the evolution of all federal laws affecting business enterprise would comprise a textbook within itself. An effort will be made here to mention some of the more common legislative acts that have a bearing on the daily conduct of business. The laws mentioned are representative, and perhaps many others of equal importance have been omitted. As the student pursues his business education, he will have occasion to study these measures, and others, in more detail.

The Interstate Commerce Act. This act of Congress passed in 1887 was among the first of the legislative acts having a far-reaching influence on business enterprise. The railroads had emerged as perhaps the most powerful industry in the United States. High-handed financial practices and abuses and discrimination among shippers had stirred public resentment against the industry. The Interstate Commerce Act was the first of several federal statutes regulating interstate transportation. The law forbade pools by rail carriers, prohibited special rates and rebates, and required railways to publish rate schedules. The act also created the Interstate Commerce Commission and gave it certain powers to investigate and regulate certain activities of the railways. When first created, the Commission was subjected to legal assaults that rendered it impotent for almost twenty years.[3] However, the Commission withstood the test of the courts and emerged a functioning body.

The Sherman Antitrust Act. The Sherman Antitrust Act of 1890 was another milestone in the growth of government regulation of business. It appears that the law may have been passed initially as a political move to appease the agrarian interest that had come to resent big business as exemplified in the "trusts." At the time of its passage, the law was not treated as major legislation, and it now appears that the impact and importance of the law was not realized by those who were responsible for its passage.[4] At the time the law was passed, the controlling interests in Congress were actually favorable to the trusts; and had the true nature of the law been recognized, it is doubtful that it would have been enacted.

---

[3] Merle Fainsod, Lincoln Gordon and J. C. Palamountain, *Government and the American Economy* (3d ed.; New York: W. W. Norton & Co., Inc., 1959), pp. 27–28.
[4] *Ibid.*, pp. 449–466.

The Sherman Antitrust Act prohibits the formation of combinations, or conspiracies, that act in restraint of interstate or foreign commerce. It is essentially an antimonopoly measure. If a person violates the act and in so doing damages another party, that party may sue for damages; and if sustained, the damaged party may collect three times the ascertained damages. In its initial form, the law could not be said to be very effective; but it has served as the basis for more specific laws in the antitrust field.

The Pure Food and Drugs Act. This was a law passed by Congress in 1906, and it is notable because it was perhaps the first law that attempted directly to aid and protect the consumer. The law prohibited interstate trade in foods and drugs that were adulterated or misbranded. The initial law met with powerful opposition from vested interests, and as a consequence its objectives were seldom realized. The original law was strengthened by the passage of the Federal Food, Drug, and Cosmetic Act of 1938. The latter act proved to be very valuable legislation in behalf of the consumer. In addition to prohibiting adulteration and misbranding, the present law specifies certain descriptive information that must be placed on labels.

The Clayton Act. The Clayton Act, passed by Congress in 1914, was designed to supplement and strengthen the Sherman Act; specifically, it sought to condemn certain practices as being unlawful and to clarify certain aspects of the Sherman Act. The act specifically forbids price discrimination, tying clauses in contracts (a contract in which the buyer of an item is forbidden to use the goods of competitors in connection with the item), interlocking directorates, and the holding of the stock of one corporation by another when the purpose is to lessen competition. Also, an important provision of the act was to exempt organized labor from antitrust action under the Sherman Act. The Clayton Act was perhaps the first major step in building upon the foundation laid by the Sherman Act.

The Federal Trade Commission Act. This act, also passed in 1914, created the Federal Trade Commission. The act sought to provide the machinery necessary to accomplish the objectives of the Sherman and Clayton Acts. The Commission was empowered to prevent unfair methods of competition, conspiracies in restraint of trade, price-fixing, and similar violations. The Commission is a quasi-judicial agency empowered to investigate and issue cease and desist orders. If the accused party challenges the cease and desist order, the issue is then taken to the courts for further action. In 1938, the act was supplemented by the Wheeler-Lea Act, which authorized the Federal Trade Commission to control false advertising of foods, drugs, and other commodities and to prevent deceptive practices where such items are sold in interstate commerce.

The National Labor Relations Act. This act, passed in 1935, is important in that it is sometimes referred to as the "bill of rights" for labor. Certainly, the passage of the law facilitated the rapid growth of unionized labor in the late 1930's and since. In effect, the act guarantees the right of certain employees to full freedom in self-organization and in the designation of their representatives for collective bargaining purposes. Under the law, the employer was enjoined from interfering with the organizational efforts of his employees or from attempting in any way to influence his employees against joining a union. After World War II, there developed some sentiment to the effect that the National Labor Relations Act had gone too far in its desire to assure labor the freedom to organize. In 1947, the Labor-Management Relations Act (Taft-Hartley Law) was passed. An objective of this law was to establish what was considered a more equitable balance in the labor-management relationship.

The Securities Exchange Act. This act, passed by Congress in 1934, is a supplement to the Securities Act of 1933. Its primary purpose is to protect investors who buy securities through brokers. In brief, the seller of securities must make available to the buyer full information on the nature of the security offered. The act also provided for the creation of the Securities and Exchange Commission, a quasi-judicial agency with the purpose of protecting the public against fraudulent practices.

The Robinson-Patman Act. This law, passed in 1936, was designed to strengthen the section of the Clayton Act dealing with price discrimination. In brief, the Robinson-Patman Act prohibits sellers from discriminating in the prices (discounts) quoted to buyers who are in competition, who are dealing in interstate commerce, and who are on the same level of trade. A seller may charge different prices to customers if he can show that it costs him less to do business with one than another, but the extent of the price differential given cannot exceed the differential in the cost of doing business. The purpose of the act is to prevent price discrimination by a seller when the intention is to enable one buyer to injure another. The law has been reasonably successful, and it is interesting to note that it is another in the series of laws with beginnings traceable back to the Sherman Act.

The Wheeler-Lea Act. This law, passed in 1938, extended the duties of the Federal Trade Commission to include the prohibition of *unfair or deceptive practices in commerce.* Previously, the Commission had concerned itself primarily with unfair methods of competition. One important aspect of the Wheeler-Lea Act is that it affords the basis for policing and punishing violators in the area of false and deceptive advertising. Action against a deceptive advertiser may be initiated by a competitor who feels that he is being injured, or the Commission may observe such a practice and initiate action directly.

Additional Laws Affecting Transportation and Communications. In addition to the Interstate Commerce Act of 1887, other areas affected with the public interest have been made subject to regulatory commissions. The Federal Communications Commission was created in 1934. This agency has jurisdiction over telephones, telegraph, radio, and television. The Federal Power Commission was created in 1918 and has authority over interstate electricity and gas. The Civil Aeronautics Board exercises authority over routes and rates in the aviation field. The various commissions charged with the regulation of industries affected with the public interest constitute a major sphere in which the government finds it necessary to have a voice in the operation of business.

State Laws

The foregoing discussion has dealt with federal legislation. The individual states have laws affecting business enterprise, but such laws are usually of less magnitude than the federal regulations. The police power of the states may be exercised in areas that affect the health, safety, and morals of its citizens. The states through their public utility commissions regulate certain businesses that operate on an intrastate basis. In providing public roads, states may establish regulations governing load limits and charge license fees to carriers who use the roads. Individual states have passed laws affecting labor-management relations and are apparently quite free to operate in this area as long as the laws passed do not conflict with federal law. It is also within the power of the states to prohibit the sale of certain commodities—usually items considered dangerous to health, safety, or morals. The authority of the states to exercise power through taxation is recognized, and this will be discussed more fully in the next section of this chapter.

FEDERAL AND STATE POWER OF TAXATION

Federal Taxation

The power of the federal government to levy taxes has always had an important effect upon business enterprise. The taxing power can be used to collect revenue, or it can be used as a part of the police power to discourage certain practices. The high taxes placed on alcoholic beverages stems in part from the belief that it is socially desirable to discourage the consumption of the product. The taxing power may also be used for such purposes as discouraging foreign competition with home industry through the levying of tariffs. The taxing power of the federal government is found in Article I, Section 8 of the Constitution. This Article states that Congress shall have the power to collect revenues to pay debts and provide for the common defense and general welfare of the nation. The so-called "general welfare clause" in the Article has been broadly interpreted and has opened the way for the federal government to collect revenues for an unlimited range of purposes,

During the past twenty-five years, there has been an enormous cost incurred in providing for the national defense. Coupled with this has been a growing demand by the public for governmental services. The rising cost of government has been accompanied by increasing rates of taxation. Table 3–1 shows the internal revenue collections for 1964. It

Table 3–1. Internal Revenue Collections for the United States, 1964

Source of Revenue	1964 (dollars)
Corporation income and profit taxes	24,300,863,000
Individual income and employment taxes	70,148,137,000
Unemployment insurance	850,858,000
Estate and gift taxes	2,416,304,000
Excise taxes	13,950,232,000
Total, all sources	111,666,394,000

Source: Internal Revenue Service, Treasury Department.

may be noted that the largest single source of revenue consists of individual income and employment taxes. It is perhaps a reasonable estimate to assume that the average taxpayer, in paying income, excise, property, and other taxes, pays as much as one-third of his gross income in taxes. Figure 3–1 is a graphic illustration showing the source of our tax dollar and also the way in which it is expended. The individual income tax is a progressive tax, and this has had the effect of eliminating some of the wide disparity that once existed in the disposable income received by the individuals. Table 3–2 shows the leveling effect of a high progressive tax rate, especially as it affects the very-high-income groups. Progressive taxation affects the business community in many ways. By placing a heavy burden upon those in the medium- and high-income groups, the lower-income groups are left with a larger share of their income to spend in the market place. This has undoubtedly widened the market for many items produced and sold in our economy.

WHERE IT COMES FROM: WHERE IT GOES:

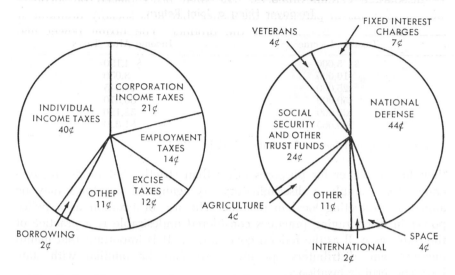

Fig. 3–1. The source of our tax dollar and the way in which it is expended, fiscal year 1965 estimate.

On the other hand, progressive taxation has been criticized on the grounds that the individual is no longer able to accumulate funds for investment purposes.

Corporation income and profit taxes rank second to individual income and employment taxes as a source of revenue. Corporations pay a *normal tax* and a *surtax* on income over $25,000. The normal tax rate is 22 per cent on all net income. The surtax rate is 26 per cent. Thus, a corporation with a net income in excess of $25,000 will pay 22 per cent on the first $25,000 and 48 per cent on net income in excess of that amount. High corporate tax rates are defended on the basis of the government's need for revenue and the ability of the corporations to pay. Opponents of high corporate taxation maintain that the tax prevents the corporation from accumulating funds for the proper maintenance and expansion of facilities.

State Taxation

Generally speaking, the individual states are free to levy taxes on activities within their borders. States may utilize an income tax, sales tax, an excise tax on various products and services, and a variety of business and property taxes. The power of the states to tax has affected the location of business relative to corporation taxes levied, the extent of business property tax, and similar levies. The states may also use

Table 3–2. Example Showing the Application of Tax Rates for a Married Taxpayer Filing a Joint Return

Taxable Income	Income After Taxes
$ 5,000	$ 4,120
10,000	8,050
25,000	18,545
50,000	30,870
100,000	52,120
200,000	81,320

SOURCE: Federal Income Tax Rate Schedules, 1964.

their taxing power for purposes other than strictly that of raising revenue. For example, a discriminatory tax against chain stores may be aimed at protecting local merchants. The use of taxation as a police power in discouraging practices considered undesirable is a practice of the states as well as the federal government. It is important that manufacturers and distributors operating nationally be familiar with state laws concerning taxation.[5]

PASSAGE AND ADMINISTRATION OF REGULATORY LAW

The Genesis of Regulatory Law

In the preceding pages, reference has been made to the fact that much of our regulatory law came into being as a result of public demands. Perhaps this should be qualified by pointing out that various segments of the public, or interest groups, often initiate the demand for regulatory measures. An interest group may demand legislative protection when its position is threatened by other segments of the economy. Many of the groups that decry government intervention into their affairs are first in line in demanding that laws be passed to protect their own interest. Generally speaking, a regulatory measure is designed to protect the majority from exploitation by a minority, but undoubtedly there are some laws that have been passed that protect special interests at the expense of the general public. Since interest groups are frequently well organized, they are able to bring strong pressure to bear upon legislative bodies.

When regulatory legislation is proposed, it signifies that opposing interests are involved. Were this not the case there would be no need for such legislation. Those who are "regulated against" will invariably seek to defeat the measures that impose restraints upon them. There

[5] Sydney Prerau, ed., *J. K. Lasser's Business Management Handbook* (2d ed.; New York: McGraw-Hill Book Co., 1960).

are at least three ways in which this opposition will manifest itself, and all regulatory laws will generally run this gamut. When a bill proposing regulation is introduced before a legislative body, efforts will be made through lobbying, advertising appeals to the public, and similar measures to achieve the defeat of the bill. If it appears that the passage of the bill cannot be prevented, the second stage of the attack is an attempt to get amendments introduced to the extent of making the law ineffective. If this strategy fails and the law is passed, the opponents of the measure still have a third and last chance to get the law nullified through the courts. If the courts uphold the law as valid, or constitutional, it then becomes the law of the land.[6] The effectiveness of the measure will then depend upon the adequacy of the law itself and the adequacy of the machinery provided for its execution.

Administration of Regulatory Law

The administration of regulatory measures affecting business are, as a rule, entrusted to a commission. There are numerous federal commissions as well as state commissions. Many of them are permanent organizations, although some are temporary and terminate with the accomplishment of a stated objective. Typical of the federal commissions are the Interstate Commerce Commission, the Federal Trade Commission, the Federal Communications Commission, and the Federal Power Commission. Most of the commissions are quasi-judicial in that they have policing powers but do not have the authority of courts. In broad terms, it is the purpose of a commission to see that industry observes those regulatory measures that have been entrusted to the commission to enforce. A commission works closely with interested parties, and much of its time is devoted to preventive rather than punitive actions. Commissions are usually appointed by the executive branch of the government, subject to the approval of the legislative branch.

Looking Ahead

In the foregoing pages, the extent to which government has come to play a part in business operations has been emphasized. Business still retains the essential freedoms—such as the freedom of entry, freedom in the choice of the manner of organization and operation, and the freedom to make a profit. But these freedoms are operative within a framework established through the evolutionary processes of government regulation. The increasing role of government in business has come as the result of war, depression, and the insatiable demand of the public

[6] Fainsod *et al.*, *op. cit.*, Chaps. 1 and 2.

for increasing amounts of service. There is evidence that the government will continue to play a vital role in the conduct of business. The demands of national defense, the instability of labor-management relationships, and the demands of the American people for increasing economic security all point to increasing rather than diminishing government participation in the operation of business enterprise.

YOUR CAREER IN GOVERNMENT SERVICE

Preparation

The student aspiring to a career in government service may prepare himself through a broad, fundamental education, or he may prepare as a specialist. If he follows the approach of a general education, he would do well to take courses in economics, political science, and statistics. If he chooses the route of the specialist, he will find that the government employs the counterpart to the specialists found in industry and the professions. In the area of business administration, he might consider majoring in accounting, statistics, finance, marketing, transportation, or industrial and personnel management. Specialists in these areas are employed by both the federal and state governments. Some branches of the federal government have organized management training programs, resembling in some respects those found in industry. These programs may be of special interest to students pursuing a general business education.

Job Opportunities

As of June 30, 1964, the federal government employed 2,370,000 civilians. Of this number, 2,202,000 were employed in the continental United States, and 168,000 were employed outside the country.[7] More than three out of every one hundred employed persons in the country were in federal employment. Add to this those persons employed by the various state governments, and one can see the significance of federal and state employment. The scale of government operations would indicate a continuing need for personnel. Thus, the person who desires a career in government service, and who has good qualifications to offer, should not find it difficult to secure a position. The needs of the government as to specialties may vary from time to time, but in general there is a constant demand for business students who have had training in accounting, statistics, marketing research, and the various transportation specialties.

[7] United States Civil Service Commission, Federal Employment Statistics Bulletin.

Civil service employment offers security and the chance to do work that is vital to the welfare of the nation. Salaries, while still somewhat lower than industrial counterparts, have been increased in recent years. College students are usually able to begin work at salaries comparable to those paid by private industry. Salaries are paid according to *grade,* and the various positions specify the grade accorded the person who fills the position.

TOPICS FOR DISCUSSION

1. Do you feel that the United States government influences business through its expenditures? What examples can you cite?

2. What do you feel are the main purposes for which government applies controls to business?

3. When you deposit funds in your local bank, are your funds protected by the federal government?

4. What are some of the economic powers delegated to the federal government by the Constitution?

5. Many people feel that the Sherman Act in substance contained nothing that was new when passed in 1890. Comment.

6. If the federal government guaranteed you an average income until you are sixty-five years of age, would you be willing for the government to tell you the kind of work you must do, the hours you must work, and where you must live?

7. Do you feel that the federal laws regulating false and deceptive advertising are doing a good job?

8. Should the federal government pay its employees salaries equal to those received by comparable personnel in industry?

9. Our present tax laws tend to have a leveling effect on the incomes received by individuals. Discuss the social and economic implications of this.

10. How have special interest groups such as organized labor, management, and the farmer influenced the role of government as a regulator?

CASE 3–1

THE PURITAN STORM WINDOW COMPANY

The Puritan Storm Window Company was one of three manufacturers producing and selling storm windows in a six-state area. In a normal year, the Puritan firm sold about 55 per cent of the storm windows marketed in the area. The Folsom Window Company and the Alden Company accounted for the remainder of sales. Puritan was clearly the leader in the market, and the prices quoted by the firm were adopted by Folsom and Alden. From time to time, the smaller competitors had complained of the hardship encountered in meeting price competition from the Puritan Company.

Early in the 1960's, the Folsom Window Company began experiencing financial difficulties. In 1965, the directors of the company approached the Puritan Storm Window Company with the suggestion that Puritan take over the Folsom Company through a merger. Puritan studied the financial condition of Folsom, and also made an evaluation of the production and marketing facilities owned by the firm. Puritan directors decided that a merger with Folsom would offer certain advantages. In brief, it was felt that, with the added capacity and facilities of Folsom, the economy of scale benefiting Puritan would be such that it could reduce its prices on storm windows by as much as 10 per cent and still show increased profits.

The Alden Company was greatly disturbed on learning of merger negotiations between the Puritan and Folsom companies. The Alden executives felt that the present predominating position of Puritan would be further enhanced and that the merger would give them a virtual monopoly in the six-state area. Furthermore, they were of the opinion that they could not reduce prices further in competition with Puritan. Attorneys for Alden visited Washington, D.C., and appealed to the Antitrust Division to intervene and prohibit the merger of the Folsom Window Company with the Puritan Storm Window Company.

In the hearings held by the Antitrust Division, Puritan based its case on the contention that Folsom could not survive if the merger should be denied. Attorneys for Puritan pointed out that, if the Folsom Company disappeared from the field, the Puritan Company stood to gain most of the Folsom market anyway. They also pointed out that the merger would enable the Folsom facilities to continue in operation, thus preserving the employment of about 75 per cent of the present Folsom work force of 500 employees. And finally, the attorneys stressed that the merger would permit economies in production and marketing to the extent that Puritan products would be reduced in price to the public by upward of 10 per cent.

Attorneys for the Alden Company based their case on the contention that approval of the merger would put the Alden Company out of business, since the firm could not meet the 10 per cent price reduction referred to by the Puritan firm. They stressed that the disappearance of Alden would result in the Puritan Company achieving a complete monopoly in the six-state area. Attorneys further charged that, once Puritan gained a complete monopoly, prices would be raised, and the public would be exploited.

The Antitrust Division continued consideration of the proposed merger and the Alden objection.

1. Should the Puritan Storm Window Company be permitted to absorb the Folsom Company through a merger? Support your argument with reasons.

2. In what way does this case illustrate the dilemma of protecting competition and acting in the best interest of the public? Or do you feel that such a dilemma does not exist?

SELECTED REFERENCES

Fainsod, Merle, Lincoln Gordon, and J. C. Palamountain. *Government and the American Economy.* 3d ed. New York: W. W. Norton & Co., Inc., 1959.

Krislov, Samuel, and L. D. Musolf. *The Politics of Regulation.* Boston: The Houghton Mifflin Co., 1964.

Mund, V. A. *Government and Business.* 4th ed. New York: Harper & Row, 1965.

Russell, R. R. *A History of the American Economic System.* New York: Appleton-Century-Crofts, Inc., 1964.

Wernette, J. P. *Government and Business.* New York: The Macmillan Co., 1964.

4

Expanding Dimensions of Management Strategy

THE INTERDISCIPLINARY APPROACH

In recent years, we have seen an increasing trend in the use of quantitative analysis in business management. It is notable also that management has begun to place more emphasis on the data and methodologies of the behavioral sciences such as psychology, sociology, and cultural anthropology. In educational circles, the tendency of management to integrate materials and methods from other fields such as quantitative and behavioral areas has been described as the *interdisciplinary approach*.

In the broader sense, the "quantitative area" may be said to embrace accounting and statistics as well as mathematical applications. It is true that the accountant and the statistician provide management with information in a quantified form. We shall, however, in this brief discussion use the term *quantitative analysis* in its more restricted sense, i.e., to refer to applications and methods associated more directly with the areas of mathematics and mathematical statistics. A similar problem of definition presents itself in relation to the behavioral sciences. In its broader sense, *behavioral science* may include, in addition to psychology, sociology, and cultural anthropology, such areas as political science, economics, and many others. Comments in this brief discussion will be concerned with a few of the developments and ideas usually associated with the first three of the above-named areas of study.

The decision-making function in business management has always been dependent on the availability of information. Recent developments drawing upon what has been described as quantitative analysis and the behavioral sciences do not represent something totally new to the business manager. Management has always sought to quantify information—most often within the scope of traditional accounting and statistics—and areas such as personnel management and marketing research have always utilized methods and data common to the behavioral sciences. The developments of recent years may be best described as an expansion and extension of the quantitative and behavioral methodologies as applied to business management. The development of the electronic computer initiated a revolution in the collection and processing of information. The capacity of the computer has made available to management within a very short time period a scope and depth of information heretofore unattainable. The utilization of mathematical techniques has developed, to a considerable extent, as a result of the quantities of information available for analysis. In a similar manner, the interest of management in the behavioral aspects of customers and employees has accelerated with the access to information that has been made possible by the computer.

THE QUANTITATIVE AREA

Scope of Quantitative Analysis

In the preceding section, an effort was made to define the area of interest associated with quantitative analysis. Developments have occurred at a rapid rate, and the scope of the area is continually expanding. Mathematical techniques are employed in the design of information systems, and, once data are accumulated, the skills of the mathematician and the statistician are used to analyze and interpret. While the techniques of quantitative analysis are involved deeply with information collection and interpretation, they are by no means restricted to these functions. Techniques involving the application of mathematics in decision making are growing in importance. The computer has made possible the development and use of models that are enabling management, through a process of simultation, to pretest the effects of a series of decisions, or alternative decisions, on the ultimate objective of productivity. The processes of simulation involve the making of assumptions, usually based on historical data, and the application of mathematical concepts such as those of probability. The scope of quantitative analysis in business management has developed rapidly, and no one can say at this time just how far we may be able to go in substituting the methods and precision of mathematics for the intuitive judgment of the business manager.

The Concept of Models

One of the more important ways in which mathematics has contributed to the solution of management problems has been through the development of models. A model has been defined as an abstraction of reality.[1] A toy airplane is a simple physical model that conveys the outward appearance of a real plane. A more sophisticated model of an airplane might be designed for testing certain principles in a wind tunnel. A mathematical model may be looked upon as an extension of the concept of the physical models mentioned above. In the mathematical model, symbolism carries the idea of abstraction into a new dimension. One source comments on the abstract model as follows:

Mathematical models are frequently criticized because the resemblance between the real world and the model is not apparent. It is true that a stringent set of assumptions is needed to go from the real world to an abstract model. Naturally, these assumptions do not describe the real world; if they did there would be little purpose in making them at all. A model should be examined to see if it is consistent with the assumptions made. Its usefulness, then, depends on whether the results which it gives will hold when the assumptions underlying it are modified to fit the many facts existing in the real world.[2]

The use of mathematical models is in no sense a new development in the study of economics and business management. Many well-known "formulas" are in themselves simplified models. The familiar *equation of exchange* that is looked upon as one approach to defining the general price level is an example of such a model. The equation states that

$$P = \frac{MV + M'V'}{T}$$

P represents the general *price level,* or the average price of goods and services exchanged in a given period. *M* represents the amount of *money in circulation,* and *M'* represents the amount of *credit* in circulation for the period. *V* represents the *velocity* of circulation for money, and *V'* stands for the velocity for credit (that is, the turnover of money and credit). *T* represents the *volume of trade* for the given period. This is frequently called the cash-transaction type of equation.[3] Stu-

---

[1] D. L. Gentry and D. L. Shawver, *Fundamentals of Managerial Marketing* (Boston: D. C. Heath & Co., 1964), Chap. 14.

[2] *Ibid.,* p. 275.

[3] H. S. Sloan and A. J. Zurcher, *A Dictionary of Economics* (4th ed.; New York: Barnes & Noble, Inc., 1961), pp. 115–16.

dents, in studying this simplified model, should find it easy to visualize changes in the price level that would arise from varying the supply of money and credit without corresponding changes in the volume of trade (the total number of units sold during the period).

A primary contribution of models to decision making derives from the facts that one is able to "abstract" from a very complex set of relationships certain very pertinent parts and that the relationship of these parts to one another then may be studied. The *equation of exchange* mentioned above abstracts and summarizes a number of important factors bearing on the general price level. In reality, there are numerous factors that go into determining just what the price level will be at a given time. The construction of a simple model, however, enables us to see the relationship between the basic components of money and credit, the velocity, and the volume of trade. The use of the electronic computer has made possible the design of very sophisticated models that contain hundreds, and even thousands, of variables. Given a more sophisticated model, one is able to "plug in" data and, through a process of simulation, gain insight into the outcome of various decision alternatives. Another important advantage of the mathematical model is that, once designed, it often lends itself to manipulation. One may solve equations for unknown quantities and thus gain insights that may not be available through intuitive judgment.

Mathematics in Management

Mathematical techniques have been used in attacking a great variety of problems in business management. It is possible here to mention only a few of the more common and simplified usages. Many business problems may be approached through solutions of equations and inequalities. An example would be the allocation of production quotas among plants owned by a single company. If some plants are better suited for producing some products than others, the position of the company is at an optimum when production is allocated to take advantage of special capacities and at the same time permit the company to achieve the total production desired and in the allotted time. The techniques of matrix algebra may be used in determining optimal shipments between factories and warehouses in serving a given market. A wide range of relationships involving costs, productivity, and the size of the firm may be analyzed through various applications of the calculus.[4]

The concepts of mathematical probability have been used in considering a variety of business problems. Probability analysis is of especial

[4] R. C. Meier and S. H. Archer, *An Introduction to Mathematics for Business Analysis* (New York: McGraw-Hill Book Co., 1960).

importance in the area of decision theory. In applying the concept of probability in decision making, the firm is likely to be concerned with determining the *mathematical expectation* that may be associated with the outcome of an event, or number of events. The approach has been described as follows:

In many situations the probability distribution cannot be determined by analysis of logically existent cases. In these situations the value to be used for a probability is often determined by a statistical analysis of data pertaining to past operations. For example, the Marketing Manager may be interested in trying to predetermine the probable results of applying a certain advertising expenditure in a given market. From analysis of past experience he may conclude that given a certain set of circumstances, i.e., population, income, and age distribution, he may, on occasion, expect X dollars in advertising to produce Y dollars of sales volume. In this example the case in which there is a positive sales response to advertising may be called an *event*. The Marketing Manager is interested in knowing the probability of the *frequency of occurrence* of the event. Based upon an historical study of a large number of cases, the relative frequency may approach a limit, and if so, this limit is called the statistical or empirical probability. In short, it may be possible to surmise that if the set of circumstances prevailing in a new territory is the same as that existing in previous territories studied, the probability is two out of three (as an example) that X amount of advertising will produce Y amount of sales.[5]

Linear programming is a mathematical method used in developing a solution that may be to minimize costs, maximize profits, determine the number of machines necessary to meet a particular schedule, or achieve some other clearly stated objective. The problems solved in linear programming involve the maximizing or minimizing of some quantity. "Linear" refers to straight-line mathematical relationships. The mathematical equations used are always expressed in the first power so that the variables in the equation develop in direct proportion to each other; that is, the influence of each element must be directly proportional to the quantity of the element involved in the problem. For example, as a result of increasing by 75 per cent the quantity of corn in cattle feed, 75 per cent more proteins, minerals, or calories will be added, or the doubling of labor will result in an approximate doubling of output. Linear programming may be used when the problem to be solved in a production process involves straight-line relationships and is made up of an objective, a number of alternative methods for reaching the objective, and restrictions in resources or controls, and when the answer required is not a negative quantity. The restrictions referred to may be that there is only a certain amount of raw materials, or that a certain amount of finished product must be supplied by a particular time, or

[5] Gentry and Shawver, *op. cit.*, p. 52.

restrictions as to amount of machines or floor space, or other types of restrictions such as marketing quotas in agriculture. Each alternative method developed in equation form yields a particular input-output ratio, and, by comparison of the ratios, the best procedure can be selected. Care is required in formulating the equations, since numbers are assigned to factors that are not ordinarily quantified. The problem must be stated in such a way that a mathematical solution is possible.

Operations Research

The term *operations research* refers to a methodology that draws upon many disciplines including mathematics and the behavioral sciences. It is group research and depends on a team of specialists. A mathematical model using empirical relations that are relevant to the problem being studied, the assumptions that are to be employed, and the objective that is sought is constructed as an aid to understanding the problem and working out the solution. The model can be manipulated to test the probable effects of contemplated changes in methods or conditions, the idea being that this can be done with a model without disturbing the existing order of things, thus avoiding the possibility of costly failures that could result from experimenting with the actual operations of a business. As in other types of research, the validity of conclusions will be no greater than the validity of the premises and assumptions that make up the model. Operations research seeks to understand the effect of various operations through observation, controlled experimentation, and theoretical analysis that will enable the researchers to predict the result of changes in operating rules or equipment and thereby better control the operation. The operations-research team, composed of management specialists, economists, statisticians, mathematicians, and behavioral scientists, attempts to study every possible course of action and then to rank the best courses of action in terms of maximum benefits to be derived.

Conclusions on Quantitative Analysis

Since World War II, the techniques of quantitative analysis have gained increasing significance in business management. As mentioned previously, the development of the computer has been a primary factor underlying the greater use of quantitative methods. At this point in time, it is impossible to say just how far we may be able to go in replacing conventional management approaches with those having a quantitative orientation. Perhaps we should look on the use of quantitative techniques as merely a refinement of traditional management methodology rather than regard it as a totally new concept. If we take this point of view, we may regard quantitative developments as means of placing new tools in the hands of the manager. There will remain, of course, areas of management in which judgment must be based on qualitative factors alone. The business manager will always prefer to have the exactness of information that derives from the quantitative methods; however, he must guard against the temptation to alter and shape qualitative data to fit the quantitative mold.

THE BEHAVIORAL SCIENCES

Management and the Behavior of People

We live in an economy that regards the will of the people as a guiding force. The success of a producer depends on his ability to turn out a product that will be acceptable to the consumer. Faced with competitive sources of supply, the consumer is in a position to accept the product of one and reject that of another. Operating in this environment, the firm must strive to anticipate consumer wants and to plan production accordingly. This entails studying the consumer in terms of motivations, habits, and customs—as well as collecting information of the more objective sort, such as statistics on population and income. Also, as an employer, the business firm may profit from an understanding of the aspirations, likes, and dislikes of the employee. A well-managed personnel program rests in no small part upon a knowledge of human behavior. As the business firm deals with people—both as employees and as customers—the need for knowledge from the areas of the behavioral sciences becomes evident.

The Study of Motivation

Underlying human behavior is motivation. The things we do, the things we like and dislike, are influenced by our motives. In addition to the basic drives of hunger, fear, sex, and anger, there are motives of a secondary nature. We are all aware of the desires for health, for security, and for an element of prestige and status. As consumers, we respond to the firm that offers us a way to satisfy our desires. The business firm, in turn, must fathom the motives of the consumer, and often this must be done in advance of the time at which the product will be available for sale. Automobile manufacturers may be faced with predicting style trends as much as two or three years in advance of the sales date. Consumer tastes are somewhat fickle and subject to frequent change. Continuous research goes on in an effort to understand the actions of the consumer, and to predict what he will prefer next.

In studying consumer motivation, the firm may employ the methods of conventional research or of *motivational research*. Conventional research proceeds on the assumption that people are aware of their motives, and are able and willing to reveal motivation when questioned. The motivational research approach takes the position that people are usually not aware of the true motives underlying their actions, and that, if they were aware, they would not willingly reveal the true motives. The advocates of motivational research employ clinical approaches in an effort to get at the hidden motives. Both the conventional and motivational approaches have their advocates. It is now generally felt that the two approaches are not necessarily competitive and that the approach used is a matter of the circumstances of the individual case. Firms are often able to combine the two research approaches in a single project.

In addition to studying motivation as it relates to the consumer in the market, business management is interested in the motivation of employees. The contentment of the worker, his willingness to learn new methods, and his productivity on the job are all influenced by the things that motivate him. While wages are vitally important, they may not be sufficient as a sole motivating factor. Opportunities for advancement, the chance to exhibit skills, and the fellowship of a pleasant work environment are all considerations in motivating the worker to perform at his best. While it may appear to some that modern management-labor negotiations tend to depersonalize the relationship of the employee to his firm, it is still desirable for management to exercise an awareness of the goals and aspirations of the employee.

Tests and Measurement

Psychological testing is used extensively by business management in the selection and placement of employees, in the planning of retraining programs, and in the counseling of employees in problems of adjustment to the work situation. Various tests applied to a sample of consumers may reveal information of importance in the design of the product and in deciding its manner of distribution. College graduates, in applying for positions, may expect to encounter a variety of testing as a part of the selection process. Companies vary in the number and types of tests used. Many will use some version of the basic intelligence test, and it is also quite common to find some use of aptitude tests. The weight assigned to testing as a factor in employee selection is a matter of company policy. Perhaps the most usual approach is for the firm to base selection on a combination of factors: the applicant's background, the results of testing, and the impressions gained in interviews. Once the individual is employed, his progress in training may be guided through the use of tests as measuring devices. In some situations, an employee may advance from one job level to a higher one on the strength of test scores. Certain testing programs may be administered by the personnel department of the firm, while others, of a more complex nature, may be handled by outside consultants.

The Group Concept

Many behavioral scientists have a particular interest in the study of cultural groups, and in the identification of groups as they relate to the market for specific product or service. We are a nation of hundreds of subgroups that tend in many respects to overlap one another. A group may be defined as a collection of people with something in common. Very few products or services are purchased by all people; there are, of course, mass markets for basic foods, medicines, clothing, etc. For a greater number of products, the market consists of some identifiable group. The group that will purchase a product may be identified by characteristics such as age, sex, income, education, family status, religion and others. Some markets are highly selective in terms of the people who will purchase the product. The market for a certain automobile might be defined as consisting primarily of men over forty years of age who are married and who have relatively high incomes. On the other hand, membership in a particular group—a religious affiliation, for example—might exclude people as customers for certain products. Anthropologists and sociologists have a great interest in studying the characteristics of groups, how they are formed, and the effect that the attitudes emerging from the group may have on the individual. Business firms are interested in groups, because groups are often a key factor in identifying a market.

The Family in Society

The family (household) is the basic purchasing unit for consumer goods. Products and services are often designed with the needs, and the attitudes, of the family in mind. Most of our marketing statistics are collected with the family as the basic reporting unit. The sociologist is especially interested in the structure and organization of the family, the lines of authority in the family, and the effects of parental behavior on the offspring. The business manager is interested in knowing how decisions are made in the family unit. This knowledge helps in dealing with problems such as the design and direction of the advertising message. There is also interest in such factors as the way in which the family spends its income and how the family reacts as it moves from one income level to another. The typical family passes through stages, beginning with the young couple. Then there is the stage of the couple with young children, followed by the stage of the couple with teen-age children. The cycle is completed with the return of the family to that of the couple alone—a much older couple, of course. The particular stage of the family has great bearing on the types and quantity of products purchased.

Population

Behavioral scientists, especially sociologists, are interested in demography—the statistical study of populations. This encompasses the study of birth rates, death rates, population distribution by age and sex, and the movements of population from one region to another. Business management is interested in forecasting the future state of population in order to capitalize on market opportunities as they arise. The high birth rate of 1947 leads us to expect that a great many marriages will take place in the years 1967–1972. Marriages indicate the formation of new families, and the creation of customers for the furnishings and appliances needed to begin housekeeping. Those who study population trends are able to predict with reasonable accuracy the size of future populations by age groups, and the geographical concentrations that reflect the movement of people. There is also great interest in the effects of the urbanization movement as people shift from rural to urban areas. As people move from one environment to another, they are faced with the need to adjust their living habits and patterns of consumption. Business managers who have an appreciation of sociological problems may be in a better position to serve these changing markets.

Age and Behavior

A productive area of study has to do with the relationship of age to behavior. The nature of many of our wants changes as we move from one age level to another, and our attitudes are likely to change as we grow older. Perhaps it is safe to say that people become more conservative in their outlook as the years pass, although the exceptions are numerous. Business firms often design products with certain age groups in mind. The Ford Motor Company designed the Ford Mustang car with the younger market in mind. This involved designing a car that would sell within the price range of the younger person who might be within his first few years of employment. It also meant designing a car that would have a "smart sportscar image." This is a good example of a company that developed a product compatible with the attitudes of a

segment of the market. The way in which we respond to certain motives also may vary with age. Teen-agers are intensely concerned with
the problem of "belonging," or being accepted by their peers. In terms
of motivation we may express this as the *desire for security and status.*
People of all ages desire to be accepted socially and to possess a degree of status, but at certain stages in our development we are more
keenly aware of these needs. An array of products is produced and
sold to teen-agers on the basis of appeals to the desire for security and
status.

Continuing Need for Behavioral Studies

Business management is exhibiting a keen awareness of the contributions of the behavioral sciences. Research efforts are active in seeking
ways to integrate knowledge from these areas into the practice of business management. Although the behavioral areas tend to overlap to
some degree, in other respects they stand alone. Sociologists, psychol-
ogists, and others may each have their own domain, and, in fact, there
may be several "schools of thought" within any one of these disciplines.
As is true in all areas of knowledge, it is not uncommon to find behavioral scientists in the same field of study who disagree with one
another relative to theories and methods. There is yet to emerge a
unified set of principles that might have the common label of "behavioral
science." Undoubtedly, in time, certain principles and concepts acceptable to the many disciplines will emerge, and a unified body of
knowledge may be placed at the disposal of those who need such guidance. In the meantime, the business manager seeks to gain a general
knowledge of the behavioral area through background studies in areas
such as psychology, sociology, and anthropology. He may learn enough
to appreciate what these areas have to offer, and, if need be, he may
obtain the services of specialists as staff officers in the employ of the
firm, or he may use consulting services.

YOUR CAREER IN THE QUANTITATIVE AND BEHAVIORAL AREAS

Opportunities

Persons who are able to combine a knowledge of business management with competence in quantitative techniques are in great demand
by employers. The use of the electronic computer tends to expand and
to involve more and more of the segments of the enterprise. The development of computers of various sizes and costs, and the establishment of centers that provide computer service on a contract, or job-lot,

basis have placed the computer within reach of firms of all sizes. Access to electronic information processing has stimulated the development and application of quantitative methods. The quantitative specialist is in great demand as a staff employee. It is also becoming apparent that the prospective line executive will need a certain familiarity with the quantitative approach. Some companies regard their computer department as the nerve center of the firm and are assigning all management trainees to this center for a part of their in-company training. Perhaps we shall never see the time when all those employed in management have a degree of proficiency in areas such as mathematics and statistics. The fact that these areas do require certain abilities, and specialized training, will continue to restrict the number of qualified people. Limitations on the supply of the qualified, coupled with increasing demands, indicate a most promising future for those who can develop a quantitative capacity.

The environment of the business firm as it exists today seems to be such as to contribute to problems in human relations. Automation alone is a significant factor contributing to adjustment problems for both management and employees. The need for the services of the behavioral scientist has never been more apparent. The complex nature of our industrial society seems to generate personnel problems. Employees need guidance in retraining for new jobs, and, as machines create more leisure, the employees may need assistance in adjusting to problems in this area. The business firm will continue to need the counsel of the behavioral expert in studying the needs and wants of the consumer. Persons trained in areas such as psychology and sociology are currently employed in marketing research and advertising, as well as in the personnel departments of firms.

Educational Background

The educational experience of the individual is of particular importance as it relates to quantitative analysis and the behavioral sciences. The person who becomes proficient in computer technology, or who becomes a "systems analyst" in industry or government, must have a substantial background in mathematics, as well as specialized courses relating to the computer and its application. The student who aspires to be an executive in business management may not have to have the training in depth of the "staff expert," but he will encounter great handicaps unless he is able to appreciate quantitative applications and to communicate with those who do have this ability. The student going into business management would do well to have a good background in mathematics, including, if possible, calculus. In addition, substantial course work in statistics is desirable, plus introductory courses dealing with computer application. This is not intended to imply that those who do not have this background will necessarily be excluded from management positions. It does mean that the person who has not had quantitative training as a part of his education may be faced with greater problems of self-education on the job, and that he may be handicapped in competing with those who have a more extensive background.

The person with an interest in the behavioral sciences will find ample demands for his services. If he aspires to become a "specialist," he should plan for graduate work. Those in a staff position, or who render services as consultants, often have the Ph.D. degree. Undergraduate majors in the behavioral areas are employed in sales, research, advertising, and areas of personnel management. Interest in the behavioral sciences should not cause one to neglect to develop capacities in quantitative analysis. Much of the research in behavioral science makes use of the computer and quantitative techniques.

TOPICS FOR DISCUSSION

1. Walter Wayne expects to accept a position with a large company as a sales trainee, after his graduation from college. He has asked to be excused from taking a course in business statistics, on the grounds that "I will have no need for it." Do you agree?

2. Discuss the contributions of quantitative models to the processes of decision making.

3. In business management, decisions are made on the basis of information available to the manager. Would you expect that the manager would have a preference for quantitative information? Why?

4. Can you cite examples of several kinds of information that are used in decision making and that cannot be quantified?

5. Why might an operations-research team include people from diverse areas of learning?

6. "There is a motive underlying every decision that we make." Do you agree?

7. Motives have been classed as *rational* and *emotional*. Can you cite an example of a motive that you would consider rational? Emotional?

8. Do you believe that test scores such as the College Board scores are a sound basis for admitting students to college?

9. How would you define the consumer group that would represent the potential customers for motorcycles?

10. If you were a manufacturer of juvenile furniture—playpens and cribs, etc.—what population statistics would you need to aid in forecasting future operations of your company?

CASE 4–1

THE TURNER MANUFACTURING COMPANY

The Turner Manufacturing Company produced a line of household items made of metals and plastics. The executives of the company have been trying to decide which of two possible items might best be produced to utilize slack production capacity. The items under consideration are an attic fan and a large outdoor plastic swimming pool. The items present a similarity in marketing in that they are both sold primarily during the months of June, July, and August. This poses a problem in that the company must forecast sales for the summer and then produce a number of units that is based on this estimate. The company feels that it cannot produce both items; however, there exists considerable flexibility in the number that may be produced of the item chosen. Cost studies reveal that production costs should decline sharply as the number of units produced increases. The company proposed to restrict the marketing of the item to within a radius of 100 miles of the plant.

An executive of the Turner Company visited several companies that produced and sold the two items in question and were outside the proposed marketing area for the Turner product. The executive was shown figures of sales going back over a number of years, and it was pointed out to him that sales varied directly with the intensity of the summer heat. One company, operating in a climate similar to that of Turner's area, had collected weather statistics over a number of years and was able to show a relationship between the number of units sold and the number of days in which the temperature rose above 90 degrees. The Turner executive was given copies of this statistical study.

The production department of the Turner Company made the following estimate of the relationship between sales volume and profit or loss for the two items:

Sales Volume for 3 Months		Profit or Loss	
Fans	Pools	Fans	Pools
$150,000	$175,000	$7,500 (loss)	$12,500 (loss)
225,000	250,000	1,000	6,500 (loss)
300,000	325,000	8,500	14,500
375,000	400,000	12,500	19,500

After studying the above figures, the executive who had visited the company making comparable products reported that a study of the relationship of summer climate to sales indicated that the following climatic conditions would have to exist in the Turner market in order to achieve the various sales estimates listed:

Number Days Temperature Above 90 Degrees	Estimated Sales	
	Fans	Pools
5–10	$150,000	$175,000
10–15	225,000	250,000
15–20	300,000	325,000
20–25	375,000	400,000

The Turner Company next sought information from a weather bureau located near the center of the market. Statistics were available on the number of 90-degree days for the months of June, July, and August and over a period of thirty years. A study of these statistics revealed that for each ten-year period there had been one year in which the 90-degree days were from five to ten in number, two years in which the 90-degree days were from ten to fifteen in number, four years in which the 90-degree days were from fifteen to twenty in number, and three years in which the 90-degree days were from twenty to twenty-five in number.

At this point, a statistician in the company suggested that the mathematical expectation of profit for the two items should be computed. He pointed out that the weather statistics extending over a period of thirty years might not be entirely satisfactory for estimating the probability of occurrence for the various degree-day periods, but he felt that such probabilities would be reasonably accurate. In explaining the method of computation, he pointed out that over the thirty-year period there had been no summer with less than five 90-degree days, and that there had been no summer having more than twenty-five such days. He regarded the expectation that there would be between five and twenty-five days of 90-degree weather as a certainty, and he proposed to represent this certainty of events with the figure 1. The "probabilities" of each of the aforementioned 90-degree-day periods would then be *represented as a fraction of 1.* Using this method, he suggested the following:

90-Degree Days	Probability of Occurrence
5–10	.1
10–15	.2
15–20	.4
20–25	.3

The statistician suggested that the decision to produce fans be regarded as strategy A and that the decision to produce pools be regarded as strategy B. He then constructed the following table of expected values:

	90-Degree Days			Expected Value
5–10	10–15	15–20	20–25	
Strategy A (fans) − 7,500 (.1) +	1,000 (.2) +	8,500 (.4) +	12,500 (.3) =	$6,200
Strategy B (pools) −12,500 (.1) +	−6,500 (.2) +	14,500 (.4) +	19,500 (.3) =	$9,100

Expected value was computed for each strategy by taking the profit or loss associated with each degree-day period and multiplying that by the probability of the degree-day period occurring. The total of the negative values was then subtracted from the total of the positive values to give the net expected value arising from each strategy.

Certain of the executives felt that, on the basis of this calculation of expected value, the strategy calling for the decision to produce pools was the correct one. Other executives demurred, pointing out that, while the possibilities of gain were higher from producing pools, the chance of loss resulting from cooler weather was much greater for pools than fans.

1. Discuss the pros and cons of using this approach in making a decision involving management strategy.

2. What does this example tell you about the relationship of profits to risk?

SELECTED REFERENCES

Bierman, Harold, L. E. Fouraker, and R. K. Jaedicke. *Quantitative Analysis for Business Decisions.* Homewood, Ill.: Richard D. Irwin, Inc., 1961.

Dudycha, G. J. *Applied Psychology.* New York: The Ronald Press Co., 1963.

Gentry, D. L., and D. L. Shawver. *Fundamentals of Managerial Marketing.* Boston: D. C. Heath & Co., 1964.

Meier, R. C., and S. H. Archer. *An Introduction to Mathematics for Business Analysis.* New York: McGraw-Hill Book Co., 1960.

Scott, W. G. *Human Relations in Management: A Behavioral Science Approach.* Homewood, Ill.: Richard D. Irwin, Inc., 1962.

5

Ethical Conduct in Business Management

A GUIDE TO CONDUCT

In an age when prominent business firms have been prosecuted for price fixing, when legislation has been introduced to protect the consumer from deceptive packaging, and when the public shows signs of becoming aroused over the conduct of advertisers, we may well wonder about ethics in business management. Actually, the history of ethical conduct in commerce has been one of improvement through the ages. With vigilant regulatory agencies, articulate spokesmen for the consumer, and improved communication, we now are made more aware of unethical conduct when it arises. However, to say that commerce is more ethical today than three centuries ago does not alter the need for continued effort to improve ethical conduct in the marketplace. In fact, ethical concepts in business are in many ways a reflection of the behavior prevailing throughout our society. We are living in an age when traditional values and mores are being examined and questioned. Perhaps it is well that we try to explore this subject, especially the place of ethics in business management. The study of man's efforts to determine right from wrong is the province of *ethics*. More specifically, ethics has been defined as "that branch of the theory of conduct which is concerned with the formation and use of judgments of right and wrong, and with the intellectual, emotional, and executive, or overt, phenomena, which are associated with such judgments, either as antecedents or consequents." [1] Ethics is regarded as a branch of philosophy when it is concerned with the ideal—as distinct from that which may actually exist. It has the characteristics of a science when it is concerned with collecting and describing the facts of experience in which judgments of right and wrong are actually embodied or to which they apply. Ethics as an art is concerned with discovering and setting forth rules of conduct that may guide men in the attainment of their ends. [2]

The evolution of ethical concepts reflects the demands of a changing civilization. Early codes of conduct were often grounded in superstitious beliefs. As these beliefs crumbled in the path of advancing civilization, existing codes disintegrated and chaos prevailed. Out of this chaos—especially as it prevailed in the Greek and Roman civilizations—emerged the efforts to discover guiding principles of conduct. The search for these guides led in many directions. Some sought a force inherent in the nature of man, which when discovered would provide the all-inclusive guide. Some felt that the concepts of *right* and *wrong* could be arrived at through a process of reasoning and laws could be derived with the preciseness of mathematics. Others looked to an external force as a fountainhead from which man must receive his rules to live by. The search to find the key that would lead to the discovery of universal laws goes on. [3]

It is far beyond the scope of this limited discussion to probe the philosophy of ethics. But as individuals living in the twentieth century, we may at least look backward upon the struggles of civilization and indulge in a moment of speculation. It is obvious that somewhere in the dim past man found himself endowed with an intelligence that was to mark his ascent from the level of the lower animals. Early man, faced with problems of survival, evidently succeeded through the power of his intellect. It is reasonable to surmise that early man, in his fight for survival, fathomed the advantage to be gained from an elementary group relationship (archeological evidence would indicate as much) and thus evolved the family, clan, and tribe. In fact, it may be argued that group behavior is instinctive to the extent that certain of the lower animals may engage in cooperative behavior for mutual protection (witness the crows that post sentinels while the flock is feeding). If early man had the intelligence to see the advantages of group cooperation, surely he must have had the intelligence to realize that group activity could not exist without some element of direction. True, it may simply have been

---

[1] See the discussion by John Dewey, *The Encyclopedia Americana*, Vol. 10 (1957), pp. 540–46.

[2] *Ibid.*

[3] See Benjamin Selekman, *A Moral Philosophy for Management* (New York: McGraw-Hill Book Co., 1959).

a matter of the individual with the greatest physical strength directing the group; but even so, the process of "directing" must have involved the establishment of certain rules by which the group had to abide. The point to be made is that group activity could not exist without rules or codes whereby each member of the group to some extent subjugated his individuality to the group objective. This "concern for others" perhaps started at the family level and later enlarged to encompass the clan or tribe. Primitive tribes today often have a rather highly developed sense of ethical responsibility within the tribe while having no such sense of responsibility in dealing with those foreign to the tribe.

From the foregoing, we may assume that man's first concept of ethical behavior developed as a product of his intelligence and was prompted by the necessity of group participation as a means to survival. As man developed from the primitive to the more complex social patterns, the need for a more complex structure of ethical codes developed. Step by step man saw his individual interest become identified with the group interest; and at each step in this development, he drew upon his intelligence to recognize and accept the necessity for codes of behavior to guide the group in its objectives. It is obvious that there would have been differences of opinion as to the codes that should guide the group. The varying concepts of right and wrong that have existed throughout the ages attest to these differences. Nations have lived and nations have perished in providing the world with a laboratory of experimentation in ethical concepts. Today, we are the beneficiaries of ethical concepts emerging from the cauldron of the ages. In our civilization, the philosophy of the *Golden Rule* and the wisdom of the concepts set forth in the *Ten Commandments* shine forth to provide a foundation for the ethical practices of our society. Our ethical concepts emerged as manifestations of man's urge for survival, and in many ways they are the product of man's experience in group living. They are also great monuments to the intelligence of mankind—an intelligence that has so far guided man through trials of success and failure but always forward to new plateaus.

Ours is not a civilization in search for rules of conduct. We have rules of conduct that the vast majority of us, even those who break the rules, agree are essential to our ultimate survival. Those who flaunt recognized ethical concepts do so with the belief that others who adhere to ethical principles will provide a protective wall around them. We pride ourselves upon having an advanced civilization, and our laws refuse to accept the contention that a mature and sane individual does not know right from wrong. Yet the lack of ethical conduct on the part of some members of society remains a frightening thing. We know that those who are devoid of ethical standards go their devious ways thinking that those with standards will not only furnish the host for their parasitic endeavor but will also provide and safeguard the pasture in which they roam. The potential tragedy lies in the possibility that more and more of the hosts will join the ranks of the parasites, and the pasture will grow up in weeds and the fences will tumble down. The fall of ancient civilizations could well be a lesson for many of us living in the twentieth century.

Business Ethics

The purpose of this chapter is to focus attention upon the problems of business ethics. In our society, everyone is either engaged in, or serviced by, activities coming under the broad concept of "business." We have specific ethical codes designed to guide the practice of medical doctors, lawyers, and others, but these groups are also parties to business practice. Some may have an interest as investors in business, and all are interested in business practice from the viewpoint of their role as consumers. In early societies, business was not the pervasive factor that it is today. Units of society were self-sufficient and relied very little upon the element of trade with others. The feudal estates of medieval times were largely self-sustaining. In fact, the tradesman was often looked down upon and considered somewhat inferior to the landowner. It was not until the eighteenth century that the social status of the trades-man began to rise.

The fact that business activity, and the trader, were initially held in low regard may account for the low state of ethical practice in early periods. The trader lived by his wits; and in dealing with fellow traders and the public, it was often "every man for himself and the devil take the hindmost." The doctrine of *caveat emptor* (let the buyer beware) emerged from this background. Examples of advertisements and other business communications preserved from early times indicate an absence of ethical standards in business practice. It is difficult to say just when business became concerned with ethics, or when the consumer began demanding improvement. But it was perhaps well into the nineteenth century before concerted efforts to improve ethical standards gained much headway. By that time the social status of the trader had risen, and the businessman had probably become aware of notions of social responsibility. In studying the ethics of business today, it is well that we keep in mind the background from which the practice of commerce has emerged. By comparison with earlier periods, we are able to note an encouraging trend in the development of ethical standards. While pointing to the need for further improvement in the ethical conduct of business, we are able to draw encouragement from that which has already been accomplished.

Historical Pattern in the United States

Religion played a very important role in the establishment of the early American colonies. Religious practices extended to the establishment of codes of conduct that reached into all aspects of daily life. Colonial families were largely self-sustaining, but such commerce as existed must have been influenced by religious practice. Also, such domestic trade as existed initially was between individuals living in close proximity and personally acquainted with one another. This would have served to discourage unethical conduct. As the colonies prospered and the population grew, business relationships became less personal; and it is probable that the tendency toward sharp business practices grew. Traders used firewater to purchase furs from the Indians, and we read of those who disguised the furs of certain animals to mislead the buyer and obtain a higher price. Such episodes were perhaps relatively minor, and the over-all conduct of business in colonial America was an improvement over that existing in the old world.

The American Revolution was an age of ideology in our country. The men who founded our government were men of high moral character and a strong religious conviction, and undoubtedly these men exerted an influence on their contemporaries. This influence has been described by one source as follows:

About the time of the American revolution, itself engendered in large part by men of interest broader than the turning of a pious dollar, there began to emerge a group of men fully conscious, on the one hand, of the duty of hard work for the glory of God and, on the other, of leisurely meditation and helpfulness to others.[4]

The effect of the industrial revolution in America was to intensify trade. The United States was gaining population and spreading westward. The growth of commerce gained unprecedented momentum following the Civil War. The race to exploit the vast resources of the nation soon developed into a competitive struggle with the ethics of business conduct largely discarded. The source quoted above has this to say:

If men like Thomas Mellon separated business and worship to some degree, other denizens of the Gilded Age separated them entirely. The maraudings of Jay Gould and other robber barons are too familiar to need recounting

[4] Maurice Baum (ed.), *Readings in Business Ethics* (Dubuque, Iowa: W. C. Brown Co., 1950), p. 1.

here. . . . Such men were almost uniquely innocent of any moral motivation. They were small boys joyous in chicanery. They did not even practice capitalism; their maneuvers lacked any element of rationality, any close computation of gain and risk, even lacked bookkeeping. Neither Drew nor his opponent Cornelius Vanderbilt kept any books at all. What they practiced resembled, in fact, juvenile warfare. Mercenaries were dispatched for pitched battles, and at one time Drew, Gould, and James Fisk barricaded themselves with three cannons and a private army in the Taylor hotel in Jersey City, all to avoid the forces of law that Vanderbilt had bribed to act against them.[5]

The growth of ruthless competition accompanied by a decline in business ethics led to certain changes that slowly emerged with the twentieth century. The government began to assume a role in the regulation of business conduct, and various groups within industry began movements to improve and police their own ethical conduct.

WHAT CONSTITUTES UNETHICAL BUSINESS CONDUCT?

The Multiple Responsibility of Business

Our society is characterized by specialization. Each may trade the product of his talents for the products produced by the talents of others. In a highly industrialized state, everyone becomes, to some extent, a part of the great mosaic of business. This places a particular responsibility upon those who compose the mainstream of business practice. To preserve an environment in which business practice can be carried on by individuals with reasonable freedom and respect for one another is to preserve what we so often refer to as the "American way of life." The business firm that now operates in a free society has a responsibility to that society. First, there is a responsibility to the consumer who deserves fair value in exchange. The firm that cheats the public undermines the very system that affords it freedom to operate. Second, a business firm has a responsibility to other firms, competitors included, to deal fairly and observe the ethical standards of fair play. This implies the willingness to compete honestly and to avoid taking unfair advantages through actions that are in conflict with the basic precepts of *right* and *wrong*. Third, the firm has a responsibility to its employees to provide honorable employment. And fourth, and of equal importance, a business firm has a responsibility to the nation of which it is a part. By accepting the responsibilities in the first three categories cited, the firm will have gone far in discharging its responsibility to the nation. The business firm that discharges its responsibility will, in so doing, demonstrate a high standard of ethical conduct; conversely, the firm devoid of ethical standards can-

[5] *Ibid.*

not assume a responsible role and is accordingly parasitic upon the public, its fellow business firms, and upon the nation.

Unethical Conduct in Selling

We normally live in an economic environment where there is great competition among sellers. Along with the blessings of an economy in which the consumer has a freedom of choice, we frequently find certain sellers resorting to deceptive practices. In earlier times, the seller often operated under a philosophy of "let the buyer beware"; and there prevailed, in general, a tolerance for the chicanery of the salesman. Falsehoods, exaggerations, and deceptions were shrugged off as inherent parts of the system. The attitude was similar to our present regard for the spiel of the side-show barker; we don't accept what he says at face value, but rather consider it as a part of the atmosphere of the carnival. Some of this ancient attitude toward the salesman has been handed down to us and can be noted in the attitudes of the courts toward verbal claims made in the course of selling. The courts have been inclined to allow a certain amount of "trade puffing." This trade puffing or "poetic license" is often observed on the part of the salesman as he proclaims the merits of his product.

Reliable business firms have been quick to realize the benefits to be gained from truthful and honest salesmanship. Buyers have rejected the deceptive salesman and his product. Honest business firms have also suffered from the practice of dishonest competitors, and this has led to cooperative action to counter the dishonest. The courts, while allowing some "trade puffing," have taken a dim view of salesmanship that is deceptive to the point of perpetrating fraud. Salesmen, and their companies, have been held responsible for giving misleading information when such as resulted in injury to the buyer. In the areas of industrial selling, or in other areas where the buyer is relatively well informed, deceptive selling practices are seldom found. It is simply not good business to be unreliable, as the deceptive firm will find its overtures rejected. To a great extent, fraudulent selling schemes are directed at the gullible—the uninformed and often the helpless. It is this factor that makes the unethical operator even more despicable than he might otherwise be.

A good part of the unethical selling practiced is aimed at the person in his home. Business firms are usually capable of detecting and dealing with deception, but the household consumer may not be as alert to the danger. So it is not surprising that these vultures would ring the door-bells of the unsuspecting. It is not intended to imply that all house-to-house selling is fraudulent, as there are reputable firms using this method of distribution. But the practices of the unethical sellers have continually made it difficult for the reliable firms to sell directly. Homeowners, once deceived, are likely to condemn all door-to-door selling. Typical of the deception sometimes found is the "research racket" used by some unethical seller to gain admission to the home. In this situation the salesman introduces himself as a research employee taking a survey. When admitted to the home, he very soon abandons the survey and goes into his sales presentation.

Deception in Advertising

From its infancy, the advertising industry has been plagued by those who seek to exploit through giving misleading information. In our country, advertising has developed on a grand scale as an integral part of our system of mass distribution. The fact that it has developed as one of the major tools of selling is a tribute to those in business who have worked to raise advertising standards. Just as firms realized the fallacy in deceptive selling, they realized the ultimate weaknesses in deceptive advertising. If advertising was to produce profitable sales, the buyer had to have confidence in it. Business associations, associations of publishers, and associated groups within the advertising industry worked to raise ethical standards. The efforts of reputable firms, coupled with consumer discontent with faulty advertising, eventually led to government action in the form of regulatory laws. But as in the case of personal selling, there remain certain firms that engage in deceptive advertising and seek to exploit.

Deception in advertising has been an especially difficult problem. The mass use of advertising results in the production and distribution of a quantity of material so great as to make it difficult to detect all violators of ethical, or legal, standards. Associations and regulatory agencies are able to note the more flagrant violators and to bring pressure to bear upon them. Again, as in personal selling, the more reputable firms maintain higher ethical standards, and the firms that seek to exploit victimize the gullible. In some respects, it may be said that many firms are less ethical in their advertising than in other aspects of their sales program. There appears to be a tendency of many to tread a thin line between that which is ethical and that which is not. Unsupported claims are made, unfavorable comparisons are drawn with a competitor's product while omitting weaknesses of one's own product, and other questionable methods are used by firms under the spur of competition. There appears to be some evidence that normally ethical firms may allow themselves to be stampeded into deceptive practices through the actions of an unscrupulous competitor. An article commenting on the effects of the 1957–58 business recession on advertising had this to say:

The man doing honest advertising tends to panic when a competitor resorts to unethical practices. The fear of losing business often leads to a decision to "fight fire with fire," and the heretofore honest advertiser adopts the practices of his unethical competitor. Although conclusive evidence is lacking, it is entirely possible that one bad advertiser could set off a chain reaction that could spread through a community, or even an industry.[6]

Where the advertiser resorts to unethical practices because of a competitor, it is an indication that he does not have confidence in the ability of the public to see through the schemes of the competitor. Perhaps this is another indication that as long as we have ignorance and gullibility on the part of the consumer, there will remain the problem of his exploitation.

The more flagrant violators of advertising ethics (those that engage in practices deemed deceptive or misleading) are often faced with action from regulatory agencies. The Federal Trade Commission is the principal federal agency concerned with the regulation of advertising practices. The FTC is empowered to act under the Wheeler-Lea Act, which was passed in 1938. Although not all violators are called to account, some of the worst cases are detected; and the law does stand as a threat to would-be violators. The following quotation from an FTC News Summary indicates the type of case frequently dealt with:

A _____, Mich., retail enterprise is charged in a Federal Trade Commission complaint announced today with misrepresenting its trade status, the nature of its business, the source of its merchandise and the guarantees on it.

The complaint alleges that the trade name _____ Company and various advertising statements create the false impression that respondents are liquidators, authorized adjustors or agents engaged in the sale or disposition of bankrupt, estate, salvage, distrained or other distress or surplus merchandise for the purpose of settling indebtedness or claims.

The truth is, the complaint states, respondents are in the business of purchasing the advertised merchandise from manufacturers or suppliers and selling it at retail for their own account to the purchasing public.

. . . The respondents are granted thirty days in which to file answer to the complaint.[7]

Unfair Competition

Another area of ethical conduct is that involving the relationship of one firm to another. The federal government was first drawn into the

[6] H. A. Frey and D. L. Gentry, "The Business Decline and Advertising Ethics," *The Arkansas Economist*, Vol. I, No. 3 (Spring, 1959), 21.

[7] Federal Trade Commission, *News Summary No. 2*, Washington, D.C., January 22, 1965.

regulation of industry through the necessity of preserving competition. Certain organizations through the formation of collusive agreements among themselves had succeeded in eliminating their less powerful competitors. The process of elimination had involved price wars and other conduct that could hardly be justified as ethical behavior. Other laws have been passed with the purpose of protecting the small firm from its more powerful competitor. It is not an easy matter to determine when competition is unfair, or unethical. Basically, the more efficient firm is entitled to lower its prices and take business from the less efficient. To prevent this is to subsidize the less efficient and thus indirectly tax the public. On the other hand, one must view these matters in terms of the long-run effect. Where there is reason to feel that the firm that lowers its prices to drive out a competitor does so with the purpose of recouping its losses by raising prices when the competition has been eliminated, there are reasonable grounds to feel that an ethical principle is involved. Most of the laws that aim at protecting the small firm from the lower prices of a larger competitor seek justification in the argument that the long-run effect would be detrimental to the public interest.

We may also point out that false advertising and deceptive selling practices are elements of unfair competition. The honest firm may suffer through the tactics of the less scrupulous. We would like to think that in the long run the deceptive firm reaps its just reward in the form of public rejection. There is reason to believe that in the long run the dishonest competitor does pay the just price, but the wheels of economic justice may grind exceedingly slow in some instances. In the meantime, the honest tradesman may suffer heavy loss or be forced into bankruptcy as a result of dishonest competition. This possibility has been a factor in the passage of laws to protect the honest dealer from unscrupulous competition.

EFFORTS TO IMPROVE THE ETHICAL CONDUCT OF BUSINESS

Associations and Codes

The common-sense value of ethical conduct has long been recognized by the more progressive elements of the business community. The improvement of ethical practice was undoubtedly one of the early incentives in the formation of business associations. Honest businessmen sought protection against the dishonest through banding together in a cooperative effort. Almost all of these associations formulated *codes of ethical practice* that members were asked to accept. The establishment of codes of conduct has not been perfect protection against the unscrupulous. In establishing such codes, an association can only ask its membership to comply, and to perhaps bring some pressure to bear on violators through an element of exposure. The rules of conduct established by the association does not have the authority of the law, although some of our laws of today that have a bearing on ethical practice first appeared as a part of fair practice codes established by associations of businessmen. Some feel that ethical codes are even more effective than the laws in this area:

Codes are useful as reminders even to the most ethical of mortals, because history shows that ordinary men are seldom capable of pure unselfishness for any considerable period of time. There is assurance of progress in social life when we look at the advancement made in codes of duty, ideals, and responsibility. These codes do more than laws could ever do. They are formulated by businessmen themselves, therefore they are workable.[8]

Associations formulating codes of ethical practice may be organized along many lines. There may be associations of producers in a particular industry, or an association of dealers in a particular trade. Other associations cut across industries and are organized along functional lines, such as buying and selling. A typical example of an association that draws its membership from a broad segment of industry is the *National Association of Purchasing Agents*. Membership in this association is composed of personnel employed in the purchasing operation in all types of industries, institutions, and governments. The organization is very much aware of the problems of ethical conduct since the purchasing employee, in carrying out his duties, may be subjected to many temptations and pressures. The National Association of Purchasing Agents has formulated a code known as the "N.A.P.A. Standards of Conduct," and the quotations that follow are a part of that code.[9]

THE N.A.P.A. STANDARDS OF PURCHASING PRACTICE
(As incumbent upon the purchasing agent, or other employees in purchasing.)

1. To consider, first, the interests of his company in all transactions and to carry out and believe in its established policies.
2. To be receptive to competent counsel from his colleagues and to be guided by such counsel without impairing the dignity and responsibility of his office.
3. To buy without prejudice, seeking to obtain the maximum ultimate value for each dollar of expenditure.
4. To strive consistently for knowledge of the materials and processes of manufacture, and to establish practical methods for the conduct of his office.
5. To subscribe to and work for honesty and truth in buying and selling, and to denounce all forms and manifestations of commercial bribery.

[8] Baum, *op. cit.*, p. 28.
[9] By permission from the National Association of Purchasing Agents, New York, N.Y.

6. To accord a prompt and courteous reception, so far as conditions will permit, to all who call on a legitimate business mission.
7. To respect his obligation and to require that obligations to him and to his concern be respected, consistent with good business practice.
8. To avoid sharp practice.
9. To counsel and assist fellow purchasing agents in the performance of their duties whenever occasion permits.
10. To cooperate with all organizations and individuals engaged in activities designed to enhance the development and standing of purchasing.

Another section of the "N.A.P.A. Standards of Conduct" refers specifically to the *standards and ethics of buying and selling*. Ten principles relating to conduct in buying and selling have been set forth as follows:

1. To buy and sell on the basis of value, recognizing that value represents that combination of quality, service, and price which assures greatest ultimate economy to the user.
2. To respect our obligations and neither expressedly nor impliedly to promise a performance which we cannot reasonably expect to fulfill.
3. To avoid misrepresentation and sharp practice in our purchases and sales, recognizing that permanent business relations can be maintained only on a structure of honesty and fair dealing.
4. To be courteous and considerate of those with whom we deal, to be prompt and businesslike in our appointments, and to carry on negotiations with all reasonable expedition so as to avoid trespassing on the rights of others to the time of buyers and salesmen.
5. To avoid statements tending to injure or discredit a legitimate competitor, and to divulge no information acquired in confidence with the intent of giving or receiving an unfair advantage in a competitive business transaction.
6. To strive for simplification and standardization within the bounds of utility and industrial economy, and to further the development of products and methods which will improve industrial efficiency.
7. To recognize that character is the greatest asset in commerce, and to give it major consideration in the selection of customers and source of supply.
8. To adjust claims and settle disputes on the basis of facts and fairness, to submit the facts to arbitration if a mutual agreement cannot be reached, to abide by the decision of the arbiters and to resort to legal measures in commercial disputes only when the preceding courses prove ineffective.
9. To provide or accept no gifts or entertainment in the guise of sales expense, where the intent or effect is to unduly prejudice the recipient in favor of the donor as against legitimate competitors.
10. To give or receive no bribes, in the form of money or otherwise, in any commercial transaction and to expose commercial bribery wherever encountered for the purpose of maintaining the highest standard of ethics in industry.

In advocating the foregoing standards, the N.A.P.A. recognizes that firms are both buyers and sellers; and that if a firm expects to maintain high ethical standards in its purchasing operations, it is likewise obligated to practice comparable standards in its selling operations. Unfortunately, certain firms seem to practice a double standard in that they expect ethical conduct in their buying operations but then proceed to send their own salesmen out to use unethical tactics in attempting to sell.

The Better Business Bureaus

We have all perhaps heard of the *Better Business Bureaus.* There is a National Better Business Bureau that developed from an organization started in 1911, and the local Better Business Bureaus started in 1912. The National Better Business Bureau was established by legitimate business to protect itself and the public from practices that are unfair, misleading, or fraudulent in the field of advertising and selling and to increase public confidence in business and to further consumer education. The local bureaus have the same objectives while concerning themselves with conditions in their respective communities. The national bureau and the local bureaus are supported by business, often closely associated with Chambers of Commerce. A bureau may formulate certain codes, or guides, and elicit the cooperation of business firms in their establishment. It may serve as a "watchdog" function in detecting and investigating cases of unethical practices. The bureaus do not have legal authority, but they can bring pressure to bear on the unethical firm by threatening exposure through publicity disseminated by the bureau. If the unethical practice violates a law, the efforts of the bureau may result in the matter being brought to the attention of the proper government agency. By disseminating information to the public, the bureau may prevent the unethical firm from capitalizing on its scheme. The extent to which a Better Business Bureau is effective depends entirely upon the support given it by the business community. In some communities, the organization is very active and contributes much in the way of protecting the public and the legitimate firms from the unscrupulous. In other communities, the organization is poorly supported and its efforts amount to little more than an empty gesture.

Consumer Education

It is perhaps safe to surmise that as long as there are significant numbers of people who are gullible, there will be those who seek to profit through exploitation. As indicated previously, business firms in dealing with one another are usually able to protect themselves to a degree where ethical practices are concerned. In comparison to the household consumer, the business firm is a "professional buyer" and better able to safeguard his interest. Thus, we may conclude that in a great majority of cases, unethical business practices are perpetrated against the consumer. This is not to imply that the ethical business firm is not damaged by the unethical operator. The unethical firm may provide a type of competition that is damaging, at least in the short run, to the ethical firm. And, also, the distrust engendered by the unethical may make it more difficult for the ethical firm to serve its customers.

If we proceed on the assumption that unethical practice is aimed largely at the consumer, we may logically reason that the most effective attack upon this scourge may lie in the education of the consumer. By education we mean the dissemination of knowledge that will make the consumer a more objective and better informed buyer—a knowledge that will enable him to detect and denounce fraudulent schemes rather than fall victim to them. It is hoped that we are making progress in this direction. The general level of education is rising, and if this education is valid it should induce people to think for themselves and be less subject to exploitation. This point may be questioned in view of the contention that some of our supposedly best informed people are frequently the victims of fraudulent stock schemes and other get-rich-quick devices. If this proves anything, it proves that greed may be so strong in some cases as to overcome the efforts of education. Let us hope that the cases where this may be true will become increasingly rare.

Business Ethics and the Law

In recent years we have seen governmental control extend itself through the passage of an increasing amount of regulatory legislation. Much of this regulation came about as a result of the failure of the business community properly to govern itself. When the public is exploited through unethical conduct, it is natural that some form of protection will be demanded. If business cannot discipline the unethical in its midst, the task will fall to government. The task of regulating conduct is not an easy one, and often laws are far from successful in correcting the abuses for which they were intended. But generally speaking, we do have many effective laws that safeguard the public interest. One unfortunate effect of amassing regulatory laws is the tendency of some business firms to shift ethical responsibility entirely to the law. Faced with many regulatory measures with which they must abide, they seem to take a position that anything not specifically violating an existing regulation constitutes acceptable practice. In other words, unethical conduct becomes limited to those actions that violate the established laws. This is an unfortunate position to take for it imposes upon governing bodies a task far greater than they are able to cope with. That law cannot be a substitute for ethics has been well stated as follows:

Ethics is wider than law. The subject of ethics takes in much more than merely the punishment of acts which are wrong. An ethical man does not seek to justify himself by the plea that he keeps within the law. An act may be quite lawful and yet be immoral and unethical. "Ethics" means "what should be." It carries with it a certain feeling of the "oughtness" of things.[10]

It is reasonable to assume that those who seek to shift the burden of ethical responsibility to the law are simply searching for a means to justify their devious intentions. Perhaps they mollify their conscience by telling themselves that a renunciation of ethical responsibility is a protest against encroachments of the law. It is most likely that such people are the ones who created the conditions making the laws necessary in the first place.

Anyone familiar with the day-to-day functioning of the business enterprise will realize the impossibility of the law serving as a guide and protector in every business transaction. If each transaction took place under conditions where each party limited himself to doing just what the law demands, and each party demanded of the other a strict and literal compliance with every conceivable law relating to the situation, it is obvious that business activity would soon be at a standstill. It would be impossible to cover every business transaction with a formal contract. It would be equally impossible to go into court to handle every adjustment arising from a misunderstanding that might occur between buyer and seller. Great volumes of business are transacted in an environment where one businessman respects another and where one man has confidence in the willingness of another to "do the right thing." If one party feels that he has suffered injury, his grievance may be settled to his satisfaction in an informal conference with the party responsible for the injury. The willingness of both parties to "do the right thing" precludes the necessity for laborious legal contests. Obviously, not all grievances and misunderstandings are settled in this amicable manner, and in such situations the parties must turn to the law.

In our society, the law develops from our efforts to interpret and establish that which is ethical; consequently, there should be no conflict to the extent that the law may require "unethical" conduct. True, unethical conduct may exist without violating the law, but this is but further proof that law cannot encompass the whole of man's conduct. Such laws as exist stand as guideposts warning us of the interpretations that society has placed upon certain actions. For those who fail to heed the warnings, the law becomes the yardstick for meting out such justice

[10] Baum, *op. cit.*, p. 8.

as society may have deemed correct. In the conduct of business, the law stands by as a source to be turned to in the case of need. It is not the purpose of law to supplant the role of ethics in business.

BUSINESS ETHICS AND COMMON SENSE

The Fallacy of Shifting Responsibility

When we get right down to it and think about the matter, most of us would agree that ethical conduct is consistent with what we term "common sense." We know that to survive as a group, a society, or nation, we must rise above the laws of the jungle and adopt rules of conduct consistent with our objective of survival. We could further agree that we exist as a society only because most members of society, at least to some degree, accept and abide by the rules of conduct established. The business community is a major segment of any industrialized society. In our society, the majority of our people are employed in an endeavor that may in some way be described as commercial activity. To a great extent, the ethics of business becomes the ethics of our society; failure of ethics in the market place becomes a failure that touches all of us.

There is no greater and more constant threat to our ethical standards than that growing out of the fallacious belief that ethical conduct is nothing more than the behavior of numbers. The statement that "it must be all right because everybody is doing it" is a fallacy contradicting the very fundamentals of ethical conduct. One may point out the absurdity of this reasoning by observing that slavery must have been "a good and moral thing in Roman times" since every known society of that period practiced slavery. The business community may be especially susceptible to this "follow the crowd doctrine." The presumably honest dealer may be panicked into following the tactics of his less-honest competitor. Attempts may be made to justify the action as being essential to the survival of the business. It is to be doubted that an erstwhile honest firm may save itself from ruin by emulating the dishonest. The presence of the dishonest competitor may afford the excuse to engage in conduct that would be otherwise more distasteful. When the business firm follows this practice, it is shifting its responsibility onto the shoulders of a proven unscrupulous leader. It is tantamount to saying that "since I cannot defeat the thief I will join him and acknowledge him as my leader." It should not tax our intelligence to foresee where this type of reasoning might lead.

Individual Responsibility

The state of ethics prevailing in the world of business is nothing more than a summary of the ethical standards prevailing in the individual firms. It is incumbent upon each business firm to contribute to the improvement of ethics through keeping its own house in order. The philosophy of "let John do it" can be exceedingly dangerous. So far there have been enough "honest-Johns" to hold our business community together and to withstand the cost of carrying unethical neighbors on their backs. But there is an old adage that referred to "the straw that broke the camel's back," and who knows but what some unethical businessman may prove to be the straw that breaks the back of the "honest-Johns" upholding the structure of an ethical business society. It would be tragic for the individual businessman to fail to realize his responsibility to society and to his fellow businessmen. It is doubtful that a man capable of grasping the significance of individual responsibilty could fail to see the common sense of ethical conduct.

It is also essential that we, as consumers, practice the ethical standards that we expect of the business firm. In an effort to bargain for price, consumers have been known to go from dealer to dealer reporting fictitious price quotations. A warranty may guarantee a fountain pen against defects from normal usage, but there are those who seem to feel that normal usage includes being run over by a truck. The consumer as a buyer has an ethical responsibility to deal fairly with the seller. If we fail to observe ethical standards in our daily lives, can we expect business firms, made up of people like ourselves, to be ethical?

TOPICS FOR DISCUSSION

1. Many businessmen feel that they and their firms must be concerned with two kinds of social responsibilities. What are these two responsibilities?

2. Why do you feel that ethical codes exist in a number of industries?

3. List three major social institutions that provide the basic sources of values for individuals and organizations.

4. Do you feel that the Protestant ethic has influenced the development of capitalism?

5. Is it unethical for a student to copy from another's paper during an examination? Why?

6. Is it equally unethical for a student to copy from a textbook during an examination? Why?

7. Assume that there are two sections in the course that you are taking. Section 1 has an exam at 8 o'clock and Section 2 has an exam at 9 o'clock. You suspect that the professor will give both sections the same test. If you

were in the first section, would you report the questions asked to a friend in the second section? If you did, would your conduct be ethical?

8. Whose responsibility is it to see that business is conducted in an ethical manner?

9. Should all ethical conduct be governed by the law?

10. "It is all right to cheat in class because a majority of the people are doing it, and if I don't cheat I may suffer when the professor grades the papers on the curve." Discuss this statement from the viewpoint of the ethical standards involved.

CASE 5–1

THE BRIGHTO PRODUCTS COMPANY

The Brighto Products Company manufactures a line of products including a toothpaste. For a number of years the toothpaste has been a rather steady seller but never one of the leading brands on the market. Early in 1964, the new president of the Brighto Company decided that an intensive promotion campaign should be launched for the toothpaste.

The toothpaste had been marketed under the brand name of "Sparkle," and it was felt that this name had considerable recognition. The promotion manager, who had been placed in charge of marketing the product, felt that in order to be successful the product would have to be differentiated from others on the market in some way. He was a strong believer in the value of additives as a promotional device. Accordingly, a chemical laboratory was employed to experiment with the toothpaste.

After several months of experimentation, the laboratory reported that it had developed an additive that changed the taste of the toothpaste and left the mouth feeling fresher. In reply to questioning, the representative of the laboratory said that the cleaning quality of the product had not been changed. Tests had shown that "Sparkle" cleaned as effectively as other brands on the market.

The promotion manager doubted that the idea of a fresher taste would be sufficient to serve as a theme for a new advertising campaign. After several days of study, he suggested that the additive developed by the laboratory be called *Savident* and that a campaign be launched built around the theme "New Sparkle with Savident prevents tooth decay."

Certain executives of the company were fearful of making such a claim. They pointed out that a conviction for false advertising might do the company considerable harm. The promotion manager was of the opinion that the company need not fear the law in launching its program. He further suggested that the company lawyer study the proposed advertising program and report back to the executives.

The lawyer reported that he was of the opinion that the company could make the claim without prosecution. "In the eyes of the court we are innocent until proven guilty," he stated. "Furthermore, if the Federal Trade Commission objects to our advertising, we can voluntarily change the theme and little harm will have been done. It is my opinion that if the FTC does object and we decide to contest the issue, we would have a good chance of winning in the courts. If the issue goes before the courts, we would be in the role of the defendant and the FTC in the role of the plaintiff. It would be up to them *to prove that Savident doesn't prevent tooth decay.* I don't believe that they have the facilities to conduct the clinical tests necessary to produce proof that the courts will accept. We might not be able to prove that Savident prevents decay, but they would not be able to prove that it doesn't—and the burden of proof would be on them, not on us. It is my opinion that we can make the claim with reasonable assurance that we will not be prosecuted."

The executives of the Brighto Company were undecided as to whether the promotion manager should be permitted to go ahead with the campaign.

1. Do you feel that there are ethical principles involved in this case?

2. If you were an executive of the Brighto Company, how would you vote on this matter? Why?

SELECTED REFERENCES

Baum, Maurice (ed.). *Readings in Business Ethics.* Dubuque, Iowa: W. C. Brown Co., 1950.

Bursk, Edward C. (ed.). *Business and Religion.* New York: Harper & Row, 1959.

Garnett, A. C. *Ethics: A Critical Introduction.* New York: The Ronald Press Co., 1960.

Selekman, Benjamin. *A Moral Philosophy for Management.* New York: McGraw-Hill Book Co., 1959.

Selekman, Sylvia and Benjamin Selekman. *Power and Morality in a Business Society.* New York: McGraw-Hill Book Co., 1956.

Smith, G. A. *Business, Society, and the Individual.* Homewood, Ill.: Richard D. Irwin, Inc., 1962.

Towle, J. W. (ed.). *Ethics and Standards in American Business.* Boston: Houghton Mifflin Co., 1964.

II

ORGANIZING THE ENTERPRISE

6

Forms of
Business Ownership

TYPES OF LEGAL STRUCTURE

An important decision faced by anyone starting a business is the form of business ownership he will use. When the business is starting, he may not think this is of much consequence, because his energies are devoted to getting the firm launched and he is concerned with the myriad decisions of production, financing, securing of space, and other problems. The type he selects, however, can determine the extent to which he is liable for losses the business might incur or how the profits will be shared, as well as many other important factors. Certainly the form of business ownership can be changed from the form initially adopted, but careful thought and planning should be given to the adoption of the type that will best meet the requirements in light of the facts known at the time.

The forms of business ownership are determined by statutory law (an enacted law) or by common law (not enacted but having the status of a law because of general usage and acceptance). These forms of legal structure are classified as being *corporate* or *non-corporate*, with the primary forms of the latter being the *sole proprietorship* and the *partnership*.

THE SOLE PROPRIETORSHIP

Characteristics of the Sole Proprietorship

The oldest form of business organization is the sole proprietorship, a common-law organization. In this type of organization, the individual who forms the company is the owner. It is the simplest type of business organization and the easiest to form. From earliest times, there have been traders and merchants who were sole proprietors, and this form of business organization is the most common today. About four-fifths of our business firms which have fewer than four employees are sole proprietorships. As the size of the business organization increases, the number which are sole proprietorships falls off rapidly. Only about one-fourth of the firms having between twenty and forty-nine employees are sole proprietorships and less than 4 per cent of those firms with 100 or more employees have this form of legal structure. As indicated in Figure 6–1, the most recent data available show that approximately 72

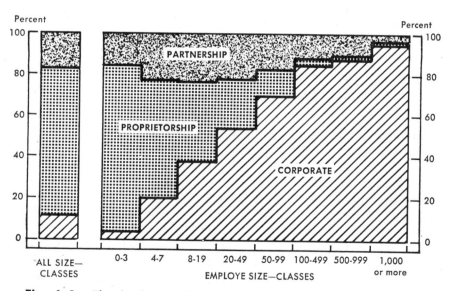

Fig. 6–1. The distribution of firms by legal form of organization for each employee size-class (U.S. Department of Commerce, Office of Business Economics).

per cent of all businesses in all size groups in the United States are sole proprietorships; 17 per cent are partnerships; and 11 per cent, corporations. The relative importance of the different types of business organizations, based on number of employees, is also shown. It can be seen from this figure that the number of sole proprietorships having over ninety-nine employees is very small, whereas the corporation assumes greater importance as the size of the firm increases. The partnership form of organization attains its greatest relative importance in those firms with four to fifty employees, in which it is the form of organization used by between one-fifth and one-fourth of the firms.

If a person has a trade or service which he wants to offer to the buying public, in many states all he has to do is find a suitable place for his business and purchase whatever stock or fixtures are necessary and he can open his doors for business. This means that he has supplied the capital, perhaps very little being necessary, and he has made contracts for the purchase or leasing of equipment or fixtures and stock. In some states and cities, in order to satisfy legal requirements, a *permit* or *license* is required if he handles certain goods or provides certain services. Examples of these are the permits necessary to sell gasoline, milk, and tobacco products. It can be seen that the sole proprietorship can be quickly formed. The cost of fulfilling any legal requirements is negligible since few of them are formal.

The sole proprietorship is sometimes called the "single proprietorship" or the "individual proprietorship." This form of business organization plays a very important part in our economy. It is a means by which widespread ownership of property is developed, which is considered to be desirable in a free economy. When a business can be handled by one person, it is an ideal form of business organization. It often happens that the sole proprietorship organization is outgrown, and another form of organization is adopted which better fulfills the needs of the changing business enterprise.

Advantages of the Sole Proprietorship

The advantages of the sole proprietorship are many, and their relative importance will vary with individuals. To one person, the fact that he is his own "boss" will be the greatest advantage of the sole proprietorship, while to another person, one of its other advantages will be of primary importance. Therefore, there is no attempt to list advantages in order of importance.

Organization Easy.   The ease with which this form of business can be organized is certainly one of its advantages. In order to form a single proprietorship, a person who has the material resources merely has to have the desire and willingness to establish the organization. There is not a lot of "red tape" in securing approval or in complying with multiple requirements. A permit or license may be required, but this is accomplished by filling out a form. This type of business organization provides the opportunity to every individual to operate a business.

Freedom of Decision. Freedom of action is another advantage of the sole proprietorship. All the managerial decisions affecting his business rest with the owner. No one tells him when and what to do about the management of his business. He is free to exercise his best judgment in all respects. He can expand his business by increasing his services or production, or he can cut back his operations. The decisions rest solely with him. To many individuals, this appears to be a major advantage of the sole proprietorship.

Need Not Share Profits. To others, the fact that all the profits of the business belong to the owner will be more important. Whatever a sole proprietorship earns goes to the owner. The product of his ingenuity, his resourcefulness, and his energy is expressed in profit, and he needs share it with no one. The prospect of profits provides a very strong motivation to go into business for oneself.

Sets Own Pace. The sole proprietorship allows the individual to set his own pace. He can work just as hard as he wants to work. He can work around the clock in performing the tasks necessary to the operation of his business, or he can lock the door and be gone for the day if he wants to do so. The usual effect, though, is that the sole proprietor works harder, and his hours of work are longer than would be the case if he were working for someone else. On the other hand, how often have we all seen such signs on doors of shops or professional offices as: "Out for lunch, back at 2:00"; "Closed Wednesday afternoons"; "Closed for the month of August."

Strong Incentives. Operating a sole proprietorship provides an *incentive*. The individual, realizing that the success of the business rests primarily upon his efforts, has a very strong incentive to do the best of which he is capable because his efforts reward him. The idea that he can become a "self-made man"—that he can start with a small business and, through his actions, make that business grow and prosper, the success reflecting favorably upon him—provides a powerful incentive.

Interest in Work. The sole proprietor is doing work in which he has an interest. He has chosen the goods he produces or the services he renders because of their particular appeal to him. His interest in the line of business he chooses provides an enthusiasm for his work. The satisfaction derived is not something which can be measured but is an extremely strong motivating force.

Individual Potential. The operation of one's own business permits the development of an individual's *full potentialities*. He is a planner, an organizer, a financier, an accountant, a salesman, an advertising man, as well as many others. He has had to visualize what the scope of his operation could be and organize it so as to fulfill his vision. In supplying capital for his business and in carrying on its operations, he has learned about financial requirements. He has learned to display his products or services to attract customers. He has had to be able to meet people readily and to sell effectively. The establishment and maintenance of records are understood by him even if the actual bookkeeping is performed by someone else. If he is an employer, he has learned the fundamentals of the employee-employer relationship. The wide range of activities which come under his direction has given him the chance to develop fully his capabilities.

Few Laws. The ease with which a business can be discontinued is another advantage. If the owner desires to discontinue his business, and his bills are paid, he does this by just closing his doors. Generally, there are no reports required nor does he have to secure approval from anyone. If he received a permit or license to operate, he must notify the issuing office of the cessation of operations; or if his bills cannot be paid, there are legal requirements which must be met, but these are exceptions rather than the rule.

Taxed as Individual. The sole proprietor is taxed as an individual, so that he pays taxes on his income and property and on his payroll if he has employees. There is no tax to be paid on the type of business organization which he has adopted, as there is for corporations which have taxes levied against the corporation in the form of franchise and incorporation fees and special state taxes. If his operation proves to be so profitable that he would be subject to federal income taxes higher than those which would be levied against a corporation earning the same amount, the federal Internal Revenue Act allows him, under certain conditions, to be taxed as a corporation if he so desires.

Secrecy Preserved. The inventor or innovator of new techniques or services does not have to disclose secret or specialized processes to anyone. He does not run the risk of someone using his secret processes to deprive him of the financial benefits derived from their development. The greater number of people in a partnership and a corporation increases the risk of secrecy being violated. The sole proprietorship enables him to become the sole developer of the products of his specialized knowledge.

Freedom of Operation. The laws which apply to the *legal rights and obligations* of a sole proprietorship provide a freedom of action in all states which the corporate form of organization does not have.

The relationships are clear between the sole owner, his agents, his creditors, and others with whom he deals in a business way. This means that a private citizen working in Missouri, for example, can carry on business in Iowa and pay no greater taxes or incur no greater obligations in Iowa than the local Iowa businessmen have. In the case of a corporation, its legal life depends on the state in which it is organized. When a corporation extends its operations into another state, it must comply with in-state requirements for corporations, such as filing certain legal papers, appointing a representative in the state to act as agent, and paying specified fees and taxes.

Disadvantages of the Sole Proprietorship

As is often true, what may be an advantage to one person may be a disadvantage to another. This is the case with some of the aspects of the sole proprietorship. Factors which will serve as a challenge to some individuals will be insurmountable to others. For that reason, some of the aspects of the sole proprietorship are both good and bad, depending upon the individual who is operating his own business.

Liability for Debts. The owner of the business is liable to the extent of his entire property for the *debts of his business*. He cannot restrict his liability in any way. This means that his liability for business debts goes beyond his business assets to personal assets. If a variety store fails, and the owner cannot pay his bills, the people whom he owes can take whatever money can be raised from the disposal of his business, and as much of his personal property—that is, his home, his automobile, and his investments—as is necessary to pay the amounts owed to them. The identity of the person who operates a business as a sole proprietor cannot be legally separated from his identity as an individual. If his business is involved in a lawsuit, the legal actions are brought for or against him as an individual.

Financing Problems. The problems of *financing the enterprise* may be greater than in some other forms of business organization. While financial institutions have funds to loan to business organizations, these are available under prescribed terms. From the borrower's point of view, one of the most important conditions in borrowing funds is that a certain percentage of the capital needed must be supplied by the owner or owners. In effect, the sole proprietor must have some money of his own if his business is going to need more capital than he can supply. For the person just starting in an untried venture, who has little or no money of his own, friends or relatives may be the only source of additional capital.

Even if the single proprietor has sufficient funds to get started in business, *working capital* is often needed to take care of remodeling expenses and for expansion, inventory, or other needs. The inability to raise necessary working capital often occurs in sole proprietorships because security for borrowed capital is based on the ability of a single individual to make repayment. The problem of capital is not worrisome for the individual who has substantial assets or who has a prosperous business. It is a problem, however, for someone who has little funds, or who has a business which makes constant demands upon him for further capital. As has often been said, money is no problem unless you do not have it. For the person who has it, additional funds are usually available from lending institutions or other sources; for the person who does not have it, securing it in sufficient quantity is sometimes a problem.

There are some businesses which require an extremely large amount of capital to start them. For example, a manufacturer of automobiles operating only one plant requires between 250 and 500 million dollars. There are not very many individuals who would have enough money to form such a company as a sole proprietor. For this reason, a business requiring large amounts for successful operations should probably not be organized as a single proprietorship.

Liability for Decisions. The sole proprietor lacks the consultative assistance of another person or persons of similar stature in the business enterprise. He cannot share his policy decisions. In other words, he does not get the benefit of other people's thinking—the exchange of ideas, the discussion of problems and policies, and informed counsel. It is true that a person may secure advice from others even if they are not connected with him in business. Since it is not based, however, upon thorough knowledge of the business and a vital interest, he may not feel secure in relying upon it.

The final decisions on the operation of his business have to be made by the sole proprietor. Since he is personally liable for the business, he cannot afford to let decisions be made which might jeopardize his business. Suppose, as sometimes happens, the sole proprietor has a manager upon whom he relies more and more until the manager is making decisions on matters which the owner should be handling himself. If this manager makes an error or two in judgment, the owner may find that he is in serious financial difficulties. It could and does happen that this delegation of responsibilities in decision-making to someone who lacks the vital interest of ownership can mean that the owner loses all that he has in his business, and his creditors also take all his non-business assets to settle matters financially.

Lack of Adequate Forethought. The ease with which a sole proprietorship can be formed may be a disadvantage as well as an advantage. This is due to the fact that, because it is so easy to go into business for oneself, not enough thought may be given to the multiple and varied problems that owning and operating a business present. The urge to be one's own "boss" is sometimes so strong that it "colors" facts and overshadows good judgment. Many people start a little business without adequately considering what may happen. They lose their savings, and perhaps borrowed capital, in a venture which would not have been undertaken if all the aspects had been thoroughly explored.

Lack of Continuity. The interruption in business operations in the event of death of the proprietor is a disadvantage of the sole proprietorship. The business and the individual who owns it are inseparable in this form of business organization, so the business actually terminates its legal existence with the death of the proprietor. The business can be continued by the heirs of the deceased if they are able to do so, but it becomes a new business with the new owners. Further, in the administration of the deceased's estate, there may be legal matters which have to be settled before the business can be taken over by new owners.

THE PARTNERSHIP

The Nature of the Partnership

Like the sole proprietorship, the partnership is a form of business organization which has existed for centuries. It developed to fulfill the needs of individuals for each other's help in some sort of business undertaking. In the Middle Ages, individual traders in the Mediterranean area who did not have adequate capital for their ventures admitted partners who furnished a part of the capital in return for a share of the profits. From that time to this, the need for additional capital to undertake a venture, or the need for another's abilities, are underlying reasons for the formation of partnerships. Examples are: business firms of doctors, architects, brokers, and lawyers, to name but a few.

Many partnerships are of only short duration, perhaps covering only one voyage or a particular venture, and others span the lifetimes of the partners. Some are for a specified period of time, like ten years. The popularity of this form of organization is not as great as it was before the advent of the corporate form of business ownership. Many partnerships change to corporations as the needs of the business organization change with growth of the enterprise or the changing business environment. Some very large corporations started as partnerships. This is true of the Great Atlantic & Pacific Tea Company, a food chain, and Swift & Company, a meat-packing firm.

A partnership is a common-law form of business organization in which two or more persons have, by means of a contract, associated themselves in common ownership of a business for profit. The agreement need not be written, although this is desirable, since a partnership can be created by either an *expressed* (written) or *implied* agreement. The partnership has the same status in law as that of the sole proprietorship. In the sole proprietorship, there is one person; in the partnership, there are two or more. Generally, a partnership is not considered to be a legal entity in itself, but one whose ownership is personal and held by the partners. However, under the provisions of the Uniform Partnership Act, which has been enacted in about thirty states, real and personal property may be held in the name of the partnership. It is also true that there are quite a number of states which have laws authorizing bringing lawsuits in the firm names of partnerships.

In this type of organization, as in the sole proprietorship, the partners are liable for the debts of the business. A partner who is dissatisfied with the partnership cannot sue the partnership, but he can sue the other partner or partners. Each of the partners is an agent for all of the partners in the business undertaking for which the partnership is formed. This means that what one partner does in the name of the partnership is binding upon all of the others, even though it was performed without their knowledge. Furthermore, they can be held liable for the acts of one partner in the conduct of the business. This authority can be restricted by a provision in the partnership agreement. In spite of such a limitation, however, the partnership is bound by contracts made by any partner unless the outside organization had been informed prior to the event that the partner had no authority to make such a contract.

The Articles of Co-partnership

Although a partnership agreement may be oral, it is more desirable to have a written agreement. The failure to record the partnership agreement in written form often causes later misunderstandings. On the other hand, many partnerships have been formed without a written agreement, and have continued without such an agreement, because the partners have complete trust in each other and are able to settle amicably any difficulties which arise.

The *written partnership agreement* is called the "articles of co-partnership." The agreement does not have to be officially approved by any government organization and, in this respect, is like the sole proprietorship. The agreement may be very brief, or it may be quite comprehensive. Generally, though, it contains clauses covering the following points:

1. The date of the agreement.
2. The names and addresses of the partners.
3. The type of business conducted by the partnership.
4. The period of time for which the agreement is effective.
5. The firm name of the partnership, and the address at which the business is to be conducted.
6. The amount of capital investment by each partner.
7. The interest, if any, which is to be paid on capital.
8. The division of profits and losses.
9. The type of bookkeeping records to be maintained.
10. The salaries to be paid to the partners, and the amount of withdrawals to be permitted.
11. The amount of time to be devoted by each partner to the partnership.
12. Whether or not any other business may be engaged in simultaneously by the individual partners and to what extent.
13. The duties of each of the partners.
14. The methods of liquidation and dissolution of the partnership.

It is generally a good practice to have a lawyer draw up articles of co-partnership, because his experience and knowledge will be of help in insuring that no matter of importance is overlooked.

Types of Partners

In the absence of any agreement, all of the partners have identical rights and duties in the partnership. The agreement may change this relationship, however, to whatever arrangement the partners desire to make. As a result, several different types of partners have developed in the partnership form of organization.

General partners are the most common. They are known to persons with whom the partnership is doing business, as well as to the general public. These partners share in the management, and they are often referred to as "active partners."

Secret partners share in the management of the partnership, but their connection with the firm is not known to the general public.

Dormant partners do not share in the management of the business, nor is the fact that they are members of the organization known to people outside the firm. In effect, they are inactive and secret partners.

Limited partners do not take an active part in the management of the firm. While it is known that they are partners in the firm, their liability is limited to the amount of their investment in the partnership.

Nominal partners are not partners by agreement, but they are partners because they are represented to the public as being partners. In effect, they have permitted other people to believe that they are partners. For example, a partner may withdraw from a firm, but he does not indicate this withdrawal in any manner to outsiders and the letterheads of the business continue to carry his name.

In some partnerships, a distinction is made in the type of partnership held by individuals according to experience, length of time in the firm, capital invested, age, or other factors. When this is done, some partners are called *senior partners* and others *junior partners*. An accounting firm, for example, may have been formed by a number of men who made the investment, built up the firm, and have primary responsibility for management. They may designate themselves senior partners. A younger man in the partnership who is elevated to partnership status may be termed a "junior partner." He has only a nominal investment and has very little to say about the way in which the business is managed.

Advantages of the Partnership

The partnership form of organization possesses a number of advantages. Some of these are similar to those of the sole proprietorship whereas others constitute improvements.

Easy To Organize. The partnership is easy to organize. All that needs to be done is to have an agreement made by the partners. A partnership may be formed by two persons or by as many more as it is desirable to have. Although the agreement may be oral, it is preferable to have a written agreement, which may involve the services of a lawyer. Other than this expense, the partnership is inexpensive to organize. Like sole proprietorships, there are no legal requirements except in those instances where a permit or license is required. It is not as simple an organization to form as a sole proprietorship because an agreement must be reached between two or more people, while this is not necessary in a sole proprietorship. It is much simpler, however, than forming a corporation.

More Capital. Capital can be raised more easily in a partnership than in a sole proprietorship, although not as easily as in a corporation. The capital of two or more individuals can be drawn upon to provide greater initial capital. The credit of more than one person is involved, so that it may be possible to operate a larger business organization than would be the case in a sole proprietorship. Some of the benefits of a larger-scale operation could thus be obtained. The partnership can also be expanded easily. Another partner or partners can be brought in at any time the present partners want to do so. The partnership may be enlarged because of the capital which a new partner can furnish, or for other reasons.

Better Credit. The *credit position* of a partnership is better than that of a sole proprietorship. Each of the partners is liable for the debts of the partnership, so that the credit of each partner, his real and personal assets, is behind the credit standing of the partnership. The debts incurred by the partnership are personal debts of the individual partners, which have to be paid.

Shared Responsibility. The partnership permits a division of management responsibilities. One person is not called upon to be personally responsible for all phases of the business. The management responsibilities are divided according to the partnership agreement between the partners. This provides a specialization in management, since each partner devotes his time to the particular areas of management for which he is responsible—the division having been made on the basis of the aptitudes and desires of the partners.

Pooling of Knowledge. Partners have the advantage of consultation with each other. A thorough discussion of business problems will often develop solutions to problems which seem insoluble to one person. Consultation also provides a sounding board for testing ideas. A sole proprietor may have a good idea for a new service or product, but be hesitant to go ahead and provide it in his business, because he feels that he may be overlooking something which could make it a costly venture for his business; or the reverse may be true. He may develop a new product on which he loses a great deal of money, the hazards of which would have been apparent to someone else. The pooling of knowledge, experience, and imagination may promote the growth of a business enterprise.

Strong Motivation. The partnership form of organization provides a strong motivation to do the best possible job, since the partners benefit both financially and in prestige from the success of their enterprise. It is their own money which has gone into the business organization and they have a high stake in its success. They are interested in insuring that the most efficient methods are employed in every phase of the business.

Complementary Abilities. The special capabilities of an individual can be secured through a partnership. Individuals often form partnerships because they have complementary abilities and interests. Partnerships are also expanded at times to admit to partnership an individual who is particularly capable in some specialized field which can be of especial value to the business.

Individual Tax Status. The partnership is taxed as an individual is taxed and not as a business organization. The same tax situation exists for a partnership as for the sole proprietorship. The partnership does not pay special state taxes or charter and incorporation fees.

Can Operate in Any State. A partnership possesses the same privileges in any state regardless of the state in which it is domiciled. The Constitution of the United States guarantees to citizens of each state all privileges and immunities provided to citizens of the other states. Thus, the partnership, a legal structure which does not involve an artificial being as the corporation does, possesses this freedom of action not available to corporations. Of course, a state may require that partnerships be licensed to carry on a particular kind of business, but the license will be equally available to businessmen of any state.

Disadvantages of Partnerships

While there are numerous advantages to the partnership, there are disadvantages as well. Before entering into a partnership agreement, an individual should carefully consider all factors.

Unlimited Liability. The *unlimited liability* of the partners is one of the disadvantages of the partnership form of business organization. If there are insufficient business assets to cover the debts of the business, the personal assets of the owners may be taken. The partners are jointly liable for the debts of the partnership, which means that if a creditor sues to collect a debt of the partnership, he would sue all of the partners jointly. If the creditor's claim could not be satisfied by the business assets, he may then bring suit against any and all of the partners individually to satisfy the debt. If one of the partners had substantial personal assets, whereas the other partner or partners did not, he would have to pay the entire debt. Of course, the partner who had to pay could bring suit against his partner or partners, but if the latter had nothing, there is very little to be accomplished by bringing such a suit. The result is, then, that one partner has sustained a much greater loss because he had greater assets than the other partner. In the event that both business and personal assets are inadequate to satisfy the claims against the partners, the debts remain personal debts, which may have to be paid sometime in the future.

Risks in Choosing Partner. The risks involved in the selection of a partner are great. Dishonesty, incompetence, or a domineering personality are some of the attributes which may be discovered in a partner after a partnership is formed. Continued disagreement among partners may cause one of them to withdraw from the firm, even against the wishes of the others. The right to choose those individuals with whom he desires to be associated in a partnership is well recognized. In the event his withdrawal causes damage to the firm, however, a partner can be held liable for any injury he may cause his former partners by his withdrawal.

Partnership Frictions. The sharing of policy authority and responsibilities may make it difficult at times to reach decisions. If each partner has an equal voice in decisions affecting company policy, there may be times when the vote for and against a proposal is a tie. If a mutually acceptable arrangement is not worked out to resolve the disagreements, perhaps by calling upon an outside party to express an opinion which would then prevail, the business of the partnership could be seriously hampered. The management of a partnership requires a "meeting of the minds," which may involve many compromises by each partner.

Binds Other Partners. Each partner is an agent for the partnership, binding the other partners by his actions in the name of the partnership. Unless the articles of co-partnership limit the power of partners to act as agents for the firm, each partner has the authority to bind the firm through contracts he makes.

Instability. There is a degree of instability in this type of organization. Changes in the make-up of a partnership can come about because of the illness or death of a partner. A partner may desire to get into some other business, or the specified lifetime of the partnership may expire, causing the partnership to be terminated and a new partnership to be formed. Sometimes, also, the form of the organization is changed to a corporation.

Difficulties in Partner Withdrawal. It is often difficult for a partner to withdraw the investment he has made in a partnership. If the withdrawing partner can find someone willing to buy his interest, the other partner or partners must agree to accept the new partner. The other partners need to exercise the same care in accepting this person as a partner as they did in the original selection of partners. If a satisfactory buyer cannot be found, the other partner or partners may purchase the interest of the withdrawing partner, but this may be at less than full value. A partner's interest in the firm can be sold to an outside buyer without the individual's being taken into the partnership. This purchaser, however, would not share in the management of the business— only in the profits which would accrue to the share he would be holding.

ADDITIONAL FORMS OF UNINCORPORATED
BUSINESS ORGANIZATIONS

The Joint Stock Company

The joint stock company resembles, in some respects, the corporation. In other respects, it is similar to the partnership. It is an unincorporated company, having members who hold transferable shares of stock represented by *stock certificates*. Unless the state statute provides for an exemption, the joint stock company shareholders have unlimited liability. The shareholders delegate the power to manage the company to a *board of directors* which, in turn, hires the management to run the business.

Although there were many joint stock companies in the early days of our country—some of them very large companies—this form was never as popular in the United States as abroad. This form of business organization has declined in importance because of the advantages of other types of organizations. It has historical significance, however, because it is a step beyond the partnership and the antecedent of the corporation.

The Mining Partnership

In mining and oil ventures, a special type of partnership has been developed. It is called a mining partnership and has the advantage of limited liability. This is particularly desirable because these ventures are quite speculative, and the person investing his money does not have to risk money beyond his investment. It is also easier to raise the larger amounts of capital which may be necessary than would be the case in the usual partnership. The members of a mining partnership do not have to approve a new member who has purchased another partner's shares, nor does the death of a partner dissolve the mining partnership. There are shares in this type of partnership, but they are not necessarily represented by certificates of stock. Special laws have been passed, particularly by western states, to sanction the formation of this type of business organization.

The Partnership Association

The partnership association is a form of business organization found in only a few states. The companies which use it are generally those whose business is conducted in the state in which they are domiciled. One of the advantages of the partnership association over the general partnership is that all of its members have limited liability. A board of directors manages the association. Shares of stock are issued, and the ownership is represented by these shares. The shares are transferable, although the purchaser of the shares must be voted upon by, and acceptable to, the other members. In the event that the purchaser is not acceptable to the other members, they must purchase the interest of the partner who is withdrawing, at a price which is mutually agreeable. Some states specify the maximum and minimum number of partners in such an organization.

The Joint Venture

The joint venture is best described as being a *temporary partnership* which is created for a specific undertaking. The joint venture, or joint adventure, as it is sometimes called, was widely used for many years in foreign trade to finance a venture in ocean shipping. For example, a group would be formed to finance the purchase and operation of a vessel for a round-trip voyage to buy and sell products in different areas of the world. Typically, it is managed by one of the partners, the others only contributing capital to the undertaking.

If a member dies during the time of the joint venture, the venture will be completed by the other members, and the deceased's share paid to his estate. Members of a joint venture have unlimited liability.

Syndicates

A syndicate is an organization which bears a strong resemblance to a joint venture. It is a group of individuals or companies joined together for a fairly short period of time, for a particular purpose. For example, a syndicate may be formed by a number of investment banks to underwrite an issue of stocks or bonds. One bank may have contracted to handle the entire amount, but in order to assist in the sale of the stocks or bonds, an underwriting syndicate may be formed with other investment banks, the liability of each being limited to the amount it has agreed to underwrite. The contracting investment bank is the manager, and the life of the syndicate is limited to the period required for the sale of the securities. There is no problem involved in the death of any member, since the members are business firms.

The syndicate is being used increasingly in financing specific purchases of real estate. Sometimes these syndicates are organized by an investor. At other times, a real estate investment company will form the syndicate. These companies find potential loan or purchase ventures, such as apartment houses and office buildings, locate investors, and have experts handle the technical problems of forming the syndicate. The tax advantages in this type of investment account for its popularity.

THE CORPORATION

What Is a Corporation?

The corporation is created by state governments through the enactment of legislation called *corporation laws*. These state laws differ widely, some states having much more lenient laws than others in regard to incorporation requirements and taxation. Because of this fact, certain states, such as Delaware, are favored over others as places in which to incorporate. Non-corporate enterprises are numerically more important than the corporate. Economically, however, the corporation has become the dominant type of business organization in the United States.

Probably the most frequently quoted definition of a corporation is that given by Chief Justice Marshall, in 1819, in the *Dartmouth College Case*, in which he stated that:

A corporation is an artificial being, invisible, intangible, and existing only in contemplation of law. Being the mere creature of law, it possesses only those properties which the charter of its creation confers upon it. . . . Among the most important are immortality and . . . individuality; properties by which a perpetual succession of many persons are considered as the same and may act as a single individual. . . .[1]

Stated simply, the corporation is an artificial person having no existence except in law; it is not a real or natural person. The rights and privileges it possesses are given it under its charter granted by the state in which it is incorporated. The most important of its characteristics are that its life is lasting and individually its own, since it is created by the specifications contained in its charter.

Historical Development of the Corporation

The use of some form of the corporation can be traced back many centuries. The Romans used it under the name of *collegium*, or college, before the fall of Rome in the fifth century. These early corporations were used extensively in non-business enterprises, such as religious organizations. Then, as municipalities grew and began furnishing services which involved the ownership of property, it became apparent that such ownership required continuous existence regardless of changes in the

---

[1] 4 Wheaton 636; 17 U.S. 518, 636.

membership of the governing body. The corporation was adopted as a form of organization for the same general uses in many European countries and gradually spread to business enterprises.

A considerable amount of public opposition to corporations existed in the United States prior to 1800, because of the experiences many people had with the trading companies formed in England under charter privileges, which gave a monopoly of trade to a company for a particular part of the world. In too many instances, these monopolistic powers were abused, and people came to associate the corporation with monopoly and special privilege.

Although the number of incorporated organizations gradually increased in the United States, restrictions were imposed by the states, limiting the use of the corporate form of business organization. The first liberalization of corporate laws came in the state of New York. In 1811, this state enacted legislation permitting liability to be limited to the amount of capital invested, and a quarter of a century later, it permitted a group to incorporate for any legitimate purpose. These changes in the New York laws made the corporate form a great deal more attractive as a form of business organization; this liberalization of the incorporation laws was soon followed in other states.

The gradual easing of corporation laws continued into the 20th century. The public's fear of monopoly and special privileges substantially lessened through the years. Greater economic activity in manufacturing and business enterprises provided a stimulus for this form of organization, in order to meet the demands of large-scale business activity requiring great amounts of capital. The modern corporation, as it has evolved, is the product of our particular business needs as they have developed through the years.

Corporations Classified as to Place of Incorporation

In the state in which a corporation is incorporated, it is referred to as a *domestic corporation*. If the corporation is not incorporated in a particular state and operates in that state, it is referred to as a *foreign corporation*. An *alien corporation* is one which is incorporated in another country.

Make-up of the Corporation

The incorporated organization issues certificates of stock, one of the types of securities issued by a corporation. (The types and classes of corporate securities are explained in Chapter 7.) Purchasers of the stock are called *shareholders* or *stockholders*. Some companies have only a few shares of stock and a few owners, while others, like General

Motors Corporation and Standard Oil of New Jersey, have millions of shares of stock and hundreds of thousands of stockholders. The owners of one form of stock, *common stock*, almost always have the right to vote in the election of the directors of the company and in certain other affairs. A stockholder is notified of meetings of the stockholders and invited to be present. If he is unable to attend and vote in person, he completes a form indicating that an officer of the company may exercise his voting right. This is called a *proxy form*. Most stockholders send in proxy forms rather than attend meetings of the company.

Stockholders may receive *dividends* on the shares of stock which they own. These are payments, usually in money, made from earnings of the corporation. *Annual reports* are made to stockholders, as well as periodic reports, to keep them informed of the progress of the corporation.

Technically, the stockholders are the owners of the corporation. As a legal entity or being, however, the corporation is the owner of the property of the business for which it was chartered. The ownership of the corporation and the ownership of the corporation's property are distinct and separate matters. Since the corporation is an artificial person, the debts of the corporation are the debts of the separate legal person, which means that the stockholders ordinarily cannot be held liable for the debts or the acts of the corporation.

A *board of directors* is entrusted with direction of the affairs of a corporation. State laws usually fix the minimum number of board members, whereas company bylaws specify the maximum number of directors. Generally, a board of directors will be composed of seven to nine persons, although there are some that have as many as thirty. Many corporations try to provide a balance in their board of directors by securing representation of company management, outside interests, representatives of large ownership interests in the corporation, and general management experts. For many years, a $20 gold piece was a common fee for directors for taking part in a board meeting. Today, director's fees are usually $50, $100, or more for each meeting attended.

Factors in Incorporation

There are requirements in most states that three or more persons are necessary to form a corporation. The persons who desire to form a corporation must decide upon the state in which to incorporate. Certain types of business organizations, such as public utilities, may be required to be incorporated in the state in which their operations are conducted. However, this is not generally true of other businesses. For small corporations or those whose business will be conducted within one state, there is little advantage to be gained by incorporating in a state other than the one in which the business will be conducted.

The organizers evaluate the incorporation requirements of the different states in such matters as: incorporation fees; taxes upon the corporations; requirements regarding securities to be issued; the qualifications required of those individuals who are forming the corporation; the rights of the stockholders; the corporation's powers; and the framework of law which has been established through court cases involving the state's corporation requirements. One or more of these factors may be controlling to one incorporating group, while different factors may be of major concern to other groups. Lawyers who specialize in incorporation of companies know which states best satisfy the needs of the group seeking incorporation.

The *capitalization requirements* (the monetary total of securities which will be required) of the corporation must be carefully examined. The financial needs of the company have to be considered as to the present and the future. The amount and kinds of securities the corporation will want to issue have to be stipulated. Since these matters have to be authorized in the corporate charter and cannot be increased without securing approval of both the stockholders and the state, great care has to be exercised in setting the capitalization needs of the corporation. The capitalization of a public utility corporation is shown in Table 6–1. In this company, 45 per cent of the capitalization is bonds, 21 per cent preferred stock, and 34 per cent common stock. These different types of securities are explained in Chapter 7.

Certificate of Incorporation

Generally with the help of a lawyer, the group organizing the corporation prepares a Certificate of Incorporation, which is the application for a corporate charter. The contents of the Certificate of Incorporation depend upon the state in which incorporation is sought, but usually include the following information:

1. The name of the corporation.
2. The purpose of the corporation.
3. The location of its principal office.
4. The duration of the corporation.
5. The amount of capital stock.
6. The voting rights of the stockholders.
7. The maximum indebtedness.
8. The names and addresses of the board of directors and their powers.
9. The names and addresses of the incorporators.

Table 6–1. Capital Structure of a Large Corporation

	Authorized	Outstanding	Ratio
FIRST MORTGAGE BONDS	Unlimited		
Series due February 1, 1974, 2¾%		$ 5 000 000	
Series due October 1, 1975, 2¾%		75 000 000	
Series due July 1, 1978, 3%		10 000 000	
Series due August 1, 1979, 2⅞%		15 000 000	
Series due June 1, 1982, 3¼%		21 500 000	
Series due October 1, 1984, 3⅛%		20 000 000	
Series due September 1, 1986, 4¼% . . .		15 000 000	
Series due July 1, 1988, 4%		30 000 000	
Total First Mortgage Bonds		$191 500 000	45%
PREFERRED STOCK, par value $100 per share	$100 000 000		
Cumulative Preferred Stock, $3.60 series		$ 27 500 000	
Cumulative Preferred Stock, $4.08 series		15 000 000	
Cumulative Preferred Stock, $4.10 series		17 500 000	
Cumulative Preferred Stock, $4.11 series		20 000 000	
Cumulative Preferred Stock, $4.16 series		10 000 000	
Total Preferred Stock		$ 90 000 000	
Premium on Preferred Stock		311 225	
Total Preferred Stock and Premium		$ 90 311 225	21%
COMMON STOCK, par value $5 per share .	$ 75 000 000	$ 71 402 445	
Premium on Common Stock		36 805 011	
Earned Surplus		37 615 505	
Total Common Stock, Premium and Earned Surplus		$145 822 961	34%
Total		$427 634 186	100%

The Certificate of Incorporation is sent to the Secretary of State in the state in which incorporation is sought, together with the amount required to cover the incorporation fees. If the Certificate is accepted and filed, it becomes the *articles of incorporation* or the *corporate charter*.

Corporation Bylaws

Although the charter is a rather complete document, it does not cover many of the administrative details of the organization. These are included in a set of bylaws. The bylaws must adhere to state incorporation laws and to the corporate charter in furnishing additional details of the administrative organization and its powers. Although many state incorporation laws do not specify what must be contained in the bylaws, typical provisions are:

1. The date and location of the annual meeting of the stockholders, including the procedure to be followed at the meeting.

2. The location of the principal office and other offices of the corporation.
3. The number, powers, term of office, and compensation of the directors.
4. The location and dates of meetings of the board of directors, and procedure at meetings.
5. The designation of the officers and the manner of their appointment; their duties and their terms of office.
6. Details regarding capital stock issued, such as the form of the stock certificates, the manner in which they can be transferred, and provisions for the replacement of lost certificates; and the manner of inspection of stock record books by stockholders.
7. Designation of the corporate seal.
8. The procedure for amending the bylaws.

The stockholders have the power to make and to amend the bylaws, but this can be delegated to the board of directors. In addition to these provisions, which are common to most bylaws, many others may be included. Some bylaws include provisions that certain actions must be submitted to the stockholders for their approval. An example is that of having stockholders vote on the public accounting firm to make the annual audit of the company's records.

Advantages of the Corporation

There are a number of advantages that corporations have which will help in understanding why they have become such an important form of business organization.

Limited Liability. One of the foremost advantages of the corporation is that its stockholders have limited liability. An investor can purchase shares of stock, and if the business should fail, he will lose only his investment. The creditors of the corporation cannot take his other assets to settle the claims they may have against the corporation, even if corporate assets are insufficient to meet the creditors' claims. This enables a stockholder to invest money in the shares of a number of companies at the same time, since his risk is limited only to the amount of money he is investing.

Varied Financing. The ability of the corporate form of business organization to raise capital is a significant advantage. Many people can be drawn into the ownership because of the number and kinds of shares that are offered. Essentially, this means that, in most corporations, the shares are available to the general public, and anyone who has the price of a share can invest in the corporation. The different kinds of securities offered meet the investment desires of a wide range of investors. There are different denominations of securities and varying degrees of powers and participation in the business, based on the type of securities purchased. Some carry voting rights and others do not. Some have a fixed dividend which is paid to the investor before the holders of another class of stock can be paid. The various classes of stock sell for different prices, thus satisfying individual investment demands. Appealing as they are to a vast number of people, the investment opportunities offered by a single corporation can raise millions of dollars in initial capital to launch the enterprise. Additional capital funds for expansion and development in later years can also be readily raised. In contrast, partnerships and sole proprietorships, as has been explained earlier, are limited in ability to raise capital. This is one of the reasons why these enterprises operate on a comparatively small scale.

Share Ownership Easily Transferred. The ease with which shares of stock can be transferred adds to the investment attractiveness of corporations. Unlike the partnership, in which the sale of a partner's share must be approved, the owner of stocks in a corporation can sell his shares of stock at any time without having the approval of anyone.

More Permanent. The existence of the corporation is uninterrupted by changes in the ownership of its stock. Even though there is constant change in the ownership of a corporation's stock, its business life continues because it is a legal entity in itself. It continues to make contracts and carry on its business in the usual way while shares are bought and sold. Corporate charters generally are granted for a specified period of time, for example, for 99 years. Some of them contain the phrase "in perpetuity," thus having no termination date. Because there is no uncertainty concerning its legal existence, it tends to be a more permanent form of organization than the partnership or sole proprietorship, which is directly affected by the death or illness of a partner or individual owner.

Stockholder Restrictions. The stockholders do not have the power to act as agents for the corporation. This is in contrast to partnerships, in which the partners generally act as agents for the business and bind the other partners by their actions. Stockholders would be unwilling to buy stock in a corporation if they were to be bound by the actions of all other stockholders, since the only qualification required to purchase stock is the necessary money.

Investors Need Not Manage. The owners or stockholders do not have to conduct the business affairs of the corporation. This is done by hired management, which is responsible to the board of directors for efficient conduct of the corporation's affairs. The investor does not need to know anything about managing a company in which he buys shares. Since he has no management responsibilities, he can invest in a number of corporations.

Specialists.   Management specialization is possible in corporations. In the corporation, management areas of responsibility are headed by specialists. These specialists, such as an advertising manager, a sales manager, a finance manager, purchasing manager, and traffic manager, bring their technical knowledge to bear on problems and policies in their particular fields. Within these areas, also, there are additional specialists who, through education, training, and experience, have developed substantial ability in their fields. Specialization permits more intensive management control than in a partnership or sole proprietorship, in which management, in some areas, may be largely of the "trial and error" type. Some management areas receive little or no attention in the non-corporate forms of business organizations.

Has Separate Legal Existence.   The corporation is a legal entity. As such, it can sue or be sued in its own name without any reference to the actual owners of the corporation—the stockholders. This is not true of the sole proprietorship or the partnership where, even if a firm name is used, the individual names of the owners are listed in any legal action. As a separate legal entity, the corporation can hold title to property, being able to acquire or transfer property in its own name.

Disadvantages of the Corporation

The corporation has become a widely accepted form of business organization. In terms of income produced, it has also become a dominant form in all fields of endeavor. In addition, in the field of manufacturing, the corporate form of business enterprise far surpasses other forms in the personnel it employs, the salaries and wages it pays, and the value added to products by manufacturing. In spite of the important role played by the corporation, however, it does have certain disadvantages.

Higher Taxes.   The taxes on corporations are higher than those for partnerships and sole proprietorships. Every corporation must pay *incorporation fees* in the state in which it secures its charter. The amount of these fees varies widely among the states, but it is a substantial figure. It is a fee that applies only to corporations and is required in forming a corporation. If the corporation desires to conduct its business in other states, most of these states will require the payment of fees from the corporation before it can do business in those states. The corporation is also subject to both *state and federal income taxes* and to *property taxes* in the areas in which it owns property. There are a number of municipalities, too, which assess income taxes on income earned within their confines. The corporation, because of its reputation of making a great deal of money, is a good target for special taxes as well, when states are looking for additional sources of revenue. Figure 6–2 graphi-

Billions of dollars

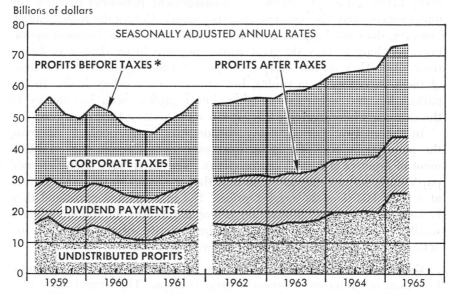

* Excluding inventory valuation adjustment. Data beginning 1962 adjusted for effects of new depreciation guidelines and therefore not comparable with previous data.

Fig. 6–2. The importance of taxes in the corporate profit picture (U.S. Department of Commerce, Council of Economic Advisers).

cally illustrates the significance of taxes in the profit picture of all corporations in the United States. As can be seen, corporate taxes amount to almost as much as dividends and undistributed, or retained, profits combined.

The federal income taxes upon corporations are taxes graduated according to the amount of income earned. For example, on the first $25,000 earned by a corporation, a tax of $5,500 might be paid, or approximately 22 per cent of the income. If the corporation earned $75,000, the tax is $5,500 for the first $25,000 and an additional tax of 48 per cent on the amount over $25,000 of income. Thus, a total tax of $29,500 is paid on earnings of $75,000.

The Technical Amendments Act of 1958, amending the Internal Revenue Code of 1954, provides in Section 64 that certain small domestic business corporations may elect the tax status of partnerships, subject to certain limitations, one of which is that the corporation must not have more than ten shareholders.

Motivation Problems.   Management personnel of a corporation lack the high degree of personal motivation which exists in the management of a partnership or a sole proprietorship. In the noncorporate forms, every action intimately affects the management personnel because the management and the owners are the same. Corporate management, however, does not have as great a financial stake in the business operations. As long as they do good work, they are in no danger of losing their jobs. They do not suffer financially if profits go down, since most of them do not share in profits, but are paid on a salary basis. In the partnership and sole proprietorship, lower profits mean less money to the owners, while greater profits mean more money to the owners.

In the postwar period, many corporations have sought to increase the personal interest of management executives through the establishment of *bonuses* and *stock option plans*. The latter have been designed particularly for top executives, so that they may purchase shares of stock at a price less than the market price. The management personnel then become owners, also. Motivation is not a problem, of course, when a small number of people own all, or the majority, of the stock and are active in the management of the corporation.

Organization Difficulties.   It is more difficult to organize a corporation than other forms of business organizations. The organization of a corporation requires a study of the corporate laws of different states and a decision on the state in which to incorporate. The articles of incorporation have to be completed and submitted to the state for a charter. The *par value* (an amount in dollars assigned to the share by the company's charter) and amount of stock to be authorized have to be determined. Bylaws must be drawn and adopted, upon receipt of the charter, which means that a board of directors must have been selected, and many other formalities completed. The process of organization is time-consuming, and special care has to be taken that specific legal requirements are followed in the organization of the corporation and in its operations. The services of a good corporation lawyer are needed from the time that a group decides it wants to organize until the corporation is a "going" concern. Most corporations retain permanent legal counsel. The expenses involved in the organization of a corporation, with the necessity of handling the many legal aspects, the filing of a charter, and payments of fees, are much greater than for other forms of business organization.

Lack of Flexibility.   The corporate form of organization is less flexible than the non-corporate forms. Since the corporation charter specifies the powers and purposes of the corporation, the business of the corporation must be conducted within this framework. If the corporation wants to modify its charter, it is necessary to secure an amendment having stockholders' approval, with the change in the charter having to be approved by the state in which it is incorporated. Changes can be made in the charter of a corporation, but they take time, and they must be in conformance with legal requirements. A sole proprietor, on the other hand, can make any change in his business that he wants to make, provided it is within the law; he does not have to secure the approval of anyone. The partners in a partnership have only to get agreement among the partners, which involves no legal formalities.

Reports Public. The public nature of the corporation may be a disadvantage. States and the federal government require corporations to provide information in the form of reports on a periodic and regular basis. If a corporation plans to issue additional shares of stock available for purchase by the general public, and the corporation operates in more than one state, the facts regarding the new issue, the financial position of the corporation, and many other facts must be submitted to an agency of the federal government, the Securities and Exchange Commission. An annual report must be issued to stockholders, and this publication is generally available to anyone when the stock of the corporation is publicly issued. This report gives a financial picture of the corporation. Competitors can easily learn the total sales of the company and its manufacturing costs, check employment data, and secure a great deal of other information which would not be available about a sole proprietorship or partnership.

In the case of small corporations, limited liability may weaken the ability of the corporation to borrow funds. Investors and lending institutions may be hesitant to provide funds when liability is limited to the assets of the corporation.

VARIATIONS IN THE CORPORATE FORM OF BUSINESS ORGANIZATION

The Holding Company

The holding company is sometimes referred to as a "super-corporation." Actually, it is a corporation which controls other corporations through the ownership of some of their stock. It is not necessary for the holding company to own a majority of the stock of a company to control it, but just sufficient voting stock to be able to exercise control over the management of the corporation. Stock in a corporation widely held by the public will not be voted as a block; therefore, if a holding company owns perhaps 20 per cent of the stock, it is very likely to have a controlling vote in management. Further, a relatively small investment may be required on the part of the people who form a holding company, since they may use the common stock of one corporation as the basis for financing the holding company. One of the large holding companies of recent years controlled $2 billion of property with an investment of about $255,000.

Some holding companies do not engage in any business activity of their own, but do control, through stock ownership, numerous other companies which are the operating companies. This type of holding company is sometimes called a *pure holding company*. The Standard Oil Company of New Jersey is an example of this type of holding company. Other companies are operating companies and holding companies as well. There are even instances where one holding company is controlled by another holding company, the former then being termed a *subholding company*. The holding company as a super-corporation was first used to combine railways and later was used in industrial and public utility corporations. Many abuses in holding companies of public utilities led, in 1935, to the enactment of federal legislation to control public utility holding companies.

The Close Corporation

The earlier description of corporations covers those whose stock is offered for purchase to the general public. This type is often called an *open corporation,* in that its stock is open for purchase by anyone. The majority of corporations are of this kind. Some corporations, however, have stock which is closely held by a very small number of people, possibly just one person. This is referred to as a *close corporation.* These are generally smaller and are sometimes formed by business organizations that previously operated as sole proprietorships or partnerships, although there are a number of very large ones that gross as much as $1 billion annually. The Ford Motor Company was a close corporation for many years, until it sold some of its stock to the public.

Non-Profit Corporations

Most corporate business organizations have been formed to make money, both for the people organizing the corporation and for the people who invest money in it. Investors do not put their money into the stock of a corporation unless it is making a profit or there is anticipation of profit. There are some organizations, however, which use the corporate form of organization but do not operate for profit. Typical examples are hospitals, colleges, universities, and charitable institutions. Organizations of this nature are incorporated under special state statutes governing their existence. Like business corporations, they are legal entities. They are granted charters and must have bylaws which contain the specifications for members, directors and officers, meetings, elections, committees, and procedures of amendment. Organizations like these usually issue no stock and are sometimes called *non-stock corporations*. The management is generally vested in an appointed or elected board of directors or board of trustees.

Many associations, such as trade associations, which represent a particular industry, are also organized as non-profit or non-stock organizations. Each member of the association has one vote, and matters of importance are referred to the membership by the board of directors for a vote.

Mutual Companies

There are many companies, called mutual companies, which supply the capital for a business and are also the clients of the business. These organizations ordinarily do not have capital stock, but they do secure a charter from the state. If the organization is a mutual insurance company, the members have supplied the capital for the business and are also the insured. In acting as a group, they insure each member against a loss. The risks of the business venture are assumed by them, and they share in the profits. A board of directors hires a management group, which is responsible to the members, to run the business. Some of the largest insurance companies in the United States are mutual companies. About 62 per cent of the life insurance in force in our nation is written by mutual life insurance companies. Cooperative societies are also mutual companies. They may be composed of consumers who operate a retail store, or of a group of producers marketing farm products. The California Orange Growers Cooperative which markets "Sunkist" oranges is one of these companies. There are also mutual savings banks and mutual savings and loan associations.

Government Corporations

Municipalities, states, and the federal government have, from time to time, created enterprises which furnish services to the public. Various facilties, such as canals, water systems, banks, and other enterprises, have been incorporated and operated by states and municipalities. For its part, the federal government has formed a number of government corporations. The Panama Canal Company, the St. Lawrence Seaway Development Corporation, the Tennessee Valley Authority, and the

Federal Deposit Insurance Corporation are examples of a number of federal corporations. Each of the federal government corporations was created by specific legislation and is chartered by the federal government. They differ somewhat in their operations, since they conform to the particular law which created them. These corporations do not operate for profit, but establish charges which will result in revenues covering expenses. They are given the authority to borrow money to finance the enterprise, which has included construction of the facility, of office buildings, etc., and the charges made for the services rendered will be adequate to repay this money and provide operating expenses. Some of them cannot be given operating funds through appropriations by Congress but must, in effect, earn their own expenses.

In general, there are no stockholders in government corporations, although there are exceptions to this. The Panama Canal Company, for example, has a single stockholder, who is the Secretary of the Army. Most of these government corporations have a board of directors or a commission or a similar group to whom policy and operations reports are made. In government corporations, the owners are the public and the managers are government employees. These corporations are legal entities and can enter into contracts and own property in the name of the corporation. Some of them may sue and be sued, although some courts have ruled that these corporations are agents of the United States, not liable, therefore, to suit without their own consent.

Municipal corporations are sometimes formed to supply water, electricity, or some other service to the community. A profit may be realized by these companies and often is.

Common-Law Trusts

The common-law trust is often called a *Massachusetts trust* because this form of business organization developed in Massachusetts. It is used in other states as well and is also known as a *business trust* and an *association formed under a deed of trust*. All of the property of the business is put in the hands of a board of trustees by the shareholders, giving the board legal title to it. The shareholders receive from the trustees transferable certificates of beneficial interest which, in some instances, are called certificates of stock. The shareholders usually have limited liability. The trustees manage the business activities and give an accounting to the beneficiaries (shareholders) periodically. Profits are distributed to them whenever it is feasible.

The duration of the trust is limited by state law. Generally, it cannot last more than twenty-one years after the death of a certain member of the board of trustees named in the corporate charter. These trusts can engage in business activities, just as any other business does. This form of organization has not been used as widely as other forms, since some states refuse to recognize it as a form of business organization. Other states recognize it, but treat it as a partnership or as a corporation.

The Growth and Nature of Our Business Enterprises

The average annual increase in business firms for the past decade has been 60,000 a year. There has been a rather steady increase in the number of business firms except during the depression years of the 1930's and the war years. The retail trade and service industries, like dry cleaners, which serve the ultimate customer, account for three-fifths of all the business firms in operation. The bulk of our business population is made up of small businesses, about two-fifths of all firms having no employees and three-fourths having fewer than four. Furthermore, only one firm in twenty employs as many as twenty or more persons.

A very large percentage of our business firms, then, are "small" by any measure used, with the predominant number of these firms being sole proprietorships. This is a desirable form of business enterprise providing, as it does, widespread ownership and an opportunity for individual initiative and resourcefulness.

The position of corporations in the United States can best be described as dominant. Even though they comprise but one-eighth of the total number of operating businesses, exclusive of agriculture and the professions, corporations account for approximately three-fourths of the national income and employment. There are many billion-dollar corporate enterprises. For example, the sales of General Motors in 1964 were over $16 billion and profits after taxes were over $1 billion, and this corporation employed more than 660,000 people and had some 1,186,000 stockholders. There were fifty-five industrial corporations with sales of more than $1 billion each during that year. About 33 per cent of manufacturing firms are corporations; and, in a recent year, these enterprises originated about 95 per cent of corporate income. This indicates that the largest manufacturing firms are incorporated.

The opposite is true among retail food businesses, filling stations, and firms engaged in personal services, of which only 2 or 3 per cent are incorporated. In the transportation, communications, and other public utilities division, the proportion of incorporated firms is a little higher than average—about one-sixth. Although practically all railroads and public utilities in this division are incorporated, business firms engaged in trucking and services allied to transportation are more numerous and are predominantly unincorporated.

Following the rapid growth in the number of corporations during the formative period in the nineteenth century, the rate of growth since the early 1900's has been only a little higher than that of the other forms of business organization. The ease with which corporations are able to raise necessary capital was a significant factor in their early growth. However, since World War I, corporate income taxes have impeded the incorporation of small and medium-sized firms. This factor has not slowed the development of the large corporations, because incorporation is the only way in which they can raise the capital needed. The percentage of corporations has increased from about 9 per cent of all business organizations, in 1910, to a little over 12 per cent at the present time, which is not a very large increase. Currently there are an estimated 500,000 corporations of which 50,000 have stock available for public investment.

Breadth of Ownership in Corporations

In business corporations, ownership by stockholders has become a great deal broader in the past ten years. By 1965, there were over 20 million stockholders. There were nearly 50 per cent more shareholders than five years earlier. *Employee stock-purchase plans* were the means by which one out of five shareholders first acquired stock. The largest single group of shareowners was housewives, and 1,335,000 labor union members owned shares. Of the individual shareholders, more than one-half were women. On the average, shareowners hold stock in three or four corporations. The 18 billion shares outstanding in 1965 had a market value of $650 billion, of which $400 billion were owned by individuals and the remainder by banks, insurance company trusts, and corporations.

The substantial increase in stock ownership during the last few years has been influenced by many factors. A high level of personal income, better public understanding of investments, rising stock prices, the arrangement whereby stock can be purchased on the installment plan, and the concern over inflation have all contributed to expansion in the ownership of stock. The median income of families who own stocks was $8,500 in 1965.

Turnover in Business Organizations

Most of us realize that many new businesses are formed each year and many are discontinued. The actual figures, however, are rather staggering. During 1964, there were 197,724 new businesses incorporated. During the same year, there were 13,501 business failures. Although we hear of the success stories in business, the failures do not receive as much publicity.

During the years after World War II, from 1946 until 1954, about half of the businesses which were newly established or acquired by transfer were sold or liquidated within two years. In other words, there was an even chance during that time that a newly acquired firm would last only about two years under the same management. Firms in the wholesale trade had the best record of survival. About three-fourths of them operated through their first full year of operation, half operated about three years, and about 30 per cent survived ten years. Firms classified as being in retail trade did not have as high a survival record. Only about 16 per cent of retail concerns during that period reached the age of ten years.

The Small Business Administration

The concern over the future of the small businessman resulted in the establishment by the federal government of an agency, the Small Business Administration, to be of assistance to small business. This agency attempts to help small business enterprises obtain a fair share of government purchases and sales; obtain competent management and technical and production counsel; and gain access to adequate capital and credit through financial counseling, including government loans. The Small Business Administration also helps, by means of disaster loans, those whose homes or businesses have been damaged by storms, floods, or other disasters; and small business concerns which have suffered substantial economic injury because of excessive rainfall or drought conditions in their areas. Currently, it is estimated that small business firms employ 40 per cent of our labor force, provide a livelihood for 75 million Americans, and account for 70 per cent of the nation's dollar volume in construction and retail and wholesale trade and services and more than 30 per cent of the value added in manufacturing.

TOPICS FOR DISCUSSION

1. "A business may start as a sole proprietorship, but, as it increases in size, it is likely to change to some other form of organization." Why?

2. "In this country it is relatively easy for one to start a business—a fact that may explain why many new businesses fail. There should be a law requiring a person to establish his capacity before starting a business." Comment, agreeing or disagreeing.

3. "Operating a business as a sole proprietor affords the maximum incentives to succeed." Do you agree?

4. "To open a small business as a sole proprietorship requires courage and sacrifice. Therefore, the person doing this should be rewarded with certain tax exemptions." Discuss.

5. The federal government subsidizes the prices of certain farm commodi-

ties, and the law establishes minimum wages for labor in certain types of employment. Should the government subsidize the sole proprietor who starts a business?

6. What action should a partnership take in order to assure the continuation of the business upon the death of one of the partners?

7. Why is it considered inadvisable to start a partnership on the basis of an oral agreement?

8. Does one encounter legal risks in functioning as a *nominal* partner in a business?

9. Cite and describe what you feel is the outstanding advantage the corporation has for the businessman forming a corporation; for the investor.

10. What information is required by states for the Certificate of Incorporation? As one of the organizers of a corporation, would you recommend the employment of a lawyer to assist in securing a charter? Why?

11. What are some of the typical provisions which are found in corporation bylaws? Why are these matters not covered in the charter?

12. How do you explain the fact that certain taxes on corporations are higher than for partnerships and sole proprietorships and yet corporations are the dominant form of business organization?

13. What is a holding company? What benefits would the public receive from holding companies? What benefits might owners of holding company securities derive from such an organization?

14. Are there any advantages of a close corporation as compared to the partnership or sole proprietorship? Why do not some close corporations eventually become open corporations?

15. From the *Statistical Abstract of the United States,* or another reliable reference work, secure a list of the twenty-five largest corporations, and rank them according to assets; according to number of employees; and according to sales. What type of business do they conduct?

16. Why do some individual businessmen in a partnership sign their personal property over to their wives?

17. Comment on the following statement: "American business corporations have a monopoly on business transacted in the United States."

18. Consult the annual reports of two firms in one of the following industries: oil, steel, automobiles, transportation, and food. Compare these organizations for last year. What are the sales revenues, foreign-market plans, and over-all future plans?

19. Do the owners of a company such as the United States Steel Corporation have a voice in management decisions?

CASE 6–1

PROBLEMS IN ORGANIZING A BUSINESS

Mr. George Shaw had been employed by a clothing manufacturer for a period of ten years. During this time, Mr. Shaw had become experienced in the buying of fabrics and in the organization and management of production. Recently, Mr. Shaw has contemplated the ownership of his own manufacturing firm. It is his feeling that he could be successful in the manufacture and sale of high-quality men's sport shirts. He believes that the shirts could be sold under his own brand and also to department stores for private branding.

The problem of financing a business has always been the major deterrent to Mr. Shaw's ambition. Within the past year, however, he has received an inheritance of $25,000. Investigation has led him to believe that he would need at least $125,000 to launch his manufacturing firm. Conferences with banks have revealed that, if he could raise slightly over $50,000 in cash, the remainder of funds needed might be obtained through loans. Mr. Shaw has considered the possibility of organizing a partnership with persons who could supply some of the initial capital. Relative to the partnership, he has two prospective partners in mind. One of these, Mr. Arthur, is a fellow employee in the firm where Mr. Shaw now works. Mr. Arthur is skilled in production management in clothing and would perhaps make a good plant manager for the new company. Although Mr. Arthur's financial capacity was not specifically known to Mr. Shaw, the latter was of the opinion that Mr. Arthur could raise a reasonable amount of capital. The other prospective partner was Mr. Hepner, a salesman for a competitor of Mr. Shaw's present employer. Mr. Shaw thought that Mr. Hepner could also raise some capital. It was not known whether Mr. Arthur and Mr. Hepner would be willing to come into the business as partners with Mr. Shaw, and to put up a part of the initial capital, but there was a distinct possibility that they would be interested.

The possibility of organizing as a corporation had also occurred to Mr. Shaw. If this form of organization was chosen, Mr. Arthur and Mr. Hepner could be brought into the firm as stockholders. The corporate form of organization appealed to Mr. Shaw in many ways, although he was aware of certain limitations that might be encountered.

In seeking a location for the proposed plant, Mr. Shaw was considering the town of Summerton. He had visited relatives in this town and was aware of the fact that it was located in an area that had an unemployment problem. The only industry in the town was a hosiery mill, and the going wage rate in the community was about 60 per cent of that earned by garment workers in the northeastern metropolitan centers. A surplus of labor and a favorable wage rate were factors attracting Mr. Shaw. He had also considered discussing his plans with the Summerton Chamber of Commerce to ascertain what aid they might be able to give him in getting the plant started. He expected that he would be able to employ upward of a hundred people to begin, with more to be added if the venture proved successful. A lawyer friend had told Mr. Shaw that the federal government might also give him assistance in financing the company in view of the fact that Summerton was classified as a surplus-labor area.

In considering possible forms of organization, Mr. Shaw was weighing the pros and cons of the sole proprietorship, the partnership, and the corporation. He was aware of the needs to raise capital and to secure the assistance of qualified management; however, he was reluctant to dilute his ownership to the point that he would not be the controlling factor in the operation of the company.

Discuss the pros and cons of the various forms of ownership as they may relate to the proposed company.

SELECTED REFERENCES

Bogen, J. I. *Financial Handbook*. 4th ed. New York: The Ronald Press Co., 1965.
Dewing, A. S. *The Financial Policy of Corporations*. 5th ed. 2 vols. New York: The Ronald Press Co., 1953. Chap. 1–4.
Donaldson, E. F., and J. K. Pfahl. *Corporate Finance*. 2d ed. New York: The Ronald Press Co., 1963. Chap. 2 and 3.
Guthmann, H. G., and H. E. Dougall. *Corporate Financial Policy*. 4th ed. Englewood Cliffs, N.J.: Prentice-Hall, Inc., 1962.
Husband, W. H., and J. C. Dockeray. *Modern Corporation Finance*. 5th ed. Homewood, Ill.: Richard D. Irwin, Inc., 1962.
Owens, R. N. *Business Organization and Combination*. 5th ed. Englewood Cliffs, N.J.: Prentice-Hall, Inc., 1965.
Paton, William A. *Corporate Profits*. Homewood, Ill.: Richard D. Irwin, Inc., 1965.

7

Financing the Enterprise

CAPITAL NEEDS

In large business organizations, manufacturers have about $22,000 of capital invested for each production worker employed. The highest investment is in the petroleum industry, where it is about $111,000 per production worker. New plant and equipment accounted for an expenditure of over $50 billion in 1965. Clearly, such capital investments require financing from a variety of different sources—investors, loans, and company surplus among others. Small companies or ones just getting started often find that financing is the most vexing of all their problems. In many surveys made of businesses that have failed, the reason most frequently cited has been inadequate capital. Certainly, the need for capital varies with the type of business, but understanding of the sources, types, and terms of capital, regardless of the size of the business firm, is extremely important to the prospective success of an enterprise. Should a firm buy equipment, lease it, or use a combination of these two methods? What is the real cost of each method? These are some of the questions that must be considered.

The particular financial needs of a business govern the methods to be used in seeking necessary capital. The length of time the money will be required, the amount of money needed, the price that has to be paid for the use of the money, and the general financial picture of the company are some of the factors that are considered by a business enterprise when it is "shopping" for money.

USE OF CREDIT

Credit is the sale of goods, services, or money claims in the present in exchange for a promise to pay in the future. Credit is sought by borrowers and extended by lenders because each believes that he will profit through the exchange of credit. The borrower believes that he will be able to use the money, goods, or services he secures on credit to make a profit in his operations; and the lender believes that the payment he receives for the use of the money or the profit on the goods or services sold on credit will be sufficiently lucrative to warrant the extension of credit. Credit is spoken of as being *short-term credit, intermediate credit* (sometimes called *term loans*), and *long-term credit.* Short-term credit is usually for a period of one year or less and is often used by businessmen in securing working capital. Intermediate credit is customarily from one to five years, and long-term credit is for a period of five or more years. *Interest* is the price or rate of premium paid per month, per quarter, semiannually, or annually for the use of money. When interest is deducted from the amount borrowed at the time that credit is arranged, it is generally called a *discount.* Short-term credit is frequently discounted. For example, a person borrows $1,000 at 6 per cent for a period of one year. If the loan is discounted, he receives only $940 instead of $1,000. The $60 in interest is deducted immediately, and he receives only the balance. He has paid $60 for the use of $940 rather than $60 for the use of $1,000. He repays $1,000 at the time the loan is due. The actual interest rate has amounted to 6.3 per cent rather than 6 per cent. If he repays in monthly installments, the rate will be even higher. Long-term loans will have an interest charge to be paid at stated intervals or at the time the entire amount of the loan is due, so the borrower has the use of the entire amount borrowed until he has to repay the loan on the date it is due (referred to as *maturity*).

Credit Instruments

The word "instrument" is used in the legal sense to mean a written document. Credit instruments, then, would be written documents used in securing credit. The *promissory note* is one form of credit instrument that is used a great deal in financing, especially short-term. This is a written promise made by a borrower to a lender agreeing to pay, either on demand or at a certain time, a specified sum of money. When only one signature, that of the person or firm borrowing the money, is on a promissory note, it is sometimes called a *single-name paper.* When two names are signed on the note, the second name being a cosigner, it is sometimes called a *two-name paper* or *double-name paper.*

Factors Considered in Extending Credit

Regardless of the length of time for which a loan is sought and regardless of whether the businessman is an individual or a corporation, the factors considered by a lender in deciding whether or not to loan money to a person requesting a loan are much the same. These factors are often called the "5 C's of credit." The first of these is *character*. Does the individual or business have a good reputation? Have its debts been paid when due? Another factor in credit standing is *capacity*. Does an examination of financial statements of the company or individual indicate a capacity for growth and continued profit? Another factor is *capital*, which means the amount of the owner's own money invested in his business. Unless the person seeking credit has a good amount of his own capital invested in a business, financial institutions are hesitant to extend credit. *Collateral* is the fourth factor. Collateral is the pledging of a marketable asset, such as land or equipment, to be available to the lending institution in the event that the borrower is unable to repay a loan. When collateral is pledged on a loan, the loan is referred to as *secured*. Collateral may also be referred to as security. If the borrower can satisfy the lender regarding character, capacity, and capital, an *unsecured loan,* that is a loan without the pledging of collateral, may be granted. A fifth factor that is considered is the use of *cosigners*. If the business position of the borrower, as well as the collateral he is going to put up, are inadequate, it may be necessary for him to get one or more persons who have good financial ratings to sign his note. These people become cosigners and, as such, are responsible for the repayment of the loan if the borrower cannot repay.

Methods of Raising Business Capital

Business organizations, and particularly corporations, are able to finance some of their operations without going to outside sources for capital. This is because they retain a portion of their earnings in the business rather than distributing all of them in dividends or salaries. When profits are high, corporations ordinarily retain a larger percentage of their earnings than when profits are low. The amount of retained profits varies considerably from year to year; but immediately following World War II, the retained earnings of manufacturing corporations represented about 43 per cent of the total sources of funds for manufacturing corporations at that time. Retained earnings currently are about 25 per cent of the total sources of funds for manufacturing corporations.

Another source of financing for businesses is that of *depreciation*. In order to replace equipment and buildings when they are worn out, businesses establish depreciation allowances. The life of the equipment or buildings is determined. The cost of the equipment or buildings is then divided by the years of life to determine the amount to be set aside each year. Suppose that a piece of equipment when it was purchased cost $11,000, and it has a useful life of ten years. At the end of that period, it is estimated that it would be worth $1,000. The amount to be set aside each year in depreciation allowance for this piece of equipment then would be $1,000. At the end of ten years, the money in this depreciation account would be sufficient, with the salvage value of the old piece of equipment, to purchase new equipment.

While businesses are able to provide for some of their financial needs through internal sources, most of them have to turn frequently to outside sources in raising capital. There are several methods of securing additional capital used by business organizations. All the types of business organizations—the sole proprietorship, the partnership, and the corporation—may raise needed capital by borrowing and by purchasing on credit. In addition, the corporation through sale of certificates of ownership (shares of stock) in the corporation to the public is able to raise large amounts of money. Each of these methods of raising business capital and the principal sources of capital will be discussed.

BORROWED FUNDS

Providing Collateral by Pledging Assets

Probably the most common method of raising capital used by the sole proprietorship and the partnership is that of borrowing money. Since these forms of legal structure hold the owner or partners to be personally liable for all the debts of their business, the lender will look carefully at the personal assets of the owner or partners as well as at the business assets. The money that will be available through loans to these forms of organizations will always be limited by the owner's or partners' own circumstances. When money is loaned to a business, the lender often requires that assets of the business be pledged to the payment of the loan. This is providing collateral for the loan and is assurance to the lender that if the loan is not repaid, the pledged assets can be sold to cover the amount of the loan.

Instruments Used in Borrowing Money

Promissory notes are a form of credit instrument extensively used in securing capital, especially for short-term uses. In a promissory note, the borrower promises to pay the lender the amount that has been loaned to him either at a specified time or when the lender requests it. The rate of interest charged for the money loaned will be stated in the note. These notes may have marketable assets of the company pledged for their payment. As stated earlier, these notes are referred to as secured loans; or if no assets are pledged, the note is said to be unsecured. Usually, only the signature of the person borrowing money is required by the lender, but when the lender has some hesitancy about loaning the money, another signature may be required on the note.

Mortgage loans are another type of credit instrument widely used in raising capital. These loans are secured by the pledging of some real estate, such as buildings or other property. The mortgagor, the owner of the property, secures money by placing a mortgage on the particular piece of property. The lender is the mortgagee. The mortgage transfers the property from the mortgagor to the mortgagee under certain conditions as security for the payment of the debt. The mortgage is void when the debt has been repaid.

The *long-term note* is used in long-term financing. This is also secured by the pledging of assets or not, as required by the lender. This type of note usually matures within ten years.

Line of Credit

Most business firms will arrange with a financial institution, usually a bank, for a line of credit. Instead of the businessman waiting until he needs the money for a loan, he files the necessary statements concerning his business with the bank in order that credit will be available whenever it is needed. The bank establishes a loan limit on which it will loan money to the businessman. It is sometimes necessary for him to request a bank to increase the loan limit, in which case the businessman has to show why the additional funds are needed as well as the ability of the business to repay. Banks that establish a line of credit for the businessman usually require that he use the bank for depositing his money. A deposit by the businessman of what is called a compensating balance of from 10 to 20 per cent of unsecured loans outstanding under the line of credit is required by most banks.

It is possible to arrange for a revolving credit agreement with a bank which assures the borrower of funds regardless of business conditions; but there is a charge, in addition to interest, for this arrangement.

Financial Institutions as Sources of Credit

There are a number of kinds of financial institutions from which the businessman may secure money in loans. Undoubtedly, the most important of these are our nation's banks. They are indispensable to **our** economic welfare, providing, as they do, a depository for the accumulation and lending of money, and for the transfer and safekeeping of funds. The main types of banks, commercial and savings, the central banking system, and the investment bank will be discussed. Other institutional sources of credit—savings and loan associations, insurance companies, sales finance companies, commercial paper houses, and others—are also of significance to businessmen seeking capital. Their operations will be briefly described to show how the businessman may make use of these sources of funds.

Banks.   The title *commercial bank* is applied to a bank that accepts money from people in the form of demand deposits—in other words, the amount deposited is subject to withdrawal by the owner on demand. Any part or all of it can be transferred to a third party by means of a check. The distinguishing feature of the commercial bank is the checking account, although it may also have a savings department. An important function of the commercial bank is to grant loans to qualified borrowers.

There are two broad types of commercial banks: the *national bank,* which can be formed after being granted a charter by the federal government, and the *state bank,* which is chartered by a state government. Many banks have but a single office. However, there are bank corporations that own and operate two or more banking offices. This is termed *branch banking.* There is also *group banking* in which a holding company controls several independent banks.

Mutual savings banks receive the savings of individuals and invest them. They pay the depositors of the money interest, or dividends, on the money they have put into the bank. This type of bank does not provide checking-account facilities. The mutual savings banks invest the depositor's money in bonds and assets on the so-called "legal list," which is a list prepared by the state in which the bank is authorized to do business. Most of the funds of these banks are put in bonds and mortgages. They loan money to businessmen, usually for long-term investment purposes.

To the businessman, the type of bank is not as important as the matter of whether he can secure a loan from it.

Federal Reserve System.   Because the stability of our monetary system is tied so closely to our banking system, the federal government has always had an interest in the operation of our banks. In 1913, Congress, by the passage of the Federal Reserve Act, created a central banking system called the *Federal Reserve System.* Under the Act, twelve federal reserve districts were established in the United States. Each of the districts is served by a Federal Reserve Bank. Since that time, twenty-four branches have also been established. Each Federal Reserve Bank is managed by its own board of directors, and a board of governors in Washington, D.C. supervises the Federal Reserve System. All national banks have to become members of the Federal Reserve System. State-chartered banks are also permitted to join the System upon presentation of evidence of a satisfactory financial condition. Currently, about half of all commercial banks are members of the System.

Member banks are required to purchase a certain amount of stock in the Federal Reserve Bank in their district. They are also required to maintain a fixed reserve, that is, a certain amount of money that cannot be used in day-to-day operations but must be held in reserve. The amount of this reserve can be increased or decreased by the Federal Reserve Board, and thereby it can expand or contract the amount of money member banks have available for credit financing. Each Federal Reserve Bank is a clearinghouse for all banks in its district in the clearance and collection of checks, which greatly facilitates the interchange of checks among banks. Federal Reserve Banks are private banks owned by the member banks in their districts. Basically, they are bankers' banks.

Reserve Banks influence the availability of bank funds for credit. A bank in making a loan on a promissory note discounts the note at the time the money is loaned. As has been explained, this means that the bank deducts the amount of interest that would be due for the use of the money before giving the balance of the money to the borrower. Then, a member bank, which has made a loan to an individual on a promissory note and discounted the note, can take it to the Federal Reserve Bank, if it wishes, and have it rediscounted by that bank and receive the balance of the note. This enables the bank to have additional funds with which to carry on its business. Rediscounting is limited to what is called *eligible paper*. Notes that are due within a stated period of time and certain other types of financial documents are eligible paper. A member bank can also receive an "advance," which is secured by the promissory note of the bank itself, together with eligible paper owned by the bank. These are ways in which more funds can be made available to the member banks.

The Reserve Banks also influence the interest rate charged by banks for the use of money. By raising or lowering the rediscount rate Federal Reserve Banks pay to member banks, they make it easier or more difficult for member banks to secure funds. When rediscount rates are raised, which is in effect the interest rate taken in advance, the member banks will have to raise their interest rates on money loaned or their profit will be less. When member banks raise interest rates, this has the effect of making it less desirable for businesses to borrow money. When

Federal Reserve Banks lower rates, on the other hand, the reverse is true; and more money is likely to be borrowed by businesses from member banks.

Although they are bankers' banks, the Federal Reserve Banks can loan directly to industry in exceptional circumstances if the borrowers cannot be financed by regular banking at reasonable rates.

An important function of the Federal Reserve System for purposes of credit control is its *open market operations.* If the Open Market Committee of the System believes that it has become too easy for money to be borrowed and there is too much money in circulation, which could have the effect of lowering the purchasing power of our money, it will sell large quantities of United States government securities in the open market, thus withdrawing money from circulation. For example, the purchasers of the government securities pay for them by drawing checks on their balances with member banks. This reduces the reserves or deposits that the member banks have in the Federal Reserve Banks. The member banks then have to decrease their loans to the lower level of reserves on deposit with the Federal Reserve Bank, thereby reducing the amount of funds that they will lend. When the Committee wants to increase the money in circulation, it will purchase government securities from banks, individuals, or investing institutions. A member bank then presents the check for payment to its Federal Reserve Bank, which credits the bank's reserve account and increases its reserve balance. This enables the bank to effect a more lenient credit policy because it has more funds available.

Investment Banking House. Another type of bank is the investment banking house. This type of bank undertakes to float security issues for corporations and federal and state governments by underwriting or guaranteeing the sale of the issues of the securities at a stated price. The banking house then sells these securities to banks, individuals, and others. In this way, investment banking houses make it possible to float very large issues of securities.

Non-Bank Institutions. Savings of individuals are put into savings and loan associations as shares of ownership; whereas when individuals deposit their funds in commercial banks, these funds are liabilities of the bank. The payments that are made on savings and loan shares are dividends and not interest. There are many savings and loan associations scattered all over the United States, and they provide a very substantial portion of loans on homes and on some commercial property. A builder who wants to build a house but has no purchaser for the house at the time he starts the construction is very often able to finance construction through a loan by a savings and loan association. Often this type of loan, called a construction loan, is converted after the home is sold to a mortgage loan by the purchaser of the home.

Life insurance companies have vast sums of money at their disposal, and they have become one of the most important sources of business financing. They loan money to business organizations for construction purposes, for purchase of equipment, and for many other purposes. They may make loans directly to businesses or they may purchase mortgages that are held by other companies. A regular source of funds for smaller businesses is provided by life insurance companies which loan money to individuals based upon the security provided by the payments the person has made on his insurance policies.

There are a number of specialized financial institutions that are important in business financing. Sales finance companies finance both businesses and consumers. As an example, sales finance companies will finance the inventory of a dealer in automobiles and also finance the dealer's sales through purchase of his customer's retail installment contracts. Much inventory financing is handled by sales finance companies. Inventory financing is used particularly by seasonal businesses that have to accumulate a large inventory and are pressed for cash. These finance companies, as well as banks, will advance funds for which the security is the inventory. Another means of business financing is through *factoring*, which is the practice whereby a business sells its accounts receivable (the amounts that are owed to it by individuals or businesses) to a financial company. This is handled on the basis of no recourse against the seller of the accounts—in other words, the financial company assumes the credit and collection function for the business, purchases its accounts receivable as they arise, and takes whatever credit losses there are without asking the seller of the accounts receivable to make up the loss. The people who owe the accounts receivable of the business are notified of the sale and pay the new holder (the factoring company) directly. The use of factoring developed in the textile business and spread to many other fields of business. There are about twenty well-known factoring companies concentrated in New York City. Subsidiaries of some of the sales finance companies also engage in factoring operations.

A little different method of financing through the use of accounts receivable is where a commercial financing institution advances to its customer loans, which are secured by the assignment of accounts receivable, with recourse to the customer for credit losses but without notice to the people who owe him.

In financial circles, reference is frequently made to *commercial paper houses* as a source of financing. Commercial paper, or eligible paper, is promissory notes. The commercial paper house will purchase the promissory notes of reliable business firms in order to resell them to banks and other lenders such as managers of pension funds and others. A fee based on the amount of the note purchased is the income on which the commercial paper house operates. The notes are generally prepared in denominations of $5,000, $10,000, and $25,000 so that they can be resold in amounts that are convenient to the purchasing bank or other lending institutions. The business organization that wants to use the commercial paper house must have an excellent reputation. The reason for the use of the services of the commercial paper houses is that the cost of borrowing from them is generally $\frac{1}{8}$ to $\frac{3}{8}$ of 1 per cent less than the interest rates of banks.

Miscellaneous Sources. Another long-term financing source is that of endowment funds of many colleges and universities. These funds, which have been given them by many persons, are invested in different types of activity. They may purchase corporate securities or real estate mortgages, or make other investments with them.

Some cities have urban development companies, composed of local business firms and associations. The development company will make loans to assist individuals or corporations that want to start a business in the city. In the over-all picture of financing, the number of companies that are financed in this way is not large. Another source is the investment development company. Since 1946, a number of these investment companies have been formed by a few wealthy persons. Their primary purpose is to provide venture capital for new and growing business firms for which there might not otherwise be funds available. Such organizations usually invest in enterprises that have new processes or products and generally take an active part in the companies they finance in addition to providing the financial backing.

The Small Business Administration and other government programs also provide financial assistance to some businesses. The Small Business Administration is authorized to make loans up to $250,000 to small business firms, as defined by it. Essentially, an applicant for a loan must show that the funds are not available from private lending sources on reasonable terms and that the business cannot raise the funds needed in any other way. The Small Business Administration can make direct loans to small businesses and can participate jointly with private banks in extending loans to businesses.

There are several guaranteed loan programs that are administered by various government agencies. These programs exist in the fields of air, water, and rail transportation and in commercial fishing. Under these programs, if the borrower is unable to obtain loans from private sources, the government will guarantee the loan (that is, if the borrower was unable to repay the loan, the government would repay it). By guaranteeing the loan, the government enables the borrower to borrow the money from private financial institutions at favorable interest rates. For example, a small airline operating on a route authorized by a government regulatory body, the Civil Aeronautics Board, can secure a government-guaranteed loan in order to purchase new aircraft.

Small businessmen may occasionally seek short-term funds from industrial banks, or Morris Plan Banks as they are called. Actually, these banks specialize in loans to individuals, and the loans are repaid on an installment basis. These banks obtain the money that they loan from depositors of the bank.

Small loan companies are another source of funds for financing on a short-term basis. They specialize in providing cash loans to individuals. The interest rates are quite high, and it would be only in unusual circumstances that a small businessman would borrow from such a company.

PURCHASING ON CREDIT

Interbusiness Financing

Purchasing on credit is one of the methods of raising additional money that may be used by all the types of business organizations—the sole proprietorship, the partnership, and the corporation. Extensive use is made of this kind of financing of purchases. It is interbusiness financing since it occurs between non-financial firms. Ordinarily, the borrower and the lender in interbusiness financing are in a buyer-seller relationship. There need not be a direct money loan in this type of financing, although there may be. One kind, that of trade credit, usually arises from the purchase of merchandise. The seller does not require immediate payment for the shipped goods and carries the purchase as an account receivable. This is the most common form of credit extended by a business and is a factor in the selling of its products. This is also called *open book* or *accounts receivable credit* because the practice of billing for the product shipped to a customer permits a certain number of days within which payment may be made. Some companies require a minimum weight or dollar amount per order or delivery. In other instances, the volume of business of the purchasing firm has to be enough to show some promise of the credit extension being profitable to the supplier. For example, a grain mill may require that a turkey raiser have at least five hundred turkeys on feed to qualify for feed credit.

Business firms extending open book credit rely upon many factors in extending credit. One of these is the financial information about the purchaser supplied by a general rating service such as *Dun & Bradstreet*. This service is available to subscribers.

There is no formal agreement between buyer and seller, such as a promissory note, for payment of the money involved—just the credit terms on the sales invoice. Discounts are usually allowed for early payment. These range from ½ of 1 per cent for certain products in the metals industry to 8 per cent in the apparel industry. Two per cent is the most frequent figure used. Thus, terms may be, "2/10, net/60." In other words, if payment is made within ten days, 2 per cent may be deducted from the bill. No discount is allowed beyond that time, and the bill must be paid within sixty days. Terms are subject to traditional practices that, in the past, have had a direct relationship to the perishability of the product. For example, meat is generally sold on about a one-week maximum credit term. Credit terms of sixty or more days exist in the furniture field.

As far as the purchaser is concerned, discount terms are very important in determining what the interest cost of this credit is to him. For example, if the customer waits the full sixty days, he is paying 2 per cent for a credit extension of fifty days. Computed on an annual basis, this is equivalent to an interest rate of 14.3 per cent. The seller extends trade credit because it is a means of aiding him in selling his product, and it is possible for him to sell more by extending credit than otherwise would be the case. The additional volume of sales that results from the extension of credit may bring greater profits because of larger scale production made possible by the higher volume of sales. The seller may be able to borrow at lower rates than the buyer since the seller ordinarily has a higher credit rating. The buyer accepts the cost of trade credit in some instances because he has no other alternative. He may not use these credit terms if the purchase can be financed in a cheaper way, such as borrowing from a bank at a lower rate of interest. Statistics show that smaller companies use trade credit more than larger companies. Trade credit terms can be used to encourage off-season buying. A toy manufacturer, for example, may sell toys in July with billing at favorable discount terms beginning October 1. Thus, the company has used a deferred dating of its trade credit.

Another type of interbusiness financing is that of merchandise suppliers who guarantee loans for customers or make direct cash loans to their customers. There are times when larger companies who want to maintain business relationships with smaller companies will guarantee the credit of the small firm. This enables the latter to have access to funds on terms that would not otherwise be available to it. There are other examples of large companies that have provided cash loans to smaller companies who serve as suppliers to them.

The provision of equipment and supplies also occurs in interbusiness financing. In many instances, suppliers provide equipment needed to merchandise the products they sell. This equipment may be loaned or it may be leased or sold. If it is sold, it is usually financed by the merchandising supplier on installment-plan buying. A beverage distributor, for example, may supply coolers for his customers. The customer is sometimes permitted to use the equipment without charge as long as he continues to purchase the merchandise from the supplier. If this equipment were not supplied, the customer would have to purchase and finance the equipment himself.

Equipment financing is a type of financing in which there is a transfer of capital equipment. Such a transfer may take the form of an installment sale or a lease. Leases have been widely used in recent years by equipment manufacturers in the handling of machine tools, automobiles, trucks, and office equipment. It is a means by which a company can secure equipment necessary in the operation of its business, such as a truck, and make payments on an agreed basis, usually monthly, for the use of it. Depending on the terms and conditions of the lease agreement entered into, the party who is leasing equipment may build up an equity in the equipment and, under certain arrangements, acquire ownership of the leased equipment. Leasing arrangements allow the money that would have been used to purchase equipment to be used in some other way in the operation of the business. Some equipment manufacturers have created their own subsidiary financing company to handle the financing arrangements.

In the petroleum industry, a company-owned filling station may be leased by the operator. He signs a note for the movable equipment and obtains working capital under another note. The repayment is then made by charging him more than the actual price on his petroleum purchases. The excess is charged to the debt reduction over a three-to-five year period.

Commercial Drafts.   A business, in the sale of its products, may sometimes use a commercial draft. This is a promise to pay either on sight (when the draft is received) or on time (the date specified in the draft). These are called *time drafts* or *sight drafts*. The business firm preparing the draft is the drawer, and the individual or organization who is supposed to pay the draft to the drawer or to his bank is the drawee. If the drawee accepts the draft, he writes his name across the face of it. This type of document is used particularly when a business organization receives an order from a customer whose financial status is unknown to it. When goods are shipped and a time draft is used in connection with the shipment, it may also be called a *trade acceptance*.

Fig. 7–1. A specimen certificate of common stock (Potomac Electric Power Company, Inc.).

SELLING SECURITIES

Kinds of Corporate Securities

The corporation has a further method of raising capital that is not available to the sole proprietorship and the partnership. This method —the sale of corporate securities—is capable of producing vast sums of money, particularly when the corporation offering securities for sale is well known. Smaller corporations or those just incorporating do not always find ready purchasers for their securities. When a company first offers its securities so that it can raise money to begin operations, a specific price is set on the securities. Once these original securities have been sold to the public and are freely traded, their price is determined solely by what the buyer is willing to pay and the seller to accept. The earnings of the company largely determine this price—what it has earned, what it is earning, and what it may earn—and its prospects for the future.

When a company wants to issue securities to sell to the public, it will prepare a *prospectus*. This is a statement that gives information about such matters as the capital structure, the nature of the business, its earnings, properties, and management. The prospectus is designed to arouse interest in the security issuance.

There are two primary kinds of corporate securities: stocks and bonds. Each of these types of securities is offered in a variety of forms or classes, which have different rights and limitations. In its corporate charter, a company specifies the types of capital stock and the amounts of each that it will issue over a period of time. The amount of capital needed by the corporation, the amount of control to be retained by the organizers, the profits expected from the enterprise, and other factors will determine the type and class of securities to be issued at a particular time. The amount of stock that is authorized to be issued but is not yet issued is called *unissued stock*. The purchaser of stocks is a part owner of the corporation. The purchaser of bonds, though, has merely loaned the corporation money that it has agreed to pay back at a certain time.

Common Stock

The kind of stock most widely purchased is common stock, which represents simple ownership in a corporation. The stock certificate is the actual piece of paper that is evidence of ownership. Watermarked paper is used, and it is finely engraved with delicate etchings to discourage forgery. A specimen certificate is shown in Figure 7–1. For many years, corporations have issued common stock that has a par value, which represents an arbitrary value of the stock at the time of issuance. At the present time, the use of no-par stock is widespread. Since the actual price to be paid for stocks—the market price—shows little relationship to par value, the latter has come to mean very little in the consideration of the value of a stock. For example, the par value of a stock may be set by the corporation at $50 a share, but the actual or market price of the stock at the time that it is purchased by an investor may be $140 a share. The market price of a stock reflects the demand for a stock and general business conditions.

Common stock can be divided into two different classes: Class A, or voting stock, or Class B, or non-voting stock. Most common stock has the right to vote although there are many well-known corporations that have non-voting common stock. If a company makes a profit, it is expected to pay out a part of its profits on a regular basis as dividends to the stockholders. The dividends on common shares vary with the profits of the company and the amount of cash on hand. Dividends may be omitted if business is poor, and earnings are withheld to invest in plant and equipment. Dividends may be paid in stock rather than in cash. Additional shares of the company stock may be distributed, such as a 5 per cent stock dividend. The owner of 100 shares of stock would receive an additional 5 shares as a stock dividend. When a stockholder holds a number of shares that result in a fractional share being due him, he is issued fractional rights. For example, if a stockholder owns 110 shares of stock, he is entitled to 5 full shares and one half share. He receives fractional rights for 50/100's of a share, and he may either purchase the additional 50/100's to make a full share or he may sell his fractional rights.

Stock dividends allow the company to conserve cash since it is not issuing a cash dividend. Sometimes, companies combine the two in one dividend, that is, part stock and part cash. Companies also vote stock splits to broaden the market for the corporation's stock by reducing the price, which results in a wider distribution of shares. A stock split is the division of the outstanding shares of a corporation into a larger number of shares and must be voted on by directors and approved by stockholders. A three-for-one split by a company with one million shares outstanding would result in three million shares outstanding. Each holder of one hundred shares before the split would have three hundred shares after the split, although his proportionate equity in the company would remain the same since one hundred parts of one million are the equivalent of three hundred parts of three million. Stock with a par value of $25 a share before the stock split would have a par value of $8.33⅓ after the split. The split would likewise affect the market price of the stock. The lower market price would make it easier for people to purchase the stock, thus resulting in wider sale of the stock.

In the case of common stock, there is no guarantee of any kind that dividends will be paid even if the profits are adequate since the board of directors may want to use the earnings in some other way in the development of the company. The Erie Railroad from 1895 until 1942 issued no dividends to its common stockholders.

Treasury stock is stock that has been issued and then repurchased by the corporation from its owners. This cannot be done until a company has a surplus.

Preferred Stock

Preferred stock also represents ownership, but the term *preferred* indicates some preference or better status than in the case of common stock. Usually, the stock is preferred as to dividends, which means that the preferred stockholders will receive their dividends before any dividends can be paid on the common stock. The dividends on preferred stock are usually a fixed amount, such as $5.00 a year on a $100-par value share of preferred stock. They do not increase as profits of the corporation increase, as dividends on common stock frequently do. Preferred stock dividends are paid only as long as the company operates profitably. Most preferred stock is cumulative preferred stock, which accumulates dividends in years in which dividends are not paid. When the company resumes payment of dividends, it must pay all the back dividends to owners of cumulative preferred stock before any dividends are paid to holders of non-cumulative preferred stock and to holders of common stock.

Participating preferred stock is stock that is entitled to receive dividends up to a specified amount, and it then shares with common stock in any further dividends distributed after the common stock has received an equal or prearranged amount. Non-participating preferred stock is eligible to receive the preferred dividend and no more. Generally, preferred stock does not have voting rights.

When a company issues more than one class of preferred stock, it may be referred to as *1st Preferred, 2d Preferred, 3d Preferred,* and so on. Another term used is that of *prior preferred stock.* Preferred stock may have conversion rights in which case it is called *convertible,* and it may not have conversion rights and be called *non-convertible.* If it is convertible, the preferred stock can be exchanged for common stock within a stated period of time at a set price. For example, if the common stock of a company is selling at $15 a share, preferred stock might be issued at a par value of $100, convertible at the owner's option for five years into five shares of common stock. If the price of the common stock were to rise above $20 a share during that five years, it would be profitable for the owner to convert his preferred stock into common, assuming that he will get as good a dividend return from the five shares of common as from the one share of preferred.

A corporation in issuing preferred stocks may issue redeemable stock. If the corporation wants to redeem the stock, it notifies the stockholder who is paid a specified sum, and the stock is retired. A corporation may desire to redeem its preferred stock in order to reduce the amount being paid in relatively high dividends to preferred stock.

Preferred stock is often referred to as "preferred as to assets," which means that the preferred stockholder is entitled to receive payment up to a specified amount, usually par value, before common stockholders receive any payment, should the company be dissolved. There is no guarantee, however, that the preferred stockholder will receive anything.

Stock Rights

A company that wants to raise more funds by issuing additional securities may give its stockholders, both preferred and common, the opportunity ahead of others to buy the new securities in proportion to the number of shares each owns. This is called a *subscription right* and is evidenced by a subscription warrant filled out by the stockholder. The rights must be exercised within a comparatively short period of time. Because the stock is usually offered to stockholders at a price below the current market price, the rights ordinarily have a market value and are actively traded in the market. An example of the use of subscription rights is that of a company that gave its stockholders the right to subscribe to shares of additional common stock on the basis of one share for each fifteen shares of common stock held at a subscription price of $22 per share at a time when the market price was $23.75 per share.

Bonds

Money secured from the sale of bonds is a loan to the corporation. A bond carries a due date, or maturity date, at which time the amount of the bond must be paid. A stated amount of interest must be paid on certain dates prior to the date the bond is due, regardless of whether the corporation has made a profit or runs the risk of being forced out of business. While a few state incorporation laws permit bondholders to vote, this is not generally true. The bondholder does not have the same role as the common stockholder who is a part owner of the corporation.

The purchaser of bonds has simply loaned the corporation money, which it is obligated to repay.

Some corporations, like railroads and natural gas pipelines, raise very large amounts of their capital through bond issues while others engaged in manufacturing issue comparatively small amounts or none at all. Corporations make use of bonds because it is possible for them to attract additional capital from some investors, individual and institutional, who prefer bonds to stocks. Further, the financial position of some companies may be such that they would have difficulty selling common stock whereas they can borrow money through the issuance of bonds. If the corporation can earn more on the capital it secures from bonds than it has to pay bondholders in interest, it is advantageous to secure money in this fashion. This is one form of what is termed *trading on the equity*. All forms of doing business on funds obtained on contracts in which limited payments are made to those who supply the funds, with the expectation by the borrower of using the funds to produce more revenue than is paid to the lenders in interest, is trading on the equity because the loans are secured by the value of the assets of the enterprise.

When a corporation issues bonds, this indebtedness of the corporation is said to be a *funded debt*. Funds that corporations raise in this manner are usually used for capital purposes, that is, to expand plant facilities, to buy machinery, and for similar purposes. Bonds are frequently issued in denominations of $1,000. However, there are bonds issued in smaller denominations such as $500, $100, or less. Those of less than $100 are sometimes called "baby bonds." For the convenience of institutional investors, some bonds may be issued in denominations of $5,000 or $10,000. There are many kinds of bonds, the most common of which are discussed here.

Bonds Classified as to Interest.   Bonds are often classified as to the way in which interest is paid to the bondholders. Payment of interest on bonds differs between registered and coupon bonds. A registered bond has the name of the bondholder on the face of the bond, as does the stock certificate. The interest on this kind of bond is sent by check to the registered bondholder. If a bond is sold, the bondholder endorses the bond and surrenders the bond certificate to the corporation or a transfer agent acting for the corporation. A new certificate is issued in the name of the purchaser. Coupon bonds are not registered. They have interest coupons attached to the bond, which are clipped by the owner and deposited in a bank for payment. A specimen coupon bond is shown in Figure 7–2. Each of these coupons constitutes an obligation of the corporation to pay to the bearer the amount of interest due on the date specified on the coupon. Most bonds are coupon bonds. Some corporations have issued registered coupon bonds that are registered as to principal only.

Most bonds have a given rate of interest, such as 3⅝ per cent, that does not change regardless of changes in the company's earnings. It can be seen that this constitutes a fixed charge that the company has to pay. There are other bonds, both registered and coupon, that carry an interest payment only if the earnings of the corporation are adequate to pay it, and these are called *income bonds.*

Bonds Classified as to Kind of Security. Bonds, like other kinds of indebtedness, may be backed by the pledge of company assets, in which case the bond is secured. If no specific assets are pledged, the debt is unsecured. The majority of bonds issued are secured. Another way in which bonds are classified is according to the security that is pledged. One of the more common types of such a bond is a mortgage bond, which is a charge, or lien, against the property named for payment of the bond. It may be a first mortgage that must be paid first or a second mortgage that is paid only after the first mortgage holder's lien is satisfied. A first mortgage bond is sometimes called a *prior lien bond,* whereas second and other mortgage bonds are then called *junior bonds.*

A corporation that has in its possession stocks issued by other business organizations may pledge them as securities for the issuance of its own bonds. These bonds are known as *collateral trust bonds.* One of the reasons that a corporation that needs additional capital would borrow money through a bond issue rather than selling the stocks it is using as collateral is that the corporation feels that the market price of these stocks is likely to improve.

Equipment trust bonds have been extensively used by railroads in the purchase of new equipment such as locomotives, tank cars, boxcars, and passenger cars. These bonds have a lien against the equipment purchased. The reason that this type of bond has been very successful in attracting investors is that a railroad has to have equipment to operate and therefore is not going to default on this kind of bond. Railroad equipment, too, tends to be standardized so that if one railroad were to default, the equipment could be sold to another railroad. There are many variations of equipment trust plans that are used.

Bonds are also issued that are secured by a particular facility. Often, bonds are issued in the construction of a bridge or a dock. The security for the bond is the bridge, or the dock, or the particular piece of property that is named.

Corporations may also issue bonds that have a lien on no specific property of the corporation; in other words, the bonds are unsecured but are based on the general credit of the corporation issuing them. These are called *debenture bonds.* Strong corporations that do not need

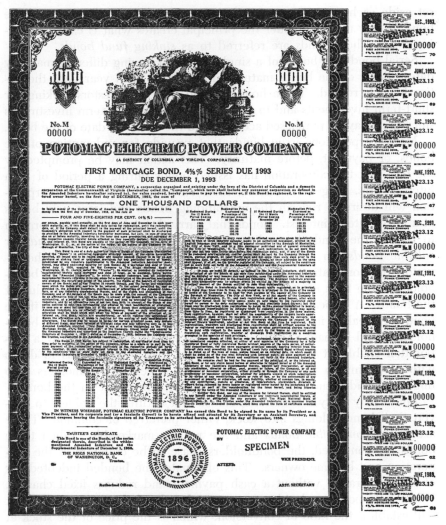

Fig. 7–2. A specimen corporation bond. The coupons on the right, of which there were 70, provide for semiannual interest payments of a little more than $23. The holder of the bond clips each coupon and turns it in on or after the date shown on the coupon in order to collect his interest (Potomac Electric Power Company, Inc.).

to pledge any property use this type of bond. Other corporations use them when they have no property that has not already been pledged.

Bonds Classified as to the Manner of Payment of Principal. A corporation may retire its bonded indebtedness by the payment of the face value of the bond upon its maturity date. A corporation that agrees to set aside each year an amount that is sufficient, upon maturity of the bond, to pay the bondholder the principal creates what is called a *sinking fund*. These bonds are referred to as *sinking fund bonds*.

Serial bonds are bonds of a single issue but having different maturity dates. Some of the bonds mature and are paid each year until the entire issue is retired. These bonds appeal both to investors looking for short-term investments and to those looking for longer-term investments since they may be purchased according to the maturity date of the bond.

Many corporations issue bonds that provide for redemption of the bonds, or payment, before maturity. This action may be prompted by the fact that the corporation has issued bonds during a period of high interest rates. If general interest rates on money decline, the corporation will desire to redeem the outstanding bonds and issue new bonds at a lower rate of interest. Bonds that carry the right of the corporation to call in the bonds for redemption are called *redeemable bonds* or *callable bonds*. In order to make callable bonds attractive to the investor, the corporation will generally provide a premium to the bondholder in the form of a higher redemption price than the face value of the bonds. A typical premium on a $1,000 bond is $50; so that if the bond were called in by the corporation before its maturity, the bondholder would be paid $1,050. The issuance of callable bonds by a corporation enables it to redeem bonds when it is advantageous to do so without having to pay unreasonably high prices to bondholders who might demand them if there were no redemption clause in the bond.

Bonds may carry a conversion clause that entitles the holders to convert their bond holdings into stock, either preferred or common. These are called *convertible bonds* and are readily marketable. When these bonds are converted, the bondholders cease to be creditors of the corporation and become owners. This eliminates the bonded indebtedness of the corporation without a cash payment and reduces fixed charges. When a corporation decides to convert bonds of this type to stock, it will establish the ratio of conversion, which is the price of the stock at the time of the exchange. The market value of convertible bonds is influenced by the market price of the stock into which the bonds can be converted. If the stock increases in the market to a high price, the convertible bond will rise in price also. If the stock sells at a lower figure, the bond does not follow the price of the stock to the same degree but will sell at a price reflecting the bond's investment value.

The Role of the Trustee. Bonds are held by many investors who are widely scattered. They are not in a position individually to make certain that the corporation is meeting all of its obligations as far as the bond issue is concerned. At the same time, the corporation issuing the bonds would have to spend a great deal of time and money if it dealt with individual investors and with the changes in investors as bonds are bought and sold. Therefore, when secured bonds are issued, a trustee is appointed who represents the bondholders and holds the mortgage for the bonds. The appointed trustee may be a person, although a trust company or the trust department of a bank is usually the trustee. A trust indenture is drawn up, which is a contract between the corporation and the trustee acting on the behalf of the bondholders. This legal document stipulates the obligations of the corporation and contains a covenant (an agreement) covering the protection of the bondholders.

Securities Exchanges or Stock Exchanges

A *securities exchange*, or as it is more commonly called a *stock exchange*, is a market place for securities. It is here that the sale of stocks and bonds of corporations takes place. A stock exchange is a non-profit, unincorporated organization formed by an association of dealers or brokers in securities. There are seventeen of these exchanges located throughout the United States. Rooms and other facilities for the transaction of business by the members of the stock exchange are provided.

The New York Stock Exchange is the oldest and the most important exchange. Trading on this Exchange is sometimes called "trading on the Big Board." Membership is limited to 1,375 members. About half of the members are partners or officers in brokerage firms doing business with the public—the so-called commission houses. Such members execute customers' orders to buy and sell on the Exchange, and the firms receive the commissions on the transactions. About one-fourth of all members of the Exchange are "specialists" because they specialize in the purchase and sale of one security. Other members may be odd-lot dealers. They arrange for the purchase or sale of a few shares at a time, from one to ninety-nine, rather than in the conventional one hundred-share unit known as a round lot. A member of the New York Stock Exchange must own a "seat" on the Exchange, a term that originated in the early days of the Exchange when members remained seated for the transactions. The price of a stock exchange membership is determined by the amount a candidate for membership will pay and the amount the owner of the membership will accept for sale of the membership. Since 1950, the prices of memberships on the New York Stock Exchange have ranged from $38,000 to $230,000. The initiation fee for new members is $4,000 and dues are about $750 annually.

In addition to those who are members of the Exchange, there are about 3,100 partners in member firms, and these partners are known as "allied members." Members only are permitted to buy and sell securities on the Exchange. The rules and regulations governing the conduct of members are set by a thirty-three-man board of governors. The

Exchange's revenues come primarily from members in dues and charges for services and facilities and from fees paid by corporations whose securities are listed on the Exchange. The member brokerage firms have offices in many cities and, although banks are not members of the Exchange, most of them have contacts with one or more of the member firms so that securities can be bought and sold at virtually any point in the United States.

Purchasers of securities compete with each other to buy securities at the lowest possible cost, and those selling securities compete with each other to get the highest possible price for the securities they are offering for sale. Those people who feel that the stock market is going up are referred to as *bulls* while those who feel it is going down are called *bears*. A bull market is an advancing market; that is, the general level of stocks is going up. A bear market is a declining market as shown in Figure 7–3. The stock exchange is a market place where shares in American industries can be bought and sold almost as easily as money can be deposited in a bank. Regardless of where a person lives, whether near a stock exchange or far removed from one, a telephone call to a member brokerage firm or bank to place an order and the payment of a commission, in addition to the price of the securities, is all that has to be done.

Fig. 7–3. The "bear" market is a declining market; the "bull" market an advancing market.

The Handling of Orders for Securities

Many people are hesitant to purchase stocks or bonds because they do not understand how to go about it. In order to show how the purchase of securities is handled, we will follow an order from the time that the prospective purchaser of stocks contacts a brokerage firm, or bank until the purchase is completed. Suppose Mr. Brown of Atlanta is interested in purchasing some securities. He telephones or goes to a member brokerage firm in Atlanta. After talking things over with a representative of the firm, he decides to buy common shares of General Motors Corporation and asks the representative to find out what General Motors common shares are selling for on the Exchange. Over a direct wire to his New York office, the representative asks for a "quote" or quotation on General Motors. A clerk in the firm's New York office dials the Quotation Department at the Exchange and hears, over an automatic tape announcer, the quotation on General Motors. Current quotations on all listed securities are received by the Quotation Department over direct wires from each trading location on the floor. Each stock is assigned a particular location, called a trading post, at one of the eighteen posts on the trading floor. All bids and offers for a stock must take place at that location. There are about eighty stocks traded at each of the trading posts.

The clerk in the New York office immediately reports to Atlanta that General Motors common stock is quoted "45 to a quarter." This means that, at that moment, the highest bid to buy this stock is $45 a share and the lowest offer to sell is $45.25 a share. Therefore, one hundred shares will cost Mr. Brown approximately $4,500, plus a commission of 1.26 per cent of the purchase price. Mr. Brown tells the registered representative to go ahead and buy. The latter writes out an order to buy one hundred shares of General Motors "at the market" and has it wired to his New York office where it is telephoned to his firm's partner on the floor of the Exchange. *At the market* means at the best price possible at the time the purchase is made. The floor partner hurries over to the trading post where General Motors is traded.

About the same time, someone decides to sell General Motors stock. Suppose James Smith of Seattle owns one hundred shares of General Motors that he has decided to sell. He calls his broker to get a "quote," and tells his broker to sell. That order, too, is wired to the floor of the Exchange. Smith's broker also hurries to the trading post where General Motors is traded. Just as he enters the General Motors group, he hears Brown's broker calling out: "How's Motors?" Someone—usually the specialist—answers, "45 to a quarter." Brown's broker could, without further thought, buy the one hundred shares offered at 45¼, and Smith's broker could sell his one hundred shares at 45. If they had done this, their customers would have been entitled to wonder why they did not try to get a better price for them.

Instead, Brown's broker thinks: "I cannot buy my one hundred at

45. Someone has already bid 45, and no one will sell at that price. I guess I had better bid 45⅛."

Smith's broker thinks: "It looks like I cannot sell my one hundred at 45¼; someone has already tried to get that price. I had better try to get 45⅛."

Smith's broker hears Brown's broker bid 45⅛ and instantly shouts: "Sold one hundred at 45⅛." They have agreed on a price, and the transaction takes place. Over and over again every day this procedure is repeated on the floor. The two brokers complete their verbal agreement by noting each other's firm name and reporting the transaction back to their telephone clerks so that their customers can be notified.

In the meantime, an Exchange employee has sent a record of the transaction to the ticker department for transmission over the ticker network. It is printed simultaneously on 2,688 stock tickers in 477 cities in this country and Canada. It would appear like this: GM45⅛. The number of shares in a round lot transaction is specified only when more than one hundred shares are involved—otherwise only the stock's symbol and price are printed.

Stock Market Averages

There are several different stock market averages that report advances or declines in the market. These are based on a limited number of stocks. One of the best known is the *Dow-Jones Industrial Average*. This average is compiled by adding the price of thirty selected stocks. This total is then divided by a divisor that is designed to compensate for past stock splits and stock dividends. In other words, the total is not divided by thirty. The reason for this is that a stock split or stock dividend of any one of the stocks can reduce the price of that stock and lower the average so an adjustment is made to reflect the effect of a stock split or stock dividend. The answer, or the average, is expressed in points, not dollars. The primary value of an average is in gauging the course of the market over a period of time rather than in measuring daily fluctuations. Some investors carefully follow these averages in making investments in securities.

Stock and Bond Quotations

Most of our newspapers contain on the financial page stock and bond tables listing all the securities that are traded on the New York Stock Exchange and often other exchanges, information about the day's prices, and quantities sold. The stocks are listed in alphabetical order so it is a simple matter to find the particular security for which you are looking. The following example shows how a stock listing for a mythical company would appear in a newspaper under columnar headings:

Stock and Div. in $	Sales in 100's	Open	High	Low	Close	Net Chg.
Typ. Mfg.2	29	25¼	25⅝	25	25½	+½

Reading from left to right, this shows that Typical Manufacturing Company is currently paying an annual dividend of $2.00 on each share of common stock (if the stock is preferred, "pf" is shown), and that 2,900 shares of the stock were bought and sold during the day in question. The first sale of the day was at 25¼ or $25.25 a share; the highest price for which any of the stock sold during the day was 25⅝ or $25.63 per share; the lowest was 25 or $25; and the last sale for the day was at 25½ or $25.50, which is a half-point, or 50¢ a share, above the closing price on the last day it was traded. In addition, some papers also show the highest price and lowest price recorded for Typical Manufacturing Company in the preceding year and the current year to date. Such figures usually appear just before the name of the stock.

Bonds, like stocks, are listed alphabetically on the financial page in many newspapers. However, bonds are separated as to different types, such as domestic corporate bonds, foreign bonds, and United States government bonds. When a corporation has more than one issue outstanding, each of them is listed because the prices will vary. Bond prices are quoted in relationship to $100 even though the denomination of the bonds is quite different, usually $1,000. Thus, a bond selling for 95½ would cost $955.

Margin Requirements in the Purchase of Securities

An individual purchasing stock can pay the full amount and thereby buy the stock outright, or he can make partial payment and borrow the balance from his broker, which is termed *buying on margin*. The United States Federal Reserve Board has, since 1934, established the margin requirements, or the percentage of the purchase price that must be supplied by the purchaser. The requirements have ranged from 40 per cent of the purchase price to 100 per cent, depending upon whether the Reserve Board wants to encourage trading in securities or discourage it. Currently, the margin rate is 70 per cent.

Selling Short

A person who believes that the price of a particular stock will decline sometimes enters into a short sale transaction whereby he hopes to make money from the fall in the price of the stock. He actually sells stock that he does not own. For example, he instructs his broker to sell short one hundred shares of ABC. His broker borrows the stock so he can deliver the one hundred shares to a buyer of the stock. The money value of the shares borrowed is deposited by the broker with the lender. Sooner or later, the person who is selling short must cover the short sale by buying the same amount of stock he borrowed in order to return it to the lender. If he is able to buy ABC at a lower price than he sold it, his profit is the difference between the two prices, less commissions. If he has to pay more for the stock than the price he received, he loses rather than gains. In order for him to make a profit on a short sale, then, the price of the stock has to decline. There are regulations that govern and limit the conditions under which a short sale may be made.

Businessmen sometimes use short sale transactions as a means of hedging. Perhaps a manufacturer desires to protect himself from loss on raw materials to be used in manufacturing. If the price on the raw materials should fall before his goods are ready for sale, the price on his finished products would be lower also; and he would stand to lose a profit on his manufactured goods. He may choose to protect himself from this possible loss by placing an order to sell short the same amount of raw materials at approximately the same time as the finished products will be ready for sale. If the price of raw materials falls during the manufacturing period, he will make a speculative profit on his short sale. If the price of raw materials does not fall, he will not lose on the raw materials used in manufacturing and will make his customary manufacturing profit, less the amount lost on the short sale.

Monthly Investment Plan for Purchasing Securities

A monthly investment plan is also available for the purchase of stocks listed on the New York Stock Exchange. Under this plan, monthly payments from $40 a month and higher can be made. If the individual decided to invest $100 a month in a stock of his choice that sells at $45 a share, the $100 will buy two shares. The commission is paid by him, which amounts to $6.00 on purchases or sales of less than $100 plus a nominal charge for buying less than one hundred shares. The remainder is used to purchase part of another share of stock. The $100 he pays the next month will be used to purchase shares at whatever price they are selling on the market at that time, and commission and charges will be paid on this purchase in the same manner as they were on his first purchase.

Over-the-Counter Stock Transactions

The over-the-counter market is a market in securities that, for the most part, are not listed on the stock exchanges. The over-the-counter market is not a place but a method of doing business by private negotiation among security dealers who use the telephone rather than a trading floor to buy and sell securities. Over-the-counter transactions are very large since the stock of all but 6 per cent of the more than 500,000 corporations are traded in this way. Most bank and insurance company stocks, United States government bonds, and municipal bonds are traded in this market. Although some large corporations like Dictaphone Corporation are traded here, it is mostly small companies that are traded.

Commodity Exchanges

Commodities that can be stored and of which there is large-scale production are bought and sold on commodity exchanges. Included are such commodities as corn, wheat, soy beans, cotton, sugar, and coffee. There are a number of commodity exchanges that specialize in a single item whereas others, like the *Chicago Board of Trade,* have many commodities that are traded. Since the items that are bought and sold are standardized as to grade and quantity, or weight, it is possible to buy and sell freely such commodities through a commodity exchange. Members of exchanges or their brokers handle the orders to buy and sell. They perform these services for a commission in a manner similar to the handling of orders on the stock exchange. It is the buying and selling on the commodity exchanges that really determines the market prices at which these commodities will be sold. It has been said that the difference between speculating in stocks and speculating in commodities can be compared to traveling in a car vs. traveling in an airplane, i.e., since the airplane travels at greater speed, if something goes wrong, the results are usually disastrous.

YOUR CAREER IN FINANCE

Career Opportunities

In our economy, we have a highly developed financial system. Personal and business savings are put to work through the medium of financial institutions as there is a great need for capital with which to provide financial assistance in expanding facilities and carrying inventories. The many career opportunities in finance are unusually good.

Banks offer employment possibilities that have strong appeal for many students. While starting salaries for the college graduate are not as high as in some other fields of business, many fringe benefits are provided that add materially to the attractiveness of this employment. In addition, the personnel in banks are highly respected citizens of their community. Banks are also expanding fast so that there are numerous managerial positions opening up all the time. Banking is interesting work because the financial needs of individuals, of businesses, and of communities are so diverse; and the banker feels that he shares in the achievement of personal and business goals. The Federal Reserve System, too, provides job opportunities for students who are interested in a career in banking. Banking is an area in which the career opportunities for women are very good.

Investment companies, insurance companies, and industrial organizations have need for persons who have specialized in finance. The capital needs of business organizations are constantly increasing and more technical in nature. Corporations need financial experts to work in their finance departments. Such matters as whether to issue stocks or bonds, or secure long-term or short-term bank loans, or a combination of these require people who are well trained in finance. Investment companies purchase many stocks and bonds from corporations so there are career opportunities in these companies for persons interested in the financial aspects of business. Insurance companies have large sums of money to invest, and so a part of their staff devotes its time to analyses of investment opportunities ranging from securities to the financing of shopping centers. Positions with any of these business organizations should be well paying and possess good future expectations.

The Securities and Exchange Commission, which exercises certain control over the issuance and sale of securities, offers job opportunities for financial experts. There are also some financial corporations owned and operated or controlled by the federal government in which there are good career positions. The Treasury Department of the federal government, too, holds possibilities for promising careers in finance.

Educational Background

A program of study for a student interested in the field of finance is based first on a general background of liberal arts subjects. He then builds upon this foundation with courses in business and economics. A course in money and banking will help him to understand better the banking institutions and financing methods. Courses in business finance are necessary to provide a knowledge of corporate structure, of capital requirements, of financial instruments, and additional aspects of finance. Investment management, statistics, credit, and accounting, beyond the principles course, are desirable areas of study. The student interested in a career in finance should develop a knowledge of local, state, and federal taxation methods and borrowing. A course in public finance would be of value in this regard. For those who want to specialize in the financial aspects of insurance, courses in insurance would be desirable. Government and politics courses are also valuable in developing a sense of public responsibility.

TOPICS FOR DISCUSSION

1. Would you advise businessmen to use financial ratios calculated by Dun and Bradstreet?

2. Do you feel that the size of an organization will be a factor in securing additional financial resources?

3. What do you feel are the three main functions of the financial manager of a business corporation?

4. Do personal income taxes affect the payment of dividends by corporations?

5. Who prepares a prospectus? If you are issuing securities in a publicly held company, do you have to have a prospectus?

6. Why might a newly formed company have difficulty raising capital from the public despite its being incorporated?

7. A businessman who has not heretofore found it necessary to seek outside financial assistance in his business finds that now, after three years of operation, he has to do so. He would like your suggestions as to what he will need in order to establish a "line of credit." Help him in any way that you can.

8. What is a sale-lease-back arrangement? Does it have any financial advantage from the seller's point of view?

9. In what way is depreciation a source of financing?

10. As a member of a corporation's board of directors, what recommendations would you make on the amount of retained earnings that should be kept in a company whose sales volume has increased 15 per cent each year for the past five years?

CASE 7–1

FINANCING THE EXPANSION OF A LAUNDRY SERVICE

Robert Lockman operated an industrial laundry service in the town of Hillsville, which had a population of approximately 10,000 and was the trading center serving an agricultural area. Mr. Lockman's method of operation was to contract with drugstores, food markets, restaurants, service stations, clinics, and doctors and dentists to launder uniforms. The uniforms were picked up, laundered, and delivered, in weekly cycles. Unlike the operators of many laundry services of this type, Mr. Lockman did not own the uniforms. Companies in this type of business frequently own uniforms that are furnished on a rental basis. Mr. Lockman had thought of operating in this manner but had never acquired the necessary capital to convert from his present operation. In the spring of 1965, Mr. Lockman employed six people in his plant. He owned a single panel truck, which handled the pickup and delivery service. On occasion, he would use the family car to supplement the efforts of the truck. The business was a small-scale operation, but it enabled Mr. Lockman to earn what he considered a "fair living."

In 1965, a national company decided to open a food-processing plant in Hillsville. This was to be an enterprise employing 500 people, and the nature of the work was such that uniforms were to be worn by all employees associated with the production processes. Since Mr. Lockman operated the only industrial laundry service within fifty miles of Hillsville, a representative of the company called on him to discuss the possibility of having him provide the laundry service. Mr. Lockman was told that he would have to furnish the uniforms and launder them according to a schedule to be established by the processing company. He would be paid a monthly rental based on the number of uniforms used.

Mr. Lockman was anxious to take on this new volume of business. He realized that, if he did not service the processing company, an outside laundry service might be brought in to do the job, or a competing business might be organized in Hillsville. Either way, he felt that a competitor who served the processing plant would be a threat to take the customers that he was presently serving.

A review of his present facilities in relation to what would be needed to take on the new business revealed to Mr. Lockman that he would need capital to the extent of at least $30,000 to finance the equipment and other costs of expansion involved in servicing the processing plant. He faced unusual problems in raising the necessary capital. The present assets of the laundry were not such as to afford a significant basis for borrowing capital. His home was covered by both a first and a second mortgage. Added to this was the fact that Mr. Lockman had a history of financial reverses prior to the operation of his present business. Unfortunately, certain of these reverses had resulted in considerable loss to creditors.

Mr. Lockman took his problem to the local banks. They were interested in seeing a local firm service the processing plant but were unwilling to advance capital to Mr. Lockman without some type of security to back up the loans. Finally, it was suggested that he talk to a representative of the processing plant to determine if they would be willing to guarantee a part of the loan. Conferences with the plant revealed that they would act as a cosigner for a part of the loan, but only if there would be a written agreement that the processing company would have authority to place a manager in charge of the laundry if the service proved unsatisfactory, or if the financial affairs of the business seemed in danger. Mr. Lockman did not look on this arrangement with enthusiasm.

Mr. Lockman visited a field office of the Small Business Administration with the hope that he could arrange financing through this agency of the federal government. After investigating Mr. Lockman's background, and his present financial situation, the agency could not offer much encouragement. At this stage in the situation, Mr. Barton who owned and operated the town's largest consumer laundry and dry-cleaning service approached Mr. Lockman with a proposition. He proposed that a partnership be established in which Mr. Barton would own 55 per cent of the business and Mr. Lockman, 45 per cent. With Mr. Barton as the controlling interest in the business, the local banks would supply the capital for the needed expansion. Under the proposal, Mr. Lockman would serve as general manager of the industrial laundry, but all decisions involving financial matters would be made in conference with Mr. Barton and subject to his approval.

Neither the proposal of Mr. Barton nor that of the processing plant appealed to Mr. Lockman as being entirely satisfactory. He realized, however, that his financial history was such as to preclude borrowing the necessary capital while retaining sole ownership and control of the business. He could give up the idea of serving the processing plant and hope that this would not endanger his present business, but this seemed to involve a large element of risk.

1. Do you feel that lenders are justified in placing so much emphasis on Mr. Lockman's past financial failures?
2. If you were in Mr. Lockman's place, what would you do?

SELECTED REFERENCES

Bogen, J. I. *Financial Handbook.* 4th ed. New York: The Ronald Press Co., 1965.
Brandt, L. K. *Business Finance.* Englewood Cliffs, N.J.: Prentice-Hall, Inc., 1965.
Donaldson, E. F., and J. K. Pfahl. *Corporate Finance.* 2d ed. New York: The Ronald Press Co., 1963.
Gerstenberg, C. W. *Financial Organization and Management of Business.* 4th ed. Englewood Cliffs, N.J.: Prentice-Hall, Inc., 1959.
Guthmann, H. G., and H. E. Dougall. *Corporate Financial Policy.* 4th ed. Englewood Cliffs, N.J.: Prentice-Hall, Inc., 1962.
Hunt, P., C. M. Williams, and G. Donaldson. *Basic Business Finance.* Homewood, Ill.: Richard D. Irwin, Inc., 1957.
Kent, R. P. *Corporate Financial Management.* Rev. ed. Homewood, Ill.: Richard D. Irwin, Inc., 1964.

8

Organizing the Management of the Firm

THE CONCEPT OF ORGANIZATION

In an earlier chapter we discussed the legal forms of business organizations—the sole proprietorship, the partnership, and the corporation. These are the exterior forms of organization with which businesses are conducted. We are concerned in this chapter with the internal organizational structure of the enterprise that enables it to operate more efficiently. This binds together the various parts of the business enterprise by specifying the authority and responsibility of everyone from the president down to the workman in the plant. The most modern physical facilities and well-trained personnel may be ineffectual without adequate planning and coordination of all activities of the business enterprise.

The sole proprietor who performs all the business functions himself has no organizational problems except insofar as his time is concerned. He does all the work himself and, in his own mind, he probably has some sort of plan by which he performs tasks in the order of their importance. If his business grows so that he is unable to handle it by himself, he may hire an employee. In order to prevent overlapping, it is now necessary that he divide duties between the employee and himself, as well as making certain that the work for the employee will be planned in such a way that the maximum will be accomplished. This is the beginning of the separation of management from operational functions. As more employees are hired, the need for coordination of activities becomes more pronounced.

PROBLEMS ENCOUNTERED IN COMPANY GROWTH

The growth of a business enterprise brings particular problems at various stages of company expansion. In the very small business with less than ten employees, the organizational problem is that of deciding what the objectives of the business activities are and dividing the work among the employees. As additional employees are hired, the problem of delegation of responsibility becomes the organizational problem. At this stage, people who have been in the organization longest may feel that on the basis of seniority, responsibility should be delegated to them. The delegation of authority, however, should go to the personnel who are best qualified. This may mean hiring outside people for the positions of responsibility. The delegation of more management functions becomes the organizational problem as the size of the company further increases. Top management's burden must be lessened, and this is usually accomplished through the employment of a person or persons to assist him. The addition of staff specialists for purchasing, personnel, traffic, and other functions is the next step in organization. By the time the company has grown to the size where it employs one to five hundred people, a single executive may not be called upon to make decisions, but this will be done by means of committees of top management.

Steps in Creating the Organization

Creating the organization of the enterprise is a function of management. The work to be performed must be grouped and divided among various necessary positions. Personnel with qualifications to fill the positions should then be found. As far as possible, similar functions should be combined in one position. In larger companies, it is necessary to group the work into departments. By creating departments and delegating authority to individuals to head the departments, the president relieves himself of much of the burden of management. With many people holding management positions, there has to be a clear picture of exactly what each person is to do, what he is responsible for, and to whom he reports. The lines of authority must be clearly delineated through the establishment of an organizational structure. Management has to decide on the authority relationships at the various levels, that is, the relationships between departments at the same level in the management organization. Ideally, the organizational structure should be balanced with no top-heavy departments that have been assigned more activities and authority than other departments. A department should not be overexpanded because it has high periodic peaks of work. It sometimes happens, however, that executives are more interested in certain departments than in others because of their own experience or training and tend to emphasize the importance of these departments.

The Organization Chart

The organization chart is a useful management tool in developing and maintaining an effective organization. Not all companies, though, make use of a chart. Its principal purpose is to present a graphic picture of the organizational structure. The organization chart is especially helpful in showing basic relationships and the grouping of positions and functions. It is significant also as a means of providing information for employees. The value of the organization chart is limited to the period during which there are no changes in the organizational structure. Another limitation of the chart is that it is able to show only a restricted amount of information.

Ordinarily, the chart is made up of interconnected rectangular boxes, each of which represents one position. Thus, the basic unit of the chart is the individual unit. The grouping of the boxes shows the groupings of activities that make up the departments, divisions, sections, and other components of the organization. By referring to the chart, it is easy to determine who reports to whom and what direct relationship one position bears to another. It will also reveal the lack of balance and overlapping positions if any exist. For example, a manufacturing firm that had trebled its volume in a five-year period found upon preparing an organization chart that the company had a treasurer, a controller, an auditor, a chief accountant, and a budget director, all of whom reported to the president on the same level. A weakness of the organization chart is that companies often design the charts to accommodate "personalities," that is, take care of certain individuals, rather than develop a chart to secure effective organization.

Most companies use vertical structure charts, which are usually scalar in form, which means that the different levels of the organization are shown in step arrangement as seen in Figure 8–1. The vertical chart is arranged from top to bottom with primary management at the top and successive levels shown vertically. The horizontal chart, as shown in Figure 8–2, is not as widely used as the vertical structure. It does have the advantage of making it possible to put more positions on it. This type of chart also minimizes the importance of levels. The functional chart is another chart in use. It is generally a vertical chart that

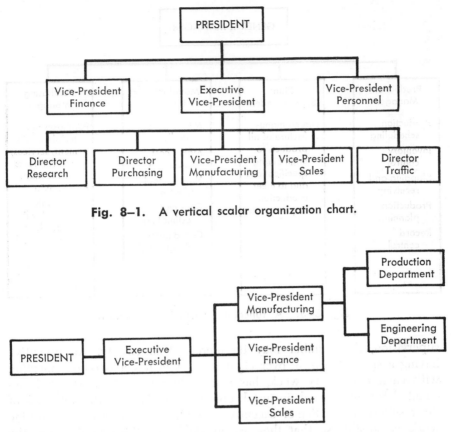

Fig. 8–1. A vertical scalar organization chart.

Fig. 8–2. A horizontal organization chart.

lists the responsibilities for the positions shown. This enables a person to see what functions have been assigned to each position and what is expected. A functional chart for a manufacturing plant is shown in Figure 8–3.

Span of Control

The problem that exists in many medium-sized and large companies is what is referred to as *span of control* or *span of management*. This means the number of persons who report to any one supervisor or executive. An organization should be planned so that the fewest practical number of junior executives report to each senior executive. In top management, some authorities suggest that there should be no more than eight people reporting to one executive. At the lower levels of

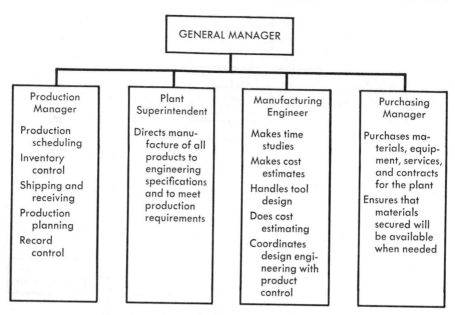

Fig. 8–3. A functional organization chart.

supervision, this number may be increased to twenty. An executive having a span of control over eight men, who has a two-hour meeting with each man every week, has sixteen hours of his work week accounted for every week in just keeping up to date on the activities of these subordinates. Senior executives should be kept as free of routine work as possible so that they are available for the planning and the solution of broad management problems.

Centralized and Decentralized Organizations

One of the questions that companies must decide as they grow in size is whether to continue management that is centralized in one individual or to decentralize management through delegation of authority to subordinates. Where there are multiple plants owned by a company, there may be centralized authority in the headquarters office with regard to policy making but decentralized management operations within the framework of the headquarters management policies. For example, General Motors has established about thirty operating divisions. Each is operated much as if it were an independent business. The general manager of each of these divisions has charge of designing, developing, manufacturing, and marketing the products of his division. He purchases his own materials and parts either from other divisions of the company or from outside suppliers. Each of the divisions is competing with other companies making similar products as well as with divisions within the company itself. Operations are carried on within the policy framework of the centralized General Motors organization with regard to planning, coordination, and control. General Electric has also decentralized in a similar manner. It has many departments each with management-assigned responsibility and accountability for the successful conduct of its business. One of the advantages of decentralization of management is the development of management potential because subordinates have to make decisions and are responsible for the success or failure of their division.

TYPES OF ORGANIZATIONAL STRUCTURES

Primary Types of Organizations

A number of types of internal management organization exist. These types are not confined to a particular kind of business enterprise, such as banking or manufacturing, but some of each type will be found in every field of business. The three primary forms of internal organizational structure are line, functional, and line-and-staff. The type of management organization used by a particular company will depend upon the size of the company, the nature of the business, and the number and complexity of problems.

The Line Organization

The oldest and the simplest form of organization is the line organization. As the word "line" implies, there is a direct line of authority from the president, or top management executive, to the workers. There are usually considered to be three levels in management organization: the management level (or executive, or administrative level), the supervisory level, and the working level. The management level is often divided into top management and middle management, or senior and junior executives. The direct line of authority in a line organization goes from the top position to the bottom, as shown in Figure 8–4. The flow of responsibility returns along the same lines. The levels of the foreman and the plant superintendent are intermediate levels in the line organization in this figure. In business organizations smaller than the one in this chart, the line organization would consist only of the workers who report to the owner. Figure 8–4 shows the departmental organization by functions—foundry shop foreman, machine shop foreman, and assembly shop foreman. Some companies establish departments on the

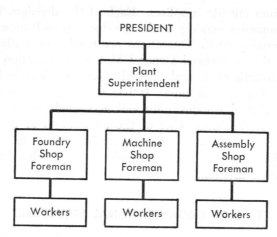

Fig. 8–4. A line organization in a small plant.

basis of products produced by the company rather than functions. As the size of this company increases, the president might select certain executives to handle selling and financing, and other functions. These people would be at a management level just below the president and would formulate plans, give advice, or render service to other executives and foremen and workers. This, however, would still be a line organization.

Under this type of organization, sections or departments on the same level of authority are completely self-contained units. The head of the section or department has charge of everything under him and is responsible only to the executive who is directly above him. The line organization is often referred to as the military organization in that the commands go down from the highest officer to the private soldier. The most precise application of the line principle is made in the military organizations where the line of command is rigidly followed. The line organization is one that is used in small businesses although many large organizations make use of the basic characteristics of this type of organization.

The primary advantage of the line organization is that it is easy to ascertain if each person is performing his job as he should since each person is responsible for certain duties and is given authority to accomplish the assigned tasks. Other advantages of this type of internal organization are that control over personnel is simplified since each person receives instructions or orders from his immediate superior; decisions can be made quickly with a minimum of red tape, and relationships are very easily understood as each person is responsible to the person above with the chain of command going upward to the top.

On the other hand, there are disadvantages to the line organization, and these limitations will be particularly noticeable as the company grows in size. The problem that arises immediately is a lack of specialization. Each supervisor is responsible for a number of duties and cannot be an expert in all of them. The result is that there may be more inefficiency than would exist if matters were handled by specialists in each area of operation. The emphasis in the line organization is on individual action, so there is little cooperation between departments or sections on the same organizational level. Another limitation is the fact that the loss of one individual can have a great effect upon company operations. Since so much authority can be delegated to one person, his loss through illness or death may seriously disrupt operations. There is also a tendency under this system to give inadequate consideration to the line of succession by management, especially to top management positions. It often happens, also, that top management in a line organization become so involved in day-to-day operations that they do not have sufficient time to devote to planning.

The Functional Organization

Another type of management organization, the functional organization, was developed by Frederick W. Taylor who was a pioneer in the development of scientific management about the end of the nineteenth century. As formulated by him, the functional organization was designed to correct weaknesses in the line of organization at the level of the foreman in the shop. Taylor had found it difficult to find supervisors who could carry out the many duties of the foreman's position in the line organization. He, therefore, divided the responsibilities of shop supervision, based on the functions performed, among several foremen, each especially qualified and in charge of a certain aspect of the work. In his functional organization, workers were to take orders from more than one superior but only with regard to the particular function over which each foreman had control, as shown in Figure 8–5. Taylor's plan was to establish more foremen who would have greater knowledge of the function for which each was responsible. This functionalization was then extended by him to office personnel.

The emphasis in functionalization is upon the development of specialists who devote their time to very limited areas of activity. Under a functional organization, the activities of the business are divided into functions and assigned to specialists so that each person who has control of a specific function exercises his authority not only over his own staff but also over the area of his specialization wherever it is found in the business. This type of organization was tried by a comparatively

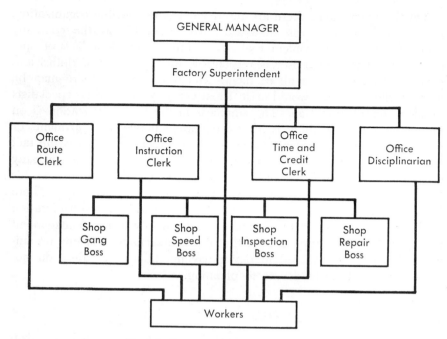

Fig. 8–5. Functional organization.

small number of companies, and many of them abandoned it because it was unworkable. However, its development was important because it showed the desirability of specialization in the management organization and was of value in the development of a type of business organization widely used today—the line-and-staff organization. It also made it possible to have skilled supervisory attention given to the workmen.

Probably the greatest disadvantage of the functional organization is that the workers have more than one boss because the separation of functions and division of authority result in each supervisor having authority over his particular function. Another disadvantage is that the foremen do not cooperate as they should, which makes it difficult to fix responsibility and eliminate poor performance, which, in turn, lowers morale. In addition, the emphasis upon specialization does not allow the specialists to develop sufficient knowledge of areas outside their specialization so as to obtain a broad background for positions of greater responsibility.

The Line-and-Staff Organization

In the development of the internal organizations, there has emerged an organization called the *line-and-staff-organization.* To the basic line organization are added separate staff departments of technical specialists and staff assistants to be of assistance to executives. When separate staff departments are created, they are manned by specialists who study and make recommendations on problems assigned to them or which they develop themselves when they see opportunities for improvement. They might develop plans and methods for assisting operating departments in purchase of materials, or study the purchase of transportation service, or recommend changes in the selection of personnel, or any other phase of the operations in which their knowledge and experience would be of value to the company at any of the levels from top to bottom. Their recommendations are made to their superior, who then makes the decision on whether or not their recommendations will be adopted.

Where separate staff departments are created, the head of each department has line control only over the people in his department. If he is the head of the personnel department, he will relieve the line executives of all the details of recruiting, testing, and interviewing people, and will even hire them subject to the line executive's approval. The line executive retains control over his department but does not have to handle many of the specialized matters that had previously claimed much of his attention. Figure 8–6 is a chart of a line-and-staff organization.

Conflicts may develop between line and staff executives unless the authority and responsibilities are clear cut and cooperative relationships

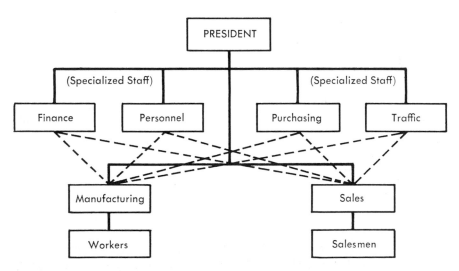

Fig. 8–6. Line-and-staff organization. Broken lines indicate staff functions of providing advice and service to the line personnel.

are fostered between line and staff. The functions of line and staff must be kept separate, and competitive attitudes between line and staff people should not be allowed to develop. Line executives need the help of staff specialists, and staff groups cannot gather facts and be of technical assistance without the cooperation of the line personnel. Each group should be encouraged to discuss with each other the objectives, duties, and problems of their respective jobs.

Also used in the line-and-staff organization are staff assistants appointed to help the top executive in the particular fields of their specialization. They do not make decisions, and aid in only those matters in which they possess special knowledge.

The advantage of the line-and-staff organization is that it possesses the same straight-line authority from top to bottom that the line organization has and to this has been added the specialized knowledge of experts in particular fields in which management feels the need for help. The line-and-staff organization has usually developed at the stage in company growth where the need for specialized help in particular areas, such as wage administration, work and time measurement, basic research, and other areas has developed.

Use of Committees in Line-and-Staff Organizations

We have seen how the continued expansion of a company has resulted in the need for more detailed management organization and the addition of special help in areas of the business that merit particular attention. These were the staff departments and staff specialists that were added when a company changed from a line organization to a line-and-staff organization. Many large companies reach a stage where the line-and-staff organization needs to be modified in order to fulfill the management requirements of their companies. This is usually accomplished by the formulation of committees that are not a form of management organization in themselves but are fitted into the management organization at different levels.

Committees are established for different purposes. A number of standing committees are set up, usually one for each level of authority. For example, a committee of top management, usually called an executive committee, may be instituted in order to keep the executives informed of the happenings in all departments of the company and to assist the president in the formulation of company policies and in planning major projects and programs. Committees, such as a production planning committee, may be formed at lower levels to promote cooperation and to solve operational problems. A plant safety committee might be formed in which there would be labor representatives as well as management. These standing committees tend to become an established and accepted part of the organization structure. In addition, there may be temporary committees created to deal with special problems or projects. Committees set up to study a particular problem are dissolved when the study is completed.

Generally, a committee does not have authority to make decisions. There is a discussion of the problem, and the committee makes a recommendation, which is passed to the executive who is responsible for making the decision. There are times when an executive refers a matter to a committee in order that the committee will have to share the responsibility in the decision he reaches. The most effective use of committees depends upon a number of factors: adequate representation on the committee but not so many members as to become unwieldy; advance notice of the matters to be discussed; a clear definition of the duties, responsibility, and authority of the committee; and appointment to the committee of persons directly concerned with the matter assigned to the committee.

The use of committees provides a good training ground for younger executives. Assignments may be given to younger men to work up material and report to a committee. They gain a better insight into company problems and learn to work with others.

FUNCTIONS OF MANAGEMENT

Planning and Policy Formulation

Profitable operations in which products or services are made available to the public to satisfy their requirements are the objective of business enterprises. In order to have a successful business enterprise, many factors are necessary; but perhaps the paramount one is good management. Regardless of the type of business, the tasks confronting management are much the same. What are the managerial functions that must be performed in order to have a successful enterprise?

Of primary importance is planning and policy formulation. Planning is thinking through what is hoped to be accomplished. Through planning, the manager evaluates various possibilities and decides upon a future course of action. Planning sets up a mental picture of what management wants for the enterprise, and policy formulation is the framework within which planning can be realized. A wide range of subjects, including such things as future production, pricing, the addition of new products, the location of new plants, and many others are embraced. Unless planning is done in an orderly manner, the desired results will not materialize.

Planning requires imagination and analytical ability. Essentially, it is economic in nature because it attempts to choose from among many alternatives the course that will accomplish the objectives of the enterprise, and at the same time minimize costs. Planning of necessity involves forecasting. Many different techniques are used in forecasting—some are mathematical, others statistical, and still others economic. Planning also embraces programs that are used in carrying out the objectives and policies of the company. They are set up to carry out the goals of the company in a step-by-step sequence and include the specific projects or activities.

Many businesses establish over-all company objectives and then break down for each level of management the objectives for that level. This means that the objectives at the top may be broad and general in nature whereas at lower levels they are specific and detailed. The petroleum industry is a good example of the manner in which companies plan the scope of their operations. Some companies operate solely in the exploration of new fields and in the production of crude oil that they sell at the well where it was produced. The objective of other companies is to be completely integrated, that is, to control the product from extraction to the customer. Standard Oil Company of Indiana is such a company. It is an explorer and crude oil producer and has pipelines for the distribution of the petroleum. It owns refineries and markets its products through stations that the company builds and leases to people who operate them. It is their desire to control the petroleum at every stage from the time it is drawn from the ground until it is sold at the filling station. For the petroleum company that sells its product at the well, the objectives at the lower levels of management would be different from those that exist at the corresponding levels in the Standard Oil Company of Indiana, which carries its operations all the way through to the consumer. There are also some petroleum companies that have embarked upon the development of petrochemicals—chemicals that are derived from petroleum. This means that their plans have had to involve the amount of capital to be needed, the location and building of plants, the employment of people, the marketing of the product, the calculation of risks, and many other aspects. It all had to be thought through before the company went into this area. This is sometimes called the "occupational" phase of objectives.

Companies sometimes find it advisable to change the occupational phase of objectives. One area may not prove to be as profitable as had been anticipated, or the expansion of the business into another area may be more desirable so that the objective will be changed. Also included in company objectives may be the amount of profits, the competitive position to be maintained, and the reputation of the company.

The establishment of policies by management is a part of the planning function. Policies serve as guides that govern some portion of the activities of a business. They set forth the proper course of action to be followed under certain circumstances. For example, the management may establish a policy that states that company traffic will be distributed among the various transportation carriers with consideration to cost and service. Management may have developed this particular policy after an analysis of whether the company should engage in transportation itself by buying equipment in which to do it or whether reliance should be placed upon commercial transportation carriers. Management has established the policy of using commercial carriers but has left the choice of the carriers—whether rail, motor, water, or air—to a lower level of management that will base their choice upon the guiding policy of consideration of cost and service of each type of carrier. Policies must be definite, clear, and understandable. They should be readily translatable into procedures and practices. There should not be too many policies and, as a rule, they should not prescribe detailed procedure.

Direction

Direction is another of the functions of management. The principal problem involving direction by management is that of getting people to put their best effort into the job and to work cooperatively with others in accomplishing company objectives. Subordinates must be guided and supervised by management. In directing people in a business organization, the success in getting things accomplished through people depends in considerable measure upon the management's ability to provide leadership.

We all recognize that there are differences between individuals, and this fact must be acknowledged and dealt with in the management approach to the direction of personnel. Direction must be flexible so that it can be adapted to different personalities. The technique used in directing one person may be ineffective in getting the best efforts from another individual. Direction by management may range from that of complete direction with little freedom being given subordinates to act without prior approval to a free-rein method in which individuals are allowed to think and act independently to assist in achieving the general objectives of the company.

The use of conferences, both formal and informal, between management and subordinates has been found by some companies to be an effective means of management direction. Informal conferences are utilized to a great extent and are called as the need for them develops. In this way, matters can be discussed and cooperation secured when it is needed rather than having to wait for a conference, which occurs only at stated intervals. The informal conference also helps in promoting an understanding of company policies and operations and helps personnel to feel that they are an important part of a team.

An important aspect of direction is communication between management and subordinates. Communication is the transmission of information, orders, and ideas to individuals or groups of individuals. Management must insure that the way is kept open all along the line for suggestions, complaints, recommendations, and comments from all personnel. Supervisory personnel need to feel that they can go to top management with their problems and that they are an essential part of the organization. Good communication means that information goes from top to bottom in the company vertically and horizontally, as well, through departments on the same level of management.

Staffing

The function of staffing has assumed an increasingly significant role in management. If management is to perform the actual function of managing and this is to be accomplished through other people, it should be apparent how important the selection of management personnel from the foreman up to the president should be. Management should recognize that the starting point in the function of staffing is the selection of individuals with management potential. Certain qualities are looked for in these persons, among them: intelligence, leadership, initiative, judgment, and the ability to work with others. The source of management personnel may be within the company or outside the company, or a combination of the two.

Staffing also involves some type of promotion pattern so that personnel can see the opportunities that exist for them at the various levels. Until recently, a somewhat neglected part of staffing was that of management training. That which was conducted was often at the lowest level of supervisory management, such as the foreman. It has been proved many times that management training can be of value at every level. Some of the many training methods are informal with the trainee assigned to observe a member of the management team and ask questions about his work. There is formal training, also, with time set aside to deal with subjects in a stated sequence. The management trainee may be given assignments of background material as well as being assigned typical problems and cases that he might be called upon to discuss, which would be similar to actual problems of management.

Control

Top management needs to give responsibility and authority to capable assistants in order to have time for planning, directing, and coordinating the activities of the enterprise. On the other hand, he must have a means of assurance that performance at all levels in the organization is satisfactory. Control, as a function of managment, is a means by which management insures that the business is measuring up to the objectives that have been set in the plans of the company. In order to establish effective control, the executive must decide first what the goals are; then he decides the procedure to be followed in attaining the goals that will specify how and when and by whom something will be done and what constitutes satisfactory performance. The checkup is the last element of control that will show how well the job has been done. Efficient control detects any fall-off in performance, thus forewarning while there is time to do something about it. Immediate action can be taken to rectify the matter wherever it occurs. Control can also provide a means to steadier and higher profits.

It is necessary to establish standards of comparison in order to control. The standards that are established can be of a wide variety, and a number are generally used by a company. They must be realistic standards and ones that are measurable. They can be expressed in terms of the number of man-hours required to perform a certain task, the quantity of product produced in an hour, the assignment of costs on a per-unit basis, the ratio of return on investment on each product, and a number of others. Control has to be effectively exercised at every level of management from the foreman up to the top executive. The top executive will be primarily concerned with over-all control of such items as costs, wages, methods, profitability, etc., while lower management levels will be more concerned with control of specific actions, such as reordering of stock, filling of orders, etc. Control attempts to anticipate any lowering of standards in any phase of the business.

The budget is a control device. It may be stated in financial terms, such as a budget dealing with anticipated expenses and revenues, or it may be in non-financial terms, such as a sales budget or a budget of the units to be produced.

The appraisal or checkup compares the performance to the established standards. On the assembly line where standards have been set through timing performance, it is relatively easy to appraise performance. In other areas of the business, however, management deals with performance that is not precisely measurable, and the basis for judging performance becomes more general. It can be seen that it would not be a simple matter to measure results when considering the performance of individuals in managerial positions, such as the vice-president of finance. Often an appraisal is based on the absence of trouble rather than on any definite achievement. If the comparison of performance with established standards indicates that it does not measure up to the standards, corrective action must be taken immediately.

Issuance of Manuals

In larger organizations, it becomes necessary to prepare and distribute manuals to inform and to guide personnel. These manuals may be organization manuals, production manuals, personnel manuals, traffic manuals, and others. These manuals make it possible for executives and subordinates to have a complete understanding of the role of each in accomplishing company objectives. The typical organization manual, for example, will contain a statement of company objectives, a list of company policies, the principles of organization, titles of organizational units and positions, procedures for making organizational changes, organization charts, and job descriptions. The organization charts give a graphic breakdown of the company, but they do not stipulate how each unit of the organization should function. The organization manual will contain written specifications for each of the key jobs and supplements the organization chart.

TOPICS FOR DISCUSSION

1. Do you agree with the often stated view that management is a universal process in all organized living?

2. Do you feel that much of our internal-organization practice has come directly from the military organization concepts?

3. In a typical hierarchical pattern of a business enterprise, communications can be viewed as proceeding in what directions?

4. Do you feel that the organization structures of firms are static? Why?

5. How would you define "decentralization of authority"?

6. Why do some companies refuse to release a copy of their organization chart? What purpose does an organization chart serve?

7. What problems are encountered in company growth that affect internal organization? How can such problems be most easily solved?

8. How important is the function of policy formulation by management? How would you define business policy? Where could you expect to find a company's policy statements?

9. What information would you put in a management manual? How would the manual be of benefit to top management?

10. In what ways can a business firm improve its internal organization? Carefully consider and report upon practical measures you would recommend.

CASE 8–1

THE CHEROKEE MANUFACTURING COMPANY

The Cherokee Manufacturing Company was an old, established producer of a line including tents, camp stoves, lanterns, and a number of other items used in camping. Its "Skyline" brand had wide recognition and acceptance. The company sold ,its line through a network of brokers who called upon hardware and sporting-goods stores.

In 1964, the Monelli Trailer Corporation purchased a controlling interest in the Cherokee Manufacturing Company. The Monelli firm was an aggressive organization that had experienced rapid growth since the early 1950's. In acquiring control of the Cherokee Manufacturing Company, its officers felt that the move gave them access to something of a related line. The sale of family trailers had increased with the boom in outdoor living. The Monelli management saw an opportunity to improve the marketing of the Cherokee line of products by making them available through the same outlets that sold certain of the Monelli trailers. They also felt that some of the dealers such as the larger sporting-goods stores presently handling the Cherokee products might be induced to handle the smaller family-type trailers. Before acquiring control of the Cherokee Manufacturing Company, the Monelli people had studied its financial position. Cherokee had made a consistent profit throughout the years. The company was in good shape financially, but the Monelli management felt that the Cherokee management had been overly conservative and had not exploited the market to the fullest extent.

Soon after acquiring control of the Cherokee Manufacturing Company, the Monelli firm sent a team of executives to make a study of Cherokee operations and management. The study turned up some startling developments from the viewpoint of some of the visiting Monelli executives. The organization chart of the Cherokee firm did not reveal the centers of authority in the company or the relationships between executives as they really existed. As an example, purchases of materials and supplies other than routine items were made subject to the approval of the advertising manager. The executive with the title of "purchasing director" did little more than serve as office manager of the purchasing department. An accountant with the title of "assistant comptroller" was really the center of authority in the production department. The production manager, who didn't care for all the computations involved in cost analysis, spent all of his time supervising the work force on the production line. In a discussion with the president of the Cherokee Manufacturing Company, it became apparent that a conflict in organizational philosophy existed between the president and one of the senior executives of Monelli. The views were summarized as follows:

The president of Cherokee:

Organization charts don't mean anything. In operating a company, you soon learn who has the ability to get things done and who doesn't have that ability. Because of seniority and other factors, you can't move people in and out of positions like checkers on a board. If we can't move the man without creating conflict, we move responsibility to the man. The fact that we are successful speaks pretty well for the system.

The Monelli executive:

I will agree that you can't always move people like checkers on a board. But the organization of your company on paper should be a reasonable approximation of how it operates in practice. If your advertising manager has time to do your purchasing, it means that you don't need an advertising manager. Your assistant comptroller obviously can't do his job in controllership while serving as production manager. Why spread a good man too thinly to compensate for carrying one that doesn't have the ability to do the job? The fact that Cherokee has enjoyed some success doesn't prove anything. Who knows but what the company might have been twice as successful with better-organized management.

Comment on the views expressed by the president of the Cherokee Manufacturing Company and those expressed by the executive from the Monelli Corporation.

SELECTED REFERENCES

Koontz, H., and C. O'Donnell. *Principles of Management.* 3d ed. New York: McGraw-Hill Book Co., Inc., 1964.

Moore, F. G. *Management: Organization and Practice.* New York: Harper & Row, 1964.

McDonough, A. M., and L. J. Garrett. *Management Systems Working Concepts and Practices.* Homewood, Ill.: Richard D. Irwin, Inc., 1965.

Owens, R. N. *Business Organization and Combination.* 5th ed. Englewood Cliffs, N.J.: Prentice-Hall, Inc., 1965.

Terry, G. R. *Principles of Management.* 4th ed. Homewood, Ill.: Richard D. Irwin, Inc., 1964.

III

INDUSTRIAL
PRODUCTION AND
EMPLOYEE RELATIONS

III

9

Industrial Location
and Plant Layout

THE MATTER OF PERSPECTIVE

In the preceding chapters, we have considered certain areas of background information of importance to the businessman, and we have examined some of the factors in the organization of the enterprise. We are now ready to move on to some of the more specific areas of knowledge that are dealt with in the world of business management. In this chapter, and in those immediately following, we will consider some of the problems associated with industrial production. Later chapters will deal with the equally important job of distributing the goods produced. In the course of his study, the student of business management will come to realize that all business activities are interrelated, and, although we may "cut the pie" into slices to digest it with greater ease, we must remember that the slices have much in common and in reality the individual parts function as a whole. In the following discussion of industrial location and layout, certain of the factors mentioned will have application to the wholesale and retail trades. When we come to the chapters on distribution, locational problems and other factors may be discussed as they relate to these trades.

EARLY INDUSTRIAL LOCATION

In its early stages, the United States was primarily an agrarian economy. Such early examples of manufacturing as existed developed from the efforts of individual communities to satisfy their needs by utilizing those raw materials that were available. As the nation grew and transportation obstacles became less formidable, certain patterns of industry began to emerge. Where soil and climate permitted, agriculture flourished. Fortunately, areas not well suited to agriculture possessed compensating features in the form of abundant water power and certain other resources. As a result of these conditions, the South and Southwest became agricultural while New England forged ahead in manufacturing. Waterways and port facilities encouraged the spread of industry into the Middle Atlantic States, and later both agriculture and manufacturing were to spread westward. It is important to remember that limitations in transportation and communication, and in sources of power, restricted the mobility of the manufacturing industries for many generations. While these factors are still important, progress—especially in transportation and power—has permitted more flexibility in the location of industry.

LOCATION BY CHANCE

It is perhaps wise to pause at this time and to point out that not all industrial concerns are located through a process of rational analysis. Many large firms develop from the humble beginning of a small shop. The small shop may have started in a certain place simply because the owner was born there. As the shop grew, people seeking employment may have moved in, and thus the community grew. One may point out that the small firms that succeeded in becoming large companies were benefactors of accidentally hitting upon good locations. To a large degree, this is perhaps true; but there are examples of firms that started small and grew into large concerns while overcoming certain negative locational factors. Obviously, the firm that starts with too many negative factors arising from location will not survive a competitive struggle.

IMPORTANCE OF LOCATION

In a competitive economy, the ability of an individual firm to meet the level of others in terms of price and quality of goods offered is vital to the firm's survival. Transportation, power, and labor are typical of the many items that enter into the cost of producing a product, and these cost factors along with many others are often influenced by the matter of plant location. Deciding upon a location involves balancing the different aspects of location in such a way as to emerge competitive. For example, the source of raw materials and the prospective market for the finished product may be hundreds of miles apart. The objective then might be one of seeking a location that would minimize the cost of transporting both the raw materials and the finished product. Of course, in some situations other cost factors may be relatively more important than transportation, and thus the problem would become that of balancing many factors.

Once a location has been decided and a plant put into operation, the expectation is that the operation will continue for a very long time. Although manufacturing enterprises do move from one section of the country to another, it is a very costly venture. When this does occur, it is often at a time when the original plant and equipment have become obsolete. In recent years, our population has demonstrated increasing mobility. As people move, so move the markets for most of the goods produced. Should pronounced shifts in population occur, a plant may find itself at a disadvantage relative to its market. This means that in evaluating a plant location, one might well consider the trends in population movement. This is only one of the many reasons why the decisions on plant location are so important.

FACTORS INFLUENCING THE SELECTION OF AN AREA

The Nature of the Product

In considering the location of a plant, one may first think in terms of a general area, for example, a region, a state, or a particular section of a state. When the area has been decided, attention may then turn to the selection of a specific site within the area. In accord with this approach, we will first consider factors in selecting an *area* and then discuss problems in selecting a *specific site*.

It is impossible to assign any rank of importance to the factors in selecting a plant location. The type of product, the nature of its production, current economic conditions, and many other things may make one factor more important than another at a given time. Thus, the order in which the factors are discussed in the following pages do not imply relative importance.

Perhaps it is safe to say that the nature of the product is one of the more fundamental factors in plant location. In the location of a plant that manufactures watches, one would not expect the transportation of raw materials or the finished product to be a major consideration. On the other hand, the location of a steel mill would be vitally concerned with the transportation of raw materials, fuel, and of the finished product to the market. In the production of some items, a large quantity of raw materials must be processed in order to produce a relatively small quantity of the finished product. Other things being equal, this would indicate the advisability of locating near the source of raw materials.

The production of some products may be influenced by factors such as climate or the nature of the water supply.

Raw Materials and the Market

Raw materials are seldom equally dispersed throughout a country. We find iron ore in the Great Lakes region, timber in the Northwest, and many agricultural products in the South and Southwest. The markets for the finished products made from these materials may be widely dispersed. Should the manufacturer locate his plant near the raw materials or should he locate near the market to be served? As previously indicated, the nature of the product may be a fundamental consideration, but other factors must also be considered. Markets consist of people, and people comprise the source of labor. Raw materials may be located in regions where the climate, terrain, and man-made facilities are not conducive to the attraction of labor. This may make it necessary to transport the raw materials to a location where labor may be obtained. In the production of certain products, it is desirable to be near the market, especially where an element of perishability is present. In the final analysis, factors such as transportation, power, and labor may enter heavily into the location decision as it pertains to raw materials and the market.

Power and Water Supply

An early dependence upon water power was a factor in the industrial development of the New England area. Later the use of steam power coupled with the discovery of abundant coal added flexibility to our industrialization. But the dependence of steam power upon coal as a fuel tended to encourage the development of industry near the source of fuel. With the development of electricity as a power source, the flexibility of power was further extended. Electric power could be generated near the source of fuel and transmitted over power lines to the point of use. The development of hydroelectric projects such as that associated with the Tennessee Valley Authority has further extended the availability of electric power for both home and industrial use. With the anticipated development of atomic power facilities, no section of the nation should be remote from electric power facilities. If this possibility is realized, the availability of power may no longer be a major consideration in plant location. However, until such advances are realized, the availability of power will continue to be a factor in plant location.

The availability of an adequate water supply is a foremost consideration in the location of certain enterprises. In industries such as brewing and in certain parts of the chemical industry, it is not only necessary to have plentiful water but the "type" of water is important. The chemical analysis of the natural water in different parts of the country may vary. It is advantageous to those plants requiring a certain type of water to locate near a natural supply. Where water is needed in large quantities, the problem of transporting it over a great distance may involve prohibitive costs. Streams have also been utilized as natural conduits for the disposal and transportation of waste. Unfortunately, certain manufacturing concerns have carelessly contributed to the pollution of streams and in so doing have caused extensive damage to water resources in the area.

Labor Resources

Labor has always been an important consideration in plant location. Despite the mobility of our present age, labor does not shift quickly from one area to another. It is much easier for the employer to locate a plant near the supply of labor than to induce labor to move into a new area. We must also keep in mind that people represent markets; and many times in moving to the source of labor, the employer is moving nearer a market. In recent years, there has been a significant movement of industry into areas previously regarded as agricultural. In some cases, this has represented the outright movement of a company; in others, the construction of branch plants.

In evaluating the labor resources of an area, many considerations must be taken into account. The presence of suitable numbers of people does not in itself imply an adequate labor resource. In areas where some manufacturing already exists, there may be a surplus of trained, or semitrained, labor. In such an area, the workers may be accustomed to an industrial life and thus quick to adjust to the demands of reporting to work five days each week and at a specified hour. Workers with no industrial experience may prove more difficult to train, and they may have some trouble adjusting to the discipline of industrial life. On the other hand, the worker with no industrial experience may approach the job with an open mind and be receptive to training in the techniques that the employer considers most suitable.

Transportation Facilities

Transportation has always been a paramount consideration in plant location. The presence of a type of transportation suitable for the production concerned would perhaps be a first consideration for many plants. Products having great weight relative to value must have access to water or rail transportation, or if possible, access to both. As value increases relative to weight, the motor carrier becomes an alternative.

The flexibility of the motor carrier brings a corresponding flexibility in the problem of plant location. But even the motor carrier may be hampered by the lack of adequate highways serving a particular area. The ultimate in transportation flexibility might arise in the case of those products whose value in relation to bulk is such as to justify the cost of air transportation. The cost of air transportation remains such that relatively few products are in a suitable category to enjoy its use. In considering the location of a plant, it is highly desirable that the area under consideration be served by at least two of the major forms of transportation. This affords protection against strikes and certain natural calamities that might interrupt service. The presence of such competition may also be helpful to the manufacturer in negotiating transportation rates and services.

Related Enterprises

Efforts are sometimes made to locate plants near others of a similar type. Mention has been made of the fact that some access to trained labor may be had in this way. It is also to be expected that the factors that prove inviting to one manufacturer in a certain line may prove inviting to another. A slightly different reason for locating near a related producer arises when a company is dependent upon that producer for crude or semiprocessed materials. It is not uncommon, especially in the chemical industry, to find a situation in which the basic material used in one plant is a by-product, or even a waste product, of production in another plant. A plant using such materials may find it advantageous to locate near the plant from which it receives the materials. Still another situation exists when a plant produces a material, or product, purchased by other plants for use in their production. In this case the supplier-plant may locate near his market—i.e., the one plant (or very few) that he serves.

Climate

The factor of climate deserves some comment in a discussion of plant location. With modern air conditioning and heating facilities, the importance of climate to the actual production processes has diminished. However, the cost of controlling temperatures within a plant may depend considerably upon the natural climatic conditions. If products are perishable and subject to early damage by heat, there is the problem of handling such products in a hot climate. Even the handling required to remove the item from storage and to load it onto a refrigerated carrier may pose a problem. Also, the cost of transportation under these conditions would be increased.

Another aspect of climate relative to plant location concerns the problem of attracting desirable labor. A favorable climate has proved to be a big factor in inducing labor to migrate. Firms located in California and Florida have used the climate appeal to attract engineers and other professionals to their employ. Apparently, the lure of a milder climate has been an effective inducement.

State Laws

If we are to consider several states as possibilities in the search for a plant location, we must take into account the fact that state laws affecting our operations vary. Some states, eager to attract industry, have passed provisions calculated to prove attractive. These provisions are usually in the form of a tax exemption or the lessening of a tax rate. States may, and do, tax such things as a corporation charter and the annual earnings of the corporate enterprise. Since state taxes are often low in comparison to federal taxes, some may be inclined to overlook their importance. It is not only advisable to investigate present state laws, but an analysis of trends over recent years may point to trouble ahead. Under growing pressures to provide more and better public services, the states are being hard pressed to find sources of revenue. While there may be a reluctance to tax business firms for fear of keeping new industries out, some states have found it necessary to increase business taxation.

In addition to tax laws, there are others that must be considered. Individual states legislate in the area of minimum wages, unemployment compensation, and management-labor relations. The individual states have authority over the permission granted to a "foreign" corporation (one chartered in another state) to do business within their territory. The states are also given considerable freedom in judging whether a corporation is classed as doing an *intrastate* as well as an *interstate* business. By making proper application, it is usually possible for a corporation to "qualify" under the laws of the state in which it hopes to locate a plant. By thus qualifying, it has the advantage of protection in the courts in contracting. By qualifying as a "domestic" corporation, the firm becomes subject to state taxes. If the firm does not seek qualification within the state and if it is then found to be engaged in intrastate commerce, the state may levy heavy fines. There are many other state laws—such as those governing highway load limits—that should be considered in evaluating a location.[1]

It is also important to investigate state laws relating to individual

[1] Sydney Prerau (ed.), *J. K. Lasser's Business Management Handbook* (New York: McGraw-Hill Book Co., 1960).

income taxes. Real estate and other taxes levied on the individual may have some importance if you hope to have employees from other states transfer to the new location. Community codes and regulations are important to look into. Zoning laws and building restrictions, and the cost of services such as utilities in the area, may become factors in your obtaining and holding a labor force.

SELECTING A SPECIFIC SITE

Construction vs. Renting

When a company has decided upon the area in which it hopes to locate, the problem then shifts to that of finding a specific site. If an enterprise hopes to move into an existing building, the choice of site will be restricted. In such a situation, the availability of a building may take precedence over other considerations. If the proposal is to start with the purchase of land and the construction of a building, there may be much more freedom in selecting a site. Relatively few companies are able to utilize existing buildings. The design and condition of old buildings seldom lend themselves to economical plant layout. New construction offers flexibility in site selection and the opportunity to design the building to suit the needs of the occupant.

It should be mentioned that some communities have sought to attract industry by offering to construct buildings. Where this is done, the building is constructed according to the designs of the occupant and is then leased to the occupant under a long-term agreement. This arrangement enables a company to operate its plant with less fixed capital, but in the meantime the choice of site is thereby restricted.

Real Estate Values

The value of land becomes important in deciding upon a particular site. Land close to towns or cities and with access to transportation may be very costly. As a rule, real estate values decline as one moves away from the city. But the advantage of cheaper land may be offset by the added cost of securing transportation, power, and purified water. Abundant parking areas may partially offset the disadvantages to employees in driving to and from work. The out-of-town plant may have problems in securing good public transportation. The importance of land may also depend upon the type of construction that the plant hopes to occupy. The over-all tendency in plant construction has favored the single-story building. With all operations on a single floor, the amount of land occupied by such a building is relatively large. The multistory building provides more floor space for a given amount of land, and such buildings are often found in areas where real estate values are very high. As in other location problems, the choice of the land used is often the result of compromises between cost and convenience.

Connections with Transportation, Power, and Water

The specific plant site chosen must have access to transportation, power, and water suitable for use by personnel—as well as the water often used in the industrial processes. If possible, a company in picking a site would like to take advantage of existing facilities. If the plant site is near a railroad and highway, access spur tracks and roads may be built at reasonable costs. Also, if the plant is near existing power lines and water mains, it may be possible to "tap into" these services. If the site is removed from existing facilities, considerable cost may be incurred in obtaining access roads and lines. Some help may be expected from railroads and utilities in obtaining these services, but there is still a significant element of cost to the builder.

Community Facilities

An industrial plant employing a thousand or more persons becomes a very significant part of the community. It usually hopes to use local labor and to attract a certain amount of its labor from other communities. "Personnel minded companies" like to feel that their employees have access to good schools and other public services. The state of the community becomes very important when one hopes to attract labor from other areas. It is also obvious that a pleasant community may be a factor in preventing a costly turnover of labor. The availability of adequate housing, or the assurance that such housing will be constructed, may be one of the primary factors in picking a specific location. Medical and hospital facilities are carefully considered, as are the availability and quality of school facilities.

Community Cooperation

An enterprise, in seeking a location, hopes to find a suitable site in a community where it will be welcomed. In most cases, communities welcome industry for the economic benefits that it brings to the existing population. Greater employment and bigger payrolls mean greater prosperity for merchants, service people (plumbers, electricians, etc.), and others in the community. So great is the desire to attract industry, communities often organize to actively seek the enterprise looking for a place to locate. As previously mentioned, the community sometimes raises funds for the construction of buildings and other facilities, which are then leased to the company. Communities may build new schools, housing projects, and other improvements in order to prove more attractive.

While it is true that most communities welcome new enterprises, it should be mentioned that cases do exist where a community actively opposes the location of a plant. This opposition may arise from the fear that the plant will be a source of odors, smoke, or similar nuisances that may damage the community as a desirable place in which to live. If the production processes are such that these undesirable side effects are unavoidable, the company should seek to locate a sufficient distance from residential areas to eliminate the nuisance. It would be poor policy for a plant to locate against the will of the community, even should this be possible. It would then find itself operating in a hostile environment; and if the community objections were strong enough, the location of the plant might mark the start of a decline in the community as a whole. This deterioration of the community might well create conditions undesirable to the plant. It is perhaps safe to say that in cases where community opposition is encountered, it is most often found to be a matter of misunderstanding; and this can be cleared up through a friendly exchange of information.

PLANT LAYOUT

Layout Defined

Plant layout refers to the manner in which the work processes are arranged. It encompasses the idea of locating machines and work stations in such a way that the production operations are carried out in the most expeditious manner. It seeks to minimize waste motion in the movement of men and materials and to maximize the productive time of men and equipment. While this section will deal with plant layout, it is desirable to note that basically all work processes involve some scheme of layout. In the design of your classroom, someone considered layout in determining the location of your desks, the blackboard, maps, and a pencil sharpener. Kitchens are constructed with sinks and appliances so arranged as to minimize the distance the housewife must walk and with attention paid to the working relationship of appliances; i.e., the dishwasher is near the sink. When an individual is assigned a task, he will often begin by "laying out" the job. If the student is assigned to write a theme, he may begin by placing his typewriter on a table convenient to a light; he secures a chair of the proper height and then places his paper and reference books where they may be easily reached.

In making these arrangements, he has "organized" his work place. In a way, plant layout may be thought of as "organizing the work place."

The Factory Building

The problem of plant layout may begin with an existing building, or it may precede the construction of the building—in which case the building may be designed to accommodate the layout. The functional approach to the design of the factory building would begin with a consideration of the work processes and the layout necessary to carry out the processes. A building would then be designed. The building is often thought of as having been "built around" the work processes. In recent decades, industrial architecture has emphasized functional design. One aspect of this has been the trend toward the single-story building. Increasing mechanization and the assembly-line type of production make good use of the one-level floor space. Also, there is the rather obvious principle that it requires less effort to move materials laterally than to move them vertically.

When erecting a new building, it is assumed that attention to the problem of layout will precede the construction. But not all factories move into new buildings. Often the problem is to take an existing building and accommodate the processes to the building. Frequently, partitions may be moved or erected, floors strengthened, and similar changes made; but, basically, the design of the building remains a fixed element. The design of the plant layout then becomes a job of fitting the work processes into a pattern suitable to the building. Regardless of whether the layout precedes the planning of the building or whether it must be fitted to an existing building, there are compromises that must be made. To erect a building to fit the ideal layout may entail prohibitive cost; thus, an adjustment in the layout may be considered. On the other hand, to fit a layout to an existing building may result in costly production; therefore, a major alteration in the building may be justified.

Manufacturing Processes

A basic consideration in plant layout is the type of manufacturing process involved. Some manufacturing involves the combination of large amounts of labor with relatively few materials, while in other types the reverse is true. The movement of large quantities of heavy materials through the production processes may be a primary influence in plant layout. One may classify the common types of manufacturing processes as follows:

1. *Continuous-Process Industries.* As related to plant layout, the

continuous process industries are thought of as those involving a production process in which there is a somewhat steady and continuous flow of materials through the work processes. An example would be the grain milling industry in which the flow of grain into the various grinding and sifting machines would be in the form of a steady but controlled flow. In this type of operation, the various machines are fed the materials through pipes and tubes varying in size and subject to the pressures necessary to control the rate at which the materials are moved. Much of the control over the movement of materials in process is achieved through the variations in the size of the pipes, tubes, and other conveyance devices used. The determination of the factors governing the flow of materials represents advanced planning and is a part of the layout function.

2. *Repetitive-Process Industries.* In this process, the flow of materials is not rigidly controlled as in the continuous process. However, there is a flow of materials through a sequence of operations. Workmen stationed along the path of the flow may perform a repetitive task. For example, the material entering the line may be a block of metal. The first workman drills a hole in the block, the next workman positions a bolt in the hole, a third places a nut on the bolt, and so on through the line with each work-station contributing to the process. The automobile industry is perhaps the best example of this type of manufacturing.

3. *Intermittent-Process Industries.* These concerns are typified by the small job-lot shop. The production operations may vary from day to day as a result of the variety of work undertaken. It may be difficult to standardize operations or to assign workmen to certain repetitive tasks. In planning the shop layout, one is not concerned so much with the flow of materials as with the positioning of certain equipment used by the workers as a group.[2]

The nature of the manufacturing process indicates the emphasis to be placed on plant layout. It should be obvious to the student at this point that in those processes where there is a movement of materials through a sequence of operations, the layout becomes an important factor in controlling this movement. Unless the steps in the sequence are properly coordinated, certain men and machines may remain idle at intervals while awaiting the arrival of the material from other work-stations. Certain "bottlenecks" develop and thus the entire production line is slowed. It is the responsibility of layout to place men and machines in such a way that the flow of work is steady and continuous and the burden of labor is fairly shared. Of course, this is the ideal, and

[2] Richard N. Owens, *Management of Industrial Enterprises.* 4th ed.; Homewood, Ill.: Richard D. Irwin, Inc., 1961), Chap. 11.

the nature of the product and the production process may not permit the achievement of perfect layout.

Approaching the Layout Problem

Needless to say, the layout-planning engineer must be thoroughly familiar with the production processes involved before he attempts the layout. This does not mean that he must be able to operate all the machines and to perform all the jobs to be done in the plant. But he must know the steps involved in the production of the product, the machines to be used, the time required for each operation, and the personnel to be utilized. He must also understand the materials used and just what is needed to facilitate their movement through the processes. He must have a great familiarity with machines and what they will do; and he must know the skills of labor, safety requirements, and the rate at which the worker will perform. With this background of knowledge, he is ready to begin an analysis of possible layouts.

At this point, the layout-planning engineer will begin to put his problem on paper. He may start with blueprints, sketches of floor space, and other aids. From this level, he will progress to the drawing of flow charts. This will enable him to visualize the lines of flow through the various stages in the manufacturing process. Here he begins to come to grips with the problem of coordinating the various steps in the sequence of production. After working with flow lines, he then converts the flow lines to machine lines. He may use templets (cardboard cutouts) to represent machines and thus move them about as he tries different arrangements. The process of refinement continues; and if the layout engineer is successful, the end result will be a layout that achieves the best possible arrangement of machines and work-stations to accommodate the production operations.[3]

Basic Types of Plant Layout

Rarely would one find two plants having identical layouts. Variations in layout derive from the production processes, the shape of the building, and the ideas—or lack of ideas—of those designing the layout. For those especially interested in plant layout, there are books on the subject that show and explain numerous layout variations. Here we will refer to two fundamental layout situations. First, there is the small, job-shop type of layout. As previously mentioned, this shop is not characterized by continuous or highly repetitive processes. The individual worker may do several, or all, of the operations in turning out a product; or a group may turn out the product—each doing a half dozen

[3] Ibid., Chap. 11.

or more of the operations involved. Characteristic of this type of shop is the fact that several workers may share a single tool or machine. This is very likely to be true regarding items such as drill presses, boring machines, grinders, etc. Thus, a principle in laying out such a shop would be to place the "group-used" equipment in the best position to be accessible to those who will use it. Figure 9–1 shows a sketch of a very

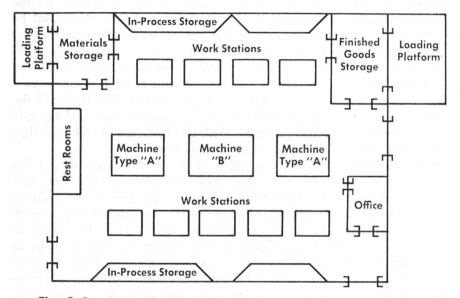

Fig. 9–1. A simplified sketch showing the layout of a small shop.

simplified shop layout. Unfortunately, the small shop operator may feel that layout is relatively unimportant and thus fail to realize advantages that could be his. There are many principles of layout that can be modified to apply to the small shop, for example, storing of materials; reducing materials movement to the minimum necessary; and avoidance of duplication in the movement of materials, equipment, and machines. Something as simple as the location of a water cooler may reduce man-hours wasted.

The second type of basic layout refers to the assembly-line method of operation. In this process, the material enters one end of the line and undergoes successive operations, eventually emerging as a finished product at the other end of the line. A single operation is performed by an individual, or group, and the operation is repeated as each piece of material arrives at the workplace. An ideal example would be a layout to accommodate straight-line production. Straight-line production does not necessarily mean a straight line on the factory floor; in fact, the flow of materials may double back and make several turns before reaching the finished stage. Straight-line production does mean, however, that the work in process does not double back to the same machines or cross other production lines.[4]

Figure 9–2 shows a factory floor and a layout illustrative of straight-

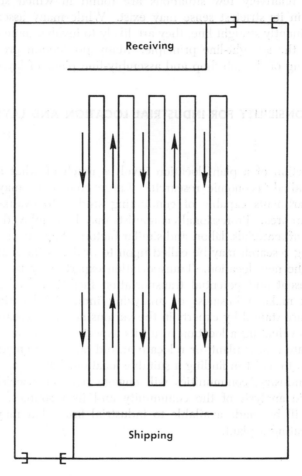

Receiving

Shipping

Fig. 9–2. A simplified sketch showing a layout plan for straight-line production.

line production. In this example, we may assume that materials enter the line and follow the route indicated by the arrows; the work process terminating at a point near the finished goods storage. As the material moves from one work-station to another along the line, it may be moved

[4] *Ibid.*, p. 222.

by the aid of overhead cranes, conveyor belts, or other devices, depending upon the nature of the material. As previously mentioned, the most difficult problem in this layout is the positioning of men and machines in such a way that the flow of work-in-process will be continuous and free of bottlenecks.

Perhaps, relatively few situations are found in which straight-line production in its strictest sense may exist. While many assembly lines are predominantly straight line, they are likely to involve some operations that violate the straight-line principle. Many production processes call for a blending of the job-shop and assembly-line plans of layout.

RESPONSIBILITY FOR INDUSTRIAL LOCATION AND LAYOUT

Location

The selection of a plant location involves much of what might generally be called "economic research." Large companies may have research departments capable of conducting studies to evaluate the resources of an area. Professional economists may be employed to analyze the sources of materials, labor, and similar factors. Specialists in the area of marketing research may be called upon to evaluate the markets to be served by the new location. Transportation experts may be engaged to analyze present and potential transportation facilities. There are companies that make a business of analyzing industrial locations. These companies are staffed by experts in the various areas of research and are capable of evaluating a location in all its aspects. A business firm planning to locate a new plant, or relocate an old one, may engage such an organization to assist in finding a suitable location. Often, as a means of attracting industry, communities will engage research specialists to do an economic analysis of the community and its resources. Data thus compiled will be made available to industrial firms that may be interested in locating a plant.

Layout

Plant layout usually requires the technical knowledge of an engineer, or at least someone with a knowledge of industrial engineering. The growth of automation and the use of more complex machines will undoubtedly make the layout job an even more technical one. Layout may best be handled by someone with an intimate knowledge of the particular production processes to be utilized. Thus, someone from within the company may be in the best position to handle the problem. There are, however, specialists in the area of plant layout, and these people are sometimes engaged to plan the layout. When a company is entering production for the first time, the layout specialist may offer the company a background of experience that it cannot find in its own ranks. Often, the small company may not be aware of the benefits to be derived from careful layout planning; and in these cases, the layout specialist, in the role of a consultant, may render valuable service.

TOPICS FOR DISCUSSION

1. Specify what you feel to be one of the more fundamental factors in plant location. Why is it fundamental?

2. Should population trends be considered in evaluating a plant location?

3. Comment on the following statement: "Employers generally do not encounter much difficulty in inducing workers to move into a new area."

4. What is generally involved in plant-location "economic research"?

5. Why would one rarely find two plants having identical layouts?

6. The rapid development of motor transportation has minimized the importance of transportation as a factor in plant location. Do you agree?

7. To what extent has labor-management strife been a factor in the growing industrialization of the South and Southwest?

8. "A community desiring to attract industry should construct a factory building and then seek an occupant." Is this sound advice?

9. Discuss ways in which you think the layout of your classroom might be improved.

10. What problems are encountered in a plant layout based upon the concept of straight-line production?

Case 9–1

LOCATING A BRANCH PLANT

In 1964, the Dale Woolen Products Corporation decided to locate a branch plant in the southeastern section of the United States. A primary factor in the company's decision to locate a branch in this area was the growing importance of the Southeast as a market for its products. When it became generally known that the Dale firm was considering plant locations, several states actively sought the branch plant. Various interested states sent representatives to visit the Dale home offices, and these representatives, in turn, invited Dale executives to visit their localities.

The Dale Corporation was aware of the fact that most states have an active program of soliciting industry. They also knew that it was not uncommon for states in search of industry to offer inducements in the form of free land for location sites, a favorable treatment relative to local taxes, and, in some cases, assistance in financing. Dale executives had discussed all factors involved in selecting a location. While not averse to considering special inducements, the firm was on guard against picking an undesirable location because of attractive initial offers.

After several months of exploration, the firm had reduced the list of possible locations to two. These two, located in different but adjoining states, seemed equal in most respects. In terms of accessibility to the market and availability of transportation facilities, they were equal. Some differences were noted as follows:

Location A. Location A offered accessibility to the market, good transportation, a good supply of labor, and a good climate. The local community had offered to donate a tract of land on which the plant could be built. The community offered good schools and a stable population. A junior college located in the town offered training in several technical areas. The community offered no tax concessions, although the local tax rate was a very reasonable one.

Location B. Location B offered accessibility to the market, good transportation, and a good climate. Numerically, the supply of labor was plentiful; however, the over-all quality of the labor in terms of education and work experience seemed somewhat lower than that found in location A. Schools were considered average for the state, although the expenditure per pupil in the state of location B was considerably less than that in the state of location A. With state assistance, the local community at location B went much beyond location A in terms of the inducements offered the Dale Corporation. The community offered to furnish the land and to erect a building for the plant. This would be done according to the specifications of the Dale firm. The plant thus erected would be leased to the Dale company on a long-term option. The terms of the lease were very favorable.

Dale executives were split over the choice of the location. Some wanted to take advantage of the financial inducements offered by location B, while others thought that the negative factors of location B were more than enough to offset any savings resulting from the building arrangement. One executive was opposed to accepting any sort of financial inducement to locate the plant. He argued that these inducements might, in the long run, cause ill feelings between the company and the community. He felt that, when a company enters a community by accepting various financial inducements, it enters with the community feeling that the firm is indebted to it. Ill will would result if the company failed to deliver all that was expected of it.

Give your opinion of the issues raised in this case.

SELECTED REFERENCES

Apple, James M. *Plant Layout and Materials Handling.* New York: The Ronald Press Co., 1963.

Owen, Richard N. *Management Industrial Enterprises.* 4th ed. Homewood, Ill.: Richard D. Irwin, Inc., 1961.

Prerau, Sydney (ed.). *J. K. Lasser's Business Management Handbook.* New York: McGraw-Hill Book Co., 1960.

Reed, Ruddell, Jr. *Plant Layout: Factors, Principles, and Techniques.* Homewood, Ill.: Richard D. Irwin, Inc., 1961.

Voris, W. *The Management of Production.* New York: The Ronald Press Co., 1960.

10

Purchasing Management in Materials Control

THE BROAD VIEW

In recent years, there has developed some tendency to view the flow of materials through the firm as an integrated and continuous movement. This concept would visualize materials control as beginning with the initial purchase of materials and supplies, continuing through the production processes, and extending on to the control and management of finished-goods inventory. While it may be difficult to employ this concept under a centralized authority such as a "materials manager," it does afford us a valuable approach to the study of a group of related functions. It is the objective of management to minimize investments in inventory without incurring undue risks of shortages. This applies to the inventory of purchased materials awaiting production, to the quantity (inventory) of goods moving through the production processes at a given time, and to the inventory of finished goods residing in warehouses and awaiting distribution. Thus, as goods move from the initial purchase of materials through production and into the hands of distributors, the firm seeks to minimize the size of the stream and to coordinate its flow in such a way that sales are maximized at minimum costs.

In this text, we shall study the activities associated with the flow of materials by examining the functional areas most directly concerned with this flow. In this chapter, we will deal with the purchasing function including the control of purchased-goods inventory. In the chapter following, on production control in the manufacturing process, we will have occasion to note the activities that occur as materials move through the production processes. In Chapter 19, on transportation and other aspects of physical distribution, we shall have occasion to study other activities related to the movement, handling, and storage of goods.

THE PURCHASING FUNCTION

Industrial purchasing includes all those activities necessary in the buying of materials, parts, and supplies for use in production. The industrial firm purchases goods for use in further production; whereas, the distributive firm such as the wholesaler or retailer buys goods for resale. In the manufacturing plant, the acquisition of materials and supplies is referred to as "purchasing" while in the retail store the acquisition of goods is referred to as "buying." The manufacturing plant may employ a *Purchasing Agent;* the retail store a *Buyer.* In the manufacturing plant having a purchasing department, the head of the department may have a title such as "Director of Purchases" while his subordinates specializing in different types of materials or supplies are known as "Buyers." The student of business management will soon learn that the terminology of the business world is not standard.

In the industrial plant, the purchasing function includes such activities as selecting sources of supply, determining the quality and quantity to purchase, the negotiation of price and terms, and the control of inventory. The purchasing function is important in all manufacturing, but it is especially important where the value of the materials and supplies purchased account for a large share of the total value of the product produced. One study based on an analysis of one hundred large manufacturing firms showed that approximately 51 per cent of the sales value of the products produced could be accounted for by the cost of materials and supplies.[1] In some companies, the cost of the materials and supplies purchased may absorb as much as 50 to 60 per cent of the sales dollar. In such cases, a savings of 5 to 10 per cent in the cost of purchases would be equivalent to a savings of $2\frac{1}{2}$ to 5 per cent of the sales dollar.[2] Factors of production cost such as wages and salaries, depreciation, and taxes are becoming increasingly difficult to control. In fact, the trend of cost elements such as wages and taxation has been steadily upward. Caught between the pressures of rising production

---

[1] S. F. Heinritz, and P. V. Farrell, *Purchasing* (4th ed.; Englewood Cliffs, N.J.: Prentice-Hall, Inc., 1965), p. 2.

[2] W. B. England, *Procurement* (4th ed.; Homewood, Ill.: Richard D. Irwin, Inc., 1962), p. 2.

costs and increasing consumer resistance to higher prices, the producer has sought to counter rising production cost through achieving greater efficiency in his operations. Since the cost of purchased materials and supplies may represent a major item in the total cost of the product, the purchasing operation affords an opportunity to reduce costs through greater efficiency. The realization of this opportunity has caused companies to place increasing emphasis upon purchasing and to recognize it as one of the most important areas of business management.

PURCHASING ORGANIZATION

Centralized vs. Decentralized Purchasing

In small shops, or in plants where the cost of materials and supplies may be small in comparison to other costs, the purchasing function may be decentralized. In decentralized purchasing, each department of the company would have the responsibility of buying its own materials and supplies. In decades past, decentralized purchasing was practiced more widely than at present. It was often argued that if a production superintendent was to be held responsible for the cost of production, he should have control over the cost of materials and supplies. It was also often argued that the using departments were the ones capable of buying to suit their needs. The many weaknesses in a system of decentralized purchasing are not difficult to detect. Where several departments may be using some of the same materials and supplies there is an obvious duplication of the purchasing effort. The administrative cost of placing a small order is apt to be as great as placing a large one. Through buying in small lots, the purchaser may forego the opportunity to realize quantity discounts; also, he may lose the chance to negotiate price and terms more favorably. Transportation and handling costs are usually higher where small quantities are involved. Where purchasing is delegated to departments, the department superintendent may treat it as a function incidental to what he considers his major responsibility. In a production department, he may be concerned with the supervision of labor and not have the time or the inclination to investigate sources of supply and negotiate carefully.

Centralized purchasing calls for the establishment of a purchasing department. Purchases used repetitively are ordered in quantity and kept in stock. The using department may obtain these items by sending a requisition to the stores room. In the case of items not used repetitively, the using department may send a requisition to the purchasing department which will in turn investigate sources and make the purchase. Centralized purchasing offers the advantage of buying in larger quantities. The requests from using departments may be consolidated to achieve this aim. Most suppliers give quantity discounts varying with the quantity purchased; also, the prompt handling of invoices by the purchasing department may enable the company to take advantage of any cash discounts that are offered. Perhaps of greatest importance is the fact that the purchasing agent is a specialist in buying and is thus able to select better sources and secure better terms than would be possible in a decentralized system. The vast majority of sizable companies practice some form of centralized purchasing.

The Purchasing Department

The position of the purchasing department in the organization structure of the company will depend upon the importance given the purchasing function. In a typical company practicing centralized purchasing, the purchasing department will be given status comparable to production, sales, finance, and other key operations. In this position, the head of the purchasing department will have the authority to report directly to top management. In a large company, the head of the purchasing department may be a vice-president. Figure 10–1 shows the position of the purchasing department in a company emphasizing the importance of procurement. Also shown is a simplified chart of the organization of the department.

A purchasing department may vary from a very few employees to several hundred, depending, of course, on the size of the company. The size of the company and the variety of its activities will indicate the specialization found in the department. Buyers will usually specialize in certain commodities. Various clerical specialists may be employed, and companies using electronic data processing equipment may employ specialists to operate the equipment. The head of the purchasing department has line authority in the supervision of the employees within the department.

Although the purchasing officer may report directly to the president, the relationship of purchasing to other operations is that of a staff department. In the operations of the firm, it is well that the authority of the purchasing department be understood. While this authority may vary from company to company, it may be generally summarized as follows: The using departments have the right to specify what is needed. The needs of these departments reach the purchasing department in the form of requisitions. The purchasing department does not have the authority to change a requisition or alter the specifications contained therein in any way. The purchasing department does have the right to question a requisition and to discuss it with the issuing party. If a

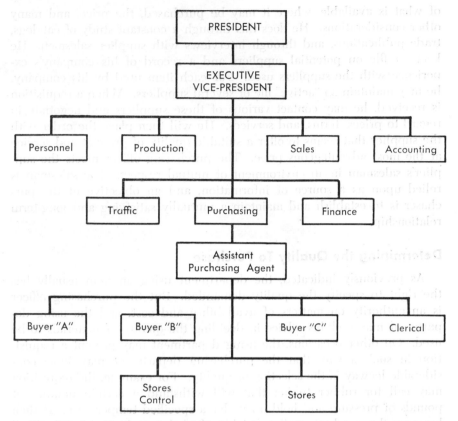

Fig. 10–1. Organization of the purchasing function in a medium-size company.

difference of opinion arises between an operating department and the purchasing department, the matter may be taken to a higher level of management for a decision. Once the materials to be purchased have been specified by the using department, the purchasing department normally should have the authority to select the source of supply. It is highly essential that the purchasing department work in harmony with other departments and the capable purchasing officer is tactful in dealing with any conflicts that may arise.

THE PURCHASING OPERATIONS

Selecting and Maintaining Sources of Supply

A fundamental part of the purchasing job is the selection and maintenance of adequate suppliers. The purchasing officer must keep abreast of what is available, where it may be purchased, the price, and many other considerations. He does this through a constant study of catalogs, trade publications, and through interviews with supplier salesmen. He keeps a file on potential suppliers and a record of his company's experience with the suppliers used. For each item used by his company, he may maintain an "active" file of several suppliers. When a requisition is received, he may contact various of these suppliers and negotiate in regard to prices, terms, and services. He will then place the order with the supplier that seems to offer a suitable quality of product and service at the most advantageous price. The purchasing officer meets the supplier's salesman in an environment of mutual respect. The salesman is relied upon as a source of information, and an objective of the purchaser is to establish and maintain a mutually satisfying and long-term relationship.

Determining the Quality To Purchase

As previously indicated, the department using an item usually has the right to specify the quality demanded. But the purchasing officer is an authority on matters of availability and cost, and the using department may seek his advice in deciding the quality of materials to be used. On other occasions, the using department may present a requisition in such a way that the purchasing department may have considerable leeway in the selection of quality. For example, the requisition may call for rubber tubing that will withstand a certain number of pounds of pressure and hold up under a specified temperature. It then becomes the purchasing officer's job to find the quality tubing that will meet these requirements. *Suitability for the purpose specified* is the creed of the purchasing officer. This means that he must guard against purchasing a quality too low to serve the specified use; it also means that he must guard against buying a higher quality, and hence paying a higher price, than is necessary.

Buying the Right Quantity

There are many factors that enter into the cost of a product besides the quoted price. Most sellers offer quantity discounts to encourage the purchase of large lots. Also, from the buyers' viewpoint, the cost of processing and handling large orders may be no more than that incurred in handling small orders. These possible savings from quantity purchasing must be weighed against the cost of carrying the larger inventory. The company that buys in small quantities (called "hand-to-mouth" buying) has less money tied up in the inventory on hand. Buying in large quantities means an investment in inventory, and consequently one may regard the interest on money so invested as an expense. It is usually necessary to carry insurance against fire and theft when quantities of goods are held in storage. Then there is a cost incurred in providing the storage space itself. As a factor in determining the quantity to buy, the purchaser may seek to balance the savings from quantity buying against the costs of carrying the larger inventory. There are considerations other than cost that must enter into the decision on quantity. If a shortage of a certain material is anticipated, it may be advisable to buy a larger quantity than usual as a protection against short supply. The price outlook may also be a factor to consider.

From the foregoing, we see that there are many variable factors that enter into the decision on the quantity to buy. Some companies have developed *buying quantity formulas,* which assign weights to the variable factors and relate them mathematically. With the advent of electronic computers, it has become practical to include more variables and in other ways refine the formula concept. The buying quantity formula seems most suitable in those cases where the item to be purchased is relatively standard, where the price is stable, and where the rate of use is fairly constant. For such items, the formula may lead to the establishment of maximum-minimum inventory levels and the establishment of automatic reorder points. In the purchase of items that have a varying price in the market, that do not have a constant rate of usage, and are subject to obsolescence through frequently changing technology, the quantity to buy is a decision based upon the judgment and experience of the executives concerned.

Negotiating Price and Terms

The purchasing department may issue invitations to bid to certain selected suppliers, or prices may be negotiated through individual correspondence and interviews. Where bids are solicited, the industrial purchaser may reserve the right to refuse all bids. He also has the privilege of accepting any of the bids submitted, not being bound to accept the lowest quotation. Bids are often used in the purchase of large unit items and in the initiating of term contracts with a supplier. In government purchasing, the buyer operates as a public servant, and it is often considered desirable that his actions be open for all to see. In certain types of purchasing, the bid system may be mandatory. When a purchase is contemplated, it is advertised in order that qualified suppliers may have an opportunity to bid. Sealed bids are submitted, and these are opened and made public at a specified time. The order automatically goes to the lowest responsible bidder. If none of the bids are deemed acceptable, the buyer must discard them all and start over by calling for new bids. If identical bids are submitted, the buyer may divide the business or decide the supplier by the flip of a coin or some other chance method—the entire procedure becoming a matter of public record. In the case of certain defense needs, technical equipment of a complex nature for example, the bid system may be impractical; and the government buyer may be permitted a certain freedom of negotiation. As a matter of fact, there has been recent consideration of legislation that would permit the government buyer more freedom in the selection of the supplier even though bids are invited.

In a competitive market, the prices offered by suppliers may not vary greatly; however, there is enough variation to make negotiation profitable to the purchaser. On a large order, a price variation of 1 per cent may be significant. The purchasing officer is concerned with many factors in addition to the supplier's quoted price.[3] He is interested in such things as discount structures, services offered by the seller, and in the seller's reputation for reliability. Thus, the buyer, in negotiating price, hopes to obtain the best "package" consisting of many factors.

Forward Buying and Speculation

If a company buys a larger quantity than normal to protect itself against an anticipated shortage, we say the company is practicing forward buying. But if a company varies the quantity normally purchased in an effort to capitalize upon a possible price change—and thus make a profit over the normal operating profit—we refer to this as speculative purchasing. Speculative purchasing is thus distinguished from forward buying in that the motive is to realize a profit through correctly anticipating a price movement. It goes without saying that all companies engage in forward buying from time to time, and many companies engage in speculative purchasing. It is not considered good policy when a company speculates in materials far in excess of the quantity needed in its production. In such a case, the company is "playing the market" with its own needs an incidental factor.

In some cases, the purchasing officer may have authority to do a degree of forward buying without consulting higher management. When considerable outlays are involved in forward buying, and in all cases of speculative buying, the purchasing officer usually consults with his superiors. In such cases, the decision may be made by a committee of top management, the purchasing officer being a member of the committee.

---

[3] J. H. Westing and I. V. Fine, *Industrial Purchasing* (2d ed.; New York: John Wiley & Sons, Inc., 1962), Chap. 8.

PURCHASING PROCEDURES

The Requisition and Purchase Order

The purchasing of an item is usually initiated in one of two ways: (1) Some items subject to repetitive use are carried in stock. When the stock on hand is reduced to a pre-established minimum (reorder point), the purchasing department places orders to bring the stock back up to the desired inventory level. (2) For those items not carried in stock, the purchasing process begins with a requisition from the using department desiring the item. The requisition (request to purchase) is made out using a standard form supplied by the purchasing department. The requisition form has space for the description of the item, dates, etc. and is signed by the responsible officer of the department requesting the order. In some cases the description of what is needed may be detailed and lengthy; in which case, *specifications* in the form of a document may be furnished the purchasing department. Where the more complex items are ordered repetitively, specifications may be kept on file in the purchasing department. This permits the requisitioning party to refer to the specification by number and thus avoid having to forward a lengthy description each time an order is requested. The requisition is the basis for placing the purchase order. A company will usually have a standard purchase order form that it will use in placing all orders. The form will bear the company name, contain space for the name of the supplier, a description of the item to be purchased, terms and prices, and also stipulations of a legal nature outlining the conditions under which the offer to buy is made.

Expediting the Order

When the supplier accepts an order from the purchaser, he obligates himself to deliver on the date requested in the order. Unfortunately, business practice is often rather loose on this matter and late delivery is not uncommon. If the order is not delivered when promised, the purchaser begins the follow-up action known as expediting. This may take the form of letters, or telegrams to the supplier reminding him that the order has not arrived. If goods are not delivered as promised, and as a result a loss is suffered by the purchaser, there may be grounds for legal action against the seller.

While most expediting begins with the failure of the goods to arrive on the promised date, there are cases where expediting begins well before the delivery date. In certain types of work—the construction industry for example—the failure to deliver materials as promised may idle labor and machines and lead to costly disruptions. In such situations, the purchaser may start "checking up" on the supplier to be sure that he will meet the promised delivery date; or at least, his inability to meet promised delivery will be known far enough in advance to make other arrangements for materials needed.

Clearing the Order

In brief, clearing the order involves receiving the shipment and identifying it as that ordered, inspecting and accepting the goods as satisfactory, and authorizing payment to the supplier. When the shipment arrives at the receiving department, the shipping ticket may be checked against a copy of the purchase order. If the purchase order indicates that the goods are to be inspected upon arrival, the goods are set aside and the inspectors notified. The purchasing department will also have been notified of the arrival of the goods. If the goods are inspected and accepted, they are moved to the proper storage area. The purchasing department will be notified that the goods have met inspection; the purchasing officer then authorizes payment of the invoice. The seller's invoice should have reached the buyer before, or concurrent with, the arrival of the order.

The inspection of items ordered usually takes place upon arrival at the buyer's place of business, but there are occasions when it is advisable to inspect the goods before they leave the supplier's plant. This is likely to be so if the item in question is something of very great weight. This saves the cost of transportation that would otherwise be lost if the item fails to meet a legitimate inspection at the buyer's location. If goods fail to meet the agreed standards and are rejected by the buyer, the seller may take the goods back or negotiate a price adjustment to the satisfaction of the buyer.

Legal Considerations

Mention has been made of the fact that the purchase order, when accepted by the seller, assumes the status of a contract. In accepting the order, the seller agrees to deliver the items as described and to deliver them on the agreed date and at the agreed price. The buyer in turn agrees to accept the goods if delivered on the promised date and if the quality is as described in the order. The failure of either party to live up to the agreement releases the other from responsibility. In case of default, the injured party may sue to recover the extent of the damages suffered.

In reality, buyers and sellers do not stand firmly on every legal right they may possess. Many times, orders are delivered late and the buyer accepts the seller's explanations for the delay. On other occasions, a buyer may ask to be released from the acceptance of an order that he has placed. As a gesture of goodwill, the seller may willingly release him from his contract. The law remains as a recourse to those who suffer loss through the carelessness, or wilful deception, of another in a business transaction. But if every businessman exercised his rights under the law on every possible occasion, it is doubtful that he would have enough time left from attending court to do much business.

THE PURCHASE OF CAPITAL EQUIPMENT

The Role of the Purchasing Department

Generally speaking, the term *capital equipment* refers to large-unit items such as heavy machines. Equipment of this type is characterized by the large investment required, the long life of the equipment, and the inherent problem of obsolescence. The purchase of capital equipment represents a decision to be made by the higher levels of management in the company. Some companies have a special committee designated to evaluate the requests for the purchase of items in this category and to make recommendations. The committee will usually be made up of representatives from the engineering department, the operating departments concerned, finance, sales, and purchasing. The purchasing officer is an important member of this committee since he is an authority on sources of supply and costs. When the committee recommends the purchase of an item of capital equipment, management must still make the decision to buy. Often, the nature of capital equipment is such that the purchase may be temporarily delayed, thus giving management a chance to pick an opportune time to buy in regard to the price of the item, the company's ability to finance, and the state of technology. The state of technology is important in that the company does not want to invest in something that may soon become obsolete. Of course, in an emergency, the decision to buy cannot be delayed.

When the decision to purchase capital equipment has been made, the purchasing department may be given the responsibility of selecting a source and negotiating a price. The nature of capital equipment is such that there may exist relatively few sources for a given item; for example, two or three qualified suppliers would be typical. When the potential suppliers have been determined, the usual procedure is to issue bids.[4] The supplier chosen will be selected not only in terms of price but in terms of his reputation for service and reliability as well. The element of service is especially important in the purchase of capital

4 England, *op. cit.*, Chap. 13.

equipment. It should be noted that in the purchase of capital equipment, as in other purchases, the purchasing department does not determine *what* is to be bought. The operating department initiating the request for equipment, and the committee for the purchase of capital equipment, establishes specifications that the item must meet. Given the specifications, the purchasing department may then seek to buy the item from the best qualified source in terms of price, service, and reliability.

Financing Capital Equipment

A major problem in the purchase of capital equipment is that of finance. Heavy installations may represent an investment of hundreds of thousands of dollars. The long life of this equipment may mean that its value will be depreciated over many years. It may also be necessary for the purchaser to finance the equipment over a long period. In evaluating the cost of capital equipment, one considers *initial cost* and *final cost*. Among the items making up final cost would be that of the interest on money invested in the equipment. Whether the item of equipment is bought outright or purchased through some form of credit, there is a cost of financing involved.

A company may finance the purchase of capital equipment in many ways: It may finance the purchase out of its own cash reserves if such are available. A company may find it more advisable to use its cash as "working capital" and finance equipment purchases through some form of credit. A corporation may borrow through selling bonds, which pay the lender (purchaser of the bonds) a stipulated rate of interest. It may also sell stock as a source of funds. The sale of stock is equivalent to selling part ownership in the company. The holders of stock share in the company earnings. The corporation may also find occasions where the seller of equipment is willing to accept stock in the purchasing company in payment for the equipment. There are also occasions where the seller will extend credit to the buyer and accept a lien (form of mortgage) on the equipment. The alternatives available to the purchaser in financing capital equipment will depend heavily upon the financial soundness of his company. The cost of credit tends to vary directly with the element of risk involved.

Leasing of Equipment

In some fields, there is an opportunity to lease equipment rather than purchase it outright. The manufacturer of the equipment (lessor) places it in the user's plant (lessee). The user is then charged a "rental" for the use of the equipment. The fee charged the user may be based on the rate at which the equipment is used. Leasing is common in the shoe manufacturing industry, and here the fee may be a certain amount for each pair of shoes produced. The leasing of equipment enables the user to gain access to the equipment without the initial capital outlay that may be necessary in purchasing it. Manufacturers unable to raise the necessary capital, or secure credit, may find leasing an alternative. It is also common for the lessor to assume the responsibility of service and maintenance of the equipment. This is an advantage in cases where the user does not have adequate service facilities of his own. It is also possible that the leasing of equipment may free capital for other uses by the lessee. The disadvantages of leasing lie in the fact that the user does not, as a rule, have complete freedom in the use of the equipment. He does not acquire ownership, and in the long run leasing of equipment may prove expensive.

ETHICS IN PURCHASING

The Acceptance of Gratuities

The purchasing officer is often in the position of having to make decisions in the selection of a source of supply. If he performs his job adequately, he will select the source of supply after a thorough and objective evaluation. The purchasing officer is an agent, and as such it is his obligation to serve the best interest of his employer. In well-organized purchasing departments, care is exercised, through the establishment of policies and their enforcement, to see that this obligation is observed. Unfortunately, there have developed situations in which the seller seeks to influence the purchaser by means outside the ethics of good business practice. The practice of personal gifts to the purchasing officer is an example. It is equally unfortunate that some purchasing officers allow themselves to be influenced by this practice. Many states have laws against commercial bribery, often aimed at preventing an agent from acting against the interest of his principal. It is probable that sellers who offer gifts and purchasing officers who accept them do not think of this as a form of bribery. But in the final analysis, business gifts do represent a form of bribery. The firm offering the gift is motivated by the desire to receive future business, and the buyer accepting the gift may find it extremely difficult to escape a feeling of obligation. The reputation of a firm is not enhanced when it seeks to influence others by actions outside the sphere of normal business activity. When a firm allows itself to be influenced by such actions, its reputation is likewise undermined.

Personal Purchases for Employees

The purchasing department of a company may, upon occasion, make personal purchases for employees. This may occur when the safety regulations of the company require the employees to purchase certain items, for example, shoes of a certain type. The purchasing department might be able to buy in quantity and obtain the shoes at a lower price. Personal purchases do not become a question of ethics unless the purchasing department misleads the supplier who may have a policy against selling directly to the consumer. A coal company may sell to industrial users in quantity and at lower rates. The same company might sell to retail coal dealers who in turn would sell to consumers. If an industrial plant buys coal at the industrial rate and then turns over part of the purchase to its employees for personal use, the local retail coal dealer would not be able to compete. The coal mining company may have a policy of protecting its retail dealers by not selling to household consumers. When subterfuge is used to defeat the policy of the seller, the practice is not ethical.

THE CONTROL OF PURCHASED-GOODS INVENTORY

Objectives

The carrying of purchased-goods inventory involves a cost to the company. Inventory costs include the interest on the money invested in inventory, insurance cost, the cost of storage space, and other costs such as fire protection and guard service. Obviously, it is in the interest of the firm to minimize these costs, and one way of doing this is to maintain inventories at the minimum safety level. The safety level implies having enough of the item on hand to insure against production shutdowns resulting from shortages. Of course, the firm must balance the savings resulting from minimizing inventory against certain savings that may result from buying in larger quantities. Cost items such as those mentioned above are referred to as *carrying costs*. Ideally, the firm should carry inventory at a level where the savings from quantity purchasing are exactly equal to the carrying costs.

Control Procedures

Progress continues to be made in devising methods of controlling the purchased-goods inventory. In an earlier section of this chapter, reference was made to the development of purchase-quantity formulas. Many companies have developed some version of the formula to be used in the purchase of items that are used repeatedly and at a constant rate. The short case at the end of this chapter will illustrate one such formula. The advent of the electronic computer added a new dimension to the use of the order-quantity formula. The computer may be supplied with data regarding the inventory on hand and the predetermined re-order point. As each unit of the item is removed from storage, the information is fed to the computer. The computer may be programmed to initiate and print out the purchase order at the proper time, and to handle the routine work involved in processing the order. This may include printing out a follow-up to be used in expediting the order, checking the invoice against the purchase order on delivery, and printing the check to pay for the purchase.

In a few industries, the computer has been used to achieve what might be termed a "continuous-flow" management of materials. Sales orders received are instantly programmed into the computer, which, in turn, produces production schedules and specifies bills of materials. The objective is to permit the firm to operate without warehousing a finished-goods inventory and also to operate with a minimum purchased-goods inventory. Goods are delivered to the market directly from the production line. The system envisions a "pipe-line" type of operation in which raw materials enter the company and flow through production and out into the market without the usual inventories accumulating anywhere along the line. It should be obvious to the student that this system would be applicable to relatively few industries. It would have to be an industry in which the rate of use for the product was constant over time, and one in which the source of materials and supplies was also constant. Where there is a seasonal factor affecting production or consumption, the system would not be applicable.

YOUR CAREER IN PURCHASING

Opportunities

Business firms have long been aware of the critical importance of purchasing. As previously indicated, most firms of considerable size practice centralized purchasing. The typical purchasing department is headed by a director of purchases (or similar title) who in turn supervises various commodity buyers and possibly assistant buyers. In conjunction with the buying operations, there are numerous administrative and clerical jobs. Many companies maintain a training program and make a practice of hiring college graduates. The purchasing department is regarded as an excellent training ground for future executives at the company-management level. In purchasing, one gets to know and work with the many operating departments throughout the firm. Interest in college-trained personnel has been exemplified by the National Association of Purchasing Agents. This very active organization has been instrumental in influencing colleges and universities to devote attention to purchasing in the business courses taught.

In industrial purchasing, the type of college training considered desirable varies with the particular industry. Firms manufacturing machines and electronic equipment normally prefer to hire engineers for training in purchasing. Firms in the chemical industry would prefer chemistry majors. Firms in other areas prefer business-administration majors. While these preferences may be described as general, they are by no means exclusive. Many non-technical graduates are hired and trained to become proficient in technical purchasing.

Government and Institutional Purchasing

Although this chapter has dealt with industrial purchasing, in discussing career opportunities one should not overlook the broad fields of government and institutional purchasing. Colleges and universities, hospitals, and many other institutions demand the services of a purchasing department. The federal government is the largest buyer in the nation, and thousands of people are employed in the many aspects of government purchasing. State governments also maintain purchasing facilities necessary to school operation, road building, etc.

Educational Background

The program of the engineering student is pretty well limited to the required fundamental arts and sciences and to courses in his area of specialization. The business administration, or arts and science, major may have the opportunity of a somewhat wider course selection. For students in business and in the arts, there are certain courses that would be desirable as a background to purchasing. Some knowledge of accounting is desirable. The purchasing officer must work with cost figures and be able to make cost analyses. A knowledge of economics is desirable in helping the purchasing executive to study and interpret price trends. Courses in marketing are desirable as they relate to buying and selling. A knowledge of transportation is helpful, as is a knowledge of industrial organization and management. The purchasing officer is constantly in communication with others, thus he must be able to speak and write with clarity. In fact, there are few areas of knowledge that will not contribute in some way to the needs of the purchasing executive.

Salarywise, the trainee in purchasing may expect to begin at a salary comparable to those who enter industrial management or sales. It is not uncommon for employees to enter purchasing after having worked in other departments of the firm. In this case, salaries would be commensurate with experience.

TOPICS FOR DISCUSSION

1. Distinguish between the terms *purchasing* and *buying*.

2. In most industrial organizations, the purchasing function will consist of four main activities. List these activities.

3. What is meant by "control of inventory"?

4. Why does the purchase of capital equipment usually receive special attention?

5. What is the main advantage of leasing equipment? The main disadvantage?

6. When a supplier accepts an order, he becomes party to a contract in which he obligates himself to deliver on the promised date. If this is so, why should *expediting* be necessary?

7. When does an item of equipment become obsolete?

8. A few years ago, the federal government changed the tax laws to permit the rapid depreciation (on paper) of capital equipment. It was thought that this would encourage the purchase of such equipment. Why might this be so?

9. Why is it considered poor policy for a company to permit its purchasing employees to accept gifts from sellers?

10. Would you rather be a purchasing officer or a salesman? Why?

CASE 10–1

THE SHAW MANUFACTURING COMPANY

Mr. Charles Shaw, president of the Shaw Manufacturing Company, had long been concerned with what he felt to be the excessive cost of carrying purchased-goods inventory. Purchasing in the Shaw company was done on a judgmental basis; that is, needs were estimated on the basis of past experience, and orders were placed with some consideration given to quantity discounts.

Mr. Shaw attended a trade association conference and heard an address delivered by an executive from a company that had successfully used purchase-order-quantity formulas. The company using this system was in the same line of business as Mr. Shaw and was of approximately the same size. After hearing the discussion of this method, Mr. Shaw sought out the speaker and discussed the matter in more detail. Mr. Shaw was told that the purchase-order formula worked well in the case of certain items that were used at a fairly constant rate, that were standard in quality, and that were of a type not subject to widely fluctuating prices.

The executive with whom Mr. Shaw talked explained that the purpose of an order-quantity formula was to afford a means of equating the carrying costs of inventory with savings that might be associated with the size of the order. The formula explained to Mr. Shaw was as follows:

$$Q = \sqrt{\frac{2\ DK}{C}}$$

where D = the number of units demanded during the year,
Q = the number of units to be ordered in each lot,
K = the costs involved in processing each order, and
C = the carrying cost per unit per year.

As an example, suppose that 600 units of an item are normally used each year. Further, suppose that it cost $10 to process each order and that the carrying cost of each unit in stock is $5 per year. In terms of the formula, D would equal 600, K would equal $10, and C would equal $5. Substituting these quantities into the formula and completing the calculations reveal that the most economical order quantity for the item in question would be a lot of approximately 49 units (practically speaking, an order of 50 units per month).

As Mr. Shaw studied the possibilities of applying the formula to the purchase of certain products by his own company, he realized that his firm would need certain information relative to the cost involved in handling an order and also the carrying costs associated with the items to be considered. Upon his return to the company, he held a conference with the accounting department to determine if the information needed could be obtained. The accountants felt that both information on the cost of processing an order and information on carrying costs could be arranged, but they pointed out that these cost estimates would involve a considerable amount of judgmental allocation in areas such as that of overhead costs. Mr. Shaw ordered a study to be made of purchase orders over the past year to determine which items had been used with a high degree of regularity. He was of a mind to try the formula approach in an effort to reduce the cost of maintaining an inventory of purchased goods.

1. Do you feel that there may be advantages in using the purchase-order-quantity formula?
2. What limitations does one face in using such a formula?

SELECTED REFERENCES

Ammer, D. S. *Materials Management.* Homewood, Ill.: Richard D. Irwin, Inc., 1962.

England, W. B. *Procurement.* 4th ed. Homewood, Ill.: Richard D. Irwin, Inc., 1962.

Henritz, Stuart F., and P. V. Farrell. *Purchasing.* 4th ed. Englewood Cliffs, N.J.: Prentice-Hall, Inc., 1965.

Lee, Lamar, Jr., and Donald W. Dobler. *Purchasing and Materials Management Text and Cases.* New York: McGraw-Hill Book Co., 1965.

Voris, W. *The Management of Production.* New York: The Ronald Press Co., 1960. Chap. 12.

Westing, J. H., and I. V. Fine. *Industrial Purchasing.* 2d ed. New York: John Wiley & Sons, Inc., 1962.

11

Production Control in the Manufacturing Process

BROADER CONCEPTS OF CONTROL

In its usual context, production control is most often thought of in relation to the organization of the work processes in the factory. It is not uncommon, however, to find those who think of production control in a broader sense. The following definition of production control, given by Charles A. Koepke, illustrates:

Production control is a major system for controlling a number of things in most manufacturing organizations. It is the coordinating agent between sales, engineering design or specification, pilot production, manufacturing and sales. It is responsible for ordering the correct raw, semifinished and finished materials as specified by design and industrial engineers. . . . Other major systems, such as design engineering, industrial engineering, manufacturing, sales, finance and top management, also have their specific controls to insure good performance.[1]

One must agree that in any successful enterprise an over-all control must exist in coordinating the activities involved in producing a product and delivering it to the consumer. Whether control at the topmost level should be referred to as "production control" or something else is of small consequence. In this chapter, we shall discuss production control in a more restricted sense and use the term as it specifically relates to the manufacturing processes.

[1] Charles A. Koepke, *Plant Production Control* (3d ed.; New York: John Wiley & Sons, Inc., 1961), pp. 1–2.

Production Control in Manufacturing

A manufacturing plant consists of men and machines arranged in a manner to deliver some degree of concerted effort in producing a product. Normally, we think of factory production as a process of bringing together materials that are worked upon by men and machines and ultimately combined into the finished item. The working process may consist of heating, cutting, machining, chemical treatment, fitting, painting, etc. In a simplified form, we may visualize this as a situation in which materials enter production at one end of the plant and emerge as a finished product at the other end. As the materials make the trip through the plant, they are transformed by the efforts of workmen performing specialized tasks. At one station, the materials may be worked upon by five men using ten machines; at another station, one man and one machine may perform an operation on each piece; and at still another station, three men may be assembling the materials as cut and shaped at preceding stations. The problem here is to coordinate the flow of work to achieve the most economical utilization of men and machines, while assuring the maintenance of the desired quality of production. This is essentially the problem of production control.

In the days preceding the development of the factory system, production control was scarcely a problem. In the small shop, each workman labored as an independent craftsman. For instance, in the production of shoes, each man performed all the operations in the making of a shoe from the cutting of the leather to the final stitching. Each man used his own tools and was largely independent of his fellow workmen. Such control as existed may have been in the determination of the days of work, the length of the work day, and possibly some exhortation to the individual to work faster.

The factory system gave rise to the specialization of labor and the use of machines. It was found that an individual could develop expertness in the performance of a single task, and that some individuals had skill in one type of work while others were skilled in something else. By having each man do the job at which he was most skilled, and through the combination of individual skills, a better product could be turned out in less time. The introduction of machinery meant that it was often necessary for several workmen to share a single machine. This made it necessary to plan the flow of work to the machine. The rate at which an individual worked was now dependent upon several others who performed operations on the product before it reached his hands, and his rate also depended upon having access to machines when needed. Obviously, there existed a need to control the flow of work in this situation. Unfortunately, in the early days of industry, little thought was given to formal plans of production control. When an order was received, the shop foreman was told to produce a certain quantity as specified. He was then left to his own devices in getting the job done. The manner in which men and machines were utilized depended upon the skill of the particular foreman and the workers concerned. Management remained aloof from shop problems.

Historical Development

Production control, as we know it today, may be said to have begun with the work of Frederick W. Taylor. Taylor, an engineer with the Midvale Steel Company of Philadelphia in the 1880's, began a series of experiments that were to develop into what became known as "scientific management." While working in the machine shop of the company, Taylor became aware of certain facts that disturbed him. He noted that neither management nor the worker seemed to know what constituted a fair day's work. He also noted that the details of performing a job were left entirely to the individual worker. He set about trying to solve these problems, and in the process he developed certain procedures. He advocated determining the one best method of doing the job, then training the worker to do the job according to the method, establishing standards to measure a fair day's work, and offering the worker a wage incentive to meet or exceed the standard. Others contributed to, and refined, the work of Taylor; and from this we derived the modern tools of time study, methods analysis, job evaluation, and other techniques. The term *scientific management* is no longer widely used in describing modern industrial practice, but the developments growing out of the early movement provided the fundamentals for what might be described today as *systematic management*. Production control as we know it would not be possible without the approaches and tools pioneered by Taylor and his contemporaries. It is generally agreed that very little in the way of control existed before the advent of Taylor.

Although Taylor and his associates were able to produce dramatic results by applying methods that are now common in production control, the application of his techniques were slow to spread. As stated, management had not concerned itself with shop procedures and was ignorant of the full import of the new developments. A practical difficulty lay in the fact that industrial engineers capable of putting Taylor's methods into practice were not available. Taylor himself was not a good salesman in advancing the philosophy of management, which he had derived. Controversy arose when it was contended that Taylor's methods robbed the worker of his individuality and contributed to the creating of "sweat-shop" conditions. Some employers did seize upon

Taylor's methods as a means of exploiting the worker. Undoubtedly, Taylor, in introducing his methods, did have as his goal a greater efficiency that would benefit both employer and the worker. In spite of controversy, the validity of the approach introduced by Taylor was such that it could not be ignored. Once the benefits of the systematic planning and control of production were known, the development of industrial management as a specialized function was assured.

Organization for Production Control

It is probable that no two manufacturing plants are organized in exactly the same way. The type of product produced, the personnel employed, and many other factors influence organization. The size of the plant may indicate the degree of specialization in performing the various functions, and this would contribute to a more complicated organization structure. The function of production control is concerned with every activity of the company; but in practice, production control is concerned most directly with the flow of the work in process. In a typical plant, there will be both line departments and staff departments. The production-control department is most likely to be in the position of a line department reporting to the production superintendent or plant manager. The various specialists that may be found in the production-control department usually function in a staff capacity; that is, they plan work, determine schedules, and route the work in process, while it remains the responsibility of the works manager and his line foremen to see that the plans are executed. It is a necessity that close cooperation exist between the planning and the work-supervisory personnel. Figure 11–1 shows a possible organization of the production-control function.

SCOPE OF PRODUCTION CONTROL

Forecasting Sales, a Prerequisite to Control

Adequate production control must give consideration to long-range planning. The long-range planning of production begins with a consideration of what the company will be able to sell during a forthcoming period of time. This is commonly referred to as *sales forecasting*. Normally, sales forecasting is a function of the company's marketing division working in conjunction with top management and such staff specialists as economists and statisticians. This is especially true where the emphasis is on "what can be sold" rather than on "how much can be produced." Regardless of where emphasis is placed, the production department should be represented in sales forecasting. Those charged

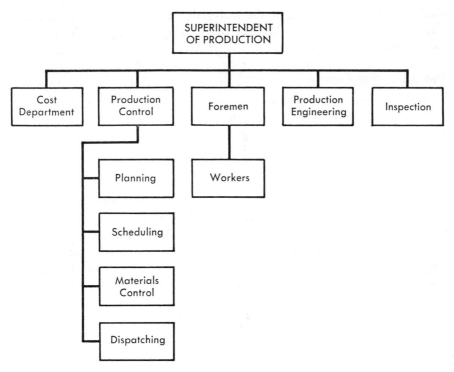

Fig. 11–1. The production-control function in the organization structure.

with production control will have to use the sales forecast as a basis for planning; and if they have a voice in making the forecast, they are likely to have more confidence in it. Sales forecasts must take into consideration future costs of production and the price at which the product will sell. Those concerned with production control are in a position to advise on matters relating to the cost of production.

Material Control

The material-control function may include the placing of requisitions with the purchasing department, the storing of materials until they are needed, and the control of materials on hand to avoid overstocking and loss from deterioration or obsolescence. As indicated in Chapter 10, the term "inventory control" involves the broad problem of determining the proper quantity to order and the most desirable quantity to keep in stock. The term "stores control" generally refers to the management of the materials on hand. The stores function is an inherent part of inventory control, and this has led in some cases to making stores control a responsibility of the purchasing department. There is, however, a lack of uniformity among companies in the matter of materials control. The management of the materials on hand, and in some cases the purchasing function itself, may be the responsibility of the production department.

Planning Production

In its narrow sense, production control is often thought of as those activities centering around planning, scheduling, routing, and dispatching. We have seen, however, that production control in manufacturing may begin as far back as sales forecasting and extend as far forward as the storage of the finished product. The student should keep this in mind as we discuss the central activities enumerated above.

There are several types of production plans. First, there are those plans that prescribe quantities and seek to coordinate production plans with sales requirements. Second, there are those plans that relate to the method to be employed in accomplishing production goals. And third, there are those plans concerned with the detailed timing of the various operations in production. The first type of planning begins well in advance of production and is concerned with seeing that materials and facilities are available and ready when needed. The second and third types become more detailed as they move toward becoming an actual blueprint describing what is to be done. The manufacturing of a product may be a very complex operation bringing together dozens of materials and fabricated parts that must be worked by men and machines. If costs are to be minimized, materials of the right type must be at the right place and processed by the right men and machines without loss of time. This can be accomplished only through advanced and detailed planning. Given a product to be produced, planning may start with the drawing of a bill of materials that specifies in detail just what will be needed. The engineering department supplies drawings of the designs of all parts, or models of the various components may be made and used to convey the idea of what is wanted. The production department then supplies information on the number and type of machines that will be required. If new, or additional, tools are required, steps are taken to see that they are ordered. These are but a few of the steps included in the planning stage of production control.

Routing

The term "routing" as a part of production control has several meanings.[2] Some define it as those activities beginning with machine anal-

[2] H. N. Broom, *Production Management* (Homewood, Ill.: Richard D. Irwin, Inc., 1962), Chaps. 7, 11, 12.

ysis and a study of operations and terminating with the preparation of documents—the release of which starts production. Another concept refers to routing as the planning designed to indicate the path that work shall follow and the sequence of operations that will prevail as it moves through the production processes. In this simplified treatment, we will use the term as it refers to the flow of work. Thus, routing becomes the job of planning where the work will be done, who shall do it, and the machines and equipment to be used. In an assembly line type of production where a single product is in production over an extended period of time, the problem of routing is less pressing. The routing of the work in process is a basic part of planning the assembly line; and once routing is satisfactorily achieved, the flow of work through the processes becomes repetitive. In custom-type production where a parade of different products are produced, routing must be accomplished anew with each production job undertaken. Routing is a detailed operation contributing to the over-all function of production planning.

Scheduling

The planning and routing phases of production control are concerned with the *what* and *how* of getting the job done. Scheduling introduces the time element into the picture. If we visualize routing as indicating the path along which the work will flow, we may think of scheduling in terms of releasing the work loads to move along the path. Just as the trains moving over a railroad must operate on schedule, so must the various jobs be on schedule in moving through the work processes. The failure of one train to move on time may delay many others; the failure of one job to move through production on time may delay others. Thus, scheduling in a production process has much in common with scheduling the flow of traffic over a railroad.

Production schedules begin with the general and work toward the specific. *Master schedules* assign the dates upon which important production goals are to be met. *Operation schedules* assign the total time required to accomplish a piece of work with a certain machine or process. *Detailed operation schedules* may assign the time required for the performance of each detailed operation of a given job. The master schedule is based upon sales orders or prospective orders and thus has to remain flexible. As the time to begin production nears, the schedules become more specific. Scheduling involves not only the assignment of starting times for the jobs to be done, but it must be concerned with keeping a careful watch over the work as it moves through the production process. This is accomplished through the use of devices such as progress charts and control boards. Charts show time along the horizontal axis with operations listed from top to bottom along the vertical axis. Control boards are similar, with machines and operators shown on the vertical axis. From the chart, one can observe the day-to-day progress of an operation as well as the amount of work scheduled for the days and weeks ahead. The control board shows the work scheduled in terms of machines and operators. By keeping these control devices up-to-date, planners are able to note if schedules are being met on time. If a job is not completed as scheduled, adjustments may be made all along the line.

Dispatching

Dispatching involves the releasing of work orders to the various employees with the authorization that the job be started. The analogy with the railroad is again applicable. The train does not leave the terminal until it receives specific orders to proceed. The worker does not start the scheduled job until he receives specific orders to do so. In production, the dispatching function extends beyond the mere initiating of the work order. It includes certain follow-up and reporting duties. In its broad sense, dispatching may include the release of work orders, the checkup on the work preparatory to the start of the job (delivery of materials at the work station), a checkup on the progress of production, the maintenance of progress records, and reports to management when deviations from schedules are encountered. Dispatching is usually conducted at a center near the work stations, and in some cases it may be little more than a clerical operation. But when the dispatching center is made responsible for follow-up and the reporting on work in progress, it becomes a vital link in plant communications.

Inspection

Production control is responsible for more than just turning out a specified quantity in the scheduled time. It is equally concerned with the maintenance of quality. Workers are instructed and machines are adjusted to produce the quality called for in the designs for the product. But seldom are men and machines infallible. Imperfections in production occur for various reasons. Sometimes faults in the material cannot be detected in advance. Machines may deviate from previous settings despite the best supervision. Workers are subject to human error. All these contingencies mean that some type of inspection is usually necessary to assure quality.

The components of a product may be inspected while in process. The early detection of faulty material or workmanship may prevent the further spoilage of materials or the waste of labor expended in machining and handling unsuitable materials. There is usually a final inspection of the finished product before it leaves the production area. The nature of the final inspection may vary, depending upon the way in which the product will be used. Brake cylinders for airplanes would be thoroughly inspected because a faulty cylinder might lead to an accident. In such cases, every cylinder would be inspected before the item was shipped to the buyer. This would be what is known as "100 per cent" inspection. Where the element of quality is less crucial, an inspection by sample might be satisfactory. Every tenth product completing the production cycle might be inspected. If rejections exceed a pre-established percentage, production would be halted until the cause of trouble has been found and corrected. Frequently, quality control procedures are established to keep a constant check on work in process. For example, a machine may be turning out bolts that are 2 inches long with a deviation of plus or minus 1/100 inch allowable. A continuous sample may be taken from the production of the machine; and when measurements indicate that the deviations are exceeding the allowable amount, the machine may be stopped until adjustments are made.

Finished-Goods Storage

The interests of production control extend all the way to include the finished-goods inventory. The actual supervision of warehouse stocks may fall within the scope of the sales division, but production is interested in reports on the level of stocks. The advanced planning necessary for effective production control causes the production-control department to want constant information on the movement of goods into the market. The failure of an item to sell as anticipated may call for instant adjustments on the production line. Thus, it becomes necessary for production to keep constantly advised on the status of finished-goods inventory.

THE HUMAN ELEMENT IN PRODUCTION CONTROL

A Problem in Coordination

From the foregoing discussion, it is apparent that production control is fundamentally a problem in coordinating the efforts of the many people that may be involved in the production of a product. Modern industrial production has been characterized by an increasing development of specialization at both management and work levels. The old craftsman who used to turn out a product by performing all of the many operations himself now finds a dozen workmen engaged in turning out the product, each performing a single operation. The shop foreman of the old days used to be responsible for the hiring and training of workers, planning the work, supervising work in process, and any other management function required. Now, the management function has been divided into a number of specialties, and several managers may be engaged in carrying out the duties that were once heaped upon a single individual. This development of specialization has brought to production an ever increasing record of efficiency.

The worker specializing in performing a single operation in the production of a product develops a skill in that operation that was not possible with the old craftsman. Furthermore, it means that a worker may be trained to perform a single operation in a matter of weeks or months; while the old craftsman, in learning to perform many operations, required an apprenticeship of several years. A manager may become proficient in a specialized area through concentrated study over a relatively short period. It would require years for a manager to become proficient in all the areas now comprising modern management. It is also important to remember that people possess varying degrees of aptitude relative to the jobs to be performed. Specialization has permitted concentration upon the job that one does best. While specialization has brought with it many advantages, it has created the difficult problem of combining the specialists into a functioning unit. A football player may specialize in playing a certain position on the team, but a team of eleven specialists each performing independently of the others would be a failure. Success depends upon coordinating the efforts of individuals to function according to a predetermined plan. Each player has an assigned role contributing to the systematic functioning of the team. Each specialist in the production of a product must function as a component of a well-organized team.

Managing Men and Machines

The problem of coordination in production control centers around the management of men and machines. The industrial engineer may approach the problem of managing his machines in an objective and detached manner. He may move the machines around the factory and experiment in his search for the best possible layout. But the machine and the men operating it must often be regarded as a unit. We cannot move men from place to place, change their methods of operating, speed them up or slow them down with the same detachment that machines are handled. F. W. Taylor, in his drive to find the best way of doing a job, was often accused of treating the worker as a machine to be moved around and fitted into a slot without too much awareness of the human factors involved. The industrial engineers that followed Taylor showed more concern for the worker as an individual. The personnel-management function became an important part of industrial management. The control of production today requires the coordination of the efforts of many people who perform specialized tasks. One does not secure coordination without the cooperation of those concerned. To obtain the needed cooperation, one must be a good manager of men as well as a good manager of machines.

Industrial Engineering

The pioneering work of F. W. Taylor and others in the development of systematic management led to the emergence of certain techniques or "tools" that are now an essential part of production control. These new tools in the area of industrial management required specialists to take charge of their refinement and use. Thus, the specialty of *industrial engineering* came into prominence. The industrial engineer performs a variety of tasks. Some of the functions of industrial engineering that are of especial concern in production control will be cited.

One of the preliminary steps in the establishment of production control is the accomplishment of *job studies.* A job study, or job analysis, involves a study of the work to be done, the workplace, the machines to be used, and the workers employed. The basic purpose goes back to Taylor's idea of finding the one best way to accomplish the task. When the best method of performing the work is determined, the method is standardized and thus becomes a basis for establishing rates. A job analysis may begin by improving the workplace to eliminate unnecessary walking or lifting. Then it may proceed to more specific areas such as *motion study.* Motion study centers around the movements of the worker in performing the task. Efforts are made to eliminate the unnecessary motions and thus enable the worker to do more work with less effort. When the essential motions in the performance of the operation have been determined, *time study* may be employed to arrive at the establishment of a standard time. The standard time allowed for the performance of a task may become the basis for administering the wage plan. Wage incentive systems usually involve the determination of a certain quantity to be produced as the "standard," with the idea of normal quantity dependent upon time study, along with other factors. Although there are many variations, a typical wage plan may pay the worker a certain rate for achieving the standard set and then pay a bonus for exceeding the standard.

The industrial engineer may be concerned with a program of *job evaluation* in which he strives to establish the relative worth of jobs within the plant. This is a continuing study since methods and ma-chines change from time to time. Unless jobs are evaluated, and re-evaluated, a situation may develop in which an unskilled performer is receiving higher wages than a man with greater skill. Workers like to be treated fairly, and good job evaluation contributes toward this end. Without the contributions of the industrial engineer, the coordination of activities required in effective production control would be difficult, if not impossible.

YOUR CAREER IN PRODUCTION MANAGEMENT

A Variety of Jobs

There are a variety of jobs in the area broadly described as produc-tion management. Many jobs at the management level involve the di-rect supervision of others engaged in the production processes. There are also jobs often described as staff positions. The staff executive is often a specialist who performs certain facilitating functions. The in-dustrial engineer is likely to function in this capacity. There are many management positions in the area that we have specifically described as *production control*. People skilled in production management are re-quired to carry out the functions of planning, routing, scheduling, dis-patching, and related activities. The best-laid plans would come to naught if adequate line supervision was not present. Line positions range from that of a section foreman to that of a plant manager, and upward to that of the company presidency itself. Staff positions may include those expert in job analysis, motion and time study, job evalua-tion, etc. The larger the company, the more highly specialized staff positions may become. Studies have shown that, in general, about an equal number of top executives in company management advance through the production department and through the sales department. Some companies are "production oriented," and a majority of the higher executives will have advanced through production. Other companies are said to be "marketing minded" to the extent of placing heavy em-phasis on sales and advertising. In such companies, a majority of the top executives may have advanced through the marketing organization. It is probable that most companies strive for a balance in their top management with executives having advanced from all functional divi-sions.

Training for a Career in Production

Many companies, especially the larger ones, follow a policy of re-cruiting potential production executives from colleges and universities.

However, few companies would close the door of advancement to a capable man who has not had the privilege of formal education. In the old days, it was common for a man to begin work with a company at an early age and then to work his way up in a step-by-step process. There will always be some executives who rise to the top over this route, but present-day conditions tend to relegate such cases to the minority. There are many reasons for this. For one thing, modern production management has become very complex, and a fundamental education beyond the secondary level has come to be regarded as highly essential. It is also recognized that college courses in engineering, industrial engineering, and production management are able to equip the student with tools and background information that contribute to a rapid adjustment on the job. The background of the college graduate also contributes to the rapidity with which he is able to advance through the learning stages. The vast expansion of industry has created a need for executives at a much faster rate than the old system of "up-through-the-ranks" could supply them. The college student employed in production usually goes through an extensive on-the-job training program before being assigned to a lower-level management job. But his college training often enables him to absorb more in his company training and to advance faster through the lower levels of management than would otherwise be the case.

Students hoping for a career in industrial production may choose one of several college programs that lead to such an objective. Many production executives are trained as engineers; others have specialized in industrial engineering. A large segment of production management will usually be drawn from Schools of Business Administration. The business administration student may have a major in *industrial management* or a similar concentration. The arts and science student should by no means consider himself left out. There are many courses in the arts and science curriculum that afford a good background for production. In the area of basic education, one might recommend mathematics to the level of calculus; at least two years of English grammar and literature; the principles of economics; and such courses in history, psychology, and sociology as time will permit. In the business area, accounting through the level of *cost accounting* is almost a must for the production man. Courses in industrial and personnel management should be taken. Courses in marketing, transportation, statistics, and finance are suggested to give the potential production executive an understanding of management in the broader sense.

Salary-wise, the production-management trainee may be able to start at a better salary than that paid the average graduate. The starting salary may prevail throughout the training program, or periodic increases may be given. When the training program is finished and the erstwhile trainee assumes a management position, his promotions and salary increases will generally depend upon merit.

TOPICS FOR DISCUSSION

1. How can management use production plans?
2. Would the production manager of a firm be more useful if he utilized mathematical tools? Explain.
3. In what type of organization would the production manager be considered more valuable to a firm than the financial manager?
4. Before the days of F. W. Taylor, management appeared not to concern itself with "shop procedures." To what extent was this attitude of management caused by social attitudes?
5. Assume that you have a friend who is considering the idea of opening a factory to produce pencils. What is the first thing that you would advise him to investigate?
6. Can you enumerate some of the things that must be taken into account in planning production?
7. Can you explain the analogy between production control in a plant and the operation of a railroad?
8. Is the present day worker, doing a specialized operation on a product, happier than the old-time craftsman who performed all the operations? Explain your answer.
9. From the standpoint of employment, what features do you think that you would like about a job in production management? What features might you dislike?
10. Why don't more of the students who desire to go into production management take courses in cost accounting, statistics, and mathematics?

CASE 11–1

THE ENGLAND MOTOR CORPORATION

Production control is not only a matter of organizing work processes and providing the right equipment at the right place; it is also a matter of organizing and maintaining the human effort. This fact was well demonstrated in the problem that faced the England Motor Corporation. The England firm produced a rather standard gasoline motor. The production process was organized into three subdivisions. Two of the subdivisions produced components, each producing one of the two major components that went into the finished product. These two subdivisions routed the components as they were completed to a third subdivision, where minor components were added and the complete motor was assembled. The England plant was divided into three areas of floor space, each accommodating a subdivision of the operation. The equipment and employees assigned to each subdivision had been organized in such a way that the flow of components into the assembly subdivision and the flow of the finished product from assembly was a coordinated and continuous one. The three subdivisions were linked in such a way that a failure in any one subdivision would have a slowing effect on production throughout the plant.

Studies made in 1964 showed that the plant was operating at 10 per cent below expected capacity. Efforts to determine the cause of this failure revealed an inability to maintain a coordinated flow through the three work areas described above. Employee absenteeism in any one part of the operation would slow down productivity in the other subdivisions. Equipment failures would have the same effect. A continued study of the day-to-day productivity over the past year showed clearly that employee absenteeism was a major source of the problem. Consideration was given to reorganizing the flow of work in such a way that the various subdivisions would not be completely interdependent. It was found that this would require a major reorganization of the production process as well as the purchase of additional equipment. It was decided that for the time being it would be more economical for the company to improve the situation by providing a means to remedy the problem of the absentee worker.

Study of the work force showed that absenteeism in the England plant was fairly typical of that found in similar operations. The company operated with a minimum labor force, and, each time that a man was out, his absence was evident in the slowing down of operations in his subdivision. Several suggestions were made for solving the absentee problem. The company employed forty-four men in one division, thirty-eight in another, and forty-two in the third. Records showed that, during the previous year, there had been twenty-two days on which as many as nine men had been absent. The average absenteeism was approximately three employees per workday. One suggestion was for the company to maintain a "flying squad" of nine men who would be trained to step into any job anywhere in the three subdivisions. Examination of the nature of all the jobs performed in the plant made it obvious that it would not be practical to train an employee to handle all of them. Another suggestion called for the training of three men in each subdivision who would be trained to handle any of the jobs in the subdivision. This still meant that a single man would have to learn several different jobs, but it was felt that men who were experienced workers could be selected and trained to perform other operations in the subdivision. If this plan could be put into effect, it would involve hiring nine new people to take the places of those who would be released to act as "floaters" filling in for absentees.

The England firm was unionized, and the union agreed to the proposal to have three floaters in each subdivision, providing the floaters were paid at a wage rate in keeping with the added skills they would have to acquire. The firm did not oppose the higher wage rate, feeling that considerable inducement would be necessary to obtain volunteers for the added training that would be required. The company hoped that, given the circumstances, enough men would volunteer to give the foreman of the subdivision some choice in the selection of the three men for the additional training. After considerable bargaining, the union agreed to waive seniority rights in the selection of these men.

1. The proposal to train "floaters" to solve the absenteeism problem calls for increasing the labor force by about 7 per cent. What will determine whether this is an economical solution to the problem?

2. Can you see any additional advantages to be derived from the proposal?

SELECTED REFERENCES

Buffa, E. S. *Modern Production Management.* 2d ed. New York: John Wiley & Sons, Inc., 1965.

Hodges, H. G., and R. J. Ziegler. *Managing the Industrial Concern.* Boston: Houghton Mifflin Co., 1963.

Koepke, C. A. *Plant Production Control.* 3d ed. New York: John Wiley & Sons, Inc., 1961.

Moore, Franklin G. *Manufacturing Management.* 3d ed. Homewood, Ill.: Richard D. Irwin, Inc., 1961.

Roscoe, E. S. *Organization for Production.* 3d ed. Homewood, Ill.: Richard D. Irwin, Inc., 1963.

Voris, W. *The Management of Production.* New York: The Ronald Press Co., 1960.

12

Personnel Management

HUMAN RESOURCES

The management of human resources is a key to successful accomplishment of company objectives. The establishment of a good work environment and satisfactory employee and employee-employer relationships is one of the primary responsibilities of the operation of a business. The degree to which the personnel-management process assists in effective management can influence company sales, the quality of company products, and service to the public. As a company expands, owners and managers tend to be diverted from the worker and his problems because their time is devoted to the more pressing matters of finance, production, and distribution. The problem of identifying the individual with the company becomes more complex in a growing company. Because employees are human beings, there will always be problems that arise from their working relationships. There are individual differences created by varied educational, economic, political, and religious backgrounds. An understanding of human behavior—of individual needs and aspirations—is basic to the management of the personnel functions.

Personnel management seeks to accomplish and maintain harmonious and cooperative working relationships through the establishment of job standards, careful recruitment and selection of employees who can meet such standards (with training opportunities for those who cannot), and fair compensation and promotion practices based on unbiased employee appraisals.

PERSONNEL POLICIES AND PROGRAMS

Functions of Personnel Management

The functions of personnel management vary among companies depending upon the size of the company, its interest in personnel management, its ability to support personnel programs, the number of employees, the number of plants, and other factors. The primary functions of personnel management are similar for all types of organizations, although the techniques used to carry them out will vary substantially among organizations. These functions and techniques of personnel management as they are performed in a business organization of sufficient size to need and support a personnel department will be described briefly. Some of these functions will be treated in more detail in later chapters while others will be discussed further in this chapter.

The formulation of personnel-management policy is one of the most important of personnel functions. The establishment of broad policies provides guideposts for all phases of personnel matters. The personnel department can then institute programs to carry the policies into effect. The policies are written statements so that there can be no misunderstanding about them. They indicate the course of action that the company will follow insofar as the actions of the personnel department are concerned.

Every company is faced with the job of hiring personnel. This is a primary function of personnel management. It requires an analysis of the job openings, recruiting of qualified personnel, and their selection and placement in positions best suited to their qualifications. The applicants are interviewed, tested, and counseled in regard to the requirements and opportunities. The personnel department also provides orientation for the employee concerning the company, its products or the service it renders, and the importance of the individual to the company.

The procedures for promotions and transfers are set up by the personnel department. Promotions usually carry with them additional earnings for employees, so it is necessary that a fair method be used as a basis for promotions.

The training of employees so that they may perform their jobs better or to help them to prepare themselves for more skilled tasks is a function of personnel management. The groups trained may be rank-and-file employees and managerial personnel as well. The type and length of training depends upon the nature of the training programs. In some instances, training may be in how to operate a machine, while in other cases it may be in how to manage people or something entirely different.

Another function is that of wage administration. Since people are compensated for the job performed, the amount of money they receive is of vital concern to them. It is likewise of vital concern to the company since it represents an important element of cost in the conduct of business. Wage administration includes the determination of what the wage scale should be for various jobs and involves constant surveys in the company's plants. Included in wage administration are different forms of employee participation in the profits of the business.

Administration of Programs. The administration of employee health and safety programs is one of the significant functions of personnel management. It has become increasingly common for companies to control working conditions and to provide specific programs that will benefit the health of their employees as well as providing safety programs. This often means the provision of limited medical services for employees if they are injured or become ill while they are working.

The safety program that a company has is usually handled by the personnel department. Safety is a field in which there has been and continues to be a great deal of activity. Much of it is aimed at accident prevention.

Personnel management also includes the administration of other employee benefits and services. These cover such activities as counseling, both personal and legal, employee insurance, savings programs, loans, pensions, retirement, and even housing. The amount of these services and benefits that are furnished depend on many factors and vary widely among companies. Many personnel departments handle recreational facilities for employees in the form of baseball fields, athletic equipment, sponsorship of bowling teams, and similar activities.

Other Functions. Handling labor relations for the company is often a function of the personnel department. In other companies, the handling of collective bargaining with employees is taken care of by a separate division. Of our over 70 million workers, about 18 million are represented by labor unions. The bargaining process between company management and unions requires the preparation for negotiations, the bargaining, and the interpretation and carrying out of the agreements.

Appraisal of the performance of employees in their jobs is a periodic function of personnel management. These evaluations are of help in determining how well the employee is performing his work and also are a means of discovering the potential of employees.

Conducting of research is an important part of personnel functions. Much of the basic data that can be used in research is developed from records of the personnel department. Facts must be analyzed in order to assist in the solution of many personnel problems. Frequently, there are research projects conducted by other departments of the company in which the personnel department will also participate.

Organization of the Personnel Department

The personnel department is a service department that performs numerous functions. In small companies, one person may handle all personnel matters; but in larger companies, it is necessary to have a large personnel department to serve the growing personnel needs of the company. The work areas and areas of responsibility must be clearly assigned. This is accomplished through setting up the organizational structure of the personnel department. In the larger companies with a single plant, the personnel department may be centralized in a single office. A typical personnel department in a large company will be headed by a director of personnel or a personnel relations director or, sometimes, an industrial relations director. He is responsible for the formulation of the personnel programs and the carrying out of personnel policies. He is a staff officer who will work closely with other staff officers and with the line organization. Usually, the functions of the personnel department will be grouped under branch or division chiefs. There may be such divisions as employment, training, safety and health, wage and salary administration, labor relations, and research, as shown in Figure 12–1. In many large organizations, separate departments may be created to handle labor relations and wage and salary administration. The division chiefs report directly to the director of the department.

When additional plants are operated, the question arises as to whether or not there should be decentralization of the personnel functions, as well as other specialized functions, or a continuation of centralization. If it is decided to decentralize, there may be a personnel department established at each plant location. The headquarters personnel department, however, will formulate the plans and policies within which plant departments must operate.

The effectiveness and the ability of the personnel department to serve other departments depends, in large measure, upon the support it receives from top management.

Policies of the Personnel Department

Personnel policies are established in broad, long-range terms that reflect the philosophy, or thinking, of top management in its relations with its employees. Policies serve as guides for management in their

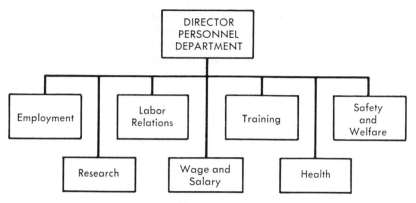

Fig. 12–1. A personnel-department organization chart.

dealings with human resources—people. Personnel policies are one aspect of company policies. As personnel policies cover the personnel activities, other policies, such as traffic or purchasing, cover other specialized departments. It is necessary, therefore, that policies be properly integrated so as to fit into the over-all company policies. For example, if a company has a production policy that calls for manufacturing goods only when it receives orders, this can conflict with a personnel policy that has stated that the company plans to provide stable employment for its workers.

The Importance of Human Relationships in Personnel Management

Throughout personnel management runs the thread of human relations. An individual is a composite of many influences: social, political, economic, and religious. When he is hired to fill a job, it is difficult to separate him while he is at work from the various attitudes that are a part of him. The result is that dealing with people is a most delicate task. The individual must be considered as a human being, as a worker performing a job, and as a part of a group of workers making up a labor force of a company. The labor force cannot be regarded as a standard package but as a changing group of individuals whose individual needs, desires, and attitudes must be included as a basic part of personnel management. The behavioral aspects of personnel management are very important.

It stands to reason that not every type of individual difference can be accommodated in an organization. If a person is hired who has difficulty getting along with people with whom he associates, he is going to be a source of trouble and discontent in the group with which he works in an organization. The human element of personnel management, then, begins in the hiring of individuals. A selection process must involve careful screening of applicants. Interviewing and testing should reveal that an individual has the ability to work amicably with others and that he has sufficient technical qualifications to enable him to fill the job requirements. The selection process should also be able to discover if the prospective employee has enough ambition to wish to progress beyond the job for which he is being hired.

Human relations in personnel management continues from the selection of employees to their working conditions. Employee dissatisfaction should be watched for, and a means of airing grievances should be established with a procedure for actions. Procedures to be followed in promotion of employees should be well known so that employees can derive satisfaction from the knowledge that there is reward for good work performance.

Motivation. One of the most important aspects of human relations is that of motivation. Motivation is a means of stimulating someone to take a desired course of action. Able leadership in management may provide the stimulus for the workers to get more accomplished. Obviously, a stimulus to work is the fact that wages are paid. However, there are many other ways in which people can be motivated. Because the same factors do not bring results in different groups of people, it is necessary that personnel management use a variety of motivation plans in order to secure optimum benefits. In addition to financial gain, a pleasant environment in which to work is a motivating factor for some people. The use of praise for good work motivates certain employees to better efforts. Another type of motivation is that provided by many trucking companies that have instituted safety programs with rewards for the family of the driver. The prizes given for each month of accident-free operation range from those that can be obtained after a month, or several months, of maintaining a good driving record to more valuable prizes that require many months of accident-free driving. The participation of his family in the choice of a much-desired prize provides a motivation for the driver in maintaining a safe driving record in order to obtain the coveted article.

Motivation must establish attainable goals—goals that most employees can attain if it is to bring about the desired results of better job performance. Otherwise, the inability to attain the goals may result in frustration that will produce the opposite effect. The desired results from employees will not be obtained when goals are too high for the majority. On the other hand, such goals should present a real challenge if employees are to realize a sense of accomplishment from their attainment.

The personnel department should be prepared to suggest means of motivation at all levels of the business organization. What factors will motivate salesmen? What motivations are there for the officers of the company? Certainly there are financial motivations; but, at certain levels of management, the prestige accompanying a certain position may be more important than financial rewards. For example, membership in exclusive clubs may go with a particular management position in the company.

Employee Morale

The morale, or state of mind, of employees is a major factor affecting their willingness to put forth their best efforts. The attainment of company objectives is affected by it. How does the personnel department contribute to high employee morale? It has fair and stable employment policies that give the employee a feeling of security in his work; it works to provide a clean and reasonably pleasant environment for employees; its procedures help the employee to feel that his complaints, if he has any, will receive consideration and that his efforts are appreciated. The working conditions that bring about a feeling like this among workers are the result of company policies and personnel planning in which the human element has been given top consideration. In this kind of situation, employees are likely to have high morale and work cooperatively and industriously.

Planning Personnel Programs

A program is a means by which a personnel policy can be carried out. It is a plan of action. All divisions, branches, and levels of the company organization that will participate in a particular program must be made aware of it. A program will assign the responsibility for its accomplishment. It will indicate objectives that are sought as a result of undertaking the program.

For each of the functions of personnel management, a program should be established. For many of the functions, numerous programs will have to be administered in order to cover the varous aspects of the functions. For example, in training employees there will be several training programs. On-the-job training may be the subject of one program, training in the field of management may be another, or training for supervisory positions may be still another.

In creating a program, the personnel department is interested not only in what it hopes to accomplish but also in what the cost of the program will be. A budget is prepared that will give the information on the program by budget periods: monthly, quarterly, or annually. In the preparation of such a budget, the extent of the program will need to be known. In a recruiting program, for example, it will be necessary to know how many people will be hired and what the costs will be per person.

The personnel department must constantly review the effectiveness of the programs in accomplishing objectives. In order to review and appraise a program, some yardsticks must be established. In a management recruiting program these are some of the points that might be checked: Have the people who have been recruited from colleges dropped out of the program? Have they made progress in their employment with the company? Is management well satisfied with the program? Is the program offering the management possibilities that were planned for it? Is it helping the company in reaching its over-all objectives?

Job Analysis and Job Specifications

The owner of a company having few employees knows what his requirements are and, when he has an opening, he will try to find the right person for the job. In larger organizations, however, there are too many positions and their requirements are too varied for them to be handled in this way. The types of jobs that exist in a company and the employees who will be required to fill them are determined by making a careful job analysis. The personnel department conducts a thorough study of the tasks, processes, and responsibilities of each job. This results in an outline of information about each particular job, which is termed a *job description*. Job descriptions are made for every type of job in the company.

Information concerning jobs is secured by observation, questionnaires, and/or personal interviews. In analyzing jobs, the basic information can be secured by ascertaining: (1) what the worker does, (2) how he does it, (3) why he does it, and (4) the skill involved in doing the job. If a questionnaire is used, a standard form is prepared and sent to each worker or to his supervisor to be completed. Upon receiving the completed questionnaires, the job analyst will group the jobs and go through each of the completed questionnaires. This method has the advantage of surveying the jobs very quickly. Sometimes the supervisors are asked to analyze the jobs under them and furnish the information to the job analyst. The best method, however, is to have the job analyst observe and interview each of the workers, because more information can be secured. Work-sampling techniques have recently been used to provide a broader time period for collecting information, thus placing less reliance on the memories and opinions of employees. In getting job information, it is important to emphasize that the analysis refers to the job and not the individual employee who holds the job.

After going over the questionnaires or upon the completion of his work sheets as a result of personal interviews, the job analyst studies records of performance and output and all other aspects of the job. He then prepares tentative job descriptions that are submitted to supervisory and management personnel under whom the jobs are performed for their review and approval. The approved job description describes the work involved in each job as well as the most suitable kind of worker for the job. It gives a great deal of detailed information about the job including the title of the job, the work performed, a description of the material or tools to be used, the qualifications necessary, the working conditions, amount and type of compensation, and opportunities for promotion. The minimum standards that are considered acceptable in employment for the job are contained in the job descriptions. A job description has to be carefully drawn so that workers do not get into arguments about which one is to do particular parts of a job.

The term *job specifications* is also widely used in personnel work and is also based on job analysis. The job specification gives a more detailed description of the personal characteristics required of the person to fill the job—his age; experience; skill and aptitudes; and perhaps physical requirements demanded for the job such as height, weight, and any other special requirement. It will also indicate the working conditions involved in the job. The "job spec," as it is sometimes called, is usually developed to facilitate the recruitment-and-selection function, since the information contained in it is necessary for determining what kind of people are needed.

Quite often, the job descriptions that have been assembled are improved by the use of time and motion studies. These studies use stop watches, or movie cameras, or other equipment in timing and studying in detail the motions of the worker in performing his task. This enables the job analyst to set up standards of performance for a particular job using the best techniques. From the facts that he has in the job descriptions and the time and motion studies, the job analyst can then figure the number of positions and the number of employees for each job. This is called a *manning table*. Also included in this table will be a breakdown of jobs in each department by title and number and the number of employees currently in each job.

Estimating Labor Needs for a Company

In some companies, it is only after a vacancy occurs that management will seek to secure a replacement. In other companies, the personnel manager cannot let production be interrupted by a vacancy. He needs to have a procedure established whereby he has a reserve of people who have been interviewed for various jobs and can be called to report for work on short notice. Essentially, the personnel department has to make an estimate of what future needs will be. This is not a simple thing to do because fluctuations in production can change manpower needs. However, the personnel manager finds that the forecasts of sales of the company are very helpful in estimating the amount of labor that will be required. Another source of help are the schedules established by the production department as to how much is expected to be produced in the near future. After the personnel manager determines what the total labor requirements are, he must determine the amount of skilled and unskilled labor needed to produce the goods for the stated period.

Labor Turnover

One of the problems confronting the personnel department is that of employees leaving the company, or the turnover of labor. Labor turnover is an indication of dissatisfaction or labor unrest, and it is, therefore, a subject of intensive study by the personnel department. Since the rate of labor turnover can be computed and expressed in percentage form or ratio form, it is possible to compare the labor turnover rates of various periods, past and present. Standard methods of computing the rate also make it possible for the personnel department to compare the company's rate with that of other companies in the same line of business.

Labor turnover rates may be computed in several ways. One is to use the *accession rate,* which is based on the number of employees hired during the month. Suppose that a company has an average of 1,200 employees during the month. The average figure is found by adding the number employed at the beginning of the month to the number employed at the end of the month and dividing by 2 to get an average. During the month, the company has hired 100 employees. The accession rate would be found by dividing the number of employees hired (100) by the average number of employees (1,200) and multiplying by 100:

$$\text{Accession rate} = \frac{100}{1,200} \times 100 = 8.33 \text{ per cent}$$

Another way of expressing labor turnover is by the number of employees who are separated from the company, that is, those who quit, are discharged, or are laid off during the month. This is called the *separation rate*. Suppose that there were 40 employees who had left during the month. The separation rate would be found by dividing the number of employees who left (40) by the average number for the month (1,200) and multiplying by 100:

$$\text{Separation rate} = \frac{40}{1,200} \times 100 = 3.33 \text{ per cent}$$

When the turnover rate is high, the personnel department tries to find out the reasons for the high rate and takes necessary steps to reduce the rate since a high turnover rate is costly to a company. The personnel department conducts interviews with employees who are leaving to find out the reasons for their separation from the company. An analysis is made of all the reasons that are causing the high turnover rate. Recommendations are then made to attempt to rectify the underlying factors.

The turnover rate varies among different types of workers. It is higher among unskilled employees than among skilled. On the other hand, it is lower among older employees than among younger employees since many older employees have built up retirement rights that they are reluctant to lose.

RECRUITING AND SELECTION OF PERSONNEL

Sources of Labor Supply

When the personnel department is filling vacancies, it may do so from among employees of the company. This is said to be an *internal source of labor* since it is within the company. If the personnel department goes to sources outside the company when it needs to fill positions, it is using *external sources*. Persons already working for the company are often selected to fill a vacancy. The transfer of the employee from one job to another can be made quickly, and the personnel department has a record of the employee's past achievements with the company that can be quickly evaluated. Too, there may be a policy of selecting people who are in the employ of the company to fill vacancies as part of the plan to build morale. Offsetting these advantages, however, are the possibilities that the person selected for the job may not be well qualified, and new ideas may be lacking when outside sources are seldom used.

Recruiting Personnel

In recruiting personnel, the number and types of jobs to be filled must be known. Other necessary information can be secured from the job descriptions of the particular openings to be filled. More applicants will be required than there are openings so that a selection of qualified people can be made. The departments of the company needing employees may file with the personnel department a requisition for personnel that indicates the basic information about the jobs and the kind of persons necessary to fill the jobs.

The most common type of recruiting is done by advertising, primarily in newspapers. Files are kept, also, of people who apply for work with the company; and when openings occur, these people may be called for interviews. There are some instances in which the labor agreement between the management of a company and the labor organization requires that the union be the first source of supply of labor. This means then that the personnel department would contact the union office, which would send out applicants for the job openings.

The type of job opening influences the type of recruiting that is undertaken. High schools and vocational schools are excellent sources of employees for many types of jobs. Many companies send recruiters to colleges and universities as well, to secure qualified candidates who have majored in fields of business administration, engineering, and others. To fill a vacancy in top or middle management, the personnel department may go to employment agencies specializing in top-management personnel; or someone working for a competitor or in a different line of business who is known to the management may be directly approached about the opening. There are other means of recruiting also, such as asking employees to suggest people with whom they have contacts or inquiring of fraternal organizatoins and even churches, and other business organizations.

Selection of Employees

After recruiting personnel, the next step is to select the individuals for the jobs. One of the first tasks involving selection is a preliminary interview. If an application blank has not been completed by the applicant, this is done. The application blank is designed to secure personal information such as age, marital status, physical characteristics, education, experience, and similar information. References are usually of two kinds: character references and work references. The latter are considered to be of greater value to the personnel department than the character references.

It is in the *interviewing* that most of the decisions are made whether or not to hire an applicant for a job. Many kinds of interviews and interviewing techniques are used in personnel management. One of the widely used methods is that of planned interviews. This means that the interviewer decides in advance the kind of information that he is seeking and how he will go about securing it. Research evidence indicates that the planned interview is the most effective approach. However, in general, the interview should be only one of the factors in selection.

After examining the application blank and interviewing the applicant, the personnel department checks the references that are given. It then interprets its findings and decides what candidates meet the requirements of the positions. Physical examinations are usually used in selection. Each applicant is asked to take one to insure that he is physically qualified before he is offered employment with the company.

The use of tests as a part of selection has become more and more common. In some companies, very heavy reliance is placed on test scores in the selection of personnel. In other companies, tests are used but they are looked upon as only one of the factors that assist in the selection of personnel. There are a number of different tests used that measure physical characteristics, skills, interests, and personality. Tests to measure skills are often referred to as *trade tests* or *performance tests*. Other tests may also measure the intelligence or mental ability of a person. Personality tests seek to measure the temperament of the individual and the amount of motivation he possesses. Although this is a difficult and complex thing to do, some indication is secured of what the individual will accomplish in his job. Many tests are standard and can be secured from testing services. Others are formulated by a company on the basis of its experience in testing.

Many personnel departments establish an *induction procedure* to be used when the applicant has been accepted for employment and is assigned to a job. He is taken to the place where he will be working in the company and introduced to fellow workers and supervisory personnel. One of the reasons for this orientation of the employee is to make him feel that others have an interest in him and in his adjustment to his new job. Every effort is made to ease this adjustment.

TRAINING OF EMPLOYEES

Shop Employees

Practically all companies give their employees training of some sort although they may not have formal training programs. New employees have to be trained for the jobs they fill and, in some instances, jobs change, which requires training of the employees so that they are able to perform the tasks. All employees should have training of some type, but the usual approach has been to establish training programs where the needs are the greatest. Some of the training is given by the personnel department; but, in other instances, it is performed in the departments in which the people are or will be working.

A number of different training methods are used. One of these is *on-the-job training*, which, as the name indicates, is training that takes place on the job in the company. In some on-the-job training programs, there will be additional classroom instruction for which employees are paid while they are learning. Larger business firms have sometimes established *vestibule training*. This is a course that is given prior to the actual performance of the job, but the training is performed in a room in which the working conditions are about the same as the shop or office conditions under which the employee will be working. In this type of training, the people being trained do not interfere with shop or office work as is the case with on-the-job training. There are about fifty trades and crafts in which the beginning worker must serve an apprenticeship or have apprenticeship training, that is, a period in service as an assistant to a qualified craftsman. Business firms and high schools sometimes institute a program of joint training, with the student attending school part of the time and working part of the time. This is called *internship training* and is a method by which students may study the principles in school and the practices on the job. Employees are often encouraged to take courses outside their company in order to give them a better background or to add to their knowledge of a particular subject. Some of these are vocational courses, evening school courses, and correspondence courses.

Supervisory Training

Another phase of training is that which is set up for supervisors by the personnel department. In general, these courses are designed to improve the supervisor's leadership qualities and his ability to handle labor grievances. This may be done on the job, but it is more commonly done in the classroom. Supervisory training programs are often of a conference type in which all the participants actively engage in a discussion of many subjects. During World War II, *training within industry* of supervisors was begun. It was widely used at that time and continues to be quite popular. The TWI program utilizes short courses in which the supervisors can acquire necessary skills in various fields through four ten-hour programs of job instruction, job methods, job relations, and program-development training. The instruction materials are supplied to industries for their use.

Management-Development Programs

Executive-training programs are used quite often in connection with bringing college graduates into a company. They are rotated through various departments and positions in the company in order that they may become familiar with policies, practices, and procedures. They are then assigned specific jobs but are "earmarked" for managerial positions. Executive-development programs often use a conference method of training. A conference leader guides discussion on actual problems that have confronted the company in the past or on hypothetical cases.

There is a growing amount of management-development programs being offered at universities of one-, two-, or four-weeks duration. They generally cover a particular area such as industrial relations or finance. Some are "refresher" courses, while others are intended to broaden the perspective of the participants and to develop new management concepts.

CHANGES IN EMPLOYMENT STATUS

Employee Rating

The personnel department frequently institutes a system of employee rating, or as it is sometimes termed *merit rating,* based on certain standards of job performance. This serves to assist supervisors in evaluating the work of employees under their supervision. Most of the rating of employees is that of shop or office employees and excludes executive and professional groups. While some rating of the latter groups is done, it is more difficult to establish standards to be used in rating. In many companies, employee rating serves as a basis for selecting individuals for promotion or for increases in wage rates. In small companies, there is no formal rating plan, but the employer rates employees in his own mind. When he promotes or raises salaries, he does so on the basis of the merit of the employees.

A typical rating form covers such items as the employee's influence on others, his ability to concentrate, acceptance of responsibility, quality of work, quantity of work, imagination, initiative, and organizing ability. There is some objection from employees and unions to a rating system that gives equal weight to each of the factors being considered—the feeling being that the quantity and quality of work should have greater value in the rating of an employee than some of the other factors. A rating system should be checked periodically to determine how accurately the ratings measure the factors they are supposed to rate. Since the human element is involved in rating, it is also recognized that some raters are much more generous than others. A successful rating program requires that the raters be completely familiar with all of the factors being rated and the purposes of the rating program.

Promotions

One of the most effective means of recognizing ability among workers is that of promotion. Promotion means higher pay, greater prestige or privileges, and greater responsibilities. Larger business organizations provide charts showing the steps in the promotion ladder. This enables the workers to see the avenue of promotion and serves as an incentive to achieve advancements. One of the methods of selection is through merit rating. However, the problem of seniority (the employee having the longest period of service to the company is said to have "seniority") has to be faced. Many labor contracts provide that seniority, in some form, is one of the elements that must be considered in determining eligibility for promotion. The employee with seniority often has the first chance at a promotion regardless of the fact that there may be others better qualified. Exceptions may be made in such contracts to promotions by seniority in the case of skilled workers or management personnel.

In trying to determine what employees are best qualified for promotion, the job descriptions and specifications are used. The records and reports of the personnel department concerning employees are also used in ascertaining the qualifications of employees. Although the personnel department assists other departments in establishing a promotion procedure, it does not promote people except in its own department. It is very helpful to all departments in any matter involving promotions and may be asked by other departments to advise on which employees should be promoted.

Transfers

Transfers are changes in which the pay and status of the new position are about the same as those of the old position. They may be necessitated because the workload in a department has been increased or decreased, and the affected employees are transferred to or from other jobs. These transfers are occasioned as a result of company operations. Another type of transfer may occur because of actions of the employee. Personnel problems may arise in the employee's work with others that reduce the effectiveness of the employee and possibly of others, or the employee might have been placed in a job to which he is unsuited, or his physical condition may require a transfer to some other type of work. There are many reasons for transfers, and the personnel department has to be prepared to transfer people as the need arises. With its knowledge of all the vacancies in a company, it is in a good position to work out transfers. The subject of transfers is often covered in the contract between labor and management, with provisions on how they will be carried out.

Separations

Separations include employees who quit, those who are laid off, and those who are fired. When an employee quits, the employee may lose a valued employee. Therefore, companies seek to determine why people leave. Is the compensation inadequate? Were there better offers from another employer? Was there dissatisfaction with the job? The answers to these questions can help management in establishing good personnel practices.

Employees are sometimes laid off because of reduced demand for a company's services or products. When this occurs, it is anticipated that they will be rehired when the conditions have changed for the better. There must be a plan developed for layoffs that takes into consideration any labor agreement provisions affecting this matter. Almost all layoff plans are based on seniority, with the employees having the least service in the company being laid off first. Layoff plans are well known by supervisors so that when the word comes to lay off a certain number of workers, the supervisors know exactly what workers will be laid off.

In order to avoid laying off skilled employees, companies sometimes seek to downgrade them and have them perform jobs for less pay and requiring less skill. If they accept the downgrading, it is usually because they feel it will be for only a short time. They are willing to put up with it, therefore, rather than seek a job with some other firm. Some companies reduce the hours of work for all employees rather than laying off any employees. This may enable the company to maintain all of its employees on a two- or three-day work week. Most employers try to minimize layoffs. It is an expensive bookkeeping procedure to lay off and later rehire people. During the period when these employees are out of work, some may find other jobs, which means selection and training of some new employees, which is additional expense.

Management may discharge employees because of violation of company rules or due to inefficiency in performing their jobs. This is often referred to as "involuntary separation." Where discharges are made because of matters of discipline, there may have been previous warnings issued. Disciplinary discharges may permit the discharged employee to appeal through a grievance procedure.

EMPLOYEE WELFARE AND SAFETY

Purpose of Welfare and Safety Programs

Employers are providing more and more services that contribute to employee welfare and safety. These programs are not a substitute for good personnel relations but supplement it. The purpose is to provide a safe and desirable place to work because this contributes to employee morale and to a stable labor force. The services that are provided by companies vary but cover such needs as insurance, housing, health services, safety measures, recreation, and food services. The tendency has been for employers to expand these services when it is hard to get and keep employees. For many years, employees and their unions argued that the costs of benefits should be paid to employees in wages, and these programs were looked upon by these groups as being paternalistic. The view of unions today is that those services that the majority feel they need should be provided by management.

Health and Safety Measures

Companies are providing medical services of various kinds to employees. A medical examination by company doctors is usually required in hiring personnel. This service may be extended to include annual physical examinations and periodic examinations for those who are engaged in any part of a company's operations that is considered hazardous. Medical and health records are maintained by the personnel department. In large business organizations, nurses and doctors are on duty so that accidents or illnesses that occur on the job can be treated immediately. As an additional service, some companies have extended a visiting nurse service to families of employees.

A medical unit is used in making regular surveys of plant conditions in order to insure that healthy working conditions prevail. Dust counts are taken where the amount of dust might be an occupational hazard. The amount of gases in the air is measured. Masks are required in certain kinds of work such as in spray painting, and ventilation is checked to see that a sufficient amount is provided. Other special surveys are made where conditions necessitate them.

Probably, there has been no other area of activity by management emphasized as much as that involving safety measures. The general improvement of safety standards on the part of companies has been due both to management's concern for employee safety while on the job and also to the cost of accidents. In spite of the efforts that have been made, the frequency and severity of accidents is still high in some industries such as coal mining, lumbering, and the construction industry.

The personnel department concentrates on two principal areas in connection with safety: (1) the employees, and (2) the mechanical facilities and workroom areas. Employees and their supervisors must be made safety conscious. An examination of the record of accidents of individuals shows that in every plant a few employees have more accidents than others. These people are referred to as *accident prone* because they are believed to be individuals who, despite efforts to train them, continue to have more accidents than their fellow employees. However, the importance of this phenomenon as a significant contributor to industrial accidents has recently been seriously questioned.

One of the most effective methods of improving safety is through training. Experience has shown that it is more effective to have safety training when a new worker is put on the job because he is in a more receptive frame of mind at that time. Lectures, demonstrations, and conferences are typical kinds of training activities. Widespread use is also made of bulletin boards to call attention of employees to necessary safety precautions. Safety rules are made for employees' protection, and there must be strict enforcement of them. Violations usually result in warnings or loss of pay. In the case of serious or continued violations, discharge may result.

The other area in safety programs, that of mechanical facilities and workroom areas, must be made as safe as possible. Many mechanical devices are used to protect employees such as those that prevent machines from operating when the worker's hands or arms are in danger zones. The areas have to be inspected to see that safety devices are used and that hazards are removed.

Insurance Programs

The safety and health programs are concerned with the physical well-being of the employees. The insurance plans and other security programs are concerned with their economic well-being. Insurance plans may cover losses due to death, illness, or accident and may provide for unemployment and retirement. Life insurance programs are very common. They provide coverage that is geared to the employee's annual earnings. A substantial part of the cost is borne by the employer and, at times, the complete cost. The employee does not have to take a physical examination to be eligible for the life insurance.

Insurance for illness and accidents wherever they occur is often provided by companies. In some of the plans, the family of the employee is also included. The employer and employees share the cost of some plans; but for other plans, the entire cost is borne by the company. The amount of surgical fees and the total amount of hospitalization expense that will be paid to an individual are limited to a stated maximum. There are state laws, called *Workmen's Compensation laws,* that provide for compensation of employees who are injured while at work. The employer pays for this special insurance. The amount of his premium is a percentage of his payroll and is adjusted to the claims made by his company against the insurance during the previous year and to the hazards of the business.

Unemployment compensation gives the worker a guarantee of at least a part of the wages he loses when he is out of work. This unemployment insurance, administered by the states, is provided by law under the Federal Social Security Act, passed in 1935, from funds paid by employers in the form of a payroll tax. In most states, the tax applies to employers with four or more employees; but in other states, all employers, regardless of the number of employees, are taxed. The tax rate is 3.1 per cent of each employee's wages up to $3,000, although proposals have been made in Congress to increase this amount. The benefits paid are determined by state legislation, and the maximum amount usually does not exceed 50 per cent of the employee's normal wage. The number of weeks for which benefits can be paid vary from fifteen to thirty, depending upon state laws. Employers who stabilize employment are taxed at a lower rate than those who have a high rate of unemployment.

Social security benefits pertaining to retirement are of particular significance to employees. Under the Social Security Act, the wage earner is eligible for retirement benefits at sixty-two years of age. Survivor benefits are payable to the insured's family regardless of the age of the wage earner at the time of his death. Disability benefits are available to the worker if he becomes totally disabled between the ages of fifty and sixty-five. There are also other forms of assistance under this Act. Over nineteen million people are drawing social security benefits.

These benefits are financed through taxes that are paid by the employee and the employer. The tax rate is collected on earnings up to $6,600 a year, and currently is 4.2 per cent for each. The rate for self-employed people is 6.15 per cent since their contribution is not matched by an employer. These rates are scheduled to be increased every few years until they reach, in 1987, 5.65 per cent each for employees and employers and 7.8 per cent for self-employed people. The employer collects the taxes and makes the payment to the government. The payment is credited to the account of each employee for whom the government has assigned a social security number.

Private *pension plans* in which the employer contributes the premium have been made a part of many of the contracts between management and labor as a result of union demands. There are over 20,000 of these plans in effect at the present time covering about five million employees. Some plans are jointly supported by employers and employees. Others are tied in with social security so that the combination of the two plans provides for retirement.

Recreational Services

Recreational services are provided by many companies. Such programs are undertaken because companies feel that provision of recreational facilities helps to maintain high morale among employees and thus justifies the cost of the programs. Basketball, volleyball, softball, and other activities are often provided. The company may participate in an industrial league with other companies. Musical groups and drama clubs, picnics, and dances are activities that are frequently sponsored.

Additional Services

Additional services are furnished by many companies to assist employees in satisfying many of their needs as conveniently as possible. A very common service is the operation of a company cafeteria. Often, companies operate mobile and automatic dispensing food units to serve employees who are located at some distance from the regular company cafeteria. Inexpensive meals are provided and, if the food service loses money, the company makes up the difference.

The encouragement of the formation of credit unions is another convenience for employees. A credit union is operated by employees with its officers chosen from their ranks. Employees invest in the credit union and receive interest on their savings. They may obtain loans at rates far below those charged by commercial loan companies. The company provides a place for the credit union to maintain its office and supplies equipment and clerical assistance.

Employers may also provide advice on a number of matters from the specialists on their staff. These include legal aid and help in completing income tax forms and citizenship papers.

YOUR CAREER IN PERSONNEL MANAGEMENT

Career Opportunities

The task of personnel management in trying to make the most effective use of manpower is one that offers many challenges and rewards. In industry, personnel management provides many different types of job possibilities. The recruiting and selection of employees is a field that appeals to many persons and in which there are numerous jobs. Many companies have training programs for employees that must be directed and administered. These are interesting and well-paying jobs since numerous companies have positions for directors of training. The handling of employee welfare and safety programs is another area in which there are good opportunities in personnel work. The welfare programs are an important part of the fringe benefits that are incorporated in labor agreements, and the job opportunities in this area have expanded rapidly. The student interested in personnel management may also find opportunities in job analysis and in making up job specifications and other phases of personnel work. The starting salaries in personnel management are about the same as those in other fields of specialized management, and college graduates usually find them to be attractive.

The federal and state governments have become very conscious of the importance of personnel management and are seeking to get qualified people. Although government positions may not pay as much initially, they offer a considerable amount of stability, and the retirement provisions of government work are quite good.

Educational Background

Students entering personnel management will find it advantageous to have a good background in human behavior. There are numerous psychology courses that are particularly helpful in this connection, and the student should take some of these courses. Of course, the courses in personnel management, industrial relations, industrial management, and labor legislation should be taken. In addition, courses in economics, and particularly labor economics, would be desirable. Since the compilation and analysis of data comprise a good deal of the work in personnel management, statistics is a course that should be included. For the person who wishes to specialize in the welfare aspects of personnel work, a course in insurance would provide valuable background for the various insurance and retirement programs. If there is time in a personnel management curriculum, a course in office management would be beneficial. Anyone who wishes to get into government work in management would find it worthwhile to take courses in political science as a means to a better understanding of the workings of our government.

TOPICS FOR DISCUSSION

1. Do you feel that psychology and sociology have contributed to the growth of personnel management in the last decade?

2. What are some of the available sources of manpower supply that a personnel manager could use to secure workers?

3. How would you distinguish between management development and training?

4. Discuss the line and staff duties in the management of personnel in the area of supervision. Use the personnel manager and the foreman in your discussion of these duties.

5. Do you feel that personnel management meets the criteria of a profession? Why?

6. How important should tests be in the selection process? What different types of tests are used? How should they be administered?

7. What are the different types of training that the personnel department may administer? How would it be possible to give an executive-training program that would benefit the company?

8. Seniority has long been an established basis for transfers and promotions in many companies. Is this sound personnel policy? If a company uses this as the basis for promotion, what personnel practices could you suggest that might encourage the most efficient work force?

9. What is the interest of the personnel department in the separation rate? What can the personnel department do to reduce this rate?

10. How important can employee welfare programs be in promoting employee satisfaction with his job? What is the trend in the development of such programs by management for its employees?

CASE 12–1

PERSONAL ADJUSTMENTS IN THE WORK SITUATION

A well-known personnel text (Walter Dill Scott *et al.*, *Personnel Management*, McGraw-Hill Book Co.) set forth the concept of the "worker in his work unit." The concept may be graphically illustrated as follows:

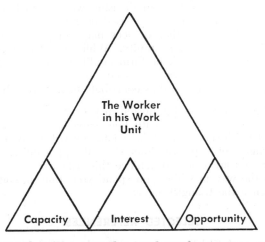

The large triangle represents the total work situation, or environment. The small triangles within the larger one represent the worker's *capacity,*

interest, and *opportunity.* If the worker is well adjusted and happy on the job, the three triangles are in balance—as shown in the above illustration. But if the triangles are not in balance, the worker is likely to be dissatisfied. For example, suppose the triangle representing capacity is small in relation to interest and opportunity. Here, we would find a person interested in the job, and the job would offer opportunity for growth and advancement, but the type of work would demand more ability than the individual possesses. Thus, he would be under a constant strain from attempting to carry out duties that are "over his head." Now, suppose the middle triangle is small in relation to the other two. Here, the individual would have the capacity to do the job, and the job would afford opportunity, but he would be doing something in which he has little or no interest. If the third triangle is small in relation to the other two, we find a situation in which the person has capacity, and he finds the work interesting, but there is no opportunity for advancement. In either of the three cases described, the individual is likely to become dissatisfied with his position.

It might be said that it is the job of the personnel administrator to see that people are placed in positions that will enable them to achieve a degree of balance among the factors of capacity, interest, and opportunity. This is a very difficult job to accomplish. Many people are not aware of the limitations on their capacity, or they may find it very difficult to face up to such limitations. Others have not been able to develop concrete interests; they may shift from position to position not knowing what they really want. To such people, the pasture is always greener on the other side of the fence. Then there are certain jobs that are, by their very nature, dead-end positions. Such jobs may require a person with considerable capacity, but not be able to offer much in the way of advancement. In each of these situations, the personnel specialist has a function to perform. In the first situation, he can help the man with limited capacity face the reality of the situation and make the necessary adjustments. He can work with the man who has not developed an area of interest and try to help such a person to find himself. Modern testing and counseling has application in this situation. In the third situation, the personnel specialist may help in devising ways of making the dead-end jobs more attractive. Wage increases based on seniority, fringe benefits, certificates of recognition, and other devices may compensate in some degree for the lack of advancement opportunity. While it is true that a person dissatisfied with his work may still perform creditably, it is generally held that a satisfied employee is the more preferred. It is thought that satisfied employees are more productive and thus contribute to the profitability of the firm.

1. As a student, are you well adjusted in your work unit? Are you following a course of study in keeping with your capacity? Your interest?

2. When you finish school and take a job, you will be concerned with balancing the triangles of capacity, interest, and opportunity. Have you any plans as to how you are going to achieve this balance?

3. How will the way in which you spend your time in college affect your capacity to balance the triangles later?

SELECTED REFERENCES

Beach, D. S. *Personnel: The Management of People at Work.* New York: The Macmillan Co., 1965.

Chruden, H. J., and A. W. Sherman, Jr. *Personnel Management.* 2d ed. Cincinnati: South-Western Publishing Co., 1963.

Flippo, E. B. *Principles of Personnel Management.* New York: McGraw-Hill Book Co., 1961.

French, W. *The Personnel Management Process: Human Resources Administration.* Boston: Houghton Mifflin Co., 1964.

Jucius, J. *Personnel Management.* 5th ed. Homewood, Ill.: Richard D. Irwin, Inc., 1963.

Pigors, P., and C. A. Myers. *Personnel Administration.* 5th ed. New York: McGraw-Hill Book Co., 1965.

Sartain, Aaron Q., and Alton W. Baker. *The Supervisor and His Job.* New York: McGraw-Hill Book Co., 1965.

Strauss, G., and L. R. Sayles. *Personnel: The Human Problems of Management.* Englewood Cliffs, N.J.: Prentice-Hall, Inc., 1960.

Voris, W. *The Management of Production.* New York: The Ronald Press Co., 1960. Chaps. 21 and 22.

Yoder, D. *Personnel Management and Industrial Relations.* 5th ed. Englewood Cliffs, N.J.: Prentice-Hall, Inc., 1962.

13

Wage and Salary Administration

THE IMPORTANCE OF WAGES AND SALARIES

The amount of compensation a person receives for his work is of vital importance to him. In addition, there are non-financial rewards that may also be motivating factors, such as recognition, privileges, promotion, security, and appreciation. The increasing use of behavioral science is helping management to obtain a better understanding of the causes of individual attitudes and of the relevant courses of action that are available to management. Why do employees react the way they do? What really motivates people?

Employers can motivate employees by the amount of wages or the system of payment that is used. The amount paid also affects the ease with which a company can recruit workers and its ability to retain them. A very difficult but important part of wage and salary administration is the establishment of levels of wages and salaries to be paid for different types of work and varying degrees of responsibility. Even the methods of payment and the frequency of payment are significant factors in the development of morale.

The personnel department is vitally concerned with the administration of wages and salaries from the standpoint of its own company and of other companies in the same employment area and in the same and competitive industries. Since wages and salaries represent a major cost to employers, the personnel department has the factor of cost to consider as well. The ability to control the costs of wages and salaries has a definite effect upon the financial condition of the company. In its advisory capacity to management, the personnel department has to weigh carefully the effect of the wage and salary level on employees and the effect of this level on over-all operating costs. In very large companies, the administration of wages and salaries may be handled by an industrial relations department, which is responsible for labor negotiations among other things. Computers are being increasingly used to handle such matters as payroll records. This not only facilitates the record-keeping aspects but also provides management with more complete data for analysis.

The administration of wages involving many employees is not merely a matter to be decided by the employer and the employees. Labor unions, in many instances, represent employees and, through agreements, a basic wage structure may be created. The personnel department has to work with any wage structure that is established in this way. It has the added responsibility of seeing that fair wage levels are established for employees who are not covered by the union agreement.

Employees who are paid on an hourly, or piece basis, are said to receive "wages." Other employees are said to be "salaried." The various aspects of wages will be considered first in this chapter.

THEORIES OF WAGES

The Subsistence Theory

A *wage theory* is a method of relating the various factors that affect wages. It is an explanation of why wages are as they are; that is, what conditions exist that cause wages to be as they are. There have been many different theories of wages advanced by economists since medieval times. One of the early theories was the *subsistence theory,* developed during the seventeenth century. This theory maintained that since food supply could not increase as rapidly as the population, the population would tend to sustain itself at that level that enabled it to subsist. If wages fell below the amount necessary for subsistence, not as much labor would be offered on the labor market; therefore, the wage level would rise. If, on the other hand, wages rose above the amount that was necessary for subsistence, more labor would be offered and wages would fall. In the short-run period, wages would be above or below the subsistence level; but in the long-run, the subsistence level would be the prevailing wage level. This was called the *iron law of wages* because wages under this theory tended to be inflexible. This theory did not recognize that the level of subsistence depended upon customs, habits, and standards; therefore, if the standards were to rise, the subsistence wage should also rise. The subsistence-wage theory was an explanation of wage conditions in a predominently agricultural economy.

The Wages-Fund Theory

Economists found numerous shortcomings in the subsistence theory, particularly the fact that, in the short run, wages would vary from the subsistence level. This led to the formulation of a *wages-fund theory* in the early part of the nineteenth century. This theory held that the amount of money that was available to pay wages at any time was determined by the amount of capital remaining in a fund made up of previously earned profits and savings after payment of rent and raw materials. Thus, it was maintained that if labor sought to secure higher wages at the expense of profits, the savings would be reduced and the amount going to rent and raw materials would have to be reduced. This theory was not considered to be valid because it did not recognize that employers balance labor costs against other costs, and that an increase in productivity could balance the increase in costs. The theory was in error also in assuming that the supply of labor is fixed and that wages had to come from past profits and savings without taking current production into account.

Marginal-Productivity Theory

The *marginal-productivity theory*, developed the latter part of the nineteenth century, is an accepted wage theory. It holds that employers will hire additional workers at any particular wage so long as the incremental (increasing) value in the total product resulting from the labor of each new worker hired is at least equal to his wage. In other words, the addition of a new worker must at least add sufficient units of production to pay his wages, in which case the employer will hire the worker. This theory is based on the assumption that there is *perfect competition* in the labor market. This means that there are as many buyers (employers who are hiring) as there are sellers (employees offering their services) so that no one person can affect the price of a unit of labor, that both buyers and sellers have a complete knowledge of market conditions, that the market is freely accessible to both buyers and sellers, and that the units of labor are standardized and homogeneous.

Under this theory, the element of competition will keep wage rates at the level of the value of the marginal product; that is, an employer will not pay more than that because to do so would mean lower total profits. On the other hand, if the employer tries to pay less than the value of the marginal product, the workers will shift to other firms paying higher rates. This is a theory that has wide acceptance but it has weaknesses. One of the weaknesses is that it assumes that there is perfect competition, and this is not characteristic of our economy. Another incorrect assumption is that we have full employment of all our resources.

Bargaining Theory

Because the marginal-productivity theory did not establish the actual wage set in any particular labor market, the *bargaining theory* of wages was formulated. Essentially, this theory holds that within a range of possible wages, the actual wage set by the employer depends upon the relative bargaining strength of the employees and employers. Wage rates tend to rise as individual bargaining is superseded by collective bargaining, since through unions the relative power of labor increases. The threat of strike (complete stoppage of work) or an actual strike by the employees who are union members will often raise wages even if other conditions do not merit the raise. Employers' strength increases as the size of the business firm grows and as employers establish trade associations (associations of business organizations). The bargaining theory is not a completely satisfactory explanation of how wages are set since there are unorganized industries (those that have no unions of employees) that have high wages. However, it does explain one phase of wage setting.

Factors Affecting Wage Determination

The representative theories just discussed provide a partial explanation of how wages are determined. There are many different factors, though, that affect the establishment of wages. Obviously, the demand for different classes of labor and the supply of different classes of labor will have an important role in determining wages. Other factors, such as the cost of living, the ease with which labor can move from one area to another, the prestige of a job, the ability of a business firm to pay wages, the state of business conditions (whether good or poor), and the amount of skill required for a job, are considered in the establishment of a wage.

WAGE STRUCTURES

Wage Levels

The general wage level of a company is an average of all the wage rates paid to the workers in the company. Wage levels can be established also for different jobs in the company. In order to prevent inequities from occurring in the wage level, the personnel department uses a number of different methods. One of these is to determine what "going wages" are, which means the amount being paid for the particular job in a given labor market. The information about the going wage is secured by a *wage survey*. In making this survey, key jobs in a company are selected and information secured on them rather than on all jobs. These are jobs that are common to the different industries being surveyed and ones that account for quite large numbers of employees in the company. Some companies, as a result of past wage surveys, have decided to exchange information on a voluntary basis each year. In some cases, the firms included in the survey are selected as being representative companies. The wage survey will then be on a sample basis since only some of the many companies are actually contacted. The jobs selected to be studied in the survey must be comparable in each company if the survey is to have any value. A job analysis can be used by the people making the survey to see what tasks are being performed and to make comparisons with similar jobs in the other companies.

The amount of information that is sought in a wage survey varies, depending upon the purposes of the survey and the number of companies included in the survey. It should include the base hourly rate for hourly workers; and, for those who are on an incentive type of wage, the wage rate used is that of the straight-time hourly earnings. The survey also secures the beginning rates at which people are hired. If jobs have a minimum and maximum rate, this information is secured because this is what is called a *structure rate*. Variations of individual wages within the range usually reflect tenure and merit considerations. Another item that is sought in the wage survey is that of wage changes. An employer is interested in the type of increase or decrease, whether it is in cents per hour or a flat percentage, and whether it applies to everyone or to a group of employees. Another item included in the survey covers wage practices involving fringe benefits such as sick leave, rest periods, pensions, and retirement funds. The wage-survey information can be secured by telephone, by mail, or by questionnaire. These surveys are sometimes conducted by unions.

Factors Affecting Wage Levels. After the wage survey has been completed and the data compiled, it is then used to check the wage structure of the company against those of other companies and to check rates for particular jobs against those being paid by other companies. If differences are discovered in the rates paid by the company, the personnel department tries to ascertain the reasons for the differences. The wage survey that gives the going wages is very helpful in setting the wage levels. Another factor that is considered in setting a wage level is existing legislation. Minimum wages of employees of organizations engaged in interstate commerce (business conducted in more than one state) were established in the Fair Labor Standards Act of 1938 and subsequent amendments. Another federal Act, the Walsh-Healey Act of 1936, makes it possible for the Secretary of Labor to fix the prevailing minimum wage in any industry that holds a government contract of more than $10,000. The effect of federal legislation establishing a minimum wage level is bringing those below the minimum wage up to that level. There have been occasions, such as during World War II and the Korean War, in which federal legislation authorized the President to issue a general order stabilizing prices, wages, and salaries. State legislation also influences wage levels since about half the states have minimum wage laws applying to women employees.

The level of wages and salaries are also affected by the bargaining of unions with management and union wage scales. An employer who does not have union members working for him may equal or exceed the union scale as a means of avoiding unionization of his employees. If we assume that the union scale is higher than the non-union scale, such action on the part of a non-union employer shows the effect of unionization on the wage level of his employees. To an employer whose employees are unionized, the wage scales used by the union in their bargaining are an important factor in the determination of the wage level that will be maintained in his company. During times of prosperity, some national labor contracts covering a particular industry establish wage patterns that are followed by other industries, both union and nonunion. For example, the labor contract settlement in the steel industry has often set the pattern for settlements in other industries.

Another element in wage-level administration is the attitude of company management on the proper wage level to be maintained. Even if company management has the ability to raise the wage level, management must have the willingness to do so since it will raise the costs of operation and affect the profits of the company unless there is an increase in productivity or unless savings can be made in some way to offset the increase in wages and salaries. The adequacy of the labor force is another factor that is considered since management recognizes that the wage level has to be sufficiently high to attract and maintain an adequate labor force.

Job Evaluation

One of the problems in the administration of wages and salaries is to devise a fair and equitable wage structure, that is, the amounts that will be paid for the various jobs in the organization. Job evaluation is the first step in building a wage structure. It tries to measure the comparative value of jobs within a business organization or among similar business organizations. The particular duties that are performed in a job and the importance of the job to the organization are considered. Job evaluation does not place a price on a job but rather seeks to determine the value of that job in relation to other jobs in the organization. As is true in employee rating, the objectivity of the rater has a great deal of influence in the outcome of the evaluation.

Job evaluation first requires that an analysis be made of the jobs in a company. This covers the duties and responsibilities of the job and the employee requirements to perform the job successfully. With this information, an analysis is made of the factors that cause one job to be at a higher level than another. These factors are called *compensable factors*. The next step in job evaluation is that of using a system to appraise jobs in the company according to the compensable factors chosen to measure the jobs. One system is the *point system*, which assigns points to each of the job elements, with varying weight given to the elements. The wage structure is then established with rates given for all the jobs.

TYPES OF WAGE PAYMENTS

Time Wages

The method of wage payment may be that of paying the employee for the time he spends on the job or for the amount of work that he does. Sometimes, combinations of these two methods are used. The most common method is paying *time wages;* that is, rates are paid on a time basis—per hour, per day, or per week—and do not vary with individual output. They are sometimes called *non-incentive plans* because they do not result in larger earnings regardless of how hard employees work during a given time period. Time wages are relatively easy to determine. The average hourly and weekly earnings of workers in various fields are shown in Figure 13–1.

An amount that is called *premium pay* is often added to the basic wage. This has become quite common for certain types of work. For example, a higher amount is paid for the night shift from 4:00 P.M. until 12:00 midnight and still higher amounts for the "graveyard shift" from 12:00 midnight to 8:00 A.M. This is often called a *shift differential* and is usually about 10 per cent or more above day-shift work. A higher amount is also paid for overtime work beyond the normal work week, which is ordinarily forty hours, and a higher amount, too, for holiday work and work on week ends.

AVERAGE HOURLY EARNINGS   AVERAGE WEEKLY EARNINGS

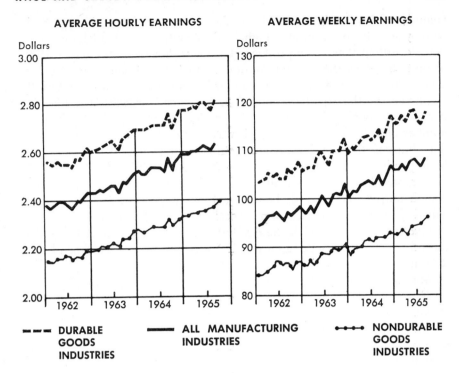

DURABLE
GOODS
INDUSTRIES

ALL MANUFACTURING
INDUSTRIES

NONDURABLE
GOODS
INDUSTRIES

Fig. 13–1. The average hourly and weekly earnings of production workers and other workers (U.S. Department of Labor, Council of Economic Advisers).

Output or Incentive Wages

Output wages are those in which pay depends upon the output of the worker, or on factors related to output. They are sometimes called *incentive wages*. Where the flow of work is regular and the job is standardized, output wages are used in many plants. The best known and most extensively used of the incentive or output wage plans is payment on a *piecework rate*. Under this plan, an employee gets a specified amount for each item that he produces. If he gets 5¢ for each unit and produces two hundred units a day, he receives $10.00. If he can increase the amount he is producing to three hundred a day, he will make $15.00. The more he produces, the more he makes. Piece rates are set for each job by making a time study to see how long it takes to perform each job. A rate is then set that will allow the employee to earn a good day's pay.

The piece rate has sometimes been modified by guaranteeing a minimum hourly amount. The *Taylor Differential Piecework Plan*, developed by Frederick Taylor, is another piecework plan. Under it, the employees who perform at a high level of output are paid higher rates per piece than those who produce at a lower level. A standard number of units is set as the amount considered to be minimum for a job, and a lower piece rate is paid if the standard number is not produced by the employee. If the standard number is produced or exceeded, the rate per piece is increased on all the units produced. Suppose that a standard number of units for a particular job was fifty units. If the employee produced any number of units less than fifty, his rate would be 5¢ per unit. If he produced fifty units or more, on the other hand, his rate would be higher, say 6¢ per unit, for all the units he produced. This encourages a high output and rewards better workers. Plans of this type are also called *production bonus plans.* Another type of bonus is the *nonproduction bonus* in which the employee is given a bonus at the end of the year. This is something on which the employee cannot depend since it is not a definite part of his wage or salary.

Another wage incentive plan is the *Halsey Premium Plan,* developed by F. A. Halsey. This plan establishes a standard time, generally based on past production records, that is allotted to complete a piece of work or job. Those employees who take the amount of time that is set as the standard time are paid a wage equal to the time rate for the time actually spent performing the task. If the job is completed in less than the standard time, however, the employee is paid his time rate for the amount of time he actually took, plus a bonus based on his time rate for the time he saved. The bonus is usually set so that the employee gets from one-third to two-thirds of the time he saves, but the most common percentage is 50 per cent. The employer's share is the other 50 per cent. For example, suppose that the employee's hourly rate is $2.00, and the standard time for a particular task is established at five hours. If the task is completed in three hours, he would be paid $6.00 for the three hours he worked. Assuming that his bonus is on a 50-50 sharing basis, he would get a bonus of $2.00, making a total of $8.00 for three hours' work, or $2.66⅔ an hour.

The *Gantt Plan,* developed by H. L. Gantt, is called a *task and bonus system.* The employee, under this plan, is guaranteed his time rate for output below a standard, based upon a time study for the particular task. If the worker reaches the standard, a bonus of 20 per cent or more is provided. If his output exceeds the standard, high piece rates are paid on the excess. As can be seen, this is somewhat similar to Taylor's plan but differs in that it is a time-saving bonus plan. As compared to the Halsey plan, it pays a much higher bonus for reaching or surpassing the time standard. There are other piecework plans, but these are representative ones.

Profit-Sharing Plans

Profit sharing is another wage-payment method used by some companies. This is an arrangement whereby the employees receive a share of the profits, the exact percentage being determined in advance before the profits are known. The actual payment is usually in cash as the profits are earned. A certain amount is set aside for company needs and then a percentage is allocated to the employees. This is known as a *current-distribution plan*. There is another profit-sharing plan, known as the *deferred-distribution plan*. Under this plan, the distribution of profits is deferred until retirement, disability, death, or other termination of employment. This type has grown very rapidly during the past twenty years.

The amount allocated to labor in a profit-sharing plan is generally divided according to seniority of employees: those with five years or more getting a full share; and those under five years getting a part of a share, depending upon the length of time they have been employed.

Another type of plan is called a *wage-dividend plan*. Profits are divided between employees and stockholders according to an established formula. This plan provides that whenever the annual dividend on common stock exceeds a certain amount, like 70¢ a share, a wage dividend is declared. This type of plan is designed to show that employees and stockholders have the same interests in the profitable operations of a company.

Employee Stock Ownership

Some companies have provided a means by which employees can purchase shares of stock in the company under an arrangement that constitutes a form of wage payment. For example, employees are given the opportunity regularly to buy stock in the company, the price of which may be 85 per cent of the closing market price on the day that the stock is offered to them. They are given a maximum number of days, such as twenty days, in which to decide whether or not to purchase the stock. If the employee purchases the stock, he is saving 15 per cent of the price of the stock through the purchase plan. The motive of the plan is to give employees a greater stake in the company and to identify them more closely with its ownership.

Guaranteed Annual Wages

Some companies have sought to provide an assured income on a year-round basis. This is felt to be a method by which the anxiety related to lack of income because of production fluctuations can be eliminated.

One of the best-known guaranteed wage plans is that of George A. Hormel & Company. Under this plan, each employee is paid his full wage for a thirty-eight-hour work week. During some weeks, the employees will not work thirty-eight hours, but in other weeks they may work more than forty hours without payment for overtime. Labor organizations have, from time to time, proposed the guaranteed wage on an industry-wide basis, especially during the early 1950's. There have been some instances in which the guaranteed wage has become a part of the agreement between management and labor. The Ford Motor Company, in its agreement in 1955 with the United Auto Workers, agreed that the company would make a 5¢ an hour contribution for each hour worked by the hourly rated employees to a trust fund out of which supplementary payments would be made to laid-off employees who had at least one year's seniority. This agreement provides a 60-65 per cent guarantee of weekly straight-time earnings for half a year, and differs from the guaranteed annual wage since it guarantees a certain income for a stated period of unemployment.

Fringe Benefits

For many years, there have been a number of different payments made to employees that are supplementary to the direct-wage payment. These supplementary payments became common during World War II when wages were controlled as a part of wage and price stabilization at that time. Labor organizations sought increased fringe benefits, and this practice became widespread and continues as a part of our national wage structure. Sometimes these payments are extra payments for time that is worked, such as a premium for working on a holiday or on a week end. In other instances, they are payments for time not worked. Examples of this are pay for rest periods, lunch periods, cleanup time and many others. Some of the fringe payments are in the nature of providing employee security in which the company pays all or a part of life insurance, accident insurance, and hospitalization. Other benefits include loan aids, provision of recreation facilities, and low-cost meals.

The cost of fringe payments has increased rapidly, until now it is estimated that it amounts to approximately 20 per cent of the payroll. There are companies that have reported fringe costs of 50 per cent of their payroll, which did not include premium pay for night, overtime, and holiday work.

Payment of Management Personnel

The salaries of management personnel are paid on a biweekly basis. Supervisor's pay is from 5 to 35 per cent higher than that of the workers they supervise. The salaries of middle-management personnel are higher than those of supervisory personnel but by no stated percentage. Top management salaries are supplemented by many other benefits. Some of these are of an incentive type to motivate management personnel to their best efforts. The option to buy stock at substantially less than the market value is a typical type of incentive. The example that follows was taken from a report to stockholders in 1966 of a large corporation. The officers had been permitted to acquire their shares of stock after October 1, 1963. The president acquired 2,000 shares at $25.18 a share, whereas the market price on the stock at the time of acquisition was $76. The value of the stock he acquired was over $100,000 more than he was required to pay for it. The other officers of the company exercised their options to buy, and their stock was also worth substantially more than the amount that they had paid, as follows:

Name	Shares Acquired	Acquisition Price Per Share	Market Price Per Share
President	2,000	$25.18	$76.00
Executive Vice-President ..	548	44.94	86.63
Vice-President	570	25.18	78.38
Treasurer	{ 1,000	{ 25.18	{ 63.75
	{ 1,000	{ 25.18	{ 71.75
	{ 781	{ 25.18	{ 80.75

Some companies provide automobiles, expense accounts, payment of club dues and memberships in organizations, and large pension and insurance funds. With our income tax structure as it is, the take-home pay of an executive may be a relatively small part of his total salary. Company management tries to devise ways to pay management supplementary benefits that will not be subject to high taxes as salaries are. In the example that follows, the president of a corporation received a gross income of over $161,000, but after deduction of federal income tax his net income was $79,258.88. To make the position more attractive and give him benefits that are not taxable as current income, the corporation has provided that if he continues in his present position until his normal retirement date at age sixty-five, he will receive a retirement of $36,939 annually. As can be seen in the table on the next page, the retirement plans for some of the other officers are also very desirable.

Another kind of incentive used by some companies for their executives is that of *deferred compensation*. This is a method of increasing a key executive's pay in the future rather than in the present. The purpose is to provide a way through which, after retirement, the executive continues to receive pay from the company as a reward for past services rendered. The deferred compensation is at a reduced amount, such as

Capacities in Which Remuneration Was Received	Aggregate Remuneration (Salary, Supplemental Compensation and Directors' Fees)	Approximate Net Remuneration after Deduction of Federal Income Tax Applicable to the Remuneration Received (Assuming 2 Dependents)	Estimated Annual Benefits upon Retirement
President and director of the corporation	$161,749.96	$79,258.88	$36,937.00
Vice-president and director of the corporation	66,633.21	42,619.61	17,784.00
Vice-president and director of the corporation	77,549.92	47,547.46	28,160.00
Vice-president, treasurer, and director of the corporation	88,562.00	52,228.04	20,987.00
Vice-president and director of the corporation	92,800.00	53,980.00	30,203.00
Vice-president and director of the corporation	99,500.00	56,660.00	14,974.00

one-half or one-fourth of the salary he received during his active years. Deferred pay can be given in addition to a current increase in pay if the company wants to do so.

YOUR CAREER IN WAGE AND SALARY ADMINISTRATION

Career Opportunities

There are many good career opportunities in wage and salary administration. Most industrial firms have personnel who deal with this aspect of personnel management. Specialists in this field may handle incentive plans for wage earners, such as the establishment of piece-rate pay. The scale of pay for different jobs is a vital part of the wage structure. Since labor contracts include the various scales of pay, there is a need for people who are interested and qualified for this work. Much of the other technical information included in wage contracts is also prepared by experts in wages and salaries. Job evaluation is one of the phases of wage and salary administration that pays well and is an important part of this field.

Unions also employ specialists who work in wage and salary administration. They compile statistics and compare wages between business organizations. They prepare suggested changes in the level of wages. The government, too, has a great deal of interest in wage and salary administration both as it affects industry in management-labor relations and as it applies to positions in the government. The agencies that administer the laws involving labor have openings in this area, and the Civil Service Commission has positions dealing with wage administration for government employees. Other opportunities are found in trade associations that compile data concerning wage structures for their industry members.

Educational Background

Some students who want to specialize in wage and salary administration will pursue courses in business administration and will major in personnel, industrial management, or production management. Others may enroll in a College of Engineering and major in industrial engineering. There are many college courses that give a student a good background in wage administration. A course in industrial relations is beneficial in supplying the student with a better understanding of the importance of good industrial relations and how they can be accomplished. A number of other courses should be taken in labor, including labor legislation and collective bargaining. A course in statistics would be very desirable. A course in production analysis study is of benefit since many of the incentive-wage systems are geared to productivity. An understanding of production management and industrial management is helpful in this work. Some universities encourage business-administration students to take certain courses in engineering, which would be of help to them.

TOPICS FOR DISCUSSION

1. What are some of the major influences affecting the wage levels for workers and for a business firm as a whole?

2. How often should organizations conduct wage surveys?

3. Would centralized control of wage and salary administration be good company policy? Why?

4. Do you feel that wages mean more to men or women, older people or younger people, married or single people?

5. From an employee's point of view, which incentive-pay plan would you favor—Gantt or Halsey? Why?

6. Many union contracts contain an escalator clause so that with an increase in the cost of living, employees automatically receive an increase in hourly pay. Under these circumstances, how can labor costs be estimated for a six- or nine-month period in advance as may be necessary in bidding on a contract that the company hopes to secure?

7. Fringe benefits have been growing rapidly during the past decade. Ascertain how important this cost is in total labor cost in a company or industry.

8. What types of salary incentives are often offered to top management?

9. What is the first step in developing an equitable wage structure? Who usually performs this job?

10. What are some of the common problems encountered in the use of profit-sharing plans?

CASE 13–1

THE BECKER MANUFACTURING COMPANY

The Becker Manufacturing Company, which produced a line of office supplies, was an old, established firm and enjoyed an excellent reputation for quality and service. Beginning in the early 1950's, the company began experiencing difficulty in maintaining satisfactory levels of production. By the early 1960's, it was customary for the production departments to fall short of the quotas established. Studies by an outside consultant affirmed that the quotas were realistically set. The consultant blamed poor performance on a somewhat higher than normal rate of turnover in labor, and on what he described as a "prevailing sense of disinterest" on the part of many employees.

The Becker Company paid its workers wages that were competitive for the area in which the plant was located. Fringe benefits offered were significant, although less than those offered by certain of the larger firms in the community. Labor relations of the firm and its 500 employees were thought to be reasonably good. The employees had voted in a union in the mid-1950's but, after five years, had voted to abandon the union. Management had not greeted the union with enthusiasm but had not fought the issue. The labor-turnover problem was blamed on the fact that many young workers in the area resigned from jobs in local industries to migrate to metropolitan areas where wages were higher.

In exploration of methods to improve production, two suggestions were given serious consideration. One suggestion was for the company to adopt an incentive method of wage payment. Throughout its history, the Becker firm had paid hourly rates to production workers. These were straight hourly rates that were in no way dependent on productivity. It was suggested that the firm adopt some version of a "piece-rate" system in which wages would be directly based on productivity. Certain of the company executives opposed such a system, pointing out that the highly diversified nature of the jobs to be performed would make it difficult to establish and administer the plan. They also felt that employees would resent a wage plan of this type and that labor turnover would be further aggravated.

The other suggestion was for the company to adopt a profit-sharing plan. Under such a plan, the company would distribute a bonus at the end of the year, the size of the bonus depending on the financial success of the firm. It was felt that, if production levels could be raised, sales would increase in proportion, and, since the plant was not used to full capacity at present, there would be a spreading of overhead costs and increased profits. The pros and cons of a profit-sharing plan were discussed among the company officials. Those favoring the plan based their primary argument on the contention that the plan would provide incentive to improve production, that it would not be unduly difficult to administer, and that the cost of the plan would come out of added profits and would thus not impose a great risk for the company.

Those opposing a profit-sharing plan contended that it would not provide a strong incentive, since the reward for extra effort was a delayed one, and one on which there was uncertainty. They feared that, if workers received bonuses for one year and did not receive them the next, there would be a sharp decline in morale. It was also argued that, if workers received extra pay under profit sharing for several years consecutively, they would come to take the extra income for granted and thus any effect as an incentive would be lost.

Do you feel that the Becker Company might benefit from a profit-sharing plan? Give the advantages and limitations of such a plan.

SELECTED REFERENCES

Belcher, David W. *Wage and Salary Administration.* 2d ed. Englewood Cliffs, N.J.: Prentice-Hall, Inc., 1962.

Langsner, A., and H. G. Zollitsch. *Wage and Salary Administration.* Cincinnati: South-Western Publishing Co., 1961.

Lovejoy, L. C. *Wage and Salary Administration.* New York: The Ronald Press Co., 1959.

Patton, J. A., C. L. Littlefield, and S. A. Self. *Job Evaluation: Text and Cases.* 3d ed. Homewood, Ill.: Richard D. Irwin, Inc., 1964.

Toedt, T. A., L. C. Lovejoy, R. M. Story, and D. Shainin. *Managing Manpower in the Industrial Environment.* Dubuque, Iowa: W. C. Brown Co., 1962.

Voris, W. *The Management of Production.* New York: The Ronald Press Co., 1960.

14

Management and Organized Labor

EXPANSION OF OUR LABOR FORCE

Our labor force has greatly expanded with the economic growth of our country. There were about 74 million workers employed in 1965, and the United States Department of Labor estimates that this force will increase by 1975 to 94 million. This does not include those in military service (currently 2.5 million), nor does it include the unemployed, estimated at 4 per cent of the labor force. It is interesting in this connection to note that a prediction made less than twenty years ago of a labor force in the future of 60 million was ridiculed at that time as being far more than the number that would actually find employment.

More and more of the jobs in the future will require education and training both of non-production workers (white collar) and of production workers (blue collar). One of the most dramatic occupational shifts in the expansion of our economy has been the growth of employment in service industries. Far more workers are engaged in furnishing services and fewer produce goods, as shown in Figure 14–1. This is a sign of our steadily rising standard of living. To some extent, the ability we have to enjoy services such as travel, recreation, and better medical care is a reflection of our progress in raising productivity in goods-producing activities.

It is expected that in the future, 45 per cent of all jobs will be white collar, 36 per cent will be blue collar, and the remainder of the labor

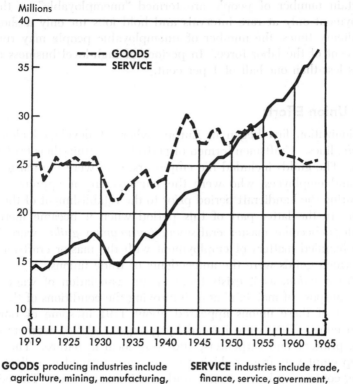

GOODS producing industries include agriculture, mining, manufacturing, and construction.

SERVICE industries include trade, finance, service, government, transportation, and public utilities.

Fig. 14–1. Employment in goods-producing industries as compared with employment in service industries (U.S. Department of Labor).

force will be in farming and miscellaneous activities, according to the U.S. Department of Labor. White-collar personnel has increased with expanded clerical, sales, and supervisory personnel and with the employment of professional and technical workers. This growth gives a degree of stability to employment. In each of our three recessions since the end of World War II, non-production employment was maintained, with the bulk of unemployment concentrated among production workers.

As hours for the worker have been shortened, an increasing number of persons have held two or more jobs. These people are often called "moonlighters." A special study made in 1964 by the Department of Labor showed that 5 per cent of the total people employed, approximately 3.7 million persons, had two or more jobs at that time.

Not everyone who desires a job, however, finds employment. Since 1946, unemployment has averaged about 4½ per cent of the labor force.

A certain number of people are termed "unemployable" as they find employment only at rare intervals and hold jobs for only a short time. In ordinary times, the number of unemployable people may run about 1 per cent of the labor force. In periods of high-level business activity, it runs less than one-half of 1 per cent.

Early Union Efforts

Unionization first began in Europe where it developed along *craft*, or *trade*, lines. Craftsmen formed organizations within their trades called guilds. The guilds included the employers, who were the master craftsmen, and employees, who were the journeymen, or apprentices. This was during the handicraft period prior to the establishment of the factory system. In the latter part of this period when it became increasingly difficult to become master craftsmen, *journeymen guilds* were formed, which handled matters of employment with the master craftsmen. The journeymen guilds were the antecedents of trade unions.

A *trade union,* as it exists today, is an association of wage earners for the purpose of maintaining or improving the conditions of their work. The first of these unions appeared about 1791 in some of our larger eastern cities. They were formed by groups of skilled workers such as tailors, printers, and carpenters, and were local in nature. They sought to keep employers from reducing wages and engaged in collective bargaining concerning hours, wages, and working conditions. The economic pressure used by the workers was the threat of strike, or the strike, when their demands were not satisfactorily met. However, many employers refused to bargain with them and brought in strike breakers to replace the striking workers. These unions, being local in nature, were often not strong enough to survive during adverse conditions.

Early efforts to link local unions into a national organization were not successful. During the period from 1852 until after the Civil War, however, national trade unions were successfully established on a single-trade basis. The rise of national unions during this period was due in part to the broadening of markets. Employers' associations had also been formed by this time, and the unions felt they could better meet the challenge of these organizations by organizing on a national scale. Some of the national unions formed during the latter stages of the Civil War sought to create organizations that would tie together different trades. At that time, there was a membership of about 300,000 in trade unions.

The end of the Civil War brought an increased amount of industrialization. With improved transportation and widening markets, labor organizations intensified their efforts to add to their membership. There were many conflicts between management and labor, which reached a peak in 1877. At that time, the railroads proposed to reduce wages, and there was strong resistance by the workers to this proposal. This disagreement led to considerable violence, with rioting by the workers and the use of strike breakers by railroad management. Federal troops were ordered in to restore order, but substantial property damage resulted. The violence of this incident and others produced a wave of reaction against unions that was reflected in the enactment of state laws and in court actions opposing union growth.

The Knights of Labor had been formed by the garment cutters in 1869. This union was not along trade lines but organized men and women of every craft, creed, and color among skilled and unskilled workers on a nation-wide basis. After the turn of the century, the union declined and was dissolved in 1917, following a number of unsuccessful strikes. It was not able to support such a diverse membership in time of need.

NATIONAL AND INTERNATIONAL LABOR ORGANIZATIONS

American Federation of Labor

The American Federation of Labor was formed in 1886 as an outgrowth of a union formed in 1881 by carpenters and printers. It was organized as a voluntary federation of craft unions. The membership of the A.F. of L. grew steadily until it became one of the dominant labor organizations. It now consists of *international unions,* which is a term used in describing a union having local branches or members outside the United States—usually in Canada. In most instances, these international unions have a local organization, which is the organization the worker joins. There are international unions for the different trades such as the metal trades. Although the A.F. of L. originally was an association of craft unions, it permitted *industrial unions* to begin affiliating with it in 1901. Industrial unions take in all workers in an industry—skilled and unskilled.

Railway Operating Brotherhoods

The railway labor movement has consisted of strong organizations since its beginning. Employees who operated trains, such as firemen, engineers, and conductors, formed unions, or brotherhoods as they called them, that embraced all the employees of a particular craft, such as railroad engineers. These organizations began more in the nature of fraternal organizations rather than trade unions as we think of them today. Their activities gradually changed to those of trade unions. The Brotherhood of Locomotive Engineers was formed in 1863, the Order of Railway Conductors in 1869, the Brotherhood of Locomotive Firemen and Enginemen in 1863, and the Brotherhood of Railway Trainmen in 1883. These operating brotherhoods are national unions.

A number of other nationwide organizations made up exclusively of railroad workers were formed in the early 1900's, such as railroad signalmen, dining-car employees, station employees, and others. They are non-operating unions, which represent their members.

Industrial Workers of the World

In 1905, a group of workers formed the Industrial Workers of the World, which favored direct action by means of strikes, restricted output, and other methods of harassing employers. Its membership was based on an industrial unionization approach, but it was never very successful. Its aggressive actions produced very great public hostility toward it. Although it continued to exist after World War I, its membership declined and it became relatively unimportant.

Congress of Industrial Organizations

During the 1920's, the expansion of mass-production techniques reduced the relative importance of skilled work in many productive processes. Furthermore, the mass-production industries, such as automobile and steel, had not engaged in collective bargaining with labor organizations. There were large numbers of industrial workers who were not members of any labor organization. The depression of the early 1930's, resulting in widespread unemployment, caused a further reduction in union membership in these and other industries. The passage of the National Labor Relations Act in 1935 stated that the public policy of the United States is to encourage and facilitate collective bargaining through unions in which employees select representatives of their own choice. It defined the rights of employees to organize and prohibited certain actions on the part of employers that were defined as "unfair labor practices."

A substantial growth of craft unions occurred following the enactment of this legislation. Industrial unionism also experienced a tremendous expansion. Dissatisfied with the A.F. of L.'s efforts to organize semiskilled and unskilled employees, eight national unions that were affiliated with the A.F. of L. formed a Committee for Industrial Organization. This group was joined by several newly formed organizations and initiated a campaign to organize the mass-production industries. Their organizing efforts were especially successful in the steel, rubber, and automobile industries. In 1938, the informal organization was changed to the Congress of Industrial Organizations, which is a federation of unions. The C.I.O. became a rival of the A.F. of L., and its membership increased very rapidly. These two organizations accounted for four-fifths of all the employees who were members of labor organizations. For a number of years, there were many organizational and jurisdictional disputes between these two federated unions. In 1955, the two groups were merged and are now called the AFL-CIO.

Independent Unions

Currently, there are some independent unions both international and national, that is, unions that are not affiliated with the AFL-CIO. Some of them were members of the C.I.O. or A.F. of L. at one time but left voluntarily or were expelled. The largest and best known of these independent unions are the United Mine Workers, the International Brotherhood of Teamsters, and the Operating Railroad Brotherhoods. Another group of independent unions is often referred to as *company unions*. This is a union whose membership is usually limited to the employees of a single plant or company. Originally, they were dominated by management. Since the enactment of the National Labor Relations Act, however, the company union must be completely free of the employer's influence in order to be lawful.

ORGANIZATIONAL STRUCTURE OF UNIONS

Local Unions

The basic unit in most labor organizations is the local union. The local holds regular meetings, collects dues, disciplines members, and administers its funds. It elects its officers annually and establishes its committees. The president, assisted by an executive board composed of the rest of the elected officers, has charge of the local organization. The important actions or decisions of the officers usually require approval of the membership. If the local union is affiliated with a national or international union, as is usually the case, its activities must be within the scope defined by the Constitution of the international or national union. Local unions are supported by monthly dues and fees that may be assessed for specific purposes. A few unions in the highly skilled trades have very high initiation fees, sometimes as high as $250, thereby limiting the number of workers who enter the trade. A portion of the dues and fees collected by locals is remitted to the national or international union with which the local is affiliated. In the larger locals, an official devotes all his time to the business of the union and is paid a regular salary. Locals usually undertake collective bargaining and work to secure new members. The locals call strikes if they feel it necessary in order to accomplish their demands, although the calling of a strike may require approval of the international. They also handle the workers' grievances.

International or National Unions

The international or national unions usually issue charters to the unions that are affiliated with them. The fact that the charters can be withdrawn gives the international or national some control over the actions of local unions. A convention consisting of a representative body of the locals is held by the international or national unions at intervals from one to five years. At these meetings, policies are determined, and the international officers and executive board are elected. Unlike local unions, the elected officials of the international or national unions are generally in office for a long period of time. The international union usually controls strike funds and will participate in the administration of health and welfare trust funds, as well as any other benefit funds the unions have so that it has a good deal of control over the locals.

The AFL-CIO Organization

The AFL-CIO organization is a federation of international and national unions. Its total membership is about fifteen million. An organization chart of this union organization is shown in Figure 14–2. There are about 130 unions that are voluntary members, or nearly 85 per cent of the total union membership. The AFL-CIO also organizes local unions where none exist. When there are enough of these unions in related trades, the AFL-CIO establishes a national union. A number of departments have been established in the AFL-CIO organization in order that the affiliated unions can work out jurisdictional disputes and other problems that may arise. Each of these departments has established local councils, whose purpose is to integrate the affairs of member locals in the affected trades within a locality. In many of our metropolitan areas, local unions of the various internationals have formed a "city central." These are sometimes called "trades and labor assembly" or "industrial council." They often become active in politics by endorsing certain candidates.

The executive officers who are elected every two years at the convention by a majority vote consist of the president, secretary-treasurer, and twenty-seven vice-presidents. The executive council is the govern-

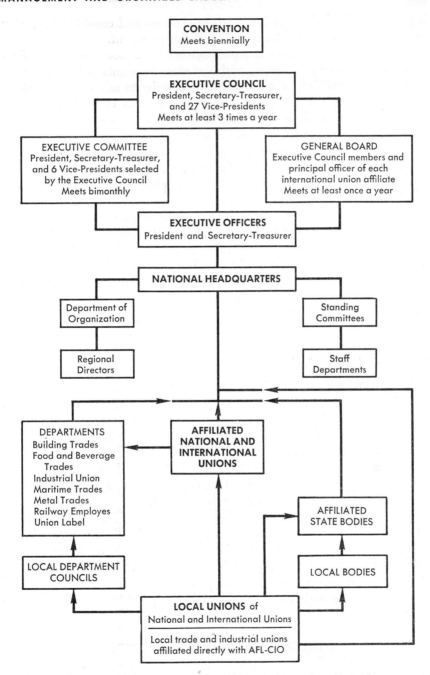

Fig. 14–2. The organizational structure of the AFL-CIO (U.S. Department of Labor, Bureau of Labor Statistics).

ing body of the federation between conventions and consists of the vice-presidents, the secretary-treasurer, and the president. It meets at least three times a year. There is an executive committee comprised of the president, secretary-treasurer, and six vice-presidents selected by the executive council that meets every two months to advise the president and secretary-treasurer on policy matters. A great deal of the work is carried on by committees that are set up under the Constitution. Some of these are concerned with legislation, political education, ethical practices, education, social security, research, and economic policy.

Each of the states has a state federation of labor that is chartered by the AFL-CIO. Their principal activity is lobbying in connection with legislation and educational activities.

The AFL-CIO has been critical at times of the actions of its member unions and has appeared to exercise more control over its members than when they were separate organizations. The organization is constantly watching for practices that might develop in its member unions or their officers that would be detrimental to the reputation of the AFL-CIO or might jeopardize public acceptance of the labor movement. Its income is secured from a monthly per capita tax of 7¢ per member per month on each affiliated national and international union.

Employers' Associations

Employers' associations have been performing various functions for their members for many years, such as research, lobbying, providing information, and advertising. With the rise of unionism, they very often have added labor negotiations to their responsibilities. Some were specifically formed for this purpose. An important reason for this is to provide a united front in negotiations. Unions with nationwide membership have frequently sought to negotiate industry-wide contracts, which almost requires an employer association.

An employers' association may be local in nature, such as that formed by general building contractors in a city to deal with employees in the building trades—carpenters, plumbers, electricians, and others. Where unions have city centrals, industry has formed a parallel employers' association. A few associations have gone beyond the negotiation aspect of labor agreements and engage in day-to-day administration of the agreements.

COLLECTIVE BARGAINING OF UNIONS

Nature of Collective Bargaining

There are many cases of companies that have several groups of employees organized on a craft basis. This may mean that the employer will negotiate with two or as many as ten different unions. Under these circumstances, unions sometimes get together and negotiate a joint contract. Much of the early collective bargaining was concerned with wages and hours. Although this is still of paramount importance in labor negotiations, unions are interested in all phases of company operations.

Pattern bargaining is often followed in collective bargaining. The agreement reached with one company sets the pattern for the agreement with others. As a result, there is a good deal of uniformity in contracts. Contracts are written for one year or longer. The trend in recent years has been to longer contracts, from three to five years. When longer contracts are entered into, certain provisions of the agreement cannot be reopened until the end of the second year of the contract.

Major Union Objectives in Collective Bargaining

There are many things that unions seek to achieve through collective bargaining. The major objectives of unions, though, are: (1) recognition of the union and union security, (2) higher wages and shorter hours, (3) improved working conditions, and (4) adjustment of grievances.

A union has to secure *recognition* from the employer in order for the union to represent the employees. Our federal and state laws require certain employers to bargain with representatives of their workers under certain conditions. When recognition has been secured, the union seeks to insure *union security* so that the membership will support the union program. One type of union security is the *closed shop*. Under the provisions of the closed shop, the employer must hire union members to fill the vacancies in his plant. The union, in effect, becomes the supplier of labor. The closed shop was forbidden in 1947 where interstate commerce is involved by the provisions of the Labor-Management Relations Act. The *union shop*, another type of union security, is one in which the employer may hire any employee; but, after working for a probationary period of usually thirty days, the employee must join the union. In some instances, the employees who were on the job at the time a union shop agreement became effective are permitted to decide whether or not they want to join the union. However, all new workers are required to join. The *preferential shop* is one in which union members are given preference in the hiring. In addition, when there are layoffs of employees, the union members are given preference in re-employment. Another form of union security is *maintenance of membership shop*. Under an agreement of this kind, all employees who are union members at the time the agreement is signed must continue in good standing in the union for the duration of the contract. The *open shop* is the one in which there is the least union security. Both union and non-union men are employed, but union membership is not required for employment. A plant in which there is an open shop may or may not have a collective-bargaining agreement with a labor organization. In the event the union workers do not constitute a majority of all the workers, the employer can still deal with the union but as the representative of its members only.

Union security is also advanced by use of the *check off* of union dues. Under this arrangement, the employer deducts the dues from workers' wages and gives them to the union. The terms of some agreements require that the worker must authorize the deduction before the employer can make it. In other agreements, only those members who are in arrears in their dues are subject to the check off. A study made by the United States Bureau of Labor Statistics covering major contracts showed that 77 per cent of the workers under these contracts were subject to check-off provisions.

Seniority is another aspect of union security. Under seniority, the employee with the longest service is given preference in promotions, transfers, the choice of shifts, choice of vacations, and in layoffs.

Higher Wages and Improved Working Conditions. Historically, higher wages and shorter hours are high on the list of union aims. During recent years when living costs have been rising, many unions have negotiated contracts in which they have attempted to maintain th purchasing power of wages by including *escalator clauses*, giving automatic increases generally proportionate to the rise in consumer prices. Most such agreements provide that for every 0.5 of a point increase in the Consumer Price Index, the wage rate increases by 1¢ an hour. The Consumer Price Index is prepared by the Bureau of Labor Statistics and is designed to measure the change in the cost of a "market basket" of goods and services as bought by single persons and a city family of moderate income. It is based on 400 items that are priced in fifty cities. Each price is multiplied by a weight representing its importance in family budgets, and the sum is the cost of the "market basket." This sum is expressed as a percentage of the average cost of the basket in 1960–1961.

Unions have also pressed for productivity increases in order to permit their members to share in the productivity of the company. The term "productivity" refers to output per man-hour of labor employed. The unions maintain that employees should share in any profits from increased productivity and that this would result in added purchasing power and greater demand for the products and services of industry. When labor seeks to share in productivity increases, it should be pointed out that the labor factor is not the only factor influencing productivity. There are also a number of non-labor factors that influence productivity such as the degree of technology, the vigor of management, the quality of business organization and management, the savings and investment that provide tools and equipment that make the individual worker more productive, our free competitive institutions, and the actions and policies of the government that affect our economic and material resources.

The President of the United States, in his economic report in January, 1962, provided for price-wage guideposts that his administration felt would help avoid inflation. The guideposts were designed for evaluating those price and wage decisions where the public has an interest in their content and consequences. They do not replace the normal process of collective bargaining.

The general guidepost for wages states that, in a particular firm or industry, the appropriate non-inflationary standard for annual percentage increases in total employee compensation per man-hour (not just in straight-time hourly rates) is the annual increase in national trend output per man-hour. It must be a national trend and would not apply to a single industry or to a single year.

The general guidepost for prices specifies that, when an industry's trend productivity is growing less rapidly than the national trend, prices can rise enough to accommodate the labor-cost increases indicated by the general wage guidepost. Similarly, in an industry whose trend productivity is growing more rapidly than the national average, product prices should be lowered enough to distribute to the industry's customers the labor-cost savings it would make under the general wage guidepost.

The guideposts are not mandatory but are being emphasized by the President as representing recommended guidelines.

The improvement of working conditions has always been of concern to unions. In their bargaining, they have sought to improve these conditions through the collective agreement. Bargaining in regard to this factor has become secondary to other matters in recent years.

Adjustment of Grievances. A grievance is a written complaint filed by an employee who claims that he has been treated unfairly. Collective bargaining includes provisions for adjustment of grievances that arise during the life of the contract. The agreement usually establishes procedures to be followed when questions arise concerning interpretation of the agreement or dissatisfaction among workers. The worker who has a grievance presents it in writing to the union shop steward, a worker in the plant who acts as the union representative. If the matter cannot be resolved by him and the foreman, the shop steward takes it to a special grievance committee of higher management and union representatives. A panel of top employer and union officials is the next step in the procedure if the special grievance committee is not able to handle the matter. If this is unsuccessful, the matter is taken to arbitration where an outside arbiter decides the issue.

Union Methods of Securing Demands

The economic weapon most widely used by unions when they feel it necessary in order to secure their demands is the *strike* or *walkout*. This is a basic right of free workers. There are certain employees who, it is felt, give up their right to strike when they take particular jobs, such as federal employees, members of the police forces, and members of the armed forces.

Certain kinds of strikes are outlawed, such as the *sitdown strike* in which the workers refuse to leave the plant and the *slowdown strike*, in which workers deliberately slow down in the amount that they produce. The *sympathy strike* is one in which the workers have no grievance against their employer but are merely expressing support for other workers who are out on strike. Courts have often found such strikes to be illegal.

Another technique used by unions is that of *picketing*. This is a method used by which the public is notified that there is a labor dispute between the management and employees of the plant. It is used to support strikes and to organize employees. Union members with signs on their backs walk back and forth at the entrance to a business that is being picketed. This is often called peaceful picketing. Ordinarily, union members will not cross a picket line of any union organization. Mass picketing, in which there are so many pickets that it is virtually impossible to get into or out of a place of business, has generally been considered to be illegal. Where mass picketing is used, violence often results.

Boycotts are another method used by unions in labor disputes. This is a refusal by union members to deal with someone until he changes the practice to which the union members are objecting. Unions urge members to refuse to buy the products of the employer with whom they have a dispute. Primary boycotts are those in which the local members of a union refuse to buy things produced by an employer with whom they have a dispute. These boycotts are generally not very effective. The secondary boycott is an effort by the union to have an employer refuse to deal with another party against whom the union has a grievance. Secondary boycotts have usually been considered to be illegal.

The Union Attitude Toward Technological Changes

Constant improvements are being made in our technology. Many inventions and technological advances have an adverse effect upon individual groups of workers. Management has sought, where feasible, to introduce the technique of making a process or system automatic, which is termed *automation*. This has particular application in mass-production industries and in the performance of routine clerical functions. Unions have been fearful that machines will replace great numbers of workers. The union attitude toward automation has varied among unions. Some try to cooperate with employers in introducing new machines and automatic processes and to have the workers operate the new machines. Where the process displaces workers, they have tried to have the machines introduced slowly and have the employer pay sufficient separation pay to provide for the worker while he is seeking other employment. Other unions have tried to block the introduction of new techniques. Still other unions have encouraged the employer to reduce wages sufficiently to eliminate the need for changes. Over a short period of time, opposition to technological advances may be successful, but experience shows that in a competitive economy such as ours the advantages of technological changes are so great that adjustments have to be made to permit their use. Furthermore, while technological changes may displace a certain group of workers, they often create jobs for other workers. Automation has developed to an increased degree through the years, and yet we have an increasing number of people employed.

Featherbedding

A practice that has developed to some extent in many industries is that of featherbedding, or make-work practices. The term is said to have originated in the railroad industry about fifty years ago when some railroaders complained of the corncob-filled mattresses they had in the cabooses on the freight trains. After hearing of their complaint, one of their superiors is said to have remarked: "What do they want— featherbeds?" Since that time, the term has been used to describe the spreading out of work to make jobs. Featherbedding practices are especially prevalent in the printing and railroad industries where there has been a decline in the demand for the service of skilled workers.

There are many different forms of featherbedding. As examples, painters establish the maximum width of brush that can be used, or the minimum number of workers required in a work crew will be a larger number than necessary under modern conditions. Another example is that of a union requiring certain work to be done or redone locally so that it provides work for local employees.

Extent of Union Membership

Union membership during the present century showed a gradual increase until the 1920's. After the passage of the National Labor Relations Act of 1935 (which was generally favorable to labor and is explained later in the chapter), there was a very sharp increase in union membership. This growth continued during the 1940's but slowed down during the last decade. For the first time in two decades, there was a decline in union membership in 1957 and 1958. By 1965, approximately eighteen million workers were members of national and international unions. This is about 20 per cent of the total number of employed people in the United States and about 30 per cent of the total when agricultural employees are not included, as shown in Figure 14–3. In addition, unions confining their activities to a single employer or a single locality account for about 500,000 more union members. The percentage relationship of union members to the total number of people employed in industries other than agriculture has changed very little since 1945.

The sharp rise that occurred after the passage of the National Labor Relations Act in 1935, as shown in Figure 14–3, was due not only to the passage of the Act, which assured the right of collective bargaining, but also to the increasing spread of industrial unionization that embraced many mass producing industries such as the automobile, steel, and farm machinery industries. In recent years, it has become more difficult to organize workers because of the cost involved in such organization. More and more of our workers have shifted from the production of goods to the provision of services. Almost three-fifths of the labor force are engaged in service activities such as trade, finance, recreation, and transportation. When unions are organizing workers in mass-production industries, they are working with vast numbers of people in a limited area. The cost per capita of organizing them is relatively low because of the large number of workers and the high percentage that will join the union. The situation is quite different in organizing employees in service industries. The people are harder to organize; the groups of workers are smaller and spread over a wide area. The cost of organizing these workers is very high.

There are about 74,000 local unions in the United States that are members of 181 national and international unions. About 43 per cent

Fig. 14–3. Union membership as a percentage of the total labor force and of employees in non-agricultural activities, 1930–62 (U.S. Department of Labor).

of total union membership is in ten of the large national or international unions. There are approximately 140,000 collective-bargaining agreements in effect at the present time.

MANAGEMENT AND COLLECTIVE BARGAINING

Management Methods

Management opposition to the organized-labor movement was in evidence at the beginning of the union drives to organize. Many managements did not even recognize unions as representing employees. They felt that it was satisfactory to bargain individually with employees. In order to prevent employees from joining unions many years ago, employers frequently made use of what were termed by unions to be *yellow-dog contracts.* Under such a contract, the employee agreed, as a condition of employment, not to become a member of a union as long as he was on the payroll. Federal legislation in 1932 made these contracts illegal.

There have been instances when employers have refused to admit workers to their jobs. This is called a *lockout.* It has not been used very often by management, but there is no legal reason why they could not do so if they liked. For management to take this action, though, would mean that a very tense and unpleasant situation existed between management and its employees.

Extensively used at one time, but now illegal, was the *blacklist.* This was a method by which an employer would notify other employers about particular persons, usually active union leaders, so that it would be virtually impossible for the workers to secure jobs. The blacklist was often secret and hard to control.

Injunctions are sometimes used by employers in labor disputes. An injunction is a restraining order issued by a court and, when used by management or the government in labor disputes, is generally to prevent certain union action, such as striking or picketing. The injunction was used a great deal by management in the early days of union organizing but has had only limited use in the last thirty years. In certain labor disputes, the federal government can secure injunctions under the Labor Management Relations Act of 1947 (the Taft-Hartley Act), which is discussed later in the chapter.

Preparations for Collective Bargaining

Historically, unions are the ones that make the demands, and employers have tended to wait and see what the union proposes. Unfortunately, this has often resulted in management being wholly unprepared for negotiations. If adequate preparations for negotiations had been made, it is entirely possible that management would have had some major demands to make to the unions. Most collective agreements require that either party that proposes changes in the agreement must notify the other party of the nature of the proposals sixty days before the termination date of the agreement in force.

The preparation for negotiations should be made well in advance of the expiration of the contract, and some companies have made preparations for negotiations a continuous, year-round program. The preparation includes the assembling of necessary data, the objectives that are to be sought, provision for analysis of economic data, and the methods of briefing the bargaining committee. In smaller companies, the president is often a member of management's bargaining team; but, in companies with over 5,000 employees, he is rarely on a bargaining team. Experts in labor relations and executives in personnel management are the usual members of the team. One member is chosen as the chief spokesman. In order to insure a united front, the chief spokesman does most of the talking and often the others speak only with his permission.

Collective-Bargaining Methods

Many companies put all of the information relating to negotiations into a book known as a *bargaining book*. The book will contain the clauses in the existing contract. If a change is proposed, it will be placed beside the existing clause, and a third column may be used to state the reason for the proposed change. This makes for more orderly bargaining. If both union and management make use of a bargaining book, each clause can be considered in order. If it is impossible to agree on one clause, this can be noted in the bargaining book and the discussion can move on to another clause, returning later to the unresolved clause or clauses. Following each clause, there is sufficient space to insert a chronological account of the discussions about the clause. Stenographic records or machine-recorded records are not usually made of the bargaining sessions because of the feeling that this would inhibit discussion. However, upon the completion of each session, each of the parties will record the general discussion as it is recalled.

When agreement is reached, the parties call in a secretary who records drafts of the contract clauses to which they have agreed. Each of the parties will go over the drafts and make such corrections as they feel necessary. The final agreement is then prepared and signed.

Unions and Antitrust Provisions

Since unions are voluntary associations, they have maintained that they do not hold monopolistic control of the labor supply. They have strongly opposed the application of antitrust regulations to their activities. They feel that since negotiation of wages is done for individuals who can think and act for themselves, labor cannot be considered to be a commodity on which a price can be set. The Sherman Anti-Trust Act applies in connection with setting a price on a commodity. On the other hand, many people believe that unions are a form of monopoly and should be subject to the antitrust laws as a business monopoly. Although unions are subject to some degree of regulation as explained later, there has been no legislation enacted to require that they be regulated under the antitrust provisions.

THE GOVERNMENT'S ROLE IN MANAGEMENT-LABOR RELATIONSHIPS

Railway Labor Legislation

Broad government regulation of collective bargaining did not materialize until 1935, except in the case of the railroad industry. As early as 1888, Congress passed a law regarding the adjustment of labor disputes between railroad management and their employees when the threat of work stoppage would interrupt interstate commerce. A number of subsequent acts dealt with railway labor and, in 1926, the Railway Labor Act was passed. This is still applicable to railway labor and, since 1936, has applied to airline labor as well. This Act creates a procedure for the settlement of labor disputes in the fields of rail and, later, air transportation in order to avoid interruption in essential transportation service. The Act provides also for the creation of the National Mediation Board, composed of three members, which attempts to mediate disputes before a strike develops.

Under the Act, the procedure established requires that a conference be held first between the disputants. If this is not successful in producing a settlement, they can seek the mediation services of the National Mediation Board, which tries to get the parties to settle the differences. Should this prove to be impossible, the Board can propose arbitration of the dispute. The recommendation of the arbiters is binding upon both parties if they agree to arbitration. However, the parties do not have to agree to this action. If they refuse, the Board can notify the President of the United States of this fact. The President may appoint an Emergency Fact Finding Board to make recommendations if, in his opinion, the threatened strike would create a national emergency. During the thirty-day period in which the Emergency Board meets and for thirty days thereafter, the terms and conditions of employment cannot be changed by either management or labor. The recommendations of the Emergency Board, however, are not binding on either party. It is felt that the force of public opinion would be strong enough to cause the parties to accept the Emergency Fact Finding Board's recommendations, but this has not always been the case.

The Railway Labor Act also provides for the creation of a National Railroad Adjustment Board of thirty-six members divided equally between management and labor. This Board handles the settlement of grievances and interpretation of existing contracts for railroads but not for airlines. If the Board is unable to agree, a neutral referee is appointed when necessary. The decisions of this Board are final and legally binding upon employers.

In spite of the elaborate and detailed procedure that has been established by law, we have had several strikes in rail transportation in the last twenty years. These have lasted for but a short time because the railroads were taken over and operated by the federal government until an agreement was reached between management and labor after which the government relinquished control.

The National Labor Relations Act

During World War I, the federal government established procedures to encourage collective bargaining. In 1935, the National Labor Relations Act was passed. Under this law, employees were encouraged to organize unions, and employers could not interfere with their efforts to organize. The Act outlawed specific employer unfair labor practices, such as refusing to bargain collectively with representatives of employees. The National Labor Relations Board was created to administer the provisions of the Act and to insure the right of employees to bargain collectively.

The Labor-Management Relations Act

After the National Labor Relations Act had been in operation for a time, employers and other groups felt that the Act favored unions and sought to eliminate or modify its provisions. In 1947, the Labor-Management Relations Act (called the Taft-Hartley Act for the two men who sponsored it) was passed. Whereas the National Labor Relations Act listed unfair labor practices of employers, the Taft-Hartley Act listed unfair labor practices of unions, such as coercing employers or employees, charging excessive initiation fees, or practicing featherbedding. The Act brought about a greater degree of balance in the position of the federal government in regard to collective bargaining. The right to collective bargaining was unchanged as well as the right of employees to join unions of their own choice. However, both employers and unions have to recognize one another's rights under law, and both parties must observe the rights of individual employees and the general public, as well as other provisions.

The Act established a procedure requiring a cooling-off period when strikes threaten national health and safety. If such a dispute threatens to develop into a strike or a lockout and there is a labor contract between management and labor, sixty days' notice has to be given by the party that desires to change or terminate the conditions of employment. During this cooling-off period, the Federal Mediation and Conciliation Service (created by this Act) can try to bring the two parties to an agreement. At the end of the period, if there has been no agreement, the employees can go on strike. If the dispute is one in which the cessation of production might result in a national emergency by jeopardizing the national health and welfare, a Board of Inquiry can be appointed by the President to investigate and report the facts. If the President, on the basis of this report, decides the strike affects national health and safety, he can direct the Attorney General of the United States to ask a United States Court for an injunction to stop the strike. The workers must go back to work for eighty days if the injunction is granted. It is hoped that during that time the parties will reach an agreement. The injunction is not used unless a strike actually threatens national health or safety. A dock workers' strike in 1959 that threatened the tieup of ships at East Coast ports caused the President to invoke the emergency Taft-Hartley provision within five days after the strike began; whereas, the steel strike in the same year went on for almost three months before the President sought an injunction to end the strike under the Taft-Hartley Act.

The Labor-Management Reporting and Disclosure Act of 1959

After the passage of the Taft-Hartley Act, which unions refer to as the "slave labor act," efforts were made to modify the Act both by management and by labor groups. Very few amendments, though, were made to the Act. Extensive Congressional hearings were held over a period of several years that brought to the public's attention practices of labor and management that were detrimental to the public's interest. There was considerable evidence of infiltration of union ranks by racketeers and of employers paying off individuals to avoid work stoppages. It was shown that some labor leaders had used union funds for their personal expenses and, in some unions, there was little or no accounting of union funds. As a result of these disclosures, there was a strong move to enact corrective legislation. After a bitter legislative battle, the Labor-Management Reporting and Disclosure Act of 1959 was passed, which was the first major labor legislation since the Taft-Hartley Act of 1947 was enacted. This Act provides for the reporting and disclosure of certain transactions of labor organizations and employers. All unions have to file annual detailed financial reports with the Secretary of Labor. The employer must also report to the Secretary any instances in which he makes payments or loans to unions or union officials and employees. It establishes a Bill of Rights for union members so that all of them have equal rights to nominate candidates, vote, and attend membership meetings. An employment ban is placed on Communists and convicts holding office in, or being in the employ of, a labor union for a period of five years after termination of Communist Party membership or after the conviction of crimes or after release from prison. It also contains provisions having to do with union elections, boycotts, organizational picketing, and others.

The Federal Mediation and Conciliation Service

The federal government provides mediation facilities for other than rail and airline disputes through the Federal Mediation and Conciliation Service, which was reconstituted under the Taft-Hartley Act. This government agency is set up to encourage the settlement of labor disputes through collective bargaining by mediating labor disputes that involve interstate commerce. If its mediation efforts are not successful, it tries to get the parties to use arbitration. A party that desires to modify or terminate a collective agreement must notify the Mediation Service of its intentions sixty days before the expiration of the contract.

State Legislation

Since 1937, a number of states have enacted legislation applicable to labor relations and collective bargaining within the state. A number of them have patterned their state laws after the National Labor Relations Act. These state laws encourage free collective bargaining and seek to reduce the conflict between employers and unions. They list unfair employer practices such as domination of unions, interference with unions, blacklisting, and discrimination due to union activity. Some of them also indicate unfair union practices such as forcing employees to join unions, breaking labor contracts, and intimidating employees. In some states, agencies or boards have been created with a number of duties. Since 1959, these agencies can take jurisdiction over any case involving a labor dispute that is rejected by the National Labor Relations Board. The Board had not assumed jurisdiction over many of the small labor disputes because of inadequate staff and funds.

YOUR CAREER IN INDUSTRIAL RELATIONS

Career Opportunities

In larger business organizations, the industrial relations function is very often set up in a department that is separate from personnel management. The field of labor relations has become of sufficient importance and is so time consuming that a group of specialists often handle these matters. Accordingly, there are many opportunities in this field. Business organizations hire lawyers, economists, statisticians, and persons who have majored in personnel or industrial-relations work. The labor contracts are often in such detail that it is necessary to have management personnel serving on grievance committees to interpret the contracts, and so there are good job possibilities in the administering of contracts. These are staff positions.

There are also opportunities with labor organizations, although there is a tendency in some of these organizations to rely primarily upon individuals who are members of the organizations. Labor organizations hire statisticians, economists, and lawyers and pay them very good salaries. With the growth and importance of organized labor, the number of jobs in this field has steadily increased. The government offers career opportunities in industrial relations as there are many positions in government that deal with some aspect of labor relations. There are people who handle arbitration and mediation matters, and the administration of labor laws that Congress has passed is handled by agencies of the government, such as the National Labor Relations Board.

Educational Background

The importance of understanding human relations cannot be overemphasized for those who are preparing themselves for careers in industrial relations. Courses in psychology and sociology should be included. A course in labor legislation will provide a background of the laws that affect collective bargaining. Since bargaining must be within the framework of law, a course of this type is necessary for those who want to enter this field. Courses in industrial relations and labor economics enable a student to understand the historical development, wage theories, the labor movement, and the process of collective bargaining. A course that would be beneficial to the person interested in labor relations is time and motion study, for this is often a problem in negotiations due to the differing attitudes concerning it on the part of the parties to the negotiation. The advantages and limitations of time and motion studies should be understood by the student who plans to enter the field of industrial relations. Industrial management and business policies are courses that provide a good background of sound management principles and the formulation and execution of business policies. Those persons who are particularly interested in the legal aspects of industrial relations often go on to study law.

TOPICS FOR DISCUSSION

1. The union is viewed as a power organization. Where does the power originate in the union?

2. Are unions in the United States democratic?

3. List some union and management goals in collective bargaining?

4. What is the key function of the union shop steward?

5. Will government wage-price guidelines lessen the role of union negotiators in collective bargaining in the basic industries? Justify your answer.

6. Why does labor usually present its "demands" to management and not vice versa?

7. Do you feel a labor organization can become too powerful?

8. Why have more white-collar workers not been organized?

9. Can you give any examples of "make-work" rules? Can they be justified? Why would management agree to them?

10. Is there any evidence that you can cite to show that the effects of collective bargaining extend beyond the parties involved? How can the unorganized benefit from such bargaining?

CASE 14–1

INTERVENTION OF THE PRESIDENCY IN LABOR-MANAGEMENT DISPUTES

In the summer of 1965, labor-management negotiations in the steel industry were deadlocked over a contract. The strike deadline was approaching, and federal mediators reported that no prospects for a settlement were in sight. At this stage of the development, the President of the United States called representatives from both sides to conferences in Washington. It was reported that the President, attending these conferences in person, had "suggested" to each side certain guidelines to agreement. Immediately after the conferences in Washington, agreement was reached on a contract and a strike was averted. The action of the President in bringing the power of the presidency to bear on the negotiations was both applauded and condemned. The following are the opposing views that were frequently stated:

Favoring intervention—

The President has an obligation to protect the welfare of the economy. A prolonged steel strike could have been damaging to the health of the economy, as industries other than the steel industry would have been directly affected. The public should not be made to pay the cost of labor-management conflict in a basic industry such as steel. The President is the representative of the people, and he did right in using his influence to encourage a settlement.

Opposing intervention—

The action of the President was a major step toward the death of free collective bargaining in the United States. Once a pattern of intervention is established, every major strike will require such intervention before a settlement is reached. If a presidential administration has a reputation of being partial to organized labor, the unions will always hold out for intervention, feeling that the power of the presidency will operate in their behalf. Conversely, if an administration is partial to management, the companies will all hold out for intervention, feeling that a better settlement will result. Under these circumstances, the settlement of labor-management conflicts becomes more of a political matter than an economic matter. It may be very dangerous to lose sight of the economic factors involved.

Do you feel that a president should apply pressure to settle major strikes? If so, how far should he go in applying this pressure?

SELECTED REFERENCES

Beal, E. F., and E. D. Wickersham. *The Practice of Collective Bargaining.* Rev. ed. Homewood, Ill.: Richard D. Irwin, Inc., 1963.

Bloom, G. F., and H. R. Northrup. *Economics of Labor Relations.* 4th ed. Homewood, Ill.: Richard D. Irwin, Inc., 1961.

Davey, H. W. *Contemporary Collective Bargaining.* 2d ed. Englewood Cliffs, N.J.: Prentice-Hall, Inc., 1959.

Dunlop, J. T. *Industrial Relations Systems.* New York: Henry Holt & Co., Inc., 1958.

Gregory, C. O. *Labor and The Law.* 2d ed. New York: W. W. Norton & Co., Inc., 1961.

Harbison, F. H., and J. R. Coleman. *Goals and Strategy in Collective Bargaining.* New York: Harper & Bros., 1951.

Lester, R. A. *Economics of Labor.* 2d ed. New York: The Macmillan Co., 1964.

National Industrial Conference Board, Inc. *Preparing for Collective Bargaining.* New York: National Industrial Conference Board, Inc., 1959.

Reynolds, L. G. *Labor Economics and Labor Relations.* 3d ed. Englewood Cliffs, N.J.: Prentice-Hall, Inc., 1959.

Shostak, A. B., and W. Gomberg. *Blue Collar World.* Englewood Cliffs, N.J.: Prentice-Hall, Inc., 1964.

Slichter, S. H., J. J. Healey, and E. R. Livernash. *The Impact of Collective Bargaining on Management.* Washington, D.C.: Brookings Institution, 1960.

IV

DISTRIBUTING GOODS AND SERVICES

15

Marketing in Our Economy

Marketing Defined

Now that we have had an opportunity to study the organization and operation of the production function, we are ready to turn our attention to the problem of distributing the goods produced. In business terminology, the terms *marketing* and *distribution* are usually regarded as synonymous terms.[1] Simply defined, marketing refers to all those activities essential in the flow of goods from a producer to the next consumer. A more comprehensive definition states that marketing is

. . . the performance of all activities necessary for ascertaining the needs and wants of markets, planning product availability, effecting transfer in ownership of products, providing for their physical distribution, and facilitating the entire marketing process.[2]

This definition emphasizes the fact that marketing includes those activities in distribution other than those that *change the form of the product.* In marketing terminology, activities that change the form of the product are regarded as *production,* and the production and dis-

---

[1] The economist may use the term *distribution* to describe the breakdown of total income among the factors of production.

[2] T. N. Beckman, and W. R. Davidson, *Principles of Marketing* (7th ed.; New York: The Ronald Press Co., 1962), p. 4; also see Dwight L. Gentry and Donald L. Shawver, *Fundamentals of Managerial Marketing* (Boston: D. C. Heath & Co., 1964), Chap. 1.

tribution activities are treated separately.[3] The student should be reminded that the economist may use the term *production* to include all the activities in *making* and *distributing* a product. A certain amount of confusion over terminology is inescapable, and it is advisable that the student reconcile himself to the task of remembering these distinctions.

Early Historical Development in the United States

Our first settlers had very few marketing problems. The family was largely self-sufficient in producing its needs. Such exchange as occurred was usually in the form of direct barter. Survival was largely a matter of producing the necessary food and fiber.

The growth of the colonies brought forth simple beginnings in marketing. The early "peddlers" walked from settlement to settlement offering to sell or trade a line of simple housewares. The few manufactured items carried by the peddler were obtained through trade with the ships that visited the colonies. As settlements grew, the early storekeeper came upon the scene. He often combined certain types of production with his retailing; for example, the shoemaker who tried making shoes for "stock" found it necessary to sell the shoes. Those who combined production and selling soon found it advisable, in some cases, to separate the two functions.

As the country developed, the separation of the production and distribution functions became more evident. Several factors contributed to this separation. It developed that certain areas were especially suitable to production in terms of materials and resources. As the population spread, the distance between these production areas and the people to be served increased. The producer could no longer meet his customers face-to-face, thus the need for a "middleman" emerged. The merchant stepped in to bridge the gap. The concept of "economy of scale" in production was another factor contributing to the separation of the functions. The producer who sold directly to his customers was often a small enterprise. In certain instances, it developed that he could lower the cost of producing an item by increasing the quantity produced. We know this principle today as that of "spreading the overhead." When the producer sought to increase his output, he found that his marketing problems increased accordingly. To market his increased output, he found it necessary to sell over a wider area. This created several difficulties: One was the problem of serving customers at a distance, as mentioned above. Another was the fact that the pro-

---

[3] A possible exception might occur in the marketing activity of *storage*. Here it is possible that some products may change their form and increase in value through aging—the curing of meats, for example.

ducer in certain lines found it unprofitable to attempt direct selling. Let us suppose, for example, that he produced neckties. He could not afford to operate retail stores selling nothing but ties, so the obvious solution was to sell to a middleman who could combine the sale of ties with other items of clothing. We still have examples of producers who do their own consumer selling through producer-operated retail stores and through direct selling on a house-to-house basis, but such producers are in a minority. In the distribution of consumer goods, it is typical for producers to solicit the aid of others in marketing the product.

Importance of Marketing

The people of the United States have experienced a rising standard of living over a long period of time; the rise being especially significant since 1929. Between 1929 and 1960 personal consumption expenditures, when adjusted for inflation, experienced a real increase of more than 140 per cent.[4] During the same period, the population itself increased by approximately 47 per cent. Thus, the size of our markets is increasing, and the individual consumer is, on an average, demanding more goods and services. This has placed increased emphasis on the importance of marketing. The United States economy has the capacity to produce huge quantities of goods; and with constantly improving production techniques, this capacity continues to grow. However, if production is to continue uninterrupted and if high employment is to be sustained, a market must exist for the goods produced. At the present time, the average American family has an income enabling them to live above the *necessity level;* that is, they have a choice to either spend or save a part of their earnings. Income above the necessity level is often referred to as *discretionary buying power.* It is difficult to say just how much of our income could be earmarked as discretionary buying power, but it is probable that most middle-class families could reduce their expenditures by as much as one-third and still have a standard of living better than that enjoyed by most people throughout the world. But if all families reduced their spending to the basic necessities, the effect would be to produce chaos in our economy. Markets would shrink, production would decline, unemployment would rise, and the vicious circle characteristic of depression would be initiated. This indicates the importance of a marketing system that can maintain a high level of consumption. Executives have recognized the importance of the marketing function as evidenced by the fact that they have become much more market minded and more research minded than in the 1930's.

4 Beckman, and Davidson, *op. cit.,* p. 28.

In undeveloped countries, it is customary to find major emphasis placed upon the problems of producing goods. In situations where the available goods are insufficient to meet demand, there is said to exist a *sellers' market*. When the economy of a country advances to a point where the capacity to produce is greater than the immediate demand, there is said to exist a *buyers' market*. Except for periods of emergency such as war, the United States may be characterized as having a buyers' market. Of course, there may from time to time exist a sellers' market in certain lines of goods; but from an over-all viewpoint, a buyers' market is common. In a buyers' market, the customer has a choice of many brands of similar products, and this encourages competition among sellers. It is only in a buyers' market that the consumer is *King*. Competition for markets has been a major factor contributing to the increased emphasis placed upon marketing. The increasing emphasis placed upon marketing is further indicated by the fact that between 1870 and 1900 the number of people engaged in producing goods showed a relative decline of 35 per cent, while the relative share employed in distribution more than doubled.[5]

Over a period of years, consumers have demanded more in the way of marketing services. More variety, better packaging, more convenient outlets, and more services such as credit and delivery have added to the cost of marketing. It is now estimated that roughly half the price paid by the consumer, on the average, can be attributed to marketing cost. The number of people employed in marketing is conservatively estimated as one-fourth of our total gainfully employed labor force.[6] While marketing costs are partially explained by the many services demanded, one should not conclude that our marketing system is entirely satisfactory. There is much inefficiency in marketing, and companies are continually striving to reduce waste and improve their systems of distribution. The share of the consumer's dollar that is now necessary to pay the cost of marketing indicates the desirability of finding ways to make marketing more efficient.

THE MARKET FOR CONSUMERS' GOODS

Consumers' Goods Classified

Consumers' goods are defined as those items purchased and consumed by the ultimate consumer. This is in contrast to *industrial goods,* which we define as those that are used in further production. When we buy a tube of toothpaste, we are purchasing a consumer good; when

[5] Gentry and Shawver, *op. cit.,* Chap. 1.
[6] *Ibid.*

a manufacturer buys steel to be used in making auto bodies, he is purchasing an industrial good.

Consumer goods may be classified as *convenience goods, shopping goods,* or *bulk goods.* Convenience goods are those items that we might normally purchase at the most convenient location. They are usually relatively standard in quality, identifiable by brand, and uniform in price among dealers. Cigarettes, candy, and gasoline are typical of such purchases. Shopping goods are those items for which the purchaser is willing to "shop" or search for before making a purchase. They are items offering a variation in quality and price and are often of such a nature that the customer needs assistance from sales clerks in making a choice. Fashion clothing, furniture, and heavy appliances are examples. Bulk goods are usually items the quality of which may be designated by brand or grade. Prices are likely to be uniform within a market area, and the consumer often buys in sizable quantities. Coal and fuel oil are typical examples.

Markets and Population

For items in the consumer-goods category, we may say that markets exist wherever there are people with money and the inclination to buy. With few exceptions, the potential market for consumer goods will vary with the population of an area. An exception may be found in the case of certain high-priced purchases. The number of persons able to afford Rolls-Royce cars may not always vary directly with the population. But for the thousands of items that make up the bulk of retail sales, population is a primary indicator of the potential sales volume.

In the past thirty years, we have experienced remarkable changes in the growth, composition, and geographical distribution of our population. These changes have been of great significance in the marketing of goods and service. Our total estimated population has increased from less than 122 million in 1929 to approximately 190 million in 1965.[7] Accompanying this growth have been striking changes in the age composition of the population. There has been a sharp increase in the percentage of people under fifteen years and in the percentage over forty-five. In 1930 approximately 5 per cent of our population was in the over sixty-five group; by 1965, 9 per cent were over sixty-five.[8] The sharp increase in the birthrate occurring after World War II has meant expanding markets in juvenile furniture, children's clothing, school supplies, and many other products used by children. An increasing percentage of our people in the sixty years and above age group has

[7] Bureau of the Census data.
[8] Bureau of the Census, Current Population Reports.

created growing markets for products appealing to elderly people. The market for recreation equipment suited to the retired person is a good example.

The geographical movement of population has had a profound effect on our marketing system. Perhaps most striking has been the shift from rural to urban areas. In 1930, our estimated farm population was 30,529,000; by 1963 the estimate was 13,367,000.[9] There has also been a shift from the smaller towns and cities to the larger metropolitan areas. Concurrent with the urbanization movement have been geographical shifts between regions. There has been a flow of population from the south and southwest into the middle Atlantic states and especially toward the west coast. California, Washington, and Oregon experienced heavy population increases between 1940 and 1960, as did Arizona, Utah, Nevada, and New Mexico. On the East Coast, Florida saw its population increase by more than 40 per cent during this period.[10] Despite migrations, very few states experienced a decline in population. Increasing birthrates in certain states were enough to offset losses through migration. These shifts in population called for rapid readjustments in our marketing system. Sales territories had to be realigned to conform to the changing values of markets. The urbanization movement swelled our large cities and triggered the flight to the suburbs. The retailing facilities followed people to the suburbs through the opening of branch stores and by the development of the now well-known suburban shopping centers. Population shifts often cause changes in patterns of living, and in so doing open new markets for many products.

Income and Its Distribution

Since emerging from the depression of the 1930's, the American people have enjoyed a steadily rising standard of living. This has been a period marked by an increasing level of income and by significant changes in the pattern of the distribution of income. Per capita disposable personal income in the United States rose from approximately $682 in 1929 to approximately $2,100 in 1963. A part of this increase in dollar income is accounted for by inflation, but, when placed on a 1954 basis (constant dollars), we see that per-capita disposable personal income increased from $1,107 in 1929 to approximately $1,873 in 1963.[11] From a marketing viewpoint, the manner in which family income is distributed is of immense importance. We cannot sell stoves,

[9] Estimates from the Bureau of Census and the Bureau of Agriculture Economics.
[10] Bureau of the Census data.
[11] U.S. Department of Commerce, Office of Business Economics, 1964.

refrigerators, and television sets in mass quantities unless buying power is widely dispersed. Table 15–1 shows changes that occurred in the pattern of the distribution of family income from 1947 to 1962. The percentages shown refer to the distribution of *real income;* i.e., they have been adjusted to make 1947 and 1962 dollars comparable. This period has been marked by striking changes in our economy.

Table 15–1. Percentage Distribution of Families by Income Group, 1947–1962, Constant (1962) Dollars

Families	Under $3,000	$3,000–4,999	$5,000–6,999	$7,000–9,999	$10,000 and Over
1947	32	32	18	11	7
1950	32	31	19	12	6
1955	25	25	24	17	9
1959	22	21	23	20	14
1960	21	20	23	21	15
1961	21	20	22	21	16
1962	20	19	22	21	18

SOURCE: Department of Commerce, Bureau of the Census.

It is of particular interest to note that, in 1947, about 68 per cent of the families in the country had an income of more than $3,000, whereas, by 1962, 80 per cent of the families had real income in excess of $3,000. In 1947, only 36 per cent had an income of more than $5,000, but, by 1962, 61 per cent were in the over-$5,000 category. Between 1947 and 1962, there occurred a "leveling of income" that saw the continued emergence of a great middle-class group. This has led to a greater proportion of the nation's spendable income finding its way into the hands of the masses of the people. In the face of progressive taxation, the high individual incomes characteristic of the 1920's have lost much of their significance. It is probable that no industrialized nation has ever experienced the equality in the distribution of income now found in the United States.

How Income Is Spent

Various studies have been made in an effort to show how family income is allocated among types of products and services. One of the most authoritative studies of family spending has been made by *Life* magazine, and the results of one phase of this study are shown in Table 15–2.

An examination of the breakdown shown in Table 15–2 shows that as the household income increases, a smaller percentage of that income is spent on the basic food category. For other categories, the relative percentages are amazingly constant. It seems that the lower income families and the higher income families allocate their spendable income in about the same way. They buy the same products and services —the difference being that the higher income family probably buys better quality and in larger amounts. The family in the four to five thousand dollar bracket spends 14 per cent of its income on the automotive category while the family in the ten thousand dollar category spends 15 per cent. But the higher income family may own a bigger car or a later model.

Who Does the Family Buying?

In the early days of our economy, the husband did most of the family buying. Travel conditions were such that the housewife found it difficult to visit markets and do the family shopping. With the coming of the twentieth century, our marketing system developed to the point that retail outlets were accessible to all, and the housewife assumed more and more of the responsibility for family buying. After World War I, it was frequently estimated that women did as much as 85 per cent of the family purchasing. The wife is still regarded as the family purchasing agent, and much of our advertising and selling is directed toward influencing her. While the wife may still do better than half of the family shopping, the husband is regaining importance in this respect. The suburban movement may have, in some respects, made it more difficult for the wife to do the bulk of the shopping. Regardless of who does the actual buying, all members of the family exert an influence in the choice of the goods and services purchased.

Buying Problems Faced by the Consumer

As a nation, we are blessed with an unequalled variety of goods. We have a choice of an almost limitless variety of products—with dozens, even hundreds, of brands within each product class. It is almost impossible for the individual to become well informed regarding all the items that may be purchased. Advertising, if used properly, may become a primary means of educating the consumer but has often contributed to the buyer's confusion. Reckless claims and counterclaims are all too prevalent. However, reliable business firms through their advertising do a commendable job in keeping the consumer informed. The consumer often comes to rely upon certain widely advertised brands as being indicative of quality. In some product lines, grade labeling has been used with a fair degree of success. For those products that can be graded, the use of the grade may be a valuable guide to the consumer. Products that have a fashion element, or food products in

Table 15–2. Household Expenditures by Types of Goods and Services (Percentages)

	All House- holds	Annual Household Income						
		Under $2,000	$2,000 2,999	$3,000 3,999	$4,000 4,999	$5,000 6,999	$7,000 9,999	$10,000 and more
All Goods and Services	100%	100%	100%	100%	100%	100%	100%	100%
Food, beverages and tobacco	29	36	33	30	29	28	26	24
Clothing and accessories	12	11	11	13	12	11	13	14
Medical and personal care	5	7	5	5	5	5	5	6
Home operation and improvement ..	19	17	20	18	19	19	18	18
Home furnishing and equipment	9	7	8	8	8	9	9	10
Recreation and recreation equipment	5	5	5	5	6	5	5	6
Automotive	14	11	13	15	14	16	15	15
Other goods and services	7	6	5	6	7	7	9	7

SOURCE: *A New Background for Marketing Decisions* (booklet distributed by *Life* magazine, 1957). (This remains the most definitive study of consumer expenditures.)

309

which taste is paramount, cannot be easily graded. In the absence of grade labeling (such as A, B, C), more descriptive labeling would aid the consumer. High-school courses in home economics and distributive education have also contributed to the ability of the consumer as a buyer. Private rating organizations such as *Consumers Union* carry on a program of testing and evaluating products. Various agencies of the federal government are also active in providing information and in the enforcement of laws for the benefit of the consumer.

THE MARKET FOR INDUSTRIAL GOODS

Industrial Goods Defined

Industrial goods have been defined as those goods purchased for use in the production of other goods and services. Some products are used exclusively in further production, for example, iron ore, automobile bodies, and certain chemicals. On the other hand, there are many products that may be classified as industrial or consumer goods depending upon their use. Fuel oil purchased by the family for heating the home is a consumer purchase, but fuel oil purchased for use in an industrial plant would be an industrial purchase.

Methods of Selling Industrial Goods

The sale of industrial goods differs significantly from that of consumer goods. Both emotional and rational motives enter into the decision to purchase goods. Household consumers as a rule are not "professional" buyers, and their decisions are often emotional ones. When we enter a supermarket to purchase three items but end up by buying six, we have engaged in what is termed "impulse buying." The industrial purchaser is more likely to be a professional buyer and much less likely to buy on impulse or for emotional reasons. Much of our industrial buying is done by purchasing agents who rely upon rational analysis in making buying decisions. This is not to imply that emotional appeals are never used in industrial selling; however, the rational appeals are predominant. The industrial purchaser is not so much interested in how an item will look; he is more likely to be interested in its cost, its performance, and its durability.

Compared to consumer purchases, industrial goods are purchased in large quantities. This enables the producer of such goods to often sell directly to the user of his product. Middlemen are much less prominent in the distribution of industrial goods, although wholesalers usually known as *industrial distributors* do play an important role in servicing small purchasers and in selling items normally bought in small lots. Items of major equipment are sold directly since it is often necessary that they be designed and built on a custom basis. Such equipment also may require complex servicing after installation, and it is necessary for the manufacturer to retain this responsibility. The fact that long-term financing is usually involved is another factor contributing to the practice of direct selling.

The Importance of Financing

In selling industrial goods, especially items of major equipment and some of the more important accessory items, the problem of financing looms large. Installations of heavy equipment often run into hundreds of thousands of dollars. Few companies are able to make such pur-chases outright; in fact, they may feel that money can be more produc-tively used as working capital rather than as an investment in fixed assets. When faced with the necessity of raising capital to purchase equipment, a corporation may borrow through the sale of bonds or sell stock, which amounts to selling an interest in the firm. Sometimes the seller of industrial goods will accept stock in the buyer's firm in pay-ment for the goods. It is also possible that the seller may extend credit and accept a lien on the equipment. An alternative to the purchase of equipment may permit the user to lease the equipment and pay a rental for its use. The fee may be based on a period of time or it may be a certain amount for each item produced on the machine.

A Fluctuating Market

Many consumer goods are absorbed by the market at fairly regular rates. Food sales, for example, tend to remain steady unless very severe declines in consumer income are experienced. In the industrial-goods market, sales tend to fluctuate from year to year, depending upon general business conditions or the conditions in a particular industry. There are many reasons for this fluctuation. New equipment is often purchased when existing equipment is considered obsolete. Equipment may be considered obsolete when newer equipment of a more economical type becomes available. Thus, not all obsolete equipment is worn out; in fact, virtually new equipment may be adjudged obsolete. This means that the firm often has some freedom in selecting a favorable time to purchase equipment. They might like to purchase a new machine, but the old one can be made to serve for a year or two more. Therefore, a company can often delay a purchase until its financial condition im-proves or until the equipment can be obtained at a better price. The demand for an industrial product is largely a derived demand; that is, the industrial firm purchases in anticipation of the demand for the product that it produces. An appliance manufacturer will expand his facilities and buy new equipment as the consumer demand for appliances rises. Fluctuations in the demand for consumer products contribute to fluctuations in the demand for industrial products. These fluctuations may be especially pronounced in the industrial market.

IMPORTANT MARKETING FUNCTIONS

Buying and Selling

Buying and selling might well be considered the primary marketing functions. All marketing activity points toward the exchange of goods and services. The following chapters dealing with wholesaling, retailing, personal selling, and advertising will introduce us to the selling function and the institutions through which sales are accomplished. The success of our marketing system depends upon the combined efforts of all those engaged in carrying out the many operations. There is such interdependence among those involved that failure in the performance of any function may seriously hamper the flow of goods from producer to consumer.

Determining Price

In Chapter 2 dealing with *economics,* we discussed some of the more fundamental concepts dealing with the theory of price determination. Price theory is a very complex area of economic analysis, and a detailed treatment of the subject is usually reserved for the more advanced courses in economics. In this chapter, we are concerned with price determination from the *applied,* or operational, point of view. The freedom that the individual seller has in determining his price will depend upon such factors as the degree of competition present and the elasticity of the demand for the product being sold. Competition tends to put a ceiling upon the maximum price that the seller may charge. In the absence of competition, the nature of demand poses a restrictive influence. Where demand is highly elastic, the buyer may be able to forego use of the product or use a substitute. Of course, if the demand is inelastic and if the product is a necessity, the seller may exercise more freedom in pricing. Fortunately, very few products and services are in this latter category. When conditions naturally favorable to monopoly are present, prices may be subject to government regulation. In our economy, elements of both competition and monopoly are influential in establishing prices. It is believed that existing competition plus regulatory measures tend to limit the opportunity of the individual seller to exploit the consumer through excessive prices.

From a practical viewpoint, the typical seller has a degree of freedom in fixing his price, but this freedom is likely to be restricted to a certain range. The cost of producing, or purchasing, the item to be sold places a floor below which the item cannot be sold except at a loss. On the other end of the scale, the presence of competitive sellers, or the presence of substitute products, places a ceiling above which the product cannot be marketed. Thus, our seller finds his price range described as a "bracket." While the bracket may establish maximum and minimum prices, there is still opportunity for the exercise of *pricing policy*.

Pricing Policies Vary

Sellers in the same market may follow different policies in pricing. One man may decide to price for volume, that is, make a small profit on each item but hope that the lower prices charged will result in the sale of a great many items. This man may minimize services to the buyer and operate on a cash-and-carry basis. His competitor may decide to forego the volume policy and operate a *prestige-type* establishment. He would charge higher prices but would offer the consumer a more elaborate shopping facility and extensive services such as credit and delivery.

There are many other factors that bear upon the specific price that a merchant may charge his customers. Manufacturers normally offer various discounts to middlemen who purchase for resale. A *trade discount* may be given according to the position of the middleman in the trade channel. A manufacturer may, upon occasion, sell to both wholesalers and retailers. The wholesaler would be given a larger discount from list price than would the retailer, the assumption being that the manufacturer who sells directly to the retailer has to perform some of the wholesaling functions himself. *Quantity discounts* are also commonly granted by manufacturers to middlemen. It is cheaper for the manufacturer to sell in large quantities, and he may pass part of the savings along to the buyer. As a rule, *cash discounts* may be offered buyers who pay their bills within a specified period, such as ten days from the date of invoice. It is not uncommon for a seller to offer the buyer certain *functional discounts*. A functional discount is allowed the buyer in return for the performance of some extraordinary service. For example, the buyer may be given such a discount if he agrees to advertise the manufacturer's product locally. The ability of middlemen (or industrial purchasers) to take advantage of these discounts will have a direct bearing on their costs of doing business and, hence, upon the prices that they must charge. Generally speaking, large firms are better able to benefit from discount structures, and this is one of the factors that frequently enable the larger firm to undersell a smaller competitor. A body of legislation has developed to preserve competition in pricing and to prevent collusion between sellers and buyers when the purpose is to enable one buyer to drive another out of business.

Transportation

In a later chapter of this text, transportation will be discussed in some detail. At this point we need to emphasize the basic role of transportation in our marketing system. Transportation creates *place utility*, and it is recognized that products to be of use must be available where needed. The development of our marketing system has paralleled the development of our transportation facilities. The movement of goods constitute a major cost of marketing, and improvements in transportation permitting faster movement at lower cost have enabled the development of extensive distribution outlets at great distances from the point of production. There remains, however, certain products the distribution of which are limited to areas near the point of production. Limitations may occur because the value of the product is low in relation to the cost of transporting it—the distribution of cement, for example. In other cases, the perishability of the product may demand a type of transportation that is costly and thus impractical. As transportation facilities are further improved, the ability to extend markets will keep pace.

Storage

As a marketing function, storage creates *time utility*. To be of use, goods must be available not only at the right place but at the right time. Transportation has enabled us to move goods to the market, and improved storage now enables us to hold the goods on hand and feed them into the market as needed. Developments in cold storage warehousing now permit the consumer to enjoy perishable products that were previously available only during the production season. Products such as butter and eggs may be stored and sold as needed. Before the development of modern storage facilities, the price of these products fluctuated widely. In the spring and summer when production was high, the price of butter would drop to a very low level. In the fall and winter when production was low, the price would be extremely high. As a result of storage, the price of butter is now relatively stable throughout the year. Both the producer and the consumer benefits from this stability.

Grading

As a marketing function, *grading* is closely related to the establishment of standards. The process of standardization establishes certain specifications that a product must meet in order to be given a certain quality designation. Quality may be expressed by a letter grade (A, B, C, etc.) as in grade labeling or it may be expressed by a numerical designation—number 2 wheat, for example. We may define *grading* as the act of separating goods into lots according to predetermined specifications. The apples gathered from a single tree may show considerable variation in quality, such as differences in size, shape, and color. The grower may pick the apples and place them in a barrel for movement to the packing house. At the packing house, the barrel of apples would be graded. The process of grading enables the grower to get a better over-all price for his product; it enables the consumer to get the quality suitable for a particular purpose; it also lowers marketing costs by eliminating the inferior products at the source of production.

There is considerable controversy over the question of *grade labeling*. Some maintain that uniform grade labeling would be of great assistance to the consumer in buying. For example, canned food products could be designated as A, B, or C grade; and, assuming the grades would be uniform, the consumer could come to rely upon them as an indication of quality. It is further argued that this would save time in buying, would eliminate the necessity for extensive advertising, would give the small producer a better chance, and would reduce competition largely to a price basis. Critics of grade labeling maintain that it could not be done accurately because intangible characteristics such as taste could not be graded. They contend that uniform grade labeling would have to be politically administered through the federal government and thus subject to interference by pressure groups and special interests. They also point out that no great need exists for grade labeling since brand names and descriptive labeling now furnish the consumer with adequate buying guides.

Packing and Packaging

Packing refers to the wrapping or crating of a product to facilitate its storage or shipment. Packaging takes place at the point of production and is often considered both a production and marketing operation. In a production sense, the purpose of the package is to contain and protect the product from deterioration. But when the package assumes the function of display through having a decorative design or by carrying consumer information and advertising, it performs a role in the marketing of the product. Packing, as defined above, is clearly a marketing function. In the case of products that are perishable, or highly fragile, packing may represent a significant marketing cost. This cost varies in relation to the distance the product is to be shipped and in relation to the manner of transportation used. In air freight transportation, for example, where the goods are handled carefully and not subjected to the jolts and jarring common to surface movement, less extensive packing is required.

Marketing Research

One of the most important marketing functions is that of marketing research, or as it is sometimes called, the *information function.* In a complex economy such as ours, the producer must identify his customer, determine his location, investigate his income, and study his buying habits. Marketing research has often been compared to military intelligence, in that the seller must have information about the market in order to plan his strategy just as the military commander needs information in order to plan operations. Business firms have research departments that study the market on a continuing basis. There are also private research agencies that conduct market studies for clients. A wealth of basic market information is collected by agencies of the federal and state governments, and this is usually made available to the public. The United States Census data comprise the most extensive collection of market information available.

The term "marketing research" covers at least three specific areas of study. These areas are identifiable by the objectives that they seek to accomplish. There is the area of *market analysis* in which one seeks to locate the market and to determine its potential worth. We may seek to locate the market in a geographical sense as would be shown by drawing a circle on a map, or where the potential customers are dispersed throughout the population, we may identify them (hence locate them) by certain characteristics that they possess in common. When the market has been located, its worth may be estimated by studying potential customers in terms of their income, their knowledge of the product, and the acuteness of their need for it. A second area of marketing research is *consumer analysis.* In consumer analysis, emphasis is on the individual in terms of his habits, likes, and dislikes. It is in this area that we study consumer motivation and attempt to understand the behavior of the consumer. Consumers buy products for reasons that we call buying motives. Often, these motives are easily detected by the seller; but in some cases, the motives may be hidden from the investigator, or perhaps the customer himself is not aware of the true motive for his actions. In recent years, "motivation research" has developed to explore the areas of hidden motives. Researchers using clinical techniques strive to find the underlying causes for certain aspects of consumer behavior. If the seller can discover the needs and desires of the consumer, and understand the motives that may prompt the consumer to act, he is in a better position to direct his sales and advertising strategy.

The third area of marketing research is that of *product analysis*. Here, the producer is studying his product in relation to the market with the objective of fitting the product to the desires of the consumer. In some cases, product analysis may take the form of laboratory research in which scientists work to improve the quality of the product, or to make it easier to use. In other cases, product analysis may involve going to the consumer and finding out what changes are desired in the product, and then making the changes where such are possible. As a rule, the business man uses the term *marketing research* to embrace the three specific areas of analyses mentioned here. In practice, it is often difficult to separate the study of the market, the consumer, and the product. An investigation in one area will invariably turn up information usable in other areas.

Market Management

The managerial function in marketing is not unlike its counterpart in production. It involves the assembly and management of men, money, and machines. The essence of market management centers around the planning and execution of the marketing operations. The successful market manager must interpret the needs and desires of the consumer so that production may translate those needs and desires into products. It then becomes the market manager's job to supervise the flow of goods to the consumer. The elements in the marketing of a product are often thought of as comprising a "marketing mix." The marketing mix includes elements such as personal salesmanship, advertising, dealer promotion, packaging, and research. The market manager strives to get the best combination of these elements; i.e., he wants the most productive allocation of his sales expense dollar.

As in all phases of management, market management is concerned with cost. The market manager strives constantly to reduce marketing cost. He may approach the problem of costs in several ways: He may attempt a *functional analysis* in which he tries to break down total cost along functional lines. For example, he might try to separate transportation cost, storage cost, selling cost, and other expenses. Functional analysis often encounters difficulty in that certain functions cannot be clearly distinguished. *Territorial analysis* has been an effective approach to cost reduction. The sales potential for territories may be established; and on the basis of this, salesmen may be reassigned and advertising expenditures more properly directed. The *analysis of product lines* is another productive approach. Through analyzing product lines, the more profitable products may be identified and singled out for promotion. Less profitable lines may be eliminated or reduced in inventory. These are but a few of the approaches that the market manager uses in his efforts to reduce costs.

TRADE CHANNELS

Trade Channels Defined

Simply defined, a *trade channel* may be thought of as the path along which title to goods travels in moving from a producer to the next consumer. Each product has its own trade channel; and when significant changes take place in the form of the product, that is, changes sufficient to alter the identity of the product, a new channel begins. Figure 15–1 illustrates this point. The trade channel for cattle is from

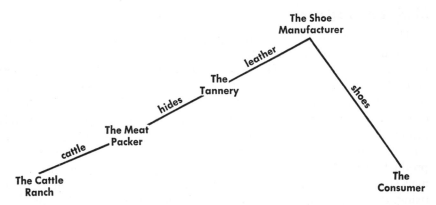

Fig. 15–1. Trade channels illustrated.

the ranch to the meat packer; the channel for leather from the tannery to the shoe manufacturer; and the channel for shoes from the manufacturer to the consumer. Thus, we may discuss the marketing of cattle, hides, leather, and shoes and point out the trade channel for each product. The trade channel is made up of the various middlemen who perform functions in the movement of goods from producer to consumer.

Variations in Channels

The producer often has a choice among several possible methods of marketing his product. His choice may center around the question of the middlemen to be employed. He may attempt to sell directly to the consumer using his own sales staff, or he may distribute through a number of independent middlemen. In the marketing process, there are certain functions to be performed, and the producer who attempts direct sales does so on the assumption that he can perform the functions as well, if not better, than the middleman. It may also happen that middlemen are unwilling to take on the distribution of a new product, in which case the producer may decide to assume the functions himself. Direct selling may eliminate certain middlemen, but it *does not* eliminate the functions normally performed by middlemen. Producers of similar products may employ different middlemen in the course of reaching the consumer. This creates variations in the channel of distribution used. We may illustrate these variations in the following manner:

Producer ⟶ Consumer
Producer ⟶ Retailer ⟶ Consumer
Producer ⟶ Wholesaler ⟶ Retailer ⟶ Consumer
Producer ⟶ Broker ⟶ Wholesaler ⟶ Retailer ⟶ Consumer

Relatively few consumer products are sold by the producer directly to the consumer. The farmer who operates a roadside market is perhaps the simplest illustration of direct selling. Normally, the producers who sell over a wide area need the assistance of middlemen. The retailer is especially important as a means of reaching consumers who buy in small quantities. The nature of the product, and the market, indicates the number, and type, of middlemen commonly used. For example, wholesalers are very vital in the distribution of *convenience goods,* while the manufacturer may prefer to go around the wholesaler and deal directly with the retailer in the distribution of *fashion goods.* In the industrial goods market, direct sale is predominant. The technical nature of many industrial items, and the fact that they are bought in relatively large quantities, are factors contributing to a direct relationship between producer and buyer.

Integrated Distribution

A manufacturing firm may become *integrated* to the extent that it owns its source of raw materials, plants for making fabricated parts, and the facilities for transporting materials and parts from the source. This is referred to as integrating *backward,* i.e., toward the source of supplies.

The same company may do its own wholesaling and operate its own retail stores. This would be known as *forward* integration, i.e., toward the market. Very few, if any, firms are completely integrated both forward and backward from the manufacturing level. On the other hand, many firms are partially integrated. Also, marketing firms may be integrated in the sense that they assume functions back toward and including the manufacturing operations. Here, we are interested in the process of integration as it affects marketing.

Many manufacturers have assumed marketing functions commonly associated with middlemen. Perhaps the best example is the manufacturer who assumes the wholesaling function by choosing to deal directly with retailers. The manufacturer may resort to direct dealing with the retailer in order to obtain more aggressive promotion than the wholesaler is able to give. There are a few cases in which the manufacturer may also take over the operation of retail outlets. When this occurs, the manufacturer often produces a line of related products that will comprise the main part of his inventory. In addition to his own products, he may retail products of other manufacturers. A wholesaler may integrate by acquiring manufacturing facilities or by opening a chain of retail outlets. The development of chain stores, and the development of large volume independents, created situations in which retailers took over their own wholesaling. A few very large retailers have taken steps to acquire certain manufacturing facilities. The size of the retailer is often an indication of the extent to which he may be integrated. The type of integration discussed in this section is *vertical* in contrast to *horizontal*. In vertical integration, a company expands by assuming functions at different levels of operation. In horizontal integration, expansion occurs through absorbing other similar companies at the same level of operation. Vertical integration is usually attempted in an effort to assure sources of supply and to acquire supplies and inventory more economically. The company that absorbs the marketing function through vertical integration does so in an effort to attain more efficient distribution. Vertical integration brings with it many management problems, the coordination of the various activities at different levels being a good example.

YOUR CAREER IN MARKETING MANAGEMENT

The Marketing Executive

In a competitive economy, the emphasis placed upon distribution makes the marketing executive a key man. The top-level management of most companies will be made up of men who come up through both the production and marketing areas. There is reason to feel that an increasing percentage of top managers may be men with a market orientation. The fact that our economy is normally characterized as a *buyers' market* would tend to support this assumption. To advance in management, the marketing man must not be too narrowly trained. In fact, to perform as a marketing executive, one must display a broad range of capabilities. He needs a knowledge of economics to understand changes and shifts in the economy as they affect his firm. Markets are composed of people, and our executive must have a firm grounding in the humanities and social sciences. His specific line of work may require knowledge of the physical sciences and engineering. The capable student willing to acquire an expert knowledge of our distribution system will find the business world anxious to provide both opportunity and challenge.

Opportunities in Research

In many respects, marketing research could be considered the nerve center of marketing as practiced today. This is perhaps the most professional of all the areas open to the marketing student. The student aspiring to an executive position in marketing will find it necessary to acquire a knowledge of marketing-research techniques and the ability to interpret the results of market studies. If one seeks a career in advertising, he will, in most cases, find a need for marketing research. Those in creative advertising must make use of marketing-research data, and often they may be required to obtain the data themselves. In deciding where one is to advertise, the choice of a medium is basically a matter of market research. In sales management, marketing research is vital to the sales manager in his day-to-day decision making. There is no aspect of marketing in which marketing research, or the data gained through such research, is not fundamental.

It is now common for most large- and medium-sized firms to have a marketing-research department. Advertising agencies have marketing-research departments—as do large newspapers, magazines, and broadcast stations. The federal government carries on extensive marketing-research activity; also, state governments frequently sponsor such research. Large universities maintain research bureaus that employ persons trained in marketing research. There are marketing-research agencies that specialize in conducting research for clients. This should indicate to the student the scope of employment opportunity for those who become proficient in this area.

The college student desiring to go into marketing research as a career can do much to prepare himself while in school. In the business area, he would do well to take certain courses in marketing. Supplementing his marketing courses should be courses in mathematics and business statistics. If possible, he should take math courses through the level of calculus and have at least three courses in statistics. If at all possible, he should have courses in psychology and sociology. The liberal-arts student may major in psychology and supplement this with business courses, especially marketing courses. He, too, will find mathematics and statistics excellent tool courses. The student familiar with college curricula will realize the impossibility of covering all the suggested courses in a normal four-year program. If possible, the student interested in a career in marketing research should plan to continue his education to the level of at least the master's degree. Many students do this by going to school on a part-time basis after obtaining an initial job. Opportunities for increased salary and advancement are excellent for those who prove their worth in research.

TOPICS FOR DISCUSSION

1. "In primitive countries, the failure to develop a system of production has been partially due to the absence of a workable system of distribution." Explain.

2. An economic doctrine of the early nineteenth century held that "the process of production automatically creates a demand for the goods produced." Why is it that in a modern economy, production does not automatically create a market?

3. Discuss the factors that have contributed to the growing importance of marketing over the past one hundred years.

4. Discuss the *marketing significance* of the fact that more people are now living past the normal retirement age.

5. Do you believe that the changes that have occurred in the pattern of the distribution of income since 1929 are desirable changes?

6. The 1920's and 1930's have often been referred to as the "decades of production," and the 1940's and 1950's, as the "decades of marketing." Comment on this observation.

7. "Marketing begins at the shipping platform and ends with the ringing of the cash register." Comment, agreeing or disagreeing.

8. Why are markets important?

9. In what way does the industrial purchaser differ from the household consumer?

10. Why has so much attention been given to motivational research by marketers?

CASE 15–1

CHANGING CONSUMER HABITS

Early in the 1960's, evidence was revealed that linked excessive cigarette smoking to diseases affecting the respiratory system. The problem was thought to be caused by the inhalation of cigarette smoke. Pipe smoking and cigar smoking were not singled out for indictment along with cigarette smoking. It was generally assumed that smokers did not inhale pipes and cigars in the same way as cigarettes. As a result of the evidence on cigarette smoking, it was thought that a significant number of smokers would begin smoking a pipe or turn to cigars. Sales of cigars and pipe tobaccos in the years following the "cigarette controversy" seem to have borne out this expectation.

A very important part of the cigarette market consists of women smokers. It was expected that women smokers might be influenced to cut down their consumption of cigarettes, but, unlike the situation of men smokers, for whom pipes and cigars were available substitutes, there appeared to be no ready substitutes to attract women. Although women in some parts of the world smoke pipes and cigars, this has not been the custom in the United States.

Faced with an apparent opportunity to cut into the cigarette market, cigar producers stepped up activity to influence men to switch to cigars. These producers also looked longingly at the huge segment of the cigarette market composed of women smokers. The strength of custom against women's smoking of cigars undoubtedly seemed too formidable to attack in an outright manner. By the mid-1960's, at least one cigar manufacturer was presenting a small cigar with a white plastic tip and was advertising this, albeit indirectly, to the woman smoker. At this point in time, it is impossible to predict if this firm, or any other company, will be successful in converting women smokers to cigar-type products.

Do you feel that women can be induced to smoke cigar-type products? How would you go about changing customs in this area?

SELECTED REFERENCES

Beckman, T. N., and W. R. Davidson. *Principles of Marketing*. 7th ed. New York: The Ronald Press Co., 1962.

Davis, Kenneth R. *Marketing Management*. 2d ed. New York: The Ronald Press Co., 1966.

Frey, A. W. *Marketing Handbook*. 2d ed. New York: The Ronald Press Co., 1965.

Gentry, D. L., and D. L. Shawver. *Fundamentals of Managerial Marketing*. Boston: D. C. Heath & Co., 1964.

Phillips, C. F., and D. J. Duncan. *Marketing Principles and Methods*. 5th ed. Homewood, Ill.: Richard D. Irwin, Inc., 1964.

Stewart, P. W., and J. F. Dewhurst. *Does Distribution Cost Too Much?* New York: Twentieth Century Fund, 1939.

16

Distribution Channels in Marketing

DISTRIBUTION CHANNELS AND MARKETING INSTITUTIONS

A *distribution channel* (trade channel) has been defined as the route taken by the title to goods as they move from a producer to the consumer. As an example, the trade channel for shoes may be thought of as extending from the shoe manufacturer to the consumer. As the goods move from producer to consumer, various middlemen may be operative along the channel. The term *marketing institution* is often considered synonymous with the term *middleman*. In the example cited above, wholesalers and retailers are institutions, or middlemen, who may be involved in the distribution of shoes. For convenience of discussion, middlemen may be thought of as *merchant middlemen*, who buy goods for the purpose of resale, and *functional middlemen*, who assist in the performance of marketing functions. The merchant middleman may be identified by the fact that he takes legal title to the goods that he handles. The functional middleman renders a marketing service without taking title, usually acting as an agent and receiving his compensation in the form of a commission. In this chapter, we will consider some of the activities of middlemen, with particular reference to the areas of wholesaling and retailing.

WHOLESALING

Wholesaling Defined

There has always been considerable confusion over just what the term "wholesaling" should include. The term is often defined as including all those marketing transactions other than the retailing function. A somewhat broader definition would place in the category of wholesaling all purchases except those bought for use by the ultimate consumer.[1] For the purpose of this discussion, we may consider wholesaling as including those activities other than the ones commonly identified as retailing. Thus, wholesaling would embrace the transactions necessary in getting the goods from the point of production to the industrial user, or to the retail outlet. We may clarify the picture still further by distinguishing the terms *wholesaling, wholesaler,* and *wholesale merchant.* The wholesale merchant is but one of many engaged in accomplishing the task of wholesaling. As previously mentioned, the wholesale merchant is a middleman who takes title in contrast to the functional middleman who does not take title. But "wholesaling" is carried on by both merchant middlemen and functional middlemen. To avoid confusion, it is thought best to use the term "wholesaler" only in connection with the wholesale merchant. However, the student may find the term used in a broader sense in certain texts.

Wholesaling Consumer Goods and Industrial Goods

The bulk of industrial goods are sold by the producer directly to the consumer. The merchant middleman plays a relatively small role in distributing industrial goods. The merchant wholesaler—often known as an *industrial distributor*—does perform a service through supplying those accounts too small to justify direct selling. He also renders a service in supplying small-unit items, or replacement parts, the volume of which would not justify direct sale. Concentration of the market is one of many factors encouraging direct selling in the field of industrial goods. In contrast, a widely dispersed market is a prime factor in making indirect sales characteristic of the consumer-goods market.

TYPES OF WHOLESALERS

The Service Wholesaler

The wholesaler who buys for resale to the retailer, and in the process extends a variety of services to his customer, is known as a *service wholesaler.* Service wholesalers may be classified as general line or specialty. General-line wholesalers carry a complete line in some field, such as groceries; the specialty wholesaler carries a limited line within one field—hosiery and lingerie, for example. Geographically, service wholesalers

---

[1] T. N. Beckman, N. H. Engle, and R. D. Buzzell, *Wholesaling* (3d ed.; New York: The Ronald Press Co., 1959), chap. 2. This standard text gives a full discussion of the various concepts of wholesaling.

may be classed as national, regional, or local. There are relatively few national wholesalers, with a majority operating regionally and locally. The nature of the goods carried is a clue to the size of the area served. The hardware wholesaler may serve a larger area than would the grocery wholesaler. The grocery market is somewhat concentrated in comparison to the hardware market, and the relative bulkiness of many food items further restricts the grocery wholesaler. National and regional wholesalers have been very active in developing their own brands. Private brands afford the distributor a degree of security in his market. The service wholesaler has much to offer both the manufacturer and the retailer. In serving the retailer, the service wholesaler performs the function of buying from producers. He also carries inventory, assists the retailer in selecting a suitable stock, makes deliveries, gives advice on pricing and merchandising, extends credit, and aids the retailer in many other ways.

Cash-and-Carry Wholesalers

Not all merchant wholesalers offer a full range of services. Certain wholesalers, known as *limited-function* wholesalers, specialize primarily in buying and selling. The cash-and-carry wholesaler buys in carlots, takes full advantage of discounts, sells to the retailer for cash, and requires the retailer to pick up the merchandise at the point of sale. Salesmen are not widely used to visit retailers. This wholesaler operates on a low margin and emphasizes a rapid turnover of inventory. He usually serves the cash-and-carry retailer.

Drop Shippers

Drop shippers, sometimes known as *desk jobbers,* qualify as wholesale merchants in that they take title to the goods while in transit from producer to buyer. The buyer places his order with the drop shipper who in turn forwards the order to the seller. When the order is placed, the drop shipper instructs the seller to ship directly to the buyer. Thus, the drop shipper does not handle the goods or perform any storage function. His service is in offering a knowledge of certain markets and through having established contacts with sources. He operates in the area of bulk commodities such as coal and lumber where carlot shipments are common. In terms of total volume of sales transacted, drop shippers are relatively unimportant.

Miscellaneous Types

There are several other types of wholesale merchants, most of whom are in the limited-service category. *Truck jobbers* are wholesale merchants who combine the selling and delivery functions. They often distribute perishable goods in situations where small lots are purchased by the retailer. Bakery and tobacco products are examples. Such jobbers are frequently small-scale operators. The *rack jobber* has come into prominence with the development of self-service retailing—especially the self-service food stores. The store supplies the space and the jobber sets up the racks, displays the merchandise, and keeps the racks filled. He receives payment for the merchandise as it is sold. The rack jobber tends to specialize in lines such as housewares, drugs, toiletries, and small tools. The *mail-order wholesaler* receives and fills orders by mail. He tends to deal in staple goods and to avoid items where style and fashion are important. The development of fast transportation and communications has contributed to the declining importance of this type of wholesaling.

FUNCTIONAL MIDDLEMEN

General Brokers

There are many types of functional middlemen who facilitate the distribution of goods. They usually operate in the capacity of agents who represent the owner of goods in selling to wholesalers, retailers, or to industrial users. In business terminology, all types of agent middlemen may upon occasion be collectively referred to as "brokers." In this discussion, it will be necessary to distinguish the more important types of functional middlemen and to indicate differences in their manner of operation.

The *general broker*—sometimes called a *pure broker*—is an important agent middleman. He does not maintain a continuous relationship with a principal but tends to operate on a job-lot basis. Over a period of time, such brokers may assist in selling a variety of goods for a number of owners. General brokers perform primarily a sales function, and they are active in distributing manufactured food products, meats and meat products, seafoods, forestry and mine products, and many others. Their commission averages from 2 per cent to 5 per cent of sales.[2] The general broker has a specialized knowledge of certain markets, and he is usually experienced in selling. He performs a valuable service for those producers who do not have sales organizations of their own, or who may not have a sufficient knowledge of the market to do a satisfactory selling job.

[2] D. L. Gentry and D. L. Shawver, *Fundamentals of Managerial Marketing* (Boston: D. C. Heath & Co., 1964), Chap. 8.

Manufacturers' Agents

The manufacturers' agent is an important functional middleman in the distribution of certain lines—notably grocery and dry-goods specialties, machinery, electrical goods, drugs, metals, and building supplies. He normally represents a limited number of manufacturers—three or four being typical—and he handles non-competing lines. The products handled are related to the extent of being purchased by the same buyer; thus, the agent may handle four drug items, all of which may be sold to the firm upon which he calls. Unlike the general broker, the manufacturers' agent maintains a continuous relationship with a the manufacturer more intensive selling than he would expect to receive a commission of from 5 to 8 per cent, depending upon the services performed. Some manufacturers' agents carry inventory, extend credit to buyers, and maintain a customer-service organization. This agent offers the manufacturer more intensive selling than he would expect to receive through the merchant wholesaler, while at the same time he spreads the cost of selling over the number of items sold. In a sense, he offers the manufacturer a compromise between having his own sales force (which may be too expensive) and distributing through a merchant wholesaler. The manufacturers' agent may be organized as a company with a staff of salesmen and service people. Such companies usually refer to themselves as "distributors" rather than as agents.

Selling Agents

Selling agents, sometimes referred to as *sales agents,* represent another type of functional middleman. The selling agent is organized as a company to provide the sales function for those principals that seek his services. The selling agent is characterized by the fact that he takes over the entire sales function for a company. He operates in an unrestricted territory, and he normally has more control in establishing prices and terms than does the manufacturers' agent. He may render extensive service to his client such as that of financing and in handling advertising and sales promotion. The selling agent tends to operate in the area of bulk goods such as textiles, canned goods, machinery, and lumber. His commission may be slightly less than that received by the manufacturers' agent, often varying from 3 to 5 per cent, depending upon the services performed. The selling agent renders an important service, especially to those producers who are too small to justify their own sales organization. Also, producers who have a seasonal output find the selling agent convenient.

Commission Merchants

The commission merchant is an agent, although he may have some of the authority normally held by a merchant. He differs from some of the other agents discussed in that the seller often delegates the control over price to him. He is most active in the sale of farm commodities—notably grains, produce, and livestock. He frequently operates in central markets such as New York and Chicago, and growers at distant points will ship products to these markets consigned to the commission merchant. The commission merchant will take charge of the product in the central market and negotiate a sale. The cost of handling plus the agent's commission is deducted from the selling price, and the remainder is returned to the grower. The commission will vary depending upon the type of product, the commission on produce normally being about 5 per cent.[3] In recent years, the commission merchant has declined somewhat in importance, probably as a result of the seller finding it difficult to control the activity of this agent.

Auctions

The auction company represents a type of functional middleman. Auction companies provide a place where buyers and sellers may meet, and they furnish the facilities for the conduct of auction selling. They publicize the auction, furnish the display space, provide the auctioneer and the clerical service, and often assist in preparing the product for sale. Auctions are of the regular scheduled type, such as those used in the sale of most tobacco, and the intermittent type, such as the auction arranged for a special sale. In the merchandise category, everything from rare antiques to automobiles may be sold at auction. The auction method of selling is very prominent in the marketing of agricultural products. Tobacco, livestock, and produce are among the commodities that utilize this method. The auction company may be paid a commission by the seller, or in some cases the commission may be paid jointly by the seller and the buyer. Commissions are thought to vary from 3 to 6 per cent.

Other Agents

There are other agents that perform functions in the distribution of goods. A service that should perhaps be mentioned is that of *factoring*. The factor is a company engaged in performing the credit function for

[3] Beckman, Engle, and Buzzell, *op. cit.*, p. 288.

the seller. The manufacturer selling on account to wholesalers and re-tailers may turn the credit function over to the factor. The factor approves the accounts to be sold; and when the sale is made, the account is turned over to the factoring company. The factor may then pay the seller the amount of the account less the cost of the factoring service and then collect directly from the customer. For example, the factor may pay the seller 97¢ on the dollar and then collect the full account from the customer. The difference is the factor's "commission" for as-suming the credit function. Factors are active in the clothing and tex-tile trades and generally restrict themselves to large-volume accounts. The factor relieves the seller of the necessity of operating a credit-and-collections department, and he enables the seller to receive payment for merchandise as soon as it is sold. Factoring may be especially valuable to those sellers who may be short of working capital.

Most of the agent middlemen discussed in this section are primarily engaged in representing the seller. However, there are agents who represent the buyer in seeking sources and negotiating prices. One such agent would be the *resident buyer*. Resident buyers are prominent in the clothing trades, and many such agents operate out of New York City. The small merchant who cannot make frequent buying trips to the central markets may engage the services of the resident buyer. The merchant may visit the market once each year, at which time he is advised and assisted by the resident buyer. Between visits, the resident buyer may make such purchases as are necessary to keep the merchant's inventory in good shape. The merchant pays the resident buyer a com-mission for this service. Resident buyers may function as companies representing a great many merchants located around the country. They are often able to spot items that are good sellers and to advise their clients accordingly.

INTEGRATED WHOLESALING

Manufacturers' Branch Warehouses

The manufacturer may choose to take on the performance of the wholesaling function himself. In the field of consumer goods, this would entail selling directly to retail outlets. The fact that retail outlets are widely scattered, and that many of them buy in small lots, may complicate direct sale by the manufacturer. In the area of industrial goods where purchases are normally larger, and where buyers are less scattered, direct selling is less difficult. In spite of the difficulty en-countered, many manufacturers of consumer goods have assumed the wholesaling function. This represents what we have referred to previously as forward integration. This has occurred largely among those manufacturers who market products in the *shopping-goods* class. These items may be large enough to justify the cost of direct selling, and the manufacturer may feel that more intensive selling is needed than that normally provided by the wholesale merchant. Sometimes, he solves this problem by using some of the functional middlemen discussed in the preceding section; but in other cases, he decides to do the wholesaling himself. Branch warehouses may be established to maintain inventory and serve retailers in a particular market.

Manufacturers' Sales Offices

In some lines, the manufacturer may establish sales offices in strategic market areas. A sales force may operate out of such an office, but no inventory is carried. In the case of some products, sales are made in sufficient volume to justify direct shipment from the nearest plant. In serving customers who buy in smaller lots, public warehouses may be used. Inventory may be carried in the public warehouse and deliveries made from this stock. The sales office is primarily an administrative unit and has the advantage of locating a territorial sales manager and his sales staff near the market.

Retailer-owned Wholesale Operations

It has become quite common for large-scale retailers to integrate backward to assume their own wholesaling. Large chain organizations do their own wholesaling and supply their retail stores out of regional warehouses. Large-volume, independent retailers—such as the independent department store—are able to buy directly from the manufacturer. They buy in quantities large enough to justify such direct selling on the part of the manufacturer. As a defense measure against the quantity buying advantages of the chains, the smaller independent retailers have often combined to form so-called *cooperative* chains. In this situation, the smaller retailers combine forces and establish their own wholesaling operation. They often rent warehouse space, hire a manager, and thereby gain some of the advantages of direct buying from the manufacturer. Such a cooperative group would not have the full range of services available through the merchant wholesaler.

The Future of the Wholesale Merchant

It should now be apparent to the student that wholesaling is an indispensable part of marketing. The question of who should perform the wholesaling function remains a matter of debate. Large firms in both manufacturing and retailing may assume the wholesaling function; however, the wholesale merchant continues to play a prominent role. In the distribution of many items, especially those in the convenience category, there seems to be no economical substitute for the wholesale merchant. The wholesaler handles an extensive line and services many retail outlets. This enables him to spread his costs among the many firms that he represents. Also, he can offer the firm a ready-made market in that he has established contacts at a given time with a number of retailers. In fact, many small retailers depend on the wholesaler as a source of credit, and as a source of advice in operating their stores. For these and other reasons, the wholesale merchant seems assured of a place in our system of distribution.

THE RETAILING PHASE OF MARKETING

Importance of Retailing

On an average, we spend approximately two-thirds of our disposable income on retail sales. Although there are varying definitions of retailing, it is generally agreed that a retail sale is one in which the buyer is the ultimate consumer; in other words, he is buying for personal use rather than for industrial or institutional purposes. Thus defined, the field of retailing is somewhat broader than is commonly recognized. In 1964, retail sales in the United States were in excess of 250 billion dollars. About 67 per cent of this amount represented expenditures for non-durables, while the remaining 33 per cent was spent for items in the durable-goods category.[4] Food and clothing are typical of the non-durable goods, while furniture and appliances are examples of durable goods.

Retail establishments represent our most numerous type of business enterprise. In 1961, there were about 2,000,000 retail establishments in the country. These had an annual average sales volume per store of approximately $110,000.[5] The preponderance of small stores is exemplified by the fact that less than one-third of the larger stores do more than two-thirds of total volume. Some small retailers have annual sales amounting to only a few thousand dollars, while giants in the industry such as A & P or Sears, Roebuck and Company may have an annual volume of sales measured in billions. In 1963, approximately 9 million people were employed in retailing.[6] This was equivalent to approximately 12 per cent of our employed labor force at that time.

[4] U.S. Department of Commerce, Office of Business Economics and the Bureau of the Census, 1964.

[5] U.S. Department of Commerce, 1962.

[6] U.S. Department of Labor, Bureau of Labor Statistics, 1964.

Method of Retailing

The retailing function is accomplished in a number of ways. It is quite common to discuss retailing according to the manner chosen to reach the consumer. Consumers may be reached through stores, by mail, through house-to-house selling, and by way of vending machines. The bulk of retail sales, an estimated 97 per cent, is made through stores. Of the remaining types, vending machines are gaining importance in the distribution of certain items.[7] The many ways of accomplishing the retailing function will be discussed in later sections of this chapter.

THE STRUCTURE OF RETAILING

The Independent Retailer

The independent operator is generally thought of as operating a single store; although in certain classifications, he may operate three or more stores and still be counted as an independent. As a rule, the independent retailer doubles as owner and manager of the establishment, especially if the operation is a small-scale one. We should bear in mind that the term "independent" refers primarily to ownership, and independents may vary in size from the one-man store to a department store doing an annual volume of millions. Numerically speaking, the independents vastly outnumber the non-independents, and the majority of independents are small operators. Typical of the independent is the family-operated store.

Over-all, the independently owned and operated retail store has held its own against the development of corporate chains. There are many reasons for this tendency of the independent to hold his ground. Perhaps of most importance is the fact that certain types of retailing apparently do not adapt well to the chain-store method. In lines such as farm equipment, hardware, building materials, drugs, and appliances, the independent overshadows the chain. The independent has an advantage where personal service and a close relationship with the customer is essential. It should also be noted that newcomers into the field of retailing will usually enter as independents. Chain-store systems generally develop from a start as successful independents. The fact that those entering retailing usually start as independents contributes to the large number of small stores in that category and also contributes to the high failure rate among independents. The nature of retailing would seem to

[7] D. J. Duncan and C. F. Phillips, *Retailing Principles and Methods* (6th ed.; Homewood, Ill.: Richard D. Irwin, Inc., 1963), Chap. 1.

assure the continuation of the independently owned store as a primary element in our retail structure.

Corporate Chains

Corporate chains are multiunit systems organized as business corporations. The Bureau of the Census has classified as chains those organizations having four or more units that are centrally owned, which practice a degree of centralized control in management and merchandising. Chains may vary in size from the local chain with less than a half-dozen stores to the giants such as A & P Stores with approximately 5,000 units and with annual sales in excess of four billion dollars. Chains are very strong in certain areas of retailing, especially in categories such as variety stores, department stores, shoe stores, and grocery stores. But when all forms of retailing are considered, the chains still account for less than 25 per cent of the total annual retail volume.[8] The corporate chain developed rapidly during the 1920's, but since 1929 the chain's share of the retail market seems to have stabilized.

There are certain inherent advantages in the chain-store method of retailing. Chains are able to buy in large quantities and thus effect certain savings in that respect. They are able to take advantage of a division of labor in that they are often large enough to justify the hiring of specialists. Buyers who specialize in certain merchandise categories and management specialists in areas such as advertising and personnel administration may be employed. This is in contrast to the small independent store where we often find one man responsible for many different tasks. The chains have also been comparatively progressive in their management. They utilize marketing research in selecting store sites and in planning store layout. They may be able to acquire capital more readily and thus be able to adopt new innovations ahead of the small independent. The corporate chain also faces certain limitations. It is generally thought of as an impersonal store and less able to offer the type of service desired by some customers. The corporate form of ownership often means that the store is owned by interests outside the market in which it operates. Some customers tend to voice prejudice against absentee ownership in contrast to local ownership. Public hostility toward chains was evidenced in the 1920's and 1930's and this even led to the passage of discriminatory taxation in some states. During this period, the independents were struggling to combat the development of chain stores, and it is probable that hostility was a by-product of this struggle. In recent years, there seems to be little resentment directed toward the chain as a method of retailing.

[8] U.S. Department of Commerce, Bureau of the Census, 1964.

Voluntary and Cooperative Chains

The development of the chain stores in the 1920's, especially in the food field, threatened the existence of the merchant wholesaler and the independent retailer. The chain was usually large enough to buy directly from the manufacturer, and this left the merchant wholesaler dependent upon the independent retailer for a market. As the independent retailers declined, the wholesaler found his market dwindling. He met this challenge through the organization of *voluntary chains*. The wholesaler in this situation took the initiative in organizing independent retailers into a group operation. The group often adopted a common name, standardized inventory, and in other ways adopted the characteristics of the chain. The wholesaler in turn was able to cut his costs since he was assured of a market. He also worked with the retailers to achieve other ways of reducing costs. This arrangement worked to the advantage of both the merchant wholesaler and the independent retailer, and it has been a factor in sustaining both—especially in the food field.

Similar to the voluntary chain is the *cooperative chain*. The cooperative chain is organized by a group of independent retailers. They establish their own wholesaling operation, often adopt a common name, standardize inventory, and employ specialists. Thus, by adopting the methods of the corporate chain, they are in a better position to compete. In the case of the voluntary and the cooperative chain, the ownership of the individual store remains with the independent.

Consumer Cooperatives

In a consumer cooperative, the customer "owns" the retail store. Such cooperatives are started by customers who subscribe to stock as a means of raising the initial capital. The store is established and a manager employed. At the end of the year, any profit made by the store is rebated to the customers in proportion to their purchases. Most consumer cooperatives are organized according to the Rochdale principles. These principles were derived by a group that organized a cooperative in England in the nineteenth century. In brief, the principles advocate open membership, democractic control, sales at prevailing prices with patronage dividends (rebates), limited interest on capital, sales for cash, and educational activities. Stores organized according to the Rochdale principles welcome all customers who care to trade at the store. Those who subscribe to the stock have only one vote each in determining management decisions. This is in contrast to the business corporation in which the stockholder casts a number of votes in direct proportion to

the shares of stock held. Since the profits of the cooperative are rebated to the customers, the cooperative is not required to pay taxes on
its earnings.

The consumer cooperative has not assumed great importance as a
form of retailing in the United States. In certain of the European countries, the consumer cooperative has become an important retail institution. Cooperatives operate primarily in the food field; and in the
United States, the chain stores have been able to market food at a cost
sufficiently low to make it difficult for the cooperative to offer its patrons
a price advantage. It is estimated that in the United States, consumer
cooperatives account for less than 1 per cent of our annual retail sales
volume.[9]

TYPES OF RETAIL OPERATIONS

The General Store

In the United States, the *trading post* was perhaps our earliest type
of retail store. As the early settlements grew, the trading posts gave
way to the general store. The general store carried a food line supplemented by a wide range of items such as clothing, shoes, hardware, farm
supplies, drugs, and medicines.[10] These stores were located in villages
and rural communities and due to transportation limitations were often
the sole retail outlets available to many consumers. The merchant who
operated the general store was often a leader in the community and
an important part of his function was the extension of credit when
needed. In addition to its merchandising function, the general store
often served as a public forum and civic center. The general store remained an important retail institution well into the twentieth century.
With the advent of the automobile and a network of roads, the general
store began to decline. Customers preferred to visit towns and cities
where variety and more up-to-date merchandise could be found. In
rural areas, the general store has given way to the modified grocery
store-gas station, and there are very few examples of the old type
general store left.

Limited-Line Stores

Limited-line retailing is represented by those stores that specialize
in a restricted line of products, for example, shoe stores, dress shops,
and millinery stores. Limited-line retailing is dependent upon popula-

[9] U.S. Department of Commerce, Bureau of the Census, 1964.
[10] W. R. Davidson and A. F. Doody, *Retailing Management* (3d ed.; New York:
The Ronald Press Co., 1966).

tion concentrations. The more specialized the store, the larger must be the market served. It is doubtful that a store selling only neckties could survive in a small town, but such a store might do very well in New York or Chicago. The limited-line store offers its customers a wide selection within the lines carried. As a rule, such stores emphasize personal service and are relied upon by their customers for advice in the selection of the items to be purchased. In the area of fashion goods, the limited-line store often operates as a prestige establishment and prides itself on having the latest fashions before they are available through other outlets.

Department Stores

Department stores are generally large stores offering a variety of merchandise under one roof. A principal distinguishing characteristic is the departmental organization. While department stores may offer everything from cosmetics to building materials, they do tend to cater to the needs of women and children. Services such as credit and delivery are emphasized; and facilities such as restaurants, tea rooms, and beauty parlors are provided for the convenience of shoppers. Some department stores are independently owned while others are units in corporate chains. Not all department stores aim at serving the same market; some emphasize price appeal and become known as bargain stores, while others may emphasize higher quality and operate as prestige establishments.

Variety and shopping convenience have long been the department store's principal competitive advantage. Traditionally, department stores have been centrally located in downtown areas for shopping convenience. In recent years, a location that was once an advantage has, in some cases, lost much of its appeal. An increasing number of automobiles in use has resulted in serious parking problems for the downtown store. The flight of the city population to the suburbs has also added to the problems of downtown operators. This problem has been met by taking the store to the suburbs in the form of branch stores. At the same time, efforts are being made to alleviate the downtown parking problem by constructing new parking lots and the organization of "park-and-shop" services. In recent years, department store sales volume has continued to increase, but the increase has been at a slower rate than that of retailing in general. There seems to be clear evidence that the department store is declining as a retail institution. Prior to World War II, department stores were thought to account for 8 to 10 per cent of the total retail sales. By 1963, they were accounting for approximately 7 per cent of total retail volume.[11]

[11] U.S. Department of Commerce, Bureau of the Census, 1964.

Other Forms of Retailing

The *supermarket* is unique to the extent that it may be mentioned as a "method" of retailing. The supermarket is a development growing out of the Depression of the 1930's. Originally, it represented an effort to bring together under one roof a wide variety of merchandise and to offer the goods in the most economical manner possible. Markets were located in low-rent areas; buildings and fixtures were utilitarian rather than fancy; and the merchandise was offered on a self-service basis. The supermarket as we know it has changed drastically from its predecessor. It is today primarily a departmentalized food store, although non-food items are growing in importance. Economy is still an appeal in drawing customers, along with convenience and variety, which are also strong appeals. Buildings and fixtures rank with the most modern in retailing.

Mail-order retailing is still in evidence. By the 1960's, there were approximately 2,500 mail-order establishments that did a combined total of less than 1 per cent of our retail sales.[12] Of these firms, Sears, Roebuck and Company and Montgomery Ward and Company are the best known. Both of these companies operate retail stores in addition to their mail-order business. Mail-order firms apparently reached their peak of importance in the 1920's. The development of the automobile and good roads has served to limit the growth of this form of retailing.

Discount houses are often mentioned as an innovation in retailing. These establishments are something of a throwback to the original idea of the supermarket in that they often attempt to minimize fixtures, services, etc., and to compete primarily in the area of price. House-to-house selling is also a type of retailing. House-to-house salesmen account for less than 1 per cent of retail sales, although they are prominent in some lines. Products that require extensive demonstration as a part of the sales technique are often sold in this manner. Automatic vending continues to grow as a method of retailing, and, in 1963, sales were estimated at $3.2 billion.[13]

PROBLEMS IN RETAILING

Selecting a Location

The establishment of a retail firm begins with a consideration of the location. Stores stressing the sale of convenience items, as in the case of

---

[12] U.S. Department of Commerce, Bureau of the Census, 1964.
[13] *Vending in 1963* (Chicago: National Automatic Vending Association).

the variety stores, must depend upon customer traffic. They must seek locations with a maximum exposure to pedestrian traffic. Stores handling shopping goods may be able to utilize locations away from the main flow of traffic. The customer for shopping goods is more willing to go out of his way a bit to visit a particular store. It is considered good policy for stores handling shopping goods to locate near one another, thus making it convenient for the customer to do comparative shopping. A cluster of shops will in themselves attract a flow of traffic. It is not always possible for the prospective retailer to get the type of location desired. If he is seeking a building to rent, he is limited to those vacancies available. There is more flexibility in the construction of a building, but initial capital requirements may preclude this.

Deciding the Manner of Operation

A variety of techniques are used in making merchandise available to the retail-store customer. Clerks may be employed to serve customers, or one may operate utilizing self-service. The nature of the merchandise sold often indicates the type of service to be offered. Staple items that are relatively standard in quality and price and well known to the consumer lend themselves well to self-service retailing. Developments in packaging have been very important in the growth of the self-service method. When the customer requires considerable information before buying an item, or when fitting or alteration is necessary, clerk-service is essential. Generally speaking, self-service has developed most widely in the grocery, hardware, variety, and drug and sundry lines. The question of customer service involves important operating decisions. In addition to the services of sales clerks, some retailers offer credit and delivery services. Large retailers frequently offer customer advisory services in areas such as home decoration, landscaping, and building improvement. Services are expensive, and stores that offer liberal services must price the merchandise to cover the added costs. Some customers demand service and are willing to pay for it, while others prefer to forego the service in order to obtain lower prices.

Choosing the Merchandise

Selecting the merchandise to be stocked calls for crucial decisions on the part of the retailer, especially if he is operating in the area of shopping goods rather than the convenience category. He must decide the variety to be carried, that is, the completeness of his stock. Sometimes this is a question of breadth of inventory versus depth; for example, should the shoe retailer carry two brands with all sizes in each brand and many pairs of each size or should he carry many brands and concentrate upon the most popular sizes with comparatively few pairs in each size? The quality of the merchandise stocked represents another major decision. Shall our retailer carry only the best quality and appeal to a prestige market or stock merchandise of lower quality and appeal to the lower income segment of the market? Many retailers attempt to reach a wide segment of the market by appealing to the middle-income groups. They handle merchandise that varies widely in quality and price. Some retailers have been successful in appealing to a wide market, while others have found success in appealing to a more restricted and specific market. The leveling of income that has occurred in the United States since the 1920's has caused the emergence of a large middle-income group, and most retailers seem dedicated to serving this market. One must remember, however, that income alone is not the sole criterion for stratifying a market. Factors such as education and occupation may lead certain customers to patronize the prestige retailer, while many people of high income derive satisfaction from practicing the thrift exemplified in shopping at the bargain store.

Inventory Control

After the retailer has made the decision on what to stock, he must deal with the problem of managing the quantity of goods carried. Decisions regarding the quantity to buy and the amount to keep in stock are often referred to as *inventory control.* There are two basic methods of inventory control: One method known as *dollars control* reports the dollar value at retail of the inventory on hand. The other method known as *unit control* reports the inventory on hand in terms of the individual items of merchandise. Dollar control may provide the buyer with information on the quantity of inventory "in dollars" in a department, or in a certain product line, at a given time. If a department stocks a very few items, the total dollar value (at retail) of each class of items may be furnished the buyer. Where a department stocks a great number of different items, dollar control that reports the value of the inventory in the entire department may fail to give a clear picture of the status of the individual items. Dollar control may be more applicable for retailers handling a relatively small number of products and in cases where the control can be applied to product lines.

Unit control enables the retailer to keep records of his inventory in terms of physical units rather than in dollars. Unit control is often used in conjunction with, and as a supplement to, dollar control. Unit control may report the exact number of items on hand, but it may not report the dollar value. While dollar control reports the current investment in inventory, unit control reports the number of physical units. Both inventory methods may be essential in providing the retailer with the information needed in making decisions.

Inventory control, whether dollar control or unit control, may be administered through physical counts or through book controls. Where physical counts are used, the items of merchandise on hand at a given time are counted and reported in dollars, units, or both. Large stores carrying a great variety of merchandise may find frequent physical counts very expensive in terms of time and labor. Book controls usually involve a record of goods on hand at the beginning of the period, a record of purchases, and a record of sales and markdowns. By subtracting the goods sold from beginning inventory and purchases, the resulting figure should represent the goods presently on hand. Book inventories do not show losses through theft and breakage, and it is usually necessary to take a physical count at intervals to correct these deficiencies.

Pricing Policies

The pricing of merchandise poses one of the most difficult problems faced by retailers. The retailer is normally in a competitive market, and this places a ceiling upon the prices that he may charge. He finds that he must price goods high enough to cover the cost of merchandise and the operating expenses, and to provide a profit. Thus, the cost of doing business places a "floor" under his prices, and the competitive situation places a "ceiling" above which he cannot price. These factors limit the range within which the retailer may safely vary his prices, but within this range there remains considerable freedom in the adoption of price policies. He may adopt a policy of pricing below competition, of meeting competition, or of pricing above competition—of course, keeping in mind the fact that his range of variation may not be wide. He may attempt to underprice competition and develop a volume business. Up to a point, retailing is a decreasing-cost industry; that is, as sales volume increases, the per unit cost of doing business declines. The retailer has certain relatively fixed costs such as rent or maintenance of the building, heat, light, power, and the maintenance of fixtures. Even his labor force to some degree may be a fixed cost. Until facilities are utilized to the maximum, an increase in sales will spread fixed costs and thus reduce such costs as a percentage of the sales dollar. It becomes the objective of the retailer to obtain an optimum sales volume that will enable him to reduce costs but at the same time maintain a price that will produce maximum profits. As long as a reduction in the price charged the customer is more than offset by the savings in cost realized from increased volume, the retailer can afford to reduce his prices. But eventually a point is reached where a savings from increased volume is not enough to offset the loss of revenue from reduced prices. The retailer who embarks upon a program of pricing-for-volume must assume considerable risks in doing so. The adjustments between costs and prices may require experimentation, and it may be necessary to continue this over a period of time. It may require time for a price reduction to produce volume, and the retailer may have to absorb a loss while waiting for this volume to materialize. There is also risk in that one does not know in advance if a price reduction will be significant enough to produce new volume.

Pricing at the Market Level

In an effort to avoid risks in pricing, many retailers establish prices by taking a cue from their competitors. They price "at the market" rather than undertake volume pricing or pricing above competition. Retailers who price at competitive levels strive to increase their operating profits through reducing costs. Such retailers may forego the buying advantages of the volume retailer, but they may reduce costs through greater efficiency in the handling and sale of merchandise. Small retailers, and newcomers into the retailing field, often price according to the competitive level prevailing in the market.

While the volume retailer may price below the market level, the so-called "prestige store" may move in the opposite direction and price at a level above the market. The prestige store attempts to build a reputation for distinctive merchandise and outstanding service to the customer. Such stores frequently feature their own labels, and a certain social significance may be attached to the possession of items purchased from these establishments. The prestige store features top quality merchandise, and the location and layout of the store are designed for comfortable, leisurely shopping. Prestige stores do not, as a rule, stress volume; thus, they must price at a higher level to compensate. Customers are drawn from the higher income levels for the most part; and consequently, the market may be thinly dispersed. For this reason, the prestige store is usually found in the larger cities.

The Mechanics of Pricing

Students interested in the mechanics of retail pricing may find detailed information in any of the standard text on the subject of retailing. In brief, we may point out that retail markup is usually figured as a percentage of the proposed selling price. The majority of medium- and large-scale retailers base the percentage markup on selling price rather than cost. In analyzing the cost of doing business, retailers frequently express their cost items as a percentage of net sales. Thus, if expenses, and markdowns, are shown as a percentage of sales, it becomes desirable to show the percentage markup as related to the same base. This facilitates comparisons between items of cost and the gross margin (the realized markup). One may use a simple formula for figuring selling price when markup is based on sales:

$$\text{Selling price} = \frac{\text{Cost of item}}{100 \text{ per cent minus per cent of desired markup}} \times 100$$

Through using the above formula we may determine that if a retailer buys an item for $3.00 and desires to realize a 40 per cent markup on the selling price, he will sell the item for $5.00. Tables have been computed that enable the retailer to determine rapidly the selling price of an item to be displayed. The percentage markup applied by the retailer will depend upon the type of business he operates. Retailers handling staples will normally operate with a smaller markup than those who handle fashion goods. Grocery supermarkets frequently operate on a gross margin of 18 to 20 per cent of sales. A high-fashion ladies' dress shop may operate on a gross margin in excess of 50 per cent of the selling price of the merchandise.

Retail Sales and Advertising

Customers frequently complain of the quality of the saleshelp employed in retail stores. Some departments in retail stores have very capable retail salesmen, while other departments employ saleshelp that could be more aptly described as salesclerks. The typical clerk makes change and bags the merchandise but does very little selling. Traditionally, retail clerks have received relatively low wages. They are often people with very little prior training or experience, and the rate of turnover on such jobs is high. Stores are frequently handicapped in paying higher wages by having to meet prevailing competition in pricing goods to the consumer. It is reasonable to assume that stores would be willing to pay higher wages if the added costs could be passed along to the customer. In many retail operations, the margin is so close that any added costs would have to result in higher prices. Although customers complain of poor service, it is doubtful that great numbers would be willing to pay higher prices in return for better saleshelp.

Advertising is a very vital part of retail selling. Stores vary in the extent to which they utilize advertising as a part of the sales-promotion program. It is not uncommon to find retail stores that do no advertising, but the majority of stores use it to some degree. The advertising appropriation may vary from a fraction of 1 per cent of sales to a high in excess of 10 per cent of sales. The typical department store may have an advertising appropriation of from 3 to 5 per cent of net sales. The newspaper is the principal medium used by the retailer, although radio, television, and direct-mail advertising are used. The basic objective of retail advertising is to bring the customer to the store in a frame of mind predisposed to buy the merchandise. It is up to personal selling to take over and complete the sale. An exception exists in the case of self-service retailing where personal selling is non-existent or held to a minimum. Many of the items featured in the self-service store are nationally advertised through a program of brand promotion. National advertising by the manufacturer and local retail advertising should be complementary, and many manufacturers work out cooperative advertising programs with the local retailer.

Trends in Retailing

Retailing has undergone tremendous changes since the early 1900's. Self-service had its beginning just prior to World War I and has continued to grow in importance. Developments in the prepackaging of products have made self-service possible and have revolutionized many phases of retailing. The shift of population from rural to urban areas was accelerated during World War II and has continued. The overflowing of cities and the resulting suburban movement brought the development of the suburban shopping center. The shopping center often centers around a large department store (often a branch store) and contains a wide representation of retail outlets. Some shopping centers are controlled in that a representation of outlets are sought and the number of stores in each category are restricted. The centers vary in size from the local center to the much larger regional center. Regional shopping centers have a wide representation of stores and draw trade from a relatively wide area. Over-all, there has been a tendency toward large-volume outlets at the expense of small-scale outlets.

Although self-service has reduced labor costs in some types of retailing, labor still remains a major cost item in retail store operation. As in the production industries, efforts to reduce costs in retailing are often aimed at reducing the labor required. Some progress has been made in the use of machines in the handling and lifting of goods in retail stores. The introduction of electronic-data-processing equipment promises to achieve significant reductions in the labor required in clerical and record-keeping operations. In addition to reducing labor costs, this equipment shows promise of being able to provide management with more reliable and up-to-date information on operations than was previously possible. Automation will undoubtedly find application in many phases of retailing, but the prospects for substituting machines for manpower face definite limitations. Much of retailing involves a personal service that falls outside the scope of the machine. As the standard of living continues to rise, customers are likely to demand more, rather than less, personal service from the retailer.

YOUR CAREER IN THE DISTRIBUTION TRADES

A Variety of Jobs

Perhaps as many as one-quarter of our employed population are in distribution, or activities directly related to it. It is obvious that a wide range of abilities is necessary to get the job done. Both wholesaling and retailing require management personnel at various levels of operation. Staff employees are required in areas such as personnel, advertising, and research. The advances of automation have not been as dramatic in the distribution trades as in the production side of business. Accordingly, distribution provides job opportunities for an increasing proportion of our people. Wherever large numbers of people are employed, there is a demand for supervisory personnel and for staff specialists.

Wholesaling and retailing traditionally have emphasized the importance of on-the-job training. College graduates who enter these fields may begin at slightly lower salaries than in certain other areas, but studies tend to show that the salary differential soon disappears. In fact, graduates who have been in retailing for ten years or more tend to earn salaries higher than those earned in most competing areas of employment.

The student who is interested in the areas of distribution discussed in this chapter will do well to pursue a sound basic education. The ability to communicate with people is important in distribution, as it is in all areas of work. Computer technology has made contributions in the larger wholesale and retail firms. Problems in areas such as inventory management are suited to the application of the computer. The prospective executive needs a good basic education in mathematics in order to function in an area that uses the computer as a tool. The behavioral sciences such as psychology, sociology, and anthropology are also important in helping one to understand the customers that he must serve. The breadth of the demand for abilities and skills in distribution is such that one is likely to find an outlet for his talents whatever they may be.

TOPICS FOR DISCUSSION

1. Although there are numerous types of middlemen involved in carrying on marketing operations, they are usually divided into two categories. What are these two categories, and what is the distinctive feature of each?

2. What advantages do you see for a manufacturer of stereo units who assumes the wholesaling function himself?

3. According to a recent survey, the American housewife spends an average of twenty-eight minutes on each visit to the supermarket. Of what value would this information be to you as a good retailer?

4. What do you feel is the main reason for the tremendous growth of point-of-purchase displays in retail stores?

5. Show one incident within the last ten years in which changing characteristics of the consumer market have forced changes in the pattern of retailing.

6. Why have the mail-order houses continued to do a certain volume of business in this age of modern travel?

7. Discuss some of the changes in our methods of marketing that have contributed to the development of supermarkets.

8. Do you feel that discount houses are desirable marketing institutions?

9. "Customers will often pay higher prices for the privilege of buying ordinary merchandise from a prestige store." Do you agree?

10. "Retail advertising that doesn't give the consumer information is worthless." Discuss.

CASE 16–1

THE MORRISON WATCH COMPANY, INC.

The Morrison Watch Company has been an importer of Swiss watch movements for more than twenty years. The company has specialized in importing low- to medium-price movements that were cased here in the United States and marketed under several brand names. The watches thus cased and branded have been sold through drugstores, variety stores, and jewelry stores specializing in lower-price lines. The Morrison line of watches generally retailed at prices between $10.40 and $22.50.

In 1965, Mr. Gedman, an executive of the Morrison Watch Company, presented to the management of the company a radical proposal for marketing a high-quality watch. In brief, Mr. Gedman proposed that quality movements be imported and incased in a manner consistent with this quality. The watches would be marketed under a new brand name, and they would be sold at retail primarily through drugstores. He contended that a watch of comparable quality to that retailing through conventional jewelry stores for $95 could be marketed through the drugstores at a retail price of $45 and return a good profit to the Morrison Company. He felt that a written guaranty could be inclosed in the box with each watch, and this would overcome the customer's concern for service in case the product did not perform as expected. He felt that the high quality of the watch would prevent the company from having a problem with repairs. In concluding his proposal, he maintained that, within five years, the reputation of the watch for quality would overcome any reluctance that customers might have to buy a watch in an unaccustomed outlet.

Mr. Greene expressed doubts regarding Mr. Gedman's proposal. He felt that the consumer develops a reliance on familiar distribution patterns. People expect to buy a quality watch from a store that specializes in fine jewelry. They not only have confidence in the outlet's support of warranties; they also associate the prestige of the outlet with the quality of the product. Furthermore, he contended, people associate price and quality. Few people would believe that a $45 watch was equal in quality to a $95 one, and they would not cherish the cheaper watch as they would the more expensive one. In short, he did not believe that one could be successful in revamping the existing distribution channel for quality watches.

Do you feel that the Morrison Watch Company would be successful in selling the higher-quality watch through drugstores? Support your answer.

SELECTED REFERENCES

Alexander, R. S., J. S. Cross, and R. M. Cunningham, *Industrial Marketing*. Rev. ed. Homewood, Ill.: Richard D. Irwin, Inc., 1961.

Beckman, T N., N. H. Engle, and R. D. Buzzell. *Wholesaling*. 3d ed. New York: The Ronald Press Co., 1959.

Davidson, W. R., and A. F. Doody. *Retailing Management*. 3d ed. New York: The Ronald Press Co., 1966.

Duncan, D. J., and C. F. Phillips. *Retailing: Principles and Methods*. 6th ed. Homewood, Ill.: Richard D. Irwin, Inc., 1963.

Hill, Richard M. *Wholesaling Management*. Homewood, Ill.: Richard D. Irwin, Inc., 1963.

17

The Role of Personal
Selling in Distribution

IMPORTANCE OF THE SALES FUNCTION

If our economy is to function successfully, someone must interpret consumer wants and produce the goods and services to satisfy these wants. The producer, in his dealings with the consumer, may represent himself in a personal manner or in a non-personal manner. Personal representation takes the form of some type of salesmanship, whereas non-personal selling may be represented by means such as advertising. In our country, where consumer choice dictates what is to be produced and marketed, producers attribute great importance to understanding the consumer and conveying his wants and desires to the decision centers of the firm. The personal salesman stands as an indispensable link between producer and consumer.

The salesman conveys information about his product or service to the consumer, and relays to his employer the demands of the consumer. In addition, he has the important task of stimulating the consumer to buy. It has been variously estimated that in prosperous times as much as 40 per cent of the consumer goods bought are in the non-necessity class. This is significant when we realize that most consumers could drastically reduce their purchasing and still get along. But, if such a reduction did occur, the consumption-production cycle would be disrupted, and we would find ourselves faced with economic depression. It is the job of our selling forces to see that the goods produced move steadily through the channels of distribution. To maintain high-level employment, we must maintain high-level consumption of the goods produced, and personal selling remains a vital cog in achieving this task. A well-known book summarizes the importance of the sales function in these words.

Salesmen are an economic institution in our society; selling is a vital function which our society obviously has found must be performed if our order is to continue on its present course. Society is both ruthless and benevolent; ruthless in eliminating unwanted firms, activities, or people; benevolent in rewarding those who give it what it wants. Hence, the salesman must be performing functions which society values, or he would have been eliminated.[1]

An early economic doctrine maintained that goods produced would automatically create their own markets. It is doubtful that this doctrine was very valid except in the most far-fetched theoretical sense, but any validity which it may have possessed surely must have expired with the advent of the industrial revolution. With the advent of the industrial revolution, technology advanced rapidly. Man's ability to produce moved forward by leaps and bounds, and this has continued until today we are no longer worried about our ability to produce most items but are very much concerned with our ability to provide markets. The maintenance of a market is a very complex thing. In an exchange economy, people must possess money to become active purchasers. Economists are concerned with patterns in the distribution of income and in the maintenance of employment as a prerequisite to an effective distribution. The salesman alone does not control the destiny of the market, but he plays a vital role through inducing the consumer to purchase rather than engage in the excessive hoarding of his buying power. It might also be said that he is a factor in inducing the consumer to work harder to earn the income with which to purchase the desired goods.

What Is Salesmanship?

There are many definitions of salesmanship, some more comprehensive than others. A simplified definition would be that *salesmanship* includes "The arts of personal persuasion employed by the seller to induce others to buy what he wishes to sell."[2] There continues to exist a certain confusion in the minds of the public over the salesman and his job. Many people may still picture the salesman as described in the literature of the last century. Traditionally, he was described as a man in a derby hat, with a gold watch chain and a big black cigar, and a roving

---

[1] F. A. Russell, F. H. Beach, and R. H. Buskirk, *Textbook of Salesmanship* (7th ed.; New York: McGraw-Hill Book Co., 1963), p. 13.

[2] *Ibid.*, Chap. 1. (This chapter develops in detail the concept of selling.)

eye for the farmer's daughter. It is just as unrealistic to compare the salesman of today with his counterpart of the last century as it would be to compare the medical doctor of today with his nineteenth-century predecessor. There are still hucksters in selling, and there are still quacks in the medical profession. But neither the doctor nor the salesman should be characterized by the unscrupulous found among them. How can we describe the modern salesman and the practice of modern salesmanship?

To begin with, salesmanship is a broad term. It may include door-to-door peddlers, retail clerks, telephone solicitors, and a host of others. Unfortunately, the public meets the least well-trained element of salesmanship in that they are exposed to the house-to-house caller and the retail clerk. As was stated in Chapter 16, house-to-house selling is relatively unimportant in the total sales picture; and by definition, we may exclude retail clerks as salesmen. The salesman in the retail store is distinguished from the clerk who makes change and bags merchandise. As discussed in this chapter, salesmanship will be thought of as embracing that area of selling requiring training, skill, and the exercise of responsibility on the part of its practitioners. The heart of this category would consist of industrial salesmen who represent a producer in calling upon another producer; salesmen who represent the manufacturer in calling upon the wholesale and the retail trade; and certain direct-to-consumer sellers in areas such as insurance, investments, and certain of the heavy durable goods. Undoubtedly, there are salesmen in other categories who merit recognition, but the above categories may be considered representative. In terms of the above categories, one may observe that the general public seldom meets the industrial salesman or the salesman selling to the trade. A knowledge of salesmanship on this level would do much to change the public's conception of selling.

Personal Selling and the Marketing Mix

The marketing strategy used by a company involves a combination of elements. The nature of the product, its position in the market, and the type of market to be served are factors influencing the marketing mix. The elements of the marketing mix may include, in addition to personal selling, various types of advertising, characteristics of product and package design, dealer promotions to secure cooperation at the retail level, and the use of marketing research. Personal selling and advertising are primary elements in the marketing of consumer goods. Emphasis may be placed upon one or the other, or occasionally the emphasis may be equally placed. New products, and products requiring consumer education as a factor in purchasing, may emphasize personal selling. Products that are non-standard and products that require technical assistance in installation and servicing may also rely heavily upon personal selling. Products in the convenience class that are well known to the consumer, and where brand acceptance is a major factor in purchase, will often emphasize advertising. It should be emphasized that in most cases, products are marketed through a combination of personal selling and advertising effort. The two elements are complimentary rather than competitive with one another. Figure 17–1 illustrates the manner in which personal selling and advertising may join to facilitate the flow of goods from producer to consumer. Study of the diagram shows that the manufacturer has many alternatives in the application of his selling effort. He may sell directly to the consumer utilizing a combination of personal selling and advertising, or he may distribute through middlemen and use both personal selling and adver-

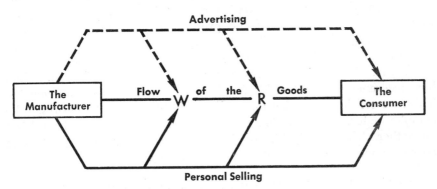

Fig. 17–1. Personal selling and advertising join forces in facilitating the flow of goods (the channel shown is the traditional wholesale-retail channel).

tising to reach them and secure their cooperation. It is not uncommon for a manufacturer to distribute through middlemen and to use personal selling and advertising to stimulate the middlemen and the consumer. In the latter situation, personal selling and advertising may be directed to middlemen, while the manufacturer takes his message to the consumer through advertising alone. There is no formula for determining the best marketing mix. It is a matter of the individual situation and the judgment of the seller. We often see identical products successfully marketed with a difference in the emphasis placed on the separate elements of the marketing mix.

FUNDAMENTALS OF SELLING

Buying Motives

Normally, one does not make a purchase without having a reason for doing so. The reason for buying may not always be valid; but if we are to understand the consumer, we must try to understand that which motivates him to act. As individuals, we are driven to act in response to motives grounded within our being. Certain motivating forces such as hunger, fear, sex, and anger are innate; while other motives may derive from our environmental conditions. The concept of motivation is a rather complex study, and much remains to be learned about what causes us to act as we do. As a rule, the salesman is not a trained psychologist, and he is not expected to be an exceptional authority on human behavior. But the salesman must deal with people, and he must be able to comprehend their needs and desires. The art of selling lies in sensing the consumer's reasons (motives) for wanting the product and then in presenting the features of the product in a manner to appeal to those reasons. If we are selling insurance to a young father, we may be reasonably sure that he is motivated by the parental desire to protect his family. Being aware of this motive, we may proceed to show him how insurance will protect his family against unforeseen contingencies. Thus, we sell him a service that will satisfy his protective desires. The complex nature of motivation tempts the layman to avoid the subject altogether. The impossibility of the salesman avoiding the question of consumer motivation has been stated as follows:

The impossibility of avoiding the question of motivation in the process of selling may be shown by a simple illustration. Suppose that Mr. Smith has a bushel of apples which he desires to sell to Mr. Brown. Obviously, Mr. Smith wants to sell the apples because there is something else which he wants more than apples. It is equally obvious that if Mr. Brown buys the apples he must be willing to give up something which he considers to be less desirable at the moment than apples. Smith might approach Brown and give him all the reasons why he would like to get rid of the bushel of apples. This approach would be entirely in terms of the seller's self-interest, and, unless Brown took pity on Smith and bought the apples as a charitable gesture, it is not likely that a sale would be made. This assumes of course that Brown did not enter the transaction with a pre-disposition for apples, and that some degree of "selling" is required. It is an accepted principle of salesmanship that if Smith is to succeed in selling the apples—that is, succeed in awakening in Brown a desire for apples—he must approach the transaction in terms of Brown's self-interest. The moment Smith makes the transition from his own self-interest to the self-interest of his prospect, he must cope with the question of motives. Without some idea of what might motivate Brown to want the apples, Smith's efforts would be entirely devoid of direction, and could in no sense be classed as salesmanship.[3]

Often the salesman is able to study the prospect in his environment and arrive at some conclusion concerning his motives. In conversation with the prospect, the salesman may be able to discover the buying motives foremost in the prospect's mind.

Sellers are continually trying to gain a better understanding of consumer behavior. Much research has been devoted to the study of why consumers behave as they do. In recent years, *motivation research*, has developed as an important adjunct to the conventional approach to consumer motivation. Motivation research, or *motivation analysis* as it may be called, employs the techniques of the clinical psychologist in an effort to further understand the consumer. Essentially, it deals with the discovery of *hidden motives* that may be responsible for consumer action. Specialists in this area of research maintain that in certain instances, consumers are prompted to act by motives of which they may not be aware or by motives that they may be unwilling to admit—even to themselves. Through a process of depth interviewing, or intensive interrogation, the researcher is able to discover these hidden motives. Once discovered, these motives may then be utilized by the producer in designing and selling his product. Undoubtedly, there have been cases where hidden motives have been brought to light and products designed and sold appealing to these motives. But for the majority of products sold on the market, the conventional approach to the understanding of buying motives provides a satisfactory approach in personal selling. The salesman in dealing with the individual prospect cannot employ the tools of the motivation research specialists. He is more or less limited to discovering his prospects' motives through an analysis of the environmental situation and through the direct medium of conversation. As the salesman is able to discover the motives of his prospect, he is able to establish the fulfillment, or satisfying, of these motives as his targets. Facts about the products and what it will do afford the ammunition to be fired at these targets.

Talking Points

As the salesman goes forth to sell, he should be armed with a thorough knowledge of his product and what it will do for the purchaser. The salesman often refers to such items of knowledge as his *talking points*. A *talking point* may be defined as a characteristic of a product or service, or its use, which when made known to the prospective cus-

---

[3] H. G. Wales, D. L. Gentry, and Max Wales, *Advertising Copy, Layout, and Typography* (New York: The Ronald Press Co., 1958), p. 64.

tomer will cause him to want the product or service. In the section that follows, we will discuss how the salesman goes about obtaining the information upon which his talking points are based. It suffices to point out here that after much study, the salesman assembles and organizes vital information on his product and its uses. Equipped with this knowledge, he surveys his prospective customer and approaches him through an appeal to the buying motives. If our salesman has detected his prospect's desires (motives) and has chosen his product information wisely, he may be able to show the prospect how the product can meet his needs (fulfill his desires). The completion of the sale will depend upon the strength of the motives of the prospective consumer and upon the ability of the salesman to show that his product is better able than any other to fulfill the need. The proficiency of the talking points is not just a matter of the salesman's skill, but they rest most heavily upon the quality and suitability of the product. To be a good salesman, one must sell a good product.

THE SALES PROCESS

Knowledge of the Product

One only has to have experience in selling a product to know the value of product knowledge. The salesman who attempts to sell without adequate product knowledge may be able on occasion to bluff his way, but eventually his lack of information will catch up with him and he will stand exposed in his ignorance. The buyer expects the salesman to be an expert on the product and its uses; and to be successful, the salesman must live up to the buyer's expectation. When the buyer discovers that the salesman does not have knowledge of his product, he loses respect for him as an authority. If a sale is made under these conditions, it is the product that sells itself—for the salesman without product knowledge may be a handicap rather than an aid in completing the sale.

In acquiring knowledge of the product, the prospective salesman may be required to devote extensive time and effort. Many companies devote a large share of the sales-training program to teaching the sales trainee in the area of product knowledge. This often involves starting the trainee out as a worker in the plant and having him gain first-hand knowledge on the assembly line. Classroom and laboratory sessions are also used as a part of in-plant training relative to the product. In the latter stages of training, contacts with dealers and with users of the product further add to the trainee's understanding of the product.

Knowledge of the Market

Knowledge of the product must be supplemented with a knowledge of the market. The salesman may be required to locate and identify his prospective customers. After locating the prospective customer, he must learn something of his needs and do other preparatory work before making the sales presentation. Without a knowledge of the market, much time could be wasted in calling upon people who are not prospective users. The salesman should be able to interpret market research data and to use published directories and other sources in locating prospects. Many sales are closed only after repeated calls have been made. In making repeat calls, the salesman builds up his knowledge of the buyer. He learns the buyer's motives, his customs and habits that influence purchase. The greatest asset of the experienced salesman is his knowledge of the market served. Markets are constantly changing, and the salesman must be continually on the lookout for new customers and for changes in the status of his present customers.

Planning the Presentation

Armed with a knowledge of his product and a knowledge of his market, the salesman is ready to plan the presentation to be made to the prospect. The presentation is what we more commonly know as the "sales talk," accompanied by such demonstrations and exhibits as the salesman may use. The degree to which the presentation is planned may vary from very specific plans to the more generalized. The planning of a presentation involves consideration of the *talking points* that may be used and the order in which these points may be presented to the prospect. As indicated earlier, these talking points will have been selected with due regard for the buying motives of the prospective customer. The most rigid presentation would be a memorized sales talk. The *memorized presentation,* or "canned sales talk" as it is sometimes called, is not widely used. It is perhaps most applicable when the salesman is of limited ability and not able to organize and present a presentation in the normal manner. It may also be used when a company has to put salesmen to work without proper training and experience. There may be some companies that feel that they have developed a single most effective presentation and thus demand that the salesman deliver the talk from memory. But there are very few selling situations that would seem to justify this stereotyped manner of presentation.

The *standardized presentation* is made up of certain predetermined talking points, but it stops short of having the salesman memorize the actual sales talk. Using this plan, the salesman has certain talking points to present and a particular order in which he would like to present them. He presents the talking points in his "own words" and is therefore more natural and flexible in his conversation. If the occasion demands, he may change the order in which the points are presented, emphasizing some strongly and devoting less time to others, depending upon the prospect, and in various other ways exercise his discretion in presenting the sales talk. Most salesmen use a standardized presentation to some degree. Such a presentation assures the salesman of having the more pertinent points at his disposal, while leaving him freedom to fit his presentation to the prospect.

Making the Sales Presentation

The preparations discussed in the preceding sections are aimed at one objective: making a sale. If adequate preparations have been made, the salesman should be well equipped to make his presentation. The presentation begins the moment the salesman greets the buyer and terminates by the salesman taking his leave. The heart of the presentation is the "sales talk" in which the salesman presents his product or service as a means of meeting the needs of the buyer. The sales talk is woven into the "interview" and is in no sense a one-way communication. The sales interview may take the form of a conversation between the buyer and seller, with the buyer explaining his needs and the seller stating what his product has to offer. In the course of an interview, the parties gain information through questioning one another. Regardless of the informality that may prevail, the course of a successful sales presentation will normally follow the traditional five steps:

1. The salesman must gain the undivided attention of the prospect.
2. The salesman must arouse the interest of the prospect in what he is selling.
3. The salesman must create a desire for the product on the part of the prospect.
4. The salesman must convince the prospect that *his* product is the best available to fulfill the desire.
5. The salesman must successfully close the sale.

We may point out that a buyer may grant an interview and receive the salesman in a courteous manner and yet not give his full attention to the presentation. The experienced salesman can sense when he has the complete attention of his prospect. If he does not have the prospect's attention, he will strive to gain it. The strength of the stimulus that the salesman offers is a prime factor in gaining attention. If the prospect is a buyer for a business firm, he will be interested in helping the firm reduce costs. If the salesman is able to state that he can reduce the manufacturing cost of an item by 10 per cent, he will immediately get the attention of the prospect. The strength of the stimulus is also a vital factor in arousing the interest of the prospect. The prospective buyer is interested in bettering himself (or his company), and appeals to his self-interest will usually meet with a favorable response. Having stimulated the interest of the prospect, the salesman may then create a desire for his product by showing how it will give satisfaction. Creating desire for a product does not in itself mean a sale. There are usually competing products in the field, and the salesman through creating an awareness of the need for a "type" of product does not automatically sell his brand. After creating an awareness of need, the salesman must convince the prospect that his particular brand is best suited to fulfill the need. If he does this successfully, he should be in a position to close the sale with an order.

SALES MANAGEMENT

The Sales Manager's Job

In a large company, the sales function may be headed by a vice-president in charge of sales. He may head up a group of regional sales managers who in turn supervise a number of district sales managers. The individual salesman would then report to the district sales manager. In a smaller company, a single sales manager may supervise the field salesmen in discharging the complete sales function of the company. Whether the company is large or small, the job of the sales manager is a diverse one. He must be an all-round marketing executive, and his knowledge must extend beyond the immediate task of selling. He must know enough about marketing research to supervise market studies or to use the market information provided by others. He should be able to determine market potentials and to establish territories and sales quotas for salesmen. He must understand advertising to the extent of being able to coordinate the efforts of his sales force with those of the advertising department. In addition to the foregoing, a large part of his work with salesmen demands a knowledge of personnel relations. We may gain further insight into the sales manager's job by taking a brief look at the four basic functions of sales management. These functions are often referred to as recruiting, training, compensating, and supervising salesmen.

Selecting the Salesmen

Large companies, and many of the smaller ones, have training programs. They may prefer to select young men and train them to fit company needs. If the training programs do not provide adequate salesmen, the sales manager may try to hire experienced salesmen. Frequently, experienced salesmen of the quality desired are not available; and where available, they are often trained in methods considered undesirable by the hiring company. The present trend seems to be toward hiring young men and then training them to meet company requirements.

The process of selecting trainees has come in for a lot of attention. It is not uncommon for companies to have training programs from one to two years in length. With such a program, a company may well have an investment of thousands of dollars in the prospective salesman before he becomes productive. The cost of sales training is severely increased if a large number of trainees drop out before reaching the productive level. A simple illustration will suffice: Let us suppose that a company has a training program of eighteen months. Ten trainees are hired at an annual salary of $6,000 each. Let us also suppose that during the year an added cost of $10,000 is incurred in the training of these men. This would represent the cost of the service of training directors and others who would devote time to the trainees. If all of our trainees completed the eighteen months of training, the company investment in each man would be $10,500 ($90,000 salary plus $15,000 training cost divided by ten). Now let us suppose that one-half (five) of our trainees dropped out at the end of the first year and the remaining five went on to finish the program at the end of another six months. The five who finished the training program would represent a company investment of $17,500 in each man ($75,000 total salary investment plus $12,500 training cost divided by five). It will be noted that the cost of training the men who dropped out must be added to the cost of training the men who completed the program.

The above illustration offers a good explanation of why companies use great care in the selection of sales trainees. Many companies place major emphasis upon recruiting college graduates as trainees. They investigate the student's college record, look into his work background, and seek references from former teachers and employers. This is supplemented by extensive testing, using devices such as intelligence tests and aptitude tests. Companies vary in the type and number of tests used. The tests are used in conjunction with extensive personal interviews. Every effort is made to select trainees who are capable of doing the job and who will be satisfied with the work. Even with the utmost precaution, some drop-outs will occur during the training period. A trainee may discover that he doesn't like the work, or he thinks that he can get a better job elsewhere, or personal problems may cause him to seek other employment. The objective of the sales manager is to hold such drop-outs to a normal percentage.

Sales Training

Sales training varies with the type of product and the type of selling required. If the product line is relatively simple, the young trainee may be able to begin producing in a very short time. When the product and market are complex—as in the case of certain industrial goods—it may require two or more years of training before the young salesman is capable of proceeding independently. In the less complex fields, the young trainee may be given a few weeks in a plant, or home office, to learn something of the product and the paper work. He may then be given a short tour with an experienced salesman in order to observe field techniques. After this tour, he may be assigned a territory and put to work on his own.

In the more complex types of selling, the training may involve extensive experience in the plant to learn the technical aspects of the product. This may be combined with classroom work in which the trainee is taught by experienced training directors. This training will then be followed by a period of field work with an experienced man. The field training may last for six months or more. There are numerous variations found in the training programs used. Some companies start their trainees as salesmen in retail stores and have them gain experience here before calling upon field accounts.

Compensation Plans

There are three basic compensation plans commonly found in the sales field: the straight salary method, the salary plus commission plan, and the straight commission plan. There are many variations of these plans. One may work for a base salary with provisions for profit-sharing, or he may work on straight commission with a basic weekly or monthly amount guaranteed. The type of compensation plan in use may depend upon the nature of the product and the manner in which it is purchased. Salesmen in the industrial-goods field are often paid a straight salary. Industrial sales tend to fluctuate as a result of conditions beyond the control of the salesman; and if a commission plan was used, the earnings of the salesman might fluctuate in an undesirable manner. Commission plans are best suited to situations where the sale of the product does not fluctuate widely from year to year and where sales are evenly distributed throughout the year.

Supervising Salesmen

A part of the sales manager's time is devoted to the direct supervision of his sales force. The salesman, unlike the factory worker, is not fixed to a work station. This makes the direct supervision of his activities more difficult. While at work, the salesman is largely "on his own" and, consequently, a great deal of self-discipline is required of him. The sales manager makes frequent trips to visit the salesman in the field, and this type of supervision is supplemented by requiring the salesman to file certain reports. The reports required of the salesman vary from one company to another, but it is quite common for a company to require its salesmen to file a report on the calls made each day. These reports may be detailed to the extent of requiring a statement of the time spent with the prospect; the reaction of the prospect to the product; and if the prospect failed to buy, an indication of his objections. Another report required is the expense account. Many jokes have been made about how salesmen "knock-down" on their expense accounts. It is perhaps true that in some loosely managed situations, salesmen do pad their expense accounts and in a sense defraud their employers. A well-managed company will compensate its salesmen fairly and then demand a strict accounting of expenses. Such companies may require a statement of all monies spent, indicating where the expenditure was made and the purpose for which it was made. Some may even require that the salesman furnish a receipt for expenditures above a certain amount. If reports are required of the salesman, it is good practice to require that they be mailed to the home office at the end of each day.

YOUR CAREER IN SELLING

Opportunities

There is no area of business today that offers more opportunity, and challenge, to a young man than does a career in sales. The man with ability is given the chance to display his talents and to advance on merit. In terms of income, he is usually free to earn according to his capacity. The freedom to display his ability often means that he comes to the attention of his superiors earlier than would his counterparts in other divisions of the company. Thus, it is not surprising that many of the younger top executives of today came up through the sales division of their companies. As one might expect, a type of work that affords great opportunity will carry with it strong demands. Selling is not the job for the man who does not possess determination, drive, and self-discipline. It is pleasant work for the man who enjoys meeting people and helping them solve their problems; it can be less pleasant for the introvert who prefers solitude. Very few salesmen are ever able to limit their work to forty hours per week, and it is true that considerable traveling is often a part of the job. Modern transportation has tended to make the travel-ing factor less of a drawback than in years past.

A career in selling would seem to offer the ambitious young man two very desirable features: First, salaries are equal to, or in many cases better, than those found in non-selling jobs. Second, the opportunity to advance to executive management positions through the avenue of sales is well recognized. With growing emphasis being placed upon the distribution of goods in our economy, the task of selling will continue to be of the utmost importance. We may expect management to con-tinue to be "sales-minded," and the need for management men with a sales background will not lessen.

The young man considering sales as a career may often be concerned with the question of security. To most, security means a regular pay check. There is apprehension regarding a job where one's earnings may be tied directly to his performance. As indicated previously, many sales jobs use a straight-salary plan of compensation and others may use salary in conjunction with commission. The young salesman is seldom asked to go on a straight commission basis until he has displayed his ability and gained confidence in himself. The fact remains, how-ever, that the ineffective salesman cannot keep his performance hidden for long. It is probable that the mediocre man may become lost in the shuffle and survive longer in other jobs than would be possible in selling. The very factors that make it difficult for the incapable to survive in selling are responsible for providing outstanding earnings and oppor-tunities for the capable man. For a good salesman, selling is a depres-sion-proof job. Unless goods are sold, they will not be produced. The people in non-selling jobs will continue to work only if someone is able to sell.

Education and Experience

The wide variety existing in the types of selling jobs indicates that people from many different backgrounds may find a place in selling. It has become a common practice for the larger companies (and frequently the smaller ones) to employ college graduates as trainees. One's college training is likely to be regarded as background to be supplemented by on-the-job sales training. There are some companies, those in technical lines, who prefer college graduates with a technical education. In the electronics field, a salesman may need a knowledge of engineering; in this case, the company would like to hire an engineering graduate who would then be given sales training. Chemistry majors are often sought by companies selling chemical lines. Accountants may be hired as sales trainees by companies that sell business machines. Companies selling less technical lines may concentrate upon hiring graduates who have majored in business administration or the arts and sciences. The non-technical graduate should have a sound fundamental education in the social and physical sciences, and the humanities. Where possible, one should have some specialization in courses such as marketing, marketing research, advertising, statistics, and psychology. Many of the companies recruiting sales trainees are especially interested in the student's extra-curricular activities. The student may demonstrate his ability to work with others through his activity in campus organizations. It should be pointed out, however, that companies are interested in these activities *in addition to* the student having a good academic record. An active role in extracurricular activities will not excuse a poor academic performance.

The student who contemplates a sales career would do well to gain early experience in selling. Summer jobs in a retail store will prove good experience, as will summer work in house-to-house selling. By taking a selling job, the student may find out if he likes the type of work or if he is well suited to the demands of selling. Of course, the type of selling encountered on a summer job may not be on the level that one would desire upon graduation, but the experience gained is invaluable, and there exists certain similarities in all types of selling.

TOPICS FOR DISCUSSION

1. A firm's marketing mix is usually referred to as the total amount of demand-creating activities utilized by the firm. Discuss the various elements of the marketing mix.

2. Comment on the statement that personal selling and advertising join forces in facilitating the flow of goods.

3. "A person does not make a purchase without having a reason for doing so." Comment on this statement.

4. Must a sales manager also be an all-around marketing executive?

5. "Creating desire for a product does not in itself mean a sale." Comment.

6. You are an insurance salesman planning to call on Mr. Smith who is a business executive. Your objective is to sell Mr. Smith a large insurance policy. What would you like to know about Mr. Smith before making the call? Could you obtain this information?

7. An encyclopedia salesman calls at a home and represents himself as conducting an educational survey. When admitted into the home, he proceeds to ask a few questions about the children in school and then goes into a sales talk about the encyclopedia. What do you think of this type of selling? What would be your reaction to a salesman who uses trickery to get into your home?

8. Why do companies devote so much time and expense to the screening process in the selection of sales trainees?

9. When you graduate from college, would you be willing to take a sales job paying a straight commission? Why? Why not?

10. Why is it bad practice for a company to allow its salesmen to falsify their expense accounts?

CASE 17–1

THE WILSON DISTRIBUTING COMPANY

The Wilson Distributing Company operated in an area embracing the major part of two states. The company had a franchise granting it exclusive rights to distribute a nationally known line of home furnaces within its area. The line consisted of a variety of oil-burning furnaces for home and industrial uses. Furnaces were sold to local heating contractors, builders, and institutional and industrial users. The Wilson company did not sell directly to home owners, preferring to leave the home market to the local contractors. They did sell directly to builders, institutions, and industrial firms.

The area served by the Wilson company was divided into six sales territories. A salesman was assigned to each territory, and the salesmen reported to Mr. Daily, the sales manager. Mr. Daily was responsible to Mr. Wilson who was the founder and president of the company. Mr. Wilson had given Mr. Daily a free hand in the selection and training of the sales force. Three of the salesmen had been with the company for more than ten years; two others for seven years; and the remaining salesman had been on the job for two years. From the end of World War II until 1953, the company had shown a satisfactory profit. The decline in profits starting in 1953 continued until by 1956 the company was no longer operating at a profit. From 1948 through 1956 net sales had remained practically constant but rising operating costs had reduced profits. In 1956, the sales volume achieved by each salesman was as follows:

Mr. Winn, territory A, $245,000
Mr. Dade, territory B, $250,000
Mr. White, territory C, $210,000
Mr. Vance, territory D, $300,000
Mr. Clay, territory E, $260,000
Mr. Wills, territory F, $220,000

Mr. Daily considered Mr. Vance the most outstanding salesman employed by the company. He pointed with pride to Mr. Vance's sales volume and often held him up as an example to the other salesmen. Some of the salesmen had been heard to complain that the territory assigned to Mr. Vance was superior to the other territories in terms of potential customers. Mr. Daily had never used any type of marketing research to estimate sales potential. At the end of each year, he asked the individual salesmen to submit estimates of the volume of sales that they thought they could achieve for the coming year. He would then raise or lower these estimates according to his own feeling about business conditions. The total estimates, thus revised, became the basis for the planning of production and sales for the coming year.

Salesmen for the Wilson Company were paid a base salary of from $200 to $400 per month, plus a percentage commission on all sales. Mr. Vance in territory D earned approximately $12,000 per year, while Mr. Wills in territory F earned slightly under $7,000 per year. Each salesman furnished his own car, but the company paid operating expenses based on the mileage traveled.

The difficulties of the Wilson company came to the attention of the furnace manufacturer. The manufacturer offered to send an assistant sales manager from the company headquarters to help the Wilson company with its problems. Mr. Wilson accepted the offer and, within a few days, Mr. Clarke arrived and began work on a sales analysis.

Mr. Clarke made a detailed analysis of each of the six sales territories. He first established the total annual furnace potential for each of the territories. He next estimated what part of this total the Wilson company should expect to achieve. This was then compared with what each territory was presently producing. He presented the following data to Mr. Wilson:

Territory	Total Market Potential	Wilson Quota	Wilson Sales
A	$ 400,000	$250,000	$245,000
B	$ 800,000	$340,000	$250,000
C	$ 700,000	$300,000	$210,000
D	$1,250,000	$500,000	$300,000
E	$ 900,000	$325,000	$260,000
F	$ 650,000	$250,000	$220,000

In presenting his report, Mr. Clarke pointed out that while sales potential in the market served by the Wilson company had increased rapidly since the late 1940's, the company's sales volume had shown little increase. He felt that the failure of the Wilson company to obtain its share of the market, as indicated by the difference between the quota that he had established and the company's actual sales, was a situation calling for immediate action.

What would you suggest that Mr. Wilson do in view of the statistics presented by Mr. Clarke?

SELECTED REFERENCES

Crisp, R. D. *Sales Planning and Control.* New York: McGraw-Hill Book Co., 1961.

Gross, Alfred. *Sales Promotion: Principles and Methods.* 2d ed. New York: The Ronald Press Co., 1961.

Hattwick, M. S. *The New Psychology of Selling.* New York: McGraw-Hill Book Co., 1960.

Russell, F. A., F. H. Beach, and R. H. Buskirk. *Textbook of Salesmanship.* 7th ed. New York: McGraw-Hill Book Co., 1963.

Stanton, W. J., and R. H. Buskirk. *Management of the Sales Force.* Rev. ed. Homewood, Ill.: Richard D. Irwin, Inc., 1964.

18

Advertising and Public Relations

THE EXTENT OF ADVERTISING

In the United States, advertising is used extensively to facilitate the distribution of goods and services. At the present time, the annual expenditure on advertising is approximately $14 billion. This is about double the amount spent in 1952. As the economy has expanded, there has seemed to develop an increased reliance on advertising to stimulate demand. In 1946, advertising expenditure amounted to 2.29 per cent of personal-consumption expenditures, but, by 1961, the percentage had increased to a point where advertising amounted to 3.51 per cent of personal-consumption expenditures.[1] Firms differ in the extent to which advertising is made a part of the marketing program. Some firms do little or no advertising; others may devote to advertising an amount in excess of 50 per cent of their net sales. Generally speaking, firms engaged in the production and distribution of consumer goods often spend in the neighborhood of from 2 to 5 per cent of sales on advertising. Sellers of industrial goods, on the average, spend a smaller percentage on advertising than do sellers of consumer goods.

Next to personal salesmanship, advertising ranks as our most important means of selling. The degree to which advertising is used depends on such factors as the nature of the product, the market, the position of the

[1] C. H. Sandage and Vernon Fryburger, *Advertising Theory and Practice* (6th ed.; Homewood, Ill.: Richard D. Irwin, Inc., 1963), chap. 1.

firm, and the availability of media. Some products do not lend themselves too well to promotion through advertising—table sugar, for example. Products having hidden qualities, which are difficult for the consumer to judge, lend themselves well to brand promotion. If the market for a product is concentrated, it may be much easier to reach the market through advertising. Where the market is widely dispersed, the advertiser may be limited to a medium such as direct-mail advertising. The position of the firm relative to the availability of capital is another factor bearing on the use of advertising. Large-scale advertising calls for large outlays of capital. A single page in a national magazine may cost in excess of $25,000, and in television a half-hour network program may cost in excess of $75,000. The availability of media may also be a limiting factor for some advertisers. For example, suburban merchants may find it impractical to use metropolitan newspapers, radio, and television since the market covered by such media is far in excess of the area served. At the same time, there may be a shortage of media limited to serving a particular suburb. There does exist a wide range of media, and the local merchant can find some means of reaching his market, although he may not have access to the medium of his choice. The following is a breakdown of our total advertising expenditure according to the media used in 1963:

Medium	Per Cent of Total
Newspapers	29.0
Television	15.8
Direct mail	15.5
Magazines	7.9
Radio	5.9
Business publications	4.7
Outdoor advertising	1.3
Miscellaneous (transportation ads, matchbooks, novelty, etc.)	19.9
Total	100.0

Source: Statistical Abstracts U.S., 1964, Table 1199.

In an economy such as ours, new products are continually coming into the market. The producer needs a form of communication that will permit his reaching a large number of people in a very short time. Advertising affords such a tool of mass communications. In a *buyers' market* with strong emphasis on high-level consumption, advertising may play a very strategic role.

The Economic Effects of Advertising

As a tool of selling, advertising may play an important role through the performance of three functions:

1. The function of informing the consumer of the availability of an item and its price
2. The function of educating the consumer to use new products and in new uses for old products
3. The function of stimulating demand

The first two functions, if performed well, afford little ground for argument. These are the information functions, and most people will agree that the consumer benefits from a better knowledge of the product and where it may be obtained. Of course, if the advertiser gives misleading information, the contribution may be a negative one. Where such abuses occur, the fault is not necessarily that of the advertising tool but rather the fault of the seller whose conduct is unethical. Some economists feel that advertising is essentially an uneconomical activity. They often point to situations in which advertising results in brand switching on the part of the consumer without causing an increase in the consumption of the product as a class. For example, people switch from buying brand A shoes to brand B shoes without any increase in total shoe consumption. It is true that much advertising is directed at stimulating *selective demand,* and consumers do change brands frequently. There are few industries, however, in which the total output remains constant; and the stimulation of selective demand may, at least in part, have a beneficial effect upon the entire industry.

From the foregoing, we may gather that the advertising function most subject to debate is that of stimulating demand. To discuss the economic effects of advertising, we must consider the way in which it influences, or fails to influence, demand. But we must define the type of demand that we are talking about. In the preceding paragraph, the term *selective demand* was used. Selective demand refers to the demand for the product of a particular producer: the demand for Baby Ruth candy bars, Silvertown tires, RCA television sets, etc. In contrast to selective demand, *primary demand* refers to the demand for the output of an industry: all types of candy, all makes of tires, and all brands of television sets. It is much easier to defend the use of advertising when it has the effect of stimulating primary demand. If advertising can increase the consumption of the product of an entire industry, it means that the industry as a whole will have wider markets. This will permit increased production and lower production cost if the industry is a decreasing-cost one. A decreasing-cost industry is one in which an increase in production, up to a point, will permit lower per unit cost of production. If there exists a reasonable degree of competition, the industry that experiences lower per unit costs will pass a part of the savings along to the consumer in the form of lower prices. Figure 18–1 shows the possible effects of advertising in stimulating primary demand.

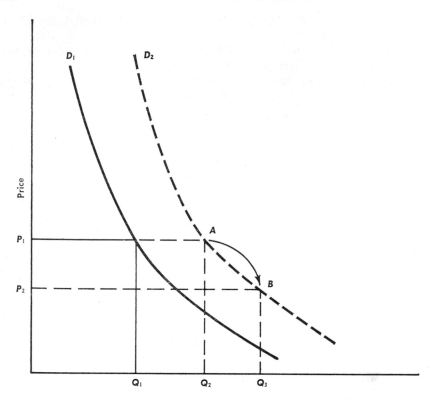

Fig. 18–1. The economic effects of advertising on the demand for the product of an industry. The demand schedule (*D₁*) is shifted to a new position (*D₂*) as a result of advertising. A subsequent reduction in price causes market demand to shift from point A to point B on the curve.

To understand the diagram, the student should recall the definitions of *schedule demand* and *market demand* as explained in Chapter 2. In viewing the diagram, we may assume that, before advertising, the schedule demand is represented by curve D_1 and that Q_1 quantity is being bought at price P_1. At this point, the industry undertakes extensive advertising, and the result is to cause the demand schedule to shift to the right (increase). We now find that Q_2 quantity is being bought, although the price remains at P_1. Thus, all producers are selling more at the same price. If the profits realized from the increased sales are greater than the advertising costs, the industry finds itself in an improved position. If we assume that increased production permitted lower per unit costs of production, then it is very probable that our sellers are in a better position.

If our sellers are in a better position costwise, *and if they are com-*

petitive, we may assume that some of the individual sellers will take the position that by reducing the price to the consumer, a larger share of the market can be obtained and even greater profits made. Thus, we have price competition that results in a lowering of price, and this in turn may increase the *market demand* for the product. This results in the lowering of the market price to P_2 and an increase in the quantity bought to Q_3. The increase in market demand is shown by the change from point A to point B on the demand schedule (D_2). It is necessary to remember that the foregoing analysis assumes that advertising is effective in increasing the primary demand for the product, that the individual industries are decreasing costs industries, and that a reasonable degree of competition exists. These assumptions are not unrealistic; in fact, we have numerous illustrations to show that the forces described are at work. A typical television set in the late 1940's would have cost as much as $500. By the late 1950's, a better set could be purchased for $150. What happened to make this possible? Certainly, improved technology was a factor. But equally important was the fact that mass-production techniques enabled low-cost production. The mass production of television sets would not have been possible had not mass markets been available. Did advertising create these mass markets? Certainly, not advertising alone; but advertising was an important element in gaining a wide market. And equally important, *advertising was a primary factor in gaining this market quickly.* Advertising is an element in the cost of distribution; but when it contributes to an increase in primary demand, it may lead to more consumers enjoying more products at a lower price, and sooner, than would otherwise be the case.

Advertising to stimulate primary demand is carried on by trade associations, associations of manufacturers, and by certain large producers within an industry. When a new product comes on the market, advertising to stimulate primary demand may be necessary. Producers may have to sell the *type* of product before attempting to build up a demand for individual brands. When a product has become well established on the market, the bulk of the advertising will very likely switch to that aimed at stimulating selective demand. If we are to have competition between producers, we must have competition in selling. Personal salesmanship and advertising are two of the many ways of competing. Perhaps, to an extent, all competition is wasteful; but the benefits of competition may far outweigh its cost. When advertising to stimulate selective demand merely results in brand switching, or in the abandonment of products before they are fully used, it undoubtedly is a factor contributing to waste. But in total, the positive economic effects of advertising that is reliable and ethical are sufficient to offset its negative aspects.

The Social Effects

While the objectives of advertising are primarily economic, the use of it does exert certain influences on our social structure. Advertising has been criticized for making people want things that they cannot afford, and thus causing unhappiness. It has also been praised for making people aware of better things and consequently causing them to work harder and be more productive. The average American is exposed to quantities of advertising, and it is doubtful if his response to advertising is of such urgency as to cause great unhappiness. It is true that we are aware of many things that we are not able to buy, but to admit that this creates a dangerous mental state would be to admit an unfortunate degree of immaturity. There are other possible social influences more important than this one.

Our system of mass communications is tied to advertising as a source of revenue. Newspapers, magazines, and broadcast stations (with few exceptions) depend upon advertising to pay the costs of operation. This is not an undesirable situation if one considers the possible alternatives. Without advertising revenue, our media of communications would have to be supported through taxation, and consequently subject to political control. It is probable that most people would not like to see our publications and broadcast stations subject to such control. There are those who contend that our mass media supported by advertising may be vulnerable to the influence of the large advertisers who pay the bills. Undoubtedly, there have been some instances of such interference, but our publications have a tradition of independence and are particularly zealous in protecting their freedom. It is also worth noting that publishing firms and broadcast companies are in themselves big enterprises and, hence, not easily dictated to by a single advertiser.

In fields such as radio and television, the advertiser may choose the content of the program as well as the advertising message. The quality of programs presented has led some to criticize the advertiser and to accuse him of not contributing to the cultural development of the nation. Advertising does follow, rather than lead, intellectual progress. The nature of advertising as a commercial activity makes this situation to a degree unavoidable. Advertising is a method of selling, and the seller will approach his market with the vehicle that produces the best results. This is not to imply that this situation is a desirable one, but rather to acknowledge the facts as they exist. If a western melodrama sells more of the product than would a program featuring a symphony orchestra, the economics of the situation may lead the advertiser to sponsor the western. As the intellectual level of the nation rises, the quality of the programs sponsored on commercial television and radio will rise accordingly. The advertiser has also been accused of presenting his selling message in a manner calculated to appeal to the ignorant. It is said that his advertising should help to educate the uninformed. Here again, we are faced with a situation in which the advertiser is seeking commercial results, and he will be tempted to create his advertising in the manner that produces sales. The advertiser does have a responsibility to the public in the programs sponsored and in the type of advertising presented. He definitely has the obligation to be truthful and to present material in keeping with the standards of good taste. Furthermore, as in the case of other industries, the advertising industry is obligated to contribute its share toward improving the level of public understanding through contributions separate and apart from its commercial endeavors. Many advertisers accomplish this through sponsoring advertising of a public-service nature. Educational material is frequently sponsored, funds are solicited for charities, and public safety campaigns are supported.

Truth in Advertising

Advertising has been haunted by those who see in its use a chance to falsify and exploit. Respectable business firms realize that the value of advertising rests to a large degree in its believability. These firms have often campaigned against the unscrupulous minority. As we delve back into the history of advertising, we are able to note the characteristics of an unfortunate youth. A coffee advertisement appearing in the seventeenth century shows that the charlatans had discovered the power of the printed word:

In Bartholomew Lane, on the back side of the Old Exchange, the drink called coffee, which is a very wholesome and physical drink, have many excellent vertues, closes the orifice of the stomach, fortifies the heat within, helpeth digestion, quickeneth the spirits, maketh the heart lightsom, is good against eye-sores, coughs or colds, thumes, consumptions, headache, dropsie, gout, scurvy, King's evil, and many others; is to be sold both in the morning and at three of the clock in the afternoon.[2]

The false and deceptive advertising occurring at an early date is better understood in the light of the status of commerce existing at that time. In this early period, business was in many respects devoid of ethical standards. "Let the buyer beware" was an accepted doctrine. Sellers and buyers may have regarded the cheating of one another as a normal part of doing business. Thus, the atrocious advertising used may have been but a reflection of the poor standards prevalent in com-

[2] Frank Presbrey, *The History and Development of Advertising* (New York: Doubleday & Co., Inc., 1929), p. 48.

merce. Against this background, one may understand why the upper classes during the seventeenth century tended to look down upon commerce as an undignified activity.

As ethical standards improved in commerce, the quality of advertising improved. Beginning in the late 1800's, business firms and publishers launched *truth crusades* aimed at improving the quality of advertising. In 1911, *Printers' Ink* proposed a model statute that amounted to a code of conduct in advertising. A majority of the states in the United States have adopted the statute, although few of them have provided effective enforcement machinery. Beginning in 1913, Better Business Bureaus were organized in many communities to perform a watchdog function over business practices, including advertising. Also media associations were formed and began campaigns to raise the ethical standards of advertising.[3]

The Federal Trade Commission was created in 1914 to provide the machinery for the enforcement of certain federal regulatory measures in the area of commerce. By the early 1930's, efforts were underway to obtain federal laws to protect business, and the consumer, from those who sought to use false and deceptive advertising. After experience with several earlier measures, the Wheeler-Lea Bill was passed in 1938. This law empowers the Federal Trade Commission to proceed against those who use false and deceptive practices. This law has achieved considerable success in moving against the unethical advertiser, but the Federal Trade Commission has not had the personnel, or the support, necessary to do a thorough job. Some of the more obvious cases of malpractice have been brought to justice, but much advertising of a questionable nature remains outside the practical reach of the Commission. In punishing deceptive advertising, the burden of proof seems to rest on the Commission. That is, to convict the offender, the Commission must produce proof that his advertising is deceiving the public. It is often difficult to produce the kind of proof acceptable to the courts. Perhaps, further laws are needed to extend the powers of the Commission in this area.

Much of the work of the Federal Trade Commission relative to advertising consists of investigating cases of apparent violation and in securing agreements from the advertiser to desist from the practice. The Commission also develops and publishes guides to help advertisers avoid violations. Such guides are designed to help the advertiser to avoid violations in advertising prices and discounts. Federal laws have helped improve the truthfulness of advertising, but the major responsibility for ethical standards still lies with business itself. Advertising in general has

---

[3] Sandage and Fryburger, *op. cit.,* Chap. 5.

improved over the last half century. One only need study the publications of fifty years ago to see evidence of this improvement. But much still remains to be done. All too many advertisers stay within "the letter of the law" while engaging in practices that are deceptive. It is believed that a very large percentage of consumers are skeptical of the advertising to which they are exposed, especially advertising in certain product lines where claims and counterclaims have been prevalent.

TYPES OF ADVERTISING

Local and National Advertising

We may begin by distinguishing advertising on the basis of the geographical coverage. Local advertising, normally sponsored by local business firms, seeks to cover an area that coincides with the market served by the firm. Retail stores are the predominant users of local advertising along with the various types of service establishments. National advertising is that sponsored by the large producer, or distributor, and is usually aimed at covering a very large area. While a national advertiser may cover the entire nation, many classed as such do not serve all markets in the country. National advertising is defined more in terms of its objective than in terms of the area covered. The national advertiser usually promotes the product, often through publicizing a brand name, and does not, as a rule, promote the particular retail store at which the item can be purchased. He says, in effect, "Buy my product at your nearest dealer." By way of contrast, the retailer doing local advertising may feature brand names in his advertising, but his major emphasis is upon the desirability of *his store as the place to buy* these brands. Efforts are made to coordinate local and national advertising in such a way that they supplement one another. Of our total advertising in the United States in 1963, approximately 62 per cent has been classed as national with 38 per cent considered local.[4]

Advertising According to the Objective

Another method of classifying advertising is to make distinctions based on the objectives that the advertiser seeks to accomplish. Perhaps, the largest segment of our advertising would be termed *promotional*. Promotional advertising is that which strives to sell a specific product or service. It may be of the direct-action type, which urges the consumer to act promptly; or it may use the soft-sell and concentrate more upon long-term objectives. Bargain advertising would be

[4] *Statistical Abstracts of the United States,* 1964, Table 1199.

illustrative of the former, while prestige advertising is more characteristic of the latter. While promotional advertising may focus attention upon the product or service, the firm may use *institutional* advertising to sell itself in terms of service and reliability. The success of some firms, insurance companies for example, depends upon the public confidence enjoyed. Through institutional advertising, these firms may stress their long history of service, their financial standing, and other factors calculated to build public confidence. Many firms combine promotional and institutional advertising in a successful program. The institutional ad is a more indirect form of promotion, but it may be used very effectively. Another form of advertising distinguished by objective is the *non-product* advertisement. Non-product advertising is used to sell an idea, or way of thinking. Religious groups may use it to popularize a particular belief; political parties use it; and management and labor groups frequently use it to present their views to the public. Although this type of advertising has grown in use in recent years, its effectiveness is still subject to debate. Often, the topics dealt with are controversial, and the name of the sponsoring organization is often enough to prejudice the reader against the advertising message. An exception to the foregoing may be the public-service type of advertisement such as those stressing highway safety. The sponsorship of such advertisements may very well generate goodwill.

Another type of advertising is that found in the *classified* sections of publications. This is a very important part of advertising, as the inspection of your daily newspaper will verify. It is unlike any other form of advertising but is in many ways comparable to a directory service. The people who read the classified section are often looking for a specific product or service, and it becomes a sort of public market for consumers who seek to buy or sell. As a rule, the classified sections do not permit extensive illustrations or elaborate copy-messages; however, skill is required in constructing an effective advertisement. It is believed that much money is wasted through the sponsorship of classified advertisements that are poorly constructed.

CREATING THE ADVERTISEMENT AND SELECTING MEDIA

The Creative Processes

Modern advertising begins with a study of the product and the market. Research is employed in an effort to *define* the market and to understand the consumer. Some of the research is statistical, as it relates to numbers of people and levels of income; other areas of research explore consumer motivation and buying habits. Given the benefit of information gathered through competent marketing research, the person creating the advertisement may deal with specifics rather than vague generalities.

The printed advertisement begins with a consideration of the consumer and the selection of the information to be included in the ad. The copy for the advertisement may be written first, with the layout being designed to accommodate the copy, or the layout may be designed first, with the copy being written to conform to the requirements of the layout. The layout is perhaps best described as a "blueprint" to be followed by those responsible for the mechanical reproduction of the advertisement. The type of advertisement to be created, and the personal preferences of those doing the work, will determine whether the job begins with the copy or with the layout. In any case, the two aspects are likely to be modified and adjusted as the ad nears completion. The mechanical reproduction of the advertisement can be a very technical matter. For example, there are many sources of artwork—such as pencil sketches, wash drawings, oil paintings, and photographs—and each of these may require its own reproduction technique. Experts in typography and photoengraving become competent craftsmen after long periods of on-the-job experience.

Creation of advertisements for broadcast media begins in much the same way as that of advertisements for the printed media. Knowledge of the product and the potential consumer leads to a choice of the information to be presented. Creation of a radio commercial has much in common with writing of the copy for a printed ad. Since the radio advertisement is heard by the consumer rather than read by him, certain modifications of the printed version may be necessary. For instance, the radio copy may utilize repetition to a greater extent than is advisable in the newspaper or magazine advertisement. The television advertisement introduces an entirely new dimension in combining sight and sound. Basically, the advertisement is still a matter of product facts directed in such a way as to appeal to consumer motives. The presentation, however, may rely on the techniques of specialists in speech and drama. The mechanical side of television advertising makes use of an array of equipment manned by experts in camera techniques. A visit to a local television studio will give one an appreciation of the production side of the art.

Advertising Media

Advertisements are created with the medium in which they will appear in mind. It is thought that the reader may devote less time to a newspaper ad than to a magazine ad, although the newspaper may make up for this by being more timely. The magazine, however, may offer a better grade of paper and the opportunity for better color work.

A medium is selected in terms of the market. *Mass media* such as newspapers, some magazines, and much of our television and radio are geared to wide audiences. Many markets are selective rather than mass, and, in such cases, *selective media* are sought. Certain magazines are very selective in that they are created to cater to the interests of a sharply defined group. Radio and television may be selective to the extent that a particular program is designed to appeal to a narrowly defined audience. The objective of the advertiser is to pick a printed medium or broadcast program that best reaches his specific market. Generally speaking, the cost of an advertising medium varies directly with the size of the audience reached. An advertiser that sells to one family out of a thousand would not want to pay for a medium that reaches the mass market, assuming that alternative media are available.

Newspaper advertising accounts for over one-quarter of total advertising expenditure.[5] Newspapers carry both local and national advertising, but emphasis is on the local. In addition to being a timely form of advertising, newspapers offer a high degree of territorial selectivity. Magazines may offer great selectivity by type of customer, and through regional editions they offer some territorial selectivity. By 1963, over 90 per cent of the households in the United States had radio and television.[6] Thus, an advertiser can get mass coverage through these media. In fact, the high cost of television advertising (the technology involved is a factor) tends to restrict this medium from the viewpoint of the selective advertiser. The comparatively low cost of radio makes the medium more adaptable on a selective basis. Direct-mail advertising affords a highly selective medium, although it can be used to reach a mass market. Direct mail is our most personal form of advertising, and its selectivity is limited only by the nature of the mailing list. Outdoor advertising plays a relatively minor role in terms of money spent—less than 2 per cent of total advertising expenditure—but some advertisers obtain good results through this medium. Miscellaneous forms of advertising, such as novelties, blotters, and calendars, account for a sizable proportion of our total advertising expenditure. These media serve primarily as a reminder type of advertising.

THE ORGANIZATION FOR ADVERTISING

The Advertising Department

A firm that does a sizable amount of advertising will usually have an advertising department headed by an advertising manager, or com-

[5] *Ibid.*
[6] *Ibid.*

parable executive. In some businesses, such as a department store, the advertising department may handle the entire advertising job. It may be responsible for research, copywriting, layout design, and handling the production of the advertisement. Specialists may be employed to function in each of these areas. In the case of firms engaged in national distribution, it is common to find the advertising agency assisting in the performance of the advertising job. When an agency is used, the advertising department of the company will work in close cooperation with the agency. In some cases, the department may function largely as the contact unit with the agency; but in other cases, the advertising department of the company may employ specialists and share some of the research and creative work with an agency. The advertising policy of a company may be a matter to be determined by the general management, but the advertising department will usually serve as the focal point in policy determination.

The Advertising Agency

The advertising agency is a professional organization that offers its services to the advertiser. The agency may be able to offer specialized service in the areas of research, copy, layout design, media selection, mechanical production, and radio and television production. In fact, a large agency may be capable of taking over the marketing of a product and carry out many of the functions of sales management as well as those of advertising. A peculiarity of the advertising agency is the manner in which it collects its compensation. The agency normally receives a 15 per cent commission from the medium with which the advertising is placed. For example, if a recognized agency places $100,000 worth of advertising in a magazine, the magazine will bill the agency for $85,000, and the agency in turn will bill the client (the advertiser) for $100,000. If the advertiser had purchased the space directly from the magazine, it would have cost him the $100,000 anyway; so by placing his advertising through the agency, he is in effect getting the services of the agency without additional cost. Of course, if the agency has to purchase art work, do an unusual amount of marketing research, or incur other "outside" expenses, the cost of such will be passed on to the advertiser (with a 15 per cent commission added). The practice of the agency drawing its commission from the medium derives from the early days in which the agency was solely a space-selling organization. As competition in space selling developed, the agency added services as an inducement to the buyer but continued to draw its commission from the medium. Publications and broadcast stations have cooperated in the maintenance of the agency system; perhaps reasoning that if the agencies disappeared, many of the services now performed would fall to the lot of the media. Although the agency receives its commission from the medium, it functions as the agent of the advertiser. Everything that the agency does is subject to approval by the client.

The Advertising Campaign

The advertising program of a firm may be referred to as an *advertising campaign*. Not all advertising is campaign advertising. A campaign is a program of advertising built around a central theme and usually involves the use of various media to achieve a common objective. An individual campaign may extend from a few weeks to a number of years. Firms that bring out new models of the product annually will often launch a new campaign when the models change, thus having yearly campaigns. To be successful, a national campaign usually must continue over a period of time. The intensity of the advertising may determine the time necessary to achieve results. If various media are used, the advertising must be coordinated in such a manner that one medium supplements another. An advertising campaign may be compared to a political campaign. In each case, a number of publicity devices are used and coordinated in the hope of achieving a desired objective. A politician may conduct a campaign for office in which he promises the voters lower taxes. An automobile company may conduct a campaign in which it promises purchasers of its cars better gas mileage. In terms of geography, an advertising campaign may be local, regional, or national. Local retailers may carry on continuous advertising, but this is seldom classified as campaign advertising. The retailer is likely to feature many products from day to day without a continuous and coordinated program on any one product.

PUBLIC RELATIONS

Public Relations Defined

We have seen that one type of advertising known as *institutional advertising* has as its objective the promotion of the firm rather than that of the product itself. The assumption is that the confidence that one has in the firm will extend to the product or service offered. Closely related to this form of advertising is the much broader area known as *public relations*. One may define public relations as being concerned with providing information to the public; influencing the public to modify its attitudes; and reconciling the attitudes of the institution and the public. One might refer to these three aspects as being the "functions" of public relations, and further add that the over-all objective of any public-relations program is to promote a favorable public attitude toward the firm. There may have been times in the past when a business firm could operate with little regard for public attitude, but certainly no such condition exists today. The modern firm is very much concerned with how the public feels toward it as an institution. We see evidence of this in the advertising efforts of some companies who seek to create a favorable "corporate image" to replace what they fear may be an unfavorable one. There are those who still think of a corporation as a greedy giant that tramples its competition underfoot in a frenzied drive for profits. Perhaps some firms may deserve to be branded with this image, but many do not deserve such hostility. The attitude of the public toward a firm may influence the sale of its product, or it may influence its ability to raise needed capital. Business firms as a group are interested in fostering a more favorable public attitude. The government regulation of business occurs when the public sentiment is strong in support of such regulation. Firms that desire to operate in an atmosphere comparatively free of regulations realize that to do so, they must have the approval of the public.

ACCOMPLISHING THE PUBLIC-RELATIONS FUNCTION

Organization

Many firms have a public-relations department. This department may be staffed with persons experienced in dealing with the press and in interpreting company attitudes and beliefs to the public. They may also have the function of gathering, summarizing, and interpreting public attitudes and the placing of this information at the disposal of the policy-making executives of the firm. Business firms stress the fact that while they may have public-relations departments, it is the job of everyone in the firm to work toward developing a sound public-relations program. A satisfied customer is still one's best ambassador of goodwill. Perhaps the greatest contribution of a public-relations department lies in its efforts to train all those in the company to be *public-relations minded*—or, stated differently, to be mindful of the public attitude and to contribute to the elevation of the firm in the estimation of the public.

Working with the Press

To become favorably known to the public, a company must have a way of conveying its actions to the people. This implies the use of mass media such as publications and broadcast stations. As noted later, one way of reaching the public is through the purchase of advertising space, but information on the company's activities carried as news stories may be more effective than a message carried in an advertisement. It is part of a public-relations man's job to see that company activities of sufficient interest to be treated as *news* are placed in the hands of publications and broadcast stations. When a company suffers an unhappy, or unfortunate, occurrence, the reporters will usually come looking for the story. But often, favorable happenings are of less dramatic interest, and the public-relations department must distribute the news and strive to see that it is given circulation. It might be added that when a company does suffer an unfortunate circumstance, it is a function of the public-relations department to see that the company is fairly represented in the news items printed. Normally, a public-relations department maintains a good working relationship with the press. News items concerning the company are prepared in the department and delivered to the proper sources. Not all releases sent out will be used, but those with content of sufficient interest to the public will be accepted. The public-relations man must be skilled in knowing the news value of an item and in the proper way of preparing and presenting it.

Using Advertising to Reach the Public

Companies desiring to express an attitude, or to inform the public of their activities, may find press releases inadequate, or too slow, to satisfy their needs. Publications and broadcast stations cannot begin to use all the news releases that come to them from business firms. They must sift through the lot and give precedence to those items that they consider to be of most interest to their audiences. Finding itself stymied in reaching the public through the "free" channels, a company may supplement its program with other methods. Advertising space may be purchased, and the company may present its views in this manner. This "non-product" type of advertising has been discussed, and it was noted at that time that such advertising may have advantages and disadvantages. The advantage lies in the fact that the company can present its message using space, illustrations, and other factors limited only by the amount of money to be spent. Faced with a strike, a company may buy space, or time, to present its side of the controversy to the public. Unions also buy advertising space and time to present their views.

Working with the Community

From the foregoing section, one might conclude that much of a company's public-relations program is taken up in representing the company in controversial situations. It is not intended to imply that this is the case. Many companies regard good community relations as the foundation of a good public-relations program. Efforts are made to establish the company as a good neighbor. Executives and employees are encouraged to take part in community affairs and to demonstrate that they are civic-minded citizens. The company may take a positive stand in promoting better schools, better public facilities, and improved recreation. The company benefits directly from being a part of a good community; better employees may be recruited and labor turnover is reduced. Furthermore, if a company has a good reputation in its own community, the news will get around. Should the company need to expand by building plants in other communities, this reputation can be a very valuable asset. Large companies with branch plants located in many communities may develop a "national" reputation as being a desirable or undesirable neighbor. Such a factor as the company's community reputation may become an influence in product acceptance, public support in labor negotiations, and in many other ways.

Other Services in the Public-Relations Category

There are many additional ways in which the company may promote public acceptance of itself as an institution, or of its policies. Some companies have developed very informative and entertaining motion-picture films for free distribution to schools and civic groups. These films may show some phase of the company's operations that is of interest to the public, or the subject of the film may be of indirect interest to the company. When companies first began to use films for this purpose, they showed a tendency to crowd the film with advertising material and thus restrict its acceptability by the public. Commercially sponsored films today are, as a rule, accomplished with a minimum of advertising. If the subject matter of the film is well chosen, and the film well done, the public acceptance is likely to be good. The production of a sound film is expensive, often running to as much as $100,000 for a half hour, but the fact that the film can be shown to many groups over a period of years helps to spread the cost over a great number of viewers. There are distributing services that make a specialty of maintaining film libraries and supplying films to interested groups. Business-sponsored films are usually free to the user, with the possible exception of return postage and insurance.

Public Relations and Employee Relations

Good employee relations are fundamental to good public relations. If the employees are antagonistic toward the company, they may very well cause the community in general to take a negative attitude. Realizing this, many companies constantly strive to sell the idea that the company is a "good place at which to work." Many companies publish a company newspaper (house organ) that has as one of its objectives the cementing of good relations between the company and the employees. Company publications, bulletin boards, and public-address systems are used to communicate with employees. In a good employee-relations program, two-way communications will exist between management and the employees. If the management-union situation is a militant one, it may be difficult for the company to avoid hostility in its relations with employees. In such a situation, the union is distrustful of the motives of the company in its attempts to win the friendship of the worker. Unfortunately, there are situations in which companies have used employee friendship to undermine the union. And there are other cases in which unions seem to promote employee hostility toward the employer as a means of assuring their own hold over the workers. In a militant labor-management situation, the public-relations job is made all the more difficult.

It is hoped that the foregoing brief discussion will give the student a general idea of some of the aspects of the public-relations program. Public relations, as a separate field of study, is comparatively recent. In an age where there is a continuous battle for the "minds of men" between factions within our country, and internationally, the role of the public-relations expert will continue to grow in importance. Perhaps we should say that the need for everyone to become a public-relations expert will become increasingly important.

YOUR CAREER IN ADVERTISING AND PUBLIC RELATIONS

Advertising

There are perhaps over 3,000,000 business firms in the United States, and the majority of these, at one time or another, use advertising. The job of carrying out the advertising function is a big one, and the authors of a leading text estimate that from 350,000 to 400,000 people hold full-time jobs in advertising.[7] If one considers the people who devote a part of their time to advertising, the above number would perhaps be doubled. In addition, many people employed in certain areas of marketing are performing functions essential to advertising. Modern advertising would not be possible without the benefit of marketing research; and, conversely,

[7] Sandage and Fryburger, *op. cit.*, pp. 13–14.

many of those employed in research owe their jobs to the fact that advertising demands the information that they provide. Much research is done by advertising agencies and advertising departments of companies and the people employed in doing this research would be included in the estimate of those directly employed in advertising. But others providing research information, such as marketing-research departments of business firms, would not be considered as advertising employees. However, research people outside of agencies and departments, along with many other types of employees, are contributing to the performance of the advertising function. It would be impossible to estimate just how many people are, in some way, contributing to the performance of the advertising function.

There is much confusion in the minds of students concerning careers in advertising. Motion pictures and popular novels have glamorized certain phases of advertising, and they have been guilty of exaggerations and the perpetuation of many misconceptions. Many students think of advertising almost entirely in terms of the creative aspects, failing to realize that the total job of advertising involves marketing research, media analysis, planning, selling, and related activities. Thus, the student interested in advertising is likely to aim at becoming a copy writer or layout designer while overlooking other phases of advertising for which he may be better suited. We point this out not to discourage the student interested in creative advertising but to emphasize the fact that a diversity of jobs are available in the field of advertising.

Another frequent misconception concerns the organization of advertising. The student hears of Madison Avenue so much that he may come to feel that all our advertising emanates from that noble street. He hears of a few nationally prominent agencies, and he sets his sights upon getting a job with one of them. Actually there are about 3,500 agencies listed in some of the directories; and while Madison Avenue may be the nerve center of the industry, it by no means predominates the employment picture. Many of the lesser known agencies are establishments of excellent reputation, although perhaps smaller than the well-known names. Many agencies specialize in product lines, or types of advertising, such as those that handle predominantly industrial advertising, and as a result, are not well known to the general public. The student seeking a career in advertising should not limit his search for a job to the nationally known agencies. It also frequently happens that the student desiring to work in advertising concentrates on getting a job with an agency to the neglect of equally attractive advertising jobs elsewhere. It is estimated that from one-third to one-half of those employed directly in advertising are working with some type of agency, while the remainder are employed in the advertising departments of firms, in the advertising departments of media, with trade associations, and others. The student should not overlook these fields in seeking employment.

Beginning salaries in advertising vary from job to job. Many agencies have extensive training programs; and generally speaking, the salary paid the trainee may be less than that offered in certain other lines. The philosophy seems to prevail that the student should be willing to sacrifice income while learning the trade. The willingness of the student to make this sacrifice is often thought to be an indication of his keen interest in advertising as a career. Some have even maintained that to succeed in advertising, one must want to do this type of work so intensely that sacrifices will be willingly made. Perhaps this is true, but it also may be true that the advertising business is losing some potentially good men who, for one reason or another, are unable or unwilling to make the initial sacrifices. For those who have the ability to advance in advertising, the income potentialities are good. But in advertising, as in other lines of business, not all of those who start at the bottom are going to reach the top. It is perhaps safe to say that the bulk of the people employed in advertising reach the medium-income level and stabilize there. Again, this is typical of other lines of employment also. If one enjoys the work, and is willing to work hard, he stands a good chance of finding a place in advertising.

Training

As previously indicated, there are many specialized jobs within the broad scope of advertising. It is difficult for the student to know which phase of advertising he may like best or be most capable of doing. One purpose of training programs conducted by agencies and other employers is to help the beginner find his proper niche. As far as college training goes, the ability of the student to fit himself for a single specialty is often limited. The student can aim for an area of specialization in a broad sense: if he is interested in research, he may study marketing research and statistics; if he is interested in design, he may take art courses; and if he is interested in television, he may take certain courses in speech and drama. If he is not sure, and most students aren't, of the specialized area in which he may be interested, a broad education is desirable. A sound grounding in the arts and sciences is fundamental. Since advertising is a part of selling, marketing courses are desirable; also, courses in areas such as psychology and public speaking are useful. In an age of growing emphasis upon research, courses in statistics and mathematics are becoming increasingly helpful.

Public Relations

The emergence of public relations as a field of employment has expanded rapidly in recent years. Like many other rapidly expanding fields, there still remains some question as to the best avenue for one to follow in getting into this line of work. So far, the public-relations and journalism fields have been very closely allied, and this would seem to be natural in view of the type of work required of the public-relations man. Many of those who have succeeded in public relations began the work after an extensive tour in the journalistic field. With the establishment of public-relations departments in companies, the practice has developed of employing graduates directly and giving them training under the direction of experienced people. It is thought, however, that public-relations departments still draw heavily upon people who have basic experience in the publication or broadcast field.

From these recommendations, one would gather that a liberal-arts education with perhaps a major in journalism or a journalism degree with strong emphasis on the arts would represent a desirable background for the public-relations man. It is believed that beginning salaries in the area of public relations would be comparable to those earned by beginners in the field of journalism.

TOPICS FOR DISCUSSION

1. In 1946, there were 8,000 television sets in American homes. Only ten years later, in 1956, there were 34,000,000. What effects do you feel this had on the advertising industry? How were the revenues of other media such as magazines and newspapers affected?

2. The degree to which advertising is used in the marketing mix depends on certain factors. Discuss these factors.

3. From your reading in recent issues of newspapers and magazines, or from your viewing of television, cite one example of advertising to stimulate primary demand and one example of advertising to stimulate selective demand.

4. Advertising has been criticized for making people want things they cannot afford, and thus causing unhappiness. Do you agree or disagree with this charge?

5. Comment on the following statement: "In a *buyer's market* with strong emphasis on high-level consumption, advertising may play a very strategic role."

6. It is a well-known fact that two out of three new products fail. Is this the fault of ineffective advertising?

7. What is the relationship between advertising copy and personal salesmanship?

8. Do you feel that present day advertising on television is effective? How many TV programs can you name? Can you name the sponsor for each of them?

9. Can you cite examples of the kind of work a public-relations department for a business firm might do?

10. Do you feel that a college or university should have a public-relations director? Can you cite some examples of the work that he might do?

CASE 18–1

A JUDGMENT ON ADVERTISING

British historian Arnold Toynbee once denounced American advertising in rather harsh terms:

> In the western world of our day the tempter's role is being played by everything we sum up under the name of Madison Avenue. A considerable part of our ability, energy, time, and material resources is being spent today on inducing us to do hard labor in order to find the money for buying material goods that we should never have dreamed of wanting had we been left to ourselves . . . disposing of the maximum quantity of consumer goods was not the purpose of the American Revolution. What is more, it is not the true end of man. . . . I would suggest that the destiny of our Western Civilization turns on the issue of our struggle with all that Madison Avenue stands for more than it turns on the issue of our struggle with Communism. [Speech at Williamsburg, Virginia, June, 1961.]

Of course, Mr. Toynbee may have been denouncing business methods in general while making a dramatic point of advertising; however, it is clear that he is not a booster of the present methods used to stimulate demand. There are others who are equally critical of advertising for some of its practices in exploiting sex (motion-picture advertising, for example), using deception, and, in some cases, disseminating false information.

When one hears the widespread indictment of advertising, and witnesses some of the excesses engaged in by some advertisers, he cannot argue that advertising is a virtuous art unjustly accused. He can ask if the practices abhorred in advertising are not a manifestation of a sickness that is not confined to the world of Madison Avenue alone. He may also ask if there are not some creditable examples of advertising, and, if so, should these not be recognized as such rather than smeared with the broad brush of universal condemnation.

What do you think?

SELECTED REFERENCES

Canfield, B. R. *Public Relations, Principles and Cases.* 4th ed. Homewood, Ill.: Richard D. Irwin, Inc., 1964.

Frey, A. W. *Advertising.* New York: The Ronald Press Co., 1961.

Marston, John. *The Nature of Public Relations.* New York: McGraw-Hill Book Co., 1963.

Sandage, C. H., and Vernon Fryburger. *Advertising: Theory and Practice.* 6th ed. Homewood, Ill.: Richard D. Irwin, Inc., 1963.

Wales, H. G., D. L. Gentry, and Max Wales. *Advertising Copy, Layout and Typography.* New York: The Ronald Press Co., 1958.

Wedding, Nugent, and R. S. Lessler. *Advertising Management.* New York: The Ronald Press Co., 1962.

Zacher, R. V. *Advertising Techniques and Management.* Homewood, Ill.: Richard D. Irwin, Inc., 1961.

19

Transportation and Other Aspects of Physical Distribution

THE SCOPE OF TRANSPORTATION

Transportation is of major importance in the satisfaction of human needs. In one form or another, it has provided the means for the development of our social and economic growth and has been reciprocally influenced by the expansion of our cultural and business horizons. Successive improvements in transportation have enabled us to enjoy unparalleled mobility, which has profoundly affected our patterns of living. Proximity to work no longer binds us in the location of homes, and, as job opportunities are available in other areas, many of us move great distances to take new employment. This mobility is evident, too, in our recreation, where continuously broadening vistas offer a wide range of pleasurable and cultural activities.

Transportation also provides us with the means for facilitating the movement of raw materials and natural resources from widely dispersed areas into processing or fabrication points. The vast quantities of finished goods are then channeled into local, national, and world markets through our network of diverse transport media. Our annual expenditures for transportation are about $120 billion—an amount equal to 20 per cent of our gross national product. About $68 billion are spent for passenger transportation, and $52 billion, for transportation of goods.

Transportation is broadly divided into the *transportation of freight or property* and the *transportation of passengers*. It is also generally spoken of as being either *intercity* or *local*. The transportation of persons and property between cities, including the pickup and delivery in connection with such transportation, is called intercity transportation. Local transportation, as the term implies, is that generally performed wholly within a city or in the area immediately adjacent to a city.

AGENCIES OR MODES OF TRANSPORTATION

The different kinds of transportation that are available—rail, motor, air, pipeline, and water—are known as *agencies* or *modes* or *fields* of transportation. A wide variety of services is offered by these transportation agencies that physically perform the service of transporting property and passengers or property only. In addition to these modes of transportation, there are business organizations that accept freight but do not physically transport it. They use one of the modes of transportation for the actual transportation of the property. This is called an *indirect method* of transportation. These indirect agencies are freight forwarders, REA, air express, and the parcel-post service of the United States Postal Service.

Some agencies of transportation are general carriers, such as the railroads. They handle all types of freight that are offered to them, and many of these carriers handle passenger traffic as well. On the other hand, there are carriers in other agencies of transportation that are specialized in their services, as the petroleum pipelines. They transport crude oil and such refined products as gasoline and are limited to the handling of liquid commodities in bulk. Many motor carriers are also specialized carriers handling only a single type of commodity, such as household goods, or a limited group of commodities.

Measurement of Traffic Transported by Various Modes

In measuring the amount of freight that is transported between cities, the statistical unit *ton-mile* is used. This unit represents the weight of the product transported multiplied by the distance it is transported so that 10 tons of freight transported 1 mile amount to 10 ton-miles. In intercity passenger transportation, the statistical unit used is *passenger-mile*. One passenger traveling 10 miles equals 10 passenger-miles. Such statistical units make it possible to compare the volume of intercity traffic of the various transportation agencies. For example, the amount of traffic transported by the railroads may be compared with that of the motor carriers.

There have been significant shifts in recent years in the amount of intercity ton-miles transported by the different agencies of transportation. From 1950 to 1965, the total volume of intercity ton-miles transported by all carriers increased from 1,063 billion to 1,650 billion; yet the share transported by railroads during this period decreased by approximately one-fourth. The share being moved by trucks, however, increased by more than one-third; pipelines by approximately one-half; while water carriers declined slightly. Although the percentage increase in air transportation was large, air carriers still transport 1.1 per cent of the total intercity ton-miles. At the present-time, our transportation system moves over twice as much freight as it did in 1940; and, by 1968, it is estimated that over 2 trillion ton-miles of freight will be transported.

In passenger transportation, approximately 90 per cent of the total intercity passenger-miles is accounted for by privately owned passenger automobiles. Of the remaining 10 per cent, air carriers account for about 55 per cent; buses, 28 per cent; and railroads, 17 per cent.

In contrast to the intercity field where distance traveled is of primary importance, local transportation of both freight and passengers is one in which mileages are relatively unimportant but the volume is very large. If the total tonnage within a city of such things as milk deliveries and deliveries from wholesale firms to retail stores, from retail stores to homes, and from warehouses to plants were computed, the figure would be tremendous. There is actually a greater tonnage moved within cities than between cities.

For-Hire Transportation and Private Transportation

Transportation is either *for-hire transportation,* which means that the transportation service is available to the public and must be paid for by the user, or it is *private transportation,* which means that it is performed by an individual or a business for his own needs and is not offered for public use. For-hire carriers operating interstate—that is, between states —are regulated by the federal government through certain regulatory bodies or agencies. The business operations of these carriers, such as their rates, accounting procedures, and the right to operate, are regulated under what is called *economic regulation.* All carriers, both for-hire and private, operating interstate must conform to *safety regulations* prescribed by the federal regulatory bodies.

For-hire carriers are sometimes called *public carriers.* They are divided into *common, contract,* and *exempt* carriers according to the type of business operation they conduct. Common carriers are found in all modes of transportation. Rail carriers are common carriers only, whereas there are common, contract, and exempt motor carriers. Common carriers possess certain characteristics. Their services are offered to the general public through holding themselves out to serve anyone who desires their service without any discrimination among their customers as to service or rates. The shipper is given a uniform bill of lading or receipt for each shipment, and the carrier will perform its service up to its ability or capacity to do so. As common carriers they have full responsibility for the safe delivery of shipments unless they have specifically limited their responsibility. While transporting the goods they are *bailees*, which is a legal term meaning that they have possession of the goods but do not own the goods. Upon completion of a shipment, a freight bill made out by the carrier is sent to the shipper showing the charge to be paid. Federal regulation requires that payment for for-hire transportation be made within a specified time with no discounts allowed.

Contract carriers do not hold themselves out to render service to everyone or issue a uniform bill of lading or receipt. They operate under long-term, individual contracts with one shipper or with a limited number of shippers. Contract carriers are found in motor, water, and air transportation.

Exempt carriers are so called because they are exempt from regulation of their business operations by the federal government. These carriers are found principally in motor and water transportation. Exempt motor carriers transport primarily agricultural commodities, livestock, and fish. In water transportation, exempt carriers transport bulk commodities, such as petroleum, coal, sand, and gravel.

Many business enterprises transport all or a part of their own freight in private transportation rather than using for-hire carriers. Since the equipment that they use may be purchased or leased under a number of different plans, it is relatively easy for business firms to transport their own goods.

FREIGHT TRANSPORTATION

Rail Transportation of Property

Railroads offer a wide variety of services and equipment to accommodate shippers. Goods may be offered to rail carriers in packages, in bulk form, or loose. Some 651 railroads operate over 220,000 mainline miles of track.

There are two basic types of freight service—*carload* and *less carload*. A carload is that amount of freight that can be loaded in or on a freight car and is entitled to a particular rate (or price) because the weight of the freight equals or exceeds that which is specified by the carrier to be a carload. A less carload is any quantity less than the amount specified by the carrier as a carload quantity. The charges or rates, as they are called, are higher per 100 pounds on less carload quantities than on carloads, averaging from 20 to 25 per cent higher. This is due to several factors. One of these is that the railroad loads and unloads less carload shipments and, in some instances, picks them up or delivers them to the shipper. It does not perform these services on carload shipments for the shipper must do the loading, unloading, and pickup and delivery. *Merchandise freight service* is a through service in which less carload shipments are loaded in rail cars equipped to run at passenger-train speeds. Such trains operate on a scheduled basis with certain departure times.

In addition to the regular freight services, there is *expedited service* available at an additional charge. Expedited service is often used in order to guarantee delivery at destination by a certain date.

In order to take advantage of the lower carload rate, a number of small shipments going to one point may be combined by a shipper and sent to one person at the destination city. This is usually a distributing agent such as a warehouseman or local trucking company who delivers the shipments to the various parties whose shipments are in the car. This is called a *pool car* or *pooling of shipments*.

The railroads formed the REA *Express* to perform express service. This agency accepts articles of all kinds for shipment by railroads as well as some articles that the railroads will not accept in regular service, such as valuable papers and currency. Generally, express service is offered in connection with passenger-train service, and therefore is a faster service than regular rail-freight service.

Motor Transportation of Property

Motor carriers of general commodities, of which there are a large number, offer services similar to those of the railroads. In addition, there are specialized carrier operations. Specialized carriers transport a limited number of commodities. The household-goods carriers, for example, transport only household goods. Over 90 per cent of the household goods moved between cities are transported in their moving vans. Other specialized carriers are tank-truck operators, which transport petroleum and similar products; haulers of explosives; heavy haulers, which transport shipments of unusual size or weight; and other specialized carriers.

Motor carriers provide *less truckload service* and *volume* or *truckload service*. Like the railroads, there is a similar differential between less truckload and volume rates. Motor carriers can perform a complete transportation service from store door to store door. They possess the advantages of flexibility and convenience in that they can go any place. In addition to rendering a complete transportation service, they also provide supplementary service to other carriers, such as railroads and airlines. Within cities, local cartage service is performed in which a very heavy volume of freight is transported. There are about 45,000 for-hire motor carriers operating over three and a half million miles of highways and streets.

Water Transportation of Property

There are 29,000 miles of improved inland waterways and 1,700 operators on these waterways. Domestic water transportation service is divided into four broad categories: *coastwise, intercoastal, Great Lakes,* and *inland water transportation.*

Coastwise service is transportation by water from and to points on the Atlantic, Gulf, or Pacific Coasts. Service over a route of this type is by deep-sea vessels that provide service for general commodities as well as bulk commodities. In addition, there is some transportation of bulk commodities by barge.

Intercoastal water transportation involves movements between the Atlantic and Gulf ports and Pacific Coast ports via the Panama Canal. The services offered by these carriers are similar to those in coastwise service.

Great Lakes shipping between Great Lakes ports primarily involves the transportation of bulk commodities such as iron ore, coal, limestone, grain, and petroleum. The ships used in this service are comparable to those used in ocean shipping.

Inland water transportation service is available on navigable rivers and canals. Barges are used to provide this service. The commodities transported are principally in bulk, with very large quantities being carried. *Integrated tows* are used to tie a number of barges together, thus moving 20,000 tons of cargo at a time. This is equal to the amount that could be hauled by four trains of one hundred cars each.

Pipeline Transportation

A very substantial quantity of petroleum is transported by pipeline. This type of transportation differs from that of the other modes in that the commodity is moved in one direction only and requires no packaging. In oil pipeline transportation, there are three kinds of pipelines. The *crude oil gathering lines* are usually laid on top of the ground and are used to bring petroleum from wells to storage points. Gathering lines are from 2 to 6 inches in diameter. *Crude oil trunk lines* are the second type. They are used to transport crude oil from producing areas to refining centers or to water terminals. These lines are from 6 to 36 inches in diameter and are buried in the ground. *Product lines* are the third type of pipelines and carry such products as gasoline and kerosene. These lines run from refineries to marketing areas. In general, the trend in pipeline construction has been to larger diameter pipe because of the more economical cost per ton-mile of transporting products. Most of the oil pipelines are affiliated with oil companies, whereas natural gas pipelines are not.

A pipeline that transports pulverized coal mixed with water—called slurry—as well as other solids, has been developed on a limited basis.

Air-Cargo Transportation

The transportation of air cargo has grown rapidly in recent years. The larger air carriers derive their principal revenue from the carrying of passengers and, in conjunction with this service, they also transport freight. Other carriers transport only cargo. Pickup and delivery of air freight is available at an extra charge.

The rates charged by air carriers average much higher than rail or motor transportation service, although the airport-to-airport speed far exceeds that of other freight carriers. The increased use of jet and turboprop planes will further speed air-freight service. The size of shipments is limited because of the space restrictions of the aircraft.

The *air-express division* of REA offers air-express service and provides pickup and delivery in larger cities with no additional charge made for the service. Air express is handled on passenger planes of the scheduled airlines. Generally, air-express charges are higher than air-cargo charges.

Freight Forwarders

Surface-freight forwarders have the obligations of common carriers, such as the railroads, yet they do not own or operate any equipment to transport the goods they handle between cities. They rely on rail, motor, and water carriers to transport their freight. Freight forwarders developed because they could consolidate the numerous less carload shipments of individual shippers into a carload. In this capacity, they act as middlemen. They charge shippers the less carload rate and make up a carload of less carload shipments destined for one city, arranging with the carrier to handle a carload shipment at the carload rate. Freight forwarders operate primarily between large cities since they need to conduct their business in areas in which there is a large volume of traffic.

Air-freight forwarders operate in a manner similar to that of surface-freight forwarders except that their shipments are transported by air carriers.

Transportation Brokers

The transportation broker arranges for transportation service by bringing the shipper and the for-hire carrier together. The broker does not physically perform a transportation service or assume responsibility for the safe delivery of goods as does the indirect carrier like the freight forwarder.

Combination Service

For a number of years, there has been *trailer-on-flatcar* or *piggyback service,* which combines motor and rail transportation. A loaded trailer is moved to a rail terminal where it is placed on a flatcar. Upon arrival at a destination, the trailer is moved from the rail terminal to the unloading point. By combining motor and rail service in this way, shipments may be transported from store door to store door without transferring the contents of the trailer until delivered at destination. Railroads render this service entirely with their own motor and rail equipment. In addition, some railroads transport trailers for regular motor carriers and trailers of shippers.

Trailership or *fishyback* is another combination service in which loaded trailers are rolled on ships. They are then transported to a destination where they are rolled off and complete their journey by motor. The same type of service, except using boxcars rather than trailers, is provided in *trainship service.*

Containerization

Increasing use is being made of cargo containers, which are shipping containers of weatherproof construction. These are transported on flatbed trucks, railroad flatcars or gondola cars, and barges and ships. They can be lifted from rail flatcars to trucks or ships by means of cranes or fork lift trucks. Containers range in size from those with a capacity of 5,000 pounds to large containers up to 40 feet in length and having a capacity of 30,000 pounds. Shipments loaded in containers are not mixed with other shipments, as is the case of less carload or less truckload lots. They are less likely to be damaged in handling and in transit.

Parcel Post

Small packages are also transported by *parcel post,* a service provided by the United States Postal Service. There are limitations on the size and weight of such shipments. These parcels must be taken to the post office to be weighed and transportation charges paid. Deliveries are made at destination. Air parcel-post service is offered at higher rates but with the same weight and size restrictions.

PASSENGER TRANSPORTATION

Automotive Transportation

Passenger transportation, like freight transportation, is either *for-hire transportation* or *private transportation*. It is similarly divided into *intercity transportation* and *local* or *urban transportation*. The majority of passenger transportation in the United States is performed by private automobiles. It is estimated that 90 per cent of our intercity passenger-miles are the result of the operation of automobiles, of which there are 74 million in the United States. This is in contrast to 1920 when about 80 per cent of our intercity passenger-miles was performed by railroads. Thus, in a comparatively short period of time, we have had a virtual revolution in the means by which people are transported between cities. In local or urban passenger transportation, there is also very heavy reliance upon the automobile to transport people to and from work. Even in large cities, such as Washington and Los Angeles, only about one-third of the persons entering the downtown area use the for-hire or local transit system.

Air Transportation Passenger Services

For many years, the intercity passenger service was performed primarily by railroads. In the last few years, however, air carriers have increased their share until they have become the dominant for-hire passenger agency. Their share is about 55 per cent of the total for-hire passenger-miles, with bus and rail carriers sharing the remainder almost equally. Scheduled air carriers have two basic services: the *deluxe* or *first-class service* and *air-coach service*. The latter, which is at a substantially lower fare than the deluxe service, developed after World War II, and the only difference is smaller seats or seats closer together. Air-coach service has become very popular and now constitutes more than 70 per cent of total air passenger-miles. Generally, reservations are required for deluxe and air-coach service.

There are eleven *trunkline air carriers* operating in the United States. These carriers engage in an express, long-haul type of service. In addition, thirteen *local service lines* render service to many small communities. There are also airlines with flights to foreign countries.

The great advantage that air service offers is that of speed. The increased use of jet planes has reduced travel time considerably, particularly between more distant points. Trips from coast to coast in 5 hours are commonplace. Technological improvements in aircraft have been made so rapidly that often equipment is obsolete long before it is worn out.

In addition to the airlines that offer transportation service between cities on a regular schedule, there are *rotary-wing aircraft,* or *helicopters,* and *air taxi operators* who operate in short-haul operations in urban areas.

Bus Transportation Services

There is an extensive network of intercity bus routes that serve many points not served by any other type of for-hire passenger carrier. It is estimated that there are over 25,000 communities served only by bus. Buses offer the advantage of flexibility since they can travel to any point where there is an adequate highway. The comparatively small size of a bus also allows more frequent schedules, thereby offering travelers many departures. Bus service is a standard service at fares lower than other for-hire carriers in most instances. On particular schedules, a "limited" type of schedule has been established in which many intermediate points are not served, thus shortening travel time. The convenience afforded by buses is great. They can pick up or discharge passengers at most any place, many passengers being discharged in front of their homes or along the highway in rural areas. Most bus schedules do not require that reservations be made.

The intercity bus is usually thirty-seven or forty-one passenger capacity. A restricted amount of mail and packages can be carried in the storage compartment of these buses. An increasing amount of revenue for bus operators is secured through the *chartering* of buses to groups that want to use the bus for special tours.

Buses transport more passengers on *urban transit lines* than are transported by commuter railroads, street railways, subways, elevated and trolley coaches. The urban bus, which has a greater seating capacity on the average than the intercity bus, is the dominant type of equipment used in passenger transportation.

Rail Passenger Services

When railroads were first constructed in this country, they derived practically all of their revenue from the transporting of passengers. Although substantial passenger service is still provided, the railroads for many years have secured over 85 per cent of their revenue from freight traffic. With the extensive ownership of private automobiles and the growth of competitive bus and air carriers, railroad passenger service has declined until, in 1966, passenger trains operated over less than one-half of the railroad trackage in the United States.

In many cities, railroads provide *commuter service*, which is a form of urban transit. This service is generally unprofitable for the railroads.

Intercity service is provided with different types of services offered. *First-class accommodations* are available in both parlor cars and Pullman cars. The charge is higher for this service than for the basic *coach service*. More space is provided each person in first-class service, and reservations must be made in advance. In most instances, reservations cannot be made for coach service. In recent years, a few railroads have instituted a service providing a small private room with sleeping accommodations at the regular coach fare, plus a nominal charge for the room. Most trains are mixed trains carrying both coach and first-class passengers.

Travel Agents in Passenger Transportation

Travel agents sell passenger tickets for different carriers and are given a commission for this service by the carrier. The price of the ticket to the passenger is the same as that which the carrier charges, so the passenger pays no more for the ticket from the travel agent than he would from the carrier. Carriers look upon travel agents as a part of their sales force. Travel agents will also arrange hotel reservations and other details and handle group tours.

Transportation Brokers in Passenger Transportation

Passenger brokers arrange transportation by bringing the passenger and the bus carrier together in a manner similar to that of brokers in freight transportation. They hold themselves out to perform this service for anyone desiring it and have been particularly active in the development of charter business. There are about one hundred passenger transportation brokers. They receive their brokerage fee from the carrier for which the transportation is arranged.

RATES AND FARES

Types of Rates in Freight Transportation

The charge for transporting freight in intercity transportation is usually computed at a stated rate per 100 pounds. Intercity rates are divided into two categories depending on the services rendered. The first charge is the *line-haul rate* and is the basic transportation rate. Carriers often render additional services, or *accessorial services* as they are called, such as providing refrigeration of commodities while enroute, for which an additional charge is made. In formulating rates, carriers are influenced by such factors as the value of the commodity to be transported, the cost of transporting it, the amount of competition from other carriers, the distance to be transported, the quantity, its susceptibility to loss and damage, the weight of the shipment in relation to the space occupied (density), and other factors.

A carrier lists its rates in publications called *tariffs*. Tariffs are essentially price lists that set the charges for the services the carriers render. In addition to containing rates, tariffs also contain any rules or requirements concerning the acceptance of freight, the packaging of freight, the application of freight charges, pickup and delivery, and other matters. Tariffs are prepared and filed with federal regulatory bodies in conformance with certain requirements.

Although there are many kinds of rates, most shippers use a relatively small number of these rates. One of the common rates is called a *class rate*. Class rates are governed by a *classification*, which is a grouping of all commodities into a limited number of classes according to their transportation characteristics. Since there are thousands of different articles or commodities to be shipped, the classifying of articles into a limited number of classes is necessary in order to simplify the determination of the rate to be applied. In rail transportation, the *Uniform Freight Classification* is the principal one in use and contains thirty-one classes. The description of articles that are to be shipped is listed in one column of the classification, and in the opposite column the rating or the class of the commodity is shown. For example, if you wanted to ship a carload of shoehorns, you would look up shoehorns in the classification. You would find the carload rating for 30,000 pounds of steel shoehorns in boxes, which is the minimum carload amount for this particular commodity, to be Class 45. This means that the rate to be applied on these shoehorns is 45 per cent of the base rate, which is called Class 100. All class rates are certain percentages of the base rate, the Class 100 rating. Class rates are based on the mileage the commodity is to be transported. These rates increase as the distance increases but in less than direct proportion to the increase in distance. Class rates are available to ship commodities in rail, motor, and water transportation to and from all points where there is carrier service. Most of the small quantity, packaged shipments are transported at class rates. These rates are often compared to retail prices in merchandising.

In contrast to class rates, there are *commodity rates*, which are lower rates. These rates are often referred to as wholesale rates since they are similar to the wholesale prices in merchandising. Commodity rates are established on specific commodities, such as coal, oranges, or rubber tires, where there is a regularity of movement of traffic and a substantial quantity to be transported. Distance is not as important a factor in setting these rates as it is in class rates. Commodity rates do not apply to nearly as many commodities as do class rates and are also limited as to origins and destinations.

When a carrier or carriers have issued a commodity rate on a specific commodity, this rate takes precedence over a class rate on this commodity. Whereas class rates in rail transportation constitute 1 per cent of the tonnage and account for 5 per cent of the revenue, commodity rates constitute 91 per cent of the tonnage and account for 79 per cent of the revenue.

Another kind of rate in frequent use is a kind called *exceptions to the classification*. As the term indicates, the carriers sometimes make an exception to the rules or ratings in the classification. This is usually done to meet competition from other carriers. Like commodity rates, an exception has limited application as to commodities and origins and destinations. The exceptions to the classification generally result in the application of a class rate that is lower than the class rate that would have applied if there had been no exception to the classification. In rail transportation, exceptions-to-the-classification traffic constitute 7 per cent of the tonnage and account for 13 per cent of the revenue.

There is some trend toward what are termed *incentive rates*. Under such arrangements, carriers establish lower rates to encourage the shipper to ship a quantity larger than ordinarily shipped.

When transportation of a shipment is completely over the lines of one carrier, the rate is referred to as a *local rate*. Often, transportation is performed from a point on the line of one carrier to a point on the line of another carrier, in which case the rate is referred to as a *joint rate*. This kind of rate may involve several carriers.

The railroads established a rate structure that is based on low rates on goods of low value and high rates on high-value goods. Furthermore, rates are relatively high on short hauls but progressively lower per mile on longer hauls. In large measure, for-hire motor common carriers have patterned their rate structure after that of the railroads. Domestic water carriers also have rates that are similar to those of rail and motor carriers. Air carriers do not use a classification, and they refer to their rates as commodity rates. Petroleum pipeline carriers also call their rates commodity rates.

Carriers use two methods of increasing their rates. One is an *across-*

the-board or *horizontal increase.* This means that all rates are increased by a stated percentage, such as 10 per cent. The other type is called a *selective* or *vertical increase* in which one commodity or a group of commodities is increased by a stipulated amount.

Types of Fares in Passenger Transportation

Passenger fares are much simpler than freight rates. They are contained in tariffs and also in time tables. Basically, rail passenger fares are established on a specified amount per mile for the passenger. As the distance increases, the fare increases proportionately. There is a differentiation in the amount of the fare per passenger-mile based on the type of accommodation used. *Coach fares* are approximately 3.0¢ per mile while *first-class fares* are about 1¢ per mile more. In addition to the latter charge, there is also a space charge for parlor and sleeping cars. Usually, there is a 10 per cent reduction for round trips.

Some railroads have established *excursion fares* applicable for only a limited period of time, perhaps thirty or sixty days, at rates that are less than the normal rates. Carriers have also set up *family-fare plans* in which a full fare is charged one adult and one-half fare or two-thirds fare charged the remaining members of the family.

Bus fares are established on the basis of a specified amount per mile, but this fare is subject to what is called the *tapering principle.* This means that the fare on a per-mile basis is less per mile the greater the distance traveled. For example, for a short journey such as 35 miles, the fare charged may be equal to 3½¢ per mile; whereas on a 1,500-mile trip, it may average about 2.2¢ per mile. The round-trip fare discount by bus is 5 per cent. Intercity bus fares have been the lowest of any of the for-hire carriers. They average 2.7¢ per passenger-mile.

When buses are used in urban transit, the fare structure is generally different from the intercity fare structure in that the fare is the same regardless of the distance except where there are *zoned fares.* The zoned fares are a system whereby the city is laid out in zones. Concentric circles are drawn outward from the center of the city, and each of the circles represents a zone. Travel solely within a zone is at a stipulated fare, but an additional amount is added when travel extends into another zone. The distance factor enters into the determination of zoned fares, but the passenger does not pay for the precise distance he travels.

Airlines have experimented with many types of fares and differentiate between *coach* and *first-class service.* The differential between these two fares was at one time 25 per cent but now is very nominal.

The *family-fare plan* was originated by the airlines and is still in effect on certain days of the week. Under this plan, one adult pays full fare, the other pays two-thirds, and the rest of the family pays one-third fare. The average fare per passenger-mile for domestic airlines is about 6.1¢. Currently, the average intercity passenger trip by rail coach is 108 miles, by rail sleeping car 456 miles, by bus 85 miles, and by air 602 miles.

REGULATION

The Role of the Federal Government in Transportation

The federal government has long played an important role in the development of transportation because of its essentiality to our national economic well-being and defense. All of our forms of for-hire transportation engaged in interstate and foreign commerce are regulated in varying degrees by federal agencies. In addition to economic and safety regulation, certain of these agencies are authorized to aid and to promote the modes of transportation that they regulate. Through other government agencies, the federal government also provides or aids in the provision of basic transportation facilities, such as airports, airways, highways, and waterways.

One of the early forms of federal aid to transportation was the construction of some of the early turnpikes; another, the granting of land to railroads before the turn of the century to aid in the settlement of the West as well as providing a means of access to and from the area. In more recent years, the federal government has provided a number of facilities to aid the development of air transportation. The *Federal Aviation Agency,* a government agency, administers the Federal Aid to Airports Act that, since 1946, has resulted in federal aid being given to cities to help them construct airports. Total federal expenditures for airports since the 1930's, including work-relief programs and World War II expenditures, have amounted to an estimated two billion dollars. The Federal Aviation Agency is also responsible for the provision of operation and maintenance of our federal airways with navigation aids for aircraft. It is estimated that over two billion dollars has been spent by the federal government on airways.

The *Bureau of Public Roads,* another federal agency, administers the Federal Aid Highway Program in cooperation with the states. Since 1920, the federal government has spent about forty billion dollars on highways. The Federal Aid Highway Act of 1956 established the National Interstate and Defense Highway System of 41,000 miles for which the federal government provides 90 per cent of the funds and the states 10 per cent. This program will require an estimated federal expenditure of about forty-six billion dollars. Under this Act, federal funds are also being provided for certain other highways.

The *Corps of Engineers* of the Army has the responsibility for developing rivers and harbors. Approximately six billion dollars has been spent in improving, operating, and maintaining our waterways. In addition, the *United States Coast Guard* provides, operates, and maintains aids to navigation and issues licenses to merchant-marine personnel.

Additional funds are provided by states, counties, townships, and cities for construction and maintenance of highways. It is expected that over one hundred billion dollars will be spent on highways between 1956 and 1971 by all levels of government. Cities also provide funds for airport construction, operation, and maintenance beyond those spent by the federal government. It can be seen that in the aggregate, at all levels of government, we spend large amounts for transportation facilities.

Both the state and federal governments levy taxes on those who use the highways. These are referred to as *user charges*. The gasoline tax is an example of a user charge. On the other hand, there are no user charges imposed for the use of inland waterways, and, until recently, there were nominal user charges in air transportation. Through the provision of basic transportation facilities without the imposition of user charges or user charges that cover only a portion of the cost and maintenance of these facilities, the government encourages use of these transportation facilities and agencies that utilize them. When basic facilities are publicly provided for three agencies of transportation, a question of fairness arises since two modes—railroads and pipelines—provide their own facilities. Unless adequate user charges are assessed for the use of government-constructed and government-maintained facilities, it can readily be seen that the modes of transportation using such facilities can establish charges that do not reflect total economic cost. This enables them to compete on a more favorable basis than those agencies that have to charge rates reflecting entire costs of construction and maintenance.

The passage of the Urban Mass Transportation Act of 1964 committed the federal government to assist in the development of urban mass transportation. The Act authorized the administrator of the federal Housing and Home Finance Agency to provide financial assistance to help develop comprehensive and coordinated mass-transportation systems, both public and private. The federal government provides aid for capital improvements such as equipment, land, and stations, which can amount to as much as two-thirds of the total cost. The local area must provide the remainder. In addition, research, development, and demonstration grants are available, under certain circumstances, for which the federal government supplies the funds. A loan program also exists to aid in the procurement of equipment.

Federal Regulation of Surface Transportation

Regulation of railroads was instituted by the Congress in 1887. The Interstate Commerce Commission, which was created by the Act to Regulate Commerce (now the Interstate Commerce Act) is an independent regulatory body consisting of eleven men given the authority to regulate the railroads under that Act. The passage of the original act was the result of general public dissatisfaction with the railroads. There were many discriminations practiced by the railroads, such as charging differing amounts to shippers for transporting the same quantity, as well as rebates or refunds being given to favored shippers. Originally, the Interstate Commerce Commission regulated rail common carriers engaged in interstate transportation. The authority was broadened in 1906 to include common carriers by pipeline transporting oil or other commodities, except water and gas; motor carriers in 1935; domestic water carriers in 1940; and freight forwarders in 1942.

The degree of regulatory authority over the different carriers varies. Regulation is divided into *economic regulation* (the regulation of business practices) and *safety regulation*. The latter establishes rules for safe operation of locomotives, trains, and all interstate buses and trucks, as well as requirements concerning packaging and transporting explosives. The Commission also prescribes the number of hours that a truck driver can operate a truck and specifies safety devices, such as fire extinguishers, the number and location of lights on trucks and buses, maintenance of drivers, logs, and many other matters. The broad areas of economic regulation include *the granting of operating authority*, which means the granting of authority to operate as a common carrier through the issuance of a *certificate* by the Commission or as a contract carrier through the issuance of a *permit*. This is frequently referred to as *control over the right of entry*. Those carriers that were operating prior to the passage of the regulatory acts were granted operating authority under a "grandfather" provision in the Acts. Under this provision, they were automatically granted operating authority to continue operating over the same routes they had been using prior to the institution of regulation.

Economic regulation also includes control over rates, fares and charges. The carriers initiate the rates through *rate bureaus* or *conferences*, which are organizations formed by the carriers to provide the means by which carriers can jointly formulate rates. This is known as the *conference method of rate making*. Rates must be published and filed with the Interstate Commerce Commission, which has authority to disapprove the rates. Generally, rates and fares must be on file with the Commission thirty days before they can be used by the carrier. This gives the public the opportunity to protest any proposed rate or fare. The Commission, on its own or if there are protests, may suspend a rate for a period of seven months during which time it conducts an investigation. During the suspension period, the old rates have to be used. Hearings may be held to determine the justness and reasonableness of new or changed rates.

Under economic regulation, the Commission also has authority to approve or disapprove all consolidations or mergers of carriers and exercises varying degrees of control over the issuance of securities by the different modes of transportation. The Commission prescribes a uniform system of accounts and, in the case of railroads and pipelines, determines the value of their properties for rate-making purposes.

All interstate rail carriers come under federal regulation, but this is not the case with motor carriers and inland water carriers. Congress exempted certain segments of motor and water transportation from economic regulation, although not from safety regulation. These carriers are called *exempt carriers*. More carriers in these two modes of transportation are exempt from economic regulation than are regulated.

Federal Regulation of Air Transportation

The *Civil Aeronautics Board* has regulated air carriers since the passage of the *Civil Aeronautics Act* in 1938 (since 1958 the *Federal Aviation Act*). The Board consists of five members appointed for six-year terms by the President, with the advice and consent of the Senate. It is an independent agency reporting to Congress as does the Interstate Commerce Commission. It has *economic regulatory jurisdiction* over domestic and international air carriers similar to that of the Interstate Commerce Commission over surface transportation. In connection with safety aspects, it has *accident investigation responsibility*. In addition, this Board may *promote* the development of air transportation. As a result, some of our air carriers receive a subsidy, whereas others have reached the stage where this is no longer necessary. The promotional aspects of this Act have no counterpart in the Interstate Commerce Act.

Federal Regulation of American Flag Carriers in International Ocean Shipping

In 1936, the Merchant Marine Act was passed, which regulates ocean carriers engaged in foreign trade. A five-man Federal Maritime Commission, appointed by the President by and with the consent of the Senate, exercises some control over rates, services, and practices and requires the filing of reports and accounts. Its regulatory control is not as comprehensive as that which applies to domestic transportation. The promotional aspects of the Act are under the Department of Commerce and take the form of what is called an *operating differential subsidy*. Because foreign operating costs are substantially less than United States costs, ship operators who can qualify may receive a subsidy in the form of a payment from the federal government. This makes it possible for them to offer their service at a rate competitive with that of foreign ship operators. The primary difference in costs between U.S. operators and foreign operators is in wages. Furthermore, in order to encourage ship replacement and ship building in the United States, a *construction differential subsidy* may be secured in the construction of a new vessel that may be as high as 50 per cent of the cost of the vessel. One of the justifications for the extensive subsidy for this mode of transportation is national defense.

State and Local Regulation of Transportation

Regulation of intrastate operations is imposed by many states, although there is considerable variation among states as to the degree of safety and economic regulation. Many states require state operating authority, regulate rates, prescribe uniform systems of accounts, and some prescribe minimum service requirements. Under the police powers of the state, most states prescribe size and weight limitations for motor vehicles. A great deal of variation exists among states on these requirements, which can act as a deterrent to the movement of vehicles in interstate operations.

In some cities, there is regulation of local passenger transportation. The right of entry is controlled, and the operating authority is in the form of a *franchise*. Rates and service are regulated. In a few instances, local truck transportation is regulated by local authorities.

TRAFFIC MANAGEMENT

What Is Traffic Management?

Traffic management is the management of the many functions involved in the purchase of transportation service and the provision of transportation for a company, including the use of facilities and equipment at a price or rate consistent with the services rendered in order to accomplish the efficient movement of persons and property from one point to another. In the purchase of intraplant and interplant transportation or in purchasing or providing transportation from or to all points needed by the business organization, a traffic manager has numerous alternative methods of transportation available to him. In addition to for-hire carriers, he may purchase or lease equipment in which transportation service can be provided by the company under his direction, in other words, private carriage. Many traffic managers, however, combine the use of different types of for-hire carriers and private carriage.

There are many variations in the title of the person who has charge of traffic-management functions in a company. "Industrial traffic manager," "general traffic manager," "director of traffic," and "vice-president of traffic" are some of the titles used in different companies. In addition to traffic management activities of individual companies, there are such activities undertaken for groups of business organizations.

The traffic department has developed because of what it can accomplish for the company and its customers in the way of controlled transportation costs and better service. For many years, top management had the feeling that since transportation rates were subject to regulation, there was very little that could be done to change rates. The advent of the newer modes of transportation gave greater flexibility in the handling of shipments and injected competitive rate and service aspects so that the skillful management of traffic functions has received greater recognition. Many companies are only now becoming aware of the amount spent to transport their raw materials and finished products. Depending upon the commodities involved, transportation costs range from 6 to 20 per cent of the cost of goods sold for many companies and can run as high as 50 per cent. Certainly, this significant expenditure should be carefully controlled.

The Traffic Department and Other Departments in the Company

The management of traffic affects many other departments of the company, so it is necessary that the traffic manager develop a department that is responsive to the particular needs of his company. The production department requires a flow of inbound and outbound traffic that, in most instances, requires that all the components necessary for an assembly line be available at the right time. On the other hand, the company does not want to maintain any larger inventory than is required. This places upon the traffic department the responsibility for careful scheduling of shipments to insure that they arrive when needed, and thus the amount of capital tied up in inventory is no greater than necessary.

The traffic department works closely with the purchasing department by showing the most advantageous purchasing areas from a transportation standpoint. Suppose that the purchasing department is considering the purchase of material at five different points. The transportation rates furnished by the traffic department will be of considerable help in evaluating the most economical sources of supplies. Information can also be furnished the purchasing department on the most economical size of purchase, since the transportation rate for small quantities is relatively greater than for large quantities. If the purchasing department is buying a number of different items in less carload quantities in one area, small shipments might be consolidated and shipped in a carload or truckload with a savings in transportation costs and better service.

The personnel department and the traffic department work cooperatively in arranging for the transportation of household goods of employees who are transferred. The traffic department will also arrange for passenger accommodations of employees traveling on official business.

The traffic department and the sales department have many areas of interest. Rate information supplied by the traffic department to salesmen is of help in determining the most desirable unit of sales on the basis of rates. The people in traffic will also supply information for prospective customers concerning transportation service and rates on the company's products. The location of warehouses for better distribution of the products may be worked out in conjunction with the sales department. The traffic department also works with the sales and production departments and material-handling personnel on packaging of the company's products to ensure safe transportation of the product and to provide an attractive exterior design to aid in the selling of the product.

Evidence to be used in rate cases and in loss-and-damage claims caused by the transportation movement is prepared in conjunction with the legal department. The traffic and legal departments also confer on contracts for securing transportation equipment used in private carriage by the company.

When the company has its own transportation equipment, such as trucks, the traffic department cooperates with the advertising department in placing appropriate advertising on these "rolling billboards."

Functions of the Traffic Department

Most of the functions of the traffic department are concerned with freight movements. Some of these include: packing and marking, loading, application of the correct classification, determination of rates, rate negotiations, rate litigation, control of carrier penalty charges for such things as holding rail cars and truck trailers beyond the free time (called *demurrage* in rail transportation, *detention* in motor transportation), consolidation of shipments, preparation of bills of lading and other shipping papers, routing of shipments, handling of claims, expediting and tracing shipments, processing transportation bills for payment, auditing freight bills, warehousing, material handling, operation of company-owned or leased transportation equipment, arranging for adequate insurance coverage, and advising on transportation aspects of new site locations.

In addition, there are special services provided by carriers that can be negotiated by the traffic department. One of these is the *transit privilege,* which permits a commodity, such as wheat, to be shipped from an origin point to an intermediate point, at which point the commodity is unloaded, stored, and processed; then it is reloaded and shipped to a final destination point. Instead of a higher local rate applying from the origin point to the intermediate point and then another local rate applying from the intermediate point to the destination point, a through rate from origin to final destination applies, plus a nominal charge called the transit charge for the stop-off at the intermediate point. The through rate, plus the nominal charge, is much lower than the two separate local rates that would apply without the transit privilege that has been secured by the traffic department from the carrier.

Another special service that can be arranged by the traffic department is called the *diversion and reconsignment privilege.* This privilege permits a shipment, such as fresh fruit, to be started in its transportation movement in the general direction of its market; and prior to its arrival at a particular market or after its arrival, its routing can be changed to a different market. Diverting the shipment to another market where the supply is not as great accomplishes a better balance of supply and demand.

Organization of a Traffic Department

As is true of other departments in a business, the organization of the traffic department depends upon such factors as the nature and size of the business and the type of organizational structure that the company has adopted. These factors will also affect the number of functions performed by the traffic department. Two general types of organizations of traffic departments exist: the *centralized* and *decentralized.* In the decentralized type of operation, the traffic department of each of the company plants operates independently. However, the headquarters traffic department establishes the traffic policies to guide the plants. They will also supply technical information when this is necessary. Many of the functions of traffic management that are of a repetitive nature can be performed at the plants, thus giving headquarters traffic personnel the opportunity to concentrate on those traffic matters that will provide greater efficiency and economy. The headquarters traffic department may assign representatives to serve as liaison between headquarters and the plants. In the centralized type of traffic operation, the more important traffic functions are performed at the headquarters office. The organization chart of such a department is shown in Figure 19–1. This type of organization maintains greater control over such matters as routing and traffic distribution, receiving and shipping per-

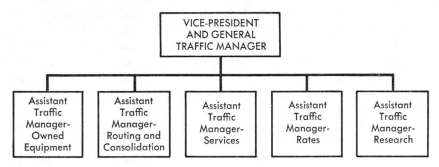

Fig. 19–1. Organization of a headquarters traffic department.

sonnel at the plants, and other functions. General traffic letters and the issuance of a *traffic manual* setting forth traffic policies and procedures are helpful in accomplishing an understanding relationship. The traffic department should make periodic reports to top management in order to keep management informed of the accomplishments of the department.

PHYSICAL-DISTRIBUTION MANAGEMENT

Transition

During the past decade, the physical-distribution concept has been appearing in some management structures. This is a somewhat broader management approach to the group of closely interrelated business functions including transportation, warehousing, inventory control, protective packaging, material handling (excluding the production line), and the communications network (computers). The emphasis in this type of managerial approach is on the *total-cost* concept in order to effectuate sound management of these elements, which are concerned with the physical aspects of distribution. Such other elements of distribution as selling or advertising are not included.

Some writers in the field have introduced the term *business logistics* to describe these functions, although this title has not as yet been used in business organization structures. The physical-distribution approach has been adopted in some companies that have recognized the value of the systems or total-cost approach in the management of the elements of the physical-distribution system, but the functions are embraced under "traffic management."

The emphasis in physical-distribution management is on service to customers and the control of costs. Physical-distribution costs are the third largest cost component in the production and merchandising of goods. By examining the flow of material from its raw state to finished goods in the hands of consumers, management is able to analyze and to effect "tradeoffs" among the different components of physical distribution. For example, a multiplant company with national distribution may have fifty warehouses. An analysis may show that savings can be effected on faster transportation carrying products directly to the customer and thereby make it possible to close twenty-five of the warehouses. Another factor of a tradeoff of this kind is that it is likely that the inventory can be reduced and so free capital for other use. Of course, within each component of physical distribution, there are alternatives. A company can own its own warehouses, or it may lease or rent space in public warehouses. A company may own and operate its own transportation service, or it may use commercial transportation. The establishment of the physical-distribution approach enables a company to determine the total cost of each component, to weigh the total effect, and to achieve a better balance and improved service to customers.

Warehousing

In most business organizations, storage, or warehousing, of products must be performed several times in the production and distribution of goods. Companies on a continuous-production basis require the maintenance of minimum amounts of materials, and these must usually be stored as raw materials prior to the production process and subsequently as finished goods, for there may not be an immediate market for them. Where a product is manufactured in advance of a seasonal market, as in the Christmas season, production takes place many months before and products have to be stored for weeks or months before going to dealers. Seasonal agricultural commodities, through storage, can be marketed over a longer period of time, and the actual value of the commodity can be enhanced.

Many business organizations use public warehouses for all or part of their storage needs rather than build their own private warehouses. Such a decision is made after consideration of the cost and service aspects of this type of storage compared with provision of facilities of their own. In some companies, a combination approach is used.

Warehousing is an integral part of physical distribution inasmuch as it involves storage aspects of physical supply and will affect cost and service. The optimal location of warehouses, the amount to be stored, and the ability to satisfy customers' needs are some of the factors to be considered.

Material Handling

With the development of mass-production techniques in industry, it became necessary to devise methods to facilitate the movement of the tremendous volume of material used in processing. This first developed on the production line and later was applied to many phases of the movement of material. The real emphasis in this area occurred during World War II when a manpower shortage caused widespread use of material-handling equipment, and the technique spread from production to distribution including warehousing and shipping and receiving.

The primary objectives of material handling are to reduce costs and increase capacity and efficiency. Surveys have shown that 20 per cent of the cost of manufacturing is for the handling of material. In some companies, the responsibility for the material-handling function, excluding the production line, has been placed in the traffic or physical-distribution department, which has responsibility for material handling up to the production line and from the production line. When this has been done, material-handling equipment can be made compatible with the transportation system to facilitate the flow of products from raw materials to customer. Specially designed containers that will meet both the producer's and the consumer's needs can be used. Orders can be unitized through the use of pallets and fork-lift trucks to reduce greatly the per-unit cost of handling. Such arrangements enhance the possibility of damage-free movement of goods at minimum cost.

There are several hundred different material-handling devices and many different unitization and containerization types. The potential for management improvement in this area is very great, particularly when it is treated as a part of the total physical-distribution system.

Packaging

There are two general types of packaging: (1) industrial, which deals with the preparation and protection of merchandise for shipment and storage and (2) consumer, which is designed to affect sales acceptance. Industrial packaging is an integral part of the management of physical distribution. It has influence on the cost of transportation, which is computed on a weight basis that also includes the weight of the package. Further, the type and manner of packaging have a bearing on the cost and choice of material-handling equipment and arrival of goods in damage-free condition. These factors must be coordinated in the selection of the type of industrial packaging to be used.

Inventory Control

The acquisition of material for processing means that a firm has acquired an inventory representing a significant capital outlay. Upon completion of production, finished goods may not readily be disposed of, so inventory costs continue. The optimal level of inventory is always a factor of great concern in business management, since it is estimated that 30 per cent of total industrial assets is in total inventories. Management is constantly seeking methods of keeping the inventory level within reasonable bounds. Different inventory standards can be used, such as the maximum-minimum stock level, the ratio of inventory to annual sales, or the number of days' supply.

The interdependence of inventory management and physical distribution is apparent in the various stages of production and distribution from acquisition of material to final delivery to the customer. The amount of material in the pipeline, that is, in storage, in transit, and in processing, can be more efficiently managed through coordination of physical distribution, production, and sales.

Organization

The close interrelationship of the physical-distribution components of inventory, transportation, warehousing, industrial packaging, and material handling can be effected through the establishment of a physical-distribution department. In companies where the executive heading it is a "vice-president of physical distribution," there will be an assistant in charge of each of the component divisions. Some companies have designated the top executive as the "director of traffic and distribution services," and others, "vice-president of distribution."

YOUR CAREER IN TRANSPORTATION AND
PHYSICAL DISTRIBUTION

Career Opportunities

A person interested in transportation and physical distribution will find career opportunities with carriers in all modes of transportation. These job opportunities may be in sales, in the claims department, in accounting, in operations, or in terminal operations. Some of the carriers have training programs for college graduates for general-management positions. Of the different modes of transportation, airlines pay the lowest starting salaries for college graduates. More job opportunities exist with motor carriers than with airlines, and the possibilities for management positions are good. Railroads tend to hire graduates of engineering colleges, and very few business-administration graduates are hired. Starting salaries with rail carriers are relatively high, but the opportunities for advancement are limited unless the person is a part of a management-training program.

Another area of job opportunities is with industrial traffic and physical-distribution departments. This area has received belated recognition as a specialized field of business management, with the result that an increasing number of good positions are available for well-qualified transportation majors in this field. Many college graduates enter this field as company trainees. The initial work of anyone entering the field of traffic management generally deals with rates. The position of traffic manager in an industrial organization is most often at the executive level except in very small companies. Even in small companies, however, a college-trained traffic manager would expect to move into an executive position ultimately.

The government offers good careers in transportation as it is a very large user of transportation. Therefore, both civilian and military agencies must have trained traffic specialists. In some instances, the government also operates its own private transportation system where there are additional job opportunities for majors in transportation. There are several regulatory bodies that have openings for persons interested in experience in different phases of regulation. Several other civilian agencies, such as the Bureau of Public Roads and the Federal Aviation Agency, provide job possibilities. In particular, those transportation majors with a knowledge of economics, general business, and statistics may find openings in these agencies that would be of interest. In general, transportation positions in industry pay more than those in government.

Transportation trade associations and chambers of commerce also employ transportation majors with well-rounded backgrounds in business administration.

Educational Background

A broad background in business subjects, including economics and political science, is of particular value to the student interested in majoring in transportation. Since transportation is a service, he must have a good understanding of what it can accomplish in all areas of business. A student majoring in transportation will take a number of transportation courses covering the different modes and industrial traffic management so that he will have a broad knowledge of the entire field. In addition, courses in accounting and marketing will be of great benefit. The principles of personnel management and industrial management should be included in his course of study. A knowledge of finance would be helpful because the student entering the field of transportation may be in a top-management position in later years. Sales, advertising, and statistics are other courses he will want to study. Statistics will be used a great deal in the interpretation of data in transportation and physical-distribution management.

There are many complexities in the transportation and physical-distribution management field, and it is not possible to cover all of them in formal classroom work. A continuation of education beyond the college degree is quite common. The American Society of Traffic and Transportation, the professional organization in this field, gives a series of tests semiannually for those who wish to take them. These cover several areas in the transportation and traffic management field and economics and general-business subjects as well. The successful completion of the examinations qualifies the applicant for membership in the organization. Its objective is to establish high standards of knowledge, technical training, and ethics for those people who are working in the field of transportation.

TOPICS FOR DISCUSSION

1. Carefully distinguish between traffic management and physical-distribution management.

2. Should the ratio of transportation cost to selling price of a product determine the degree of management control exercised by a manufacturing company over the transportation function?

3. List what you consider to be the five primary public-policy issues in transportation.

4. What organizational problems would confront you in establishing a physical-distribution department? How would you overcome them?

5. *Public carriers* are usually classified as either common, contract, or exempt carriers, according to the type of business operation they conduct. Discuss the distinguishing characteristics of each classification.

6. Domestic water transportation service is divided into four broad categories. Name and describe each category.

7. One of the fastest-growing techniques for transportation of cargo is known as "containerization." Describe this technique.

8. What is the primary function of a transportation broker?

9. Distinguish between "piggyback" service and "fishyback" service.

10. Critics frequently contend that motor carriers are subsidized because they operate over highways built by the taxpayer. The motor carriers contend that they pay for the use of highways through taxes paid. What do you think?

CASE 19–1

THE BLUE LINE RAILROAD

The Blue Line Railroad operated out of headquarters in the city of Timberlake. One branch of the line ran from Timberlake south 200 miles to Allensville. Allensville was a prominent petroleum-production center, and the Blue Line was the only railroad serving the area. A second branch of the line ran from Timberlake west for 150 miles to Barnesville. The Central Valley Railroad also operated a line between Timberlake and Barnesville.

The Blue Line Railroad had been in financial difficulty for several years. No dividends had been paid to the holders of common stock since 1962. In 1964, the Blue Line published and filed with the Interstate Commerce Commission a schedule of rate reductions to apply to the movement of certain classes of petroleum products between Allensville and Timberlake. The reductions averaged about 10 per cent. The Lockley Motor Freight Lines, Inc., filed an objection with the Commission, and hearings were held.

The Blue Line Railroad based its plea for a rate reduction on several factors. It contended that an improved traffic volume was necessary if financial disaster was to be avoided. The claim was made that any traffic that might be diverted from the motor carrier would represent goods the nature of which made them more suitable to movement by rail. And finally, it was pointed out that the rate reduction would benefit the shipper and hence the public. The motor carrier, in opposing the rate reduction, claimed that the diversion of traffic from the carrier that would result from the lower rail rate would threaten the existence of the carrier. Attorneys for the motor carrier contended that once the railroad achieved a monopoly in the transportation of petroleum products from Allensville, rates would be raised to exploit the shipper. The Commission studied the situation and denied the request of the Blue Line Railroad for lower rates. In denying the rate reduction, the Commission based its decision on the principle of the desirability of maintaining competitive transportation facilities between Timberlake and Allensville.

Late in 1964, the Blue Line Railroad approached the Central Valley Railroad with the proposal that a merger of the two lines be considered. After many conferences between officials of the two railroads, plans for a merger were worked out and presented to the Interstate Commerce Commission for approval. In presenting the request for approval, the parties concerned maintained that the merger would rescue the Blue Line Railroad from imminent financial receivership, that the financial health of the consolidated lines would be better than that of either operating independently, that wasteful duplication of services between Timberlake and Barnesville would be eliminated, and that services to the customers of both railroads would be improved as a result of the merger.

The Interstate Commerce Commission considered the proposed merger and in June, 1965, gave its approval. Attorneys representing interests in the Barnesville area had opposed the merger in appearances before the Commission. They now moved to challenge the merger in the courts. Objection to the merger was based on the contention that elimination of competition between Blue Line and Central Valley in serving the Barnesville area would work to the detriment of shippers in that area.

1. In considering the merger, the court must be mindful of all parties that have an interest at stake. Who are these parties?

2. Do you feel that the Commission was justified in denying the request of the Blue Line Railroad for a rate reduction in 1964?

SELECTED REFERENCES

Frederick, J. H. *Commercial Air Transportation.* 5th ed. Homewood, Ill.: Richard D. Irwin, Inc., 1961.

Germane, G. E., N. A. Glaskowsky, Jr., and J. L. Heskett. *Highway Transportation Management.* New York: McGraw-Hill Book Co., 1963.

Heskett, J. L., R. M. Ivie, and N. A. Glaskowsky, Jr. *Business Logistics.* New York: The Ronald Press Co., 1964.

Locklin, D. P. *Economics of Transportation.* 6th ed. Homewood, Ill.: Richard D. Irwin, Inc., 1966.

Mossman, F. H., and N. Morton. *Logistics of Distribution Systems.* Englewood Cliffs, N.J.: Allyn & Bacon, Inc., 1965.

Norton, Hugh S. *Modern Transportation Economics.* Columbus, Ohio: Charles E. Merrill Books, Inc., 1963.

Owen, Wilfred. *Strategy For Mobility.* Washington, D.C.: The Brookings Institution, 1964.

Pegrum, D. F. *Transportation: Economics and Public Policy.* Homewood, Ill.: Richard D. Irwin, Inc., 1963.

Smerk, George M. *Urban Transportation: The Federal Role.* Bloomington: Indiana University Press, 1965.

Smykay, E. W., D. J. Bowersox, and F. H. Mossman. *Physical Distribution Management.* New York: The Macmillan Co., 1961.

Taff, C. A. *Commercial Motor Transportation.* 3d ed. Homewood, Ill.: Richard D. Irwin, Inc., 1961.

————. *Management of Traffic and Physical Distribution.* 3d ed. Homewood, Ill.: Richard D. Irwin, Inc., 1964.

20

Public Utilities

PUBLIC-UTILITY SERVICES

One type of business that seems to be taken for granted by the public is that group generally referred to as "public utilities." The essential services provided by public-utility companies include electricity, gas, water, telephone, telegraph, and urban transport. Only when there is a service interruption due to adverse weather conditions or a breakdown does the public seem to show real awareness and concern about the companies rendering service for them. The managements of these companies face most of the same problems that confront other business firms but, in addition, operate in an environment of government regulation by municipal, state, and/or federal regulatory bodies, which gives rise to special responsibilities and problems. In some public utilities, the seller installs facilities on the buyer's property, such as telephone and electric lines, and gas and water connections. The services that are available can be secured, for all practical purposes, only from the seller since there is a physical connection, and the buyer cannot secure the service from someone else.

A public utility has an obligation to (1) serve everyone desiring its service up to its ability or capacity to do so, (2) render adequate service, (3) furnish service at reasonable rates, and (4) furnish service without discrimination. Government regulation assures the fulfillment of these obligations. A public utility is given the right to use the power of *eminent domain*. This means that public authority, such as the state, will grant the utility the right to acquire property for use by the utility. Although an owner may refuse to sell his property to the public utility, the right of eminent domain enables the company to acquire the property at a fair price, often established by the courts, despite the owner's refusal to sell.

Some Tests of the Public Utility Status

The public utility concept has been established largely through court decisions. A number of leading cases are often cited as having established one or more tests of what constitutes a public utility. Other tests have been a part of the public utility concept from its beginning. One of these tests of a public utility is that of *control over entry*. This is the right to operate a public utility and is accomplished by the issuance of either a *franchise* or a *certificate of public convenience and necessity*, depending upon the utility. A company cannot operate as a public utility without a franchise or a certificate. This affords protection to the public through control of the operations of the public utility and also gives the utility protection or partial protection from competition. Extension of service to areas or customers not presently receiving service may be compelled by public authority, and service cannot be abandoned without approval of the regulatory body. Thus, the public utility loses freedom of action in matters of this kind. Control over entry in the public utility field is limited by public authority. For example, a franchise that permits a utility to use the streets to provide bus service or to erect electric poles may be issued by a municipal regulatory body. In other instances, this control may rest with a state or federal regulatory body. Under such circumstances, there is a definite regulatory control over the number of companies that may operate in the field. When a local regulatory body issues a franchise that is exclusive for an electric company to operate in a city, a monopoly is thereby created. In the absence of control over entry, there might be two competing companies rendering duplicate service with parallel facilities on each street. It is deemed desirable to avoid this and have just one company perform the service.

Public utilities are industries that tend to require a *large capital investment*. This is another of the tests generally a part of the concept of a public utility. Facilities and distribution lines are very costly. The large amount of capital in the form of property investment is particularly significant when it is compared with the rate of *capital turnover*, which is the annual gross revenues of a business divided by the total capital invested in the enterprise. The capital turnover of gas, electric, water, street railway, and telephone utility companies amounts to about once every four to six years. In a chain-store business, capital may turn over eight times in a single year while a high capital industry, such as steel, does not ordinarily require capital in excess of its annual revenue. With the extensive capital investment, a large portion of the costs are relatively fixed; that is, these costs do not vary with changes in the output. High fixed costs provide an incentive to the utility industries to increase output in order to gain a greater volume of business over which the fixed costs may be spread. The greater the number of units of output over which fixed costs are distributed, the lower the fixed cost per unit of output. This is referred to as *the economies of decreasing cost.* In order to increase output, companies lower prices. If there were no public regulation of public utilities, this pressure to reduce prices to gain a larger volume of business would become cutthroat and detrimental to public interest. Competitors would be driven out so that a single monopoly would likely prevail with no regulatory control over it.

Another of the tests of a public utility is that its property is *dedicated to public use.* Its services are available to any who wants them, and it has a duty to serve without discrimination as to rates and service. Further, it cannot discontinue service, as most other businesses can, without approval of the regulatory body.

Another factor heavily relied upon in considering public utility status is that of *necessity.* The services provided by electric, gas, water, telephone, and other public utility companies are considered to be necessities of life for which there are no ready substitutes available. This is an element that causes a desire to insure that the public will be protected in the rates charged and the services provided. It is possible that a legislature could, under a given set of conditions, find most any good or service to be a necessity, but the fact is that they have not. Legislatures, as well as courts, have recognized the essential nature of public utilities.

STATE AND LOCAL REGULATION

Development of Regulation

One of the characteristics of public utilities is the extensive regulation to which they are subject. In the early development of public utilities, they were local in operations. Therefore, our first regulation of these companies was local regulation. It was not until utilities expanded to serve more than one community that state regulation was established. All of the states now have some form of public utility regulation, but there is a very marked difference among them concerning the composition, operation, and administration of state utility laws.

Counties and municipalities may regulate local utilities in their communities or areas to the extent that the state has granted them the authority. Because utilities use streets and other public property, they have to secure special permission to do so, which is granted in the franchise or certificate containing the authority to operate. In local regulation, the franchise becomes the instrument of regulation because it contains specific obligations and stipulations as to service as drawn up by the city officials. In many cities, the regulatory body is not a group especially appointed to handle this responsibility as in state and federal regulation, although it may be. Often, the regulatory commission is composed of the elected city officials.

The Franchise

The franchise is a contract entered into between the city and the public utility company. Provisions on standards of service, rates, accounts and reports, and the method for interpreting provisions and adjusting disagreements are included in the franchise. Many early franchises were of very long duration, some of them even being perpetual. It was found through experience that such franchises often led to abuses by utility companies because they had the right to operate regardless of the service they provided. This early experience resulted in the use of franchises of shorter duration. If franchises run for more than twenty-five years, they are usually referred to as *long-term franchises*—less than that, *short-term*. As the termination of a franchise approaches, it often becomes difficult for the utility to finance capital improvements because of the uncertainty of future operations, which could be terminated with the franchise being given to another company. Because of this problem, some cities issue an *indeterminate permit* rather than one with a fixed termination date. The indeterminate permit enables the public utility to continue to operate as long as the city is satisfied with its services. The city, in turn, may terminate the agreement at any time it desires to do so, giving the company fair compensation for its facilities.

Because of the problems that arise in connection with inflexible clauses concerning rates and services in franchises, particularly where franchises run over a long period of time, some cities have granted franchises that seek to adjust rates and services to changing conditions. In any rate matters, the utility and the regulatory commission must first agree on the elements of costs that will make up an *agreed base* to be used in arriving at reasonable rates. The agreed base is composed of the classification of costs, the value of the property, the reserves for contingencies, and other items. One franchise that permits adjustments in rates is the *service-at-cost franchise*. This kind of franchise stipulates that a certain *rate of return* (a percentage figure arrived at by dividing earnings by the agreed base) will be allowed on an agreed base. The *sliding-scale franchise* is another flexible franchise similar to the service-at-cost type in providing for a specified rate of return. However, if the rate of return goes above that specified in the franchise, the rates are reduced; if the rate of return falls below that amount, rates can be raised. For example, if the agreed rate of return is 7 per cent and the company does not earn this return, the rates can be increased according to a stated formula. The city of Washington, D.C. uses a plan of this type in which the basic rate of return is now set at 6 per cent. The agreement states that if earnings of the company exceed 6 per cent but are less than 7 per cent, half of the excess is to be used for reduction of rates the following year; if earnings are between $7\frac{1}{4}$ and 8 per cent of the base, 60 per cent of the excess over $7\frac{1}{4}$ per cent is to be used for reduction of rates; if earnings exceed 8 per cent, 75 per cent of the excess over 8 per cent is to be used for reduction of rates. This type of franchise provides an incentive for reducing costs.

Regulation of Service

Although regulation differs from state to state, the major areas covered in all state regulation are *service* and *rates*. Service includes the establishment of minimum standards of service by the regulatory commission. This body may require that the utility improve its service if it is not meeting the minimum standards. The utility must give equal service to all of its customers. This requirement is, of course, subject to reasonable interpretation. It also has a duty to serve all who apply for its services within its ability to do so. For example, a water company that had a diminishing supply and was not able to get additional water at reasonable cost was permitted by a regulatory commission to refuse to serve new customers. Public utilities are allowed to make reasonable rules and may refuse to serve customers when these rules are not obeyed. Telephone companies, for example, specify that the telephones can be used for legitimate purposes only. Service does not have to be continued to those who fail to pay their bills. As previously indicated, the public utility has to have permission to abandon any of its service, and it also must have authority to extend its service beyond that authorized. The utility can be required to extend service into rural areas if they are within the general region of service even though the utility does not wish to do it. When involuntary extensions are required, regulatory bodies usually specify that a part of the cost of construction must be paid by the customers, or a higher minimum bill established than for other customers, or some other similar arrangement.

Regulation of Rates

A public utility is required to serve its customers at reasonable rates. Inasmuch as the utility company is given the authority to render service that gives it a protected status, there must be regulation to insure that rates will not be exorbitant yet, at the same time, result in a fair rate of return to the utility. The method ordinarily used in determining reasonable earnings is to multiply the fair valuation of the property used for public service by a fair rate of return. The fair return is the income that is used as payment to those who contribute capital to the public utility company. It is important to the utility company, to the people who invest in the company, and to the customers. The fair return that is permitted varies from 5½ to 8 per cent depending upon the circumstances, such as the rate of return of industries that have similar risks and are in the same geographical area. An increase from 6 to 7 per cent in the rate of return allowed a utility is the equivalent of an increase of 16⅔ per cent in the income of a utility. Even though a return of 6½ per cent may be allowed, there is no guarantee that the company will earn this amount.

Equally important as the fair rate of return is what is a fair property valuation to be used in conjunction with the fair rate of return. A public utility company tends to place a high valuation upon its property while the regulatory commission usually places a considerably lower valuation upon the property. The higher the valuation upon the property, the greater will be the earnings. In arriving at a figure that constitutes reasonable earnings for a utility, a fair valuation and a fair rate of return have equal weight. A change in either of these elements results in a substantial change in the reasonable earnings that result. For example, a fair valuation of $20,000,000 and a rate of return of 6 per cent result in earnings of $1,200,000. By increasing the fair valuation to $24,000,000 with a rate of return of 6 per cent, the earnings would be $1,440,000; whereas a fair valuation of $24,000,000 and the lower rate of return of 5 per cent would yield earnings of $1,200,000.

There are several methods of determining fair property valuation. The *cost of reproduction* is one of these methods. Under this method, the cost of reproducing an existing plant is used as the measure of its valuation. There are many complexities, however, in making such a study. For example, should the cost to reproduce be based on original conditions or present conditions? Another problem involved in the use of this particular valuation standard is that in reproducing it today, the new facilities might be built in an entirely different manner. Public utilities always compute the valuation of their property on a cost of reproduction basis at a much higher figure than the regulatory bodies do.

Another method sometimes used is the *prudent investment standard.* This utilizes the amount of investment, prudently made, which is used and useful in public service, as the valuation base. This determination is made largely by reference to accounting records showing the original cost of investments and subsequent purchases. Even though this method has considerable merit, disagreement may arise over whether an investment made by the company was prudent or whether additions that are made to the original cost have been wisely made. This method is sometimes called *original cost plus additions.*

The market value of the company's outstanding securities is another method of ascertaining fair valuation of property. The weakness in this method is that market values reflect the earning power of securities. If earnings are large, investors tend to regard the securities very highly, and the market price of the securities goes even higher. If these prices are used as the valuation base, then the earnings that result from their use will be necessarily high. These high earnings will continue to affect the market price of the securities in their upward trend. The opposite would be true if company earnings were low. The company's securities would not be in as great demand, and the market price of the securities would tend to be low.

The determination of a fair valuation has been carried to the courts many times. The Supreme Court in two cases, one in 1942 and the other in 1944,[1] decided that state legislatures and regulatory bodies may employ whatever method they see fit to use in determining the general level of rates. They are not bound by any formula or any set of rules in doing so. The Court ruled that it is not the theory used in determining rate levels but the "end result" that is important. If the results of a general level of rates allows the utility to operate successfully, attract capital, maintain its financial well-being, and compensate its investors for their risks, the rates would be considered to be reasonable in the opinion of the Court.

Public Utility Rate-Making

The rates charged by utility companies are filed with the regulatory body that has jurisdiction over the company. If there are proposed changes in rates, these must be approved by the regulatory body. Public utility rate-making is quite complicated. Utilities engage in what is called *differential pricing.* This means that different customer groups—residential, commercial, street lighting, and rural customers of an electric utility, for example—are charged different rates; and within a customer group, a graduated rate scale applies according to the amount used. The rate becomes progressively lower as the amount used increases. An *electric utility company* might have a schedule of rates for residential customers as follows:

First 40 kilowatt-hours	....	4.30¢ per kw-h.
Next 210 kilowatt-hours	....	2.22¢ per kw-h.
All additional kilowatt-hours	....	1.70¢ per kw-h.

[1] *Natural Gas Pipeline Company* v. *Federal Power Commission,* 315 U.S. 575; and *Federal Power Commission* v. *Hope Natural Gas Company,* 320 U.S. 591

If a bill is not paid within a stipulated number of days, such as twenty, a 5 or 10 per cent additional charge is made. A minimum monthly charge, such as $1.00, must be paid by a customer whether or not that amount is used. This charge covers billing, collecting, and other expenses that are independent of the amount of electricity used. The rates shown above are known as *block rates*. The rates apply to a given block and decrease as consumption progresses to another block. A rate schedule set up in the three blocks as shown above will establish the last block to be a promotional type of rate that will encourage greater consumption through the installation of ranges, refrigerators, heaters, and other appliances. Since a customer can get similar service by using gas appliances, the third block of rates is made in order to get the customer to use electrical appliances and thus use more electric energy. Other groups of customers have rate schedules that are somewhat more complicated.

Gas utilities, like electric utilities, divide their customers into groups such as residential, commercial, industrial, and space heating. Residential rates are higher than industrial rates because of numerous factors, including the volume of gas consumed. Gas companies use a rate schedule in which the rates are computed on a block basis. The following is an example of a rate schedule used by a gas utility for residential customers.

First	5	Therms or less per month	$ 1.50
Next	10	Therms per month	16.0¢ per Th.
Next	15	Therms per month	14.6¢ per Th.
Next	570	Therms per month	13.0¢ per Th.
Next	5,400	Therms per month	10.6¢ per Th.
Next	94,000	Therms per month	9.5¢ per Th.
Next	100,000	Therms per month	9.0¢ per Th.
Over	200,000	Therms per month	8.5¢ per Th.

Space-heating rates of gas companies are established to encourage greater use of gas for heating and to be competitive with other methods of heating. These rates are much lower and apply if the customer uses more than a specified amount. As in electrical rates, there is a minimum monthly bill, and failure to pay the bill within a specified number of days adds 5 or 10 per cent to the amount of the bill.

In smaller communities, *water rates* are generally a flat annual or semiannual charge so that billing and collecting are simplified. In larger communities, however, rates are based on the amount consumed, which is measured by a meter, as are gas and electric consumption also. Typical rates are of a block type like that used in the preceding examples, with rates becoming lower with increased consumption. The first 10,000 gallons of water, for example, might cost 20¢ per 1,000 gallons, but the next 40,000 gallons might cost 16¢ per 1,000 gallons. Customers are billed quarterly or semiannually.

When the charge is based on the amount consumed, electric, gas, and water utility companies use meters to record the amount as it is used by each customer. These meters are read periodically, and the customer is billed from the reading. A minimum charge is often established by water utilities based on the size of the meter, which, in turn, depends upon the size of the pipe leading from the street connection into the meter.

Telephone, Telegraph, and Transit Rates. The rates charged for *telephone service* vary with different classes of customers. Residential rates may be on a single-party line or on a two-, four-, or more party line. The cost of the single-party line is the highest. For a two- or four-party line, the rates may be from $1.50 to $1.75 less per month. In many communities, the telephone rate within what is called exchange service, or calls within prescribed limits as within an urban area, is in the form of a flat rate regardless of the amount of use. Measured service rates are used in many cities. A minimum monthly rate is charged for a given number of calls, perhaps twenty, and a message rate per call added for any calls beyond that number. Both types of rates are available in some cities, and the customer chooses the type of service he desires.

The rates of *long distance telephone service* are based on *mileage blocks.* The charge for the first eight miles might be 15¢; from eight to sixteen miles, 20¢; and for each additional eight-mile block up to a distance of forty miles, the rate might be 5¢. The charge per mile will decrease rapidly beyond that distance because the mileage blocks used are larger.

Special rates are made for furnishing *program-transmission service* to radio and television broadcasting companies. *Teletypewriter services* are also provided under a contract basis for commercial purposes.

In long distance calls, the station-to-station rates where the caller talks to anyone who answers the telephone are cheaper than those calls made on a person-to-person basis in which the caller asks to talk to a particular person. The station-to-station call is a little less costly for the telephone company and is an effort on the part of the company to secure more business through the lower rate.

Urban transit rates, in most cities, were a flat rate for many years; that is, the fare was the same regardless of the distance traveled. This system of charging worked reasonably well as long as cities were comparatively small geographically. As cities increased in size and the growth of the suburban areas resulted in the average rider making longer journeys, many transit companies established *zoned fares*. These fares are more in accord with the distance the passenger travels. In the zoned fares, there is a basic fare that applies to the central city—Zone 1. Concentric circles of one, two, or three miles are then drawn outward from Zone 1 and consecutively numbered. Some transit companies give their regular riders a lower fare than the occasional rider by selling *tokens* to the regular riders. If the cash fare is 20¢, five tokens might be sold for 90¢. This practice is not as prevalent as it used to be. *Weekly passes* are used by some companies, which permit the rider who purchases a pass to ride as much as he likes during the week the pass is effective. The pass can be used going to and from work and any other times that the person wants to ride. If a single ride was 20¢, the pass might sell for $2.25. This is a slight reduction and a convenience for the regular rider.

Telegraph rates are based on the number of words in a message, the distance they are transmitted, and the type of message. The rates are lower for some types of messages than those charged for the *straight telegram,* which receives the most expeditious handling. A *day letter,* which is a deferred service and not handled as expeditiously, goes at a lower rate per word than a straight telegram. Likewise, a *night letter* that is transmitted during the night and delivered the next morning goes at a still lower rate. There are also contractual services performed for newspapers and news agencies, and private-wire service for the use of customers between certain points.

The rates of *cable companies* that provide wire service between this country and foreign countries are regulated under the Federal Communications Act. The cable rates are based on the number of words, the distance the message is sent, and the time it is transmitted, day or night. The rates of *radio-telegraph service* to foreign countries are like ocean-cable rates and depend upon the same factors.

Regulation of Financing and Consolidations

State regulation often requires that a utility must secure approval before it can authorize the issuance of new securities. In other states, there is merely a requirement that there be publicity concerning the new issue. As a part of securing approval, the company must indicate how the proceeds of the security issuance will be spent. One of the purposes of regulating financing is to prevent overcapitalization. Regulatory bodies require periodic reports and usually prescribe a uniform system of accounts to be used by utility companies, which is helpful in more effective regulation.

Regulatory bodies also have control over mergers and combinations of utility companies. The incentive for companies to consolidate when a physical integration of properties can be effected is that plants can be utilized to a greater extent and thus operated more efficiently. Regulation of combinations or mergers involves a showing by the companies that the proposal is in the public interest. Sometimes, regulatory commissions require that the consolidation cannot increase the capitalization of a new company beyond the total value of the bonds and stocks in the companies being combined.

FEDERAL REGULATION

Development of Federal Regulation of Public Utilities

The first federal regulation of public utilities appeared in 1887 with the passage of the *Act to Regulate Commerce,* which was a law enacted to regulate railroads. The Federal Power Commission was created in 1920 with authority over hydroelectric power facilities under the *Federal Water Power Act.* The real expansion of federal regulation, though, occurred during the 1930's. Many utility-company systems had been formed during the 1920's, which linked together widely scattered companies. Continued consolidation and acquisition followed, and the formation of holding companies became widespread. By 1932, the three largest holding companies controlled almost half of the electricity sales in the United States, and sixteen holding-company systems controlled 80 per cent of the total sales according to a Federal Trade Commission investigation of utility holding companies. There were many abuses that developed with the appearance of the holding company. As utility systems grew and the operations of a single system spread into many states, regulation of them by the states became less effective. As a result, a number of federal regulatory acts were passed in the 1930's to bring these operations under control. These were: The Federal Communications Act of 1934, The Federal Power Act of 1935, The Public Utility Act of 1935, and The Natural Gas Act of 1938.

The Public Utility Act of 1935

The Public Utility Act of 1935 applies to interstate holding companies in gas and electricity and was designed to control public utility holding companies. A holding company was defined as any company that had the power to control the vote of 10 per cent or more of the outstanding voting securities of a public utility company. The administration of this law was placed with the *Securities and Exchange Commission,* which was an existing government agency with other responsibilities. All such companies had to register with the Commission. One section of the Act provided that after January 1, 1938, holding companies were limited to a single integrated public utility system, that is, a system in which the companies were capable of being physically interconnected. Since many of the holding companies were not integrated, their properties being widely scattered, this section of the Act become known as the *death-sentence clause* because it meant that many of the existing holding companies would have to be drastically changed to meet the provisions of the law.

The holding companies bitterly opposed compliance with the provisions of this Act, and there was a great deal of litigation before compliance was forthcoming. As a result of the Public Utility Act, a great reorganization of the gas and electrical utility industries has been accomplished. By 1960, the job of eliminating unnecessary holding companies was largely completed. The Securities and Exchange Commission has favored a system confined to a single area with interconnected facilities. It also ruled that gas and electric interests could not be integrated in the same system unless there were substantial economies that could be shown from such combined operations.

The Federal Power Act of 1935

The Federal Power Act of 1935 amended the Federal Water Power Act of 1920, which had created the Federal Power Commission. The Federal Power Commission, by the Act of 1935, was given jurisdiction over rates charged for the sale of electric energy at wholesale and over service of interstate electric utilities. The rates charged must be just and reasonable and must be filed with the Commission and open for public inspection. Rates ordinarily cannot be made effective until after thirty days' notice has been given. They may be suspended by the Commission (that is, they do not become effective) for a period of five months, pending investigation. There is also regulation of securities, accounts, and combinations of these utilities.

The Natural Gas Act of 1938

The Natural Gas Act of 1938 gave the Federal Power Commission authority to regulate the transportation of natural gas in interstate commerce and the sale in interstate commerce of natural gas for resale. The latter provision means that the Commission can set the charges that natural-gas companies may make to those industrial users who take service directly from the company. The local distribution and the production or gathering of natural gas is now subject to Federal Power Commission regulation after a long period of controversy and litigation concerning whether or not the Commission had the power to regulate this aspect of operations. Congress has sought on several occasions to change this interpretation by exempting this phase of operations from regulation, but the opposition of the states that consume gas is very strong against such action.

The Commission can prescribe just and reasonable rates and eliminate undue preference between localities and classes of wholesale customers for the companies subject to its jurisdiction. It can suspend rate increases for five months, pending investigation, and can prescribe the accounting systems as well as set the measurement of depreciation charges. The Commission cannot regulate the issuance of securities and mergers or consolidations, and it cannot order interconnection of gas lines. As can be seen, the degree of regulation that the Commission has over the natural-gas industry is not as great as that which it has over electric and gas utility companies.

The Federal Communications Act of 1934

The Federal Communications Act of 1934 created the Federal Communications Commission and gave it authority to regulate common carriers in communications, that is, wire and wireless communication companies such as telephone and telegraph. These public utility companies are referred to as common carriers to differentiate them from radio and television. The latter are not public utilities and are regulated under the Act to a lesser extent than the public utilities are. The Federal Communications Commission requires interstate and foreign common carriers subject to its jurisdiction to furnish communication service upon reasonable request, to establish physical connections with other carriers, to establish through routes and charges, and to establish and provide facilities. Lines may not be extended or service discontinued or reduced without prior approval of the Commission. One carrier cannot acquire control of the property of another without authorization.

Federal Regulatory Commissions

The Securities and Exchange Commission, which administers the Public Utility Act, is composed of five members. The members are appointed by the President with the advice and consent of the Senate for five-year terms. This is an independent regulatory body, which reports directly to Congress.

The Commission requires that the issuance and sale of securities by holding companies and their subsidiaries must be reasonably adapted to the security structure and earning power of the issuing company; that the proposed financing is necessary; that the consideration received and the fee, commission, and other remuneration paid are fair; and that the terms and conditions of the sale are not detrimental to investors, consumers, or the public. The sale of utility assets by companies subject to the Act and all transactions among affiliates of such companies are subject to Commission rules and orders. To correct the abuses of the past, the Act requires the geographic integration and simplification of holding-company systems, the simplification of corporate-system structures, and an equitable redistribution of voting power among security holders.

Federal Power Commission. This agency administers the provisions of the Federal Power Act of 1935 and the Natural Gas Act of 1938. It is an independent agency reporting directly to Congress and consists of five commissioners.

Some of the duties of the Federal Power Commission include the study of the water-power resources of the nation and the development of plans for multipurpose river basin development. It also evaluates applications and issues permits and licenses for the construction, operation, and maintenance of water-power projects in navigable waters or on government lands. The Commission exercises jurisdiction over the transmission and sale at wholesale of electric energy in interstate commerce and over public utilities engaged in such commerce. Under the Natural Gas Act, it has regulatory responsibility and authority over the transportation and sale of natural gas in interstate commerce for resale and of the natural-gas companies engaged in such commerce.

Federal Communications Commission. This independent regulatory body administers the Federal Communications Act. It is composed of seven members appointed by the President with the approval of the Senate for a term of seven years.

In the telephone industry, monopolistic tendencies show up to a greater degree than in other public utility industries. The American Telephone and Telegraph Company (the Bell System) is one of the largest business enterprises in the United States. AT&T provides contract services, such as engineering, accounting, and legal services for subsidiary companies that are members of the Bell System. Through control of more than two hundred corporations, AT&T supervises between 80 and 90 per cent of local telephone service, 98 per cent of long-distance telephone wires, almost all of the wire facilities used for radio broadcasting, and all of the transoceanic radiotelephone service, according to a government investigation.

The Commission has jurisdiction over interstate and foreign rates and charges of wire, cable, and radiotelephone and telegraph companies, which must be just and reasonable. The common carriers subject to its supervision must file their tariffs with the Commission showing all charges. The Commission has the power to suspend tariffs for a period of three months. It also has authority to investigate the prices that communications companies pay for equipment, supplies, managerial or construction services, and research work. It conducted an investigation of the telephone industry, which was primarily concerned with AT&T because of its dominant position. It found that AT&T through its manufacturing subsidiary, Western Electric Company, accounted for 90 per cent of the nation's output of telephonic equipment. Since Western Electric was a manufacturing organization and not subject to the Act, it was not subject to regulation; yet the sale of the equipment to AT&T would have an effect upon the level of telephone operating costs. The Department of Justice filed an antitrust suit in 1949 requesting that Western Electric be separated from AT&T, and the suit was settled by consent decree in 1956. Under the provisions of the consent decree, Western Electric was required to maintain cost accounting methods for determining the cost of equipment that it sold to AT&T and the operating companies of the Bell System. Further, AT&T was not to engage in any business other than furnishing common carrier communications except that business that it conducted through Western Electric.

RADIO AND TELEVISION

Extent of Regulation

Radio and television broadcasting are not designated in the Federal Communications Act as public utilities. They do not meet the tests of public utilities, although there are some people who feel that they should be regarded as public utilities and so regulated. The regulation of these industries differs in several respects from that of telephone and telegraph communications. The Federal Communications Commission does not regulate rates of these industries. It has no control over discriminatory practices or over consolidation of radio and television companies. Control over entry, however, is regulated. The companies that engage in radio and television broadcasting must be licensed by the Commission. The power to regulate entry in this field was given to the Commission because there are a limited number of frequencies to be assigned in a given area. Another reason for control over entry is that stations must be in responsible hands. The person or company securing a license possesses a medium of great importance, which can have a profound effect upon public attitudes and behavior. The Commission inquires into the moral, financial, and technical responsibility of applicants for licenses.

Licenses are granted for a limited time. In the case of broadcasting licenses, the maximum period is three years and, in renewing old licenses as well as granting new ones, the Commission has to find that the public interest, convenience, or necessity will be served by the grant. The Commission can revoke licenses if the holder does not operate according to the conditions of his license or if he violates any of the Commission's regulations. For example, the use of obscene or profane language is prohibited. Licenses cannot be assigned or transferred except upon consent of the Commission. The Commission can designate the length of time that the broadcaster can be on the air and can prescribe the nature of service to be rendered by the various classes of stations. The location of stations can be stipulated and their minimum and maximum power, which means the range within which the broadcaster can be received. The Act provides no power of censorship over radio-television communications. The Commission, however, can develop its own criteria of what constitutes public interest. When broadcast matter is paid for or furnished, the station must announce that fact and the name of the party who is paying for it. The Commission has encouraged broadcasters to establish high standards of performance.

Inasmuch as the granting of licenses and the designation of the power rests with the Commission, some stations have been given a better channel and more power than others. The strong power stations with their range are better advertising media than other stations, so they tend to prosper. Smaller stations often leased their time to a national chain in order to secure more advertising and programs than they otherwise could. Frequently, the networks purchased an interest in the affiliated stations, and the result was a concentration of control. This threat of monopoly caused the Commission to investigate chain broadcasting in 1938. As a result of this investigation, a number of changes were required. The National Broadcasting Company had to divest itself of one of its networks, which became the basis of the American Broadcasting Company. The new rules issued in 1941 limited network contracts with stations to two years and permitted network affiliates to use programs from other stations. The networks were prevented from owning more than one station in a locality and could not control the rates charged by the affiliates in competing for advertising business.

The commercial broadcaster does not sell its service to the listener or viewer. The programs are available through the medium of advertising. For this reason, there is no regulation of rates since the public does not pay a charge for the entertainment provided.

Radio and television have industrial uses other than broadcasting to the public. Radio is used for the transmission of private messages by many companies including taxicab, trucking, and pipeline companies. Some of the equipment may be mobile transmission and receiving equipment whereas other equipment may be fixed. Motor carriers use radio communications permitting a two-way conversation between truck drivers and the truck terminal where the dispatcher is located. The Commission assigns the frequency for this type of operation. Radio is also required for safety purposes on board certain types of ships. Closed-circuit television has a number of uses. It is sometimes utilized to demonstrate a particular technique or to bring a message to a group of company employees, such as salesmen, who are holding meetings in different cities. The company using this service would pay for it.

GOVERNMENT OWNERSHIP

Municipal Public Ownership of Utilities

For the most part, the essential public utility services are furnished by companies that are private-enterprise firms. There are instances, however, in which municipalities own and operate a public utility company. This type of ownership is far more common in regard to the provision of water to a city than other public utility services. In communities of 5,000 or more population, about 67 per cent of water utilities are municipally owned. This is probably due to the strong public interest in the purity and adequacy of a water supply. The city's responsibility for fire protection is also an important factor. In addition, this type of utility company is very simple to operate. There are only a relatively small number of publicly owned utility companies in gas and urban transit, less than 2 per cent, and almost no public ownership of telephone utilities. Most of the controversy on municipal ownership versus private ownership has occurred with regard to the electric utility industry. The substantial profits made by electric utility companies make them attractive for municipalities to own and operate. About 12 per cent of the electric companies in cities of more than 5,000 are owned and operated by the city, although the number of cities operating these systems, the largest of which is Los Angeles, has been declining.

Federal Ownership of Utilities

During the depression of the early 1930's, the "New Deal," as the administration of President Roosevelt was called, instituted a number of legislative changes by which the role of the federal government in the development of public power was greatly enhanced. The *Tennessee Valley Authority,* which was created in 1933 by Congress, is a corporation created primarily to provide for flood control, navigation, and hydro-electric power in the Tennessee Valley area. The most controversial aspect of the TVA has been the production and transmission of energy. It does not engage in retail distribution of electric energy but enters into power contracts with municipalities and cooperative organizations not operated for profit. TVA and various municipalities and non-profit cooperative associations have purchased from utility companies the electric generating, transmission, and distribution facilities in the southeastern area. The power contracts under which TVA furnishes power to municipalities and cooperatives requires the purchaser to adopt a standard schedule of resale rates designed to promote the sale of electricity. In effect, TVA has become a regulatory body for those municipalities and cooperatives that have entered into contracts with it. In its earlier operation, TVA was widely hailed as being a yardstick project to be used in comparing the cost of power from a public project to its cost from private industry.

There are other regional projects such as the lower Colorado River development, the Columbia River project, and the St. Lawrence River project, which are multiple-use projects. All of these projects generate power. This is one of the reasons that the generation of power produced by privately owned utilities dropped from 92 per cent in 1937 to 76 per cent in 1957.

Rural Electrification and Telephone

Another area in which the federal government has participated in public utilities is that of *rural electrification* through the creation of the Rural Electrification Administration in 1935. At that time, private utility companies had tended to serve more populous areas first and to leave the sparsely settled rural areas without service. The REA loans money for the construction and operation of generating plants and transmission and distribution lines in order to furnish electricity to rural areas. The REA, which is under the Department of Agriculture, encourages rural electrification through farm cooperatives.

In 1949, REA was authorized through the passage of an Act by Congress to make loans for the purpose of furnishing and improving *rural telephone service.* Loans are made to independent telephone companies and cooperatives. The program must be conducted so that telephone service will be made available to the widest possible number of rural users.

Private Versus Public Ownership of Utilities

Differences of opinion are sharp between the merits of private owner-ship versus public ownership in the public utility field. There may be times when private capital cannot develop and does not want to de-velop projects of a regional nature, the development of which would be advantageous to large areas of the country. When such is the case, government development may be the only answer by which a multiple-use project involving power, navigation, conservation, and irrigation can be developed. In recent years when the government has built and oper-ated these facilities, it has been selling power at wholesale to private utilities. Under these circumstances, it is not in competition with electric companies in retail sales. On the other hand, when private capital can develop necessary facilities and provide satisfactory service, then private enterprise should be relied upon. More advanced courses will bring a fuller discussion of this subject and an opportunity for the student to analyze the pro's and con's.

YOUR CAREER IN PUBLIC UTILITIES

Career Opportunities

The industries comprising the public utilities field offer the student many employment possibilities. There is a very high degree of job stability in these industries, although salaries may not be as high as those found in non-regulated industries. Since public utilities are not subject to the wide fluctuations of the business cycle that many business enter-prises are, widespread layoffs do not occur as they do in many other fields of endeavor. The student will want to balance the greater job stability that exists in this field with the relatively higher salaries that are found in some of the other fields.

The job opportunities in public utilities cover a wide range. Many of these industries are very large corporations. They need accountants, economists, statisticians, office managers, personnel people, financial spe-cialists, traffic managers, marketing specialists, and many others. There are numerous regulatory agencies including local, state, and federal, which exercise some degree of control over public utilities. Many satis-factory careers can be found in these agencies of regulation for econ-omists, statisticians, and others. Often, people who have held good posi-tions with regulatory bodies are hired by public utilities, so employment with a regulatory agency is frequently a stepping stone to an excellent position in industry. Proceedings before regulatory commissions require extensive preparation by both the public utility and the regulatory body. Interesting careers exist for competent persons who work in preparing data and testifying before regulatory agencies.

Educational Background

The student going into the public utility field will find that in addition to a broad background in general-business subjects, a number of courses in economics will help him to attain a better understanding of our economic system and the reasons for regulation. Courses in government and political science are also of value in providing information on the role of government in our society. Courses in public utilities are of utmost importance to the student interested in this field, and he should acquire as thorough a background as possible in this subject. Courses in accounting, finance, and statistics would be highly beneficial since reports have to be filed periodically with regulatory bodies and exhibits prepared for rate hearings. The very large amounts of capital that are needed and used in the public utilities industries requires an understanding of finance. Since there are a wide variety of opportunities in public utilities, courses in any of the other specialized fields would also be of value. In addition, elective courses in engineering can be of benefit to the student in this field. A considerable amount of the public utility operations are performed by engineers, so that a course or two in a college of engineering would provide better insight into the problems encountered in operations.

TOPICS FOR DISCUSSION

1. A public utility has several obligations. What are some of these obligations? Which do you feel is the most important?

2. Explain the concept of eminent domain. Do you support it?

3. Although regulation differs from state to state, there are two major areas covered in all state regulation of utilities. What are these two areas?

4. The agreement entered into between a public-utility company and the city is known as a "franchise." What does this agreement involve?

5. Discuss the concept of economics of decreasing cost.

6. "In a system of free enterprise, the federal government has no right to engage in the production and sale of electric power except in those cases where private companies cannot, or will not, provide service." Discuss this statement, agreeing or disagreeing.

7. Do you believe that regulatory agencies are free of political control or interference?

8. Suppose a student inadvertently breaks the glass from several windows in the classroom. Should he be required to reimburse the school for the original cost of the glass plus installation, or should he be charged the replacement cost plus installation? Is this example similar to a problem faced by certain utilities?

9. Why do certain utilities that have a monopoly in an area advertise in that area?

10. Do you feel that more competition in the telephone industry would result in better service? Or less effective service?

CASE 20–1

THE EMPIRE GAS COMPANY

The Empire Gas Company, which operated within the metropolitan area of a large eastern city, furnished natural-gas service to approximately 500,000 families in the area. The company was competitive with the electric utility in the market, and with the fuel-oil industry also. For many years, Empire Gas had been a large-volume advertiser.

In 1964, the two leading newspapers in the market informed Empire Gas that, after a specified date, the company would no longer be entitled to the local advertising rate but would be charged the general, or flat rate. The general rate was almost 50 per cent higher than the local rate, and the announcement by the papers was considered a severe blow by the sales division of Empire Gas. A statement of rate policy appearing on the rate card of one of the papers read as follows:

General advertising is construed to be for an individual product or service, and is considered as general if containing a factory address or any out-of-town headquarters designation, additional or exclusive, or any advertisement containing two or more signatures, or containing any indication that the product is available through other than the retail firm whose signature appears in the advertisement. The general rates apply to advertising of manufacturers, producers, distributors, jobbers, and jobbing or distributing sales branches or representatives selling through retail outlets. General rates do not apply, however, to organized local retail groups whose copy is mainly diversified to cover miscellaneous kinds and brands of goods.

Mr. Vandenburg, vice-president of sales for Empire Gas, felt that the rate increase represented outright discrimination against the utility company. Empire Gas operated a sales room in which appliances were sold directly to the consumer. Mr. Vandenburg contended that the company's sole business consisted of retailing a service (natural gas) in the local market, and in retailing appliances in the same market. No business was transacted with customers living outside the area defined by the newspapers as the local market.

Mr. Vandenburg felt that it was a form of discrimination for the papers to sell space to department stores for 60 cents per line while charging Empire Gas a rate of 90 cents per line. The executives of Empire Gas held a conference with representatives of the publishers but were unable to get the local rate restored. The publishers, when asked to justify the higher rate charged the utility, pointed out that it was a common practice to charge utilities a general rate and to refuse to classify them as local business. They admitted to a certain lack of logic in charging the utility a higher rate than department stores when both were serving the same market; however, they refused to alter the decision to charge the general rate to the Empire Gas Company.

Executives of Empire Gas considered possible courses of action to take in view of the rate increase. Although there may have been grounds for legal action against the papers, the company decided to refrain from taking action for fear that the papers might retaliate by adopting a critical and negative editorial policy toward the utility. Finally, it was decided to discontinue advertising in the newspapers and to concentrate expenditures in radio and television. It was hoped that the newspapers might eventually reconsider and sell the utility advertising space at the local rate.

Do you feel that Empire Gas Company executives were justified in refusing to pay the higher rates for newspaper advertising?

SELECTED REFERENCES

Garfield, Paul J., and Wallace F. Lovejoy. *Public Utility Economics.* Englewood Cliffs, N.J.: Prentice-Hall, Inc., 1964.

Glaeser, M. G. *Public Utilities in American Capitalism.* New York: The Macmillan Co., 1957.

Koontz, H., and R. W. Gable. *Public Control of Economic Enterprise.* New York: McGraw-Hill Book Co., 1956.

Pegrum, D. F. *Public Regulation of Business.* Rev. ed. Homewood, Ill.: Richard D. Irwin, Inc., 1965.

Phillips, Charles F., Jr. *The Economics of Regulation.* Homewood, Ill.: Richard D. Irwin, Inc., 1965.

Wilcox, C. *Public Policies Toward Business.* Rev. ed. Homewood, Ill.: Richard D. Irwin, Inc., 1960.

21

International Trade

IMPORTANCE OF INTERNATIONAL TRADE

The United States businessman who is considering entering international trade may sometimes feel that the information he must secure and the regulations with which he must comply to enter into trade abroad are not worth the effort. Yet the thousands of United States firms successfully operating in other countries indicate that the profit potential is a strong offsetting factor. A part of the businessman's reluctance is due, no doubt, to the fact that he feels he may not be able to control his product or service in a different environment as he can when operations are confined to the United States. Recent improvements in transportation and communications and the many specialists now available to assist in international trade should remove concern about inability to control and market products efficiently.

In recent years, Western European countries and Japan have made remarkable economic growth, with the result that there has been and will continue to be shifts in the international trade of the United States. With other industrial nations advancing economically, they have become more competitive with the United States on more and more products. This provides a real challenge to United States producers to improve marketing techniques and produce new and better products.

The company new to foreign trade must become acquainted with the basic differences between foreign trade and trade within the United States. What are some of these differences? The foreign trader must have specific information about pertinent laws, regulations, practices, and current market conditions in the foreign country with which he is concerned. For example, he must be informed on the amount that can be imported into a particular country since some countries have restrictions on imports. He must be informed as to currency regulations and the methods of operation and payment customarily followed in the country with which he is dealing. The channels of distribution may vary from one foreign market to another and will be different from those in the United States. Like domestic trade, a sound foreign trade can be built by supplying a product or a service to a market that has a continuing demand.

METHODS OF EXPORTING

Direct Exporting

In determining the method to be used by a company in exporting products, two alternatives are available: *direct methods* and *indirect methods.* In the direct methods of exporting, the company sells directly to the customer. The company handles all of the details and assumes full responsibility and risk. In the indirect methods of exporting, a company conducts its export business through a *middleman* or *intermediary* who takes care of arrangements for the company. Before 1920, the majority of American companies used indirect methods of exporting because of their unfamiliarity with foreign markets. As American manufacturers grew in size and came to know more about foreign trade, many larger companies began selling directly and relying less upon indirect methods. Numerous small- and medium-sized manufacturers still use the indirect methods. In the case of agricultural products, indirect exporting is the predominant method used because the bulk of these products are grown by farmers who have no distribution organizations and must therefore channel their products through middlemen.

Business firms may use any one of a number of different types of organizations in direct exporting. Sometimes the export activities are assigned to certain personnel in the company. All financial arrangements, credit matters, and transportation arrangements are handled by these people who also have responsibilities in domestic operations. This is called a *built-in export department.* Usually, the only addition to the staff is an export manager who directs export sales. A more common type of export organization is what is termed the *separate export department.* This type of department performs all export functions and is one that controls, supervises, and conducts the export functions. Another form that has been used by larger companies is a *separate international company.* This organization may or may not establish its own manufacturing and selling facilities in foreign countries. The international company is formed as a subsidiary company for exporting.

Indirect Exporting

The second category of exporting methods is that of the indirect in which outside organizations, or export middlemen or intermediaries, are used. There are many kinds of export middlemen who will relieve the manufacturer of practically all of the business details involved in foreign trade. The extent of services performed by these middlemen will be determined by the contract that the manufacturer or producer enters into with this type of organization. Some manufacturers divide their export business so that part is handled by the direct methods and part through the indirect.

The numerous indirect methods of export selling may be classified into three broad types: (1) the buyer and seller for his own account, (2) the buyer for the foreign customer, and (3) the seller on behalf of the American supplier. Within each of these broad types, there are varying export organizations. The more important of them are described briefly so that the student may become familiar with the services performed by the indirect export organizations.

Export merchants, often termed *export houses,* buy and sell for their own account. They purchase goods outright from the American manufacturer and then export and sell the goods themselves. They handle all phases of international trade. The manufacturer who uses this channel of distribution may sell for cash at his factory and not have to handle even the domestic shipping arrangements and none of the details of the foreign transactions. W. R. Grace and Company is an export merchant. It has developed not only an export marketing and merchandising business but also transportation and financial businesses as well.

The *export commission house* acts as a buying agent for foreign customers. It does not buy for its own account but only to fill specific orders for foreign customers. Its services are paid for by commissions from the foreign purchaser. *Buyers for export,* such as foreign government purchasing commissions and purchasing agents for large foreign industries like mines and railroads, are another of the types of organizations that buy for the foreign customer.

The *combination export manager* handles the entire export function for a number of manufacturers of allied but non-competitive lines. He performs all of the operations ordinarily handled by the export department of a company. His correspondence is often on the letterhead of the firm he represents. Some combination export managers receive a monthly payment or retainer from each manufacturer they represent plus a commission on sales.

The *export agent* usually handles non-competitive but related lines for a number of manufacturers and works on a commission basis. American manufacturers may place their entire line with one export agent or place different items with different agents.

There are some *export trade associations* that are a group of business organizations selling the same or similar products and organized in a cooperative effort to handle their export trade on an industry basis. These are often called *Webb-Pomerene Corporations* since these associations have been formed under the Export Trade Act of 1918, more popularly known as the Webb-Pomerene law. One such voluntary organization has been formed to sell prunes, and another was formed to ship lumber to foreign countries.

Many large companies engaged in foreign trade and having their own export department offer to distribute non-competing products of other manufacturers in foreign trade. In instances like this, the export department of the manufacturer is capable of handling more than its own products, and the money received for handling the products of other manufacturers helps to defray the expenses of operating the export department.

METHODS OF IMPORTING

The methods used by a company in importing are classified in the same manner as they are in exporting: *direct* and *indirect*. In direct importing, the manufacturer handles all of the details involved in the purchase and shipment of imported products. The majority of companies, however, depend on middlemen, which is the indirect method. Some of the more widely used organizations in indirect importing are explained. While the titles of the organizations are different, the activities performed for importers are much the same as those performed in indirect exporting.

The *import merchant* buys abroad and imports goods for his own account. He will then sell to United States buyers at his own price. The import merchant assumes all risks. Some specialize in certain commodities while others bring in all types of products. Specialization is sometimes carried to the point where a coffee importer, for example, handles only Brazilian beans.

An *indent house* is an importer who buys only on orders received from domestic firms. An *indent* is an order or specification sent abroad for price quotation. The indent house, upon the requests of United States buyers, sends indents abroad for pricing and purchases imports on specific orders.

The *import commission house* usually sells goods shipped on consignment, receiving a commission from the foreign producer. Sometimes these commission houses will buy small amounts of goods for a commission paid by the purchaser.

A *resident agent* represents foreign producers in the United States. These agents sell on a commission basis for the account of the foreign producers they represent. The resident agent is a salesman and is usually assigned to a specific territory. He contacts wholesalers, jobbers, and retailers.

An *importing wholesaler* or *jobber* generally imports non-perishable items. He can then serve small independent retailers who require credit and a ready source of supply of imported merchandise.

The *import broker* or *factor* brings together the buyer and seller and negotiates the contract of sale. After the sale is made, the domestic buyer imports the goods in his own name and arranges for their payment directly with the foreign seller. The broker receives a stipulated fee from the company that engages him, either the foreign exporter or the domestic importer.

The Foreign-Freight Forwarder

The freight-forwarder service has become established in foreign commerce as it has in domestic trade. The technical details connected with the handling of a shipment of goods for export, such as arranging for cargo space for export shipments on ocean carriers, preparing or processing necessary shipping papers for ocean transportation, and arranging the clearance of export shipments subject to regulations of the federal government, are handled by the foreign-freight forwarder. On request, the freight forwarder will arrange for appropriate insurance and for packing of shipments.

The Customhouse Broker

The customhouse broker is a specialist in the complex official arrangements necessary for merchandise to be processed through customs in any country. He must be familiar with the constantly changing provisions of customs laws and regulations. In the United States, the customhouse broker must be licensed by the United States Department of the Treasury.

SPECIAL OPERATIONAL ASPECTS OF INTERNATIONAL TRADE

Terms of Sale

In foreign trade, the terms of sale are often different from those in domestic business. A wider range of conditions exist under which sales can be made. Terms of sale, in addition to the price of the article, indicate the place of delivery, the form and method of payment, the insurance coverage, methods of transportation, and all necessary information concerning quantity and kind of merchandise, as well as time of delivery or shipment. The terms of sale are generally expressed through the use of abbreviations, such as "C.I.F. (named port of destination)," which means that the terms of sale cover the cost of the merchandise, insurance coverage, and freight to the named foreign port of destination. Another example is that of "F.A.S. Vessel," which means "free alongside the vessel at the named port of shipment" and indicates that the conditions of sale cover the cost of merchandise plus transportation to the vessel at the United States port of shipment. These abbreviations have become well defined within a particular trade or country. Many of the terms in common usage are contained in the *Revised American Foreign Trade Definitions—1941,* found in all foreign-trade textbooks.

Transportation Services

The transportation services are those that exist in domestic transportation and, in addition, ocean transportation. Because of the greater distance goods must be transported, a longer period of time must be allowed for delivery to be accomplished. Promising of deliveries by certain dates is hazardous. Although air transportation is available, its use is not practical for many commodities because of higher cost. Most transportation is performed by ocean carriers, with about 7 per cent based on value of our exports and imports shipped by air. Special arrangements enable shippers to protect shipments of unusual value or perishable shipments by providing special facilities. Transportation companies handle the necessary shipping documents and will take care of the routing of shipments.

The basis of charges differs somewhat in ocean transportation from that in domestic transportation. For example, in domestic transportation, most charges are based on a rate per 100 pounds. In ocean shipping, the ton is the unit used. Charges are usually assessed on the basis of the *long ton* (2,240 pounds) or the *metric ton* (2,204.6 pounds), depending upon the foreign-trade area.

Marine Insurance

The liability of domestic transportation carriers is a great deal broader than that of ocean carriers. Ocean carriers are liable only for a very limited amount of the value of the goods transported. Marine insurance is available and is extensively used in international trade. Shippers purchase additional insurance from marine-insurance companies to cover the risks of ocean shipping. The services of these companies include that of determining the amount of insurance necessary to cover a particular shipment and the prompt settlement of claims.

Communications Service

The international telephone, cable, and radio services make operations in distant markets possible. In addition, international postal service is available and may be used when transactions can be handled by mail.

Financial Arrangements

Many commercial banks have an international department to handle necessary financial arrangements in the form of loans or credits to cover the value of merchandise while it is in warehouses or being transported. When merchandise is in a warehouse, the warehouse receipts issued for the merchandise provide the security that makes it possible for the banks to handle the loans rapidly. Bills of lading for the goods in transit are also used as security for loans. These and other credit arrangements are extremely important in foreign trade since a substantial part of the export trade of the United States is done on a credit basis.

A *letter of credit* is frequently utilized. This is a letter form issued by the purchaser's bank. It authorizes the seller to draw certain funds on this bank or another named bank when the terms agreed to by the purchaser and the seller have been fulfilled. Under such arrangements, the purchaser deposits the full payment in his bank; a letter of credit is then forwarded to the seller's bank, and payment is made against this letter of credit upon delivery of the goods.

There are other terms of payment used in foreign transactions. *Sight drafts* generally defer payment by the purchaser until the goods have arrived, and *time drafts* permit payment to be deferred for a period of time such as 30, 60, or 120 days after date of delivery of the goods. In the case of heavy machinery, payment may be arranged over a period of years.

ECONOMIC ASPECTS OF INTERNATIONAL TRADE

The Theory of Absolute Advantage

The economic health of a country may be dependent in large measure upon its world trade. A primary problem in world trade is to strike a balance in each country in exports and imports. If each country could sell as much as it needs to buy, a healthy economic environment would exist in the world. Obviously, this is not the case. Many countries are required to import far more than they are able to export for many reasons. Other countries, perhaps more technologically advanced or having greater productive capacity, may be exporting a great deal and importing only a small amount. There are various economic explanations of the functioning of foreign trade. One of these is the *theory of absolute advantage,* which assumes that countries will concentrate on the production of a product in which they have an absolute advantage. The example that is frequently used in explaining this theory is that of Country A, which produces article X more efficiently than Country B, while Country B produces article Y more efficiently than Country A. These two countries could profitably engage in trade, each selling to the other the product that it produces more efficiently, that is, the one in which it has the absolute advantage.

The Theory of Comparative Advantage

Another economic explanation of how world trade should be conducted is that of the theory of comparative advantage. This theory supposes that one country, Country A, can produce articles X and Y more efficiently than another country, Country B. However, the difference in advantage that Country A has over Country B in producing one article, such as article X, is greater than the difference in advantage that Country A has over Country B in the production of the other article, article Y. Therefore, under the theory of comparative advantage, Country A will concentrate on the production of article X and purchase its requirements of article Y from Country B, inasmuch as this will enable Country A to make the best use of its productive capacities. Country B, through its concentration on the production of article Y, in which it has the least comparative disadvantage, will buy its requirements of article X from Country A because by so doing it will be making the most efficient use of its productive capacity.

Although this theory and the theory of absolute advantage are helpful in explaining general tendencies in foreign trade, it must be emphasized that the relative advantages that produce a given situation may change over a period of time. For example, there may be improvements in communications and transportation facilities that reduce prices; or there may be the imposition of government barriers in the form of a tax or duty on certain imported products, thus increasing the price of these products and offering some measure of protection to the competing product locally produced. Political expediency is another factor that may obscure economic causes in foreign trade. For example, one country may buy from another for the deliberate purpose of aiding the economic development of the country, or one country may buy from another to prevent certain materials from falling into the hands of a third country.

Balance of Trade

When the value of a country's exports exceeds the value of its merchandise imports, it is said to have a favorable balance of trade. Conversely, a nation is said to have an unfavorable balance of trade when the value of its imports exceeds the value of its merchandise exports. The balance of trade, as it has been defined, contains only visible items, that is, merchandise. The true balance of trade is made up of many other items as well, referred to as invisible factors. These items are sometimes more important in the balance of international payments than the exports and imports of merchandise. Since no statistical records are kept of the invisible items, their amount is not readily available. Some of the invisible items are expenditures by tourists, payment for services rendered (such as ocean freight charges and marine insurance), investments, gold and silver bullion, and others.

The terms "favorable" or "unfavorable" as used in describing a balance of trade are misleading since they seem to indicate that nations will always strive to export more than they are importing. The flaw in this reasoning is that in order to import from other nations, each nation must receive money from its exports. No nation can expect to export more than it imports over a long period of time without impoverishing the nations with which it is trading. If a country with a favorable balance of trade does not purchase sufficient imports from the countries to which it is selling its products, those countries cannot indefinitely continue to purchase the merchandise unless their economy is sustained by gifts or loans, which is what the United States has done in a number of instances.

Balance of International Payments

A country's economic relations with other countries can be shown in its balance of international payments. The balance of international payments for an individual country represents that country's financial statement of foreign trade and investment. All of the funds received from sources outside the country are credits, and all of the funds expended to sources outside the country are debits. Both the visible and invisible items referred to earlier are included, although the inability to secure exact information on certain of the invisible items, such as tourist expenditures, makes it difficult to make up an accurate balance of international payments. An examination of a country's balance of international payments would show that country's ability to buy goods from other countries and to pay its debts to other countries. The balance of international payments of the United States, for example, is a record of money made available to foreign countries by the United States through purchases of goods, services, and investments abroad and the uses to which money is put by foreign countries in making similar purchases from the United States. The United States balance of international payments for the year 1964 is shown in Table 21–1. During that

Table 21–1. United States Balance of International Payments (Billions of Dollars)

Payments of the United States		Receipts of the United States	
Imports of non-military goods and services	$25.6	Exports of U.S. non-military goods and services	$36.3
Unilateral transfers, net	4.5	Long-term capital inflow	.4
Private-capital outflow	6.5		
Military expenditures, net	2.1		
Errors and omissions	1.1		
Total	$39.8	Total	$36.7
Deficit (Total payments, minus receipts)			$ 3.1
Settlement of the deficit was effected by:			
1. Change in U.S. reserve assets			$ .2
2. Increase in foreign acquisition of official and short-term private dollar assets			$ 2.6
3. Official debt prepayments and advances on military exports			$ .3

SOURCE: Department of Commerce, for the year 1964.

year, the payments made by the United States to other countries amounted to 3.1 billion dollars more than the amount received by the United States from other countries. This table shows the ways in which this deficit was made up.

Tariffs

All countries impose certain restrictions on the flow of international trade. Tariffs are the oldest and most general type of restriction. They were initially designed to block trade between individuals in different countries. Tariffs may exist for a variety of reasons, although their primary purpose is the protection of local industry. They may also be imposed as a means of controlling the volume and kind of imports for effect on exchange. The revenue produced by tariffs is small.

The tariff is a type of tax that is levied, and the assessment of this is called a *duty*. We have customs duties that must be paid before certain goods may be brought into the United States. These duties may be assessed on an *ad valorem basis*, which is a percentage of the value of the goods. Ad valorem duty is a percentage based either on the price

paid for the goods or on an appraised value of the goods. A wide
variance exists in the amount of duty on different articles. The duty on
plain paper envelopes is 2½ per cent, while the duty on cigarette lighters
is 55 per cent. Another basis of assessing customs duties is the *specific
method*. Specific duties are assessed by quantity, weight, or measure
without regard to value. For example, on certain printed books, the
specific duty is $3.00 per 1,000. A type of *compound duty,* which is a
combination of the specific and ad valorem methods, is also used. For a
pack of playing cards, the compound duty is 5¢ per pack plus 5 per
cent of their value. A number of other special types of duties are assessed, at times, for particular purposes. A customs declaration is required on all goods on which duties must be paid. Some items are on
what is called a "free list," which means no customs duty is assessed
on these items.

Quotas and Exchange Controls

Since the end of World War I in 1918, a growing amount of restrictions in the form of quotas and exchange controls have developed in
foreign trade, equaling in importance that of tariffs. These governmental
restrictions are often imposed for the purpose of furthering the national-
istic economic plan of individual governments. Import quotas may be
established for certain classes of goods or for all goods of a certain class
over a stated minimum. Quotas may stipulate that only certain countries may import goods under the quotas, or a stated amount may be
permitted under a quota and any country may import to the extent of
the quota. Many countries also regulate the sale of foreign exchange,
or the sale of currencies or monies of other countries, thereby controlling
their own currency. This is due in some countries to the fact that there
are very limited supplies of foreign exchange available. The majority
of foreign trade transactions are not settled in cash but through the use
of drafts drawn by the seller or exporter on the buyer or importer. The
money involved in the transaction comes to the exporter or seller from
the bank or agency designated, which gives him the cash less an amount
for handling the transaction (discount price). That bank then presents
the draft for payment to the foreign bank which pays the first bank
and then receives its money from the buyer or importer. The *rate of
exchange* in foreign exchange is the price or sum per unit at which the
currency of one country is exchanged for the currency of another
country.

The rate of exchange is set by the government using exchange control. By this method, a government more or less limits and selects imports. It is not what the individual citizen feels is the most desirable

or profitable item for him at a particular time. Rather, the government decides which items are considered to be essential and thus desirable as imports. These may then be purchased and paid for with exchange bought at the most favorable price. On the other hand, non-essentials have to be paid for with exchange bought at a much higher price.

Under foreign exchange control, the exporter must sell all or a large part of the foreign exchange he secures to his central bank or the agency designated by his government for the purpose; the importer must buy all or a large part of the foreign exchange needed to pay for his purchases from the same agency.

Some of the sellers of exchange are exporters, ocean shipping companies, sellers of foreign securities, and insurance companies and banks. Buyers of exchange are importers, buyers of foreign securities, buyers of foreign services, travelers, and banks.

Foreign-Trade Zones

In an effort to facilitate foreign trade and surmount the restrictions imposed by tariffs, a number of countries have established *foreign-trade zones,* or *free-trade zones,* at their ports. A foreign-trade zone is a fenced-off and policed area within the port. Inside this area, foreign merchandise may be landed, stored, repacked, sorted, mixed, manufactured, and displayed with a minimum of customs control. An example of the way in which foreign-trade zones may be used is in the importing of fish oil. This product may be brought by ship into the New York foreign-trade zone in large containers where it can be bottled, labeled, and its potency reduced before any customs have to be paid on it. If it were brought into any other area of the port, customs would have to be paid on it immediately, or it would have to be bonded while it was stored. Foreign merchandise held in such a zone may be re-exported without ever going through customs. If the merchandise is brought from the foreign-trade zone into any other part of the port, it is subject to all customs laws and regulations. There are four foreign-trade zones in the United States.

The Trade Expansion Act of 1962

For many years, we have had tariff laws imposing duties on certain commodities imported into the United States. In general, our tariffs have been high or low depending on the political party in power. Historically, tariff rates tended to increase until the passage, in 1934, of the *Reciprocal Trade Agreements Act.* Congress extended this act periodically, amending it at times, and subsequently changed its name to the *Trade Agreements Act.* This act had an important influence in the reduction of our tariffs. Authority was granted to the President, with certain limitations, to lower or raise tariffs.

The *Trade Expansion Act of 1962* replaced the Trade Agreements Act and its amendments and was a significant development in trade legislation. This act extended the authority of the President to enter into trade agreements and to modify import restrictions for a period of five years ending June 30, 1967. It provided that the President, under specified procedures, is authorized to reduce by as much as 50 per cent rates of duty existing on July 1, 1962, and he may reduce by any amount or completely eliminate rates of duty in trade agreements with the European Economic Community on articles for which the United States and the Common Market account for 80 per cent or more of the free-world export value. He may also reduce by any amount or completely eliminate rates of duty in trade agreements with the European Economic Community on certain agricultural commodities. Where a rate of duty on an article for which the ad valorem rate or its equivalent is 5 per cent or less, this may also be reduced or eliminated.

The President may also increase any rate of duty up to 50 per cent above the rate existing on July 1, 1934, and may also modify existing import restrictions, other than duties, and impose other import restrictions such as quotas.

Inasmuch as this legislation was enacted under President Kennedy, the tariff negotiations that have taken place since that time have become known as the "Kennedy round" of tariff negotiations. Under the requirements of the Act, a special representative for trade negotiations is appointed by the President and confirmed by the Senate. He is the chief representative of the United States in all trade negotiations authorized by the Act, and there are, in addition, two members of the House Ways and Means Committee and two members of the Senate Finance Committee who serve as members of the tariff delegation.

The Act contains the *most-favored-nation principle,* under which tariff reductions are extended to products of all foreign countries. An escape-clause procedure is also provided under which a domestic industry that feels threatened with, or is experiencing, serious injury from increased imports as a result of a tariff concession may petition the Tariff Commission for tariff-adjustment assistance. After investigation, the Tariff Commission may recommend modifications.

Adjustment assistance is available to individual firms or groups of workers in an industry that are experiencing serious hardships due to imports. If certified by the Tariff Commission, adjustment assistance can be made available to firms in the form of loans, tax relief, or technical assistance, and to workers in the form of weekly allowances for unemployment, retraining, and relocation allowances in certain cases.

General Agreement on Tariffs and Trade

Under the authority of the 1945 extension of the Trade Agreements Act, simultaneous negotiations were conducted with a large group of nations. Twenty-three nations participated in the original negotiations. The total now is thirty-seven. Out of this first negotiation came the General Agreement on Tariffs and Trade (GATT), which became operative in January, 1948. It was a means by which the President used his authority under the Trade Agreements Act to negotiate.

The General Agreement contains an important set of mutually agreeable rules of behavior for international trade. These are based largely on rules evolved from earlier negotiations of bilateral agreements by the United States. The essential principle is that each member nation agrees to apply its regulations to the trade of all other members equally so that one is not favored over another (the *unconditional most-favored-nation principle*). Almost as important is the undertaking by members to cease using quotas to regulate imports as soon as economic conditions permit. Certain exceptions to both these rules are permitted. The General Agreement includes tariff schedules showing the maximum tariff rates that each member nation has agreed to extend to all other members.

The General Agreement has been effective in carrying out the purposes of the Trade Agreements Act. Tariff negotiations under GATT auspices have generally proved more fruitful than bilateral negotiations. As a forum for settling trade disputes among members and for limiting the scope of restrictive actions by individual countries, GATT has also been valuable.

European Economic Community or Common Market

Six nations—Belgium, France, West Germany, Italy, Luxembourg, and the Netherlands—joined in forming a *European Economic Community* at the beginning of 1958. These six member nations plan to reduce and finally to abolish protective tariffs and trade quotas among them making six separate national economies into one large *Common Market*. This began in 1958 and is to be accomplished over a twelve-to-fifteen-year period. Since the United States has a substantial amount of trade with these countries, one of the questions that arises is whether we will have less trade than has been the case in the past. This question is also in the minds of European countries not members of the Common Market.

The objective of the Common Market is to increase the efficiency and raise the income of the area by providing freer competition. It is a development that will be closely watched by the rest of the world to see how the external relations of the countries will be arranged so that there will not be tariff discrimination against non-Market countries.

European Free Trade Area

Seven of the countries that are not members of the European Common Market formed the *European Free Trade Area* in 1959. It is planned that, over a ten-year period, tariffs will be abolished among these seven countries so that there will be a free or common market among the members. The Association is open for any other country to join; but, initially, membership consisted of Austria, Britain, Denmark, Norway, Portugal, Sweden, and Switzerland. The group, which has been referred to as the *Outer Seven,* began lowering tariffs on industrial goods by 20 per cent in July, 1960.

GOVERNMENT AND MULTIGOVERNMENT ORGANIZATIONS THAT FACILITATE FOREIGN TRADE AND INVESTMENT

United States Tariff Commission

The United States Tariff Commission of six members appointed by the President was created in 1916. It investigates and reports upon tariff and foreign-trade matters. An example of the kind of work it does is that of investigating the difference in costs of producing similar articles in the United States and abroad. Under the Trade Expansion Act, the law requires the Tariff Commission to determine a *peril point* for each individual tariff before any negotiations are started to lower that tariff. A peril point is the tariff level below which, in the Commission's opinion, the tariff cannot be lowered without threatened or actual injury to a domestic producer. The Commission is given up to six months to make a study and conduct a public hearing. If the President exceeds a peril point in lowering a tariff, he must explain his action to Congress.

The purpose of the peril point is to make it hard to lower any tariff below the level which, in the Commission's judgment, would cause injury to domestic producers. Under this clause (the escape clause), the Tariff Commission recommends an increase in restrictions on imports if it finds threatened or actual injury to domestic producers. The 1958 extension of the Trade Agreements Act provides for a limited Congressional review of Presidential decisions in escape-clause cases. The Trade Expansion Act of 1962 modified the use of the peril point and the escape-clause provision.

Agency for International Development

The Agency for International Development, a government agency, is in the State Department. It provides technical cooperation with less developed areas by sharing United States knowledge, techniques, and skills. This help is principally in the form of teaching, training, and exchanging of information. Through a development loan fund, A.I.D. participates in the financing of projects that will stimulate economic growth in less developed countries.

The Export-Import Bank

The Export-Import Bank is a United States government corporation created in 1934 to aid in financing exports and imports. The bank extends credit to finance purchases of material and equipment produced in the United States and to provide technical services of American firms and individuals. Its loan charges vary with individual loans. The capital stock of the bank is subscribed to by the United States Treasury, and it can borrow money from the Secretary of the Treasury. Loans up to seven billion dollars may be outstanding at one time. It does not compete with private capital since it confines its dealings to loans in which private banks are not interested because the risks are more than they want to assume. It tends to reserve its credit to productive capital equipment exports, which include agricultural, mining, transportation, and industrial machinery. The scope of its activities are limited by law.

The International Bank for Reconstruction and Development

To expand international investment activity is the aim of the International Bank for Reconstruction and Development, also called the *World Bank*. This agency was organized in 1946 with headquarters in Washington, D.C. The powers of the World Bank are vested in its board of directors, which consists of one governor appointed by each member country. There are 123 nations that are members, including the United States. Its capital stock is approximately $22 billion and is subscribed by all member nations in varying amounts. It may lend to member governments and, with the guaranty of member governments, to their agencies. It grants loans repayable in dollars and pounds as well as other "hard" currencies. These loans are made on long-term investments and are designed to promote faster economic development in the areas of electric power, transportation, communications, agriculture, and industrial expansion.

The International Finance Corporation

The International Finance Corporation is a legally separate and distinct organization from the International Bank for Reconstruction and Development, although it is closely affiliated with it since the directors are the same. However, the International Finance Corporation is an investing, not a lending, institution that deals directly with private businessmen. It will not invest in undertakings that are government owned or operated. Membership in this organization is open only to countries that are members of the World Bank. There are currently seventy-nine members. It has an authorized capital of almost $100 million, and its investments are in the form of loans. They carry some interest charges as well as limited rights to participate in the growth of the enterprise being financed.

International Development Association

The International Development Association, also closely affiliated with the World Bank, was created in 1960 with initial resources of one billion dollars to provide capital in loans for underdeveloped nations. It furnishes loans where the repayable funds are only in currency other than pounds or dollars. Loans are without interest, but a service fee of ¾ of 1 per cent is charged. There are no payments on the principal for a grace period of ten years, after which small payments are made for a forty-year period. Individual nations are not required to guarantee repayment of the loans as is true on loans from the World Bank. This Association, unlike the World Bank, may loan money on such projects as community water supplies, sanitation, and pilot housing developments.

International Monetary Fund

The International Monetary Fund is an agency whose primary function is to make short-term loans to member countries whose currencies are unstable or which are having serious deficit balance-of-payments problems. It is a specialized agency of the United Nations with headquarters in Washington, D.C. It started operations in 1947 and currently has 103 member countries, of which the United States is one. A board of governors, composed of one from each member country, directs the Fund. A pool of gold and currencies is contributed by member nations, and it is used to promote exchange stability. By 1965, this pool amounted to over $16 billion. This organization facilitates consultation and collaboration on international monetary problems.

YOUR CAREER IN INTERNATIONAL TRADE

Career Opportunities

Foreign trade has always played an important role in the success of many of our domestic companies, and there are career opportunities in this field for persons who are thoroughly trained in various aspects of foreign trade. This is a field in which most companies just opening foreign markets do not have qualified personnel. Many aspects of foreign trade are unfamiliar to the untrained in this field. The documents are more numerous, financing arrangements are more complex, and government restrictions play an important part. There is a great need for people who have a good basic knowledge of the workings of foreign trade.

The type of organization a firm has to handle its foreign trade and the extent of foreign-trade activities will influence its personnel needs in this field. United States companies that conduct their own manufacturing operations abroad require more personnel than those that conduct primarily marketing activities. Most United States firms engaged in manufacturing in a foreign country, however, prefer to employ nationals of those countries. As a result, a comparatively small percentage of the employees of such firms are United States citizens. The young man who is accepted for a position in the foreign operations of such a company enters the organization in a relatively more important position as far as responsibility and opportunity are concerned than a person of similar age, experience, and qualifications in the domestic operations of the same company.

Generally speaking, salaries are higher than those paid in the United States for performing similar work. Many companies add a fixed percentage to the base salary when living conditions abroad are less attractive. In some foreign countries where higher costs of living prevail, companies pay allowances to compensate for the higher costs. The customary arrangement regarding home leave for personnel stationed overseas is three-months' leave after three years of foreign service, with round-trip expense of the employee and his family paid by the company. Of course, the employee is usually entitled to a local vacation in those years in which home leave is not taken. There are additional fringe benefits, as well, such as housing allowances.

There are many persons who are connected with foreign-trade activities whose jobs are in the United States. Career opportunities exist with companies engaged in direct exporting, with foreign-freight-forwarder companies, indirect exporters such as export merchants, and import organizations, customhouse brokers, and the foreign departments of banks. In addition, there are government career opportunities with the Bureau of Customs of the United States Treasury, the Export-Import Bank, the Bureau of Foreign Commerce of the Department of Commerce, and the United States Tariff Commission. The work of these government agencies is concerned principally with foreign trade.

Educational Background

The person who enters the international trade field should have had a thorough background in economics, foreign-trade procedure, and international trade. Transportation courses will be of particular help because the transportation involved in foreign trade is of great importance. The monetary aspects of this field will be more readily understood if courses in finance have been taken. The insurance requirements of foreign trade and the need for a knowledge of marketing make these areas a necessary part of the preparation for a career in foreign trade. Some students who plan to enter this field will also take several years of the language spoken in the geographical area in which they may want to locate. Courses in political science are valuable also in preparing for a career in foreign trade in that the different philosophies and operations of governments in various parts of the world are studied. In addition, the student should have courses in business organization, personnel management, and communications. For those who expect to get into manufacturing, a course in industrial management is essential.

There are many complexities of foreign trade that the student will find can only be learned after he is on the job.

TOPICS FOR DISCUSSION

1. Indirect exporting is only one category of exporting methods. The numerous indirect methods of export selling may be classified into what three broad types?

2. What are Webb-Pomerene corporations?

3. One of the most widely used credit tools in export trade is the *letter of credit*. What is a letter of credit?

4. Do you feel it would be better for a nation to have a favorable or an unfavorable balance of trade?

5. It would be very difficult for the United States watch industry to compete with the Swiss watch industry without some form of protective tariff. What factors cause this situation?

6. What are some of the political factors that influence foreign trade?

7. Has the development of air-cargo transportation affected foreign trade?

8. What would have happened in the United States had not the Constitution prohibited individual states from interfering with interstate commerce?

9. The United States has accumulated vast quantities of surplus food products. Why aren't more of these products exported?

10. Would you be interested in a job in the foreign-trade field? Why?

CASE 21–1

THE SEACOAST FISHERIES, INC.

The Seacoast Fisheries, Inc., is one of the largest and most successful of the packers and canners operating on the East Coast of the United States. Seacoast markets a variety of fishery products under the "Sea Nymph" brand. In 1964, Mr. Wallis, vice-president in charge of marketing, began consideration of the export market. Investigation of this area led to the conclusion that a particular Latin American country offered an excellent export market. On a visit to the country, Mr. Wallis concluded that a market existed in a quantity to accommodate as much as Seacoast could produce for export.

While visiting the prospective market, Mr. Wallis explored possible arrangements for marketing certain canned fish products. In the course of this exploration, he met a representative of the Galagos Wholesale Company, a firm operating wholesale outlets serving an area containing approximately 75 per cent of the population of the country. The Galagos Company was a family-owned organization dating back for several generations. It specialized in handling a line of canned food products that were marketed under its own brand name. Galagos executives were interested in becoming the distributor for Seacoast products. In conference with Mr. Wallis, they offered a presentation to show the network of retail food outlets served by the company. Mr. Wallis was impressed by the extent of the company's wholesale operation.

The Galagos Company proposed that it be given the exclusive rights to the distribution of Seacoast products in the country. It further proposed to market the Seacoast products under its own brand. The Galagos firm marketed all of its food products under the "Rosa" brand. This brand name was well known throughout the market, and evidence indicated that the brand enjoyed a very satisfactory degree of acceptability. Galagos executives contended that the brand name would be a big factor in achieving instant acceptability for the canned fishery products. In addition, the Galagos firm offered both a ready-made sales force to cover the market and the physical facilities for storage and delivery. It was suggested that the firm would supply Seacoast with labels that would be applied in the Seacoast plants before shipment. In concluding its presentation, Galagos pointed out that a high feeling of nationalism existed in the country and, if the products were marketed under a brand recognized as native to the country, acceptance would be facilitated.

Mr. Wallis was impressed with the possibilities outlined by the Galagos Wholesale Company, but he had some misgivings about entering into the arrangement. He realized that, by marketing the products under the Rosa brand, Seacoast would not achieve recognition in its own right. He also realized that, if the products proved successful, the Galagos firm could switch to another source of supply if it chose to do so. Seacoast had anticipated spending considerable sums in promoting the products in the foreign market, but, by having the product sold under the brand of another company, Seacoast would not benefit except in an indirect sense.

The alternative to accepting the Galagos proposal was for Seacoast to enter the market by establishing sales offices at strategic locations and hiring a sales force to call on wholesale and chain distributors. There would also be the problems of physical distribution to cope with if Seacoast entered the market in a direct manner.

1. Do you feel that Mr. Wallis should accept the Galagos proposal?
2. Would you suggest that Mr. Wallis make a counterproposal to that offered by Galagos?

SELECTED REFERENCES

Dowd, L. P. *Principles of World Business.* Englewood Cliffs, N.J.: Allyn & Bacon, Inc., 1965.

Ewing, J. S., and F. Meissner. *International Business Management.* Belmont, Calif.: Wadsworth Publishing Co., 1964.

Horn, P. V. *International Trade Principles and Practices.* 4th ed. Englewood Cliffs, N.J.: Prentice-Hall, Inc., 1959.

Kindleberger, C. P. *International Economics.* 3d ed. Homewood, Ill.: Richard D. Irwin, Inc., 1963.

Kramer, R. L. *International Marketing.* 2d ed. Cincinnati: South-Western Publishing Co., 1964.

Martyn, H. *International Business.* New York: The Free Press of Glencoe, 1964.

Young, J. P. *The International Economy.* New York: The Ronald Press Co., 1963.

V

OTHER SPECIALIZED AREAS OF MANAGEMENT

22

Accounting: Recording and Analysis of Operational Data

ACCOUNTING INFORMATION ESSENTIAL

It is difficult to conceive of a business firm operating successfully without some system of record keeping. Even the operator of the smallest enterprise needs to have some idea of the funds that are coming in and those that are going out. Such a firm may have a very simplified system; in fact, the operator may be able to keep most of his records in his head—although the Internal Revenue Service may not be sympathetic to that manner of operation. Any firm, large enough to be referred to as such, needs some degree of formal record keeping. When goods or services are sold, an accounting of the revenue must be kept. When goods or services are purchased, an accounting of the expenditure must be recorded. Without an idea of revenue and expenditure, the operator would have no idea of profit or loss—until faced with some contingency such as being unable to meet current expenses. The larger the firm becomes, the more extensive are the needs for accounting information. In the well-managed firm, the accounting system performs a far greater function than that of simply indicating profit or loss over a period of time. Information on the operation of the firm is assembled, categorized, and analyzed to provide management with explanations of past events and to provide the basis for future decisions.

Accounting may be defined as a system for providing information concerning property and the rights to property and to show how property and the rights to it have been affected by business operations. Broken down into its component parts, the activity of accounting consists of *recording* business transactions, *classifying* these activities by placing them into groups that may be handled in a systematic manner, *summarizing* the various classes of data to further facilitate their usefulness, and interpreting the results of operations as summarized in the various reports. Accountants usually distinguished the terms *bookkeeping* and *accounting*. They regard bookkeeping as the routine recording and reporting of business transactions, while accounting is thought to involve the element of theory and interpretation. Thus, accounting is the more comprehensive term in that it includes the activity of bookkeeping but goes far beyond this mechanical operation.

Evidence of some form of accounting is as old as commerce itself. As commerce has developed, the need for accounting has kept pace. In fact, the commerce of modern civilization has accelerated the need for systems of accounting and the information that they provide. The growth in the size of the individual firm has been a primary factor. As a business grows in size, its operations embrace more transactions, and the variety of transactions tend to increase. Adequate record keeping becomes a must if intelligent management is to exist. Unfortunately, small firms frequently fail to realize the need for better accounting as they grow in size. The result of this neglect is often the first step toward poor management and subsequent failure of the business. Competition has been another factor contributing to the need for more accounting. In a highly competitive situation, the firms that survive are those fortunate enough to be well managed. Managing a firm without adequate record keeping would be comparable to navigating a ship without charts. In corporate enterprise, the ownership and the management of a firm are often separated. It has been necessary to develop more extensive accounting to protect the interests of both owners and managers in this situation. The tendency of larger firms to diversify and spread their interests over many different lines has complicated ownership and management and added to the need for accounting data. And finally, the ever increasing role of government in business activity has intensified record keeping. The various taxes levied against the business firm, the management of social security and workmen's compensation deductions, the handling of the withholding of individual income tax, and the management of private pension plans have all increased the burden of accounting. Tax laws generally require some form of record keeping to substantiate information reported by the taxpayer.

ORGANIZATION OF THE ACCOUNTING FUNCTION

A small firm may employ one individual as a bookkeeper, or accountant. As the firm grows in size, an accounting department may develop. In the larger departments, areas of specialization may develop along the lines discussed later in this chapter. It suffices to point out that such a department may have general accountants, cost accountants, auditors, tax accountants, and others. In a large company, the accounting operations may be under the direction of a controller. The controller may be a vice-president of the company and be on the same managerial level as the superintendent of production and the sales manager. In its role as a tool of management, accounting is essentially a staff function; however, within the accounting department, the line form of organization may prevail. In matters of details, the accounting organization will vary depending upon the characteristics and needs of the individual company. Accounting systems are designed to fit the needs of the individual company, and the organization of the department and the personnel employed will reflect this fact. The design of a system based upon individual need is one of the services performed by the qualified accountant.

THE FINANCIAL STATEMENTS

Accounting Objectives

In a very general sense, the accounting operations have as a goal the derivation of the financial statements. The principal financial statements are the *balance sheet* and the *income statement* (sometimes called *profit and loss statement*). Both are summary statements: the balance sheet showing the financial status of the business in terms of what is owned and what is owed, and the income statement summarizing the operations of the business in terms of the revenue and expenditures for the period. While the derivation of the statements may be the goal of many accounting operations, accounting objectives go beyond the derivation of the statements to include an analysis of the data found in the statements and an interest in the application of accounting data to business problems.

In giving the student a brief introduction to the field of accounting, it is thought best to begin with a discussion of financial statements. This will illustrate the type of information that the accounting department seeks to provide. Then, we will proceed to a brief discussion of how the accountant assembles the data necessary to derive the statements.

This will be followed by a look at the various specialized areas of accounting. And finally, a section will be devoted to a discussion of some of the ways in which management makes use of accounting data. Accounting is an extensive, and sometimes complex, field. The student should bear in mind that in a survey text, it is impossible to do more than give a vastly generalized picture. Any of the *Principles of Accounting* texts cited at the end of the chapter will provide a more comprehensive introduction to the subject.

The Balance Sheet

The balance sheet is a summary statement showing the financial status of a business as of the date upon which the statement is drawn. The fundamental balance sheet equation is as follows:

$$\text{Assets} = \text{Liabilities} + \text{Proprietorship}$$

Assets may include anything of value owned by the business. Liabilities represent the obligations of the business to pay money, other assets, or services to another now or in the future, i.e., the debts of the business. Proprietorship is the excess of assets over liabilities; it is the owner's equity in the business. For example, if you were to borrow $20,000 to start a business and supplement this amount by putting up $10,000 of your own money, the business might acquire assets valued at $30,000, but your equity in these assets would consist of the $10,000 invested. As changes occur in the financial status of the business, the changes will be reflected in the balance-sheet equation. Assets may change as a result of purchase, fabrication, sales, or depreciation. Liabilities change through buying on credit, borrowing, paying off debts, and exchanging one form of liability for another. The proprietorship will change as a result of additional investment in the business through a profit and loss from operations or through a withdrawal of earnings or part of the investment.

The balance sheet is usually present in one of two standard forms: The *account form* shows the data in two parallel columns, assets in the left-hand column and liabilities and proprietorship in the right-hand column. This follows the pattern of the balance-sheet equation shown. The *report form* lists the assets and below them the liabilities and the proprietorship. In terms of the equation, this form would indicate that assets minus liabilities equals proprietorship. The form used is of minor concern since the data remains the same in each. Figure 22–1 shows the balance sheet for a merchandising firm using the report form.

Looking further at the balance sheet shown in Figure 22–1, we may consider the separate parts of the statement. *Current assets* consist of

JOHN FISHER
Balance Sheet
December 31, 1965

Assets

CURRENT ASSETS:

Cash		$ 1,200	
Accounts Receivable	$ 6,050		
Less Allowance for Bad Debts	200	5,850	
Merchandise Inventory		8,000	
Total Current Assets			$15,050

FIXED ASSETS:

Delivery Equipment	$ 5,000		
Less Reserve for Depreciation	400	$ 4,600	
Store Fixtures and Equipment	$ 3,000		
Less Reserve for Depreciation	150	2,850	
Office Equipment	$ 600		
Less Reserve for Depreciation	50	550	
Building	$10,000		
Less Reserve for Depreciation	400	9,600	
Land		4,000	
Total Fixed Assets			$21,600
DEFERRED CHARGES TO EXPENSES			1,500
TOTAL ASSETS			$38,150

Liabilities

CURRENT LIABILITIES:

Notes Payable	$ 1,000		
Accounts Payable	2,300		
Wages Payable	300		
Total Current Liabilities		$ 3,600	

FIXED LIABILITIES:

Mortgage Payable		5,000	
TOTAL LIABILITIES			$ 8,600

PROPRIETORSHIP:

John Fisher, Capital, June 30, 1965		$26,750	
Net Profit Six-Month Period	$ 4,000		
Less Withdrawals	1,200	2,800	
John Fisher, Capital Dec. 31, 1965			$29,550
TOTAL LIABILITIES AND PROPRIETORSHIP			$38,150

Fig. 22–1. Balance sheet for a merchandising firm.

cash and other assets that will be converted to cash through normal operations and in a relatively short time. The current assets of a firm may vary from day to day as business transactions occur. *Fixed assets* are items of value whose life normally may be expected to extend over several years. Land, buildings, and equipment are examples of fixed assets. Many fixed assets are subject to depreciation or depletion, and in some cases obsolescence. The correct evaluation of fixed assets may pose a problem for the accountant. Deferred charges to expenses, sometimes called *prepaid expenses,* represents such items as supplies purchased for future use and prepaid insurance.

The liabilities sector of the statement begins with a statement of the current liabilities. *Current liabilities* are the obligations incurred by the firm and which mature within a relatively short time—often anything coming due within a year is considered in this category. As will be discussed later, current liabilities are important in relation to current assets. *Fixed liabilities* consist of long-term obligations, such as mortgages, or other instruments that become due at a future date greater than a year. In the *proprietorship* section of the statement, the equity of the owner of the business is shown. This may be thought of as the owner's claims against the business. This shows what the owner would receive were the business to be sold at its book value. In a corporate balance sheet, this section would show the kinds of stock outstanding and any surplus that might be held by the corporation. The equity of the stockholders in the corporation may be ascertained in a manner comparable to that used to ascertain the equity of the owner in a sole proprietorship.

The Income Statement

It is often said that a balance sheet shows the condition of a business at a given time, and that the income statement (sometimes called the operating statement) shows how the business got into the condition. Simply defined, the income statement summarizes the income and expenses incurred by the firm for the period of time covered in the statement. The balance sheet and the income statement may be drawn at frequent intervals as the need for such summary information may dictate. Some businesses, especially smaller firms, may require that the income statement be drawn only once each year; however, many firms require the statement as often as once each month. If the statement is to provide managerial information, it should show in detail the source of all income and also show expenses in as much detail as is practical. A good accounting system will give a breakdown of all expenses incurred, and such an itemized listing of expenses will be summarized on the income statement. A firm may keep its books on either a *cash* or an *accrual* basis. If the cash basis is used, income is regarded as earned when cash is received regardless of when sale is made or service rendered, and expenses are recorded only when cash is paid out. If the accrual basis is used, income is recorded for the period in which it is earned, regardless of whether it is received during that period. Expenses incurred are treated as expenses for that period, although they may not be paid until a future date. The accrual method of accounting provides management with more accurate and useful information since it matches the revenue earned during a period with the related expenses. The vast majority of business firms keep their accounts on an accrual basis. Professional men and very small businesses frequently keep their records on a cash basis.

As in the case of the balance sheet, the income statement may utilize two forms. The *account form* makes use of two parallel vertical columns; the cost of goods and expenses are shown on the left and incomes on the right. The *report* (or multistep) *form* arranges all items in a vertical column, segregated into sections such as sales, cost of goods, operating expenses, and profits. The report form is more commonly utilized and an example of an income statement using this form is shown in Figure 22–2. Looking at this statement, we see that *net sales* are arrived at by deducting *sales returns and allowances* from *gross sales*. It is common in a merchandising establishment for the customer to occasionally return items purchased or for one reason or another to ask for an adjustment in the price. The merchant strives to hold sales returns and allowances to a minimum. The cost of goods sold during the period is determined by taking the beginning merchandise inventory and adding the purchases made during the period plus any freight that the merchant pays on incoming shipments. From this amount is deducted the closing inventory to arrive at cost of goods sold. The cost of goods sold deducted from the net sales gives the merchant his gross profit on sales. Gross profit on sales is also referred to as the gross margin, or realized markup.

The expenses section is divided into *selling expenses* and *general expenses*. Selling expenses are those directly connected with the selling activity. They should, in a general way, vary directly with the volume of sales. General expenses are less closely related to sales volume, and certain of the items found in this category are commonly referred to as "overhead." The income statement shown does not breakdown the expenses into as many classes as might be possible. For example, tax expense, insurance expense, and the utilities are included in the miscellaneous categories. From the standpoint of analysis, it would be more desirable to have these expenses itemized. The *total expenses* deducted from the gross profit on sales gives the merchant his net profit, or loss.

In the foregoing discussion of financial statements, a merchandising firm was used for illustrative purposes. In the case of manufacturing firms and service establishments, the statements would follow the same general pattern but would vary in detail to reflect the activities peculiar to these businesses. Larger firms with accounting departments employ-

JOHN FISHER
Income Statement
For Six-Month Period Ending December 31, 1965

INCOME FROM SALES:			
Gross Sales		$120,800	
Less Sales Returns and Allowances		1,600	
Net Sales			$119,200
COST OF GOODS SOLD:			
Mdse. Inventory June 30, 1965		$ 15,600	
Purchases	$80,600		
Freight In	4,900	85,500	
Merchandise Available for Sale		$101,100	
Less Mdse. Inventory Dec. 31, 1965		7,000	
Cost of Goods Sold			94,100
Gross Profit on Sales			$ 25,100
EXPENSES:			
Selling Expenses:			
Salaries of Sales Clerks	$ 7,800		
Advertising	2,500		
Depreciation Store Equipment	900		
Store Supplies Used	400		
Miscellaneous Selling Expense	1,600		
Total Selling Expense		$ 13,200	
General Expenses:			
Office Salaries	$ 4,400		
Rent	2,000		
Depreciation Office Equipment	300		
Loss from Bad Debts	200		
Miscellaneous General Expense	1,000		
Total General Expense		$ 7,900	
TOTAL EXPENSES			$ 21,100
NET PROFIT			$ 4,000

Fig. 22–2. Income statement for a merchandising firm.

ing specialists are able to provide management with more detailed information, and this would enable the preparation of more detailed and comprehensive financial statements.

ASSEMBLING ACCOUNTING DATA

The Debit and Credit Concept

Now that we have been introduced to the financial statements, we may turn our attention to the methods used by the accountant to assemble the data from which the statements are derived. There are at least two elements to every business transaction: for instance, if something is received something is given up, and vice versa. As transactions occur, the assets, liabilities, and the proprietorship of a firm are affected. The accountant must record transactions in such a way that the effects of the transaction on the business may be readily ascertained. The method that has evolved for accomplishing this is a system based on the debit and credit concept.

To understand the debit and credit concept, we must think of the individual items appearing on the financial statements as "accounts." For example "cash" is an account—and as money is taken in, the account is increased; and as money is paid out, it is decreased. "Merchandise inventory" is an account that is increased and decreased by the purchase and sale of merchandise. It is customary to keep accounts in dual columns with the title of the account written across the top. The framework of the account so designed resembles the letter *T;* and such accounts are sometimes referred to as T-accounts. With the accounts designed to afford dual columns, the procedure is to place additions to assets on the left side of the account (left column) and additions to liabilities and proprietorship on the right side. Conversely, a decrease in the value of an asset would appear on the right side of the particular account, and a decrease in liability or proprietorship would appear on the left side of the account concerned. In accounting terminology, the left side of an account is referred to as the *debit* side and the right side of the account is referred to as the *credit* side. If we receive money, we "debit cash" for the amount; and if we pay out money, we "credit cash" for the amount. With the debit and credit sides of accounts thus established, we may observe the following effects:

Debit Indicates:	Credit Indicates:
Asset increase	Asset decrease
Liability decrease	Liability increase
Proprietorship decrease	Proprietorship increase
Income decrease	Income increase
Expense increase	Expense decrease

Through the concept of debits and credits, we are able to utilize double-entry bookkeeping. In double-entry bookkeeping, each transaction is recorded in such a way that its effect on assets, liabilities, and proprietorship is shown while maintaining the equality of debits and credits. The necessity for maintaining equality of debits and credits provides one of the primary checks against errors in bookkeeping.

The Journal

We note from the foregoing discussion that transactions are recorded in the various accounts. It might be possible to post (enter) the transactions to the accounts directly as they occur, but this would not be practical for most firms. Transactions may occur rapidly, and thus it may be advisable to record them for later posting. Furthermore, the ledger (accounts) alone may not record the complete information desired. The record supplementary to the ledger is the journal. The journal is a chronological record of the transactions of a firm. It might be compared to a diary, or a ship's log, in which events are recorded as they occur. In addition to providing a chronological history of transactions, the journal provides a brief description of each transaction. It also shows, in one place, the accounts affected by each transaction. And finally, as a descriptive record, it is a valuable aid in detecting errors that may occur in the ledger. As the book of original entry, the journal ordinarily has greater weight as legal evidence than the ledger.

Business papers used in routine transactions provide the source of information for the entries made in the journal. Incoming checks and cash received are evidence of the money taken in; check stubs may evidence the money paid out. When a firm makes a purchase, the seller will send the buyer an invoice (bill) describing the transaction and showing the indebtedness incurred. When cash sales are made, the cash-register tape may provide the data for journalizing; when credit sales are made, a copy of the sales slip will provide the data. These and other sources evidencing transactions provide the basis for making the journal entries. The form of the journal is usually a multicolumned page. A column is provided for the date, for listing the account debited or credited along with a description of the transaction, for recording the ledger page to which the transaction is posted; and a debit column and a credit column is provided for recording the amounts of the transactions. Figure 22–3 shows a simplified illustration of journal entries. In the illustration, the entries appear in print; however, in practice, journal entries, and entries in the ledger, may be handwritten.

The Ledger

The original entries made in the journal are posted to the ledger. The ledger is a collection of accounts, each identified by title and providing space for debit and credit entries. As previously indicated, each account has two columns with the title of the account imposed across the top of the columns. This gives the appearance of the letter *T* thusly:

Merchandise Inventory

Debit	Credit

JOURNAL

DATE		ACCOUNT	L.F.	DEBIT AMT.	CREDIT AMT.
1965 Jan.	1	Cash J. Fisher, Proprietorship Invested cash to establish business		20,000	20,000
Jan.	5	Building Cash Made down payment on building to be used		5,000	5,000
Jan.	7	Store Equipment Cash Purchased equipment and fixtures for cash		2,000	2,000
Jan.	10	Merchandise Inventory Cash Purchased merchandise from Smith and Co. for cash		5,000	5,000
Jan.	11	Merchandise Inventory Accounts Payable Purchased merchandise on account from Jones Wholesale Company		5,000	5,000
Jan.	15	Salary Expense Cash Paid weekly salaries		200	200
Jan.	20	Cash Sales Cash sales for week's operations		1,000	1,000

Fig. 22–3. A simplified illustration of journal entries.

As a rule, only one account is placed on each page of the ledger; and while the ledger may be bound, it is common practice to use loose-leaf forms. This permits the rearrangement of accounts and the insertion of new accounts that may arise. The number of accounts established in the ledger varies with the type of business and the accounting policy of the individual firm. If transactions are itemized in detail, many accounts will be needed. For example, one firm may record its expenses by using only six accounts while a similar firm may desire its expenses broken down into twelve classes and hence twelve accounts. From the viewpoint of management, it is desirable to have accounts itemized with as much detail as possible with due regard for accuracy. If too many accounts are used, the allocation of such costs as overhead to the individual categories becomes to some extent a matter of judgment, and the accounting data thus loses some of its objective quality. Figure 22–4

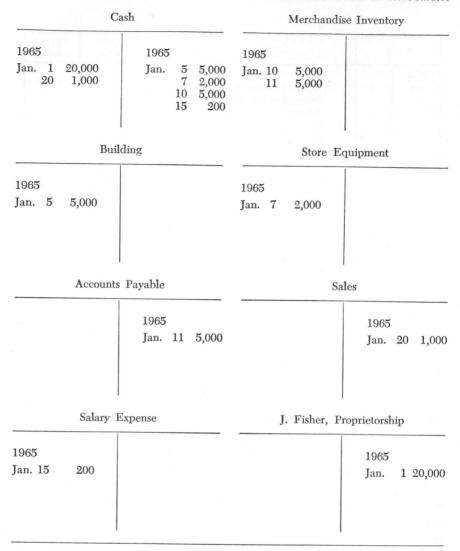

Fig. 22–4. A simplified illustration of ledger accounts. (The column for posting reference designed to show the page of the journal from which the item has been transferred was omitted for reasons of brevity.)

shows how the journal entries illustrated in Figure 22–3 might appear when posted to the ledger.

The variety of accounts found in the ledger may be classified into groups as asset accounts, liability accounts, proprietorship accounts, income accounts, expense accounts, and the summarizing accounts. By comparing the brief illustration of a journal with that of the ledger, it is hoped that the student will note the manner in which journal entries are transferred to the ledger accounts and posted. Note also that each time an account is debited or credited, an offsetting entry must take place in another account. Any transaction affecting the business must thus affect at least two accounts. It is upon this concept that the fundamentals of accounting are based.

Summarizing the Data

At intervals, it becomes desirable to summarize the data contained in the accounts and thus obtain a concise financial picture of the business. Before totaling the accounts, certain adjusting and closing entries may be necessary. Adjusting entries may be required in the merchandise-inventory, depreciation, and bad-debts accounts. For example, the merchandise-inventory account will show the inventory that should be on hand according to the records, but items lost through theft or breakage will not show on the books. A physical count of the inventory may reveal certain shortages, and thus the inventory account will have to be adjusted to bring the book inventory in line with the actual inventory. Adjustments may be necessary in other areas where the written records have not been able to reflect true conditions with complete accuracy. The accountant has prescribed procedures for handling the mechanics of adjusting entries.

At the close of the accounting period, certain accounts such as the income, expense, and summarizing accounts must be closed. These accounts serve their purpose during the accounting period; and at the end of the period, they are closed by transferring their balances, through the income statement, to the proprietorship account. When the adjusting and closing entries have been made, the accounts are balanced; and the totals thus derived afford the data for constructing the financial statements.

THE MANAGERIAL USE OF ACCOUNTING DATA

Facts for Decision-Making

Modern management is characterized by a relentless effort to gather and analyze information pertinent to a problem before a decision is made. As noted in an earlier chapter, marketing research has undergone a rapid development as the manager has realized the need for market information. Information concerning the market is often found through an analysis of the firm's own records; for example, an analysis of the sales of hats should reveal which styles and prices have proved most acceptable to the customer. The manager is also vitally concerned with the internal operations of his firm and the way in which these operations have influenced one another. A relaxation of credit policy may increase sales but at the same time increase the loss from bad debts; thus, the manager must remain vigilant concerning these relationships. Changes in the financial structure of the company as revealed through the accounting records will often detect problems in their early stages when corrections are easier to make. Trends in income and costs are revealed through an analysis of records, and decisions may be made in light of these trends. From the viewpoint of management, the accounting department may be regarded as an "internal intelligence bureau" that keeps management appraised of the continuous financial changes that affect the present and future of the firm.

Accounting records provide management with many different types of information. In addition to the general information provided, specialized branches of accounting such as *cost accounting* furnish a wealth of detailed information. If a company is making ten products, the cost-accounting department may supply data on the relative cost of making each product and the share of total income contributed by each product. In addition, the cost accountant may be able to break down the cost of producing a product into its component operations. As illustrative of the manner in which accounting information is used, we will discuss some of the ways in which the data found in the financial statements may be interpreted and utilized by management. We will deal specifically with some of the more common examples of *ratio analysis* and then discuss *comparative-statement analysis.*

Ratio Analysis

Basically, there are three kind of ratios that may be derived from the financial statements: ratios that refer to relationships between balance sheet items, ratios that show the relation of expense accounts to income (income statement), and ratios that show a relationship between an item on the income statement and one on the balance sheet. Dozens of ratios may be computed from the financial statements. There are certain ratios that are pertinent to all business firms, while others are significant to one type of firm and less significant to another. The following ratios are among those considered to be of importance to most firms.

Current Assets to Current Liabilities. This ratio is computed from data found in the balance sheet. It shows the ability of the firm to meet its short-term credit obligations. For a firm in good financial health, the current assets should exceed the current liabilities by an amount sufficient to allow for any shrinkage that may occur before the liabilities become due. A ratio of 2 to 1 is often cited, although in certain types of businesses a smaller ratio of current assets to current liabilities would be regarded as satisfactory. The ratio is obtained by dividing the current assets by the current liabilities. Creditors are particularly interested in this ratio since it indicates the degree of protection present in extending short-term loans. If current assets sufficiently exceed current liabilities, the creditor may be protected even in the event of the dissolution of the firm.

Turnover of the Tangible Net Worth. Tangible net worth is the worth of a business minus intangibles such as goodwill. It is the book value of the owner's equity in the business less any intangibles that may have been included. The ratio is obtained by dividing the average tangible net worth into the net sales for the same period. The ratio is expressed as the number of times the turnover is achieved during the period. If tangible net worth is $20,000 and net sales amount to $80,000, the turnover for the period is 4. This shows how actively the capital is being utilized; and when compared to other periods of time, or to other firms of the same size and type, it gives management another clue to efficiency.

Turnover of Working Capital. Working capital is determined by deducting the sum of current liabilities from the sum of current assets. Working capital represents assets that may be easily converted into operating funds. If current assets are $100,000 and current liabilities are $50,000, there would be a working capital of $50,000. Since a part of this working capital may be invested in merchandise and receivables that cannot be converted to cash instantly, most firms will require an excess of current assets over current liabilities sufficient to permit carrying these investments and still have funds available for current operations. The turnover of working capital is computed by dividing the working capital at the close of a period into the net sales for that period. The ratio indicates the degree to which the working capital is being utilized; and if the ratio is very low or exceedingly high, it may indicate a financial problem.

Net Profits to Tangible Net Worth. This ratio indicates the return that the business is receiving on its investment. Net profit is the amount left over from income after all costs have been paid. The ratio is determined by dividing tangible net worth at the end of a period into the profits made during the period. This ratio is expressed as a percentage. For example, if the tangible net worth is $100,000 and the net profit is $10,000, the ratio of 10 per cent indicates the return on the owner's investment. The ratio compared to what the capital would earn elsewhere, or compared to what is being earned in similar businesses, is an indication of the efficiency of the operation.

Fixed Assets to Net Worth. The fixed assets, less depreciation, are divided by the tangible net worth. This shows the extent to which net worth may be invested in fixed assets. Some types of businesses require a very high investment in plant and equipment, while others require much less. It is valuable for management to know whether its investment in fixed assets compares favorably to that of other companies of its type.

Total Debt to Tangible Net Worth. Total debt is the sum of all obligations owed by the firm—both short and long term. The relationship of total debt to net worth indicates the ability of the firm to pay its debts if faced with dissolution. The ratio is obtained by dividing the total debt by the tangible net worth. This ratio is of interest to creditors in deciding on the extension of long-term loans. It is difficult to set any standard for this ratio. Some very successful firms carry a large indebtedness; in fact, their success becomes a prime factor enabling them to borrow. The relationship between total debt and tangible net worth must be viewed with regard to other aspects of the firm's operations.

Inventory to Sales. This ratio known as the "stock turnover" is obtained by dividing the average inventory at cost into the cost of goods sold or by dividing the average inventory at selling price (cost plus proposed markup) into net sales. The ratio is expressed as a number, or in days. A stock turnover of 4 would indicate that the inventory has been turned, on an average, every ninety days. If we have a beginning inventory at cost of $20,000 and an ending inventory at cost of $24,000 and our cost of goods sold during the period was $66,000, we could compute the turnover using the cost method as follows:

Beginning inventory	$20,000
Ending inventory	24,000
Divided by 2	44,000
	$22,000 = Average inventory

Cost of goods sold, $66,000, divided by the average inventory of $22,000 would give a turnover of 3.

In computing stock turnover, it is necessary to remember that one must keep all figures at either the cost level or the selling-price level. If the average inventory is computed at cost, one must divide the average into the cost of goods sold rather than into net sales. If net sales are going to be used, then one must value the average inventory at the proposed selling price. To be accurate, the average markup applied to inventory should be the same as that realized on sales.

The significance of the rate of stock turnover depends upon other factors in the business operation. Everything remaining equal, an increase in turnover would seem to indicate greater efficiency. But there is nothing magic in the rate of turnover itself. One may reduce prices, increase sales, and increase the rate of stock turnover while rapidly going broke. Also, the rate of stock turnover is based on the entire inventory computed in dollars, and this may mask certain slow-moving items that are being compensated for by the faster sellers. Perhaps, the most profitable use of stock turnover is to enable a firm to compare its rate of turnover with other firms in the same class.

The foregoing ratios have been presented as representative of what is termed "ratio analysis." There are many other ratios such as net income to net sales, gross profit to net sales, and net sales to receivables. The experienced manager is able to compute and compare ratios and in a sense "take the pulse of his business." Banks, and other creditors, in making business loans, rely heavily upon the information revealed in ratio analysis.

Comparative-Statement Analysis

Much can be learned about the condition of a business by comparing the financial statements of one period with those of a preceding period and also by comparing the statements of the firm under study with those of firms approximately the same size and in the same line of business. We have indicated that the balance sheet gives a picture of the firm's financial status as of a particular date. In the preceding section, we saw that by comparing one part of the balance sheet with another, we are able to reach certain conclusions as to the financial health of the firm. We may gain additional insight into the firm's financial condition by comparing the current balance sheet with those immediately preceding. For example, the latest balance sheet may show a high proportion of accounts receivable. A look at previous balance sheets will show whether the receivables have been increasing over a long period or whether the increase has been in the nature of a sharp and recent upsurge. The rate at which a change has occurred may be just as important as the magnitude of the change. Bankers, in evaluating loan applications, may require the applicant to present his latest balance sheet along with several preceding ones. An analysis of this type will often enable the detection of trends that have a bearing on the firm's borrowing capacity.

A firm may also find it helpful to compare its most recent income statement with statements from a preceding period. To facilitate this comparison, the items on the income statement should be converted to percentages, each item expressed as a percentage of net sales (net sales, as a base, would be equal to 100 per cent). This comparison points up those items of cost that may be increasing or decreasing relative to preceding periods. To illustrate, the latest income statement may show loss from bad debts as 2 per cent of net sales. A look at preceding income statements may show that loss from bad debts had been running at 1 per cent of net sales. This would alert the manager of the business to check his credit policy and to determine if possible why the sudden increase in bad debts has occurred.

The Use of Average Ratios

The foregoing examples show how a business may gain helpful information by comparing the statements of one period with those of another. In making such time comparisons, the firm utilizes its own statements. A second area of statement analysis is that in which the firm compares its statements with average statements based on firms of the same type and size. These "average statements" are composites made up by soliciting statements from firms, averaging the components, and expressing the components as percentages. As an example, hardware stores having annual sales between $100,000 and $150,000 might be asked to supply a copy of their most recent income statement. Let us assume that one hundred stores supplied statements and the average net sales per store was $125,000. We check the advertising expenditures of all the stores and find that the average store spent $1,250 on advertising for the year. This average expenditure when expressed as a percentage of average net sales shows that the advertising expense was 1 per cent of sales. From the one hundred income statements supplied, a composite, or single-average statement, is made; and the components of the average statement are reduced to percentages—or "ratios" as they may be called. Organizations such as Dun and Bradstreet, trade associations, universities, and government agencies collect the data from which average statements are drawn.

Ratios may be available showing the relationship of the items on the balance sheet of the "average firm" of a certain size and type. More in evidence are ratios based on average income statements. Average ratios are more plentiful in the area of merchandising than in manufacturing. Such information is now available for practically all lines of retail trade and for many wholesale operations. Ratios have also been compiled for service establishments. The manager of a firm can make good use of comparative ratios in checking the performance of his business against the average for his size and type of firm. Ratios, however, must be used with caution. The manager must remember that he is comparing his firm against an "average," and there are perhaps successful firms both above and below this average. It is very unlikely that any firm would ever coincide exactly with the average ratios reported. The great value of ratios is that they do afford a general yardstick, or basis, for comparison.

The Different Areas of Accounting

There are many branches of accounting and many "specialists" who perform services. The *general accountant* handles the bookkeeping of the firm, does some tax work, and frequently assists in cost studies. The *cost accountant* is concerned with determining the unit costs of production and distribution. He provides management with data essential to cost control. He is concerned with breaking down total cost into its components and thus revealing the avenues to cost reduction. *Budgetary accounting* refers to the accountant's role in establishing the budget and in its maintenance. Budgets are adjusted from time to time, and much of this work centers in the accounting department. *Auditing* is the "watchdog" branch of accounting. The auditor checks upon the accuracy of reports and verifies the records of the firm. Firms may employ internal auditors to check upon the work of others and to detect errors or faulty procedures. Auditing firms are independent business organizations employed to come into a company for the purpose of checking and examining its records. The growing complexity of tax structures has demanded the development of a specialized area of accounting to deal with this problem. *Tax accounting* demands both a knowledge of accounting practices and of the tax laws. Governments and institutions have accounting problems peculiar to their operations, and this has given rise to further specialization in accounting. The foregoing represent some of the more common areas of specialization in accounting. Individual firms may have problems peculiar to their operations, which require specialists not mentioned above.

YOUR CAREER IN ACCOUNTING

Opportunities

In the past, and even today, many employees of the accounting department did not have college training. High-school graduates learned through a program of "on the job" training, and many others entered accounting after one or two years in a technical school. The trend today would seem to be toward college training for those interested in accounting. Colleges of Business Administration within universities have very active accounting departments; frequently accounting majors outnumber other categories. In this brief summary, we are interested in the opportunities available to the college or university graduate who majors in accounting. We may also point out that a distinction is often made between the *bookkeeper* and the *accountant*. Much of our routine bookkeeping may be accomplished by people without college training, while those services usually associated with the accountant are being rendered more and more by college-trained individuals.

The college or university graduate who majors in accounting may launch a career in at least two broad directions: (1) He may specialize in accounting, and (2) he may use accounting as a background for non-accounting jobs. If he decides to become an accounting specialist, he may choose public accounting and work for an accounting firm, or he may become an employee in the accounting department of a business firm. The public-accounting firm does auditing work, installs systems, and other work for clients. The young person going into public accounting will be especially interested in becoming a Certified Public Accountant. The C.P.A. certificate is awarded to those who have met certain educational and experience requirements established by the states and who have passed the C.P.A. examinations. Many schools offer accounting programs designed to enable the student to qualify for the examinations. For those desiring a job within industry, often called industrial accounting, the C.P.A. certificate may have less importance; however, it is a goal frequently sought by all accountants.

In public accounting, the opportunities for advancement and salary are determined by the capacity of the individual. The public-accounting firm may have a large number of employees and be organized along both functional and regional lines. There are administrative jobs at many different levels, and the young man who enters public accounting will usually hope to advance to an administrative position. In order to achieve this, he must serve an apprenticeship in which he masters the details of his profession. In some respects, opportunities in industrial accounting parallel those found in public accounting. The accounting function in a large corporation may be divided according to special areas, and each area may be organized into sections and divisions. There are administrative jobs ranging from that of section head up to that of controller. Generally speaking, promotion is from within, and the individual is expected to work his way up the ladder as his ability permits. At the present time, college graduates entering public and industrial accounting are receiving starting salaries at least comparable to those received by sales and industrial-management trainees. Administrative jobs carry salaries commensurate with the ability and responsibility required. Often the controller of a company is a vice-president receiving a salary comparable to other top-management people.

Training

The college or university student majoring in accounting usually takes a business-administration degree (or a B.S. in commerce, or similar degree). Small colleges may permit a concentration in accounting while giving the Bachelor of Arts degree. In all cases, the student is usually required to have a minimum of two years in the traditional liberal-arts courses. During his last two years in a College of Business Administration, he will take accounting courses along with other courses in business and economics. Over-all, his accounting major may consist of six or more accounting courses. It is essential that the accountant work with other members of management, and the value of the accountant is enhanced if he has a knowledge of business management as well as a specialized knowledge of accounting. The fact that the accountant with a college degree may have a broad knowledge of management gives him an advantage over the accounting specialist trained through a one- or two-year technical course. There is a growing realization that the accountant, in order to perform most efficiently, must have a broader knowledge of management than has been true of accountants in the past.

In recent years, much has been heard about the use of new and improved business machines in the growing trend toward automation. Machines have proved effective in eliminating much of the drudgery in the accumulation and analysis of information. The effect that this automation will have upon the demand for accountants cannot be assessed at this time, but there are those that feel that the machine will not displace the accountant. Gavin A. Pitt, in his book on career planning, has this to say:

As the use of automatic office machines comes into more general use, the need for accountants will not be diminished in the least. It is possible that the increased scope of data produced by the machines will force the men in accounting departments to take a more comprehensive view of the company's operations. This will make it necessary for them to have a broader education than is now being given in the normal business school.[1]

If the student likes to work with figures and is of an analytical bent, he may find accounting a rewarding and interesting subject. Although

---

[1] Gavin A. Pitt, *The Twenty-Minute Lifetime, A Guide to Career Planning* (Englewood Cliffs, N.J.: Prentice-Hall, Inc., 1959), p. 64.

accounting deals with figures, it should not be confused with mathematics—actually the relationship is no closer than that between mathematics and the other business subjects. The student with a background in accounting will find many opportunities to capitalize upon his knowledge.

TOPICS FOR DISCUSSION

1. Could management utilize a source-and-application-of-funds analysis prepared by an accountant?

2. Do you consider the certified public accountant a professional?

3. A business-firm balance sheet indicates the financial position of an organization with respect to asset values and the corresponding claims of creditors and owners on the assets as of a given point in time. Present this statement about the balance sheet by use of a formula.

4. How do you distinguish between a managerial accountant and a financial accountant?

5. Is there a difference between the accountant's concept of business income and the economist's concept of profit?

6. What are some of the things that a banker might learn from studying the company's balance sheet?

7. What might he learn from studying the income statement?

8. Why is it often considered necessary for an industrial-management major to study cost accounting?

9. In what ways have events of the past twenty-five years increased the importance of accounting?

10. "I wouldn't like to be an accountant. I couldn't stand to sit at a desk eight hours a day working with figures." Discuss this statement.

11. How would the following people make use of some accounting knowledge in their jobs: a businessman, lawyer, medical doctor, minister, or scientist.

CASE 22–1

THE BLUE DRUG STORE

The Blue Drug Store opened in 1958. It was located in Johnsville, a town of 5,000 population. The town has some light industry, although it is principally noted as the trading center for a farming area. Mr. Allen, operator of the store, considered his business quite successful until 1963. At the end of 1963, he felt that he had had an unsuccessful year. In an effort to determine the source of his trouble, he secured average ratios for drug stores of his size and operating in his section of the country. He converted his own income statement to percentages and then found that his ratios compared with the average as follows:

Blue Drug Income Statement		Blue Drug Ratios	Average Ratios
Net Sales	$97,090	100.00%	100.00%
Cost of Goods Sold	70,200	72.00	66.00
Gross Margin	$26,890	28.00	34.00
Expenses:			
Proprietor's salary	$ 7,540	7.8	7.0
Wages	10,153	10.5	10.0
Rent	2,291	2.4	2.0
Heat	316	0.3	0.2
Light and power	718	0.7	0.8
Taxes	813	0.8	0.9
Insurance	308	0.3	0.4
Interest paid	360	0.4	0.1
Repairs	396	0.4	0.3
Delivery	1,260	1.2	0.2
Advertising	475	0.5	1.3
Depreciation	602	0.7	1.1
Bad debts loss	1,200	1.5	0.2
Telephone	195	0.2	0.2
Miscellaneous	928	1.0	1.3
Total Expense	$27,555	28.7	26.0
Net Business Profit (loss) ...	−685	−0.7	8.0
Add Proprietor's Withdraw .	7,540	7.8	7.0
Net Accounting Income ..	$ 6,855	7.1	15.0

Average Merchandise Investment:
Blue Drug Store .... $14,040, Average Store $17,000
Stock Turnover, Blue Drug —5, Average Store, 3.5

From studying the foregoing comparative ratios, what conclusions could you draw about the operation of the Blue Drug Store?

SELECTED REFERENCES

Anthony, R. N. *Management Accounting*. 3d ed. Homewood, Ill.: Richard D. Irwin, Inc., 1964.

Dickey, R. I. (ed.). *Accountants' Cost Handbook*. 2d ed. New York: The Ronald Press Co., 1960.

Foulke, R. A. *Practical Financial Statement Analysis*. 5th ed. New York: McGraw-Hill Book Co., 1962.

Kohler, E. L. *Accounting for Management*. Englewood Cliffs, N.J.: Prentice-Hall, Inc., 1965.

Wixon, R., and R. G. Cox. *Principles of Accounting*. New York: The Ronald Press Co., 1961.

23

Budgetary Control in
Business Management

CONTROL THROUGH BUDGETING

In some respects, a business firm may be compared to a railway train. Before the train starts its journey, there must be plans regarding its destination and the time of arrival. The plans also include certain stops along the way to take on and discharge people and goods or to service the train. The business firm may look on the fiscal year as a journey. In starting on that journey, plans must be made in terms of what the firm hopes to accomplish by the end of the year, and also plans must indicate just what the situation should be at intervals throughout the year. The railway train has a schedule of operations; the business firm has a budget.

The budget is a plan summarizing the estimated future operations of the business. Budgets may be expressed in dollars, physical units to be handled, or both. A more formal definition defines budgeting as follows: "The budget is a co-ordinated financial plan for a business enterprise. It includes estimates of sales, production, purchases, labor costs, expenses, and financial operations. Its purpose is to plan, co-ordinate, and control the activities of various divisions and departments of the business." [1]

Perhaps the simplest example of a budget would be the family budget.

[1] Richard N. Owens, *Management of Industrial Enterprises* (4th ed.; Homewood, Ill.: Richard D. Irwin, Inc., 1961), p. 655.

Here, the family anticipates its monthly income and plans expenditures accordingly. Such advanced planning is helpful in preventing over-extension of buying power and in preventing overspending in certain areas at the expense of deprivation in other areas. The budget is the device whereby financial plans are formalized. Without financial planning, a business would operate in a manner comparable to a ship that sails without navigational aids. When we think of the budget as a formal statement of financial plans, it becomes a less formidable object.

In practice, a going business concern executes financial planning through a number of budgets operating concurrently. One source states that the average manufacturing firm requires as many as ten or more separate budgets to have complete budgetary control.[2] Each department of the company that receives funds, pays out funds, uses materials, or performs a service may have a budget. The plans set forth in the individual budgets may be summarized in a "master budget," which sets over-all company goals. The period of time covered by the budget varies, depending upon the nature of the company's business and its production cycle. As a rule, the budget period will correspond to the accounting cycle; a year being the most typical period used. Although the budget may be developed to cover a year's operations, it may be broken down into quarters or even months. Most business firms are to some extent seasonal, and the budget may be broken into segments reflecting the seasonal pattern. The budget is a control device, and as such the company must continually compare actual performance against the budgeted objectives. Dividing the budget period into short time segments facilitates these comparisons.

Advantages and Limitations of the Budget

Since the budget is a device used in planning, many of its advantages are evident to the student. These advantages may be summarized as follows:

1. It establishes objectives for the firm and provides a basis for evaluating performance.
2. It forces management to plan the use of money, labor, and materials.
3. It helps in defining the limits of an executive's responsibility.
4. It provides a means of predetermining financial needs.
5. It signals management when performance deviates from budget standards and calls attention to potential trouble spots.

2 *Ibid.*, Chap. 37.

6. It forces a depth of planning that would be unlikely to take place in its absence.

All of the foregoing are important contributions of a well-organized and well-managed budgeting operation. In the larger firm, formalized budgeting is usually accepted practice. In the case of the smaller firm, budgeting is often absent or very inadequate. The great contribution of budgeting to the smaller firm lies in the fact that it forces management to engage in a formal type of advanced planning and that it is a helpful device in establishing and clarifying lines of authority. Firms that attempt to operate without advanced financial planning are incurring many unnecessary risks. Of course, some financial planning may be possible without the budget as a tool; but in the case of a sizable firm, it becomes almost a necessity that such planning be formalized through the budget. The small firm can profit from budgetary control in that the budgets used may be simplified in keeping with the scope and nature of the business. All businesses, regardless of size, may benefit from adequate accounting records, and any business having such records can profit from budgetary control.

As with all control devices, the budget faces certain limitations. Close cooperation between departments is required in establishing budgets. If the budget is to be a successful control device, all departments must work together to reach the goals established in the budget. This requires respect for, and confidence in, the budget as established. Sometimes budgets are designed by higher level executives and imposed upon lower executives. When the budget is imposed in this manner, the cooperation necessary to make it a success will be hard to achieve. To install budgetary control requires a good accounting system, good personnel relations, and clearly defined lines of authority. Many companies are weak in these areas, and thus budgeting becomes difficult for them. The point to be made here is that budgeting cannot be applied to a company irrespective of its internal organization and managerial efficiency. Budgeting can never be a substitute for poor management.

If the budget is to serve its purpose, it must be properly used. The goals established in the budget are not inflexible goals or guideposts. In making the budget, management can never foresee all the events that may affect the performance of the business. Thus, it is essential that the budget be regarded as a flexible tool and that it be adjusted as events deem necessary. If a budget is established and treated as an inflexible guide, real damage to managerial efficiency may result. The budget will not be misused if management properly understands its purpose and function.

Constructing the Budget

The procedure followed in constructing budgets will vary from one company to another, depending upon such factors as size and organization. Often the procedure begins with a meeting between top management and the department heads. In this meeting, the over-all conditions of the business will be discussed. Past performance will be viewed and future trends affecting operations will be evaluated. Companywide financial objectives may be set forth and certain performance objectives studied. The break-even chart shown in Figure 23–1 is a device for

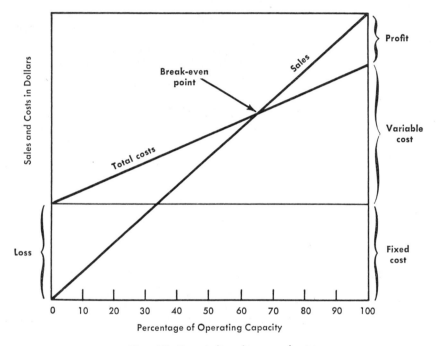

Fig. 23–1. A break-even chart.

showing the performance levels that must be sought in the broad terms of costs and sales. The chart takes into account the fixed costs and variable costs in relation to sales and shows the average percentage of capacity at which the firm must operate in order to show a profit.

After a general conference between top management and department heads, the department heads may return to their respective areas and construct the departmental budgets. Department heads will usually make use of the executives in the department to assist in preparing the budget. The department may also call on budget specialists in the accounting department for assistance in preparing a detailed presentation. When the departmental budget estimates are complete, they may be submitted to the budget officer of the company—often the controller or treasurer of the company. The budget officer may suggest changes to department heads prior to the general-budget meeting. When the general-budget meeting is called, each department head submits his budget and answers any criticisms that may arise. In this meeting, final adjustments are made, and the various budgets are submitted for approval to the president or to some other officer who has been given the authority to approve. Upon final approval, copies are made of the budgets and distributed to all interested parties.

In the course of preparing the budgets for the departments, conflicts may arise and adjustments must be made. Since the activities of the departments are interrelated, the performance of each department depends upon others. For example, the sales department cannot construct a sales budget without considering the capacity of the production department. And conversely, the production department cannot establish a budget independent of the estimates of the sales department. Thus, the budgeting process must be accompanied by a free flow of information between departments. Where differences cannot be adjusted by the departments themselves, the budgetary officer, or top management itself, may be required to render a decision.

REPRESENTATIVE TYPES OF BUDGETS

The Sales Budget

In many respects, the sales budget is the most fundamental of all company budgets. Through the sales budget, the company estimates the quantity of the product that will be sold during the coming period. This estimate becomes the basis for production planning and other key operations of the company. The term "sales budget" may include two elements: (1) the forecast of sales and (2) the budget of expenses anticipated in achieving the sales. The latter is often called the *sales-expense budget,* while the former may be referred to as the *sales forecast.* Our discussion of the sales budget will be largely in terms of its function as a forecast.

The forecast of sales volume is of such vital importance that the top management of the company, along with various staff assistants, may join the sales executives in making the estimate. There are two basic approaches to making the sales estimate, often referred to as the breakdown method and the buildup method. In the breakdown method, the estimates are made at the top of the management structure—usually by general management executives; ranking sales executives; and staff executives such as economists, statisticians, and market-research specialists. The total estimates made are broken down by territory and product line and handed down to those on the operational level. Many feel that this method is not as satisfactory as the buildup method of forecasting. In the buildup method, district sales managers—even individual salesmen—are asked to submit estimates of what they think can be achieved in the coming period. These estimates are passed upward from district managers to territorial managers to regional managers and on to the general sales manager of the company. At each level of management, the estimates may be revised in view of the wider knowledge of conditions that may prevail at that level. When the estimates reach the level of general company management, the top executives of the company in conference with staff specialists may make further refinements. When the forecast has been thus built up, it is subdivided and handed down to the operating level. A district manager who initially estimated that he could sell $500,000 worth of the product for the coming year may receive from the top his share of the volume to be achieved in the form of a quota. The quota may be very close to his original estimate of what he could do, or it may be more or less. If the quota is not too far from his original estimate, he has the satisfaction of feeling that he has participated in setting his company's goals. Of course, if the quota assigned is far removed from his original estimate, he may feel that his opinions were not valued. In general, lower-level sales executives are reasonably proficient in estimating their territorial potentials.

The Production Budget

The production budget sets forth the plan for producing the quantity of the product called for in the sales budget. A principal feature of this budget is the proposal for spreading the required production over time. The sales of many products are seasonal and this may pose a production problem. Should production be spread evenly throughout the year while the product is stored in anticipation of the selling season, or should production coincide more closely with the high and low points in the selling season? The answer to this will often depend upon the nature of the product and the characteristics of the market served. If the product is one in which storage is very costly, or one subject to very rapid style changes, it may be advisable to plan production to coincide with sales on a seasonal basis. Also, if the demand for the product is fickle and subject to change, risk can be minimized by keeping production closely tied to sales. On the other hand, seasonal production is often expensive. It is difficult to vary the labor force from season to season, and seasonal production also results in periods during which the facilities are not in use. Management likes to avoid the depreciation and investment cost on idle equipment. The production budget encourages the advanced planning necessary where decisions are to be made on the scheduling of production.

The production budget will usually be prepared in the production department and forwarded to the budget department or principal budgeting officer. The budget will indicate the plans that the production department has for meeting the requirements of the sales department. These plans may entail the purchase of new machines or the hiring of additional labor. The sales estimates may call for more production than present facilities will be able to turn out. This presents management with the problem of scaling sales estimates downward or increasing plant facilities. It is important to note that the preparation of the production budget calls attention to the capacity of the department relative to producing quantities specified in the sales budget. This planning is essential to the coordination of the production and sales functions.

The Purchase Budget

The purchase budget summarizes the purchasing department's plans for acquiring the materials and supplies needed to produce the products as outlined in the production budget. Many companies do not use a purchase budget, leaving the timing of purchases to the production department. It would seem that among the larger companies the purchase budget is generally used, while the smaller companies do not make extensive use of it.[3] If the purchasing department has the authority to select sources of supply and negotiate prices, much can be gained from the advanced planning of the purchase operation. Prices of items to be purchased may show seasonal variations, and the purchasing department may weigh the savings through purchasing at a lower price against the cost of carrying the item in storage. Also, the savings from quantity purchasing are weighed against carrying costs. If the purchasing department is to make decisions on these matters, advanced planning becomes essential.

The Labor Budget

The labor budget is based upon the production budget. It shows the amount of labor required from month to month in order to produce the quantities specified in the production budget. The extent to which the labor supply may be varied to coincide with the production schedule

[3] W. B. England, *Procurement, Principles and Cases* (4th ed.; Homewood, Ill.: Richard D. Irwin, Inc., 1962), Chap. 18.

depends upon the nature of the employment and the policies of the company. If skilled labor is required in production, the company may be reluctant to lay off such labor in slack periods for fear of losing the workers. This becomes a consideration in production planning as revealed in the production budget. Where a company makes different products, and where seasonal patterns in the demand for the products may be different, it may be possible to shift workers from one product or division of the company to another. A labor budget made out along product lines will facilitate the advanced planning needed in shifting labor.

The Advertising Budget

Effective advertising requires advanced planning. Advertising plans are often summarized in the advertising budget. Such a budget will consist of several parts: first, the amount of the appropriation will be established; second, the media to be used will be determined; and third, the time for the release of the advertising will be determined. There are several methods of determining the advertising appropriation.[4] The choice of media calls for advanced planning in that, frequently, space and time must be bought well in advance of the appearance date. Also, the necessity to coordinate the media used makes such planning essential. The release of advertising relative to time may depend upon the seasonal character of the demand for the product. This factor is also influenced by the availability of certain media. The effectiveness of an advertising program often depends upon the way in which its many components are coordinated. This often makes it desirable that the advertising "package" be complete before the first advertising appears. As a rule, an advertising program is released subject to the approval of management. The budget presents to management a summary of advertising proposals. The budget will be supplemented by other materials necessary to give management a preview of a complete program.

Other Expense Budgets

Every department in a company may have operating expenses. An expense budget may be required as a controlling device for each department. There may be administrative expense budgets, maintenance budgets, research budgets, and others. In each case, a major objective of the budget is to force advanced planning and to give the departments a goal in their efforts to control costs. If expense budgets are

---

[4] A. W. Frey, *Advertising* (3d ed.; New York: The Ronald Press Co., 1961), Chap. 18.

realistically drawn, they become a helpful tool in evaluating departmental performance.

The Cash Budget

The day-to-day operation of a business normally requires that certain transactions be handled on a cash basis. For example, the payroll usually involves a cash outlay. To meet such requirements, a certain amount of cash must be "on hand" when needed. The cash budget is a method of forecasting the cash position of the company at a future date. It may attempt to show the cash position by months and be projected several months into the future. A company may receive cash through selling its product or service for cash or through collecting receivables. At the same time, the company may be paying out cash for on-the-spot purchases of goods and services and through meeting its accounts payable (goods previously bought on credit). Thus, it is important to forecast the relationship between cash income and cash outlay and to plan accordingly. The cash budget usually forecasts:

1. The estimated cash that will be on hand at the beginning of each month.
2. The cash income anticipated during each month.
3. The cash outlay anticipated during each month.
4. The estimated cash that will be on hand at the end of each month.

Through determining in advance the anticipated cash needs, a firm may make provisions to borrow. Many firms operating a business with seasonal sales receive their income only during certain months. They may have to make cash payments on a regular basis; and to meet these obligations, borrowing is sometimes necessary.

Estimated Financial Statements

The budgets discussed in the preceding pages present income and cost estimates for the company during the period covered. Based on these estimates, summary financial statements may also be projected. A balance-sheet budget will contain estimates of assets, liabilities, and capital for the period. These estimates, when compared to past balance sheets, may forewarn of changes in the capital structure of the company. Also, the summary estimates of items on the balance sheet may call attention to inaccuracies in certain of the other budgets. For instance, the estimated credit sales as forecast in an "accounts-receivable budget" may show up as being excessive when shown as the asset *accounts receivable* on the balance sheet.

The estimated-income statement is sometimes called *the operating budget.* The items on the estimated-income statement are derived from the budgets already prepared. The estimated-sales figure is derived from the sales budget; costs are estimated from the production and expense budgets. The estimated-income statement summarizes the effects of the projections made in the various budgets. It may call attention to certain cost estimates that appear out of line when compared to other cost items or to income. Figuratively speaking, it serves the purpose of calling attention to certain rough spots in the road before such are encountered and passed. If management is warned in advance that a certain cost item threatens to be excessive, corrective action may be undertaken. Figure 23–2 shows an estimated-income statement for the John Fisher Merchandising Company mentioned in Chapter 22.

JOHN FISHER

Income Statement for Six-Month Period Ending Dec. 31, 1965

and

Estimated Income Statement for First Six Months, 1966

		Actual Statement Last Half 1960		Estimated Statement First Half 1961
Net Sales		$119,200		$128,000
Cost of goods sold		94,100		99,500
Gross profit on sales		25,100		28,500
Salaries of clerks	$7,800		$8,500	
Advertising	2,500		3,000	
Deprec. store equip.	900		900	
Store supplies used	400		500	
Misc. selling exp.	1,600		1,700	
Office salaries	4,400		4,600	
Rent	2,000		2,000	
Deprec. office equip.	300		300	
Loss from bad debts	200		250	
Misc. gen. expense	1,000		1,100	
Total expense		21,100		22,850
Net Profit		4,000		5,650

Fig. 23–2. Estimated income statement for merchandising firm.

The Master Budget

The master budget is not a budget in the strict sense of the term but rather a restatement in summary form of important figures contained in other budgets. It contains a summary of the estimated operating statement; the cash situation as revealed in the cash budget; and account balances such as receivables, payables, inventories, assets, and expenses. It serves the purpose of bringing together totals from other budgets and presenting the estimated financial structure in its broad sense.

The Budget in Operation

From the foregoing discussion, one should observe that the construction of a budget is a venture requiring the cooperation of all departments within the company. This is exemplified by the fact that a departmental budget does not stand alone but is dependent upon the accuracy of budgets in other departments for its own accuracy. As an example, the production budget is dependent upon the sales estimate, and labor and other expense budgets are dependent upon the accuracy of the sales and production budgets. One great advantage of a budgeting system is that it often forces a realization of this interdependence.

The preparation of a budget is but the beginning of a budgetary program. The value of the budget is realized when it is put to work as a control device. A certain amount of organization is required for the administration of budgetary control. Basically, the responsibility for the proper use of the system rests with the chief executive of the company. Budgetary control requires the active endorsement and support of top management. Larger companies may maintain a special department through which the budget is maintained and its controls activated. The chief budget officer may be the controller, or treasurer, of the company, or he may be an executive with a title such as that of budget director, budget supervisor, budget control officer, or manager of the control department. The budget control section is often centered within, or closely allied with, the accounting department. This is essential since the data necessary to budgetary control emanates from the accounting records. The function of the accounting department in budgetary control is indicated by one author as follows:

> The accounting department should establish an account classification corresponding to the form of the budget estimates. An account should be opened for each budget allotment, and all expenditures should be classified and entered to show the total expenditure under each classification. Monthly reports should be prepared by the accounting department to show for each income or expense item (1) the amount for the current month, (2) the amount for the same month last year, (3) the budget estimate, and (4) the amount of the current month over or under the budget. Such reports should be prepared soon after the close of each month; and copies should be furnished to department heads, foremen, and other persons in the management.[5]

As data from actual operations are compared to the budget estimates, certain discrepancies will invariably show up. The discrepancies may be the result of unavoidable budgeting errors, unforeseen events affecting operations, or faulty operations due to poor management or other forces. The maintenance of the budget requires that frequent ad-

[5] Owens, *op. cit.*, p. 668.

justments be made to correct budgeting errors and bring the estimates into line with realistic goals. When a discrepancy is traceable not to inaccurate budgeting but to faulty operations, management is able to put the finger on the source of trouble and take corrective action. This is one of the paramount objectives of budgetary control. The continuous comparisons between *actual performance* and *budgeted performance* gives management something of a "quality-control" device. Of course, the accuracy of initial budget estimates, and the manner in which the budget is revised and kept up to date, determines its true worth as a yardstick of comparison. As in the case of all control devices, authoritative support flowing from top echelons downward is indispensable to a system of budgetary control.

Institutional Budgeting

Tax-supported institutions, and most private institutions, have budgeting as a cornerstone of their financial operations. Agencies of governments, schools, and hospitals are typical examples. These institutions operate on appropriations granted by legislative or other governing bodies. In the case of such institutions, the budget may serve two fundamental purposes: (1) It is the tool through which the appropriation is requested, and (2) it is a controlling device used in the expenditure of the appropriation. Many private institutions (private in contrast to tax-supported institutions) draw financial support from religious groups, civic groups, and charitable foundations. In requesting financial support, a budget is presented to explain and justify the requests made. Also, private institutions are often governed by boards of directors who are not a part of the direct management. These directors may have the power to approve or reject financial proposals made by the institution. The active management of the institution will use the proposed budget as a basis for requesting the approval of the directors.

In the case of the tax-supported institution, the budget is the central instrument in requesting funds. As guardians of the public treasury, elected officials are not supposed to appropriate money except for justifiable needs. Frequently, public revenues may not be adequate to meet all requests, in which case the more vital needs must be distinguished from the less vital. The proposed budget, showing in detail how the funds requested will be spent, becomes an important factor in determining the relative urgency of requests. Budgets presented by agencies of the government to the legislators are often "trimmed" by legislative committees. With the approval of the budget, the requesting institution is authorized to operate with the funds thus established. Usually, the approval of a budget establishes a fixed sum for use during the budget period. On occasion, when unforeseen events arise, the institution may request additional funds through a supplementary budget.

When the budget is approved by the appropriate authority, it begins its function as a control device. The approved budget indicates the amount available to finance operations. If this is less than the initial budget requests, changes must be made to bring operations in line with the approved budget. Having been informed of the funds available, operating departments may establish monthly or weekly schedules of allowable expenditures. By comparing actual expenditures to scheduled expenditures, the department operates within the budget. In the absence of some such planning, appropriated amounts might well be expended before the end of the budget period.

Career Opportunities

From the standpoint of personnel, budgetary control and accounting are closely allied. Accordingly, much that was said about career opportunities in the area of accounting will apply to those working with budgets. In many cases, the budgetary-control section will be a division of the accounting department; and even if it should be organized as a separate department, the relationship with accounting will be very close. The maintenance of the budget and its application as an operating device involves continuous use of accounting data and thus makes it dependent upon the accounting function. In a large organization, specialists may be employed to work with the budget on a continuous basis. As to whether it is desirable for the young person to become a specialist in budgetary control would be a matter of opinion. As in the case of many specialists, he runs the risk of becoming so narrow in his area of operation that he may be handicapped in moving into administrative positions. On the other hand, the person employed in budgetary control may have an opportunity to work with many departments and become acquainted with many executives in the company. If he is an astute observer, he may learn much in addition to the technical aspects of budgeting. The value of becoming known in the company has been summarized by one author as follows:

A good rule of thumb within all of industry is that the positions that permit a young man to establish contact with a number of sections—that permit him to be seen and observed by a variety of department supervisors—afford more opportunity for advancement than do assignments that keep him within the confines of his own department.[6]

---

[6] Gavin A. Pitt, *The Twenty-Minute Lifetime: A Guide to Career Planning* (Englewood Cliffs, N.J.: Prentice-Hall, Inc., 1959), p. 67.

TOPICS FOR DISCUSSION

1. Do you believe that a family should budget its income and expenditures?

2. What are some of the general advantages of budgetary control to the business enterprise?

3. "The establishment of a sound budget at the start of a period makes the management of the business automatic for the rest of that period." Do you agree with this?

4. Why is it sometimes difficult to budget labor cost?

5. Why should the operator of a retail store bother to establish an advertising budget?

6. Can an individual, a student for example, benefit from constructing a cash budget to cover the school year?

7. "People who make out government budgets often overstate their requirements because they know that the legislators want to have something to cut in order to show the people back home that they are economy minded." What do you think about this statement?

8. "When government agencies are appropriated funds, they will always spend the full amount for fear that failure to do so will result in next year's budget being cut." Comment on this statement.

9. How is the budget used as an operation tool?

10. What do you consider to be the requirements of a budget director as outlined in the chapter?

CASE 23–1

THE ANTHONY CYCLE COMPANY, INC.

The Anthony Cycle Company manufactured a full line of bicycles along with a limited line of motor bikes and motor scooters. The firm employed 500 people, and the present owners (all the stock was owned by the Anthony family) were the third generation to operate the business. The company prided itself on the employment of skilled craftsmen, and there were numerous cases in which both fathers and sons worked in the plant. A policy of promotion from within had always been followed, and the present supervisory personnel up through the level of the plant manager were all men who had been trained on the job and had begun as hourly rated employees.

As early as 1960, the firm had begun to show a declining trend in profits. By 1965, the company was operating at a loss. The situation was frustrating to management in that for each year since 1960 the company had shown an increase in sales. In an effort to get at the root of the trouble, a management consulting firm was engaged to investigate and make recommendations.

At the completion of the investigation, the consulting firm made its recommendations to management. The consultants maintained that the major problem of the Anthony Cycle Company was the absence of effective control in both production and distribution. As a recommendation to correct the situation, it was suggested that a complete system of budgetary control should be established. Heretofore the only budgeting done by the company consisted of a sales forecast—usually a modification of the last year's sales—and a generalized financial budget that made a rough allocation of funds to be expended in the purchase of materials, on labor costs, and on advertising. Admittedly, this attempt at budgeting was used for purposes of initial planning and no effort was made to use the budget as an operations control.

Mr. Shannon, who was controller of the company, was enthusiastic in his support of the idea of a thorough system of budgetary control. In management conferences, he cited the many advantages that would derive from such a system. Other members of the company management did not question the need for more control but were skeptical of whether the Anthony company could operate under the discipline demanded in a budgetary system. Mr. Newman, a vice-president of the firm, pointed out that the management personnel in the plant at the operations level had never had experience in operating with a budget. He felt that the supervisors, who were not formally trained in management, would resist the record keeping that would be required by the budget. He also felt that many of them would look upon the assignment of quotas, and the establishment of expense budgets, as means of "checking up" on them and also as means of depriving them of a part of the authority they exercised.

The consultants agreed that the installation of budgetary control would meet with some resistance, especially at the beginning. But they pointed out that the Anthony firm had little choice in the matter if it hoped to restore its operations to a profitable level. Management accepted this view and began discussing ways of selling the idea of the budgetary system to many of those who would be involved in its operation.

How might the Anthony Cycle Company go about convincing supervisory personnel in operations of the necessity for instituting budgetary control?

SELECTED REFERENCES

Anderson, D. R., and L. A. Schmidt. *Practical Controllership*. Rev. ed. Homewood, Ill.: Richard D. Irwin, Inc., 1961.

George, C. S. *Management in Industry*. 2d ed. Englewood Cliffs, N.J.: Prentice-Hall, Inc., 1964.

Heiser, H. C. *Budgeting: Principles and Practice*. New York: The Ronald Press Co., 1959.

Owens, Richard N. *Management of Industrial Enterprises*. 4th ed. Homewood, Ill.: Richard D. Irwin, Inc., 1961.

Voris, W. *The Management of Production*. New York: The Ronald Press Co., 1960.

24

The Use of Statistics
in Business Management

IMPORTANCE OF STATISTICAL DATA

Much of the information used in decision making in business may be expressed in a quantitative form. Data on the operations of the company, the status of competitors, the conditions of the specific market for the product, and the conditions prevailing in the economy as a whole are expressed in statistical terms. The study of *statistics* is essentially concerned with procedures in the collection and analysis of information existing in the form of "figures." It is essential that the business executive have a basic knowledge of statistical techniques; it is especially important that he be able to interpret and analyze certain statistical information placed at his disposal. Business firms often employ professional statisticians to handle the more complex studies and to assist management in the interpretation and analysis of information. In this capacity, the statistician may function as a staff assistant. In smaller companies, staff specialists may not be available to assist management, and, even in the largest companies, the executive will not have a statistician at his side on every occasion. It is imperative that all executives have some knowledge of statistical analysis, as more and more information reaches him in a quantified form. The development and use of the electronic computer have been important factors in making available to management increasing quantities of statistical information. There is every reason to believe that the executive in the years ahead will need a greater knowledge of statistical procedures than that required of his predecessor.

In the foregoing, we have stressed management's need for a knowledge of statistical procedures as an aid to the intelligent use of business information. A study of the management of a modern enterprise will reveal that statistical devices are widely used as operational aids. Marketing studies gather information through a process of sampling, and statistical techniques are used in selecting the sample from the population, or group, under study. In the production department, we find statistical techniques used in maintaining quality control. The personnel or labor-relations department may make use of statistical procedures in wage-and-salary administration. In the accounting department, some aspects of auditing may be handled on a sample basis—and this again implies reliance upon statistical procedures. In recent years, advanced business machines, including electronic computers, have appeared on the scene to open up new dimensions in the collection, analysis, and interpretation of data. In many respects, these machines may be looked upon as a means of extending the capacity and scope of the statistician. If one is to understand the potentiality of a device such as the computer and to employ it as an operational tool, a knowledge of statistical procedures is essential.

THE PRESENTATION OF STATISTICAL DATA

Ratios

There are many ways of presenting statistical data. The method of presentation often depends upon the purpose that the data are to serve. Basically, statistical findings are expressed either in numerical values or as relative values. We might report that a study of family income in the United States for a certain year showed the following distribution:

> 3,500,000 families received incomes of $10,000 or more
> 17,000,000 families had incomes between $5,000 and under $10,000
> 16,000,000 families had incomes between $2,000 and under $5,000
> 7,000,000 families had incomes under $2,000

A manufacturer producing a product that would normally be purchased only by those families in the $10,000 or above bracket would be interested in the specific number of families in this category; i.e., the 3,500,000 families would indicate the scope of his market. On the other hand, a person interested in studying the pattern of the distribution of income in the country would find the data more meaningful if the number of families in each income category was expressed as a percentage of the total number of families. Expressed as percentages (figures rounded) we see that 8 per cent of the families are in the first (highest) category, 39 per cent in the second, 37 per cent in the third, and 16 per cent in the fourth, or lowest, bracket. Furthermore, with the distribution expressed as percentages, we are able to compare the pattern in the current year with that prevailing in preceding years; and it is also possible to compare the pattern existing in one region with that of another. It is very difficult for the individual to grasp the meaning of large numbers and to readily make comparisons. When numbers are expressed as relatives, they are presented in reference to a fixed base (the total number of families in the foregoing illustration) and are thus reduced to terms that demand less difficulty of comprehension.

Percentages represent perhaps the most commonly used ratio, but there are numerous other ratios used. Man-hours worked, output per hour, and income per person are examples. Each trade, or line of activity, will have its significant ratios that are in common usage. All numbers that refer to the real world are ratios in one form or another, and the problem is not one of whether to use a ratio but that of discovering a base that will be most meaningful to the user of the data.[1]

Tables

Quantitative information is most frequently presented in the form of tables. The purpose of a table is to summarize numerical data and present the findings in a form adapted to the intended use. Tables may be extensive collections of statistical data as represented by those found in the United States Census reports, or they may summarize a particular class of data. Table 24-1 shows a simplified table setting forth the estimated world production of natural rubber for the years 1957–1963 inclusive. Tables should be accurately titled, classifications properly labeled, and the source of the data in the table should be given.

Where a mass of numerical data has been assembled, it would be impossible to present in tabular form each individual statistic. To present such information in an understandable form, it is often necessary to rearrange and classify it in some manner. One way of achieving this goal is to arrange the data to form a *frequency distribution*. In constructing a frequency distribution, we divide the data into classes, usually in an array ranging from the highest class to the lowest or vice versa. If we were to interview a thousand college students to ascertain their

[1] Boyd L. Nelson, *Elements of Modern Statistics* (New York: Appleton-Century-Crofts, Inc., 1961), Chap. 2.

Table 24–1. A Simplified Statistical Table

Estimated World Production of Natural Rubber
1957–1963

Year	Far East	Tropical Africa	Africa	Total
1957	1,756,500	30,000	116,000	1,902,500
1958	1,807,500	26,250	123,750	1,957,500
1959	1,870,900	28,100	141,000	2,040,000
1960	1,829,017	29,733	141,250	2,000,000
1961	1,922,263	28,987	138,750	2,090,000
1962	1,943,971	28,289	142,000	2,115,000
1963	1,879,235	36,265	147,000	2,062,500

SOURCE: Business and Defense Services Administration (shipments in long tons).

individual weights, we would end up with a thousand statements each quoting the weight in figures. This mass of data in its original form would tell the observer very little. To present the data in a meaningful manner, we might arrange the weights in an array ranging from the lightest to the heaviest. If the lightest student weighed 90 pounds and the heaviest weighed 200 pounds, we might construct a frequency distribution establishing class-intervals of 5 pounds. We would then be able to show the number of students in each 5-pound interval. Our distribution would begin as follows:

    90– 94 lbs. .... 85 students
    95– 99 lbs. .... 91 students
    100–104 lbs. .... 110 students
    105–109 lbs. .... 115 students
        etc.

The size of the class-interval used (in the above example, 5 pounds) would depend upon the nature of the data and the specific use to be made of the findings. For example, in the above illustration, if the purpose of collecting the information was to have it serve as a guide to the determination of the necessary strength specifications required in student desks, an interval of 10 pounds might provide satisfactory information.

Perhaps a majority of our statistical tables present data in the form of a grouped frequency distribution. Without such grouping certain types of data would be much less manageable. Table 24–2 is an example of data presented through a process of grouping. The objective is to show a distribution of life expectancy according to age. Rather than attempt to show the number of persons for each yearly age group, the data is presented in summary form by establishing five-year intervals beginning at the age of one and running through the age of twenty-five. In this case, the five-year interval seems adequate to give the reader a

Table 24–2. Tabular Presentation of Grouped Data (Life Expectancy of Selected Age Groups, by Sex—1962 Data)

Age Group	Average Remaining Years	
	Male	Female
1–5 yrs.	68.4	74.9
5–10	64.6	71.1
10–15	59.8	66.2
15–20	54.9	61.3
20–25	50.2	56.4

SOURCE: U.S. Department of Health, Education, and Welfare.

quick picture of average life expectancy according to age.

The data found in tables showing individual statistics and those showing grouped frequency distribution will usually permit graphic presentation in the form of charts. Charts frequently present the identical data found in a corresponding table. The chart may lend itself to a quick and more generalized interpretation while the table may, in certain cases, provide more specific information.

Graphic Presentation

We are all to some degree familiar with the use of charts to present statistical findings. When such material is presented graphically, the reader is able to grasp the significance quickly and to comprehend certain relationships that may not be so obvious in other forms of presentation. In this respect, the chart is an "aid to visualization" in the study of data and their relationships. Another important function of the chart is its use as a "working tool." Certain classes of economic behavior may be plotted on a single chart and the statistician, through studying the relationship between the resulting curves, may be able to draw conclusions concerning the relationships of the data. Sales curves for several time periods, when superimposed upon a chart, may reveal the comparative success of sales for the several periods. In this limited treatment of graphic presentation, we will concern ourselves primarily with the chart as a means of presenting statistical information. Students will have a chance to become familiar with charts as analytical devices in the more advanced courses.

The Bar Chart

Most students will recall from the study of algebra that points are located on a chart through coordinate axes relative to a horizontal X axis and a vertical Y axis. This concept is basic to all forms of graphic presentation where quantitative relationships are concerned. If the relationship shown involves the element of time, the time span will be plotted on the horizontal X axis with the other quantity shown on the Y axis. Where time is not a factor, the measures plotted in relation to the axes is a matter of the individual situation. If the chart is clearly labeled, no confusion should arise over this point. One of the simplest forms of graphic presentation is the *bar chart*. Figure 24–1 shows such

HIGHWAY CONSTRUCTION CONTRACTS AWARDED: 1947 TO 1963

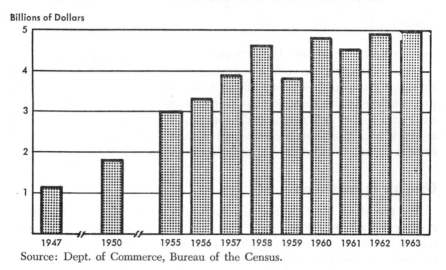

Source: Dept. of Commerce, Bureau of the Census.

Fig. 24–1. The vertical bar chart.

a chart indicating the highway construction contracts awarded 1947–1963. The height of each bar relative to the Y axis indicates the volume for that year. The simple bar chart may be elaborated to show a number of relationships on the same chart. Figure 24–2 uses the bar chart to show the relationship between federal receipts and expenditures, 1955–1965. The bars have been distinguished by a process of "cross-hatching," and an identifying legend has been included.

The Pie Chart

Another simple method of graphic presentation is the "pie chart" in which total amounts are represented as a circle (pie), and the components contributing to the total are shown as divisions of the circle (slices of the pie). Figure 24–3 shows such a chart. Cross-hatching has been used to differentiate divisions of the circle. It is also quite common to observe charts that make use of pictorial matter to drama-

RECEIPTS AND EXPENDITURES—FEDERAL BUDGET DOLLAR: 1955 TO 1965

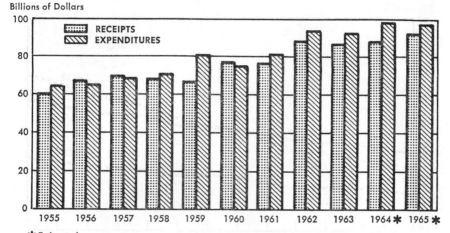

Billions of Dollars
100
80
60
40
20
0
RECEIPTS
EXPENDITURES
1955
1956
1957
1958
1959
1960
1961
1962
1963
1964 *
1965 *
* Estimated

Source: Chart prepared by Dept. of Commerce, Bureau of the Census. Data from Executive Office of the President, Bureau of the Budget.

Fig. 24–2. The bar chart used to show component relationships.

STATE AND LOCAL GOVERNMENT REVENUE AND EXPENDITURE: 1962
[In billions of dollars]

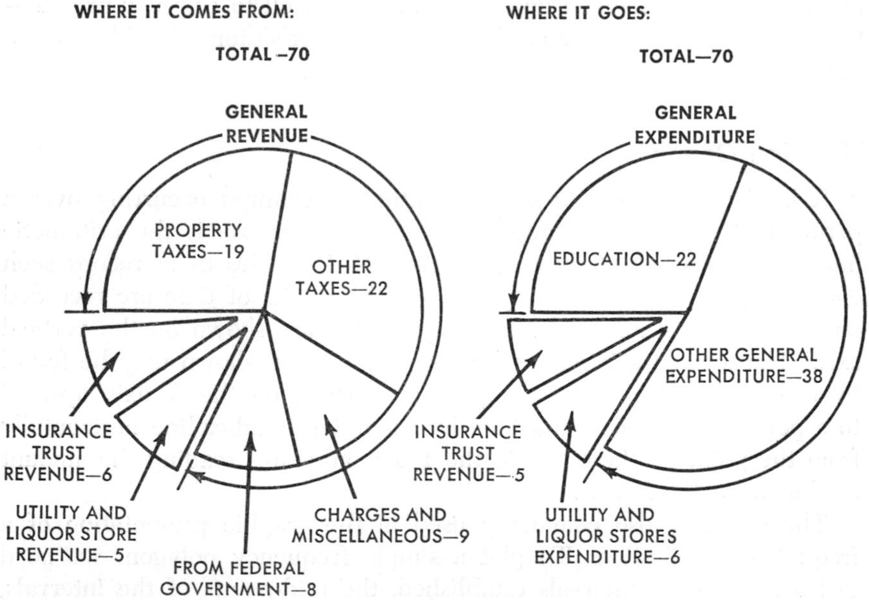

WHERE IT COMES FROM:
WHERE IT GOES:
TOTAL –70
TOTAL—70
GENERAL REVENUE
PROPERTY TAXES—19
OTHER TAXES—22
INSURANCE TRUST REVENUE—6
UTILITY AND LIQUOR STORE REVENUE—5
FROM FEDERAL GOVERNMENT—8
CHARGES AND MISCELLANEOUS—9
GENERAL EXPENDITURE
EDUCATION—22
OTHER GENERAL EXPENDITURE—38
INSURANCE TRUST REVENUE—5
UTILITY AND LIQUOR STORES EXPENDITURE—6

Fig. 24–3. The pie chart as a method of presentation (Department of Commerce, Bureau of the Census).

NATIONAL INCOME ORIGINATING IN DISTRIBUTION INDUSTRIES: 1950 TO 1963

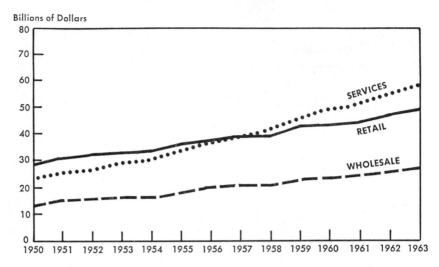

Fig. 24–4. The arithmetic line graph for a time series (Department of Commerce, Bureau of the Census).

tize the data presented. This can be very effective in presenting simplified data, but the method does not lend itself well to complex presentations of comparative data. Accuracy and precision should not be sacrificed for the mere sake of dramatic effect.

The Line Graph

It is often desirable to show quantitative changes occurring over a period of time. A chart appropriate to this purpose is the arithmetic line graph. The chart shown in Figure 24–4 enables us to record such changes in the form of a simple curve. The units of time are recorded on the horizontal axis while other quantities are shown on the vertical axis. The income originating for any of the years shown may be found by extending a line from the year as marked on the X axis upward to a point on the curve and then by extending another line horizontally from the point on the curve to the Y axis and thus reading the amount as shown on the Y axis.

The curve is also commonly used in the graphic presentation of a frequency distribution. To plot a simple frequency polygon, we need to know the class intervals established, the mid-points of the intervals, and the number of occurrences falling within each interval. The dis-

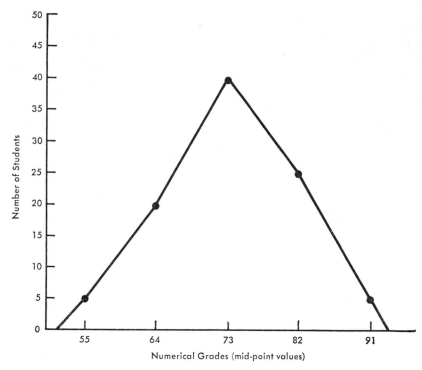

Fig. 24–5. A curve showing the distribution of the grades made by 100 students (a simplified example).

tribution of the grades made by one hundred students might be recorded as follows:

Grades (class-interval)	Mid-Point	Number of Students
51–59	55	5
60–68	64	20
69–77	73	40
78–86	82	25
87–95	91	5

The above distribution may be shown graphically in the form of a frequency polygon. The mid-point values may be indicated along the horizontal axis of the chart with the class frequencies indicated along the vertical axis. Figure 24–5 shows a frequency polygon derived in this manner. The student will realize that the smaller the class-intervals, the more closely the curve will correspond to the actual distribution of student grades.

Index Numbers

It is often necessary to present statistical data in a form that shows relative changes over time. The *index number* is a device for accomplishing this. The index number shows the relative change, if any, of prices, costs, quantities consumed, or similar factors between one period of time and some other period of time selected as the base period. Changes in the item under consideration are shown as percentage changes from the base. As an illustration, let us assume that at a certain place sugar was selling for 5¢ a pound in 1939 and that in the years following this date the price increased. We can show these changes by indicating the actual price change for selected years and also by computing an index number for each of the years selected. In computing an index number for each year, we will use 1939 as the base year and assign the price charged in that year a value of 100 (1939 = 100). Our calculations would then appear as follows:

Year	Price Per Pound	Index Number
1939	5¢	100
1943	6¢	120
1946	7¢	140
1949	8¢	160
1953	10¢	200
1956	12¢	240
1963	15¢	300

The value of computing an index number lies in the fact that it shows change as a ratio—percentage of a base period—and the significance of the change may be more readily appreciated when presented in this manner. Thus, instead of saying that between 1939 and 1949 sugar increased in price by 3¢ per pound, we may say that for this period there was a 60 per cent increase in the price of sugar, as can be ascertained by a glance at the index number computed.

The Weighted Index

The index number is even more valuable as a device to summarize the changes that have occurred in the cost of living as exemplified by the prices paid for a list of items normally purchased by the family. To show this, we will need to derive a single index number (ratio) that describes the changes that have occurred. If all the items on the list are of equal importance to the family, i.e., comparable dollars worth of each consumed per year, we would have little trouble in computing an index. We would record the price per unit for each item on the list, add the prices, and divide by the number of items. We would then select a base year to equal 100 and then express the changes relative to this base. But we know that when we consider family purchases not all items bought are of equal importance. For example, sugar and salt may have the same unit price of 15¢ per pound, and both items are bought by the family—but the family buys far more sugar than salt. If we gave sugar and salt the same importance in our index, we would not be presenting an accurate picture of family purchasing. This problem is solved by use of a "weighted index." In a weighted index, the items averaged are assigned relative weights according to their importance in the summary factor to be measured. If we are to come up with a single index that shows changes in consumer prices, we must assign relative weights to the items that are to be averaged. If we assume that the family buys 25 pounds of sugar for each pound of salt purchased, and assuming that both items sell for 15¢ per pound, we would assign sugar 25 times the weight assigned salt in our index. If the basic unit to be averaged is the pound, we would multiply the price of sugar by 25 and the price of salt by 1. With all the items in our list so weighted, they are then averaged; and the average is expressed as a relative of the base chosen. The base may be the average for a single year, or a number of years may be averaged and this used as a base. The *Consumers' Price Indexes* computed by the Bureau of Labor Statistics frequently use the years 1957–59 as a base (1957–59 = 100).

STATISTICAL AVERAGES

Importance of Averages

We have already encountered the concept of an average in discussing index numbers. More often than not, statistical data are communicated in terms of averages. If you were to ask your instructor to describe the grades made by the class on your last examination, he could do so in a number of ways. He could read off each individual grade, but this would be a cumbersome method and you might fail to get a clear picture of the class accomplishments. On the other hand, if he told you that the average for the class was a grade of C, his reply would be more meaningful. It would be even more meaningful if he were to tell you the kind of average referred to and something about the distribution of grades around the average.

The wide use of averages as a summary device in communication makes it very important that we know something of the different types of averages used. It is also important that we know how to evaluate averages, or more specifically, the type of average relative to its intended use. In our brief survey, we will mention some of the elementary approaches to the determination of averages and some of the ways in which averages are evaluated.

The Arithmetic Mean

The arithmetic mean is perhaps the most commonly used average. It is arrived at by adding a series of figures and dividing by the number in the series. Thus:

$$
\begin{array}{r}
10 \\
7 \\
5 \\
2 \\
1 \\
\hline
25 \\
\end{array}
$$
$$\frac{25}{5} = 5$$

The test of an average is whether it gives a realistic description of the data found in the series. If the numbers averaged are relatively close in value, the mean gives us a good description. But if there is a wide range in the values averaged, the mean will present a misleading picture. To use an old illustration, suppose there are ten people living on an island. One person on the island has an annual income of $100,000 and the other nine have no income. If we figure the average income per person on the island by the use of the arithmetic mean we will find that the average income is $10,000 per person (total income divided by the number of people on the island). A merchant seeing this figure would assume that each person living on the island is a good potential customer. Evidently, a surprise would be in store for him! From the foregoing, we may conclude that the mean as an average should be subject to question unless accompanied by certain explanatory data—some of which will be mentioned later.

The Median

Another type of average is the median—or as the name implies, the middle value. To find the median we arrange the data in an array ranging from the lowest to highest value:

$$
\begin{array}{c}
1 \\
3 \\
6 \\
7 \\
9 \\
\end{array}
$$

In this array, the middle figure, or median, is 6. If we had an even numbered series such as

$$1$$
$$2$$
$$3$$
$$4$$
$$5$$
$$6$$

we could determine the median by adding the *two* middle numbers (3 and 4) and dividing by two. In the above array, the median would be 3.5. The median tells us that there are just as many numbers above the average as there are below it. If you made an 80 on an examination and your teacher told you that the median grade was 78, you would know that your grade was among the top 50 per cent of the class. The median tells us something more about the distribution than could be determined from the mean, but there still might be extreme variations not apparent from either of these averages.

The Mode

The mode may be described as the item that occurs most frequently in a group of data. In a series such as

$$1$$
$$3$$
$$2$$
$$3$$
$$4$$
$$5$$
$$3$$

the mode would be 3. Obviously, as an average, the mode may be extremely misleading, especially if there exists a wide variation in the values in the series. There are occasions when on might want to know the most frequent statistic appearing in a group, and the mode would provide this information. Also, if the mean and the median are known, the mode adds further descriptive information.

There are other methods of computing averages, some of which are designed to restrict the influence of widely varying items in the series. Students will encounter these methods in courses dealing with elementary statistics.

Evaluating an Average

An average may be misleading because it is a summary statistic that provides only a very limited amount of information. Thus, it becomes necessary that we have some means of describing the manner in which the items vary from the mean average. This variability may be referred to as the *dispersion* of the data in the series or as the *deviation* from the mean. There are many ways of describing variability, some affording more precise information than others. A crude descriptive device is to cite the *range* of the data in the series. If the average grade in a class is 78, the range of grades may vary from a low of 56 to a high of 95. Since the range shows only two grades—highest and lowest—it would not be too helpful in telling us the true nature of the average. Another way of indicating dispersion would be to divide our series of values into four equal segments. By dividing the series into segments, we could ascertain how many values lie in the lowest 25 per cent and how many lie in the highest 25 per cent. Using this method, a measure known as the *quartile deviation* may be derived. The first quartile is the point on the scale of values below which 25 per cent of the values lie, and the third quartile is the point on the scale of values below which 75 per cent of the values may be found. Half the distance between the first and the third quartile is the *quartile deviation*. This measurement shows the range of values in the series after the highest 25 per cent and the lowest 25 per cent of the values have been eliminated from consideration. In a series characterized by the presence of a few very high values and a few very low values, the quartile deviation overcomes some of the limitations of the range as a measure of variation.

More Precise Measures

A more precise measure of variability would be one in which all the values in the series are considered in relation to the mean. Two such measures are the *average deviation* and the *standard deviation*. In computing the average deviation, we find the arithmetic mean for the series and then record the amount by which each value deviates from this mean. We then divide the sum of the deviations by the number of values in the series to get an average deviation. The following is a series of values with an arithmetic mean of 4 and with deviations from the mean as shown:

Values	Deviation from Mean
4	0
6	2
3	1
5	1
2	2
4	0
$\dfrac{24}{6} = 4$	$\dfrac{6}{6} = 1$

The average deviation shows the dispersion around the mean. A large deviation would indicate the presence of widely fluctuating values and would thus warn us to be cautious in accepting the arithmetic mean as being descriptive of the series. In the above example, the average deviation is 1 and the mean is 4. The intended use of the average would determine whether or not this amount of deviation would be cause for concern.

A measure of dispersion more commonly used in statistics is the *standard deviation*. This measure is used because it lends itself to certain mathematical manipulations that would not be possible with the average deviation. The standard deviation is computed by determining the arithmetic mean of the values in the series and then by recording deviations from the mean algebraically. The deviations are then squared, their mean determined, and the square root of the mean extracted. The following example will illustrate:

Values	Deviation	Deviation Squared
8	3	9
4	−1	1
6	1	1
5	0	0
2	−3	9
$\dfrac{25}{5} = 5$	0	$\dfrac{20}{5} = 4$

The arithmetic mean of the values is 5. The sum of the deviations from the mean when we add algebraically will always be zero. The deviations squared divided by the number of values gives us a mean of the squared deviations of 4. Thus, the *standard deviation* is the square root of 4, or 2. It is necessary to take the square root of the mean of the squared deviations in order to express the dispersion in terms of the units of the data. If the original values were expressed in feet, the mean of the squared deviations is in square feet; thus, taking the square root reduces the measure to the original unit of feet. The statistician may use more convenient methods to arrive at the standard deviation, but a discussion of such methods will be relegated to more advanced courses. It should also be pointed out that the same basic procedures may be used in computing deviations for grouped data. The mid-values of the class-intervals are averaged, and the deviations are shown in relation to the mean.

From the foregoing discussion, we have seen that there are several ways of computing an average. The average may not always give a representative picture of the data that it summarizes. By applying the methods discussed, we are able to determine the extent to which the average is a reasonable representation of the data as it exists. Because of the nature of averages, they are often used to convey an erroneous impression. The reader must always be on the alert to question the nature of an average cited and to examine it to determine its value as a summary descriptive device.

STATISTICAL SAMPLES

The Role of Sampling

Much of the work in statistics would not be possible without the technique of sampling. If we wanted to know the height of men in the United States, it would be impractical, if not impossible, to measure every male fourteen years of age or over. But through a process of sampling, we could reach valid conclusions about the height of men. In sampling terminology, the total group from which we seek data is called the *population* or *universe*. In the example cited above, the population would be all men in the United States that are fourteen or above. The *sample* is a small group drawn from the population in such a way that the small group contains the characteristics of the large group from which it was taken. It is a *principle of statistics* that the distribution of data existing in nature is such that small groups properly drawn will very nearly contain the characteristics of the populations from which they are drawn. For example, if we wished to determine the proportion of shoes in each size-class worn by men students in a large university, we could determine this through sampling. If we selected a suitable sample of 1,000 students and recorded the percentage that wore size 7, 8, 9, 10, etc., we would derive a distribution according to size. Assuming that our sample was a representative one, the addition of a second 1,000 students to the group measure should not materially change the percentage distribution among the shoe sizes. Thus, the distribution derived by recording the sizes worn by 1,000 students would be reasonably indicative of the distribution prevailing among all men students. This principle enables the collection and analysis of data that would otherwise remain beyond our reach.

Random Sampling

In dealing with samples, the statistician usually prefers the technique of random sampling. A random sample has been defined as follows:

When sampling from finite populations, we shall say that a sample is random if every item in the population has an equal chance of being included in the sample. This definition implies that the selection of the sample should, in some way, be left to chance, and it is, indeed, common practice to base the selection of random samples on some form of gambling device.[2]

The random sample is preferred because it lends itself to certain techniques of mathematical treatment not possible with other samples. In assessing the degree of sampling error in an estimate, a knowledge of the *normal curve* is often necessary. Most students have heard of the normal curve and probably know that it is somewhat bell shaped in structure. The concept of the normal curve derived from the observation that the distribution of the variations in certain data seemed to fluctuate around the mean of the data in a pattern describing a bell-shaped curve. The tendency for this to happen seemed to indicate that the distribution around the mean occurred in response to some "natural law of chance." A simple experiment can demonstrate this principle. We may take a bag of black and white marbles containing an equal number of each and proceed to draw samples of ten. Each time we draw a marble, we will record its color and return it to the bag, shaking the bag to see that it is properly mixed. As we draw samples of ten, we will get varying combinations of the two colors. The most probable combination would be five black marbles and five white marbles, and the least probable would be ten of one color and none of the other. If we continue drawing samples of ten and plot the frequency of each combination on a chart, and if we draw a sufficiently

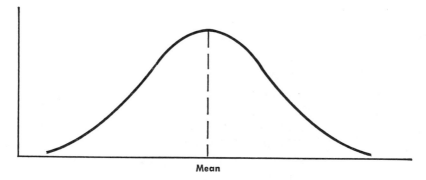

Mean

Fig. 24–6. The normal curve of distribution.

large number of samples, the results when plotted will conform rather closely to the normal curve. Figure 24–6 illustrates the normal curve.

If we knew that data existed in the population to be sampled in a pattern conforming to the normal curve, we would expect variations in our sample (if it is adequate) to conform to a like pattern. It is

[2] J. E. Freund, *Modern Elementary Statistics* (Englewood Cliffs, N.J.: Prentice-Hall, Inc., 1960), p. 193.

possible that in the area of the physical sciences, or under laboratory controlled conditions, the distribution of data in the population may approximate the normal curve. But in the area of business and economics, it is highly unlikely that very much data exists with distributions conforming to the concept of the normal curve. This, however, does not destroy the contribution of the normal curve to the study of business and economic statistics. It has been found that "errors in sampling" are distributed around their mean in a pattern described by the normal curve. One author refers to this tendency as follows:

The *normal curve* is in many respects the cornerstone of modern statistical theory. Its mathematical study dates back to the eighteenth century when scientists observed an astonishing degree of regularity in errors of measurements, that is, in repeated measurements of one and the same quantity. They found that the patterns (distributions) which they observed were closely approximated by a continuous distribution curve which they referred to as the "normal curve of errors" and attributed to the laws of chance.[3]

By using techniques based upon the properties of the normal curve, the statistician is able to cite the *probable* extent to which findings in the sample may vary from conditions existing in the population *as a result of sample error.* The student should note that mathematical techniques for determining the reliability of the sample do not in any way vouch for the reliability of the methods used to collect the data. A representative sample may be used in a survey, and yet the findings may be in error as a result of poor survey techniques (non-sampling errors) such as the improper wording of questions, errors in tabulation, and improper classification.

Other Uses of Sampling

In addition to the use of sampling as a means of gathering information, the technique has other uses. Sampling techniques are employed in production-quality control. A machine may be used to turn out bolts of a specified length. The use of the bolts may dictate that very little variation in length can be permitted. The machine may not be perfect, and from time to time it may require adjustment. Because of this, a close watch must be kept on the length of the bolts. In most cases, it would be impractical to measure each bolt turned out, so we solve the problem by measuring a sample of the bolts. Variations in the length of the bolts chosen for the sample tell us when the machine is out of adjustment. As mentioned in an earlier chapter, sampling is now being used by accountants in certain auditing procedures. Discrepancies dis-

[3] *Ibid.*, p. 168.

covered through an analysis of the sample may be projected against the population, or errors discovered in the sample may indicate the feasibility of doing a complete audit. These are but a few of the ways in which sampling is used in the area of business.

Other Forms of Sampling

While the statistician may prefer the random sample, there are times when its use may not be practical. To maintain the conditions necessary to preserve the random quality of the sample may involve prohibitive costs under certain circumstances. In some forms of marketing research deriving information through field surveys, a less precise method of sampling may provide the desired information. One such method is known as *area sampling*. In an area sample, consumers to be questioned are selected according to their area of residence. The method makes use of the technique of "probability sampling" in selecting the areas and subdivisions of areas to be surveyed. For example, a total market may be divided into counties and the counties to be surveyed are selected by using a random method. The counties may then be divided into townships and a number of townships selected. This process would continue until specific households were selected for interviewing. When properly conducted, this method can provide a satisfactory sample. The method is most applicable to a situation where a large area is to be surveyed.

Another type of sampling is the *quota sample*. In quota sampling, the population is studied to determine its characteristics that bear on the problem to be solved by the information. When these characteristics, or "controls," have been determined for the population, a sample is chosen in a manner to deliberately include the characteristics in the proper proportions. Suppose we are trying to sample a college student body to determine their preference for a certain product. We know that the student body is composed of 33 per cent freshmen, 25 per cent sophomores, 22 per cent juniors, and 20 per cent seniors. We also know that the boys in the student body outnumber the girls three to two. Using these two controls, our sample would have class representation according to the percentages shown; and in each class, there would be three boys chosen to every two girls (assuming this ratio is constant for all classes). The more pertinent the controls established, the greater should be the reliability of the sample. Of course, the quality of the sample depends upon the pertinency and completeness of the controls chosen. This type of sampling is widely used in marketing research since it takes less time, effort, personnel, and funds to plan and execute.

FURTHER STATISTICAL MEASURES

Correlation

Some types of data important to the businessman are readily accessible while other types are obtainable only through the most indirect means. If a manufacturer wants to know the number of automobiles registered in a particular state, he can usually obtain that information from the state Department of Motor Vehicles. But if he wants to predict the market for tires for the coming year, he has a much more difficult problem. Valuable insight into problems such as this one can often be gained through discovering a relationship between the measurable data and that which defies measurement. If two series of data move in the same direction, we say that a *positive correlation* exists; and if they move in opposite directions, a *negative correlation* exists. If the two series moved in the same direction, and at the same rate, a perfect or 100 per cent correlation would exist. If they moved in opposite directions but at the same rate, the negative correlation would likewise be a perfect one. If data does not move at the same rate, the extent of the correlation is measured by a value less than 100 per cent. Where there are only two factors involved in the measurements—i.e., the number of automobiles in use and expected tire sales—there is said to exist a *simple correlation*. If we discover a relationship between prospective tire sales and two factors—(1) number of cars registered and (2) number of cars two years old or more—we are employing *multiple correlation*. The statistician is able to derive mathematical formulas to assist in computing measures of correlation. Series of data are constantly being examined to detect relationships that may be helpful in areas such as forecasting. There are also graphic methods that permit us to plot the relationship between two variables on a chart and to observe the presence or absence of a degree of correlation. Such charts are often referred to as "scatter diagrams."

Time-Series Analysis

Much of the data used by business is presented in the form of changes occurring through time. For example, income statistics may be pertinent for certain purposes only when one period of time is compared to another. When measurements of data are separated by significant periods of time, the presentation is referred to as a *time series*. A typical series would be monthly department-store sales. When we study variations in data over a period of time, we are usually aware of the fact that many influences may be present in the variations. A curve showing industrial output for a certain product may show seasonal fluctuations present within each year; it may show the effect of business recessions from one year to another; the curve may also contain the long-term growth trends present in the industry. The analyst may be interested in "separating these influences" and noting the effect that any one of them may have had on output for a period of time such as ten or twenty-five years. There are statistical procedures that will enable him to single out these influences and to determine the relative effect of each on industry output for the time series under study.

Probability

In an age of electronic computers and a growing interest in the application of mathematical techniques to the solution of business problems, one hears much about *probability*. The idea of probability is sometimes referred to as the "laws of chance," although this layman's definition may not meet the technical requirements of the statistician. In the section on sampling, we discussed the distribution of certain values about the mean and indicated that this distribution seemed to be founded in a certain *principle*. This principle seemed to indicate that the factor of chance works in such a way that in certain cases, a series of events, if free of man-made interference, will produce results that conform to a predictable pattern. The drawing of marbles from a bag, or the flipping of a coin, would be examples of such events. The concept of probability extends this principle of chance to embrace many types of data in a great variety of business situations. If a business firm wished to increase its sales, a great many variable factors would have a bearing on whether the goal was achieved. The firm might employ more salesmen, spend more money on advertising, redesign its packages, and change its price. The mathematical statistician might concern himself with an effort to determine the *probability* that these methods would be successful in achieving the established goal. With the aid of modern machines, and the history of the company's past experience and that of related companies in achieving sales, he would evaluate the many variables that will be present to influence sales. The end product of his analysis would be to indicate the relative degree of certainty with which the desired goal may be expected.

SOURCES OF STATISTICAL DATA

Primary and Secondary Sources

Statistical data derived from original sources, such as a field survey, are referred to as *primary data*. If we use data that someone else has collected—that is, at least once removed from the original source—we are using *secondary data*. Quantities of primary data are compiled through enumerations and surveys. The United States Census is perhaps our greatest collection of statistical information. Private companies do original research, and there are private research companies that specialize in assembling information for clients. Colleges and universities are active in primary research. Many companies find their own records a valuable source of primary data.

In solving a problem requiring information of a statistical nature, we would always exhaust secondary sources of information before turning to primary research. It is less costly to obtain data from secondary sources, and also much valuable time can be saved. Among the principal sources of secondary data are the federal government and its many divisions, state governments, colleges and universities, private agencies, trade associations, and similar agencies. Relative to data available from government sources, there are publications, such as the booklet *Statistical Services of the U.S. Government* (Superintendent of Documents, Washington, D.C.), which explain the sources available and indicate the proper method for gaining access to the material.

Evaluating Statistical Data

Unfortunately, not all the statistical information available can be considered reliable. Some of it may simply be out of date; and although once valuable, it is no longer pertinent. In other cases, the data for one reason or another may not be trustworthy. Sometimes, the organization collecting the original data may not have had sufficient funds to do sound research, or they may not have had trained and capable personnel to collect the data. In other cases, the data may have been collected in such a way as to get a deliberately distorted result. Some advertisers have used unscrupulous methods to bias research findings to serve a promotional purpose. The American people have a certain respect for the scientific method, and research which purports to be scientific is often accepted without critical examination. One should be aware of the fact that "although figures do not lie, liars can figure." The person, or firm, that abuses research techniques in order to deceive the public is doing a great disservice to the public and to other firms that depend upon the cooperation of the consumer in the collection of statistical facts.

In evaluating statistical information, certain questions should be asked:

1. Was the information collected by capable researchers, and were sufficient funds available to do a reasonable job?

2. Who paid for the study? Did the party paying for the study have a vested interested in its outcome?
3. Were the procedures followed in conducting the research in keeping with sound methodology?
4. If the data were collected by sample, was the sample adequate?
5. How was the reliability of the sample tested?
6. Was the study sufficiently recent to still be pertinent?

Questions such as these, and others along the same line, will lead the user of statistical information into examining his sources of information. It is more dangerous to make decisions based on misleading information than to have no information at all.

YOUR CAREER AS A STATISTICIAN

Opportunities

We have emphasized the fact that all modern business managers should have a knowledge of statistical procedures sufficient to enable them to evaluate and use the quantities of data available to them. One might go further and state that all business managers should know enough about procedures to use statistical tools in the conduct of such research as they may be called upon to do. This emphasizes the importance of *statistics* as a secondary area of specialization for those who seek to major in one of the various subject areas discussed in this book. The production executive, the marketing executive, the financial administrator, and the accountant will all find a familiarity with statistical procedures to be of great help to them. Industry recognizes the value of statistical training; and as a consequence, the person who has had two, three, or more courses in statistics will find recruiters from business firms very much interested. Of course, two or three courses in the subject does not make one a statistician, but the value of such courses as a complement to other areas of specialization cannot be overemphasized.

For the person who makes the study of statistics his major area and who achieves a knowledge of the subject sufficient to qualify him as a professional statistician, the career opportunities are almost unlimited. There has long been an acute shortage of well-qualified statisticians; and those who are qualified, find their services much in demand. Needless to say, this has the effect of advancing the salaries that may be earned by those qualified. The rapidly expanding role of business and economic research as carried on by industry has created a growing need for statisticians. The expansion of government in the control of industry, and the growth of government service to the public, have created a vast need for statistical services in government. Statisticians are required to collect, analyze, and provide information to those who must make decisions. Another factor accentuating the role of the statistician has been the development of advanced business machines such as the electronic computer. The statistician is one of the specialists whose training enables him to play an important role in the utilization of this equipment. If computers are to play the important role now predicted, the future demand for statisticians will intensify. Opportunity in terms of advancement and salary should be very encouraging to the young person having the ability, and willingness to work, necessary to becoming a well-qualified statistician.

Training

Those desiring to study statistics as a complement to other specialized areas will find that most universities offer three or more courses in the subject. Some facility with mathematics is required in the study of statistics; but generally speaking, a knowledge of college algebra affords sufficient background for the first two or three courses given. As a rule, courses in business statistics are taught with the emphasis on application, and this tends to minimize the mathematical requirements.

Those desiring to specialize in the study of statistics will find it necessary to acquire a wider knowledge of mathematics. To take the advanced courses on the undergraduate level, one is perhaps well advised to study mathematics through the level of calculus. It is also well for the student desiring to be a professional statistician to plan for graduate study. The master's degree, and preferably the doctorate, is desirable for those who hope to scale the higher levels of competence. This is not to imply that the undergraduate who acquires statistical training is not in demand; but the subject embraces a wide area of knowledge, and the advanced levels are of such complexity that graduate training may be essential. Those who anticipate graduate work in statistics might do well to acquire an undergraduate major in mathematics. The statistician who hopes to work in the areas of business and economics should take sufficient courses in those areas to familiarize himself with organization, procedures, and policies common to the area. In addition to the usual grounding in the liberal arts, he should take courses in psychology, sociology, and related areas. Problems in the design of samples, and in the construction of questionnaires, will often involve a knowledge of these subjects. As with other jobs, the statistician will find that companies offer the advantages of "on-the-job" training. This may include the privilege of working under the direction of an experienced and well-qualified expert.

TOPICS FOR DISCUSSION

1. Why is it that so much statistical information is presented in terms of ratios?

2. Discuss the limitations of the arithmetic mean as an average.

3. Is it possible for statistical information to be technically accurate and yet be misleading? Can you cite an example?

4. If you wanted to know how well the members of your class had done on a recent examination, would you prefer that your instructor tell you the mean, median, or mode of the grades made?

5. Is an examination a form of sampling? In general, are exams adequate as samples?

6. How is it possible that an organization such as the Gallup Poll can question a fraction of a per cent of our population and predict an election with reasonable accuracy?

7. Do you believe that there exists a correlation between the hours studied and the grades made on an examination? What type of correlation—positive or negative?

8. Do you believe that the grades made in a typical class will have a distribution that conforms to the so-called normal curve? If not, is it justifiable for the instructor to *grade on the curve?*

9. If you desired information on the per capita income earned in your home county, where would you find such information?

10. Suppose you were asked to find out if the students in your school preferred to take three days from the Christmas vacation for the purpose of adding three days to the Easter vacation. How would you go about finding out this information?

CASE 24–1

A PROBLEM IN STATISTICAL SAMPLING

A group of 25 students at a state university was exploring the possibility of compiling and publishing a "book" that would rate professors teaching in the undergraduate program. The university had an enrolment of approximately 15,000 undergraduates, and more than 1,200 people were employed in teaching one or more undergraduate courses. It was thought that the proposed book might contain for each professor a listing similar to the following:

Jones, Robert R. Age 45, Ph.D. Columbia. Teaches English 122, 128, and special courses in English literature. Lectures are usually interesting, though often poorly organized. Tests given are usually objective type. Papers usually graded by graduate assistants. Difficult to arrange conferences after class hour. Over-all rating as teacher: average.

The students proposed to obtain data to be used in the evaluation directly from students who had been members of classes taught by the professor to be rated. It was thought that a questionnaire could be designed and distributed to students and that, on the basis of the information thus collected, the evaluation would be made. The students interested in the project admitted that it would not be practical to obtain information from all undergraduates in the university, and that some form of sampling would have to be used. A member of the group proposed that tables be set up in the student-union building and that each of these stations should be manned by a student who would pass out questionnaires that would be completed on the spot and returned. Signs would be posted directing students to the tables, and announcements would appear in the school paper inviting students to fill out a questionnaire in the student union.

When asked for an opinion of the proposed project, an administrator in the university was quoted as follows: "Such a project might have something to offer if the evaluations were accomplished in a thorough and responsible manner. If the project was not handled in a responsible way, it would be a disservice to both the students and the faculty." The interested group continued with plans to launch the project and to make the "book" available in a mimeographed form.

1. Discuss the proposed procedure for obtaining the opinions of a sample of the undergraduate students.

2. Do you think that the project will meet the standards of a "thorough and responsible" evaluation?

SELECTED REFERENCES

The following texts are representative of those found in the area of elementary statistics. An examination of any of these will afford the student an elaboration of the sections discussed in this chapter.

Leabo, D. A., and Frank Smith. *Basic Statistics for Business Economics.* Rev. ed. Homewood, Ill.: Richard D. Irwin, Inc., 1964.

Nelson, Boyd L. *Elements of Modern Statistics.* New York: Appleton-Century-Crofts, Inc., 1961.

Richmond, S. B. *Principles of Statistical Analysis.* 2d ed. New York: The Ronald Press Co., 1964.

Spurr, W. A., L. S. Kellogg, and J. H. Smith. *Business and Economic Statistics.* Homewood, Ill.: Richard D. Irwin, Inc., 1961.

25

Risk Management

OBJECTIVES OF INSURANCE

If everyone could spend his life in a germ-free vacuum, isolated from other individuals, we would be able to minimize risk, but this is not reality. So we find some risk in all of our activities. This is true of individuals as well as businessmen. It is simply not possible in the modern world to escape the constant exposure to perils of one kind or another, whether they are physical or financial. The individual, though, has a considerable amount of control over some perils. The threat of fire, for example, is always with us but, through the observance of fire prevention rules, the individual can reduce the danger. The perils that face all of us can be ignored, but this can be very costly; or we can decide to set aside savings that would absorb some of the loss from a peril, such as a fire. One of the problems in the latter plan would be the danger of a loss before there was sufficient money saved to cover it. Business firms sometimes operate under such a plan, setting aside a certain percentage of gross revenue to cover possible losses from fire and other hazards. This is called *self-insurance*. The other alternative, and the one that has led to the development of a large industry—insurance companies— is to purchase insurance protection.

Insurance can reduce the uncertainties and provide a measure of security against losses. By securing protection, the individual transfers the chance of loss to a professional risk bearer—an insurance company— through the purchase of an *insurance policy*. This is a contract between the *insured* (the person or business taking out the insurance, also called the *assured*) and the *insurer*, the insurance company or *underwriter*. The contract indemnifies the insured, or the policyholder, against losses. By paying a small amount to an insurance company at regular intervals, the individual can insure himself against a large loss. He can insure against almost any peril whether it is to his life, to his health, to his business, to his home, to his car, or to almost anything. The insurance company provides protection against the particular peril named in the policy of the insured. The amount of the insurance policy, or the limit of liability specified in the contract, is called the *face of the policy.* The insured pays a stated amount of money for this protection, which is called a *premium.*

The insurance company is able to assume the large risks for a comparatively small premium because it is dealing with a large group and has based its premiums on the expected losses for the group rather than for the individual.

Types of Risks or Hazards

Economic risks may be *speculative,* in which case there may be the chance of a gain or the chance of a loss. This kind of risk can be offset by *hedging,* which is the neutralizing of a risk. This was explained in the buying and selling of securities. The kind of loss against which insurance offers protection may be called *pure risk.* There is no chance of gain in a pure risk as there is in a speculative risk—only the chance of loss. For example, a building may be destroyed by fire. The provision of insurance on the building can offset the loss to the extent of the insurance on the building. The risks that are dealt with in this chapter are pure risks.

The businessman faces four broad categories of risks against which insurance can be secured. There are those which involve loss or damage to his own property, those involving liability and injury to the person or property of others, those involving himself, and those involving the persons of his employees. The first two categories of risks can be covered under property and liability insurance—the latter two under life, accident, and sickness insurance.

Most insurance companies handle or "write" insurance to cover only a limited range of risks. Lloyds of London is an exception. It is a corporation composed of over 2,000 underwriters. Through one or more of its underwriters, it will insure almost any risk. As a corporation, it does not subscribe to policies of insurance or issue them, but the insurance is written by individual underwriters.

Insurance companies, in general, limit their coverage to *insurable risks.* These are risks that can be measured statistically so that the amount of expected loss, called an *average of losses,* can be computed.

Over a number of years, actual losses will vary somewhat from the average, being either higher or lower. This is termed a *deviation from the average.* The probable deviation can be predicted quite closely by averaging the variations for the years under examination. When the average loss has been determined with the expected percentage of deviation, the premium can be established on an *actuarial basis.* The people who make these computations for insurance companies are called *actuaries.* Insurable risks are those in which there is a large number to be insured. There are some restrictions imposed by insurance companies on insurable risks, such as those concerning the general health of a person seeking life insurance or the imposing of higher rates for fire insurance on buildings whose location in relation to fire departments or water supply is not desirable.

INSURANCE COMPANIES

Stock Insurance Companies

There are a number of types of organizational structures in insurance companies, or as they are sometimes called, *insurance carriers.* One of the more common is that of stock insurance companies. These companies, like other corporations in the United States, are organized under the laws of a particular state. They indicate in their charter the kind or kinds of insurance that they are going to handle or write. Insurance companies of this type are organized for the purpose of making money. Capital is subscribed to by stockholders who expect to receive dividends on the money they have invested in the stock of the company. This capital constitutes a fund that, in addition to premium payments, can be used to pay losses. Under this structural organization, the company charges policyholders a fixed rate of premium for the risk that is carried. The cost is known in advance by the policyholder whose only interest in the company is that he will be paid in the event of any loss covered by his policy. He receives no dividends from the earnings of the company and has no liability for any of its debts. He cannot be assessed or held liable in any way for any additional premium if the losses of the company should exceed its income. Stock company policyholders forego the possible profits if the insurance company has a fortunate experience in order to be relieved of liability if its experience is unfortunate, which leaves the chances of a profit or a loss to the stockholders of the company. The policyholders, however, may ultimately benefit from the profitable operation of the company since not all profits are distributed in dividends. Some are placed in surplus accounts. When these accounts are built up, there may be a lowering of premiums that will be beneficial to the policyholder. Stock companies are the dominant type of company in practically all types of insurance underwriting except life insurance.

Mutual Insurance Companies

A mutual insurance company is a corporation owned and operated by its policyholders. Its purpose is to provide insurance at cost under the laws of the state in which it is incorporated for its members or policyholders. The policyholders elect the directors who, in turn, appoint the company officers. Each policyholder, with few exceptions, pays premiums. If his policy provides for it, an assessment can be made when the premium contribution is inadequate to meet the expenses of providing insurance. Although mutual companies are owned by the policyholders, few policyholders are ever very active in the affairs of the company.

Mutual insurance companies operate in all fields of insurance, but life insurance is the area in which they are used to the greatest extent. Companies of this kind handle 62 per cent of all the life insurance in the United States. Some mutual insurance companies, such as local *farm mutuals,* collect no advance premiums. They just levy assessments periodically. There are mutual companies that select risks of a particular class, such as hardware stores and milling companies. These are called *class mutuals. Factory mutuals,* also, select risks of a certain class, such as those factories that use all possible means of fire prevention so as to keep rates low.

An *interinsurance association* or *reciprocal association* is another type of mutual insurance operation. Under this form of insurance contract, each policyholder is insured by all of the others. He, in turn, insures them, usually in a stipulated amount. The liability of each policyholder or subscriber is limited. Each subscriber has an individual account into which his premiums are paid, and he pays only a stipulated share of each loss. A manager is appointed who carries on the business. This type of insurance operation is found particularly in fire insurance.

Reinsurance Companies

An insurance company wants to spread the risk it has assumed so that no single accident will upset the average. For this reason, insurance companies keep only a portion of the risk and buy insurance for the balance. This insurance is called *reinsurance.* There are some insurance companies that are reinsurance companies only, whose clients are insurance companies. Many of these reinsurance companies, in turn, do not want to assume all of the risk that they have taken from another insurance company so they will reinsure their risk with another re-insurance company. The effect of this is to spread the risk very widely. It can be seen that the risk of a catastrophe could be spread so widely that it would not hurt any one of the risk bearers. A simple type of reinsurance is one in which the reinsurer agrees to take a stated percentage of the risk involved. The reinsurer will get the same percentage of the premium as it took in risk less a commission allowed to the insuring company, and the reinsurance company will bear the same percentage of the losses that he has assumed of the risk.

Insurance Provided by the State or Federal Government

The states and the federal government also provide insurance of various types. The federal government under the Social Security Act provides old-age pensions and unemployment insurance, the latter being administered by the states. The states require Workmen's Compensation, as explained in an earlier chapter, through a premium based on employers' payrolls and administer this program. The federal government also provides life and health insurance to its employees.

Both the states and the federal government have retirement plans for employees. The federal government also insures bank deposits and deposits in savings and loan companies up to $15,000 per person through special government agencies. It provides insurance through the Postal Service on parcel post. Through an agency of the government, the Federal Crop Insurance Corporation, crop insurance is provided that guarantees the farmer a certain amount of protection against drought, flood, frost, and many other risks.

Insurance-Company Representatives

In selling insurance, companies may establish *local agents*, whether the company is a stock or a mutual company. They will appoint a local representative and pay the agent a commission on the business that he writes. Generally, the agent is an independent businessman. He may represent a number of companies in different types of insurance like life, property, and casualty; or he may sell only one kind of insurance for one company. Quite often, the insurance agent is also a realtor or engaged in some other business activity and writes insurance as one of his sources of income. The agent operates under an agency contract that specifies the amount of commission, the area of his territory, and to what extent he represents the company.

A *general agent* supervises all of a company's business within a specified territory. Such an agent may be an individual or a business firm. This kind of agent is paid a commission on all the business that passes through his hands. He may also solicit insurance business as any local agent does.

A *broker,* unlike the agent, represents no particular insurance companies, but represents his clients, the people who are going to purchase the insurance. The function of the broker is to buy the broadest available policy at the lowest possible cost consistent with sound protection. Although the service he renders is principally for the insured, he does not receive his brokerage fee from the insured but from the insurance company with which he places the business. A broker may be a person or a business firm. In the larger insurance brokerage firms, there may be many specialists who collectively provide a complete insurance service.

Some insurance companies do not have agents but engage in *direct writing.* The company representatives are called field agents, or a similar title, and are employed by the company. They are assigned to geographical territories.

Regulation of Insurance

Insurance is subject to regulation by the states. Many of the state laws were enacted to protect against insolvency of insurance companies by requiring detailed financial statements from the companies. Some states regulate the premiums that are charged and prohibit discrimination and rebating. Legal reserve requirements are also specified by states. These requirements stipulate that the insurance companies have to set up as a liability a reserve that must be maintained and is adequate to meet policy obligations upon their maturity. There are some mutual companies operating wholly within a state that are not subject to this provision in that the reserve requirement may vary depending upon the assessment provisions contained in the policies.

PROPERTY AND LIABILITY INSURANCE

Fire and Allied Insurance

Owners of property seek to indemnify themselves for losses that grow out of damage to or destruction of their property. One of the more common losses is due to fire. Therefore, fire insurance is carried. It has become common for all fire-insurance policies to include loss to property occasioned by fire and by lightning as well. The policy contracts are standardized. All that needs to be added is information concerning the owner or insured. Fire-insurance policies cover direct losses. This includes smoke damage from fire and water or chemical damage that results from attempts to extinguish the fire. The scope of the coverage of any insurance contract can be broadened or restricted by the addition of a provision to the contract called an *endorsement* or *rider*. It has become general practice to add an endorsement that broadens the fire policies to include loss by other perils, such as windstorm, hail, explosion, riot, falling aircraft, motor vehicles, and smudge from faulty heating devices. This particular combination is called *extended coverage endorsement*. In addition to the direct loss occasioned by fire or allied coverages, the same peril may create a *consequential loss*. The damage occasioned by the fire, for example, may cause an interruption of normal business operations. Fire insurance will pay the loss on the property, but the business may lose earnings as well as having to maintain personnel during the period of repairing the property. The possibility of consequential loss gives rise to *business interruption insurance*, which may be covered by endorsement to the policy. This will pay for the earnings that would have been made under normal conditions so that expenses can be covered. Another type of extended coverage insurance is *rental value insurance*. This insurance provides protection for the owner of rental property who would lose the income from rent while a building was being repaired following a fire. *Extra expense insurance* may also be added to the policy by endorsement. This coverage provides for the additional expenses incurred in order to maintain an operation at another location while the insured property is being restored. Firms that depend upon continuous operations, such as those providing services, are likely to have this kind of insurance.

A number of coverages may be put into one contract. This is termed *packaging*. Sometimes such packages are referred to as *all-risk policies;* but this may or may not be the case, depending upon what is specified in the contract. Businessmen sometimes use the *mercantile-block policy,* a package combination that includes a number of forms of coverage on two of the basic fire policies.

Factors Affecting Rates.   The rates on fire insurance are set up by rating bureaus. These are staffed by engineers, statisticians, inspectors, and others. Policies are usually written on a one-, three-, or five-year basis. Rates for the longer periods of time are lower than for the one year. For example, the five-year policy rate is four times the one-year premium. Rates generally are either *class rates,* which apply to all property that falls within a given classification, or *specific rates.* The factors that affect class rates are the construction of the building, the occupancy, and the amount and quality of fire protection. Specific rates are issued by rating bureaus for business properties and establishments. These rates are determined by a schedule designed to measure the relative quantity of fire hazard involved in each risk. Fire rates are affected by the location of the risk, proximity to the fire department, proximity to water hydrant, adequacy of public water supply, type of building construction, occupancy, and protection such as automatic sprinklers or fire alarm services.

Co-insurance. An insurance company may insert one or more clauses that will limit the liability of the insurance company. With such a limitation in liability, the amount of the premium may be lower. A *co-insurance clause* is one of the clauses that limit the liability of the insurance company. It requires that the insured carry insurance to a stipulated percentage of the property's value. At the present time, the most common co-insurance clause requires that insurance equal to 80 per cent of the value of the property be carried. This clause is inserted in fire-insurance contracts because experience has shown that when people insure their properties in varying percentages of the value, the person or persons who insure in higher percentages are bearing a proportionately greater burden for protection than those carrying less insurance in lower percentages of value since the majority of insurance losses are partial losses. For example, assume that one person insures his property for 20 per cent of its value, another for 40 per cent, and another for the full value. Each suffers a loss that is less than the face value of the least insurance carried, and each is paid the full amount of his loss. Those who are carrying the smaller percentages of insurance to total value have paid less for their insurance; and yet because the loss is partial and less than the face amounts of their policies, they have received the full amount of their loss. In order to eliminate the inequities in such a situation, the amount of loss paid is in proportion to the percentage relationship of the insurance carried to value of property insured. For example, the insured has a property valued at $40,000, and he insures at 80 per cent co-insurance, or $32,000. If he suffers a loss of $16,000, his full loss is covered. If he suffers a loss of $40,000, his loss is covered up to the face of his policy, $32,000. On the other hand, if the insurance he carries is less than the required 80 per cent, he becomes a co-insurer of his own risk and is paid only that percentage that the insurance he carries bears to the 80 per cent he should be carrying. Suppose that he carried $24,000 in insurance on his $40,000 property and has a loss of $16,000. The amount of loss that is covered is $24,000/$32,000 or ¾ of the loss—$12,000. On any loss that he has, he would be covered only to the extent of ¾ of the loss.

After the insurance company has paid the insured the amount of loss on the property insured, whether an automobile, a building, or some other property, the insurance company has the right of action against the person responsible for the loss equal to that held by the insured. Suppose you own a building that is destroyed by fire through the negligence of someone else. Your loss is paid to you by the insurance company with which the building was insured. The insurance company, then, has the same right to attempt to recover the amount of the loss from the person responsible for the fire as you held as owner of the building. This is called *subrogation*.

Ocean and Inland Marine Insurance

Businessmen often find it necessary to insure property against the perils of the sea while it is being transported by ship. This is due to the fact that ocean carriers limit their liability on property they are transporting, and so the shipper or owner of the property wants to be sure that he protects it against loss or damage by purchasing what is called marine insurance. Marine insurance is also carried by the owner of the ship for protection of the hull of the vessel. Although marine insurance is the oldest form of insurance, there has been no standard marine policy developed.

Marine insurance policies are subject to implied warranties. These are not actually a part of the written policy, but they have as much legal status as if they were included in the insurance contract. The implied warranties are that the vessel is seaworthy, that there will be no route departure from the voyage, and that the voyage is for a lawful purpose and will be carried out in a lawful manner.

Losses in marine insurance are of two types: total and partial. The total loss is when property is completely destroyed. This kind of loss may be either an actual loss or a constructive loss. The former occurs when the property is destroyed, as the loss by fire or sinking of the vessel. Constructive total loss is when the expense of recovering or repairing the goods exceeds their value after this cost has been incurred. Partial losses are referred to as average, which means a loss less than the total. There are two kinds of average losses: particular average and general average. The particular average is a loss that falls upon a single interest, such as the owner of a specific cargo shipment. General average is a loss that affects all cargo interests on board a vessel and which affects the ship as well.

Although most of our transportation companies assume the liability for property that they transport within the United States, there are some situations in which the shipper wants to carry insurance on his shipments whether they are moving by rail, truck, barge, or plane. This has given rise to what is termed *inland marine insurance*. It developed because of a need for insurance on shipments to be transported by means other than ocean shipping. Since marine insurance was the first type of insurance to be written, it was natural to turn to marine underwriters to supply insurance on shipments moving inland. As inland marine insurance exists today, it embraces many kinds of insurance on all sorts of property. The policies may be written to cover specific risks or may be on an all-risks basis. They can be written for a single trip or for a certain period of time. Bridges and tunnels are insurable under inland marine forms. They are fixed property but are insured by inland marine underwriters because they are a part of the transportation system. Merchandise shipped by parcel post can be insured by the use of inland marine insurance, and this is one of the most widely used of its forms. Many types of movable personal property are insured in inland marine insurance under policies known as personal-property floaters. These policies cover articles such as furs, silverware, and jewelry. Floater policies are under inland marine insurance because the articles do not necessarily stay in one location and are thus covered by insurance, subject to the limits of the contract, wherever they may be taken.

Automobile Insurance

With the widespread ownership of automobiles, automobile insurance has grown tremendously. Of all property and liability insurance business, more than half is automobile insurance. There are two broad types of coverage: liability or casualty coverage and physical damage. Liability insurance is the individual's responsibility toward the person or property of someone else. This is divided into bodily injury liability, property damage liability, and medical payments coverage. Bodily injury and property damage insurance requires the insurance company to pay, on behalf of the insured, the amounts that are specified in the policy that he might become legally obligated to pay as damages caused by an accident involving the insured's automobile.

The rates of automobile insurance are based on standard limits. These limits have been $5,000 for bodily injury to or death of any one person and $10,000 for bodily injuries or death involving more than one person in a single accident. A number of states require that minimum coverages of $10,000 and $20,000 be carried. These standard limits are very low in view of judgments that are awarded by juries in accident cases. Juries have been very generous in their awards so that many automobile owners carry $50,000/$100,000 in insurance or even $100,000/$300,000. Additional insurance beyond this amount can also be secured. Most of the claims that insurance companies settle are within the standard limits of $5,000/$10,000 so the base premium is set on the cost of providing insurance in these amounts. Insurance in excess of these amounts can be secured at relatively small additional cost—just a few dollars more. For example, coverage of $50,000/$100,000 in one area in 1966 was $57.65; on the same car and under the same circumstances, coverage in the amount of $100,000/$200,000 amounted to $60.00; and for $100,000/$300,000, it was $61.20. Rates vary according to the territory or area in which the automobile is garaged and used, whether it is used in business or is just a pleasure car, the age of the drivers, and other factors.

The businessman who supplies automobiles for his salesmen's use or trucks used in his business can secure fleet liability insurance applying to five or more vehicles. This insurance can be written on a deductible basis, which would provide insurance at a lower premium because the insured is assuming responsibility for losses up to the amount named as deductible, such as $250.

The liability coverage involving medical payments makes it possible for the insured to make payments in limited amounts to persons who are injured while riding with him. Typical coverages are from $250 to $5,000.

Physical damage coverage protects the insured from loss or damage to his own car and includes fire, theft, and collision. Fire and theft are written under one premium rate; and if collision insurance is also included, the premium is substantially higher. A comprehensive coverage can be secured that covers all sorts of perils and is in the form of an all-risks coverage, except for collision.

Collision insurance can be written on a full-coverage basis or a deductible basis. The deductible provisions are used when the insured wishes to protect himself from the larger losses through insurance and will take care of losses up to the amount named from his own pocket. The insured assumes liability for the damage to his car, no matter what the size of the loss, up to the amount named in the policy, such as $50 deductible and $100 deductible. The higher the amount named as deductible, the lower the premium paid by the insured for collision coverage above that amount.

Most states have enacted financial responsibility laws that require that an individual be able to pay damages, within the limits established by the statutes, that may be caused as a result of operating an automobile. When this has been done, most persons will take out insurance to comply with this requirement.

Aviation Insurance

Aviation insurance covers risks of loss or damage to the aircraft, which is coverage of the hull; liability to cover property damage and passenger liability; as well as numerous other types of coverage. Aviation insurance has developed as a specialized field. The rates in this field are not standard.

Fidelity Bonds

Fidelity bonds are designed to protect the businessman against loss that is caused by employee dishonesty. Fidelity bonds may be secured from surety companies. The employer takes out the bond and is the beneficiary, or the one to whom payment is made in event of loss. The employee is named, or the position is named, as bonded principal or bonded party. When one employee or more is named, the bond is called an individual or named schedule bond, under which employees can be insured for differing amounts. Blanket bonds automatically cover each employee up to the limit of the bond. Banks use this type of bond, which covers every employee from the president to the janitor. There are also blanket position bonds that cover only those in certain positions, such as cashiers in a supermarket.

Surety Bonds

A surety bond guarantees the performance of an obligation or a contract. The purpose of the surety bond is not to protect the businessman but is sometimes required of him as a means of protecting others. The principle underlying surety bonds is that no losses are expected, and the premium amounts to a service charge to compensate the insurance company for pledging its credit. In the construction industry, a form of the surety bond, *a performance bond,* is required by federal and state governments on projects financed from public funds. A bond of this type guarantees that the bonded party will fulfill the conditions of the contract, and the insurance company assumes the responsibility if the bonded person defaults on his obligation. The bond serves the purpose of guaranteeing to the government that the project will be completed at the contract price and helps the contracting company to secure credit from lending institutions since the bond guarantees its performance of the contract. The man who has his house constructed for him may also be protected by a performance bond. This guarantees that the plans and specifications will be followed and that all labor and material bills will be paid.

Federal, state, and local governments also require license and permit bonds in the case of certain businesses. These bonds guarantee that the bonded person will comply with the law or ordinance governing the type of operation for which the license or permit is issued. Customs bonds are required by the federal government on certain goods that are imported into the United States, which guarantee that the owner of the merchandise will pay any required taxes or duties and will comply with the applicable federal statutes. This type of bond enables him to secure immediate possession of the merchandise without waiting for determination of the amount to be paid in duties.

General Liability or Third Party Liability Insurance

General liability or third party liability insurance is usually carried by businessmen and consists of two types. Bodily injury insurance covers claims for the accidental injury or death of persons other than employees, and property damage covers accidental injury to the property of others that is not being used by the insured or in his care. General liability insurance includes all kinds of insurance that provide protection against damage claims with the exception of claims arising out of the use of automobiles and claims by employees, both of which are discussed elsewhere in this chapter under automobile liability insurance and Workmen's Compensation. The basic coverage in general liability insurance includes liability for accidents occurring on the business premises or arising out of the use of the premises for business purposes.

The liability of a manufacturer or a seller does not end when he has sold an article and delivered it to a customer. There may be accidents caused by defective electrical apparatus, poisoning from food or from dyes in textiles, as well as other matters; and law suits may be instituted because of occurrences after the merchandise has been sold. Protection against such liability hazards can be secured through products liability and completed operations coverage.

Other Types of Insurance

Some of the additional types of insurance include boiler and machinery insurance, which covers accidental explosion or breakdown of heating and power equipment; glass insurance to replace damaged glass; and burglary and robbery insurance. Businessmen can also secure credit insurance, which protects them from unusual debt losses. Every businessman who extends credit realizes that he may not be able to collect all of the payments due. Based on records of past experience, though, he can predict approximately what the percentage of uncollectible bills will be and absorbs this as a part of his cost of doing business. An abnormal credit loss, however, is quite different. The result of such an occurrence can be just as disastrous as loss from a fire or some other physical catastrophe. Credit insurance provides protection against these abnormal losses.

LIFE, ACCIDENT, AND SICKNESS INSURANCE

Accident and Sickness Insurance

Accident and sickness insurance, sometimes called disability insurance or health insurance, is a form of casualty insurance. Its use has become widespread, and it is an important factor in making it possible for individuals to meet the expenses incurred through injuries or illnesses. More than 145 million Americans had health insurance by the end of 1965. Workmen's Compensation protects an employee from financial losses from job-connected injuries, and accident and sickness insurance provides for expenses resulting from off-the-job injuries or major illnesses, as well as loss of income from inability to work. Accident and sickness insurance is obtainable on both an individual and a group basis. An increasing number of employers provide group insurance for employees in which the company bears all or part of the cost. This insurance is provided by organizations that are incorporated as non-profit organizations. An example of this is the Blue Cross plan, which provides hospital service and care. Blue Cross reimburses the hospital when one of its enrollees has been hospitalized. Blue Shield is a companion plan covering surgical payments to doctors selected by the enrollee. There are numerous insurance companies that handle the same type of insurance but operate on a profit basis and deal in individual policies rather than company policies.

Accident-and-sickness policies have tended to become broader each year so there are many items covered. The loss-of-time income insurance is a typical coverage found in the group insurance that provides against loss of income during an absence caused by a non-occupational injury or illness. Medical payments for visits to the doctor's office and accidental death and dismemberment, which covers fatal accidents or loss of arms or legs, are other coverages of this type of insurance.

Life Insurance

Life insurance was developed for family protection. It is used for a variety of purposes today, although family protection is still a very important reason for much of the life insurance written. It is a contract or agreement in which the insurer agrees to pay a stipulated sum upon the death of the insured, or at some specified time, to a designated person, called a *beneficiary*. Since death is a certainty, life insurance is not insuring against an uncertainty but against the possibility of a monetary loss should death occur before the normal life expectancy. In other types of insurance, a loss must be experienced before any payment is made as the result of an insurance agreement. In life insurance, on the other hand, the insured may live beyond his earning years and his family experiences no monetary loss upon his death, yet the amount of life insurance that he has in effect at the time of his death is paid to his beneficiary.

The premiums for life insurance are based on life expectancy and the necessary expenses of the insurance company. The younger a person is when he takes out insurance, the lower the premiums are because he has a longer life expectancy than when he is older. The premium he pays is based on his age at the time he takes out the policy, and it remains the same throughout the entire period of payment, unless the contract calls for a lower premium the first few years and then for a slightly higher stationary premium as in a modified life policy.

There are mortality tables containing tabulations on life expectancy, which are used by insurance companies in setting premiums. For example, one of the tables, The Commissioners 1958 Standard Ordinary Mortality Table, shows that 1.69 out of every 1,000 persons of the eighteen-year-old age group will die during a year and that the expectation of a person of that age is 52.19 additional years of life. Since insurance companies require a physical examination before a person can be insured, their mortality rate is generally better than the ones given in a table. This provides a margin for the insurance company, a part of which is invested by the company, thus drawing interest that helps lower the cost of the insurance. The policyholders in so-called participating companies will receive what is termed a dividend, which comes from a portion of the surplus. Other companies, which are nonparticipating companies, provide insurance at lower premiums but distribute no dividends. Premiums are based on providing insurance to a large group of people. The actuarial tables are based on averages and are valid only when they are applied to a large enough group to make the law of probabilities work.

A policyholder can cancel his life insurance contract at any time, but the insurance company may not cancel it after a specified time for any reason other than fraud or non-payment of premiums.

There are four basic types of family protection in life insurance. These are: (1) whole (or straight or ordinary) life, (2) term, (3) limited-payment life, and (4) endowment. Each of these types will be described.

Whole or Straight Life. Whole life insurance or ordinary life or straight life are interchangeable terms. This type of insurance derives its name from the fact that it provides protection for the entire lifetime of the insured person. The premiums will be paid during the entire period the policy is in effect. This insurance accumulates a cash reserve and has a cash surrender value (an amount available in cash upon surrender of a policy before death or maturity) upon which loans may be made by the insurance company for payment of premiums or for other purposes. Table 25–1 gives the approximate cost of various kinds of

Table 25–1. What Various Policies Cost

Approximate Annual Premiums for $1,000 of Insurance *

Type of Policy	Age at Which Policy Is Issued					
	20	21	22	23	24	25
Five year term (Renewable and convertible)	6.80	6.90	7.00	7.10	7.20	7.30
Ten year term (Renewable and convertible)	6.89	6.90	7.00	7.10	7.20	7.30
Straight life	14.15	14.50	14.85	15.25	15.65	16.10
Life-paid-up-at-65	16.20	16.60	17.10	17.60	18.15	18.70
20 payment life	25.85	26.30	26.75	27.25	27.75	28.30
Retirement income at 65 (Male)	25.50	26.30	27.15	28.05	29.05	30.15
20 year endowment	46.95	47.00	47.05	47.10	47.15	47.20

* Rates shown are approximate premium rates for life insurance protection. Rates of "participating" policies would be slightly higher but the cost would be lowered by annual dividends. "Non-participating" policy premium rates would be somewhat lower than those shown and no dividends would be paid.

SOURCE: Institute of Life Insurance, 1965.

insurance at different ages of the insured. A man twenty-four years of age who purchased a $10,000 straight life policy would pay an annual premium of $156.50 for this insurance, as shown in this table. At the end of ten years, the cash value of this policy, according to the Institute of Life Insurance, would be about $950. It would be $2,430 at the end of the twentieth year. If he wants to give up his policy at any time, he will receive the cash surrender value of it, or he can convert it into a smaller paid-up policy.

Term Insurance. Term insurance provides temporary protection and has the lowest premium of any life insurance. It gives protection for only a stated period of time, such as one year, five years, ten years, and so on, and has no cash surrender value. It is paid only if the insured dies within the given period. A term policy may be convertible into other types of life insurance, in which case the policy might be exchanged for straight life insurance, for example, at a higher premium without taking a medical examination. Some term policies, however, are not convertible. This type of insurance policy is often renewable. The insurance company will agree to extend the policy in the same amount for a similar period of time but, of course, at a higher premium based on the age of the individual at the time of renewal. Usually, the renewable privilege, if there is one, does not go beyond a specified age, such as sixty.

Limited-Payment Life. Limited-payment life insurance permits the insured to concentrate the payment of insurance premiums in the productive working years. It provides lifetime protection, as ordinary life insurance does, but the premium payments are made for a stipulated period of years, such as 10, 15, 20, 25, and 30 years. These insurance plans are referred to as *10-pay life, 20-pay life,* and so on. The shorter the period of payments, the higher the premiums. The same amount of protection can be secured from an ordinary life policy at a considerably lower premium than under the limited-payment life. For example, for a young man twenty-three years old, $10,000 of ordinary life would cost $152.50 (Table 25-1) per year. If he took a "20-pay" policy with $10,000 of protection at the same age, his annual premium would be $272.50. The higher premium for the same amount of protection is occasioned by the fact that he pays this premium for twenty years rather than life. The amount spent for premiums on a 20-payment policy would buy a great deal more insurance protection in an ordinary or in term life insurance.

Endowment Life Insurance. Endowment life insurance provides insurance protection but, in addition, is a savings plan. The premiums on this insurance are higher than on any of the others because a large portion of the premium constitutes a savings. At the end of a specified period, such as ten, twenty, or thirty years, when the endowment policy matures, the face value of the policy is paid to the insured, either in a lump sum or in monthly installments. If the insured dies at any time during the life of the policy, the beneficiary is paid the face value of the policy. As shown in Table 25-1, a 20-year endowment at age twenty-two would cost $470.50 a year, whereas $10,000 of ordinary life would cost $148.50 annually. As in limited-payment life, the shorter the term of the endowment policy, the higher the premium.

Annuities. Many persons purchase an annuity from a life insurance company. The annuity is a contract that provides an income for a certain period of time, such as a stated number of years or for life. A lump sum is paid at one time in purchasing the annuity, and later payments are made periodically by the insurance company during the lifetime of the annuitant (the person purchasing the annuity), which cease upon his death. Many people purchase annuities in order to be certain that the amount of money that they have will be spread out over the rest of their lifetime.

A life annuity can be purchased by means of periodic deposits extending over a number of years. The contract may provide for income payments to start immediately upon the payment of a single deposit or upon completion of a series of periodic deposits, or at some later time. In life insurance, the younger the insured when the policy is written, the lower the annual premium. The reverse is true with an annuity— the younger the annuitant, the greater the amount that must be paid in order to secure a stipulated sum. Ordinarily, there is no medical examination required in the purchase of an annuity.

Annuities can be secured in which two people are guaranteed an income during the lifetime of both. Upon the death of one, the annuity continues without reduction until the death of the survivor. This is called joint life and survivorship annuities. It is also possible to buy life insurance upon the life of one person and combine it with an annuity agreement. When the insured person dies, the proceeds of the policy are used to provide an annuity for the designated beneficiary. This is called a survivorship annuity. There are many additional variations to annuity plans.

Planning Life-Insurance Programs To Meet Varying Needs

Insurance requirements of an individual will differ widely due to earnings, size of family, the age of the family, and the purposes for which insurance is intended. A number of combinations of different types of insurance are often used, depending upon the purposes for which the insurance is designed. Typically, basic insurance in the form of ordinary life insurance would be carried. Term insurance might be added to give extra protection during particular periods when it is needed, such as when dependents are small or to cover a mortgage on a home or business establishment. Endowment insurance might be used for purposes of savings to supplement retirement or to provide college education for dependents. In recent years, insurance represent-atives have provided life insurance programs which are termed *life estates*. A program of this kind involves an analysis of the person's financial position, as well as his future obligations, and the life insurance facilities that are available to supply capital to meet his needs. This, then, makes it possible to arrange for the proper amount of life insurance at the least possible cost.

Business Life Insurance

Since a dominant factor in a business organization is the individual, the loss of a key executive through death can be as disruptive or perhaps more so than the destruction of equipment or the plant. Regardless of the form of business organization, business life insurance is often used.

In the sole proprietorship, life insurance payable at the owner's death could take care of any debts of the business and enable the family to get through the period when the business is being disposed of or survive the financial loss that sale of the business may entail. In a partnership, the death of one of the partners ordinarily dissolves the partnership. If the partnership firm carries life insurance on each of the partners, the insurance settlement at the death of one member can be used to pay heirs of the deceased partner his share in the partnership. The surviving partner or partners then do not have to try to sell the share and are relieved of the necessity of trying to raise money to buy the share.

In a closely held corporation, or a close corporation, the top executive is often a very strong leader who has delegated little authority. His death may work a real hardship upon the company. Possible conflicts between the deceased executive's family and the other stockholders can be resolved more readily with the money provided by the insurance. In any corporation, a contract may be made between the executives and the company stating that the company will make certain payments to its executives after retirement or to their beneficiaries after death. One large corporation pays a premium of $14,000 annually on an annuity for its president. Life-insurance policies on executives will help to meet these company obligations and are also a form of fringe benefit.

Credit Life Insurance

Much of our consumer sales involve sales on a credit basis. Commercial banks, finance companies, and credit unions loan money to persons to buy consumer items like furniture on time payments. If the credit purchaser dies, his heirs are confronted with this debt. This has led to the development of credit life insurance. These financial agencies have group policies that will pay the unpaid balance in event the borrower dies. Credit life insurance policies are term policies; that is, they cover a specified period of time. The premium cost is included in the individual's installment payments.

Industrial Insurance

Industrial insurance is intended to provide ordinary life insurance coverage by arranging that the premiums can be paid on a weekly or monthly basis to an insurance company representative who calls at the home each premium period to make collections. These policies are issued in small amounts, usually not over $500, for which the insured pays 10¢, 15¢, or 25¢ per week or proportionately larger amounts per month.

The amount of insurance that the premium will buy depends upon the age of the individual at the time he purchases the insurance.

Group Life Insurance

Group life insurance is issued usually without medical examination to a group of persons under a master policy. Ordinarily, it is issued to an employer for the benefit of employees. The individual members of the group hold certificates as evidence of their insurance and name their beneficiaries. Sometimes, premiums are partially paid by the employer; and at other times, the employer pays the full premium. Under the employee-contributory group plans, it is customary that at least three-fourths of the eligible employees must accept the plan.

It is estimated that over half of the nation's workers, excluding military personnel and agricultural workers, are now covered under group life insurance. It is basically in the form of one-year term insurance. Because of the new young people who are added to a company's payroll each year, it is possible to use the term-insurance basis and still keep the cost lower than it would be if each person were to take out an individual one-year term insurance policy. Some group plans provide that if an employee leaves a company's employment, the insurance company will write an individual policy for him in the same amount of insurance that he had in the group insurance plan at a premium based on his age at the time that he leaves the employment of the company.

YOUR CAREER IN INSURANCE

Career Opportunities

The field of insurance has attracted many college graduates. It will continue to do so because they find it to be a career with great potential. Persons entering the insurance field usually decide whether they will affiliate themselves with life, accident and sickness companies, or with companies that are in the property and liability insurance business.

Many people work for insurance companies as agents. The agent may be an independent businessman and receive a percentage of the premium on the contracts that he writes. In life insurance, agents usually start on a combination of salary and commissions. To be an agent, you should prefer self-employment to a payroll job since compensation will depend upon your sales and service to your clients. Some companies that are engaged in direct selling have openings for field agents who are assigned to selling in a geographical territory. These jobs would be on a combination salary and commission basis.

It takes some time to build up a good income as an agent so this should be taken into consideration. Insurance companies, however, have other positions available for college graduates. For the student who has a major interest in insurance, there are many areas of specialization from which to choose. He may specialize in foreign insurance, in marine insurance, in fire insurance, automobile insurance, aviation insurance, in bonding, in life insurance, in accident and sickness insurance, or in claims adjustments, as well as other areas. Some people are actuaries whose work is highly technical. There are very great opportunities in this work, and these are positions with very good salaries. Others are accountants, investment analysts, economists, real estate experts, sales and advertising specialists, and others. There are also job openings with the non-profit group insurance companies and with reinsurance companies. In addition, because the states regulate insurance companies, quite often there are openings with state insurance regulatory agencies.

Insurance companies are seeking college graduates because they need well-rounded individuals who can deal with the public. Employment in insurance is not materially affected by the business cycle or seasonal slumps.

Educational Background

Students who expect to enter the insurance field should prepare themselves with a general-business background. This should be supplemented with insurance courses. Many Colleges of Business Administration have courses in risk management, life insurance, and property insurance. Some colleges have a number of other insurance courses. The additional requirements for an actuary would be a concentration in mathematics and statistics. For those who expect to sell insurance, courses in marketing and sales would be valuable. Accounting beyond the principles stage should be taken, and financial management and investment management would be of particular benefit to anyone who is looking toward a future in an executive position. Insurance companies have developed very large reserves that must be invested profitably in order to keep premiums low. Since insurance deals with people and their plans for the future, courses in psychology would be beneficial. Fire insurance companies are interested in fire prevention work, and certain courses in engineering would be valuable for someone planning a career in this kind of insurance.

There is great emphasis by the insurance companies on continuing education while one is employed. Correspondence courses and short courses are offered by many companies to their employees. In order to establish insurance as a profession, the industry has established an examination program that must be successfully completed for anyone in the insurance field to be designated as *C.P.C.U.*, which is Chartered Property Casualty Underwriter, and *C.L.U.*, which is Chartered Life Underwriter.

TOPICS FOR DISCUSSION

1. Since business firms and individuals can self-insure, why is it that everyone does not become self-insured?

2. If you were going to sell life insurance, would it make any difference to you whether the company you represented was a stock or mutual company? Why?

3. Some people have proposed that insurance companies should be subject to federal regulation. Discuss.

4. Would you rather be an insurance broker or an agent? Why?

5. If businessmen would screen their prospective employees more carefully and be more selective in hiring, it would not be necessary to carry fidelity bonds. Comment.

6. What is *your* opinion of life insurance? Why?

7. We are all familiar with what is meant by "insurance." However, are we familiar with what is meant by "reinsurance"? Describe reinsurance.

8. What are some of the factors that affect the rate of fire insurance?

9. There are two types of insurance bonds used by businessmen. Name each bond, and give an example of when each type could be utilized.

10. There are two types of liability insurance that can be carried by businessmen. Name each type, and give specific examples of when each type could be used.

CASE 25–1

LIFE INSURANCE AS A FRINGE BENEFIT

In 1960, William Henderson, Thomas Johnson, and their wives formed the Cherokee Brick Company as a corporation. The Henderson and Johnson families each owned 50 per cent of the common stock of the firm. The company manufactured bricks that were sold to building contractors within a radius of 100 miles of the plant. The venture proved successful, and the firm had grown steadily since its beginning. Profits grew with the success of the firm, and, by 1965, the corporation was paying a significant amount each year in corporate income taxes.

It came to the attention of the management of the business that it might be able to establish certain fringe benefits through the corporate organization. One such possibility lay in the area of life insurance. It was learned that the tax laws would permit a corporation to establish a group term life-insurance program in which the firm would be permitted to pay the premium on up to $50,000 of life insurance on an executive, with the executive so insured given the privilege of designating his beneficiary. The corporation would be permitted to treat the cost of such premiums as a deductible expense.

With the aid of an accountant versed in the establishment of fringe-benefit programs, the firm initiated a group term life-insurance program with policies written on Mr. Henderson, Mr. Johnson, the plant manager, and the sales manager. Each man became the recipient of coverage in the amount of $50,000. The management of the corporation felt that, as the firm grew in size, other employees might be given similar benefits.

Suppose the tax provision that permitted the establishment of policies as discussed above should be up for review. Would you argue for or against the provision?

SELECTED REFERENCES

Angell, F. J. *Insurance—Principles and Practices.* 7th ed. New York: The Ronald Press Co., 1964.

Magee, J. H., and D. L. Bickelhaupt. *General Insurance.* 7th ed. Homewood, Ill.: Richard D. Irwin, Inc., 1964.

Mehr, R. I., and B. A. Hedges. *Risk Management in the Business Enterprise.* Homewood, Ill.: Richard D. Irwin, Inc., 1963.

Mowbray, A. H., and R. H. Blanchard. *Insurance.* 5th ed. New York: McGraw-Hill Book Co., 1961.

Schultz, R. E., and E. C. Bardwell. *Property Insurance.* New York: Holt, Rinehart and Winston, Inc., 1959.

26

Legal Environment of Business

THE NATURE OF BUSINESS LAW

Business operates in an organized society, and its activities must be conducted within the framework of laws that govern society. The daily operations of a businessman deal with some aspect of law. This may be in the contract he has made to buy and sell goods or services, the documents he has signed in connection with borrowing money, the checks he has endorsed, his liabilities from people who represent him, the liability of partnerships, laws affecting corporations, social security laws, and many others. At every turn, he is confronted with some action that requires a knowledge of business law. Essentially, the term *business law* refers to those laws that treat the rights and liabilities of individuals or businessmen who are parties to business transactions. Since earlier chapters have dealt with partnerships, corporations, insurance, and transportation and the legal aspects of these subjects, they will not be covered again in this chapter.

Sources of Law

An early form of law was common law, which was extensively used in England and brought to this country by the colonists. The English common law legal system consisted of principles based on tradition and custom and enforced by the courts. The early decisions of the courts were used as proof of established law, although there was no written law upon which these earlier decisions had been based. Each subsequent decision was based on preceding decisions. This practice of following earlier decisions as statements of law is termed the *doctrine of stare decisis* (meaning adherence to precedent). Common law courts could grant three legal remedies: (1) money damages, (2) recovery of possession of personal property, and (3) recovery of possession of real property.

Because the remedies that could be granted under the English common law system were so limited, the practice developed of appealing to the king who could grant special remedies. This evolved then into a separate court, which became known as the *equity court*.

Each of the states in the United States has a separate system of common law, and this is an important part of our system of law. There are about six states that have separate equity courts. In the other states, law and equity courts have been combined. The same judges serve to handle common law rights and equitable rights. Suits can be entered in the equity courts only if remedy under common law has not been adequate. This does not refer to a money judgment or the possession of personal or real property because these remedies are available at common law. The complainant might be seeking to require that a person perform some action that he had promised to do, such as living up to the terms of a contract. Further, common law cannot prevent the doing of a wrong. It can only render judgment after a wrong has been done. If the complainant can show that great harm would be done if a certain action were taken, an equity court can order that the act not be performed or equitable relief secured from the law and equity court. One of the most common forms of equitable relief is the use of the injunction. Another is the requiring of accounting of funds by the supervising court when a partner suspects that the other partners are misusing funds, which cannot be proved until an accounting is made. There are other uses as well.

In addition to common law and equity courts, there existed for many years what was called the *law merchant*. Much early trade was international in nature, and the merchants carrying on this trade developed their own usages and customs for handling the legal problems of international trade. They established their own temporary courts known as *merchant law courts* and later as the law merchants. Through long usage and court decisions, these customs became accepted as laws, and the common law courts absorbed them. The principles regarding much of our business law, such as negotiable instruments, insurance contracts, sales contracts, and surety, were those that were developed by the law merchant.

Statutory Law.   Statutory law is law that is enacted by a body that has legislative power such as the United States Congress and the legislatures of each of the states. It is a formally drawn statement of law, while common law is found only in the decisions of the courts. Statutory law is often differentiated from common law by saying that it is written law whereas common law is unwritten law. The federal laws, or statutes, must conform to the federal Constitution and state statutes to the federal and respective state Constitutions. Where the federal government has been granted certain powers, the state cannot exercise those powers unless the federal government has not done so. At one time, the lack of uniformity among state statutes caused a great deal of confusion and inconvenience to businessmen. For example, buyers and sellers did not know their legal rights and liabilities in connection with a sale in a state other than their "home" state. As a result, uniform model laws were drawn up covering many aspects of business and included in a Uniform Commercial Code. Contained in the Code are the Uniform Negotiable Instruments Law, Uniform Sales Act, Uniform Bills of Lading Act, Uniform Warehouse Receipts Act, and a number of others. A large number of states have adopted some of these statutes, and at least one state has adopted all of them.

The states can and do delegate power to cities to enact laws, or ordinances as they are called, in the conduct of their own affairs. The ordinances must conform to federal and state constitutional and statutory law. Businessmen are affected by many city ordinances because they deal with such matters as zoning, building codes, licensing, billboards, street traffic, the protection of life and property, and sanitation and health.

Our System of Courts

The system of courts in the United States consists of federal and state. The Constitution provided for the establishment of one Supreme Court and any lower courts that Congress saw fit to create. The right to a trial by jury is granted under the Constitution in criminal cases (those cases involving offenses against the public) and law, or civil, cases (those involving private rights and duties). This is the right to have a case heard by a body of not more than twelve citizens, a jury, which determines the verdict, or decision, by secret ballot that must be unanimous. Congress, under the power conferred by the Constitution, has established federal courts of general jurisdiction and courts of special jurisdiction. Those of general jurisdiction are federal District Courts having original jurisdiction and the Courts of Appeal, which are appellate courts hearing cases of appeals from decisions of the District Courts of original jurisdiction. This means that either party to a suit that has been heard in a District Court has the right to appeal the decision to a Court of Appeals. Attached to the District Courts is the Bankruptcy Court to which administration of an estate in bankruptcy is assigned. The courts of special jurisdiction are the Court of Claims, Court of Customs and Patent Appeals, and the Customs Court. The Court of Claims was created to handle certain kinds of claims against the United States. The Court of Customs and Patent Appeals was formed to decide certain questions that arise under customs law and patent and trademark cases. The Customs Court reviews appraisals of imported merchandise and decisions of Collectors of Customs.

The state court system is composed of three or four levels of courts depending on the state. The lowest of the courts is the Justice of Peace court, which has very limited jurisdiction, usually confined to hearing cases in a community. It handles only cases involving a limited amount of money. Above this court is the trial court, which may be called Circuit Court, District Court, Superior Court, and other titles. They have original jurisdiction as well as appellate jurisdiction, that is, appeal from a decision of the lower court. Some states have intermediate courts, or appellate courts, above the trial courts and another court above this that is a court of final appeal, the State Supreme Court. In other states, there is only a Court of Appeals and no intermediate Court of Appeals. Special courts have been established in some states, among which are Juvenile Courts and Small Claims Courts.

Procedures in Law

Although the laws of procedure are not the same in all of the states, there is a similarity. The legal terms used are identical regardless of the state. The person bringing the complaint or grievance is the *plaintiff*, and the person against whom he makes his claim is the *defendant*. It is customary for each party to a complaint to hire a lawyer or attorney to represent him. Large business firms have their own counsel or lawyer, and they may also retain a law firm to handle special cases for them. This firm may receive an annual amount called a retainer and additional amounts for special work. A judge presides over the hearing. During the trial, he rules on points of law and instructs the jury before it retires to deliberate on the case before reaching its verdict. In the event there is no jury, the judge renders the verdict.

The action in bringing a complaint into court is called a suit. In many states, the issuance and serving of a *summons* on the defendant is the first step in starting a suit. The summons states the nature of the suit and informs the defendant that he must appear on a certain day to defend himself against the charge named in the summons. It is served by a sheriff, constable, or police officer and is prepared by a court at the instigation of the attorney for the plaintiff. *Pleadings* are then filed with the Clerk of the court. These are written statements of the plaintiff and defendant on their positions and are handled in the following manner: The plaintiff through his attorney files a *declaration* or a *petition,* which states the claim in full. It gives the reasons why the defendant should be held liable for payment of a certain sum of money. The defendant then answers each point in the plaintiff's charge. This is called the *answer.* These pleadings are then the basis for the trial of the case in court. Sometimes it is not possible for witnesses to be present at a trial so they submit a statement made under oath concerning their knowledge of the facts in the case. This is called a *deposition* and is used when a witness is ill and cannot appear in court, when a witness lives outside the jurisdiction of the court, or when, for some other reason, the witness is unable to be present. If the case is a law case, the parties may have a jury trial, or they may agree to waive the use of a jury. A jury is not used in cases of equity.

CONTRACTS

The Nature of Contracts

In practically every business transaction and in many personal transactions, there is a contract that determines the legal rights and duties of the parties to the contract. A contract is a binding agreement. Contracts can be made orally; but, in business transactions, contracts are usually written. Many contracts are a standard form and all that needs to be done is to fill in the date, the names of the parties, the price, the article that is the subject matter of the contract, and the signatures of the parties to the contract. Contracts can also cover the performance of services, such as building a house. The parties to a contract are called the *promisor* (the person or firm who makes a promise) and the *promisee* (the person or firm to whom the promise is made). There are other terms used in describing the parties to a contract—for example, in a sales contract they are called vendee and vendor; in a transportation contract, carrier and shipper; and in an insurance contract, the insured and insurer.

Essentials of a Contract

A contract that is legally enforceable contains certain essentials. These are: (1) the offer, (2) the acceptance, (3) consideration, (4) legal capacity of the parties, and (5) legal objective. The *offer* that is made may be oral or written. A person or a firm makes an offer with the intention of creating a legal obligation. The terms of the offer must be made so that they are reasonably understandable. Because in many business transactions negotiations or bargaining are quite common, it should not be assumed that merely because there is a willingness to negotiate that an offer has been made. An offer must be definite. It must state what the person making the offer is promising to do and what he demands in return. Generally, advertisements in newspapers, magazines, and other media of goods and services are not considered to be offers but are simply invitations to deal or negotiate.

To have *acceptance* of an offer, there must be acceptance of exactly what is offered. If the party accepting the offer changes any terms of the offer, he is not accepting the offer because he has not agreed to the offer as it was made. Similarly, if the party makes an offer through a salesman or representative, which is accepted by a customer, and then changes any terms of the offer, the acceptance is not binding. If the person to whom the offer has been made wants to accept the offer, he must agree to all of the terms and conditions before the offer becomes a contract. Often, companies who have salesmen calling on customers require the salesmen to inform their customers when they receive orders that the signed orders are not enforceable contracts until the employer sends his acceptance of the orders, since the salesmen are merely soliciting orders and submitting them to their employer for his acceptance.

Where an offer has been made between parties who have had no previous transactions with each other and there is no reply from the person to whom the offer has been made, this silence does not constitute acceptance. This prevents the wording of an offer to be such that the person to whom it is made must take some action or he will be bound by a contract. For example, the seller might say, "If I do not hear from you, I shall consider that my offer has been accepted." Where parties have had previous dealings, however, the person who has been made the offer may have a duty to reject the offer. His silence may be regarded as an acceptance.

The acceptance of an offer must be communicated directly to the person by whom the offer has been made or to his agent. An offer can be terminated in a number of ways, among which are the revoking of the offer or the rejection of the offer by the person to whom it has been made.

Another essential part of a contract is what is termed *consideration*. Consideration is the price that the promisor demands for his promise. Social promises and promises to make a gift are generally not enforced by court action. It is only those promises that are sold and paid for by the surrender of legal rights or through the assumption of legal obligations that are enforceable by court action. If a student promises to take a friend to the movies but fails to do so, the friend would not have cause of action because no consideration was given for the promise. On the other hand, if a student offers to pay a friend $75 for his typewriter, and the friend accepts the offer, the $75 is the consideration in this contract. The friend has given up his ownership of the typewriter, and the student pays him $75. This contract would be enforceable by court action.

Another factor necessary to make a valid contract is the *legal capacity* of the parties to the contract. Most states require that persons must be twenty-one years of age in order to have legal capacity to enter into contracts. Until a person reaches his twenty-first birthday, he is considered to be a minor. Others who do not have legal capacity to contract are those who are insane or intoxicated at the time and those who are aliens or convicts. Some corporations also are limited by their charters as to the contracts into which they can enter.

The final factor required in an enforceable contract is the *legality of the subject matter*. This means that an agreement that would result in violation of a statute or common law or that would be detrimental to society would be illegal. For example, states have passed laws that prescribe the maximum rate of interest legally permissible for a loan of money, and a rate that exceeds this maximum is considered to be *usury*. If a contract was made under which money was loaned at a rate higher than the permissible rate, there would be no contract. Another example is a contract that would unreasonably restrain trade in violation of the antitrust laws.

Classification of Contracts

Contracts may be classified in a number of different ways, one of the most common of which is formal and informal (or simple). The formal contract is a written contract and is referred to as a contract under seal. When the formal contract is executed, or signed, by the parties to the contract, a seal is affixed or the word "seal" or the letters "L.S." (meaning legal seal) are written on the contract following the signatures of the signers. All other contracts are considered to be informal or simple contracts whether they are written or oral. Informal contracts can be *express* or *implied*. An express contract is one in which the parties to the contract make oral or written declarations of their intentions and the terms of the agreement. The implied contract is one in which neither the intention of the parties nor the terms of the contract are stated either orally or in writing, rather the terms are implied by the acts and conduct of the parties. A typical example of this is the house-wife who calls a department store to have the store send out a sweater. The sales clerk accepts the order and the sweater is delivered. Although the housewife did not say that she would pay for the sweater, there is an implied promise that she will do so.

Contracts that have been fully performed are called *executed con-tracts*. This refers to contracts in which all the terms of the contract have been carried out, and nothing remains to be done under the con-tract. Most business contracts are what are termed *bilateral contracts*, that is, contracts that involve an exchange of promises or a promise for a promise. The businessman who promises to sell a building for $70,000 and the buyer who promises to pay that amount for the building are exchanging promises, and this contract would be a bilateral contract. It is desirable that business contracts be in writing so that there is no misunderstanding of the terms of the contract.

Discharge of Contracts

Usually the performance of the terms of the contract will result in the termination of the contract since the parties have carried out their promises. This is known as discharge of the contract by performance. Contracts may also be discharged by agreement. Some contracts con-tain a stipulation that either party to a contract has the right to termi-nate it after giving thirty days' notice; other times, the agreement will contain a clause that states that the contract will be terminated upon the performance of a certain act or lack of performance regardless of whether the other terms of the contract are completed. For example, a contract might contain as one of its clauses the stipulation that a cer-tain number of units would be produced and furnished by one party to the contract to the other party. If this number is not provided, the contract could be discharged by agreement. Other methods of dis-charge are the *impossibility of performance*, such as by death or illness; by *operation of the law*, as in mergers; and the *breach of contract*. The latter occurs when one or both parties fails or refuses to perform the contract. The party who is injured as a result of the breach of contract can bring an action in the courts for damages or to require performance of the contract. The court may render a *judgment* (which is an obliga-tion to pay) against the defendant in the action for damages equal to the value of the gains the injured party would have enjoyed if there had been no breach of contract. If a money judgment for damages is not an adequate remedy, the injured party may secure an award from an equity court requiring specific performance of the contract. If a judg-ment is not paid by the person against whom it has been rendered, the amount of damages can be collected through sale of as much of the debtor's property as is necessary to pay the judgment, except for property that is exempt from such action under state law. If the debtor does not have property that can be sold, it is possible to secure a *garnishment*. A garnishment is a notice to anyone holding funds or property of the person against whom the judgment was rendered not to release the funds or property to the person but to account for them to the court. The funds or property might be bank accounts, wages, accounts receivable, or others. State statutes govern the use of garnishments. Businessmen are often served garnishments that require them to withhold a certain part of wages from an employee who has failed to pay installments on merchandise that he has purchased. Businessmen also use the garnishment to satisfy judgments when the debtor possesses no property but is a wage earner.

AGENCY

The Nature of the Agency

Businessmen are constantly faced with the need for a knowledge of agency law. This is due to the fact that so many business transactions involve an agency relationship. The *agent* is a person who is authorized to act for another, his *principal*, in business transactions with third parties. The actions of the agent obligate the principal to a third person or give him rights against third persons. An individual may appoint an agent to act on his behalf, and groups of persons can also act through agents. As a matter of fact, a group of persons organized as a corporation have to make a contract through an agent since the corporation is not a living person. Through an appointed agent, a businessman may conduct a great many more business transactions than he could otherwise. Agents can be appointed to represent companies in different parts of the country.

We have come to associate the term *agency* with a somewhat different meaning from that it possesses in law. For example, we speak of a dealer in automobiles as having an automobile agency. The dealer is not an agent for the automobile manufacturer, however, and does not represent him in making contracts with third parties.

Power of Attorney

One of the ways by which an agent is named is for him to be appointed by the principal. In some instances, this is done orally, although some states require that the appointment of an agent must be in writing. Where there is a written authorization by the principal to the agent to perform specific acts in behalf of the principal, this is usually referred to as *power of attorney*. The agent does not need to be an attorney, though. There are instances in which an agent involved in a business transaction exceeds his authority and, in such cases, his acts do not bind his principal. It is possible, under these circumstances, to have the agent's acts bind the principal if the principal ratifies, or approves, the unauthorized acts. For this to occur, the principal must be in existence at the time the acts were done, the acts must have been done in the name of the principal, and the principal must indicate that he intends to be bound by the acts of the agent. The agent cannot delegate authority by creating subagents unless the principal agrees.

Fiduciary Relationship

The relationship between the agent and the principal is fiduciary; that is, it is one of trust. The agent must not violate the trust placed in him by the principal by seeking to make a profit or obtain an advantage through his transactions as agent. He must also obey lawful instructions that are given him by the principal and must account to the principal for all money or property that belongs to the principal that comes into the agent's possession. In addition, the agent has a duty to inform his principal of all facts affecting the agency so that the principal can protect his interests.

Termination of Agency Agreements

Agents are sometimes appointed to handle one particular business transaction, such as purchasing a building for the principal. These are called *special agents*. On the other hand, a *general agent* is one who may be appointed to transact all of the business of the principal with regard to a particular type of trade or in a certain area. The relationship between the principal and the agent can be terminated by either party. In terminating an agency, it is important for the businessman to realize that he should give notice to third parties who have been dealing with the agent because if they do not have knowledge of the termination of the agency, the principal will be bound by any acts of the agent following the termination. This is the reason that one sometimes sees in newspapers an announcement that a particular person who has been an agent for a company is no longer associated with the company in that relationship. Letters are also sent to the third parties who have done business with the agent.

PROPERTY

The Nature of Property or Ownership

Property or ownership has been defined as the exclusive right to possess, enjoy, and dispose of objects or rights having economic value. The term *ownership* is used synonymously with *property*. We refer to a person or business as being the owner of a building or some other property, which means that he has certain rights or interests in the property. Title to property is evidence of ownership. Ordinarily, we think of property as having a physical existence, such as a factory building; but property, in the legal sense, may also be an item that has no physical existence. For example, if the owner of the factory building decided to lease this building to someone else, the lease is also property since the lease confers rights to use the building.

Private ownership of property is a fundamental characteristic of our society. Our Constitution recognizes the right of individuals to ownership of property. Our society has provided that the individual property owner is restricted to a certain extent in the use of his property, in order to provide protection for all of us. An owner cannot use his property, for example, in such a way as to be unduly injurious to others, such as maintaining a nuisance on his property that is detrimental to others.

Classifications of Property

The most common classification of property is that of *real property* and *personal property*. Real property is land, including everything under the surface and the space above the surface, and all things that are firmly attached to it, such as buildings. Personal property is all other property that is not real property. Generally speaking, real property is immovable while personal property is movable; although when you take a course in business law, you will find that there is some overlapping in these terms. The objects that are referred to when we speak of owning personal property, such as our automobiles or our household furniture, are referred to as *chattels.*

Another classification of property is based on the ownership of the property and that is that of *private property* and *public property*. Private property is that property that is owned by an individual or individuals or a business organization. The person owning the property has the right to do anything he wishes with the property as long as he violates no law. Even though the property may be used to serve the public, such as a railroad, it remains private property. Public property is that property that is owned by the federal government, a state government, or a political subdivision of the state. Examples of public property would include such things as a city park or a post office.

Property is also classified as being *tangible* and *intangible*. Property that has a physical existence, such as land or buildings or equipment, is tangible; whereas property with no physical existence, such as stocks or bonds or patent rights, is intangible.

Property as Security for Loans

As explained in an earlier chapter, property is often used as security for loans. This is referred to as a mortgage. The property described in the mortgage is pledged to the payment of the loan. When the loan is repaid, the mortgage is cancelled. If the debtor does not repay the loan, the property can be sold to pay the debt. When the property used as security is real property, the mortgage is known as a *real mortgage* or simply *mortgage*. The pledging of personal property as security is called a *chattel mortgage*. When the seller repossesses real property because of non-payment, the action is called *foreclosure*. In action involving a chattel mortgage on personal property, the action is called *replevin*.

Some of the Forms of Ownership

There are different legal terms used in expressing forms of ownership. Some with which the businessman should be familiar are explained here. If certain property is owned by one person alone, it is said to be held in *severalty*. When two or more persons own undivided interest in particular property a *tenancy in common* exists. Under this type of ownership, the interests of the parties in the property may not be identical. In *joint tenancy*, on the other hand, two or more persons have identical interests in certain property. Some states have statutes that provide that property acquired during the period of marriage is *community property*, or property that is owned by both husband and wife.

Bailment

Often, the owner of personal property has to entrust it to someone else for one reason or another. There are innumerable examples of this in our daily lives. A suit is taken to the dry cleaner or a watch to a jeweler for repairs, or shipments are entrusted to a transportation company for delivery, or goods are stored in a commercial warehouse. This legal relationship between the owner of the goods, the bailor, and the party to whom the goods are entrusted, the bailee, is called a bailment. This is a very common type of relationship, but most people do not associate it with its legal term. Ordinarily, the bailee does not have title to the goods even though he has possession of them because it is a transaction that does not involve transfer of ownership. Bailment is based upon an agreement or contract and is usually in writing. It applies only to personal property since real property cannot be placed in bailment. The bailee is required to take reasonable care of the property entrusted to him. He may insure the property so that if something happened to it while it was in his possession he could compensate the owner of the goods for the loss. The owner of the goods has an obligation under the terms of the contract or agreement to compensate the bailee for the services that he has performed. The bailee may stipulate in his contract with the owner, or bailor, that if the owner does not pay him for his services, he has a right of lien on the goods. As explained in an earlier chapter, a lien is a charge upon property for the payment of a debt. Statutes usually require a public sale of property subject to a lien. For example, a lien may be placed upon property transported by rail or motor when transportation charges are not paid as required.

SALES

The Sales Contract

The most common of all business transactions involves the buying and selling of goods. The sale of goods is an agreement by which the seller transfers the title of goods to the buyer for a sum of money or some other consideration, such as property. The person selling the goods is called the *vendor,* and the buyer is called the *vendee.* A *bill of sale* transfers the title of the personal property named in the bill of sale from the vendor, or seller, to the vendee. In most instances, a bill of sale is not required in the sale of personal property, but there are some states whose statutes require that one be given, or the agreement between the parties may stipulate that a bill of sale be given. The bill of sale is always signed by the vendor, or seller.

The transfer of title in the sale of real property is by *deed.* The deed is a written document by which the owner transfers or conveys an interest in land to a new owner. The *quitclaim deed* is one in which the owner transfers to the buyer whatever title or interest he has in the property. The *warranty deed* is one in which the owner transfers his interest and includes in the deed warranties to protect the purchaser in case the title to the property is not as it has been represented. Suppose that you are the purchaser of some property—a home and the land on which it stands, for example. The seller of the property provided you with only a quitclaim deed. This deed transfers to you only his interest in the property. It does not assure you that title to the property, as it pertains both to the land and the building, has passed clearly from all people who had any rights of ownership in it since the land was first recorded in the records of the county in which it is located and the house was first recorded as having been constructed on the land. As the new owner, you have the title searched; that is, you pay a Title Company to look up the records on the property you have purchased. These companies trace the record of ownership of the property to determine, in each instance, that the title passed clearly from one owner or owners to the next. They look for such things as the completeness of each signature on all documents, the fact that all persons who had any right of ownership to the property have signed the bills of sale, that there were no mortgages on the property or any liens that had not been paid, and other matters. If they find any reason why the title is not clear, your rights of ownership in the property are greatly restricted. You would have trouble when you tried to finance your purchase because the lending institutions would not loan money since the security for the loan is property on which the title is not clear. If you decided to sell the property, you could not assure a buyer of a clear title and would have difficulty in selling under a quitclaim deed. On the other hand, if you had purchased property under a warranty deed, the seller of the property guarantees that the title is clear. The title is searched and so stipulated before the sale is completed.

When Does Title Pass? It is often very important to know when title to personal property passes from the vendor to the vendee. If the property is damaged or destroyed, the matter of title to the goods at the time that the occurrence takes place is of importance to both parties. At one time, it was felt that delivery of goods was necessary in order to effect the change of title; and later, that payment of the sale price was considered to be sufficient. Today, the rule that is followed is that title to the goods passes when the parties intend that it shall pass. In cash transactions, as when a candy bar is purchased, title passes at once. In other transactions, the parties should agree as to when the title will pass. For example, manufacturers may sell products with the title passing as soon as the products leave their plant (F.O.B. origin, or free on board [i.e., loaded on the carrier's equipment] at the origin); or they may pay the transportation charges to deliver products to the buyer (F.O.B. destination), in which case the title does not pass until the goods are delivered to the buyer. When parties fail to agree as to when title passes, which often happens, the rules contained in the Uniform Sales Act are used by the courts.

There are many arrangements under which goods can be sold. Sometimes a company will handle a line of goods on *consignment*. Under this arrangement, the owner of the goods retains title, and the merchant acts as his agent to sell the goods.

Warranties

In selling goods, the seller makes statements concerning the merits of his merchandise. Some of these statements are considered to be just a part of sales technique, such as "This is a good buy." On the other hand, the seller may make a specific statement concerning the quality or capabilities of his goods, which is considered to be an *express warranty*. An express warranty may be either oral or written. If it is found to be untrue, the seller is liable to the buyer for breach of the warranty.

An *implied warranty* is one that is not made by the seller but is imposed on the seller of the goods by the operation of law. Under the law, the seller's implied warranty is that he has the right to sell the merchandise and that there are no liens against it. This means that he is assuring clear title to the goods. If the seller sells his merchandise by description or by using a sample, there is an implied warranty that the goods will be as described or will correspond to the sample. The implied warranty is not an absolute responsibility of the seller since he can, by agreement with the buyer, relieve himself of the implied warranty. In circumstances such as this, though, the buyer would certainly be wary of the purchase.

Conditional Sales

Conditional sales are those in which merchandise is purchased under the condition that the purchaser agrees to pay for it in accordance with some prearranged terms. The title to the goods does not pass to the purchaser until he has completed payment of the goods. The term *conditional sales* is also applied to transactions in which the buyer takes legal title but assumes an obligation to the seller in the form of a chattel mortgage, which is a mortgage on personal property. Conditional sales contracts are a common method of selling merchandise on credit and are widely used in the sale of durable goods, such as automobiles, radios, refrigerators, and the like, and in the sale of industrial equipment. Since the title to the goods does not pass to the buyer, except in the case of chattel mortgages, the seller can take back the merchandise whenever the purchaser fails to make his payments. The conditional sales contract cannot be rescinded by the seller and the merchandise repossessed simply because the seller becomes dissatisfied with the terms of the contract. It is only when the contract is breached by the buyer, and usually this is through failure on the buyer's part to meet the payments, that the merchandise can be repossessed. The buyer, on the other hand, has to use the property in a reasonable manner. Often, the contract restricts the buyer's use of the property and prohibits its removal from the county or state without the seller's consent. Conditional sales agreements are required, in most states, to be in writing and to be recorded in the proper records.

NEGOTIABLE INSTRUMENTS

Kinds of Negotiable Instruments

A very large part of our business activities is based on the extension of credit. This is made possible through the use of negotiable instruments, which are written promises or orders to pay money. They are transferable in the ordinary course of business. In the earliest business transactions, some form of negotiable instrument was used. As the scope of trade and commerce broadened, the need for uniformity in negotiable instruments became imperative. In an effort to establish uniformity of the law of negotiable instruments among the states, a Uniform Negotiable Instruments Law was developed and has been adopted by all of the states. The forms of negotiable instruments are: (1) bills of exchange or drafts, (2) checks, and (3) promissory notes.

The *bill of exchange* or *draft* is an order to pay money. The parties involved are the *drawer,* who is the one who draws or makes out the instrument and signs it; the *drawee,* the one to whom the order is given and who is ordered to pay the money; and the *payee,* who is the one who receives the money. A bill of exchange or draft can be drawn so that a payee is not named, and it is merely drawn to the *bearer,* who would be the person presenting the draft for payment.

There are a number of types of bills of exchange or drafts. One of these is a *bank draft,* which is a check drawn by one bank on another bank. This kind of draft may be purchased from a bank and is used when a personal check will not be accepted by the payee. Another type of a bill of exchange is the *trade acceptance.* As explained before, this is drawn by the seller on the buyer for the price of the merchandise sold. Ordinarily, the drawer of a trade acceptance names himself as payee. When accepted by the buyer, it is his obligation that is incurred because of his purchase of the goods from the seller. A *cashier's check* is another kind of bill of exchange. Such a check may be purchased from a bank for a small fee in addition to the amount of the check and may be used when a personal check is not acceptable. It is a check drawn and signed by the cashier of a bank upon the bank itself.

A *check* is an order by a depositor that is made upon his bank to pay a sum of money to another person. It is usually listed as a separate form of negotiable instrument, but it is basically a form of a bill of exchange. The depositor is the drawer and signs the check; the bank is the drawee; the person to whom the check is made out is the payee. Of the types of negotiable instruments, the check is the most widely used. It is readily accepted as payment in many personal and business transactions and often serves as evidence of payment.

A *promissory note* is a promise in writing by one person to pay money to another person. The person making the promise is called the *maker,* and the person to whom the payment is to be made is called the *payee.* The maker must sign the instrument and makes a promise to pay a certain sum of money to a named payee, or to the bearer, on demand or at some fixed future date. The promissory note is widely used when it is necessary for a person or a firm to raise money, as was explained in Chapter 7. Lending institutions often require that the borrower pledge some type of collateral as security for the money borrowed.

Requirements for Negotiable Instruments

The Uniform Negotiable Instruments Law provides that an instrument to be negotiable (1) must be in writing and signed by the maker or drawer; (2) must contain an unconditional promise or order to pay a certain sum in money; (3) must be payable on demand or at a fixed or determinable future time; (4) must be payable to order or to bearer; and (5) when the instrument is addressed to a drawee, he must be named or otherwise indicated therein with reasonable certainty. The last requirement applies only to bills of exchange, whereas the others apply to all negotiable instruments. The negotiable instrument must conform to these requirements or it is not negotiable.

Endorsements

The process of transferring a negotiable instrument from one party to another is called *negotiation.* In effect, negotiation conveys the title to the instrument from the person who possesses the negotiable instrument to another party. A negotiable instrument that is payable to the bearer requires only delivery of it to the other party for it to be negotiable. On the other hand, the negotiation of an order instrument requires the endorsement of the holder and delivery. *Endorsement* is the signing of the instrument by the holder. He must write his name exactly as it is written on the instrument. When the instrument is endorsed and delivered, title to the instrument is passed. There are several kinds of endorsements. An *endorsement in blank* is one in which the endorser simply signs his name:

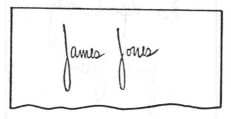

It is the most common type of endorsement and has the effect of making the instrument payable to whomever has possession of it. If a check were endorsed and then lost, the person finding it could cash the check. People usually do not endorse checks until they are ready to cash the check or to endorse it for deposit in a bank. A *special endorsement* is one in which the signature of the endorser is written and above it the name of the person to whom the endorser makes the instrument payable as follows:

A *restrictive endorsement* is one that prevents any further negotiation of the instrument. This is accomplished by an endorsement that reads as follows:

> For deposit only
>
> James Jones

or

> For deposit only
> to the account of
>
> James Jones

When a restrictive endorsement is made, it is the intention of the endorser that the bank is to collect the check and credit the endorser's account. A *qualified endorsement* is one in which the endorser assumes no liability for the check. If the maker of the check should have insufficient funds, for example, the endorser could not be held liable for the amount of the check. Such an endorsement does not affect the passage of title or the negotiability of the instrument.

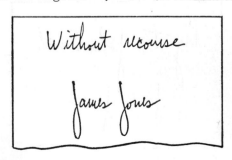

> Without recourse
>
> James Jones

A *conditional endorsement* contains a condition that must be complied with before the endorsement is effective, such as the one which follows:

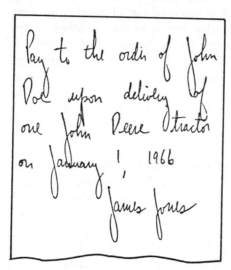

If the maker of a note refuses to pay it when it is presented to him, a *notice of dishonor* has to be given to the drawer and to each endorser. The liability of the previous endorsers, or as they are called *secondary parties*, depends upon whether certain steps were taken within the proper time, so it is important for the holder to be able to prove that he has complied with the requirements of the law. The holder can go to a notary public and inform him that upon the presentation of the negotiable instrument for payment, it was dishonored. The notary prepares a *certificate of protest* that is sent to the secondary parties and is evidence of the facts stated in the protest.

Holder in Due Course

To be a holder in due course, a person must be in possession of a negotiable instrument that is made out to bearer or to the order of a particular person that has been properly endorsed and accepted in good faith believing it to be a good instrument.

SURETYSHIP AND GUARANTY

Suretyship

Many business transactions involve the extension of credit. The person who borrows money may be required to pledge personal property as security, to give a mortgage on real property, to provide a cosigner to a note, or to have someone else agree to perform the obligation if he does not do so. The latter situation, in which one person becomes liable for the debt or undertaking of another person, is called a *surety-ship*. The person who agrees to pay another party's debts if he does not do so or to insure the performance of a duty, such as the construction of a building, is called a *surety*. The surety, who is also referred to as the third person, joins the principal (or borrower) in a contract promising to repay money or to perform a certain act. If the principal does not pay the debt, the surety has to do so.

Guaranty

Another type of agreement is called the *guaranty*. In this type of contract, the third person is the *guarantor*. A guarantor agrees to pay the debt or to perform the obligation only if the debtor fails to pay or to perform the obligation. The guarantor can be made to pay only after an attempt has been made to collect from the debtor. In the suretyship, the surety is liable for the debt or performance from the beginning. Suretyship and guaranty contracts are very common.

BANKRUPTCY

Voluntary and Involuntary Bankruptcy

When a person or several persons start a business enterprise, they anticipate that the business venture will be successful. Under our competitive system, however, there is no assurance that all business enterprises will meet with success. Some fail for one reason or another. When this occurs, the owner of the business often has debts that he is unable to pay. For the protection of the public, the federal government has passed a law that governs the distribution of the remaining assets of a business or of an individual when the business or individual is insolvent (that is, unable to pay creditors). This law is the Federal Bankruptcy Act. Under its provisions, a debtor may be declared bankrupt, or unable to pay his debts, by a court if he requests this action to be taken or if the person's creditors request it. This Act specifies that United States District Courts will serve as Courts of Bankruptcy. These courts have jurisdiction over bankruptcy proceedings within their territorial jurisdiction. When a debtor asks the court to declare him bankrupt, this is called *voluntary bankruptcy*. If the request is made by his creditors, it is called *involuntary bankruptcy*. There must be three or more creditors whose claims amount to $500 or more before a petition can be filed to have the person adjudged bankrupt, and the person must owe more than a total of $1,000 before the court declares him to be bankrupt. Wage earners whose income does not exceed $1,500 a year and farmers cannot be forced into bankruptcy on petition of their creditors.

Procedure Followed in Bankruptcy

When a petition in bankruptcy is filed, creditors may ask the court for the appointment of a *receiver*. The receiver is the custodian of the property of the bankrupt. He does not take title to the property but continues as the receiver until a *trustee* or *trustees* are selected. The Bankruptcy Act provides that a *referee* may be appointed by a Court of Bankruptcy for a term of six years. The referee calls a meeting of the creditors and presides over the meeting. At this meeting, the trustee or trustees are selected by the creditors, or they may be appointed by the court. Under the provisions of the Act, one or three trustees may be selected. They may be individuals or a corporation who takes possession of the property and converts the assets into money as quickly as possible. The trustee then distributes the proceeds among the creditors. Some creditors are *preferred creditors,* and their claims must be paid first. Such debts as taxes owed by the bankrupt and wages to workmen not to exceed $600 are examples of preferred claims against the assets. The trustee must keep accurate records and make a final accounting of the estate. The referee hears evidence and submits his findings to the court. After the preferred creditors have been paid, all other creditors, or *general creditors* as they are called, are paid.

There are many times in bankruptcy proceedings of corporations that a trustee prepares a plan whereby the corporation can be refinanced. As a rule, such reorganization plans cause all creditors to make some sacrifice. When a firm is insolvent and bankruptcy proceedings have been instituted, it is possible that the creditors may decide, through an extension agreement, to postpone the date that their bills are due until the company has a chance to recover. It may be that the assets of the company are inadequate to pay the creditors more than a portion of their claims and that there is strong likelihood that the company could get on its feet. Under these circumstances, the creditors will take over the management of the firm. Creditors can, under a *composition agreement,* agree to accept a reduction in the amount that is due them. In this case, they will have a representative of the creditors assume management of the business.

After a person has been through bankruptcy proceedings, he may start another business if he so desires. The assets of the new business cannot be claimed to cover debts that were not completely paid under the bankruptcy proceedings.

Railroad, insurance, municipal, and banking corporations and building and loan associations are not subject to the Bankruptcy Act inasmuch as other laws have been enacted that provide for the handling of the affairs of these organizations should they become insolvent.

CRIMES AND TORTS

Crimes

A crime is a wrong against the public. Criminal law, which has developed as a separate division of the law, deals with crimes against the state or society as a whole. The state brings action to enforce a penalty or punishment when a crime is committed. Crimes can be classified as *treason, felonies,* and *misdemeanors.* Treason, as most of us know, is an attempt by a person to overthrow or betray his government. Felonies are also serious crimes such as arson, homicide, and robbery. Misdemeanors are less serious and are punishable by a fine or imprisonment in a county jail. Such acts as parking an automobile illegally or disturbing the peace are misdemeanors.

There are many crimes that affect business. Forgery is one of them. A person may sign someone else's name to a document or to a check in order to secure money. The use of mails to defraud is another of the crimes that affect business. False statements made to sell stock in a corporation or dishonest statements regarding the value of goods destroyed in a fire in order to get a settlement from an insurance company are examples of this type of crime. Unfair competition, obtaining money under false pretenses, false weights and measures, and many other crimes occur that affect the operations of a businessman.

Torts

A tort is a wrong against one or more persons in contrast to a crime, which is a wrong against the state or society, as a whole. The person who has been wronged can bring an action against the wrongdoer when a tort has been committed. It is possible for a wrongful act to be both a crime and a tort. The theft of an automobile is such an example. Even though a person who has committed this act is punished by the state for his crime, he is not relieved of his tort liability to the person or persons injured by his act. The owner of the automobile could sue him for the theft of his property.

Under tort law, a person is entitled to the safety of his person, the safety of his property from trespass and conversion, his good reputation, and freedom from interference in his business relations and his domestic relations. The Federal Tort Claims Act enables an individual under certain conditions to sue the United States government for torts of its agents and employees.

YOUR CAREER IN BUSINESS LAW

Career Opportunities

Businessmen must have a basic knowledge of laws that affect them in the conduct of their business. For anything beyond the rudiments of business law, however, they need to consult a lawyer. With the laws affecting business becoming more intricate and more numerous, the businessman finds that there are some occasions on which he has to seek a lawyer's advice.

The practice of law is a respected profession and one that usually pays very well. The student who is interested in business law would have to secure a degree in law in order to pursue this line of work and pass the bar examinations in the state in which he wanted to practice. The field of business law offers many good career opportunities. Many lawyers are specializing in one phase or another of this field—in patent laws; in corporate structures; in work before government regulatory bodies dealing with power, communications, or transportation; and in other areas. Other lawyers are on the staff of a company and are consulted about any legal matter affecting the business. Such companies also retain outside law firms to represent them when the need arises. The opportunities in business law, then, would be to specialize in a particular aspect of law or to give counsel in matters covering a broader area.

Some lawyers are primarily trial lawyers and represent clients in court before a judge and jury. Others are chiefly advisers who show clients how to stay out of court and inform them of the rights and duties they have in the conduct of their affairs. Still others handle every sort of legal activity. Established law firms have junior positions for young men who have just completed their education and passed the bar examination. These positions provide good experience for young lawyers. There are also opportunities for young attorneys to open their own offices. Many do this, although it may take some years to establish a good practice. Often, they are elected to serve as county attorney or appointed to a part-time position with the city council. These positions do not pay a great deal, but they usually bring clients to the young lawyer by helping him to become better known. Many lawyers are offered good positions in industry after they have practiced law for a number of years. Some lawyers are heads of large business organizations.

Educational Background

The student who is interested in business law will have to secure a law degree from a College of Law. His first few years of college, however, are spent taking a pre-law course in liberal arts or in business administration. The student who wants to develop a good background in business law might find it a great deal more advantageous to pursue the pre-law curriculum in business administration. The first two years of this curriculum would be primarily liberal-arts courses, but his third-year work would be composed of business-administration subjects. He would, thus, acquire a good knowledge of economics, accounting, finance, marketing, personnel, and other courses he would elect to take. After he completes his pre-law course, which is usually three years but sometimes four depending upon the Law School requirements of the university where he plans to study law, he enrolls in a College of Law. In many institutions, the student receives the bachelor's degree after the successful completion of the first year of law. Two additional years are then required before he receives the Bachelor of Laws degree. After completion of the law curriculum, state administered examinations are taken. Those who are successful in passing the bar examination are admitted to the practice of law in the state.

TOPICS FOR DISCUSSION

1. What is meant when we say that an instrument is "negotiable"?

2. If someone presented you with a promissory note, what would be the first things for which you would look?

3. If you were a "holder in due course," what would you be?

4. Jones sold Smith a suit of clothes. Before the sale was completed, Jones stated that, because of the strong fiber of which the suit was made, it would "wear like iron." After one year, the suit began to show signs of wear. Smith sought recourse against Jones for breach of an expressed warranty. Will he succeed?

5. Clearly distinguish between the terms *drawer, drawee,* and *payee.*

6. To be negotiable, an instrument must meet certain requirements. What are they?

7. Compile a list of all the legal documents you think would be required in starting a manufacturing business as a partnership.

8. Carefully explain the procedure that is followed when a petition in bankruptcy is filed. What is the difference between a receiver and a referee?

9. List some of the crimes that affect business. As a businessman, how could you protect yourself against them?

10. Is a lawyer always retained by a company when its gross volume of business reaches a certain figure? Discuss.

CASE 26–1

THE RAYMOND CHEMICAL COMPANY

John Raymond, a young chemist, developed a formula for an especially effective paint to be applied to concrete. He decided to open a small manufacturing plant in which he proposed to mix the paint. He began by locating a suitable building that was for rent. Next, he designed the plant layout to accommodate the mixing machines that would be required. He had some difficulty locating the desired equipment but was finally able to locate the machines needed. Unfortunately, he was able to obtain the desired equipment only by buying individual pieces from several different sources. The manufacturing process involved the movement of the materials through several different machines during the operation of mixing and blending. This entailed a rather complicated system of pipes through which the materials must flow. It was evident that electric motors would have to be provided to power the pumps necessary to move the mixture through the pipes. Mr. Raymond noticed that the size of the pipes varied between machines; and in some cases, the mixture would be much heavier than in others. This caused him to think that different-size motors would be needed to do the job.

Mr. Raymond did not know very much about electric motors so he wrote to the Price Manufacturing Company for information. The Price company responded by sending a salesman to talk to Mr. Raymond. Mr. Raymond showed the salesman the drawings of the plant layout and the machines and pipe that had been purchased. He explained the manufacturing processes and the nature of the liquids to be piped. The salesman made detailed notes and promised Mr. Raymond that he would study the situation and advise him on the size and type of motors needed.

Three days later, Mr. Raymond received a letter from the Price salesman in which a specific electric motor was recommended for each pumping job. Prices were quoted, and Mr. Raymond was urged to order immediately. The salesman promised to assist in the installation of the motors. One week later, Mr. Raymond wired an order to the Price company requesting shipment of the motors named in the salesman's letter.

In due course, the motors arrived and the Price salesman was present when they were installed. The following week Mr. Raymond began operations. On the third day of operations, two of the electric motors burned out. This occurred at a time when a large quantity of the product was in the mixing stage. The chemical nature of the product was such that the several hours' interruption required to replace the motors ruined the mixture. In addition, several pieces of machinery were damaged when the mixture was allowed to stand in the vats for a prolonged period. A repairman called by Mr. Raymond said that the motors that had burned out were too small for the pumping job to which they had been assigned. Considering the loss of the product in process—which had to be thrown out—and the damage to the machinery, as well as the loss of time, Mr. Raymond felt that he had suffered a loss in excess of a thousand dollars due to the breakdown. Consequently, he wrote the Price company and explained what had happened. He asked for an adjustment to cover the loss suffered through the failure of the motors. The Price company refused an adjustment, contending that their guarantee covered the motors under normal usage, and that the fact that the motors had been overloaded was proof that normal usage had not occurred. Mr. Raymond instituted a suit for damages.

In your opinion, could Mr. Raymond collect? Why? Why not?

SELECTED REFERENCES

Anderson, R. A., and W. A. Kumpf. *Business Law.* 7th ed. Cincinnati: South-Western Publishing Co., 1964.

Bergh, L. O., and T. Conyngton. *Business Law.* 6th ed. New York: The Ronald Press Co., 1964.

Dillavou, E. R., C. G. Howard, P. C. Roberts, and W. J. Robert. *Principles of Business Law.* 7th ed. Englewood Cliffs, N.J.: Prentice-Hall, Inc, 1962.

Houghteling, J. L., Jr., and G. G. Pierce. *The Legal Environment of Business.* New York: Harcourt, Brace & World, Inc., 1963.

Lusk, H. F. *Business—Law Principles and Cases.* 7th ed. Homewood, Ill.: Richard D. Irwin, Inc., 1963.

Wyatt, J. W., and M. B. Wyatt. *Business Law—Principles and Cases.* 2d ed. New York: McGraw-Hill Book Co., 1963.

Zelermyer, William. *Introduction to Business Law: A Conceptual Approach.* New York: The Macmillan Co., 1964.

27

Information Management: Electronic Data Processing

THE INFORMATION SYSTEM

Information is the foundation of decision making in management. From the very beginnings of commerce, management has sought to maintain records and to use the information contained therein. The primitive trader may have kept his records by cutting notches in a stick, scratching tallies on the wall of a cave, or some equally simple method. As civilization has advanced, the procedures for handling information have kept apace, or perhaps a step ahead of the march. Until comparatively recent times, information was recorded using pen or pencil and stored in files. With the coming of the twentieth century, machines were developed to aid in the collection and handling of information. Adding machines, comptometers, bookkeeping machines, and checkwriters appeared on the scene. More recently, the electronic computer has come into use to bring to information management an entirely new dimension. A well-devised information system requires the performance of essentially four activities: (1) the collection of data, (2) processing, (3) retaining, and (4) the distribution of data.[1] In this chapter, our primary concern will be with the

[1] George R. Terry, *Office Management and Control* (4th ed.; Homewood, Ill.: Richard D. Irwin, Inc., 1962), p. 22.

way in which the computer and the development of electronic data processing have come to influence these activities.

ELECTRONIC DATA PROCESSING

Earlier chapters in this text have referred to the computer and the many ways in which it has come to influence business management. The computer has become sufficiently commonplace that most students will have seen the machine in operation. Figure 27–1 shows a computer and

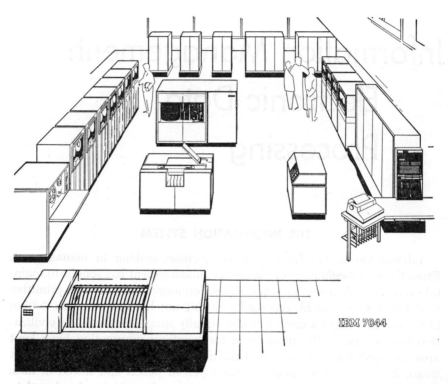

Fig. 27–1. An electronic data processing system (courtesy International Business Machines Corporation).

the auxiliary components that constitute a data processing system. Computers are marvelous devices that perform calculations at fantastic speed; in fact, it is possible to feed information into some computers at a rate of 100,000 digits per second. Calculations are performed in seconds that otherwise would require many man-hours of labor. As marvelous as it is, the computer can be only as effective as the human element controlling its operation. One author comments as follows:

The awe-inspiring electronic computers, with their fantastic accomplishments, have led some to refer to them as machines that think. This is not true. The machines do not think. They operate only as instructed and must be told what to do in the minutest detail. Decision making is not their prerogative except what decision making is given them. They must follow a predetermined pattern of action. This means that managers must still think; they cannot turn this vital requirement over to the computer. However, it must be noted that computers are capable of making simple decisions; they can modify their own instructions as dictated by progressive stages of their data processing. Erroneously, the simplification and improvement in computer operation have given rise to some calling a computer a thinking mechanical human being. It is mechanical, all right, but it is not thinking, and it is not a human being.[2]

The Concept of the Electronic Computer

The computer was developed toward the end of World War II. The need for rapid calculation arising with the development of very complex weaponry focused attention on calculating machines. The period 1944–1946 saw the development of a computer at the University of Pennsylvania. Europe's first computer was produced at Cambridge University, in England. There are two basic computer systems: digital and analog. An analog computer represents a number by some analogous physical quantity such as voltage. These computers measure one physical system against another and establish controls within predetermined limits.[3] Digital computers deal directly with numbers in processing data and in problem solving. They are thought to be more suitable for the kinds of problems and usages associated with management in industry and the administration of institutions. While they do not handle complicated mathematical problems as rapidly as analog computers, they offer greater storage capacity, and the speed of operation is satisfactory for the kind of work encountered.

Digital computers operate by using a *binary number system*. We are accustomed to using a decimal system—with 10 as a base. The binary system is based on two symbols only—the figures one and zero. In the decimal system, when we shift a digit one place to the left, its value is multiplied by 10; in the binary system, if a symbol is shifted one place to the left, its value is multiplied by two. Quantities expressed in terms of the decimal system may be converted to the binary system. For example, the number 19 in the decimal system may be expressed in binary terms as 1 0 0 1 1. As you can see, the binary system utilizes a greater quantity of number spaces, but the great speed at which the computer operates nullifies any disadvantage that might arise from this characteris-

---

[2] *Ibid.*, p. 60.

[3] C. L. Littlefield and Frank Rachel. *Office and Administrative Management* (2d ed.; Englewood Cliffs, N.J.: Prentice-Hall, Inc., 1964), Chap. 12.

tic. The adaptability of the binary system to the digital computer may be seen from the following explanation:

Computers function in what is called a binary mode. This term simply means that the computer components can indicate only two possible states or conditions. For example, the ordinary light bulb operates in a binary mode: it is either on, producing light; or it is off, not producing light. The presence or absence of light indicates whether the bulb is on or off. Likewise, within the computer, vacuum tubes or transistors are maintained either conducting or nonconducting; magnetic materials are magnetized in one direction or in an opposite direction; and specific voltage potentials are present or absent. The binary modes of operation of the components are signals to the computer, as the presence or absence of light from an electric light bulb is to a person. . . . Because binary indications represent data within a computer, a binary method of notation is used to illustrate these indications. The binary system of notation uses only two symbols, zero (0) or one (1), to represent all quantities. In any one position of binary notation, the 0 represents the absence of a related or assigned value and the 1 represents the presence of a related or assigned value.[4]

Basic Components

A computer system consists of a number of interrelated components. There are *input-output* components, *storage or memory* components, *processing components,* and *control* components. Input devices provide the ways of feeding information into the computer. The more common input methods involve the use of punched cards, punched paper tape, and magnetic tape. There are other specialized input devices to accommodate special materials. The input device used is a primary factor controlling the speed at which the computer operates. The more common output device is the high-speed printer. Some printers are able to print out the conclusions of processing at a rate of 1,000 lines per minute. Storage devices are sometimes referred to as the "memory" of the computer. The major types of storage devices are the magnetic core, magnetic drum, and magnetic disk. Information may be placed into it, contained, or removed as the need arises. The nature of the information stored may be in the form of instructions to direct the central processing unit, the data to be processed, and reference data used in processing.[5] The storage capacity of the system varies with the type and size. Some of the more recent computers have an almost unlimited storage capacity.

In processing data, the computer performs addition and subtraction, and, through repeating, it may perform multiplication and division. Also there are operations such as the logical comparison of items of information. The fundamental operations of the computer involve very simple

---

[4] International Business Machines Corporation, *General Information Manual,* 1960 —revised 1964—p. 18. (Information quoted through courtesy IBM, Poughkeepsie, New York.)

[5] *Ibid.*, p. 29.

arithmetic; however, the operations are performed with incredible speed and encompass vast quantities of data. The control unit of the computer uses the stored program of instructions and tells the machine what to do and the order in which it is to be done. The control unit, when activated by the program of instruction, can call data from the storage unit, process it, return it to storage, and cause the printer to print out the results of the operation. The control mechanism operates through a combination of switches that act on the circuitry of the machine. Figure 27–2 shows

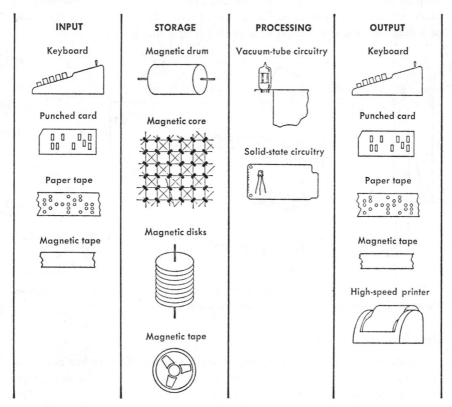

Fig. 27–2. A glossary of basic computer components.

certain of the mechanical principles associated with the basic components of the computer.

THE COMPUTER IN OPERATION

The Problem and the Data

The computer is an aid in handling almost every type of business problem. It is applicable in those situations where the data may be reduced to some symbolic form. When management studies a problem, or a production or administrative process, it soon becomes apparent to the experienced person whether the information exists, or can be converted into a form, that may make utilization of the computer possible. In a complex situation, much study and much planning go into the decision to use electronic data processing. A complete familiarity with the problem at hand, as well as a knowledge of the machine components, their manner of operation, and their limitations, is essential. It is usual for a team of individuals to combine their efforts in achieving the planning necessary to place a computer system in operation. Figure 27–3 shows, in the form of a diagram, the conversion of a problem to a machine program.

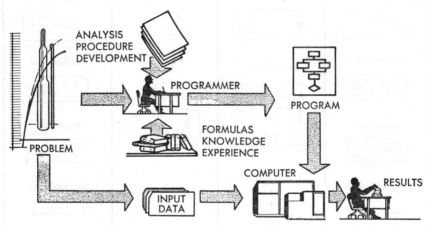

Fig. 27–3. Steps in the conversion of a problem to a machine program (courtesy International Business Machines Corporation).

Developing the Program

A data processing system involves handling a specific number and type of operations. Someone must decide the exact operations to be performed and the exact sequence in which the performance is to take place. The sequence may involve such operations as selecting the items of information to be used, locating information in storage, transferring the information, processing, returning to storage, and discharging the results through the output device. The preparation of customers' invoices by a computer may involve as many as 1,500 or more instructions.[6] As a step in the development of a program, operational flow charts are designed. Figure 27–4 shows such a chart detailing the operations involved in designing a program to handle the data processing arising through the issu-

---

[6] Terry, *op. cit.*, Chap. 5.

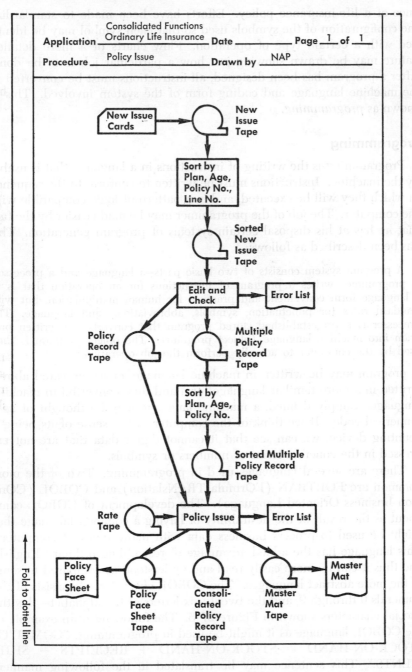

Fig. 27–4. Operational flow chart in data processing (courtesy International Business Machines Corporation).

ance of a life-insurance policy. Efforts have been made to standardize the configuration of the symbols used so that each symbol may be identified with a certain type of operation. Flow charts of a more detailed nature may be drawn showing just how a particular job is to be done. After a program has been designed, all instructions must be converted to the machine language and coding form of the system involved. This is known as *programming*.

Programming

Programming is the writing of instructions in a language that is usable by the machine. Instructions must be written to conform to the sequence in which they will be executed, and in a pattern of logic compatible with the computer. The job of the programmer may be made easier by the fact that he has at his disposal certain systems of program generation. This has been described as follows:

> A program system consists of two basic parts—a language and a processor. A programmer writes a program of instructions for an operation that is in a language form convenient and practical for human manipulation, but with standard rules for punctuation, symbols, abbreviations, and language. The processor is a pre-established stored program that converts the written program into machine language (object program). The object program is then used by the computer to actually perform the job operation.[7]

A program may be written in machine language, or as indicated above, written in a more familiar language form and then converted to machine language. Simply defined, a machine language may be thought of as a numerical code. If we think of the computer in the sense of its being a counting device, we can see that it cannot digest data that are not expressed in the concrete terms of numbers or symbols.

There are several languages used in programming. Two of the more common are FORTRAN (FOrmula TRANslation) and COBOL (COmmon Business Oriented Language). The development of COBOL came about as the result of the desirability of having a common language that might be used to process business data with many types of computers. This language has the added advantage of resembling ordinary English, and thus it can be more easily read and understood as compared to some of the more abstract languages. The COBOL *character set* consists of the numerals 0 through 9, and the twenty-six letters of the alphabet—plus the special characters shown in Figure 27–5. The following is an example of the COBOL language as it might be used in programming: "COMPUTE STOCK-ON-HAND = STOCK-ON-HAND + RECEIPTS − SHIPMENTS." This sentence may be translated in the following manner:

---

[7] Littlefield and Rachel, *op. cit.*, p. 209.

Name	Character	Card Code
Space		(blank)
Plus Sign	+	12
Minus Sign ⎱	—	11
Hyphen ⎰		
Multiplication Sign ⎱	⁕	11-4-8
Check Protection Symbol ⎰		
Division Sign	/	0-1
Left Parenthesis	(	0-4-8
Right Parenthesis	)	12-4-8
Comma	,	0-3-8
Period ⎱	.	12-3-8
Decimal Point ⎰		
Dollar Sign	$	11-3-8
Equal Sign	=	3-8
Quotation Mark	'	4-8

Fig. 27–5. Special characters used in the COBOL language (courtesy International Business Machines Corporation).

"Compute the value of the expression at the right of the equals sign (i.e., STOCK-ON-HAND + RECEIPTS — SHIPMENTS), and change the value of the item at the left of the equals sign (i.e., STOCK-ON-HAND) to equal this value." [8] The above instructions written in COBOL would then be converted by a processor to the machine-language code and then executed by the computer.

Innovations in programming and changes in the computer system itself have combined to strip the computer of some of its mystery. The ability of the executive to appreciate the computer and to communicate with those at the operational level has improved as a result of simplification in programming.

THE APPLICATION OF ELECTRONIC DATA PROCESSING

Routine and Non-routine Processing

Perhaps we most often think of electronic data processing as a system for the automation, or at least partial automation, of the records and information functions. A system may be programmed to handle a payroll, including the many types of deductions. This would represent the performance of a somewhat repetitive task for each pay period. The processing of a payroll may be viewed as a routine project. There may be other situations in which the computer system may be called on to do what has been described as "non-routine processing." For example, the

[8] IBM General Information Manual: COBOL (Poughkeepsie, N.Y.: International Business Machines Corp., 1961), Chap. 1.

system may be called on to tabulate and perform certain analytical functions relative to a marketing survey. In the following discussion of applications, the student will recognize some of these as being of the routine type and others as representing non-routine processing.

Examples of Applications

The extensive use of the computer and related equipment in the administration and control of business operations is now accepted. The examples cited here are intended to be representative of what is being done. There are now situations in which we have fully automated factories. In these plants, the production processes are scheduled, controlled, and monitored by a computer system. Machining operations may be controlled from the point of reading a blueprint to include setting and adjusting the machines as they operate. In the case of certain items, inventory management has been automated through electronic data processing. Stocks of materials are monitored; reorders are automatically printed; and, when orders are delivered, the invoices may be checked against the purchase order.

In the area of marketing, continuous sales forecasts are possible. Data on sales made and information on changes taking place in the market may be fed into the computer to make possible up-to-date sales forecasts at any time. As stated in an earlier chapter the computer may be used in making marketing decisions; the use of models in an effort to optimize advertising expenditures in relation to sales would be an example. In all phases of business management, the computer is utilized in the handling and processing of what we term "paper work." Customers are billed; credit ratings are checked; and, in correspondence, the replies to certain types of incoming mail may be produced by a computer system. Banks, insurance companies, public utilities, and other organizations having to maintain customer records and to correspond with customers at intervals find electronic data processing especially adaptable. One can well imagine the savings involved when a system can handle automatically the thousands of monthly bills and statements that such firms must send to customers. Transportation agencies have found computer systems adaptable to the problems of scheduling. Airlines are able to know instantly the number of vacant seats on flights originating at various cities within the system. Colleges and universities are now using computer systems to maintain student records, assemble and print grade reports, and bill students for financial obligations. The trend toward the use of the computer in the management of all types of organizations is continuing. Innovations in computer equipment are now placing the service within the reach of medium-size and small organizations that heretofore could not afford it.

Integrated Data Processing

The term *electronic data processing* encompasses the use of the computer plus various types of auxiliary equipment. The term *integrated data processing* refers primarily to a system that ties together different types of office machines through the use of common media and integrates their operations into a unified system.[9] In order for the computer and its auxiliary equipment to share in the handling of data, it is necessary that a common language link be maintained. A common language medium joins the various machines and permits the direct transmission of data from one to another. There are three common language media in use today. They are (1) perforated tape, (2) punched cards, and (3) edge-punched cards. The various machines constituting the "system" may be located in a single office; however, this is not a necessity. The machines may be linked by wire and dispersed over a wide area. Plants located in different geographical areas may thus feed information into a centrally located system for processing. While it is true that in many firms, especially large organizations, one will find the computer working in conjunction with items of auxiliary equipment, it should be noted that the computer frequently handles the entire job of data processing within itself.

DECISIONS FOR MANAGEMENT

Feasibility of a System

Despite the rapid growth of electronic data processing in industry and other areas, one cannot say that every business firm should own a computer. As the computer first gained prominence, it was felt that some firms bought the equipment prematurely. There was the suspicion that an element of "status" attached to the installation of the equipment. In the early days of its development, the computer was not available in the variety of "sizes" found today. Thus, it was difficult for many firms to fit the equipment to the scale of their needs. While all firms have administrative work and other activity adaptable to data processing, they may not have needs of sufficient scale to justify the installation of a system. Now, these firms often are able to "rent" computer time from agencies that specialize in providing this service. The decision to install electronic data processing should be made with very careful planning. The effect of the system is likely to bear upon all departments of the firm, not just the area of office management. If the executives of the firm have not had

[9] Terry, *op. cit.*, Chap. 7.

firsthand experience, they should perhaps employ consultants to do a feasibility study.

Cost Considerations

There are very small computers costing under $25,000, and there are large ones that cost in the neighborhood of $3 million. Most computers are utilized on a rental basis, and the typical rental for a small computer may be around $1,000 per month; a medium-size machine, around $5,000 per month; and a large one may rent for from $20,000 to $50,000 per month. These are average estimates and would vary with the type and the sophistication of the equipment used. In considering the installation of a system relative to cost, management must attempt to answer two questions: (1) "What savings may we expect through the displacement of present personnel and methods?" and (2) "What are the intangible benefits that may accrue?" Electronic data processing implies the automation of information handling. It is expected that the installation of a system will displace certain clerical workers and others presently employed in handling "paper work." If the payroll of employees in this category has been $25,000 per month, and if this can be reduced to $10,000 per month, at least a part of the rental cost may be covered through this saving. Most firms will make an effort to retain employees displaced by the new equipment, and this may involve the cost of retraining. If such is the case, this must be considered as a part of the cost of conversion to an automated system. Perhaps of equal importance are the savings of an indirect, or intangible, type that may result from the conversion to electronic data processing. Management may benefit from having more information than before and from having this information in a more up-to-date and accurate form. The influence of the system on the management of the firm, especially to the extent that it may make better management possible, should be a consideration when costs are discussed.

Personnel Considerations

As stated above, the installation of electronic data processing usually means that certain employees are displaced. Unless the firm is prepared to transfer these employees to other jobs or to retrain them, morale problems are likely to arise. If the firm is unionized, labor conflict is likely, unless displaced workers are provided for in some manner. The type of employee displaced may not be easily transferable to another division of the company. The clerical worker may not prove adaptable to a production job. The problems of retraining may be difficult, especially in regard to older employees. Certain office employees may be retrainable to work with a computerized system, while others may be unable to acquire the necessary skills. Even with the best programs of retraining, it will usually be necessary for the firm to go outside and hire certain specialists when electronic data processing is installed. Systems analysts, programmers, and others continue to be relatively scarce, and the salary cost in employing persons with these skills may be high. Management must keep in mind that even the most expensive equipment will fail to serve its purpose unless competent supervisors and operators are available. In fact, a system that is poorly manned may generate problems well in excess of the benefits that may accrue from its use.

YOUR CAREER IN ELECTRONIC DATA PROCESSING

Opportunities

The demand for persons with technical skill in the area of electronic data processing continues unabated. Job titles have not clearly emerged, although one hears reference to *systems analysts, programmers,* and *operators.* These terms may imply different degrees of skill and training, depending on the customs of the firm in question. Generally speaking, systems analysts are concerned with designing information systems and maintaining their operation. Such a person must have a thorough knowledge of the business firm, as well as a knowledge of the particular computer and auxiliary machines that are to be used. Thus he may be said to operate with "one foot in business management and the other in computer technology." The demands for the individual who can bridge the gap between the computer, on the one hand, and the typical business executive, on the other, are much in evidence. The term *programmer* varies in the degree of skill implied. In some situations, programmers become involved in designing systems, formulating problems, and doing other work requiring detailed knowledge of computer systems and how they work. There are other situations, in which the job of the programmer may become rather a matter of routine and a job performed without a high degree of technical training. In connection with electronic data processing, there are numerous jobs requiring the services of operators. These individuals may be trained for a very specific job—a job that involves some mechanical knowledge of the machine.

In the higher echelons of employment in computer-related work are a special group referred to variously as "computer scientists" or, in some cases, "computer technologists." These people often have graduate degrees in mathematics or some phase of engineering, and they are skilled in such areas as model building and the devising of intricate systems of computer application. Needless to say, these individuals are well rewarded in our technological society.

When one speaks of opportunities in relation to the computer and data processing systems, he should go beyond the scope of those directly involved in the operation of the system. Young executives in management today who have knowledge of the computer and its applications, along with some understanding of information systems, will find this a great help in advancing themselves. As mentioned earlier in this text, some companies attribute such importance to the computer and information processing that all their management trainees are placed in this department for a part of their training.

Education and Training

A student who aspires to a career in what has been referred to as "computer science" should acquire an extensive educational background in mathematics and statistics. Perhaps, the student in business administration with an interest in, and inclination toward, computer-related activities might well think in terms of developing a facility comparable to that attributed to the "systems analysts." Persons aspiring to this type of work should combine education in business management with courses in mathematics and statistics. In addition to the general courses in business management, accounting should be taken at least through the level of *cost accounting*. A combination of not less than twenty-four semester hours of mathematics and statistics is thought necessary. In recent years, colleges have begun to offer courses in integrated data processing and systems design, as well as other courses that develop an understanding of computer systems. These courses should be taken by those who hope to specialize in this work, and also by those who hope to go into executive-management training.

Companies having electronic data processing systems have developed programs for training personnel. One source states that "Most individual companies are doing their own training for computer programers and systems analysts, recognizing that trained and experienced employees are in high demand and difficult to acquire." [10] Although firms may have well-organized training programs, they will try to find employees who have an adequate background. Where promising employees are deficient in that they do not have sufficient educational background in mathematics and statistics, the firm may pay tuition rates to encourage these people to attend evening classes. In summary, the area of *information management* is an extremely promising one for the young person considering a career. For those anticipating a career in business management, a familiarity with computer systems and information processing appears indispensable.

[10] Littlefield and Rachel, *op. cit.*, p. 250.

TOPICS FOR DISCUSSION

1. Why do many people stand in awe of the electronic computer?

2. Why is the binary numbers system so adaptable to the digital computer?

3. What are the basic input media used in feeding information to the computer?

4. In what way is the information acceptable to the computer limited?

5. What is meant by the term *machine language?*

6. What is meant by *integrated data processing?*

7. What factors enter into deciding whether or not it will be profitable to install electronic data processing?

8. How might a small firm gain access to some of the advantages afforded by the larger computer systems?

9. Computers have been closely associated with automation, and automation has been associated with the idea of machines' replacing people at work. Have you any personal concern with the advances of automation? Discuss.

10. Do you agree that the advent of the computer and the development of electronic data processing have influenced the educational needs of the prospective business executive? If so, in what way? If not, why not?

CASE 27–1

AUTOMATION IN THE OFFICE

The Gilmore Manufacturing Company is a large manufacturer of men's clothing. The company has national distribution and follows a plan of selling directly to selected retailers. At the present time, the company's office force numbers 210 people. The office force is under the direction of Mr. Patrick, who has the title of Office Manager. A prominent part of Mr. Patrick's duties consists of work within the area of personnel management. At the present time, he is faced with a very difficult personnel problem.

Early in the spring of 1964, the company employed consultants to study the operations of the firm, with particular emphasis on records management and control. Upon the advice of the consultants, the company has secured plans for a system of integrated data processing, centering around the purchase and use of a medium-size electronic computer. In addition to the computer, the system will make use of other items of advanced equipment in the office-machines field. Once the system is in operation, the present office force of 210 will be reduced to approximately 125 people. The personnel problem involves determining who will be retained in the office force and also the disposition of those employees no longer needed in the office.

An analysis of employee records revealed the following breakdown in terms of years of service:

Years of Service	Per Cent of Employees
20 or more	9
15–20	12
10–15	15
5–10	17
less than 5	47

It would have simplified things if Mr. Patrick could have adhered to a policy of strict seniority in deciding who would be retained in the office, but the problem was more complicated than this. In the first place, the kind of work required in many of the positions in the integrated system would demand a degree of technical skill not presently found among the employees. At least half of the 125 employees needed in the new system would be required to take training courses. It was the hope of the company and Mr. Patrick that the employees to be trained could be selected from the present office force; however, if this proved impossible, the company would have to hire new personnel. In view of the circumstances, it was decided that seniority would not be a major consideration in assigning personnel to jobs under the new system, except for those positions not requiring specialized skills.

The policy of the Gilmore company relative to automation had always been to retain employees by shifting them to other jobs whenever possible. The company had followed a practice of retraining employees and had tried to avoid downgrading in pay when shifting from one job to another. The present office situation posed problems not encountered in other divisions of the company. The office was the only division of the company employing significant numbers of women. The office force of 210 consisted at present of 160 women and 50 men. It was probable that most of the men could be absorbed in other divisions of the company, but Mr. Patrick pointed out that some of the men now employed in the office represented preferred prospects for the technical training needed in the new system. The company was anxious to solve the displacement problem in a way that would be fair to employees and at the same time enable the company to develop a capable office force to man the new system.

1. What specific procedures might the company follow in meeting this problem?

2. To what extent would the normal rate of employee turnover assist in solving the problem?

SELECTED REFERENCES

Bierman, Harold, L. E. Fouraker, and R. K. Jaedicke. *Quantitative Analysis for Business Decisions.* Homewood, Ill.: Richard D. Irwin, Inc., 1961.

Hicks, C. B., and I. Place. *Office Management.* Englewood Cliffs, N.J.: Allyn & Bacon, Inc., 1962.

International Business Machines Corporation. *General Information Manual: Introduction to IBM Data Processing Systems.* Rev. ed. Poughkeepsie, N.Y.: International Business Machines Corp., 1964.

Littlefield, C. L., and Frank Rachel. *Office and Administrative Management.* 2d ed. Englewood Cliffs, N.J.: Prentice-Hall, Inc., 1964.

Nett, R., and S. A. Hetzler. *An Introduction to Electronic Data Processing.* New York: The Free Press of Glencoe, 1959.

Schmidt, R. N., and W. E. Meyers. *Electronic Business Data Processing.* New York: Holt, Rinehart & Winston, Inc., 1962.

Terry, G. R. *Office Management and Control.* 4th ed. Homewood, Ill.: Richard D. Irwin, Inc., 1962.

28

Business Research and
Recent Management
Developments

THE ROLE OF RESEARCH

Not too long ago, management in many business firms was prone to belittle research. Little or no funds were allocated to its support. The worth of research has been demonstrated in important technological advancements, however, and the attitudes of management generally have undergone a dramatic change. As a matter of fact, it now seems to be a part of the "image" business firms want to project to the public, as is exemplified by the increased references to it in speeches and annual reports to stockholders. Today, business is deeply immersed in all types of research and strong support is given it.

Since businessmen are considered to be "practical," it is not surprising to find that they tend to engage in *applied* research more than *basic*, or *pure*, research. The latter is concerned with basic scientific investigations directed toward the discovery or development of new fundamental facts, theories, natural laws, or relationships. The primary aim of the investigator is a fuller understanding of the subject rather than any practical application. Scientific curiosity is the motivation for basic research, and it is often performed by government agencies and by industry under contracts for the government, as well as by colleges and universities.

It sometimes happens that the facts developed from basic research are used to advantage in applied research. Some companies that engage in the former type of research do find profitable commercial items to be developed as a result. Nylon and transistors are two outstanding examples.

Applied research is the search for new scientific knowledge and the utilization of all existing knowledge to be applied to specific problems. *Development* is the systematic use of scientific knowledge directed toward the production of useful materials, devices, systems, or methods including design and development of prototypes and processes. Thus, one often finds business firms with research *and* development activities. There are a number of general areas of research and development in business operations. The principal ones are *product research, marketing research,* and *economic research.* These areas often overlap, especially in marketing and product research.

Types of Data Used in Research

Two types of data are used in research: *primary* and *secondary.* Primary data, as was explained in Chapter 24, is that which is developed by the person conducting the research in the course of his study. Data of this type might be statistics that were compiled from the results of a questionnaire that the researcher formulated or the results of laboratory tests, or other original research.

Because of the heavy cost of collecting data, extensive use is made of *sampling techniques* in many types of research. The general theory of sampling is that a moderately large number of items taken at random from a very large group are almost certain to have the characteristics of the larger group. In any sampling operation, the *universe* (the entire group of items such as people, stores, or industries to be surveyed) must be defined. There are two methods that are used: (1) the *probability sampling method* in which every item in the universe, such as every chain grocery store in a specified area, has a chance or probability of being chosen for the sample; and (2) the *non-probability sampling method,* in which there is no provision that every item in the universe with a known chance of being chosen will be included in the sample. This means that the person conducting the research will decide what items to select.

Secondary data can be secured from various company reports and from sources outside the company. Probably the most widely used secondary materials in business research are the census data compiled by the United States Bureau of the Census. There are seven different censuses made: population, housing, business, manufactures, agriculture, transportation, and minerals. Registration data, compiled by federal, state, and local government agencies and covering a wide range of subjects—births, deaths, marriages, sales-tax payments, export declarations, and others—are also used. There are guides that contain indexes to periodicals, monographs, bulletins, and even books.

Scientific Methods in Conducting Research

Research assumes that scientific methods are used rather than "hunches" or guesswork. The methods used in the laboratory where conditions make it possible to control all variables, to make exact measurements, and to have objective experimentation and testing are clearly scientific. Much of our research is of this type in the development and testing of products. On the other hand, there is a good deal of research that is not conducted in the laboratory, such as determining consumer preferences, in which it is difficult to maintain scientific methods. It is necessary that this kind of research be conducted in a scientific manner. The steps in the research process in such instances may be as follows: (1) formulation of the problem, (2) determination of sources of information, (3) preparation of the data collection forms, (4) designation of the sample, (5) collection of the information, (6) tabulation and analysis of the data, and (7) preparation of the research report.[1]

A scientific study meets certain standards. The procedure used must be objective and involve accurate measurements. Basic scientific methods that are accepted and recognized must be employed in the study. The person who conducts the research must possess a scientific mind; that is, he must be unbiased, constantly searching for new facts, and requiring logical solutions.

There are a number of basic methods used in scientific research, which are sometimes modified in their use in particular fields. The *historical method* is one in which there is analysis and interpretation of past events. These facts are then used as the basis of understanding of existing problems and future events. In the *inductive method,* general conclusions are drawn from controlled individual observations. It is necessary that there be sufficient data to make it possible to generalize. The inductive method is often referred to as the method of reasoning from the specific to the general. The *deductive method* is to arrive at logical conclusions drawn from generalizations. It is obvious that induction and deduction methods are used together. The facts are gathered and generalizations developed by using induction. From these generalizations, the logical conclusions can be drawn, which is deduction. The *analytical method* is an attempt to discover the true nature or interrelationships of an intellectual problem

[1] Harper W. Boyd, Jr. and Ralph Westfall, *Marketing Research* (rev. ed.; Homewood, Ill.: Richard D. Irwin, Inc., 1964), Chap. 6.

or a substance that does not superficially reveal them. This method divides a complex whole into components that can be more easily observed and understood. The *experimental method* is one in which a solution is sought by keeping all elements constant that will affect the result except the one being measured, which is permitted to vary. This type of controlled experiment involving a very small quantity can be applied to unlimited quantities of like material.

PRODUCT RESEARCH

Factors Considered in the Development of New Products

Companies spend large amounts on product research. This involves the development of new products that will make better use of under-utilized production facilities or the expansion of facilities to enlarge the business enterprise. Management will consider many factors in evaluating product ideas. Will the product fit into the existing line? Will it offset seasonal or irregular demands for existing products? Is there a broad or restricted market for the product? Can it be handled by the present sales force and sold, in general, to the same consumers in the same sales areas? How long would it take to develop the product and can it be patented? Will competition be copying the product and how long would it take them to do so? Are the manufacturing materials needed easily obtainable and already in use in the company? Is manpower available? What are the long-range prospects and estimated return on investment? These and other factors are considered before authorization is given to go ahead on a new product. Table 28–1 shows the steps that might be followed in a large manufacturing organization in product development.

A great deal of product research is also devoted to improvement of the products already in a company's line. Weaknesses or defects in products are analyzed, and research undertaken to correct them. New features may be added to existing products that may have been shown by marketing research to be advantageous to the sale of the products.

Sources of Product Ideas

One of the principal sources of new product ideas in a company is the sales force. Some companies go so far as to regard this as a responsibility of the sales staff. Salesmen know consumer needs and competitive or substitute products. Although products suggested by them are not always acceptable because of technical problems, salesmen are a valuable source of ideas in the development of new products.

A primary responsibility of the research department is the suggestion of new product ideas. This department is the center of a company's experimental research so that many of the problems that it seeks to solve will give rise to product ideas, or new products will be developed as by-products of work on other products. Basic research often gives rise to new product ideas, also.

Other company personnel are encouraged to submit new product ideas as well as other suggestions through established channels, like the suggestion systems. Another source of product ideas is that of sources outside the company, such as investors, stockholders, trade associations, and others. One company that does receive and appraise many ideas from outside the company is General Foods. It indicates that it has received only one promising new product idea by an outsider in years. That suggestion was developed and marketed as Minute Rice.

MARKETING RESEARCH

Methods Used in Collecting Data

Marketing research in some companies includes the gathering, recording, and analyzing of all facts about problems relating to the transfer and sale of goods and services from the company to its customers. Much of our marketing research involves the use of primary data. Data are collected for this research through (1) questioning and (2) observing. A standardized questionnaire must be developed in the questioning method with questions that are not ambiguous. Care must also be taken to insure that all the necessary information is covered and that the questionnaire is not too long. This information can be solicited by mail, telephone, and personal interview. Mail questionnaires are relatively inexpensive, but the percentage of returns may be low. Personal interviews are expensive to conduct but are more flexible. The investigator conducting the interviews has to be carefully selected, though, or his bias could substantially affect results.

Questionnaires can be *structured* or *non-structured*. When no formal questionnaire is used and the interviewer adapts his questions to each interview, the questionnaire is non-structured. Questionnaire studies that have formal, written lists of questions to be asked are called structured. Questionnaires may be constructed so that the person being asked the questions can understand what the objective is, in which case it is referred to as *non-disguised*. When the objective of the questionnaire is unknown to the person interviewed, it is said to be a *disguised questionnaire*. Questionnaires can be classified by structure and disguise into four types: (1) non-disguised structured, (2) disguised structured, (3) non-disguised non-structured, and (4) disguised non-structured.

Table 28–1. Development of a New Product

Step	Department in Charge	Department Assisting
1. Idea	(Submitted by any division or employee or by outsiders.)	
2. Preliminary appraisal and assignment of priority	Research and development	All departments provide data as requested
3. Literature search	Technical laboratory; patent	
4. Project authorization	Company management; research and development	
5. Laboratory research	Research and development	Market research
6. Product formulation and laboratory evaluation	Technical laboratory	Sales; market research
7. Technical and economic survey	Market research	
8. Appraisal and recommendations	Research and development	
9. Pilot plant authorization	Research and development; company management	
10. Pilot plant design	Research and development	
11. Pilot plant construction	Research and development	Manufacturing; outside construction company

598

12. Pilot plant operation	Research and development	Manufacturing
13. Product evaluation (field trials)	Research and development	Sales; market research
14. Tentative commercial plant design and cost estimates	Research and development	Manufacturing; sales; patent division (final patent review)
15. Final technical and economic survey	Market research	All other departments as required
16. Appraisal and recommendations	Research and development	Manufacturing; sales; company management
17. Commercial plant authorization	Company management	All departments (recommendations)
18. Commercial plant design and cost estimates	Manufacturing	Research and development
19. Commercial plant construction	Manufacturing	Outside construction company; (sales department starts to plan sales campaign)
20. Commercial manufacture—initiation	Manufacturing	Research and development
21. Sales introduction	Sales	Market research; patent division (trademark protection); research and development
22. Commercial sale	Sales	Market research; research and development (sales service)
23. Commercial plant—process study	Manufacturing	

SOURCE: National Industrial Conference Board, Inc., *New Product Development*, 1950, p. 5.

The *non-disguised structured* is the most common form used in marketing research. In this type of questioning, a formal list of questions is used, and each selected person is asked the set of questions in a given sequence. The answers range from a simple "yes" and "no" to the use of scales in which weight is attached to each of the questions. There is no attempt to disguise from the respondent the purpose of the inquiry. In the *disguised structured questionnaire,* the respondent does not know the purpose of the questions being asked and, therefore, does not bias his answers. In this type, the respondent is given questions that he is not likely to be able to answer correctly and is forced to guess. It is believed that he is influenced in guessing by his attitudes, which is of help in disclosing motivation. In the *non-disguised non-structured type,* neither the questions nor the answers are predetermined. No fixed list of questions is used, and the interviewer seeks to get the respondent to talk freely about the subject. Since the purpose of the interview is to determine basic motives, this procedure is often called *depth interviewing.* These interviews may last for an hour or more and, therefore, are costly. The tendency has been to use them for a small sample because of the cost. Depth interviews have been utilized in exploratory research, the results of which can then be tested with other methods.

In the *disguised non-structured questionnaire,* projective techniques are used in order to give the interviewer insight into the inner feelings of the respondent. These techniques include word association, sentence completion, story completion, and pictorial tests. These various projective techniques are considered to be useful in uncovering subconscious attitudes and motives.

Observational Methods. Data are also collected through observing. Instead of relying upon the answering of questions on a questionnaire, the observer may go into a store to see what brands people are buying or act as a customer to observe sales methods. The observational method cannot secure the information concerning individual attitudes or plans that can be accomplished through the questioning method. Observing a person buying soap, for example, tells only that he buys a particular brand and a particular size. For example, it does not tell why he likes this soap better than another brand. The observational method is also an expensive method. It can take place in a natural situation, or an artificial situation can be created at a more convenient time and place.

There have been a number of mechanical observational devices perfected and placed in use. Probably the best known device is the *audimeter.* This is used by the A. C. Nielsen Company, a marketing service firm, to record when radio and television sets are turned on and the stations to which they are tuned. The information is recorded on a tape that is then mailed at regular intervals to the Nielsen Company where it is analyzed.

Introducing New Products

The timing in the introduction of a new product is very important. Many companies have found that it is desirable to get in at the start of a new product's popularity because this is the time when price competition may be less than later. Too often, manufacturers enter the market with a product at a time when supply is catching up with demand and prices are weakening. The interval between the time market research is conducted and the product comes on the market may be long enough that the demand for the product has been satisfied, or the consumers' desires have changed.

Some companies use a test area or a test group before general marketing of a new product is undertaken. In some instances, the product is tested and then marketed outside the United States before it is introduced in this country. This was done, for example, when one of the soft-drink companies was introducing a "king-size" bottle.

One of the large tire manufacturers introduced the tubeless tire in a test area because the company wanted information on public reaction to the use of this kind of tire. This product represented a radical change in the concept of automobile tires because the inner tube had long been regarded as a necessary part of the tire and tube combination. The tire manufacturers had conducted extensive advertising in the past of punctureproof and blowoutproof tubes, which increased the reliance that motorists placed on inner tubes. Tire engineers, on the other hand, realized that the inner tube was the source of many tire failures. The problem then was to find out what would be the reaction of American motorists to a tire that required no inner tube, which they had been accustomed to using for such a long time. Before introducing what was considered to be a revolutionary product, it was decided to test market the tubeless tire in order that some facts could be learned before large sums had been spent trying to market it nationally.

A test was conducted, and in view of favorable attitudes toward the idea of a tubeless tire shown by the motorists in the test area and the sales results during the test marketing period, management felt justified in beginning nationwide marketing of the first tubeless passenger-car tire.

In periods of high business activity, some companies that normally would have ascertained consumer reaction to a new product have introduced products without any market research and found that they did not meet with consumer acceptance.

Naming the Product. For many products, the choice of name is very important. A great deal of research goes into the selection of just the right name for a new product. One of the large manufacturers of cake mixes developed an angel food mix that contained a variety of colors randomly spotted throughout the white angel food cake. The sales and advertising personnel, as well as the company's advertising agency, suggested various names. This list was narrowed on the basis of judgment and then further narrowed by the legal department, which eliminated those names that could not be used because they could not be registered. The final list contained six names: Carnival, Confetti, Fiesta, Rainbow, Tutti-Frutti, and Cherry-Almond. Experience in previous products had convinced this company that there was usually one proposed name that was superior to the others. It was decided that personal interviews would be conducted with a sample of housewives who bake angel food cake occasionally. Three widely separated sampling locations were chosen to determine if geographical differences in reactions to the names under consideration were likely to exist. A wide range of middle-class housewives of various ages were contacted. The questionnaire used in the personal interview was designed to determine what pleasant or unpleasant connotations the names had in the minds of consumers, with what representative consumers associated the names, and whether these associations were favorable or unfavorable in nature. In interpreting the results, the list was narrowed to three names; and it was found that "Confetti" was the choice of 59 per cent of the housewives. This was the name that was adopted, and this product became a successful addition to the company's line of cake mixes.

Motivation Research

Business concerns, in recent years, have been emphasizing motivation research as a means of determining why people buy one brand or type of product instead of another. The principal objective of motivation research is to determine the hidden or subconscious reasons for consumer behavior. The indirect research methods that have been described earlier under different types of questionnaire studies are used in connection with motivation research. It is recognized that human behavior is a very complicated thing to investigate, and yet it is felt that an understanding of it helps explain why people are motivated to buy products. This research involves the use of techniques developed in the fields of psychology and sociology. It seeks to determine the attitudes of people toward particular factors, such as the design of packages or the types of appeals that are used in advertisng. Since a product rarely pleases all consumers, it is necessary to select a part of the market and gear selling and advertising to this portion. Motivation research ascertains the positive and negative attitudes among different consumer groups.

There are many assumptions and beliefs held by consumers, which have developed over a period of years. These influence them in their acceptance and purchase of goods. The probing of these assumptions and beliefs in order to determine the bases for them is another phase of motivation research. A study of sensations is likewise important because it represents the reaction of the mind to either a mental or a physical stimulus. Sensations are of especial significance in advertising. Closely associated with sensations are images. These are the mental pictures that are formed as a result of some stimulus. Since consumers form certain images about products, an understanding of the nature of the images can be helpful in the marketing of the product. Like attitudes, images held by consumers can and do change.

Information about motives is also sought since all human behavior is motivated by some need or want. Motives are varied and complex, and our behavior usually reflects a combination of them. All of the behavioral factors, such as assumptions, attitudes, sensations, images, and motives, taken together constitute the total picture of a person. An understanding of these various factors, it is felt, will aid in the marketing of products.

ECONOMIC RESEARCH

Forecasting

Many business decisions rest upon some type of economic forecasting of future conditions. The use of varied forecasting techniques is quite common both in government and in business. The general purpose of forecasting is to provide management with reliable advance information on what future business conditions will be. Through the use of accurate forecasts, management can make sound decisions and plan for the future. *Short-term forecasts* used by business organizations are usually for a period of three months to a year in advance. This type of forecast is often used in the prediction of company sales, both by products and by territories. Based on sales forecasts, production can be determined, material purchased for processing, inventories can be increased or decreased as necessary, and expenses can be budgeted. *Long-range forecasts* are usually for five to ten years in the future. These forecasts are not as detailed as the short-term. Nevertheless, they are equally important. Here, again, sales could be forecast. This would be particularly useful in arranging for long-term financing and new plant development. Long-range forecasting is frequently of a more general kind in which an individual company attempts to predict general business conditions that will prevail in the future and influence the company's business. This type of forecast uses measures of over-all business activity, such as employment, production, price levels, gross national product, as well as other general factors.

Methods of Forecasting.   The methods of forecasting used by companies vary from opinion methods to more scientific efforts. Some companies use what is referred to as a jury of executive opinion. Top executives of the company are asked to estimate what the future demands will be for company products. This provides a variety of views by specialists. The executives draw upon their extensive experience and make future projections of what they feel will occur. By combining the estimates and averaging them, a company has a forecast that reflects the opinions of all its executives.

Opinion polling to forecast economic activity is also conducted by outside business organizations. This type is a more accurate method since it includes more opinions and covers a wider area. Some of the best known of these are the *Fortune Magazine* Poll; the McGraw-Hill Survey; and the Survey of Consumer Finances sponsored by the Board of Governors of the Federal Reserve system, which is conducted by the University of Michigan.   The *Fortune Magazine* Poll is a nationwide poll of top executives in large- and medium-size firms. The information is secured by means of a mail questionnaire that, when compiled, gives an indication as to the direction in which these businessmen expect our economy to move. The McGraw-Hill Survey covers the expenditure plans for plant and producers' durable equipment, that is, capital expenditure plans. The Survey of Consumer Finances is conducted among a limited number of consumers in order to determine the condition of consumer finances and their planned purchases.

Another forecasting technique often used as a supplement to other forecasting methods is the development of pressure indexes.   An example is the ratio of durable to non-durable goods production.   It is well known that durable goods production fluctuates more widely than non-durable goods production over the span of a business cycle. Thus, the ratio tends to increase in periods of prosperity and to decline before a downturn of the business cycle. Another type of pressure index is that of the ratio of raw materials inventories to new orders for finished goods. This is often used by purchasing agents in predicting the prices of raw materials.

The lead-lag approach to forecasting is another forecasting technique that has had a great deal of attention.   Forecasters have long tried to find an accurate index, or indicator, that would show in advance when there would be changes in the business cycle.   Many indexes have been used through the years and discarded as inaccurate. A recent study by the National Bureau of Economic Research showed that there were a number of indexes that have tended to have lead characteristics, which means that they have tended to anticipate the changes in general business cycles. The leads varied from one month to as much as ten months. One of these was common-stock prices, which have a long lead since they reflect changes in the demand for funds to finance capital goods and because investors try to predict future corporate profits in their stock trading. Another lead indicator is building construction since the materials, such as steel and lumber, are contracted for before construction is started. Each of these indexes when used separately, or in combination with other indexes, has only a tendency to lead. None is completely reliable because their lead characteristics are not sufficiently consistent. The lagging indicators such as manufacturers' inventories usually reach turning points after they are reached in aggregate economic activity. Careful study of lead and lag indicators is of material assistance in forecasting.

Econometrics

One branch of economics has developed a method of explaining past economic activity and predicting future economic activity by using mathematical equations to express the most probable interrelationship between a set of economic variables. This is called *econometrics,* or economic measurement. Some of the economic variables included in an equation are inventories, government revenues and expenditures, disposable income, and foreign trade. The economist uses past events to express in mathematical terms what seems to be a valid relationship among the variables. This model is an expression of a real situation and is used to predict the future in numerical terms. Sales can be forecast using this method as well as production, costs, and many other items. It can be applied to the *microeconomic,* or individual firm, level; or it can be used as a forecasting method at the *macroeconomic,* aggregate (total) economy, level such as the national level of employment or production of durable goods or many others.

THE ROLE OF RESEARCH IN BUSINESS

The Importance of Research

There is an increasing awareness by business firms of the importance of research. Large firms are in a better position to support systematic research activities than are small firms. The research budget of a large firm can be large enough that many projects can be supported. When a larger number of projects are undertaken, some of them are bound to succeed and compensate for the failures. The small firm with only a few projects cannot take the risks of failures. Another factor is that research often requires complex equipment that cannot be fully utilized unless a large number of research workers share in its use. The outcome of research is unpredictable, but a large firm with a diversified line of products has a good chance of finding an application for whatever its research develops. On the other hand, a small firm may be able to use only a small part of the knowledge it gains from its research.

Company-financed research expenditures are often expressed as a percentage of sales. They vary greatly among companies and among industries. The range is from 0 to over 10 per cent in some highly technical fields that are still in a developmental stage. Expenditures for research are between 2 and 3 per cent of sales in fields such as electrical equipment, professional and scientific instruments, and chemicals. For industry as a whole, company-financed expenditures average between 1 and 2 per cent of sales.

The importance of research in a company's growth and development is exemplified by the progress of the Minnesota Mining and Manufacturing Company, which manufactures Scotch tape and many other products. Large expenditures for research have been a policy of this company for a number of years. In 1965, its expenditure for research amounted to 5 per cent of its sales. The company stated that about 25 per cent of its sales in that year came from products that had been developed by its research and placed on the market during the preceding five years. The duPont Company is another firm that has devoted substantial resources to research. In 1964, it marketed a synthetic material—Corfam—that is a substitute for leather. It took an estimated $25 million and twenty-five years to get the product from the laboratory to market. During a seven-year period, duPont made 19,000 experimental pairs of shoes in 200 different shoe plants to test the product. After the extensive testing, a $2 million national advertising program was instituted to assist in marketing Corfam. It is typical of the chemical industry that half of its commercial products now in use will be supplanted within ten years by new products.

Sources of Support of Research

The financial support for research comes from a number of sources. The federal government conducts research to meet military, health, agricultural, and other requirements of the nation. This research is undertaken on behalf of society as a whole. Private industry supports research and is prompted by the prospects of profits. Colleges and universities and other non-profit institutions, including privately endowed foundations, also conduct research. Research and development expenditures have grown rapidly in recent years. In 1949, the expenditures for research throughout the United States totaled 3.1 billion dollars. At that time, 52 per cent of money spent on research was provided by the federal government; 45 per cent by private industry; and 3 per cent by colleges, universities, and other institutions. The total expenditures for research and development by 1964 amounted to an estimated $19 billion. The government's share was estimated to be 58 per cent; industry's share, 35 per cent; and the institutional share, 7 per cent. It is predicted that, by 1969, $29 billion will be expended, based on the current growth in research and development, of about 11 per cent per year. One of the principal reasons for this expansion is government-sponsored research, much of which is related to national defense and the space program. For example, industrial research in aircraft and aircraft parts was financed by the federal government to the extent of 87 per cent of the total cost. It is felt that the research needed to develop detection and warning devices required to police an effective disarmament will be more extensive than that required for weapons they are supposed to detect.

Outside Research Organizations

There are many outside research organizations that may be employed by a company to conduct all or a part of any type of research desired. Research laboratories to which problems are given for solution, or products for testing, operate on behalf of any company that will pay for the research undertaken. Similarly, there are research organizations and individual consultants that will conduct business research, market research, and economic research. This can be done on an intermittent basis, on a continuing basis, or for a single project. Firms can be hired to collect and interpret basic data, or merely collect the data. Some of these firms specialize in the kind of research performed, such as a particular branch of marketing research like psychological research, or media testing, while others provide a complete service. In some research fields, the organizations have developed a variety of continuous services, such as economic indexes, marketing indexes of food, credit information, and construction statistics, to which businesses can subscribe and which constitute the results of continuous research. Some trade associations perform research that can be used by their industry members. Colleges, universities, and agencies of the federal government also engage in extensive research activities. The educational institutions do this both independently and under contract.

RECENT MANAGEMENT DEVELOPMENTS

Collection and Analysis of Research Data

Chapter 27, "Information Management: Electronic Data Processing," discussed at some length the contributions of the electronic computer and supporting equipment to the performance of the information function. Business firms and other institutions are now able to assemble, analyze, and store vast quantities of information. Not only is this possible on an unprecedented scale, but the utilization of data may be accomplished with a speed unheard of a few years ago. We are now able to store information and sort, compare, and correlate an array of items bearing on the problems at hand.

The ability to do so much with information, and within allowable limits of cost and time, has been an encouragement to business firms to increase their research efforts. Also, government agencies, foundations, and others interested in economic data have been encouraged to further their efforts. It is probable that the decision areas faced by business management are becoming more complex as our society in general becomes more complex. The availability of sophisticated equipment for use in the processing and analysis of information may, however, help the decision maker to keep abreast of the problem.

Management-Game Theory

Since 1945, there has been a growing interest in game theory. This developed as a new analytical method in economics and sociology but has expanded to other fields including statistics, mathematics, political science, and military science. More recently, the development of management games has been used as a technique for research and for training in administration.

Game theory does not involve games in the ordinary sense. Many ordinary games contain a great deal of chance in their play, whereas management-game theory emphasizes strategy. It includes not only individual choices and preferences but also the power of individuals to enforce their desires upon others when they are participating in group action.

The individual, individuals, or team that plays a management game is given certain information about the particular situation that constitutes the problem. They are given control over certain factors, such as money. They decide whether to spend more on research, advertising, sales promotion, expand production, and so on. Rules of the game are established, and each player finds that the way he decides to commit the factors he controls is affected by the actions of others, and his decisions likewise affect the group. However, he is seeking by his choices and decisions to maximize his reward. This effort to maximize must be done in the face of competition from the others playing the game who have similar intentions, so various possibilities must be considered in a way that is like the situation in the business world. A model is generally constructed simulating a particular situation, which serves as the basis for the game. In some instances, the game is played by using an automatic data computer to assist in making some of the calculations.

It is felt that the use of management games provides a supplement to laboratory studies and field studies for research. It can be used to improve decision-making and provide a better understanding of individual and group action in dealing with simulated business situations.

Systems Analysis

Systems analysis is a method used to study any particular aspect or segment of a system and requires an understanding of the entire system. A business firm is composed of many elements such as manpower, materials, machines, customers, competitors, and others. The various components are grouped and, if necessary, subgrouped, and the control and interrelationships are studied in a systematic and analytical manner in order to ensure accomplishment of company objectives. Typically, such techniques as operations research, linear programming, and probability theory are used. Models, both mathematical and non-mathematical, may be constructed by postulating alternative types of systems, and the models can be tested. Usually, this method seeks to ensure that all elements of the business organization are examined.

In recent years, some companies have made use of a management tool termed *value analysis*. This system of techniques and planned methods is utilized to look objectively and imaginatively at a part, a material, an operation, or a project and compare the costs with the function performed. The basic concepts of this approach are simplification and standardization that will result in greater reliability and/or lower costs.

Educational Background for Research

Persons who go into research work should have analytical ability and a genuine desire to do research work. It is challenging work and requires a great deal of attention to detail. In physical-science research, such as chemistry and physics, companies usually seek persons with advanced degrees, such as the master's or Ph.D. degrees. The master's degree is the first advanced degree beyond the bachelor's degree. An additional thirty semester hours of planned graduate study or forty-five quarter hours are required for this degree and, in many universities, the successful completion of a thesis. The degree is usually a Master of Arts, a Master of Science, or a Master of Business Administration. In a few universities, this degree requires sixty semester hours of work or ninety quarter hours. The Doctor of Philosophy, or Ph.D., degree or the Doctor of Business Administration or DBA, degree consists of sixty semester hours beyond the master's degree, or ninety quarter hours, and includes a doctoral dissertation. Rigorous qualifying and final examinations, both oral and written, are also required.

In social science research fields, such as economics, marketing, or psychology, graduate training is desirable at least through the master's degree. The reason for the requirement of graduate work is that the researcher receives training in conducting research and learns to handle independent research projects. The skills and techniques he has learned in graduate study are of great benefit to him in subsequent research. There are many research jobs, however, in which a bachelor's degree is all that is necessary.

TOPICS FOR DISCUSSION

1. Cite some specific examples of how management can use the computer in making business decisions.

2. Many people associate research solely with the man in the white coat amidst the test tubes in the laboratory. Bring research into focus so as to clarify this image.

3. Define and give concrete examples of *primary data* and *secondary data*.

4. There are two main types of sampling used. Name and describe each type.

5. Do you feel it is the responsibility of business to support research in academic institutions?

6. Many people state that motivational research on the part of business is immoral because it enables the businessman to become aware of consumer buying motives of which the consumer himself is not aware, thereby giving the firm a certain power over the individual. Do you agree or disagree? Why?

7. Some companies spend an amount equal to 3 per cent or more of their gross sales on research. Can they really afford to do this, or should they take that money and increase dividends?

8. How do you account for the fact that the amount of research done in the social-science field is such a small amount compared to that carried on in the physical sciences?

9. Management-game theory has been growing in popularity as a training method in administration. Soon, it is said, every college student will have to show his prowess at playing the game or be unable to find a job. Comment.

10. Is it possible to use the scientific method in connection with many different research techniques? What limitations are there to its application in some fields?

CASE 28–1

THE ROLE OF RESEARCH IN A BUSINESS DECISION

The Greystone Petroleum Company was a large producer and distributor of gasoline. The company concentrated its marketing program in an area embracing fourteen states. In this area, the Greystone brand ranked consistently among the top five brands in sales. For several years, the company had considered the expansion of its market to include a greater number of states. Management had delayed the decision on expansion while awaiting what might be identified as an opportune time.

By 1964, certain of the company executives thought that the time was opportune for the expansion program. Greystone chemists had worked for several years on an additive to improve gasoline performance. Such a product had been developed and tested extensively under laboratory conditions. It was reported by the chemists that the additive would increase gasoline mileage by as much as 10 per cent. They also reported the possibility of some engine corrosion as a result of using gasoline with the additive, but they felt that this was a minor difficulty and that, through continued research, they might be able to eliminate it. The executives who favored immediate expansion of the market felt that the additive would give the company the push needed to become established in new territories.

Mr. Wasson, a vice-president of the company, opposed the immediate use of the additive in Greystone gasoline. He felt that the product (the additive) had not been adequately tested under actual conditions of use. If the product was used widely and proved faulty, the Greystone position in the market would be gravely threatened. He advocated extensive market tests under various climatic conditions and over a period of not less than six months. If no problems developed in the use of the fuel during the tests, he would then support the idea of announcing the discovery in an advertising program, and would also approve the opening of new markets.

The marketing research department was asked to prepare a statement on the time and cost involved in the period of testing advocated by Mr. Wasson. When completed, the report stated that the tests would require a minimum of eight months and that the costs would approximate $150,000. Several executives were strongly opposed to the program of testing. They pointed to an already large investment in chemical research. While they conceded the possibility of a problem with corrosion, they felt that the advantages to be gained by going into the market with the new additive would offset the risk of consumer dissatisfaction. They emphasized that, once the additive was on the market, it would probably be imitated in some form within less than three years.

Mr. Wasson remained adamant on his position. He argued that a bad experience with the additive could destroy in months the goodwill that Greystone gas had developed over years. He felt that $150,000 invested in research to verify the quality of the product would be money well spent.

Should Greystone use the additive immediately, or should it spend the money and time required for further research?

SELECTED REFERENCES

Boyd, Harper W., Jr., and R. Westfall. *Marketing Research*. Rev. ed. Homewood, Ill.: Richard D. Irwin, Inc., 1964.

Bright, James R. *Research, Development, and Technological Innovation*. Homewood, Ill.: Richard D. Irwin, Inc., 1964.

Enrick, N. L. *Management Operations Research*. New York: Holt, Rinehart & Winston, Inc., 1965.

McMillan, C., and R. F. Gonzalez. *Systems Analysis*. Homewood, Ill.: Richard D. Irwin, Inc., 1965.

Wasson, C. R. *The Strategy of Marketing Research*. New York: Appleton-Century-Crofts, Inc., 1964.

Index